GLOBAL CHILD POVERTY AND WELL-BEING

Measurement, concepts, policy and action

Edited by Alberto Minujin and Shailen Nandy

First published in Great Britain in 2012 by

The Policy Press
University of Bristol
Fourth Floor
Beacon House
Queen's Road
Bristol BS8 1QU
UK
t: +44 (0)117 331 4054
f: +44 (0)117 331 4093
tpp-info@bristol.ac.uk
www.policypress.co.uk

North American office:
The Policy Press
c/o The University of Chicago Press
1427 East 60th Street
Chicago, IL 60637, USA
t: +1 773 702 7700
f: +1 773-702-9756
e:sales@press.uchicago.edu
www.press.uchicago.edu

British Library Cataloguing in Publication Data
A catalogue record for this book is available from the British Library.

Library of Congress Cataloging-in-Publication Data
A catalog record for this book has been requested.

ISBN 978 1 84742 481 5 (paperback)
ISBN 978 1 84742 482 2 (hardcover)

Cover design by The Policy Press
Front cover: image kindly supplied by
Ryan W. Daniels
Printed and bound in Great Britain by
Henry Ling, Dorchester

MIX
Paper from
responsible sources
FSC
www.fsc.org
FSC® C013985

Contents

List of tables and figures

Tables

Figures

Notes on contributors

Hicham Ait Mansour has a social work degree from the National Institute of Social Work, Tangier, Morocco (1999), a BA (2005) and MPhil (2007) in sociology from the University of Rabat, Morocco (2005) and an MSc in policy research from the University of Bristol, UK (2009). Between 1999 and 2004 he worked with Save the Children UK in Morocco as a training officer, and then as a child rights programming officer. Between 2004 and 2006 he worked as a consultant on child rights including coordinating qualitative research on the situation of children in residential care institutions in Morocco. Between 2007 and 2011 he worked at UNICEF Morocco as a monitoring and evaluation and social policy analysis officer.

Sabina Alkire directs the Oxford Poverty and Human Development Initiative, a research centre within the Department of International Development, University of Oxford, UK. In addition, she is a research associate at Harvard, USA, and vice president of the Human Development and Capability Association. Her research interests include multidimensional poverty measurement and analysis, welfare economics, the capability approach, the measurement of freedoms and human development. She holds a DPhil in economics from Magdalen College, Oxford, UK.

Helen Barnes is a research fellow in the Oxford Institute of Social Policy at the Department of Social Policy and Intervention at the University of Oxford, UK. Her recent work has focused on the measurement of poverty in South Africa, including the analysis of take-up of social grants, the construction of small area level indices of deprivation (relating both to the general population and to children in particular), and the definition and measurement of child poverty using money metric approaches and the socially perceived necessities method.

Jo Boyden is director of Young Lives, a longitudinal study of childhood poverty in Ethiopia, India, Peru and Vietnam. She is a social anthropologist based at the University of Oxford's Department of International Development (UK), and has worked for many years on issues of risk and resilience in childhood.

Jonathan Bradshaw is professor of social policy at the University of York, UK. His recent work includes three books on the well-being of children in the UK, comparative studies of child well-being in the European Union (EU), Central and Eastern Europe (CEE)/ Commonwealth of Independent States (CIS) and Pacific Rim countries, and analysis of child well-being at small area level in England. He is currently working with The Children's Society on the measurement of subjective well-being. He is a consultant to UNICEF in the CEE/ CIS region and has recently completed a study for the European Commission on the measurement of extreme poverty in the EU.

Sarah Burd-Sharps is a co-director of the American Human Development Project and author (with Eduardo Martins and Kristen Lewis) of *The measure of America: American Human Development report 2008-2009* (Columbia University Press, 2008) and *A portrait of Mississippi* and *A portrait of Louisiana*. Sarah and Kristen Lewis founded the project in 2006. Previously, Sarah worked with the United Nations (UN) for over two decades. Most recently she was deputy director of the Human Development Report Office of the UN Development Program. Prior to this, she worked with UNIFEM (UN Development Fund for Women) in China and in a number of African countries on gender issues and economic empowerment. Sarah holds an MIA from Columbia University.

Enrique Delamonica is the social and economic policy adviser at the United Nations Children's Fund (UNICEF) Regional Office for Latin America and the Caribbean, dealing primarily with child poverty, equity, social expenditure analysis and social protection policies. An economist and political scientist, he was educated at the University of Buenos Aires, Argentina, the Institute for Economic and Social Development, Argentina, Columbia University, New York, USA, and The New School for Social Research, New York, USA. He was a policy analyst at UNICEF's headquarters for over 10 years, focusing on poverty reduction strategies, socioeconomic disparities, financing social services and the impact of macroeconomic trends on child welfare. He has published and co-edited books on issues of social policy and economic development, particularly as they affect children's rights, including *Eliminating human poverty* (with Santosh Mehrotra; Zed Books, 2007). He has also written several articles in journals and books, including 'Economic growth, poverty and children', in *Environment and Urbanization* (with Jan Vandemoortele and Alberto Minujin; 2002). He has taught economics, international development, policy analysis, statistics and research methods at, among other places, New York University, Columbia University, The New School and Saint Peter's College (New Jersey), USA. He is a fellow of the Comparative Research Programme on Poverty of the International Social Science Council.

Chris de Neubourg is chief of Social and Economic Research at the UNICEF Innocenti Research Centre in Florence, Italy. He has been affiliated with the Universities of Groningen and Maastricht in the Netherlands, Liège in Belgium, Denver and Harvard in the USA, Nihon University in Japan and the European University Institute in Florence, Italy. He is currently working on research projects on multidimensional deprivation analyses, social protection impact analyses and migration.

Sólrún Engilbertsdóttir is a policy analyst in the Social Policy and Economic Analysis Unit, UNICEF Policy and Practice department, New York, USA. She is part of a team promoting and advancing the Global Study on Child Poverty and Disparities in over 50 countries. Prior to this Sólrún was with UNICEF Kenya, where she was working on social policy, in particular social budgeting and social protection issues. Sólrún, an Icelandic national and graduate of Columbia University, USA, has substantive experience in her native country, working with high-risk children and adolescents.

Ernesto Espíndola Advis is an expert in social information in the Social Development Division at the Economic Commission for Latin America and the Caribbean of the United Nations, where for the past 14 years he has been a member of the team producing the *Social panorama of Latin America* report. He is a specialist on poverty, education, youth, labour market and family. He is a sociologist, with a Master's degree in social sciences of labour, and a diploma in human resources management. He is also a professor at graduate and undergraduate levels in quantitative techniques of social research and data analysis in Chile.

Gaspar Fajth is an economist and chief of the Social Policy and Economic Analysis Unit in the UNICEF Policy and Practice department, New York, USA. He is responsible for promoting UNICEF's engagement in socioeconomic analysis and advocacy, including through UNICEF's Global Study on Child Poverty and Disparities. Prior to this Gaspar, a former director of the Hungarian Central Statistical Office, was chief of the Socioeconomic Unit at the Innocenti Research Centre, Florence, Italy, the main research arm of UNICEF. He has edited, authored and co-authored several books, publications and articles on public policy, social protection and poverty, and has worked on evidence-based economic and social policy issues in a large number of countries and regions.

Franziska Gassmann has a PhD in economics (Maastricht University, the Netherlands, 2000). Since 2005, she has been working as a senior researcher and head of training and research projects at the Maastricht Graduate School of Governance, the Netherlands. She has demonstrated her skills and expertise as a consultant and researcher in the economics of poverty reduction, social policy reform, transition and development. Her research focuses on multidimensional poverty and vulnerability assessments and the effectiveness of social safety net policies.

Shirley Gatenio Gabel is associate professor at Fordham University's Graduate School of Social Service, New York, USA. Her diverse experiences include directing public policy analyses for government and non-governmental organisations, lobbying and organising community efforts. Her primary research areas are comparative child and family policies in both industrialised and developing countries, especially for young children, and on how public policies can improve the well-being of children from a child rights perspective.

David Gordon is professor of social justice at the University of Bristol, UK, and director of the Townsend Centre for International Poverty Research. He is working with UNICEF on its Global Study of Child Poverty and Disparities, with the UN Department of Economic and Social Affairs on youth poverty and hunger and with Eurostat on measuring deprivation in the European Union. He is heading the large Economic and Social Research Council-funded project on Poverty and Social Exclusion in the UK (www.poverty.ac.uk).

Abby Hardgrove is a research assistant in the Young Lives team and is currently writing her DPhil on war-affected youth at the University of Oxford, UK.

Petra Hoelscher is a social policy specialist with the UNICEF Namibia, focusing on issues around child poverty and child well-being, social protection and applied budget work. Before joining the Namibia Country Office she was holding the same position at the UNICEF Regional Office for Central and Eastern Europe/Commonwealth of Independent States in Geneva (2006-10), having worked previously as a research fellow at the University of Stirling, Scotland, UK (2004-06) and at the University of Dortmund in Germany (1997-2003). She was awarded a PhD from the University of Dortmund in 2001.

Sir Richard Jolly is honorary professor and research associate in the Institute of Development Studies at the University of Sussex, UK. As co-director of the United Nations (UN) Intellectual History Project, he is currently overseeing and working on a 16-volume history of the UN's contributions to economic and social development since 1945. Before returning to England in 2000, Sir Richard was assistant secretary general of the UN, holding senior positions at UNICEF and UN Development Programme (UNDP) for nearly 20 years. From 1996 to 2000 he was special adviser to the administrator of the UNDP, and architect of the widely acclaimed *Human development report*. Before this, he was, for 14-and-a-half years, deputy executive director of UNICEF, with responsibilities for its programmes in over 130 countries of the world, including its strategy for support to countries in reducing child mortality and implementing the goals agreed at the 1990 World Summit for Children. While working for UNICEF, he also led the agency's efforts to ensure more attention to the needs of children and women in the making of economic adjustment policies, and co-authored the book *Adjustment with a human face* (Clarendon Press, 1987).

Sheila B. Kamerman is the Compton Foundation centennial professor for the prevention of child and youth problems at the Columbia University School of Social Work, New York, USA, and director of the University-wide and interdisciplinary Institute for Child and Family Policy (ICFP). She also co-directs, with Alfred J. Kahn, the ICFP website-based Clearinghouse on International Developments in Child and Family Policies (www.childpolicyintl.org). She is the author, co-author, editor or co-editor of more than 30 books or monographs and about 200 articles and chapters. Her current research is focused on global developments in social protection policies for children and their families.

Caroline Knowles is communications manager of Young Lives, and has a background in publishing and research communication for development.

Sharmila Kurukulasuriya is a poverty specialist, formerly at the Social Policy and Economic Analysis Unit, UNICEF Policy and Practice division, New York, USA. She managed the Global Study on Child Poverty and Disparities in addition to creating UNICEF's first global community of practice on child poverty. Sharmila was previously with the UN Development Programme's Human Development Report Office where she supported the preparation of national reports. Sharmila has conducted research on human development, statistics, health economics and poverty, among other issues. She has a Bachelor's degree in quantitative economics from Tufts University, USA, and a Master's in public administration from Columbia University, USA.

Ted Lechterman previously worked as a research assistant for the American Human Development Project. He is currently pursuing a PhD in political theory at Princeton University.

Audrey Lenoel is a postgraduate researcher at the School for Policy Studies, University of Bristol, UK. Her current doctoral research aims to assess the impact of migration and remittances on women left behind in Morocco. She has previously worked as a research officer for different governmental and academic institutions in the UK.

Ruth Levitas is professor of sociology at the University of Bristol, UK. Her research straddles political theory, transformative ideas and utopianism, and poverty, inequality and social exclusion. Publications include the *Concept of utopia* (Syracuse University Press, 1990); *The inclusive society? Social exclusion and New Labour* (Macmillan, 1998); and *Poverty and social exclusion in Britain: The Millennium Survey* (edited with Christina Pantazis and David Gordon; The Policy Press, 2006). She is co-investigator on the Economic and Social Research Council-funded 2011 Poverty and Social Exclusion Survey. *Utopia as method: The imaginary reconstitution of society* is to be published by Palgrave Macmillan in 2012.

Kristen Lewis is a co-director of the American Human Development Project and author (with Eduardo Martins and Sarah Burd-Sharps) of *The measure of America: American Human Development report 2008-2009* (Columbia University Press, 2008) and *A portrait of Mississippi* and *A portrait of Louisiana*. Kristen and Sarah Burd-Sharps founded the project in 2006. Kristen also comes from an international development policy background, having worked primarily in the areas of gender equality, governance, environment and water and sanitation. Kristen is co-author, under the leadership of Jeffrey Sachs' Millennium Project, of the 2005 book *Health, dignity and development: What will it take?* (Earthscan, 2005). She worked at the United Nations (UN) for some 10 years, first with UNIFEM (UN Development Fund for Women) and then in the UN

Development Programme's policy bureau, and has served as a consultant for many international development organisations. Kristen holds an MIA from Columbia University.

Bethuel Makosso is assistant professor at Marien Ngouabi University, Brazzaville (Congo). He specialises in industrial organisation and economic development and holds a doctorate at the University of Nice Sophia Antipolis (France). He is director of the Sector Policy Analysis Department at the Centre for Studies and Research on Political and Economic Analysis (CERAPE), Brazzaville Congo. Bethuel has worked on a consultancy project for UNICEF, International Labour Organization and the United Nations Development Programme.

Isabelle Maquet-Engsted works as a policy analyst in the Directorate for Social Protection and Integration at the European Commission. She was the secretary of the Indicators Sub-Group of the Social Protection Committee (SPC) between 2004 and 2010. Her main areas of expertise are social indicators and poverty analysis. She follows policy developments in the area of social inclusion and child poverty in particular. She was the pen holder of the 2008 SPC report on *Child poverty and well-being in the EU*.

Andrés Mideros Mora is an economist (Catholic University of Ecuador, Quito). He holds Master's degrees in economics (Latin American Faculty of Social Science, FLACSO), and in public policy and human development (Maastricht University). Currently he is a research/PhD fellow at Maastricht Graduate School of Governance and United Nations University – MERIT, Maastricht University. Since 2003 he has worked as researcher and consultant in development economics, public economics and political economics, focusing on poverty and inequality, social protection, microfinance, impact evaluation and policy analysis. Previously he served in UNHCR (the UN Refugee Agency) in charge of urban refugee local integration policies in Ecuador (2008-10). He specialises in quantitative methods for social policy analysis and evaluation. He writes on poverty and inequality, socioeconomic development, social protection and public economics, with occasional excursions into governance and politics.

Alberto Minujin is a mathematician with postgraduate studies in applied statistics and demography. He currently teaches at the Graduate Program in International Affairs, The New School, New York, USA, where he conducts teaching and research on the topics of children, human rights, poverty, and monitoring, evaluation and social research methods, social protection and budgets. He is the director of Equity for Children, a programme and website (www.equityforchildren.org) at The New School in New York, with Latin American counterparts: Equidad para la Infancia (www.equidadparalainfancia.org) for Spanish speakers and Equidade para aInfancia (www.equidadeparaainfancia.org) for Portuguese speakers. Alberto provides consulting services on issues related to social policy, child poverty, design and development of projects for child well-being, and statistical analysis and monitoring and evaluation. He worked for UNICEF for many years, first as regional adviser for social policy, monitoring and evaluation for Latin America and the Caribbean, and, until 2005, as senior programme officer (New York headquarters). Alberto has also served as deputy director of the National Statistical Office of Argentina and professor of postgraduate studies of the School of Social Sciences, University of Buenos Aires, Argentina.

Alain Beltran Mpoue is a national expert for the United Nations Development Programme in the Republic of Congo and works on issues regarding the Millennium Development Goals, especially those pertaining to poverty. He has a degree in economic statistics and has worked on the development, collection and analysis of household living standard surveys for the Centre National de la Statistique et des Etudes Economiques of Congo Brazzaville. He has also participated in research projects on living standards in other Central African countries.

Shailen Nandy is currently research associate in the School for Policy Studies at the University of Bristol, UK. He is a co-author of *Child poverty in the developing world* (The Policy Press, 2003) and recently completed his PhD looking at trends in child poverty in developing countries between 1990 and 2000. Shailen has acted as a consultant to the UNICEF Global Study on Child Poverty and Disparities, as well as to UNICEF regional and country offices.

María Nieves Rico is a social affairs officer in the Social Development Division, Economic Commission for Latin America and the Caribbean, at the United Nations(UN). She is a social anthropologist (Universidad Nacional de Rosario, Argentina), and currently a PhD candidate in sociology at the Universidad Complutense de Madrid, Spain. She holds a Master's degree in development sociology (Instituto de Estudios Panibéricos, Spain), a Master's degree in urban development and local government (Instituto de Adminstración Local, Madrid, Spain) and a diploma in international relations (Universidad Complutense de Madrid, Spain). She is the author of books and papers on public policies from a gender perspective in several areas such as the labour market, unpaid work, violence and human rights, education, family, the environment and water.

Patrick Guyer is the chief statistician for the American Human Development Project. Guyer has also worked as a researcher with the Economic and Social Rights Empowerment Initiative and has served as a consultant to UNICEF and the United Nations Department of Economic and Social Affairs. He holds a BA in political science from McGill University in Montréal and an MA in international affairs from The New School, New York, USA.

Geranda Notten is assistant professor at the Graduate School of Public and International Affairs, Canada. She specialises in poverty and social policy research and holds a PhD in economics from Maastricht University (the Netherlands). Geranda has been a visiting researcher at International Networks for Studies in Technology, Environment, Alternatives, Development (Luxembourg), the Kennedy School of Government (USA) and at the Maastricht Graduate School of Governance (the Netherlands). She has worked on consultancy projects for the World Bank, the European Union and UNICEF in countries such as Mauritius, Congo Brazzaville and Russia.

Simon Pemberton is senior lecturer in social policy in the School for Policy Studies, University of Bristol, UK. He has researched the question of poverty and human rights since 2002, when he was involved in a UNICEF project exploring the relationship between child rights and child poverty in the developing world. Alongside colleagues at the Centre for the Study of Poverty and Social Justice (University of Bristol), he has published a number of texts on the topic of rights and poverty.

Dominic Richardson works at the Organisation for Economic Co-operation and Development (OECD) in Paris on issues of child well-being, in particular analysing child and family policies, and developing policy-amenable indicators of child well-being to compare children's material well-being, health, education, risk behaviours, housing and the environment, and the quality of their school lives. At the time of writing, and prior to taking up the post at the OECD, Dominic worked in the Social Policy Research Unit at the University of York where he contributed background research to the UNICEF Innocenti Report Card 7 on child well-being.

José Manuel Roche is a research officer at the Oxford Poverty and Human Development Initiative, a research centre within the Department of International Development, University of Oxford, UK. He holds a PhD in sociology and an MSc in social research methods from the University of Sussex, UK. His research interests include poverty analysis, social inequality, geographical inequality, survey analysis, human development and social indicators. He has served as a consultant and social statistics adviser in diverse projects from the United Nations Development Programme, UNICEF, the European Union, the Institute of Development Studies, the Venezuelan National Institute of Statistics and the Venezuelan Ministry of Planning and Development. He oversaw the 2011 Multidimensional Poverty Index calculation with Sabina Alkire.

Keetie Roelen is currently working as a research fellow in the Vulnerability and Poverty Reduction team at the Institute of Development Studies, University of Sussex, UK. She obtained her PhD degree at Maastricht University (the Netherlands) in the field of child poverty measurement and policy. Her research interests include (child) poverty, poverty reduction policies and social protection policies in the context of both developed and developing countries.

Peter Townsend was professor of international social policy at the London School of Economics and Political Science, UK, and emeritus professor of social policy at the University of Bristol, UK. Over the course of a long career his research interests included international social policy, the sociology of poverty, inequalities in health, and issues concerning ageing, disability and the family. His most recent publications include *Building decent societies: Rethinking the role of social security in state building* (ILO/Palgrave Macmillan, 2009); *The right to social security and national development: Lessons from OECD experience for low-income countries* (International Labour Organization, 2007); *Child poverty in the developing world* (co-authored with David Gordon and others, The Policy Press, 2003); and *World poverty: New policies to defeat an old enemy* (co-editor, The Policy Press, 2002). A tireless activist and campaigner, he was co-founder and president of the Disability Alliance, and a founding member of the Child Poverty Action Group until his death in June 2009.

Jan Vandemoortele served with various parts of the United Nations (UN) for 30 years: the UNICEF, the International Labour Organization, the UN Development Programme (UNDP) and on loan to the World Bank. His last assignment was as UN resident and humanitarian coordinator to Pakistan. As director of the Poverty Group at UNDP, he was closely involved in the creation of the Millennium Development Goals. He holds a PhD in development economics. He now works as an independent researcher, writer and lecturer.

Gemma Wright is a senior research fellow at the Oxford Institute of Social Policy in the Department of Social Policy and Intervention at the University of Oxford, UK, deputy director of the Centre for the Analysis of South African Social Policy, and senior research associate of the Department of Sociology and the Institute of Social and Economic Research at Rhodes University, South Africa. Her areas of interest include the definition and measurement of poverty, child poverty, small area level analysis of deprivation and social security policy including modelling tax and benefit arrangements using microsimulation techniques.

Sepideh Yousefzadeh Faal Deghati is currently pursuing her PhD at Maastricht Graduate School of Governance, the Netherlands, focusing on multidimensional child poverty in Iran as a middle-income country. She read for her Master's degree in public administration at Harvard University's Kennedy School of Government, USA, and her Bachelor's degree in midwifery at Shiraz University, Iran. For the past 17 years she has worked with children and women – mainly marginalised groups – in the field of reproductive health, displacement, income generation, capacity development and rights advocacy. She has worked in Iran and Afghanistan, and has experience in Lebanon and Pakistan in refugee settings. Her working experience is diverse. She has worked with government organisations, civil society organisations (Iran) and community-based organisations (Afghan and Palestinian), international non-governmental organisations (NGOs) and the United Nations. Her last experience was with UNICEF in Iran where she worked in a child rights partnership and helped in initiating a partnership with religious leaders (for child rights advocacy), the Ministry of Social Welfare (to mainstream social policy for children in national strategies and plans) and the Ministry of Interior (to enhance the social and development planning role of the Ministry and its local offices).

Acknowledgements

This book is written in tribute to Professor Peter Townsend (1928–2009) who was a source of inspiration and enlightenment for all of us who work to combat injustice and poverty around the world. Peter was politically and intellectually committed to a more equitable world, with social justice and freedom for all. He made key contributions to the conceptualisation and measurement of child poverty, and to our work on the matter. His advice and presence are greatly missed.

We would like to thank Sharmila Kurukulasuriya and Gaspar Fajth, of UNICEF, and Michael Cohen of The New School's International Affairs Program (US), for their support in helping to create the 2008 international conference entitled 'Rethinking Poverty: Making Policies that Work for Children', which was the starting point for this book. We also want to thank David Gordon for his constant encouragement and support and Louise Moreira Daniels for her valuable collaboration. We are also grateful to Karen Bowler, Laura Vickers and Dawn Rushen from The Policy Press for their support and advice. Finally, we thank all the authors for their great and innovative contributions.

Alberto Minujin and Shailen Nandy

Foreword

Sir Richard Jolly

For over more than 60 years, the United Nations Children's Fund (UNICEF) has led the way with international action for children. But UNICEF has been at its best and had most influence when the action has been combined with ideas and thinking about how best countries and the international community can give more attention to children in both national and international policies. It is the action that has usually attracted most attention and support – because of its obvious practical appeal. Indeed, UNICEF has built its reputation on 'making a difference', not just talking about what needs to be done. Nonetheless, when UNICEF's action has been directly linked to pioneering ideas, the results have been greatly multiplied.

Each of the decades of UNICEF's existence can be identified by a dominating idea:

1945:   Children recovering from war need urgent and special support.
1950s: Children in developing countries deserve and need international support as much as those in war-torn developed countries.
1960s: Children's needs must be made an integral part of national economic planning.
1970s: A country programme approach for children is essential if action is to be tailored to the specifics and capacities of each country.
1980s: Accelerated action is possible with social and political mobilisation and can lead to a veritable child survival and development revolution.
1990s: Children's rights provide moral and practical guidelines for addressing children's needs in ways which offer them respect and where their voices are heard.
2000s: The Millennium Development Goals (MDGs) provide a global agenda of meeting the needs of children alongside other human priorities.

The list is obviously an oversimplification. Although these ideas have characterised these eras of advance, there have been others. The 1980s, in particular, brought a burst of actions and global leadership. UNICEF's

The State of the World's Children report (SOWCR), each year released in 100,000 copies and a dozen languages, ensured that UNICEF's vision and ideas gathered headlines in virtually every country of the world. But action was always a central part of the message. The SOWCR provided a year-by-year commentary on how social and political mobilisation was bringing progress for children, documenting country successes in expanding immunisation, oral rehydration and the increasing use of other low-cost readily available measures to save children's lives and to reduce child mortality.

The 1980s were years of economic setbacks, and often disaster, for many developing countries, especially in Sub-Saharan Africa and Latin America. Countries were forced to adopt policies of structural adjustment with cuts in government spending as a condition for obtaining loans. UNICEF countered with ideas of 'adjustment with a human face', which showed how priorities for children could and should be maintained, even in severely constrained economic circumstances. This powerful idea gained increasing support precisely because it was not just an abstract proposal but directly linked with the demonstrable progress being made in reducing child mortality. And it made a measurable difference. Although average incomes over the 1980s fell in Sub-Saharan Africa and were stagnant in Latin America, the annual number of child deaths declined in every continent, often at a faster rate than in earlier years. Worldwide, the number of children dying each year was reduced from 15 million in 1980 to 12 million in 1990. Priority actions for children were maintained over the 1990s and child deaths fell to 10 million by 2000 and to under 9 million by 2010. Ideas linked to action can indeed have a multiplied impact.

Today – and in this volume – the authors are exploring ideas that can again lead the way with actions for reducing child poverty. The focus of the ideas has moved on. Today's agenda for action combines the country-by-country approach to action and monitoring with special attention to child rights, the girl child and environmental sustainability. There is also a new awareness of the importance of inequality, both the need for special attention to children in the poorest groups who are usually the most difficult to reach and also the need for broader actions to reduce national and international inequalities.

Some of these priorities are common to the broader agenda for meeting the MDGs. But UNICEF's approach involves some important differences. The mainstream agenda and priorities of the Bretton Woods Institutions and many donors puts greatest priority on accelerating rates of economic growth with the expansion of education and health in the second rank of priorities.

In contrast, UNICEF puts forward a broader range of ideas and approaches:

- less dominated by the need to accelerate economic growth rates; with more emphasis on child rights and participation;
- with clear recognition of the part that children and their communities can play in moving towards the MDGs – and how this is an essential part of a rights-based approach;
- with more awareness of the roles which other UN agencies are playing and how collaboration can improve 'delivering as one'.

Above all, at least in principle, UNICEF seeks to promote and explore a child-centred approach. Such an approach is closely aligned with human development – putting people at the centre, in this case putting children at the centre. The key objective is how to strengthen their capabilities and the capabilities of their families and communities, so that children grow and acquire knowledge and skills, character and confidence, culture and values, including a sense of obligation to others on which robust and democratic societies depend.

This embraces far more than a top-down results-based expansion of education and health in an economy that is growing ever faster. It is a uniquely child-focused approach, with children treated in terms of their own needs and capacities, not just as mini-adults – or, as a statistic calculation once put it, 'child consumption is taken for statistical purposes as 0.7 of an adult's consumption.'

Child poverty is similarly very different from adult poverty defined in terms of living below US$1.25 a day. Child poverty needs to be defined in terms of key deprivations – of food and nutrition, clothing and shelter, education and schooling, access to health, perhaps above all, of nurture and care. For a child, each of these is needed and the lack of adequacy must be assessed not just in terms of a child's immediate needs but in terms of what the child needs to grow in strength and capabilities so as to reach adulthood, with the basic capabilities needed for being a good citizen, within the community and beyond.

The chapters in this volume follow such an approach and already set out some of what is required. But the new thinking and approach must also be classed as work in progress – with ideas and advances which can be used to guide action but which still leave many questions unanswered and many issues yet to be discovered. This is fully in line with UNICEF's past experience. Action, however bold and farseeing, will pose new issues in the process of implementation, calling for new ideas and research. New research and thinking will in turn raise new possibilities for action. This is the heady mixture that has been at the heart of UNICEF's successful leadership for children in the past. Long may it continue in the future.

PART I

PART I

ONE

Introduction

Shailen Nandy and Alberto Minujin

In December 2006, the United Nations General Assembly (UNGA) adopted, for the first time, an international definition of child poverty. It recognised that:

> ... children living in poverty are deprived of nutrition, water and sanitation facilities, access to basic health-care services, shelter, education, participation and protection, and that while a severe lack of goods and services hurts every human being, it is most threatening and harmful to children, leaving them unable to enjoy their rights, to reach their full potential and to participate as full members of society. (UNGA, 2006, para 460)

The United Nations Children's Fund (UNICEF), the agency charged with promoting international child welfare and which had campaigned for agreement on a definition, noted:

> Measuring child poverty can no longer be lumped together with general poverty assessments which often focus solely on income levels, but must take into consideration access to basic social services, especially nutrition, water, sanitation, shelter, education and information. (UNICEF, 2007)

These internationally accepted and agreed statements and definitions were a major step forward for everyone interested in the issues of child well-being and child poverty. The definitions provided a clear and unambiguous direction to governments, advocacy groups and others interested in dealing with child poverty as to which dimensions future research and indicators needed to reflect. The measurement and analysis of child poverty requires consideration of a wide range of non-monetary dimensions and factors, all of which are known to have a well-documented impact on children's survival, well-being and development. These dimensions include, as the definitions set out:

children's living conditions, their access to basic services, their ability to participate in normal society as full citizens, the right to be free of any kind of discrimination and exclusion and their rights to protection from exploitation and abuse. In summary, this measurement and analysis addresses equal opportunities for all boys and girls in all countries and all situations. When viewed in conjunction with the sentiments expressed in the 1989 UN Convention on the Rights of the Child (UNCRC), where state parties were enjoined under Article 27 (among others) 'to recognise the right of every child to a standard of living adequate for the child's physical, mental, moral and social development' (UN, 1989), two things are apparent. First, evidence from around the world, from rich, middle-income and poor countries alike, confirms that many millions of children continue to experience deep poverty, deprivation and exclusion (Micklewright and Stewart, 2001; Gordon et al, 2003; Richardson et al, 2008). Second, that despite the binding commitments of the UNCRC over 20 years ago, the most basic rights of children continue to be infringed (van Bueren, 2002; Redmond, 2008).

This book presents a collection of work by leading international academics, researchers and policy makers concerned with the measurement and mitigation of child poverty. It brings together many of the actors involved in the development of indicators and measures of child poverty and well-being, and through a series of national and regional level case studies, demonstrates how research on child poverty has developed over the last two decades. Until 1999, few researchers concentrated on child poverty as a concern that deserved special emphasis. Poverty meant adult and household poverty, and the prevalent approach to measurement relied on income/consumption indicators. No information on child poverty was available at a global or regional level, and only a handful of countries estimated the number of children living in income-poor households. In 1999, the UN Expert Group on Poverty Statistics met in Portugal and researchers such as Alberto Minujin and Peter Townsend made the case for documenting child poverty in statistical and policy terms. The concept at that meeting was based on the over-representation of children among the poor and utilised only the money metric approach. By the end of 1999, however, UNICEF, under the leadership of Jan Vandemoortele, Enrique Delamonica and Alberto Minujin, furthered the effort by coining the phrase 'Poverty reduction starts with children' (UNICEF, 2000b) in order to influence the design and implementation of the Poverty Reduction Strategy Papers (PRSPs), which had recently been established by the World Bank. In 2003, a research team led by Professors Peter Townsend and David Gordon, produced the first ever global estimates of child poverty for UNICEF (Gordon et al, 2003) as an outgrowth of the Portugal meetings and UNICEF action plan. When data from the report were used in the *State of the World's Children 2005* report (UNICEF, 2004) to show that over one billion children were severely deprived of one or more basic needs, there was immediate and widespread recognition that more needed to be done to tackle child poverty. In the years that followed, academics and activists developed an international network of actors, all of whom were involved in developing research on child well-being and poverty. With the issue of child poverty now placed at the centre of the international stage, there was (and continues to be) a significant increase in activity and research on child poverty around the world (Boyden et al, 2003; Feeny and Boyden, 2003; Minujin and Delamonica, 2003; Seager and de Wet, 2003; White et al, 2003; Noble et al, 2004, 2006; Corak, 2005; G.A. Jones, 2005; N. Jones, 2005; Minujin et al, 2005, 2006; Delamonica and Minujin, 2007; Lyytikainen et al, 2006; Doek et al, 2009; Nandy and Gordon, 2009; Jones and Sumner, 2011).

Much of this activity built on another earlier body of work about children and poverty, typified by UNICEF's landmark study *Adjustment with a human face* (Cornia et al, 1987). The report detailed the impact on children of another global financial crisis (during the 1980s), and called for the collection and use of data on the 'human' dimensions of adjustment. Such data might include information about people's access to education and health services, rather than just conventional macroeconomic indicators. It also noted the need for status (or impact) indicators (for example, nutrition status, education level), process indicators (for example, availability of food, or education), and input indicators at three levels: household, government and community (Stewart, 1987, p 258). To assess the impacts on children of the by then widely implemented policies of structural adjustment, the report argued one would need to know how different input indicators affected the process indicators, and in turn how these affected status indicators. At the time, reliable and readily accessible household survey data for most poor countries were scarce, but *Adjustment with a human face* demonstrated that data on the 'human' dimension were available, from different sources such as nutrition surveys and hospital records. These, it argued, could be used to create a 'composite index of social stress' to serve as an early warning system to denote when conditions for children were unfavourable and likely to have a negative impact on them. Components of such an index could include indicators of malnutrition, cases of Kwashiorkor or other important diseases, the proportion of babies born with a low birth weight, food prices in regional markets and even rainfall patterns. In time, other indicators could be added, but what was key was the call to incorporate into conventional econometric and planning models those factors that directly affected children. The report concluded that 'it is important to aim at a systematic set of human accounts, on a par with the economic accounts' (p 264) and that 'information is not a luxury to be added on as an afterthought ... but an essential pre-requisite for devising good programmes' (p 262). Given the current ongoing global financial crisis, it is perhaps obvious that we recommend readers revisit the arguments and issues covered in *Adjustment with a human face* (Cornia et al, 1987), as well as other work from the era (MacPherson, 1987; Cornia et al, 1992; Kent, 1995) which examined child poverty on its own merits. UNICEF's current Global Study on Child Poverty and Disparities (see Chapter Twenty-One, this volume) is detailing the impact of the current economic crisis on children around the world (Mendoza, 2009).

The chapters of this book focus primarily on the measurement of child poverty. They provide insights into recent theoretical, methodological and policy developments, from a number of geographic and intellectual positions. In doing so, the book benefits from material from case studies on countries that might not otherwise have appeared alongside each other. Important empirical work from countries as diverse as Congo Brazzaville, Tanzania, South Africa, Vietnam, Bangladesh, Morocco, Iran and Haiti is presented, to show how, even in challenging contexts, research on children is developing in new and innovative ways. Wider regional level portraits are also presented, with analyses of the European Union (EU), the United States (US), and countries of Central and Eastern Europe/Commonwealth of Independent States (CEE/CIS), of South Asia and Sub-Saharan Africa. The methodological discussions presented in each chapter provide readers with a wide range of information about working with multidimensional child poverty measures, and may suggest analyses that could be applied in other countries. Many of the chapters present data to show changes over time, and these will no doubt form key sources of information for future studies aiming to assess progress towards the Millennium Development Goals (MDGs) and the target date of 2015. Their importance is accentuated given there is no single distinct goal or target for child poverty per se. However, given the ever-increasing availability of household survey data and developments in various methodologies, it is reasonable to expect that in the not too distant future, specific global targets for child poverty might be set and adopted as they have already been in some regions (European Commission, 2008; OECD, 2009).

Who is this book for?

Given child poverty is acknowledged to be the result of overlapping dimensions of deprivation, as well as the non-fulfilment of many basic economic, social and human rights, this book is intended for an audience from many disciplines. We hope it will be of use and interest to specialists in their fields, as well as those with a more general interest in the topic. Where relevant, each chapter sets out its working definition of child poverty, the conceptual approach taken, and relates these to the indicators developed and used. The presentation of empirical data on child poverty and disparities should give policy makers and advocates of children's rights sufficient evidence on which to challenge the shape of existing policies when they clearly appear to fail. We hope the methodologies described and tested here will encourage others to make their own forays into research, applying what is shown here to their own countries and contexts.

Outline of the book

The book has four main parts, and between each there will inevitably be some degree of overlap. The first part includes this introduction, as well as two chapters that set out some of the key debates relating to the study of child poverty and its measurement. **Chapter Two**, by Simon Pemberton and colleagues, examines international human rights frameworks and conventions to reveal their potential as mechanisms to hold key international players, both governmental and non-governmental, to account when children's basic needs are unmet and rights thus infringed. It details a series of practical obstacles which stand in the way of ensuring that rights are realised, and how these might be overcome, given sufficient political and popular will. It also shows how children's rights and child poverty are closely linked, and how, using methods similar to those used by other contributors to this book, an account can be made of how children's rights continue to be violated, despite governments having agreed clear core obligations to meet such rights.

Chapter Three, by Jan Vandemoortele, tackles the issue of economic growth, until recently depicted as the *sine qua non* for development and poverty reduction. He argues that an idea which has dominated international development discourse – that economic growth is a sufficient condition to reduce poverty – is flawed on a number of levels, and that the key international metric of international poverty – the so-called 'dollar-a-day' poverty line – is particularly problematic.

He sets out his reasons, with evidence, and builds a strong case for a greater focus on issues of equity and the need to ensure that any poverty reduction strategy considers at its core, the needs of and implications for children. Given international concerns about the global financial crisis, and growing recognition of the need to protect those least responsible for the crisis, he posits that 'child-focused policies can be a Trojan horse for introducing equity-enhancing measures in social and economic policy making' which would benefit societies as a whole.

Part 2 builds on some of the themes raised by the chapters in Part 1, and shows how different measures of child poverty, deprivation and well-being can be developed and applied. **Chapter Four**, by David Gordon and Shailen Nandy, sets out in some detail what has come to be known as the 'Bristol Approach' (Minujin et al, 2005; Roelen and Gassmann, 2008). It explains the theory and rationale behind the approach, showing how it built on the long history of poverty research in the UK and around the world. The chapter also discusses how *not* to measure child poverty, providing a critique of some other commonly used measures, including the World Bank's popular 'US$1/day' indicator, the Asset Ownership-based Wealth Index also developed by the World Bank (Filmer and Pritchett, 1998, 2001), and the recently developed Multidimensional Poverty Index (Alkire and Foster, 2008; Roche, 2009), which replaces the United Nations Development Programme's (UNDP) Human Development Index (HDI). **Chapter Five**, by Sabina Alkire and José Manuel Roche, shows how researchers are building on the 'Bristol Approach', to develop indicators that reflect the depth, intensity and composition of multidimensional poverty. Using data from Bangladesh, they set out the Alkire and Foster method for developing a multidimensional poverty indicator for children under the age of five. They experiment with varying thresholds and cut-offs to show how sensitivity analyses can be used to refine such indicators, and then present, in detail, changes in the index over a 10-year period (1997-2007) at both national and subnational level.

Chapter Six, by Helen Barnes and Gemma Wright of the University of Oxford, presents a different approach to assessing child poverty. Their work is part of a wider project on the measurement of poverty in South Africa (Noble et al, 2004, 2006), which involves, among other things, the application of the socially perceived necessities approach (Mack and Lansley, 1985; Halleröd, 1994; Gordon and Pantazis, 1997). Poverty in this instance is treated as an enforced lack (due to insufficient resources) of items and services identified by society as essential for an acceptable standard of living, and the chapter presents a fascinating account of the methodology being used to elicit children's perspectives about poverty in South Africa. The material resulting from focus groups run with children showed that children were more than capable of identifying which items and services they believed to be essential (as opposed to luxuries). While there was some overlap between what adults and children thought were necessary, there were also some significant differences. For example, school transport, school equipment, access to a doctor and having warm, dry clothing were all accorded a greater importance by children than by adults. These findings, and others in the chapter, have important implications for other similar consensus-based measures and indexes, if based solely on the responses of adults. The chapter provides an excellent example of how measures of child poverty can be augmented by consulting children about their experiences and opinions.

In **Chapter Seven**, Sarah Burd-Sharps and colleagues make the case for the development and use of a 'Tots Index' for the US. Despite having per capita incomes well in excess of most other countries, the US also has some of the highest rates of child poverty in the OECD (Organisation for Economic Co-operation and Development) (2009; see also UNICEF, 2000a). The authors, whose American HDI (Burd-Sharps et al, 2008) received international attention in 2008, show why an index focusing on children under the age of five in the US is warranted. Most of the issues raised in the chapter are universally relevant and applicable, and, as the chapters by Petra Hoelscher and colleagues (**Chapter Eight**) and Isabelle Maquet-Engsted (**Chapter Nine**) show, multidimensional indexes of child well-being, poverty and deprivation are being developed in a number of regions (the CEE/CIS states and the EU) and have begun to influence policy makers. One aim of this book is that readers might be spurred into applying some of the methods presented and eventually to develop similar indexes that focus on children. To this end, **Chapter Ten**, by Shirley Gatenio Gabel and Sheila B. Kamerman, provides a summary of the types of data available to researchers, both on outcomes and on policies for children. They propose a preliminary child policy paradigm, which encompasses the dimensions key to child survival and development, including health, family economic well-being, education, child welfare and protection and children's rights.

Part 3 presents seven cases studies of recent research on multidimensional poverty among children from around the world. Alberto Minujin and Enrique Delamonica (**Chapter Eleven**) report on work done with UNICEF colleagues in Tanzania, developing a child poverty and deprivation measure. They provide an example of how a UNICEF country office applied the methodology developed by David Gordon and Peter Townsend to examine subnational differences and disparities, and to also assess change over time. The resulting information, which shows where progress is occurring or stalling, can help in the design and targeting of future programmes and resources. The next three chapters all report on work done by academics connected to the Maastricht Graduate School of Governance in the Netherlands. In recent years, the School has been involved with UNICEF and other organisations, in developing and using multidimensional poverty indexes for a number of countries. In **Chapter Twelve**, Geranda Notten, Chris de Neubourg, Bethuel Makosso and Alain Beltran Mpoue present a profile of multidimensional child poverty in Congo Brazzaville. They use their index to go beyond the provision of a poverty headcount, instead examining the overlaps between different dimensions of deprivation. The disaggregation of results, showing which groups are most likely to experience which types of deprivation, and the use of Venn diagrams to show overlaps between key dimensions, exemplify the value and merit of a multidimensional approach to poverty assessment. **Chapter Thirteen**, by Keetie Roelen and Franziska Gassmann, discusses the results of a study on multidimensional child poverty in Vietnam. Using indicators and thresholds appropriate to the Vietnamese context, they also provide a detailed analysis of child poverty and prevailing disparities, particularly between urban and rural areas, regions and, interestingly, by ethnicity. The chapter also includes an overlap analysis of the different dimensions. Analyses of poverty from Iran are limited in number, so we consider ourselves fortunate to include the chapter by Sepideh Yousefzadeh Faal Deghati, Andrés Mideros Mora and Chris de Neubourg (**Chapter Fourteen**) on child poverty in Iran. Using a nationally representative survey on household income and expenditure, the authors develop their own index of multidimensional poverty, encompassing the three dimensions of provision, participation and protection. They report considerable regional, socioeconomic and gender disparities in various dimensions of deprivation. Unfortunately, ongoing restrictions of access to survey data on Iran means there is limited scope for others interested in following up this work, and developing it further.

  Chapter Fifteen, by David Gordon and colleagues, presents results of the first ever study of child poverty for Haiti, the poorest country in the Americas. The world is now familiar with images of the aftermath and impact of the magnitude 7.0 earthquake that struck the island on 12 January 2010. Over 200,000 people are estimated to have died, with many more losing their homes and livelihoods. Children were particularly badly affected in the days and months following, with more than 5,000 schools destroyed. The chapter shows how in the decade before the earthquake, between 2000 and 2005, there was no statistically significant decrease in child poverty in Haiti. The findings also show little or no reduction in the prevalence of severe deprivation for key basic needs among children. This information, disheartening as it is, provides some context for interpreting efforts to 'rebuild' the country.

The final two chapters of Part 3 present regional level analyses of child poverty and deprivation. Ernesto Espíndola and María Nieves Rico (**Chapter Sixteen**), from the Social Development Division of the Economic Commission for Latin America and the Caribbean (ECLAC), present results from the first ever study of multidimensional child poverty for the region (CEPAL and UNICEF, 2010). Taking advantage of national household surveys, and using a combination of both deprivation and monetary indicators, they estimate that, in 2007, around one child in six in the region (18%, or around 32 million children) experienced extreme poverty (that is, children experiencing a severe deprivation of at least one basic need). Using slightly less stringent thresholds to reflect a more moderate degree of deprivation (but arguably no less indicative of poverty), they found nearly half (45%, 81 million) of all children in the region were affected. The depth of child poverty in the region is shown to be directly linked to its prevalence, and thus also to the extent to which states have ensured the fulfilment of children's basic rights. Given the region is party to some of the greatest socioeconomic inequalities and disparities, it is no surprise the study found child poverty rates highest in rural areas, among indigenous communities, and among African-Caribbean groups. The data provide yet more evidence of the extent of unmet needs for large sections of the region's population, suggesting where future resources and programmes need to be applied. **Chapter Seventeen**, by Shailen Nandy, focuses on the two poorest regions of the world, South Asia and Sub-Saharan Africa. He provides evidence to show how these regions fared at the end of the 20th century with regard to the extent of child poverty. Using data from household surveys covering almost all children in the two regions (80% of children in South Asia in 2000, and 97% of children in Sub-Saharan Africa in 2000), he presents two rounds of estimates, for 1995 and 2000, to shed light on the dynamics of child poverty in the regions. Estimates are also presented for urban and rural areas, and for boys and girls (for specific deprivations), which provide some indication as to the direction of change regarding disparities and inequality. Nandy reports contrasting fortunes for the regions, with a decline in child poverty in South Asia and an increase in Sub-Saharan Africa between 1995 and 2000. The story is more complex than it first appears, however, with disparities between children living in urban and rural areas decreasing in Sub-Saharan Africa and increasing in South Asia. What are the drivers behind these apparently counter-intuitive results? More rapid *increases* in *urban* poverty than rural poverty in Sub-Saharan Africa, and *less rapid decreases* in *rural* poverty than urban poverty in South Asia. Sadly, as the data in the chapter show, there were roughly 30 million *more* children living in absolute poverty in Sub-Saharan Africa in 2000 than in 1995; during the same period, the number in South Asia decreased by roughly 63 million, to about 290 million children.

Moving away from a focus on measurement, the chapters in Part 4 discuss issues of causation and the nature of policies being used to tackle child poverty. Ruth Levitas (**Chapter Eighteen**) considers the principles on which societies need to be based in order to guarantee *genuine eradication* of child poverty. She shows that calls for policies which made universal provision of allowances to families with children have a long pedigree, and argues that a persistent problem with many anti-poverty policies (not just with regards child poverty) is that they are just not ambitious enough in their consistent and continuing adherence to a belief in the inevitability of at least some poverty, deprivation and inequality. Levitas sets out an architecture for the design of policies that, if implemented, would go some way to tackling the structural causes and propagators of poverty. The underlying principles of this architecture include the promotion of equality, a revaluing of care and its provision, a reconsideration of what counts as wealth and productive activity, the universal provision of child benefit and a guaranteed basic income for all, the mainstreaming of sustainability and the prioritising of human flourishing and well-being. **Chapter Nineteen** by Jo Boyden, Abby Hardgrove and Caroline Knowles provides an overview of the ongoing longitudinal study of children's lives in four poor countries (Vietnam, Ethiopia, Peru and the Indian state of Andhra Pradesh), the Young Lives project. The authors detail the project's conceptual and analytical framework, and report on some early findings concerning trends in children's welfare and the dynamics of child poverty. The project is one of the few international longitudinal studies of children and child poverty, and the lessons learned will be of real value to policy makers around the world. Based on their findings to date, they conclude that economic growth, by itself, will not solve the problems associated with poverty in childhood, and in some instances, can accentuate inequalities. They also conclude that the experience of deprivations during childhood can have longer-term impacts for children as they grow and develop, and also that properly designed social policies for children do have a protective effect against economic shocks (such as the global financial crisis). Importantly, data from the project have been deposited with the UK Data Archive and are available to researchers.

Chapter Twenty by Hicham Ait Mansour presents a case study of Morocco. He focuses on the implications for policy of using a multidimensional approach to examining child poverty. Using both monetary and non-monetary indicators, he shows (as others have) that children are far more likely to be identified as deprived (of basic needs, such as shelter etc) than income-poor. This is a key issue with regards the measurement of child poverty and is also discussed by others in this book (see Chapters Two, Three, Four, Eleven, Twelve and Thirteen, this volume). Future assessments of child poverty and well-being, intending to apply the UNGA definition set out at the start of this chapter, will almost certainly end up following the examples set in this book, including in the chapter on Morocco. Ait Mansour also provides an interesting take on counterfactuals – in a short exercise he shows how estimates of child poverty would be affected if individual deprivations were eradicated (that is, were not experienced by any children). In his example, child poverty in Morocco would fall from around 41% to 35% were sanitation deprivation to be eradicated. If, instead, overcrowding in households was tackled (that is, his indicator for shelter deprivation), child poverty rates would fall from 41% to 29%. Of course, it is not as simple as tackling a single deprivation at a time, and anti-poverty strategies need to work across many different sectors simultaneously (Mehrotra, 2004; Mehrotra and Jolly, 1997; Mehrotra and Delamonica, 2002).

Many of the chapters in this book report on work either done by, with, or for, UNICEF. Its role in international efforts to tackle child poverty is uncontested, and the Global Study on Child Poverty and Disparities is now taking place in over 50 countries, covering 1.5 billion children. **Chapter Twenty-One** by Gaspar Fajth, Sharmila Kurukulasuyria and Sólrún Engilbertsdóttir sets out the aims of the Global Study, and reflects on findings from a number of countries. By also focusing on disparities and examining national policies, the Study is producing valuable information about the determinants of child poverty in different settings, and documenting cases where policies for children have been shown to have positive effects. Importantly, at a time of international financial crises and government cuts to social and public expenditure, the Global Study is documenting the effects on children and their families. All of the countries involved in the Study are using a combination of monetary and non-monetary deprivation indicators to reflect the multidimensional aspects of child poverty. The constantly expanding network of researchers and policy makers involved that has emerged will ensure the issue of child poverty, its conceptualisation and measurement, remains a key issue on the international agenda. Qualitative methods have been used to great effect in the Global Study (and also in Young Lives) to contextualise children's experiences of poverty, and these in turn will lead to the development of better quantitative indicators.

It is only fitting that Peter Townsend (**Chapter Twenty-Two**) has the final word. In the years before his death, Peter campaigned with passion and vigour, with the International Labour Organization (ILO), for the adoption by the UN of an international child benefit (Townsend, 2007, 2008, 2009). He advocated the use and implementation of an international currency transfers tax along the lines proposed by James Tobin in the 1970s and 1990s. Peter's work throughout his life made clear the degree of real need around the world, not just among children. Many of the contributors to this book would acknowledge the considerable influence Peter had on their work, either directly or indirectly. Peter sets out in his chapter why many previous global strategies at poverty reduction (for example, the trickle-down policies of the 1980s) failed, and also how sufficient resources might be raised to ensure that every man, woman and child on the planet could still be covered by systems of social security to ensure they have a decent standard of living. A universal child benefit with an extra amount for children with a severe disability, he believed, would have an immediate and direct effect on household purchasing power, and thus reduce child poverty. He was well aware of the scale of forces (and degree of scepticism) arrayed against him, but never backed down. In an earlier report for the ILO, he sounded a forceful call to arms:

> ... the growing number of scarifying accounts of the hunger, exposure to conflict and abuse, extreme poverty and premature death still experienced by many millions of children across the world must concentrate the public mind.... It is not enough to set new goals. Finding – and agreeing – the necessary replacement policy is the top priority. New policies have to be devised to replace those that have failed. They have to have large-scale direct and positive effects. The time for elaborate pretence, with selectively helpful pilot projects for a very few children and for image-building by organisations at token cost, is over....
> (Townsend, 2008, p 3)

We hope the material in this book, and the detailed examples from around the world, contribute something to concentrating the public mind on global child poverty. We also hope that the methodologies described, and the indicators developed, will be used to demonstrate how and when policies fail or succeed. Poverty is not a law of nature. It can be eradicated, through the implementation of policies and programmes that guarantee universal and equitable access to basic social services as was nearly achieved in Europe after the Second World War. The lives and fortunes of hundreds of millions of people around the world are too important to leave to the whims of the free market.

References

Alkire, S. and Foster, J. (2008) *Counting and multidimensional poverty measurement*, Oxford: Oxford Poverty & Human Development Initiative (OPHI), University of Oxford.

Boyden, J., Eyber, C., Feeny, T. and Scott, C. (2003) *Children and poverty: Experiences and perceptions from Belarus, Bolivia, India, Kenya and Sierra Leone*, Richmond, VA: Christian Children's Fund.

Burd-Sharps, S., Lewis, K. and Martins, E.B. (2008) *The measure of America: American Human Development Report 2008-2009*, New York: Columbia University Press.

CEPAL (Comisión Económica para América Latina y el Carib) and UNICEF (United Nations Children's Fund) (2010) *Pobreza infantil en América Latina y el Caribe*, Panama City: UNICEF.

Corak, M. (2005) *Principles and practicalities in measuring child poverty for the rich countries*, Florence: UNICEF Innocenti Research Centre.

Cornia, G.A., Jolly, R. and Stewart, F. (1987) *Adjustment with a human face: Protecting the vulnerable and promoting growth*, Oxford: Oxford University Press.

Cornia, G.A., van der Hoeven, R. and Mkandawire, T. (1992) *Africa's recovery in the 1990s: From stagnation to adjustment to human development*, Florence: UNICEF International Child Development Centre.

Delamonica, E.E. and Minujin, A. (2007) 'Incidence, depth and severity of children in poverty', *Social Indicators Research*, vol 82, pp 361-74.

Doek, J.E., Shiva Kumar, A.K., Mugawe, D. and Tsegaye, S. (2009) *Child poverty: African and international perspectives*, Antwerp: Intersentia.

European Commission (2008) *Child poverty and well-being in the EU: Current status and way forward*, Luxembourg: Office for Official Publications of the European Communities.

Feeny, T. and Boyden, J. (2003) *Children and poverty – A review of contemporary literature and thought on children and poverty: Rethinking the causes, experiences and effects*, Richmond, VA: Christian Children's Fund.

Filmer, D. and Pritchett, L.H. (1998) *Estimating wealth effects without income or expenditure data – or tears: Educational enrolment in India*, World Bank Policy Research Working Paper, No 1994, Washington DC: World Bank.

Filmer, D. and Pritchett, L.H. (2001) 'Estimating wealth effects without expenditure data – or tears: an application to educational enrolments in states of India', *Demography*, no 38, pp 115-32.

Gordon, D. and Pantazis, C. (1997) *Breadline Britain in the 1990s*, Aldershot: Ashgate Publishing Ltd.

Gordon, D., Nandy, S., Pantazis, C., Pemberton, S.A. and Townsend, P. (2003) *Child poverty in the developing world*, Bristol: The Policy Press.

Halleröd, B. (1994) *A new approach to direct consensual measurement of poverty*, Sydney: Social Policy Research Centre, University of New South Wales.

Jones, G.A. (2005) 'Children and development: rights, globalisation and poverty', *Progress in Development Studies*, vol 5, pp 336-42.

Jones, N. (2005) *Mainstreaming children into national poverty strategies: A child-focused analysis of the Ethiopian Sustainable Development and Poverty Reduction Program (2002-05)*, London: Young Lives and Save the Children UK.

Jones, N. and Sumner, A. (2011) *Child poverty, evidence and policy: Mainstreaming children in international development*, Bristol: The Policy Press.

Kent, G. (1995) *Children in the international political economy*, Basingstoke: Macmillan.

Lyytikainen, K., Jones, N., Huttly, S. and Abramsky, T. (2006) *Childhood poverty, basic services and cumulative disadvantage: An international comparative analysis*, Young Lives Working Paper No 33, London: Young Lives and Save the Children, UK.

MacPherson, S. (1987) *Five hundred million children: Poverty and child welfare in the third world*, Brighton: Wheatsheaf Books.

Mack, J. and Lansley, S. (1985) *Poor Britain*, London: George Allen & Unwin Ltd.

Mehrotra, S. (2004) *Improving child wellbeing in developing countries: What do we know? What can be done?*, CHIP Report No 9, London: Childhood Poverty Research and Policy Centre (CHIP), Chronic Poverty Research Centre (CPRC), Save the Children and the Department for International Development (DFID).

Mehrotra, S. and Delamonica, E.E. (2002) 'Public spending for children: an empirical note', *Journal of International Development*, vol 14, pp 1105-16.

Mehrotra, S. and Jolly, R. (1997) *Development with a human face: Experiences in social achievement and economic growth*, Oxford: Clarendon Press.

Mendoza, R. (2009) *Aggregate shocks, poor households and children: Transmission channels and policy responses*, New York: United Nations Children's Fund.

Micklewright, J. and Stewart, K. (2001) 'Child well-being in the EU – and enlargement to the East', in K. Vleminckx and T.M. Smeeding (eds) *Child well-being, child poverty and child policy in modern nations*, Bristol: The Policy Press, pp 99-128.

Minujin, A. and Delamonica, E.E. (2003) 'Mind the gap! Widening child mortality disparities', *Journal of Human Development*, vol 4, pp 397-418.

Minujin, A., Delamonica, E.E., Davidziuk, A. and Gonzalez, E.D. (2006) 'The definition of child poverty: a discussion of concepts and measurements', *Environment and Urbanization*, vol 18, pp 481-500.

Minujin, A., Delamonica, E.E., Gonzalez, E.D. and Davidziuk, A. (2005) 'Children living in poverty: a review of child poverty definitions, measurements and policies', Paper for UNICEF conference *Children and poverty: Global context, local solutions*, New York: The New School, 25-27 April 2005.

Nandy, S. and Gordon, D. (2009) 'Children living in squalor: shelter, water and sanitation deprivations in developing countries', *Children, Youth and Environments*, vol 19, pp 202-28.

Noble, M., Ratcliffe, A. and Wright, G. (2004) *Conceptualizing, defining and measuring poverty in South Africa: An argument for a consensual approach*, Oxford: Centre for the Analysis of South African Social Policy, University of Oxford.

Noble, M., Wright, G. and Cluver, L. (2006) 'Developing a child-focused and multidimensional model of child poverty for South Africa', *Journal of Children and Poverty*, vol 12, pp 39-53.

OECD (Organisation for Economic Co-operation and Development) (2009) *Doing better for children*, Paris: OECD Publishing.

Redmond, G. (2008) 'Child poverty and child rights: edging towards a definition', *Journal of Children and Poverty*, vol 14, pp 63-82.

Richardson, D., Hoelscher, P. and Bradshaw, J. (2008) 'Child well-being in Central and Eastern European countries and the Commonwealth of Independent States', *Child Indicators Research*, vol 1, pp 211-50.

Roche, J.M. (2009) *Child poverty measurement: An assessment of methods and an application to Bangladesh: Multidimensional measures in six contexts*, Oxford: University of Oxford.

Roelen, K. and Gassmann, F. (2008) *Measuring child poverty and well-being: A literature review*, Maastricht: Maastricht University.

Seager, J. and de Wet, T. (2003) *Establishing large panel studies in developing countries: The importance of the 'Young Lives' pilot phase*, London: Save the Children.

Stewart, F. (1987) 'Monitoring and statistics for adjustment with a human face', in G. Cornia, R. Jolly and F. Stewart (eds) *Adjustment with a human face: Protecting the vulnerable and promoting growth*, Oxford: Clarendon Press, pp 257-72.

Townsend, P. (2007) *The right to social security and national development: Lessons from OECD experience for low-income countries*, Discussion Paper 18, Geneva: International Labour Organization.

Townsend, P. (2008) *The abolition of child poverty and the right to social security: A possible UN model for child benefit?*, London: London School of Economics and Political Science.

Townsend, P. (ed) (2009) *Building decent societies: Rethinking the role of social security in development*, Basingstoke: Palgrave Macmillan.

UN (United Nations) (1989) *Convention on the Rights of the Child*, New York: UN Department of Publications.

UNGA (United Nations General Assembly) (2006) *Promotion and protection of the rights of children, Report of the Third Committee*, New York: United Nations.

UNICEF (United Nations Children's Fund) (2000a) *A league table of child poverty in rich nations*, Innocenti Report Card No 1, Florence: UNICEF Innocenti Research Centre.

UNICEF (2000b) *Poverty reduction begins with children*, New York: UNICEF.

UNICEF (2004) *The State of the World's Children 2005: Childhood under threat*, New York: UNICEF.

UNICEF (2007) *UN General Assembly adopts powerful definition of child poverty*, New York: UNICEF (www.unicef.org/media/media_38003.html).

van Bueren, G. (2002) 'The minimum core obligations of states under Article 10(3) of the International Covenant on Economic, Social and Cultural Rights', in A. Chapman and R. Sage (eds) *Core obligations: Building a framework for economic, social and cultural rights*, Washington DC: American Association for the Advancement of Science – Human Rights Information and Documentation Systems, International, pp 149-60.

White, H., Leavy, J. and Masters, A. (2003) *Comparative perspectives on child poverty: A review of poverty measures*, Young Lives Working Paper No 1, Brighton: Institute of Development Studies, University of Sussex.

TWO

Child rights, child survival and child poverty: the debate

Simon Pemberton, David Gordon and Shailen Nandy[1]

Introduction

It is estimated that over eight million children under the age of five in developing countries die each year, mainly from preventable causes (Black et al, 2010). In approximately half of these deaths, malnutrition is a contributory cause (UNICEF, 2002). However, the World Health Organization (WHO) has argued that seven out of ten childhood deaths in such countries can be attributed to just five main causes or their combination. In addition to malnutrition (WHO, 2002), these causes are pneumonia, diarrhoea, measles and malaria. Many of these deaths could be prevented using readily available medical technologies at comparatively little cost (Jones et al, 2003; Tomkins, 2003). While medical interventions can, in principle, prevent most young children from dying early they cannot remove the underlying causes of poor health. The reasons why such large numbers of children die are linked directly to the severely deprived or absolutely poor living conditions in which 30% of the world's children live (UNDP, 1998; UNICEF, 2004). For example, almost a third of the world's children live in squalid housing conditions, with more than five people per room or with mud flooring. Over half a billion children (27%) have no toilet facilities whatsoever and over 400 million children (19%) are drinking from unsafe open water sources (for example, rivers, lakes, ponds) or have to walk so far to water that they cannot carry enough to meet minimum health requirements (Gordon et al, 2003; Nandy and Gordon, 2009). Thus, eliminating extreme poverty is the key to improving global child survival rates, particularly over the long term. This chapter seeks not to address the policies required to end extreme poverty, as it is our contention that the scientific knowledge required to achieve this is widely documented (Gordon, 2002). Instead, attention is focused on the potential of human rights frameworks to create mechanisms of accountability that will hopefully effect meaningful change (Pemberton et al, 2007).

History bears witness to the potential of such an approach. Over the course of the 20th century, most advanced industrial societies developed models of social citizenship, a set of social rights (rights to healthcare, education, social security and so on) that guaranteed a minimum standard of living. Social rights came to be realised, albeit often imperfectly, in the development of complex social security and healthcare systems, as well as a range of social services. Ultimately, social citizenship ensured that the economic growth experienced following the Second World War in many advanced nation states served to build better societies that significantly advanced the fulfilment of universal human needs. However, the emergence of the neoliberal 'Washington Consensus' towards the end of the 20th century articulated models of citizenship that rejected social rights in favour of civil and political rights. While the Consensus has served to persuade some advanced nation states to retrench social programmes, the impact of these ideas has been more severely felt in developing nation states who, through the structural adjustment loans and stabilisation programmes of the World Bank and the International Monetary Fund (IMF), have been required to abandon 'expensive' social rights that were felt to hinder the economic growth model and 'trickle-down' anti-poverty policies propounded by these organisations (Mehrotra and Jolly, 1997; Townsend and Gordon, 2002). Despite the rhetoric of the Consensus, advanced industrial nations, some of which have actively promoted this position, continue to witness high levels of social spending; in fact many of these states' social spending has increased during the current phase of globalisation (Townsend, 2009). Most OECD (Organisation for Economic Co-operation and Development) countries spend around 20% of gross domestic product (GDP) on public services and cash benefits; in most low-income countries the figure is less than 5% (Townsend, 2009). The rhetoric of neoliberalism for advanced nation states may indeed be persuasive to some, but the reality of relinquishing social rights is another matter, an often politically unpalatable one at that, exactly because of the devastating social harms that result when these rights are violated. Given this context, Townsend (2009, p 31) asserts: 'the restoration of the social contract is becoming urgent ... that contract must take a new form but one that invokes the institutions that have served many countries so well in the past.' This chapter seeks to contribute to the task of articulating a new social contract, through an examination of the utility and limitations of the human rights approach to child poverty.

Outlining the case for a human rights approach to child poverty

This section considers the value of a human rights approach to the reduction of child poverty. In particular, it examines the extent to which a human rights approach offers a framework to increase accountability for the policies that perpetuate impoverishment. In doing so, it also explores the ways that a human rights framework can increase societal understanding of poverty and serve to include, within policy making, the voices of those who endure poverty.

First, human rights frameworks provide universally agreed standards that are clearly violated by the existence of child poverty, as well as values that should inform policy interventions, such as models of social protection (see Townsend, 2009). However, arguments exist that doubt whether rights, as formally presented in these conventions, are in fact genuinely universal (Kallen, 2004). The critiques of cultural relativism and Asian values have suggested that human rights are 'Western' in orientation and content and, consequently, promote liberal/individualist social preferences over more 'collective' forms of organisation. While it is important for any human rights approach to be sensitive to these critiques and to acknowledge the limitations of such a framework, we support Sen (1999) and Doyal and Gough's (1991) rebuttal of both the post-modernist and Asian values culturally relativist standpoint. Moreover, it remains a fact that every country in the world (the 193 United Nations [UN] member states) has signed the Convention on the Rights of the Child (UNCRC) and only two countries are yet to ratify the UNCRC – Somalia and the US. Given that there is near-unanimous consensus on the objectives and values contained in the UNCRC, it would appear that negotiated moves towards the realisation of the agreed goals are feasible.

Second, the human rights approach establishes the relationship between those living in extreme poverty and the nation state and therefore offers a mechanism to challenge unequal power relationships. As Mary Robinson (2002) (former UN High Commissioner for Human Rights) in her speech to the 2002 World Summit on Sustainable Development in Johannesburg argued, human rights conventions are of fundamental importance because they place universal obligations on states:

> ... a human rights approach adds value because it provides a normative framework of obligations that has the legal power to render governments accountable.

When viewed in this way, poverty is 'neither natural nor inevitable but becomes something done to people, for whom certain actors bear responsibility' (Gready, 2008, p 742). Thus, what rights-based approaches to poverty offer which 'needs'-based approaches cannot, are a relational dimension that necessarily imposes a set of responsibilities on state actors and parties (CARE, 2004). Such obligations should be interpreted in their broadest sense. The Committee on the Rights of the Child (CRC) (General Comment No 5) specifies that the realisation of child rights are the responsibility of all nation states, be it within their jurisdiction or through international cooperation. Social problems, such as child poverty, are the product of an increasingly interconnected world that necessitates analyses that move beyond individual nation states to encompass global structures and interests. Indeed, there are numerous accounts that relate the living standards currently enjoyed in the 'Global North' directly to the exploitation and impoverishment of the 'Global South' (see, for example, Chossudovsky, 1997). Therefore, a 'global citizenship' that transcends the boundaries of nation states, placing clear obligations on the states of the 'Global North' to intervene to mitigate the deleterious aspects of economic globalisation, is already implicit in human rights declarations (Lister, 1998; Fraser, 2005).

Third, any comprehensive understanding of the root causes of poverty cannot ignore the legal structures that create and perpetuate income and wealth imbalances within society (Williams, 2003). One facet of the human rights approach is the challenge it offers to these legal structures. Primarily, this challenge arises through the obligations human rights frameworks place on nation states of the 'Global North' for the contexts that perpetuate poverty. This is an important counter-argument to the notion that globalisation has undermined the capacity of nation states to respond to social problems within and beyond their own boundaries. On the contrary, as Held (2000) suggests, OECD countries, rather than being weakened by the rise of transnational corporations (TNCs), have in fact become more powerful. Whether or not this is indeed the case, it remains that globalisation should not be considered to be a unidirectional phenomenon, where states purely function to attract and to accommodate global capital (Hall, 1998). Powerful nation states have played a fundamental role in shaping the current form of global markets (Weiss, 1997; Hall, 1998). Thus, TNCs rely on the political and legal systems of states – in particular, the national and supranational systems promoted by the 'North' – to create and maintain a global apparatus of wealth accumulation. It is these very structures that have facilitated the growth of TNCs over the past 30 years. Without the supranational frameworks of the IMF, World Bank, the General Agreement on Tariffs and Trade (GATT) and World Trade Organization (WTO), corporations would not have been able to operate in developing countries with the impunity they have to date (Chossudovsky, 1997; Townsend, 2002). While we acknowledge that human rights conventions contain rights which support such structures, particularly through the right to property, they also contain rights that offer the potential to realise the universal fulfilment of human needs. It is the latter that places obligations on governments to make reference to considerations that are wider than the compulsions of wealth accumulation. Moreover, as a legal discourse, human rights frameworks provide a vehicle to articulate challenges to those legal debates (TRIPS [trade-related aspects of intellectual property rights], trusts, patents, tax avoidance etc), which underpin the unequal process of wealth accumulation.

Fourth, the language of rights offers the potential to orientate current policy debates in positive directions. Primarily, the use of rights-based language shifts the focus within these debates from the personal failures of the 'poor' to a focus on the failures of macroeconomic structures and policies implemented by nation states and international bodies (WTO, World Bank, IMF, etc). Given this shift of focus, child poverty should no longer be considered by policy makers as a 'social problem' but as a 'violation of rights' that nation states have a legal obligation to remedy (Chinkin, 2001). Again, the history of poverty reduction in advanced industrial economies teaches this lesson. For example, in the UK, the development of social security systems to tackle poverty were premised on a notion of social citizenship that rejected the 19th Century moralism of the 'deserving/undeserving poor' in favour of universal entitlement to a minimum standard of living. As Lister (2004, p 159) suggests, 'even in the absence of such entitlements', human rights can provide a powerful 'symbolic rhetorical force' that prompts sharp political discussion. Moreover, a human rights framework offers a voice within such discussions because it emphasises the value of 'participation', which is not 'dependent on the whim of a benevolent outsider but rooted in institutions and procedures' (Uvin, 2007, p 603). Therefore it offers an opportunity to promote anti-poverty policies based on experiential as well as expert knowledge, thus serving to increase the chances of these policies' success.

Finally, a human rights framework facilitates definitions of poverty that are multidimensional. Clear synergies exist between the wide range of rights within conventions (to healthcare, education, food, etc) and the definition of absolute poverty adopted by 117 countries at the World Summit for Social Development in Copenhagen in 1995, as 'a condition characterised by severe deprivation of basic human needs, including food, safe drinking water, sanitation facilities, health, shelter, education and information.'[2] A human rights approach to measuring poverty, particularly child poverty, requires that age and gender-appropriate indicators are used, as children have rights which are independent and co-equal to those of adults. Moreover, such an approach serves to challenge traditional measures of poverty based on household income (like the World Bank's US$1 per day PPP [purchasing power parity] measure) are inadequate for measuring child poverty as they fail to estimate:

- the cash income children receive;
- the share of income spent solely on the child;
- the 'income' in kind children receive privately and from public services and facilities;
- the share children can be presumed to have of the remaining household resources that are spent for the joint benefit of all members of the household.

In addition, the World Bank's (1990, 2000) consumption-based poverty definition in terms of *the expenditure necessary to buy a minimum standard of nutrition* is inappropriate for measuring child poverty, particularly for young children who have low food requirements but numerous additional basic needs that require expenditure. Many academic commentators have severely criticised the World Bank's US$1 per day poverty threshold for not being an adequate definition of an adult's needs in developing countries (for example, CROP, 2001). Therefore, setting an arbitrary child poverty income threshold is unjustifiable and would likely lead to incorrect policy conclusions – a human rights approach is necessary to highlight these problems.

Child poverty: practical obstacles to the realisation of child rights

The previous section outlined the benefits associated with a human rights approach to child poverty. Here we consider some of the practical limitations to this framework. The Office of the High Commissioner for Human Rights (OHCHR) (2004, p 16) has suggested that a human rights-based approach to poverty reduction offers a system of accountability through the following mechanisms: the judiciary (through public law and judicial review of domestic legislation according to declaration commitments); quasi-judicial bodies (through special rapporteurs, human rights treaty bodies); administrative bodies (through the publication and scrutiny of human rights audits); and formal political processes (through parliamentary review). An obvious criticism of this model of accountability relates to the faith placed in formal modes of redress and scrutiny. Writers such as Ferraz (2008, p 603) doubt the extent to which social change may be engendered through 'judicial activism'. Instead, he argues 'institutions and initiatives that have had a proven significant and lasting impact on the predicament of the poor, such as universal healthcare in most Western European countries, have come about mostly through political struggles...' (Ferraz, 2008, p 603). These struggles have not just taken place within the formal political sphere, and therefore we would add a fifth mechanism, one which acknowledges informal political activity within civil society and reflects the importance of trades unions, non-governmental organisations (NGOs) and grassroots campaigns in realising rights. Drawing on this model of accountability, we consider the issues of 'progressive realisation' and 'justiciability' as potential obstacles to be negotiated in the process of holding nation states to account for the persistence of child poverty.

A consistent criticism of the human rights approach to poverty alleviation has been the extent to which social rights can be developed into effective legal mechanisms to render nation states accountable. It has long been argued that pre-legal 'moral' claims contained in human rights conventions are not easily transferred into legal systems. The difficulty posed by translating ambiguous or imprecisely defined rights into concrete legal decisions has meant that domestic courts have effectively ignored many rights contained in international conventions. It would appear that many states are prepared to place civil and political rights in the 'justiciable' section of their constitution while relegating economic, social and cultural rights to the realm of directive principles. The views of Ferraz (2008, p 602) are representative of those arguments that question the possibility of incorporating social rights into 'justiciable' legal mechanisms:

> The nub of the problem ... is this: given that the definition of the state's concrete duties arising from social and economic rights is dependent on scarce resources and, as a consequence, on how these resources are and ought to be raised and distributed by the state, it involves intractable empirical and normative issues which are much more complex and controversial than those involved in most civil and political rights.

Like many commentators, Ferraz presents the questions that poverty raises of any given society as being 'intractable'. Implicit within this position is an assumption that the judiciary would be required to make decisions that would fundamentally reorganise societies in order to eradicate child poverty. On the contrary, the reallocation of resources required to eradicate absolute child poverty, as well as relative child poverty, are relatively small. It is difficult to believe that those in the 'Global North', whether the transfers occurred via a 'Tobin tax' or domestic taxation systems, would even notice that these transfers had occurred. For example, the UN Development Programme (UNDP) (1997) estimated it would cost the equivalent of US$50 billion a year, for 10 years, to provide every person on the planet with basic social services (that is, basic healthcare, nutrition, education, adequate sanitation, clean water, etc). This is a lot of money but not when compared to what is spent annually on pizza in the US (US$30 billion a year) or pet food (US$12 billion) (Gordon, 2004). In rich countries, the economic costs of *not* eradicating child poverty are estimated to be greater than the cost of actually doing it, that is, in the long term it is cheaper to eradicate child poverty – its eradication would result in a net economic gain to the exchequer and society (Holzer et al, 2007; Blanden et al, 2008; Bramley and Watkins, 2008; Laurie, 2008).

Furthermore, as van Bueren (1999) argues, domestic courts appear adept at making complex decisions in cases relating to civil and political rights, as witnessed recently in the UK in debates on national security versus the rights of terrorist suspects. However, they have generally avoided the issues of poverty and the non-fulfilment of people's economic and social rights for reasons of 'complexity'. Admittedly, domestic courts have not been helped by the lack of international jurisprudence and effective international law. Hence van Bueren (1999) suggests that both domestic and international judiciaries follow the inventive and progressive approaches of treaty committees and special rapporteurs when addressing the question of justiciability. In the context of the UNCRC, and the economic, social and cultural rights it contains, domestic and international courts could draw inspiration from the following approaches. The UN Committee for Economic, Social and Cultural Rights (UNCESCR), in its General Comment No 3, is clear: a state where a 'significant number of individuals are deprived of essential foodstuffs, primary healthcare, of basic shelter and housing, or of the most basic forms of education is, prima facie, failing to discharge its obligations under the covenant'. These guidelines recommend that any assessment as to whether a state has discharged its 'minimum core obligations' must consider whether the state has used the 'maximum' of its 'available resources'. The CRC General Comment No 5 states that Article 4 of the Convention, 'with regard to economic, social and cultural rights, State Parties shall undertake such measures to the maximum extent of their available resources', should be seen as 'complementary' to UNCESCR General Comment No 3. Consequently, the CRC has, on a number of occasions, refused to accept the 'non-affordability' claims made in the progress reports of states. For instance, Indonesia and Egypt have been asked to justify their failure to make significant progress in implementing the UNCRC in light of their high expenditure on defence budgets (see van Bueren, 1999).

Moreover, nation states, such as India, South Africa and Finland, have placed economic and social rights into their constitutions. These rights are removed from the political sphere where they remain contested and placed into the legal sphere (Campbell, 2003). Some commentators argue that the advantage of this shift is that courts and not politicians set minimum welfare standards – through reviews of government budgets, vetoing legislation that is likely to increase rather than reduce poverty, and so on. For example, in South Africa, a number of landmark cases denote the role of judicial activism in setting such standards. In the Grootboom case, the South African Constitutional Court recognised the rights of 900 people evicted from an informal settlement to adequate housing, which the state was required to address through 'a comprehensive and co-ordinated programme progressively to realise the right' (cited in Donald and Mottershaw, 2009, p 30). While some writers have criticised the vague content of the ruling (see Bilchitz, 2007), it did provide remedial basic services for the community affected and led to a national programme of low-cost housing (Donald and Mottershaw, 2009). This prompted Sunstein (2001, p 123) to exhort 'the approach of the constitutional court serves as a powerful rejoinder to those who contended that socio-economic rights do not belong in a constitution.' The obvious limitation of enforcing rights through the courts is the onus it places on individuals from marginalised groups to bring cases – this is reliant on individual access to funding and representation. Those who have brought such actions are usually supported by the funds and expertise of NGOs, who provide invaluable assistance.

A related issue that necessarily follows from 'justiciability' is that of 'progressive realisation'. While human rights conventions like the UNCRC place clear obligations on nation states to work towards the eradication of poverty, there is not an expectation that this will be achieved immediately. Therefore, many economic and social rights contained in the UNCRC are required to be realised progressively.

Naturally these precise duties will vary according to the nation state involved and the resources available to them. Few nation states would object to the notion of 'progressive realisation' although obtaining their agreement to the milestones that they should reach and deadlines by which they should do so has proved controversial. This is a matter that domestic judiciaries have tended to avoid, although there are notable exceptions. Again, in South Africa, following the Grootboom case, where the court failed to set a clear timetable for realisation and thus relinquished oversight of this process, subsequent cases have seen direct judicial scrutiny of state performance towards specified milestones (Donald and Mottershaw, 2009). This is clearly desirable otherwise, as Bilchitz (2007) observes, further inaction of government could only be challenged by further litigation. Another example of active judicial scrutiny is provided by the Colombian Constitutional Court in a judgment relating to the rights of displaced persons, which set a clear 'time bound plan' whereby the state was ordered to reallocate budgetary resources within 54 days (Tomasevski, 2005, p 3). We share Tomasevski's (2005, p 3) assessment of the importance of such cases in highlighting '... the core purpose of enforcement: halting and reversing governmental practice of denial of basic rights to a large, dispersed, impoverished and politically voiceless population'.

Despite these encouraging developments, progressive realisation necessarily entails a discussion of prioritisation, which has caused considerable controversy and dispute within the human rights community. For many proponents, the fact that rights are indivisible militates against prioritisation. The United Nations Children's Fund (UNICEF), for example, under Carol Bellamy, adopted a position in which all the rights in the UNCRC were regarded as of equal importance and countries were obligated to realise these rights progressively, that is, that steps must be taken to implement all children's rights as no rights were unimportant. No priorities were set as to which rights should be implemented first. However, some rights are clearly more important than others and/or contingent on others. Therefore, while UNICEF recognises that children living in poverty are more likely to experience non-fulfilment of other rights (UNICEF, 2004), the right to vote is not much use to a child who has died in infancy as a result of a lack of medical care due to poverty. There is a clear need to prioritise the realisation of rights in policy so that action can be divided into successive stages according to the degree of severity of transgression and available resources. Ensuring the survival of children would provide a good basis for this prioritisation but, to be effective, actions need to tackle both the symptoms and the underlying causes.

Our position would appear to align with the OHCHR (2004, pp 24–5) principles of prioritisation, that:

- 'rights can still be given priority at different stages of progressive realisation on practical grounds';
- 'no right can be deliberately allowed to suffer';
- 'the international human rights system specifies some core obligations that require States to ensure, with immediate effect, certain minimum levels of enjoyment of various human rights.'

As the latter principle suggests, the minimum core obligations as specified by the UNCESCR lend particular credence to the prioritisation of rights. It is clear that the persistence of absolute poverty, according to these core obligations, compels nation states to prioritise the rights violated by such deprivation while observing the principles outlined by the OHCHR.

To summarise, this section has sought to outline a set of guidelines and case examples that offer to economic, social and cultural rights a greater determinacy and certainty than exists in the conventions themselves. These assist the further development of both domestic and international jurisprudence as well as equip social movements with the tools necessary to increase the likelihood of timelier implementation.

Relationship between child poverty and child rights: methodological issues

Social scientists have a specific role to play in advancing political accountability for failing socioeconomic policies and the realisation of human rights. We suggest that an important element of this role is the conduct of objective 'audits' that describe the extent and nature of rights violations caused by deprivation. If it can be shown that universally agreed standards of basic human needs remain unmet as a result of the present form of economic and social organisation, then this can only serve to increase the pressure for reform. It should be noted that important work exists that has subjected budgetary spending to human rights scrutiny in order to probe the commitments of states to 'progressive realisation' of these rights. We do not focus on such an approach here because of the inevitable limitations to this methodology. As Donald and Mottershaw (2009, p 22) highlight, budgetary approaches are essentially descriptive in nature and fail to 'establish definitive causal links between economic policies and the degree of substantive enjoyment of economic and social rights'. With this in mind we seek to provide audits that can be directly related to their policy context. The following section outlines how such an audit can be constructed by drawing on the articles of the UNCRC and an existing deprivation index. In doing so, we consider three methodological issues that arise from this exercise.

First, a significant methodological problem is that the UNCRC does not contain a specific right to freedom from poverty (Mbonda, 2004). Hence, to relate rights to the measurement of poverty, a selection process is required to match the rights contained in the UNCRC to the severe deprivations of basic human need that characterise poverty and cause ill health. As discussed above, the clustering of rights is not to suggest that rights are divisible in any ultimate or 'perfect' sense; however, for practical purposes, if the constituent elements of these conventions are to be used to alleviate specific social problems, such as child poverty, as well as offer policy guidance, these methodological exercises are entirely necessary.

Second, some rights contain clearer obligations than others. Therefore, it can make assessment of state performance difficult. Drawing a distinction between 'perfect' and 'imperfect' duties acknowledges that some rights are more precisely defined than others and that this distinction helps to clarify the fact that the fulfilment of certain rights is easier to measure than others. For example, crossing the threshold from life to death is easier to determine than access to healthcare or education. In some cases, rights may appear to be normative: a state either adheres to them or it does not and, consequently, whatever measurement results will be binary in nature. Necessarily, the approach has to be different when attempting to measure a phenomenon such as health that is often considered to be part of a continuum ranging from 'good health' to 'poor health' (Gordon, 2002). Similarly, from a social science perspective, fulfilment of rights can also be considered to be a continuum ranging from complete fulfilment to extreme violation. However, courts make judgments on individual cases on the correct threshold level at which to find that rights have been violated or fulfilled (see Figure 2.1).

Figure 2.1: Continuum of rights

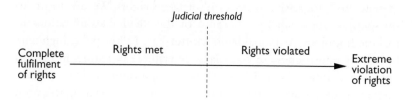

30

Unfortunately, at present, there is little international or domestic case law that would allow the location of this 'judicial' threshold with respect to most social, economic and cultural rights, such as the right to healthcare, to be determined. However, as indicated in the discussion of the UNCESCR core minimum obligations above, it would appear reasonable to assume that basic needs which remain unfulfilled (shelter, health, food etc) due to the existence of individuals in absolute poverty would represent a prima facie violation of human rights. We have proceeded on this basis.

A final issue relates to the fit between rights and indicators. As demonstrated, some rights are more prescriptive than others. The consequence for social scientists when trying to operationalise indicators of human rights fulfilment and relating them to social phenomena is that some rights and their corresponding indicators provide a better match than others. Hence, those rights that confer 'perfect' duties – due to their specificity – are more likely to find a 'direct' match to an existing social indicator (for example, girls not being allowed to attend school). We suggest that the relationship between rights and indicators should also be viewed as a continuum. Thus, associations of rights and indicators can range from those gathered at the 'perfect/direct' point through to those at the 'imperfect/indirect' point.

The 'perfect/direct' point is characterised by a right that has a prescriptive quality and an indicator that is able to quantify the essence of the duty. This category requires a minimal level of interpretation. An example of a rights/indicator closest to the 'perfect/direct' point is education. Article 28 of the UNCRC establishes 'the right of the child to education' and progresses to specify 'primary education compulsory and available free to all' and 'the development of different forms of secondary education, make them available and accessible to every child'. An indicator of the severe deprivation of the right to education might therefore be reflected by the number or proportion of children who are 'unable to attend primary or secondary education'.

It is of little surprise then that, for the more ambiguous articles of the UNCRC, indicators become more indirect. The 'imperfect/indirect' nature of such indicators for rights makes the data difficult to interpret. For instance, Article 24(1) talks of securing the right through facilities 'for the treatment of illness and rehabilitation of health' and, similarly, Article 24(2)(c) describes the need to 'combat disease and malnutrition … within the framework of healthcare, through … the application of readily available technology'. In order to provide a more comprehensive picture of rights fulfilment in the case of the 'imperfect/indirect' end of the continuum, clusters of indicators are required to cover all possible interpretations of these rights.

Table 2.1 demonstrates the relationship between indicators of severe deprivation and the infringement of specific economic and social rights. These rights are matched with indicators that demonstrate the levels of their non-fulfilment. Alongside these indicators, we have designated the nature of the fit between right/indicator; naturally those rights with indirect indicators must be treated with greater care when drawing conclusions from these results. The table contains information from two countries, India and Nigeria, and presents estimates of the numbers of children whose rights, according to the CRC, were infringed by poverty in 2005. Such estimates could be made periodically to demonstrate progress (or regress) in the meeting of child rights around the world.

The 'audit' outlined above gives a very specific measure of rights fulfilment. This must be further developed to build a more complex picture. As Green (2001) suggests, methodologies designed to capture the reality of rights fulfilment must provide 'information pyramids' to reflect the multifaceted nature of rights and the phenomena to which they relate. Therefore, we would encourage an approach that moves beyond the statistical indicators provided in this audit to consider other layers that provide important contextual information. An important aspect of such an exercise would be to provide analyses that promote an understanding of the violations detailed in the audit. Thus, a case study approach that describes the domestic policy context of these violations and, in turn, relates policy formulation of a nation state to the processes of the international policy-making and global economic structures, would provide a starting point for important public debate. Indeed, such an exercise has formed part of UNICEF's ongoing Global Study of Child Poverty and Disparities in over 50 countries around the world.

Conclusion

In creating the basis of a rights audit, it is not our intention to label certain countries as particularly culpable human rights abusers. Rather, such an exercise demonstrates the gravity of the plight of many of the world's children and, more importantly, that the deprivations these children experience are violations of their rights according to the UNCRC. Given the obligations the UNCRC places on all nation states, as stipulated by the CRC (General Comment No 5) which specifies the collective responsibility for the realisation of child rights, be it within a state's jurisdiction or through international cooperation, such

Table 2.1: The relationship between indicators of severe deprivation and rights contained in UN CRC

Deprivation	Severe deprivation	Indicators	Article/right infringed	Rights/indicators	India (2005) % children deprived/ (number)	Nigeria (2005) % children deprived/ (number)
Food	Malnutrition	Severe anthropometric failure in children under five (severe stunting, underweight, or wasting)	24(2)(c) Health	Imperfect/ indirect	27% (25,000,000)	24% (5,800,000)
Safe drinking water		Long walk to water (>200 metres) which is occasionally polluted (unsafe source) >30 minutes to water or surface water	24(2)(e) Health	Imperfect/ indirect	7% (30,400,000)	37% (26,300,000)
Sanitation facilities		No sanitation facilities in or near dwelling	No sanitation facilities	24(2)(c) Health	Imperfect/ indirect	62% (272,000,000)	28% (20,000,000)
Health		Health facilities more than one hour's travel away. No immunisation against diseases	No vaccinations or untreated diarrhoea	24(1)/(2)(c) Health	Imperfect/ indirect	13% (57,400,000)	47% (33,600,000)
Shelter		No facilities, non-permanent building, no privacy, no flooring, one or two rooms, five+ per room	Mud flooring or over five people per room (severe overcrowding)	27(3) Standard of living	Imperfect/ indirect	68% (300,200,000)	50% (35,600,000)
Education		Unable to attend primary or secondary education	Child of school age (7-18 years) and not in school or not received any education	28(1)(a)/(b) Education	Perfect/ direct	13% (34,400,000)	30% (11,400,000)
Information		No access to radio, television or books or newspaper	Combination of (a) Information access – if mother listened to radio in last week or read a newspaper or watched television; (b) Information possession – of a television or radio	13/17 Information	Perfect/ direct	14% (61,300,000)	18% (12,900,000)

exercises also ask questions of developed nations. As we have argued, human rights approaches provide important tools in a globalising world, from which a 'new social contract' and a 'global citizenship' may be articulated, to assert the obligations of powerful nation states towards those who suffer as a result of our wealth accumulation. For those convinced that the solution to eradicating absolute poverty for the developing world lies solely with economic growth, the history of struggles to realise more comprehensive forms of social citizenship in advanced nation states strongly suggests otherwise.

Notes

[1] The research for this chapter was undertaken with and inspired by our friend and colleague Peter Townsend, who died in the summer of 2009.

[2] It should also be noted that the definition of child poverty agreed by the UN General Assembly in December 2006 (mentioned in chapter one) highlights the importance of the relationship between rights and poverty.

References

Bilchitz, D. (2007) *Poverty and fundamental rights: The justification and enforcement of socio-economic rights*, Oxford: Oxford University Press.

Black, R.E., Cousens, S., Johnson, H.L., Lawn, J.E., Rudan, I., Bassani, D.G., Jha, P., Campbell, H., Fischer Walker, C., Cibulskis, R., Eisele, T., Liu, L. and Mathers, C. (2010) 'Global, regional, and national causes of child mortality in 2008: a systematic analysis', *The Lancet*, vol 375, no 9730, pp 1969–87.

Blanden, J., Hansen, K. and Machin, S. (2008) *The GDP costs of the lost earning potential of adults who grew up in poverty*, York: Joseph Rowntree Foundation.

Bramley, G. and Watkins, D. (2008) *The public service costs of child poverty*, York: Joseph Rowntree Foundation.

Campbell, T. (2003) 'Poverty is a violation of human rights: inhumanity or injustice?', in UNESCO (United Nations Educational, Scientific and Cultural Organization) (ed) *Ethical and human right dimensions of poverty: Towards a new paradigm in the fight against poverty*, Sao Paolo: UNESCO.

CARE (2004) *No rights, no justice, more war: The story of RBA in CARE Sierra Leone*, London: CARE International.

Chinkin, C. (2001) 'The United Nations decade for the elimination of poverty: what role for international law?', *Current Legal Problems*, vol 54, pp 553-89.

Chossudovsky, M. (1997) *The globalisation of poverty: Impacts of IMF and World Bank reforms*, Goa: Other India Press.

CROP (Comparative Research Programme on Poverty) (2001) *A critical review of the World Bank report: World Development Report 2000/2001. Attacking poverty*, Bergen: CROP (www.crop.org/publications/files/report/Comments_to_WDR2001_2002_ny.pdf).

Donald, A. and Mottershaw, E. (2009) *Poverty, inequality and human rights: Do rights make a difference?*, York: Joseph Rowntree Foundation.

Doyal, L. and Gough, I. (1991) *A theory of human need*, London: Macmillan.

Ferraz, O. (2008) 'Poverty and human rights', *Oxford Journal of Legal Studies*, vol 28, no 3, pp 585-603.

Fraser, N. (2005) 'Reframing justice in a globalizing world', *New Left Review*, vol 36, pp 69-88.

Gordon, D. (2002) 'The international measurement of poverty and anti-poverty policies', in P. Townsend and D. Gordon (eds) *World poverty: New policies to defeat an old enemy*, Bristol: The Policy Press, pp 53-80.

Gordon, D. (2004) 'Poverty, death and disease', in P. Hillyard, C. Pantazis, S. Tombs and D. Gordon (eds) *Beyond criminology: Taking harm seriously*, London: Pluto, pp 251-66.

Gordon, D., Nandy, S., Pantazis, C., Pemberton, S. and Townsend, P. (2003) *Child poverty in the developing world*, Bristol: The Policy Press.

Gready, P. (2008) 'Rights based approaches to development: what is the value added?', *Development in Practice*, vol 18, no 6, pp 735-47.

Green, M. (2001) 'What we talk about when we talk about indicators: current approaches to human rights measurement', *Human Rights Quarterly*, vol 23, pp 1062-97.

Hall, S. (1998) 'The great moving nowhere show', *Marxism Today*, Nov/Dec, pp 9-14.

Held, D. (2000) 'Regulating Globalisation?'. International Journal of Sociology. 15 (2) 394-408.

Holzer, H., Schanzenbach, D., Duncan, G. and Ludwig, J. (2007) *The economic cost of poverty in the United States: Subsequent effects of children growing up poor*, Washington, DC: Center for American Progress.

Jones, G., Steketee, R.W., Black, R.E., Bhutta, Z.A., Morris, S.S. and the Bellagio Child Survival Study Group (2003) 'How many child deaths can we prevent this year?', *The Lancet*, vol 362, pp 65-71.

Kallen, E. (2004) *Social inequality and social injustice: A human rights perspective*, New York: Palgrave.

Laurie, N. (2008) *The cost of poverty: An analysis of the economic cost of poverty in Ontario*, Toronto: Ontario Association of Food Banks (OAFB).

Lister, R. (1998) 'New conceptions of citizenship', in N. Ellison and C. Pierson (eds) *Developments in British social policy*, Basingstoke: Palgrave, pp 46-60.

Lister, R. (2004) *Poverty*, Cambridge: Polity Press.

Mbonda, E. (2004) 'Poverty as a violation of human rights: towards a right to non poverty', *International Social Science Journal*, vol 56, pp 277-88.

Mehrotra, S. and Jolly, R. (eds) (1997) *Development with a human face: Experiences in social achievement and economic growth*, Oxford: Oxford University Press.

Nandy, S. and Gordon, D. (2009) 'Children living in squalor: shelter, water and sanitation deprivations in developing countries', *Children, Youth and Environments*, vol 19, no 2, pp 202-28.

OHCHR (Office of the High Commissioner for Human Rights) (2004) *Human rights and poverty reduction: A conceptual framework*, Geneva: OHCHR.

Pemberton, S., Gordon, D., Nandy, S., Pantazis, C. and Townsend, P. (2007) 'Child rights and child poverty: can the international framework of children's rights be used to improve child survival rates?', *PLoS Medicine*, vol 4, no 10, e307.

Robinson, M. (2002) Speech at the World Summit for Sustainable Development, Plenary Session. World Summit for Sustainable Development, Johannesburg, South Africa, 1st September 2002.

Sen, A. (1999) *Development as freedom*, Oxford: Oxford University Press.

Sunstein, C. (2001) *Social and economic rights? Lessons from South Africa*, Public Law Working Paper No 12, Chicago, IL: University of Chicago.

Tomasevski, K. (2005) *Strengthening pro-poor law: Legal enforcement of economic and social rights*, London: Overseas Development Institute.

Tomkins, A. (2003) 'Reducing infant mortality in poor countries by 2015 – the need for critical appraisal of intervention-effectiveness', *Transactions of the Royal Society of Tropical Medicine and Hygiene*, vol 97, no 1, pp 16-17.

Townsend, P. (2002) 'Poverty, social exclusion and social polarisation: the need to construct an international welfare state', in P. Townsend and D. Gordon (eds) *World poverty: New policies to defeat an old enemy*, Bristol: The Policy Press, pp 3-24.

Townsend, P. (2009) 'Social security and human rights', in P. Townsend (ed) *Building decent societies. Rethinking the role of social security in state building*, London: International Labour Organization/Palgrave Macmillan, pp 29-59.

Townsend, P. and Gordon, D. (eds) (2002) *World poverty: New policies to defeat an old enemy*, Bristol: The Policy Press.

UNDP (United Nations Development Programme) (1997) *Human Development Report 1997*, Oxford: Oxford University Press.

UNDP (1998) *Human Development Report 1998: Consumption for human development*, New York: UNDP.

UNGA (United Nations General Assembly) (2006) *Promotion and protection of the rights of children, Report of the Third Committee*, New York: United Nations.

UNICEF (United Nations Children's Fund) (2002) *The State of the World's Children 2002: The rate of progress*, New York: UNICEF.

UNICEF (2004) *The State of the World's Children 2005: Childhood under threat*, New York: UNICEF.

Uvin, P. (2007) 'From the right to development to the rights-based approach: how "human rights" entered development', *Development in Practice*, vol 17, no 4-5, pp 597-606.

van Bueren, C. (1999) 'Combating child poverty: human rights approaches', *Human Rights Quarterly*, vol 21, pp 680-706.

Weiss, L. (1997) 'Globalisation and the myth of the powerless state', *New Left Review*, vol 225, pp 3-27.

WHO (World Health Organization) (2002) *The World Health Report 2002: Reducing risks, promoting healthy life*, Geneva: WHO.

Williams, L. (2003) 'Introduction', in L. Williams, A. Kjonstad and P. Robson (eds) *Law and poverty: The legal system and poverty reduction*, London: Zed, pp 1-7.

World Bank (1990) *World Development Report 1990: Poverty*, Washington, DC: World Bank.

World Bank (2000) *World Development Report, 2000/2001: Attacking poverty*, Washington, DC: World Bank.

THREE

Equity begins with children

Jan Vandemoortele

More than 100 years ago, Henry George – a colourful economist who ran for mayor of New York and whose brainchild is the famous board game Monopoly – noted that 'the association of poverty with progress is the great enigma of our times' (George, 1882). And so it remains today.

The recent stretch of globalisation has produced unprecedented prosperity and spectacular technological progress – not unlike that in the days of Henry George in the late 19th century. Yet, too much of the progress is bypassing the people who are most in need of it; so much so that an unacceptable high number of children continue to live in abject poverty.

Growth-mediated development

The global discourse on human development considers economic growth as the prime force for reducing poverty. The lack of growth is invariably seen as the main cause of poverty. Progress in human well-being is seen as the result of increased wealth and income. So, according to that outlook, almost everything is 'growth-mediated'.

But after a decade of rapid economic growth in India, for instance, an excessive proportion of children continue to suffer from malnutrition. *The Economist* (2010) notes, 'Since 1991 [India's] GDP [gross domestic product] has more than doubled, while malnutrition has decreased by only a few percentage points.' The usual response to such observations is that rapid growth has lifted hundreds of millions of people out of poverty in China and elsewhere. Yet that argument is not based on direct observation but on tautological reasoning. By defining poverty in terms of income alone and by using the international poverty line US$1.25/day as the metric, it is only normal to find a near-perfect correlation between growth and poverty. Unfortunately, that correlation is by and large a fiction of the mind.

All indicators are imperfect but some are more imperfect than others. The poverty indicator based on the US$1.25/day poverty line is particularly problematic. Fundamental criticism has been formulated by

Saith (2005), Reddy (2008), Kanbur (2009) and Fischer (2010) among others. Its main weakness stems from the fact that the indicator is not based on direct observation but on complex calculations that entail arbitrary assumptions. All indicators are based on two basic ingredients: observation and transformation. It can be observed quite directly, for example, whether a child is attending school or whether the child is malnourished. But direct observation cannot determine whether a child is struggling to survive on less than US$1.25/day. The latter needs a large amount of information, elaborate calculations and complex modelling, all of which are based on several assumptions, often haphazard. As the amount of transformations and the number of assumptions increase, the reliability and accuracy of the indicator decreases.

The choice of indicator and the level of aggregation invariably shapes the claims and conclusions of economic analyses. Combined, they can lead to 'misplaced concreteness', a term coined by a mathematician turned philosopher (Whitehead, 1925). Aggregates and averages are useful and helpful to understand complex realities, yet they always represent an abstraction of reality, if not a distortion of it. It is misplaced to think that one deals with a concrete reality when, in actuality, one observes the world with a high degree of abstraction.

When the poverty line is set at an exceedingly low level and when it is fixed in ways so that it moves with aggregate growth, then it is no surprise to find that growth is good for the poor. But this abstraction does not correspond with reality as measured by non-modelled indicators. It explains why non-monetary indicators of poverty – for example, health, nutrition, education – correlate poorly with the indicator based on the metric of US$1.25/day. The argument that 'growth is good for the poor' (Dollar and Kraay, 2000) is based on such abstract meta-analysis. At the time, the World Bank boasted about this research, featuring it prominently on its website for an extensive period of time. However, the analysis was not based on direct observations but on a theoretical framework that focused exclusively on the quantum of economic growth. Since then, the argument keeps popping up at regular intervals at the World Bank. Ghani (2011), for example, concludes, 'the conventional wisdom that growth is important for poverty reduction is consistent with the empirical facts in South Asia' (p. 5). In order to address such cognitive dissonance, one must distinguish between the abstract measure of income poverty and the more directly observable – and more reliable – indicators of human well-being. The former frequently yields a distorted view of reality.

After examining the role of social services in human development, Anand and Ravallion (1993) conclude 'that certain components of public spending can matter greatly in enhancing human development in poor countries, and that they matter quite independently of what they do or don't deliver in terms of reduced income poverty' (p. 147). Therefore, many consider the growth perspective as too narrow because it ignores the non-economic aspects, the historical background, the sociopolitical context and the international dimension of human poverty.

Aggregate growth versus disaggregated reality

Different groups in society typically display different levels of social and economic well-being. Data confirm that social indicators vary as much within countries as they do between countries. Evidence confirms that not all citizens benefit from *average* growth. Thus, national statistics do not only reveal, they also conceal. Some call it the *fallacy of the mean*; others consider it as a *tyranny of averages*.

The moment one ceases to realise that averages and aggregates do not exist in reality but that they are abstract concepts that originate from the human mind, one risks drawing unwarranted conclusions based on deductions from abstractions. Such conclusions suffer from 'misplaced concreteness' because they are not based on concrete observations. The poverty indicator of US$1.25/day is a prime example of misplaced concreteness. Its widespread use is mainly due to the convenience of dolarising the poverty debate and of donorising the discourse about the Millennium Development Goals (MDGs) (Vandemoortele, 2011). Yet it does not yield a better assessment or understanding of human poverty.

Economic growth is important, we agree, but as long as aggregates and averages are misused to keep growth on its pedestal, and as long as the majority of economists remain prisoners of their own assumptions and theories, the discourse on global poverty will continue to be an exercise in futility. After analysing the US economy during the boom period from 2000 to 2007, the authors of *The state of working America 2008/2009* conclude concisely, 'the economy did well, except for the people in it' (Mishel et al, 2009, p. 47, quoted in Wuyts, 2011, p. 439). Mishel et al. (2009) estimate that the top decile appropriated a staggering 91 per cent of the income growth in the USA between 1989 and 2006. Rajan (2010), a former chief economist at the International Monetary Fund (IMF) , calculates that nearly 60 per cent of the income growth that was generated in the US between 1976 and 2007 went to the top 1 per cent of households. But these trends are not limited to the USA. According to the International Labour Organization, income inequality rose in 16 out of 20 developed countries between 1990 and 2000 (ILO, 2008). The same report shows that income inequality rose in 41 out of 65 developing countries with data. Income inequality also got worse in OECD countries. Over the past 30 years, the gaps widened in 15 out of 22 nations. Two saw no change; with only 5 countries witnessing mostly modest improvements in their income inequality (OECD, 2011). In sum, the late Kenneth Boulding could be *paraphrased* as follows: Anyone who believes rapid growth will eradicate human poverty is *either a madman or a macroeconomist*.

Kenny and Williams (2001) show that our understanding of what causes economic growth remains rudimentary. Yet the orthodox school continues to prescribe deregulation, liberalisation and tax cuts as magic bullets for reducing poverty. Developing countries are told, for instance, to practise free trade and to enforce patent laws in order to accelerate growth so as to alleviate poverty. The Director-General of the World Trade Organization (WTO), for instance, writes 'Dear visitor, welcome to my website, I believe that trade opening and reducing trade barriers, has been, is and will remain, essential to promote growth and development, to improve standards of living and to tackle poverty reduction' (Lamy, 2011).

But economists cannot really explain why free trade is the best avenue to economic prosperity, simply because free trade was seldom practised by today's industrialised countries during their economic ascent. They all subsidised their economy behind protected tariffs. Instead of respecting intellectual property rights, they freely copied from one another without restrictions or costs imposed by patent laws. The fact that they now practise a high degree of free trade and enforce patent laws does not mean that free trade and copyrights are essential for fostering development and for accelerating growth. By overlooking their extensive use of protectionism, rich countries conveniently suffer from historical amnesia so that they can 'kick away the ladder' (Chang, 2007) they once climbed to reach the world's top economic position.

Thus, poverty reduction requires more than economic growth. Actually, it needs much more. The tragedy is that a single-minded pursuit of economic growth can harm human well-being, that is, impoverishing growth. A growth process that is based on the orthodox policy framework leads to entrenched inequality (UNRISD, 2010). Bhaduri (2008) calls it 'predatory growth' when growth and inequality feed on each other. The logic of 'growth-mediated' development inevitably leads to speculative bubbles and painful burst. It cannot be denied that economic instability has increased markedly in recent decades. The world is witnessing the recurrence of financial crises with greater frequency. Within a decade, we have seen financial meltdowns originate in Thailand (1997/98), in Argentina (2002) and in the US (2008), each with more devastating effects on human well-being than the preceding one.

Poverty reduction must begin with children

Since growth is far from being a panacea for reducing poverty, alternative strategies are called for. We argue that children hold the key to breaking the poverty cycle. No strategy will be more effective and efficient than to give each and every child a good start in life.

Although they hold the key, children are hardest hit by poverty. Deprivation causes lifelong damage to the mind and body of infants and small children. Child development, especially in the first years of life, is a succession of biological developments for which there is seldom a second chance. Infant malnutrition, for instance, leads to irreversible damage to health. It impedes the learning capacity of the child, which cannot be repaired later in life. In the few cases where second chances exist, they are invariably less effective and more costly than preventive action. Since poor families tend to be larger than non-poor ones, children are also disproportionately represented among the poor. No age group suffers more from human poverty than children.

Not only are they likely to live in poverty and suffer most from poverty than adults, children are also the main link for transmitting poverty to the next generation (Mehrotra and Jolly, 1997). Poverty begets poverty because child poverty perpetuates it. In this vicious circle, malnourished girls grow up to become malnourished mothers who give birth to underweight babies. Poor parents lack access to information and resources to optimally care for their children. Illiterate parents cannot adequately support children with their learning process. Hence, impoverished children become – as parents – transmitters of poverty to the next generation.

This vicious circle can be transformed, however, into a virtuous one by ensuring that poverty reduction begins with children (UNICEF, 2000). Investing in children is equivalent to laying the foundations for a stable and strong house; retrofitting the foundation is always costly but not always effective. Investing in children is a prerequisite for breaking the poverty cycle. It is not a matter of charity or of adding a soft side to economic development; it is about creating a cohesive society and a strong economy. No country has ever sustained economic growth on the basis of high levels of illiteracy, widespread malnutrition and rampant morbidity. The leaders of the now industrialised countries realised this when they established a market economy: they gave it a human face by ensuring a good start in life for each and every child through universal social services and other welfare programmes. The so-called Asian Tigers have followed the same recipe in more recent times.

Equity-mediated development

Four arguments are commonly used to justify investments in children. First, the legal argument is that the United Nations Convention on the Rights of the Child (UNCRC) is binding for member states that ratified it. It commits the state to 'use the maximum of available resources' to ensure the progressive realisation of the rights of children. Second, the ethical argument is that all children have fundamental economic and social rights, without any discrimination whatsoever. It is morally unacceptable to make children the victims of errors made by adults in politics and in policy making. Third, the economic argument is that children who get a good start in life will grow up to be productive adults who contribute to economic prosperity, so breaking the poverty cycle. The success of today's industrialised countries was the outcome of investments in children through economic ups and downs. Finally, the political argument is based on the view that widespread poverty diminishes opportunities for participation and genuine democracy in society. Investments in children are a key instrument for enhancing social cohesion.

While valid, the legal, ethical, economic and political arguments do not make explicit one fundamental premise, namely that human development must be equitable, that disparities within society must be kept within acceptable bounds, that fairness is an essential part of human well-being.

Inequity and inequality are often used interchangeably, yet they are distinct concepts. *Inequity* highlights the existence of unfair disparities. It allows for differences in outcomes that are based on the principle of fairness and caused by differences in endowments, efforts and circumstances. Inequity accepts differences that are earned fairly. *Inequality*, on the other hand, does not allow for differences in outcomes, whether earned fairly or unfairly.

Gender helps to clarify the different meaning of equity and equality. Although frequently used, *gender equity* is an incorrect term because no differences in life chances are deemed acceptable when they originate simply from being male or female. The correct terminology is *gender equality*. Differences in life chances that stem from factors that are beyond the control of a person or for which the person cannot be held responsible are deemed unacceptable.

The main concern about inequity is expressed in the human rights discourse. It also makes the case that all segments in society need to have a stake in national development for it to be sustainable. When groups feel disenfranchised and systemically excluded or ignored, they will not feel they have a stake in the national progress. When this occurs, it invariably leads to polarisation and internal conflict.

The sad reality is that the majority of countries are witnessing widening disparities. Inequality has become the ugly underbelly of global prosperity. The results of the Demographic and Health Surveys confirm that much of the social and economic progress made in recent years has bypassed the most vulnerable and the disadvantaged groups in countless cases. These surveys go beyond national aggregates and averages by providing disaggregated data. They generate information by wealth quintile (that is, a fifth of the population). Households are not grouped on the basis of income or consumption, which are exceedingly difficult to measure accurately and tend to yield unreliable results. Instead, their grouping is based on the possession of basic assets that can be directly observed – for example, radio, bicycle, electricity, tap water, types of building materials, etc (Macro International, 2009).

Minujin and Delamonica (2003) examine in detail the results of 24 such surveys. They conclude that progress in terms of child mortality during the 1980s and the 1990s for the bottom quintile was 'modest, and in most developing countries it was not statistically significant' (p. 414). Moser et al (2005) and Reidpath et al (2009) also document the growing disparities in terms of child mortality. Wilkinson and Pickett (2010) explore a mass of detailed country-level data for developed countries. They show that the most unequal ones do worse according to almost every quality of life indicator. Whether the indicator is life expectancy, infant mortality, obesity levels, drug and alcohol abuse, teenage pregnancy, mental illness, homicides or literacy scores, they find that the more equal the society is, the better its performance is in terms of human wellbeing. They argue that the best predictor of the rank of particular countries is not the differences in wealth between them but rather the differences in wealth within them.

While it is beyond doubt that the world will miss the MDGs in 2015, the explanation for it remains a matter of debate. The conventional narrative says that economic deregulation and liberalisation have been patchy; that foreign aid has been inadequate; that governance remains poor and corruption rampant. Moreover, it is often argued that it is Africa's weak performance that is keeping the world from meeting the MDGs. These arguments are either partial or incorrect. They are also missing the point.

The point is that disparities within countries have become so wide that inequities are now undermining national – and hence global – progress. The lower quintiles in countless countries have seen little or no progress in terms of human well-being in recent years. The implications of such an inequitable pattern of development are that investments in human development yield fewer and fewer results because they mostly benefit the upper quintiles whose social indicators, such as life expectancy, are already near the natural limits. At the same time, the lower quintiles see little or no benefits. Their low level of human development drags down the national and global progress. Rising inequities explain why the majority of countries have witnessed a slow down in national progress in terms of human development since 1990. As long as the people in the lower quintiles do not partake in national progress, there is little hope for meeting the global MDG targets by 2015.

Inequality is receiving increased attention. Reports by the International Labour Organization (ILO, (2004), United Nations (UN, (2005), the World Bank (2006), IMF (2007), World Health Organization (WHO, 2008), the Institute of Development Studies (Kabeer, 2010), Save the Children's International Alliance (2010), UNICEF (2010; Ortiz and Cummins, 2011) and Oxfam International (Stuart, 2011) highlight the importance of equity. In the wake of the global financial crisis, Kumhof and Rancière (2010) write in an IMF staff working paper, 'Because crises are costly, redistribution policies that prevent excessive household indebtedness and reduce crisis-risk ex-ante can be more desirable from a macroeconomic stabilization point of view than ex-post policies such as bailouts or debt restructurings' (p. 3).

But equity continues to be seen as politically divisive and socially corrosive. It is frequently dismissed as a misplaced effort in social engineering. Economic growth, by contrast, is considered as non-political and grounded in sound analyses. The term *evidence-based* policy making finds its roots in this logic. Its key message is that politics should be replaced by rational decision making, based on objective analyses. It is utopian, however, to pretend that politics can be taken out of the process of policy making. Policy making is always rooted in politics. Moreover, it is inconsistent to separate policy making from politics when the argument is made in favour of multiparty democracy. Evidence-based policy making is frequently used as a euphemism for imposing a certain world view on others. As the Commission on the Social Determinants of Health states, 'Evidence is only one part of what swings policy decisions' (WHO, 2008, p. 34). Instead of practising evidence-based policy making, some analysts and political leaders do not shy away from what can best be described as 'policy-based evidence making'.

Ripple effects

Child-focused policies can be a Trojan horse for introducing equity-enhancing measures in social and economic policy making. Apart from being legally binding, ethically imperative, economically smart and politically desirable, investments in children are also a powerful and practical way of promoting equity – in the sense of equality of opportunity. Most inequities find their roots in unequal initial conditions. Giving a good start in life to all children will considerably diminish the extent of polarisation and inequality within society.

Behind each preventable maternal and child death, behind each out-of-school child, behind each malnourished child, behind each AIDS patient who is not treated with antiretroviral medicine and behind each instance of environmental degradation lay a personal story of high inequality and deep-seated discrimination. In other words, poverty will be eradicated, not by accelerating growth or by increasing foreign aid, but by enhancing equity.

What, then, is the right sequence between poverty, growth and children? It is to start with children, thereby creating equitable ripple effects across society and the entire economy. It will engender equity, which in turn will yield a rapid reduction in poverty and sustained – green – economic growth. Any other sequence will prove less effective and less efficient, and ultimately unsustainable. Addressing equity by investing in children is doable and affordable in all countries, even in the least developed ones.

As long as the global discourse overlooks equity, as long as growing inequalities are dismissed as either anecdotal or as a passing phase, then human poverty will pervade and deepen. The equity-inducing effects of putting children first will make for a more effective and efficient approach than the strategy of 'growth-mediated' development. Drèze and Sen (1989) distinguish between 'growth-mediated' and 'supply-led' development strategies. We stress the need for an 'equity-mediated' approach. We do not consider equity only for its intrinsic value but also for its instrumental worth.

When the former US President Jimmy Carter received the Nobel Peace Prize in 2002, he stated, 'I was asked to discuss the greatest challenge that the world faces. Among all the possible choices, I decided that the most serious and universal problem is the growing chasm between the richest and poorest people on earth. The results of this disparity are root causes of most of the world's unresolved problems, including starvation, illiteracy, environmental degradation, violent conflict, and unnecessary illnesses that range from Guinea worm to HIV/AIDS' (Carter, 2002).

A sharper focus on equity is essential for shifting the discourse from private to shared well-being, from individual battles with disease to public health, from individual gains to collective dignity, from itemised freedoms to human rights, from prosperous people to a *great* society.

In short, the right sequence is to begin with children. Seeing poverty reduction as primarily 'growth-mediated' is erroneous. Human development must be child-focused for it to become 'equity-mediated'. That sequence will automatically reduce poverty and sustain economic growth while protecting the environment. Realising such a virtuous cycle is not a *mission impossible*. The key ingredient is political leadership – a rare commodity in most countries and woefully inadequate at the international level. Fortunately, the tide is gradually changing. Mainstream organisations such as the IMF are beginning to pay attention to inequality. The UN Children's Fund (UNICEF) has shifted its organisational focus to equity.

Can equity be promoted?

Once the argument about 'equity-mediated' development is accepted, the logical question is: How can equity be promoted?. Several answers are usually given, including universal coverage of basic social services, conditional cash transfers, progressive taxation, land reform, micro-credit, decentralisation, quotas for women and minorities, minimum wage, social protection, public works programmes, etc. Such recommendations, however, are of a general nature. Any specific policy recommendation risks falling victim to 'misplaced concreteness'. This is not to say that no valid lessons can be learnt from specific experiences, but that their replicability in other contexts is much smaller than what is commonly assumed. Therefore, the adage 'We know what works' is frequently incorrect.

Since there is no single-best interpretation of equity, it is not possible to precisely determine the single-best avenues for achieving it. Overall principles can be set (Sen, 2009), but the concept of equity cannot be reduced to a set of instructions or best practices because all policy making is rooted in the local context – political, cultural and historical. There are no techno-fixes for what are essentially political issues. Any set of standard policy recommendations is at risk of ignoring or overruling this basic tenet.

As noted earlier, equity is about giving a good start in life for everyone, based on fairness and on a level playing field. However, '[t]ackling inequities often requires working against the interests of national elites, challenging vested interests or dominant ideologies, or speaking for people who are excluded and ignored systematically by those making policy' (Jones, 2009, p. viii). The story of the Queen and the Mughal – drawn from the 17th century – illustrates this point.

The Mughal Shah Jahan (1592–1666) ruled a vast and powerful empire. His wife, Empress Mumtaz Mahal, bore him 14 children, half of whom died in infancy. She died in 1631 while giving birth. In her remembrance, the Mughal built a magnificent mausoleum. The shrine still exists; it is known as the Taj Mahal. Later that century, in another part of the world, Ulrika-Eleonora of Denmark, Queen of Sweden and Finland (1656-93), was the mother of seven children, of whom only three survived to adulthood. She did not die while giving birth but she observed the prevalence of maternal mortality around her and decided to establish the first-known professional midwifery school in the world. In 1685, she ordered all physicians to send one or two women from each town to Stockholm for midwifery training.

These two leaders faced the same problem – maternal mortality – yet they adopted radically different responses. In those days, they did not benefit from the advice of external partners from the World Bank, the United Nations, bilateral donors, think-tanks and consultancy firms. It is not totally inconceivable that the majority of such advisers would have supported the Mughal but not the Queen. They would have argued that his approach promoted investment, foreign exchange earnings and economic growth – which would eventually bring down maternal mortality. The Queen's response would have been dismissed as bloating the public sector, adding to the budget deficit and creating opportunities for corruption.

Most importantly it is not the precise action that each undertook but the mindset with which they did it. From the splendour of the mausoleum, it seems that the Mughal was a distraught man when he lost his beloved wife. But his mindset accepted high maternal mortality as a given – an act of God or an act of nature. The Queen's world view was very different. For her, maternal mortality was not a given; she did not see mothers as innocent victims of acts of nature or of deities. She valued the status of women enough to warrant special protection – which was then quite revolutionary. She did not consider their situation yet tolerable, albeit deplorable – as the Mughal did.

Similarly, most economists and political leaders today continue to perceive inequity as a given. Growth and efficiency are what matters, they argue – whilst showing a high degree of tolerance vis-à-vis growing inequality. Even if they acknowledge equity as a valid concern, they frequently do so superficially while maintaining the same old discourse about the growth narrative. Symptomatic of this is the translation of equity into a reference to the bottom quintile – which is a very simplistic and reductionist view of equity.

Conclusion

The equity argument considers it unacceptable that differences in life chances should originate from factors that are beyond a person's control – such as aggregate growth or strict fiscal or inflation targets. We argue that the best avenue to address human poverty is by giving each and every child a good start in life. The right sequence, thus, is to place children first, not growth. This will create a virtuous ripple effect across society and the entire economy.

The tale of the Queen and the Mughal shows how different mindsets yield different policy frameworks. Thomas Kida observes, 'We seek to confirm, not to question, our ideas' (2007, p. 18). The term 'evidence-based policy making', therefore, is a misnomer. It is the frame of mind that determines the policy framework, rather than the evidence. Ultimately, there are no facts, there are only interpretations of facts, said Nietzsche. That is why the growth narrative fails to accord priority to the social and economic rights of those who are excluded, ignored, marginalised or dispossessed. In spite of the compelling evidence of what caused the severe global financial crisis in 2008, it remains equity-blind. Just as the Mughal accepted high maternal mortality, the orthodox growth narrative takes growing inequality as a given, as a kind of unavoidable by-product of rising prosperity.

Of critical importance is the transformation of the mindset of political leaders and the thinking pattern of policy makers so as to make a quantum leap in imagination. The dual aspect of equity – its inherent and instrumental value – must be placed at the core of the discourse about human well-being and human rights. The growth narrative has yet to liberate itself from old theories, out-dated world views and 'misplaced concreteness' so as to make possible a direct, unmediated and undistorted contact with reality. Mainstream thinking ignores the 'equity-mediated' approach not because it is faulty but because it is inconvenient. It prefers to indulge in over-abstraction, over-generalisation and over-simplification. If there is any validity in the statement that 'growth is good for the poor', the evidence shows quite compellingly that equity is far better for the poor – and for everyone else.

The Lugano Report on preserving capitalism in the 21st century argues that leaders who are concerned about equity 'will learn that few votes are garnered by [focusing on] the dregs of humanity' (George, 1999, p 145). And so it remains today.

References

Anand, S. and Ravallion, M. (1993) 'Human development in poor countries: on the role of private incomes and public services', *Journal of Economic Perspectives*, vol 7, no 1, pp 133-50.

Bhaduri, A. (2008) 'Predatory growth', Development Dialogues, 23 February (http://development-dialogues.blogspot.com/2008/02/amit-bhaduri-predatory-growth.html).

Carter, J. (2002) Noble Lecture, Oslo: The Nobel Foundation (http://nobelprize.org/nobel_prizes/peace/laureates/2002/carter-lecture.html).

Chang, H.-J. (2007) *Bad Samaritans – Rich nations, poor policies and the threat to the developing world*, London: Random House.

Dollar, D. and Kraay, A. (2000) *Growth is good for the poor*, Washington, DC: Development Research Group, the World Bank.

Drèze, J. and Sen, A. (1989) *Hunger and public action*, WIDER Studies in Development Economics, Oxford: Clarendon Press.

Fischer, A. (2010) 'Towards genuine universalism within contemporary development policy', *IDS Bulletin*, vol 41, no 1, pp 36-44.

George, H. (1882) *Progress and poverty*, New York: Appleton & Co.

George, S. (1999) *The Lugano Report – On preserving capitalism in the twenty-first century*, London: Pluto Press.

Ghani, E. (2011) 'The South Asian development paradox: can social outcomes keep pace with growth?', *Economic Premise*, no 53, p 5, PREM Network (Poverty Reduction and Economic Management), Washington, DC: World Bank.

ILO (International Labour Organization) (2004) *A fair globalization: Creating opportunities for all*, Report of the World Commission on the Social Dimension of Globalization, Geneva: ILO.

ILO (2008) *The World of Work 2008 – Global income inequality gap is vast and growing*, Geneva: ILO.

IMF (International Monetary Fund) (2007) *World Economic Outlook – Globalization and inequality*, Washington, DC: IMF.

Jones, H. (2009) *Equity in development – Why it is important and how to achieve it*, Working Paper No 311, London: Overseas Development Institute.

Kabeer, N. (2010) *Can the MDGs provide a pathway to social justice? The challenges of intersecting inequalities*, Brighton: Institute of Development Studies.

Kanbur, R. (2009) 'Poverty disconnected', *Finance & Development*, vol 46, no 4, pp 32-4.

Kenny, C. and Williams, D. (2001) 'What do we know about economic growth? Or, why don't we know very much?', *World Development*, vol 29, no 1, pp 1-22.

Kida, T. (2007) *Don't believe everything you think – The 6 basic mistakes we make in thinking*, Amherst, MA: Prometheus Books.

Kumhof, M. and Rancière, R. (2010) *Inequality, leverage and crises*, IMF Working Paper WP/10/268, Washington, DC: International Monetary Fund.

Lamy, P. (2011) *Message from the Director-General*, Geneva: World Trade Organization (www.wto.org/english/theWTO_e/dg_e/dg_e.htm).

Macro International (2009) *Measure Demographic and Health Surveys*, Calverton, MD (www.measuredhs.com).

Mehrotra, S. and Jolly, R. (eds) (1997) *Development with a human face: Experiences in social achievement and economic growth*, Oxford: Clarendon Press.

Minujin, A. and Delamonica, E.E. (2003) 'Mind the gap! Widening child mortality disparities', *Journal of Human Development*, vol 4, no 3, pp 396-418.

Mishel, L., Bernstein, J. and Shierholz, H. (2009) *The state of working America 2008/2009*, Ithaca, NY: Cornell University Press (for the Economic Policy Institute).

Moser, K., Leon, D. and Gwatkin, D. (2005) 'How does progress towards the child mortality Millennium Development Goal affect inequalities between the poorest and the least poor? Analysis of Demographic and Health Survey data', *British Medical Journal*, no 331, pp 1180-3.

Ortiz, I. and Cummins, M. (2011) *Global inequality: Beyond the bottom billion – A rapid review of income distribution in 141 countries*, UNICEF Working Paper, New York: UN Children's Fund.

Rajan, R. (2010) *Fault lines: How hidden fractures still threaten the world economy*, Princeton, NJ: Princeton University Press.

Reddy, S. (2008) *The new global poverty estimates: Digging deeper into a hole*, One Pager 65, Brasilia: International Poverty Centre of the United Nations Development Programme.

Reidpath, D., Morel, C., Mecaskey, J. and Allotey, P. (2009) 'The Millennium Development Goals fail poor children: the case for equity-adjusted measures', *PLoS Medicine*, vol 6, no 4, e1000062.

Saith, A. (2005) 'Poverty lines versus the poor: method versus meaning', *Economic and Political Weekly*, Special Issue on 'The measurement of poverty', vol 40, no 43, pp 4601-10.

Save the Children (2010) *A fair chance at life: Why equity matters for child mortality*, London: International Save the Children Alliance.

Sen, A. (2009) *The idea of justice*, London: Penguin Books.

Stuart, E. (2011) *Making growth inclusive – Some lessons from countries and the literature*, Oxfam Research Report, Washington, DC: Oxfam International.

Economist, The (2010) 'Putting the smallest first', 25 September, p 31 (www.economist.com/node/17090948?story_id=17090948).

UN (United Nations) (2005) *The inequality predicament, Report on the World Social Situation 2005*, New York: Department of Economic and Social Affairs, UN.

UNICEF (United Nations Children's Fund) (2000) *Poverty reduction begins with children*, New York: UNICEF.

UNICEF (2010) *Narrowing the gaps to meet the goals*, New York: UNICEF.

UNRISD (United Nations Research Institute for Social Development) (2010) *Combating poverty and inequality: Structural change, social policy and politics*, Geneva: UNRISD.

Vandemoortele, J. (2011) 'The MDG story: intention denied', *Development & Change*, vol 42, no 1, pp 1-21.

Whitehead, A.N. (1925) *An enquiry concerning the principles of natural knowledge*, Cambridge: Cambridge University Press.

WHO (World Health Organization) (2008) *Closing the gap in a generation: Health equity through action on the social determinants of health*, Report of the Commission on Social Determinants of Health, Geneva: WHO.

Wilkinson, R. and Pickett, K. (2010) *The spirit level: Why equality is better for everyone*, London: Penguin Books.

World Bank (2006) *World Development Report 2006: Equity and development*, Washington DC: World Bank.

Wuyts, M. (2011) 'Growth, employment and the productivity-wage gap: revisiting the growth-poverty nexus', *Development & Change*, vol 42, no 1, pp 437-47.

PART 2

Measuring child poverty and deprivation

David Gordon and Shailen Nandy

Introduction

Ten years ago, the United Nations Children's Fund (UNICEF) asked the Townsend Centre for International Poverty Research at the University of Bristol, UK, to produce a scientifically valid and reliable method for measuring the extent and depth of child poverty in all the developing regions of the world. The methodology had to be socially and culturally appropriate, age and gender-specific and allow for the fact that children's needs change as they grow and develop. The methodology also needed to be consistent with agreed international definitions of poverty used for policy-making purposes and within the framework provided by international human rights conventions, particularly the UN Convention on the Rights of the Child (UNCRC).

The resulting methodology to measure child poverty (sometimes referred to as the 'Bristol' Approach by UNICEF) was briefly described by Gordon et al (2003) and was subsequently adopted by UNICEF as a core child poverty measure for the Global Study on Child Poverty and Disparities.

The 'Bristol Approach' was designed to produce meaningful scientific comparisons of child poverty *between* countries and UNICEF regions. A purpose of this chapter is to show how this methodology can be adapted and applied to produce meaningful and appropriate child poverty analyses *within* countries. The chapter also clarifies some of the myths and misconceptions that have arisen about the 'Bristol' methodology.

This chapter first briefly describes the 'Bristol' methodology. This is followed by a discussion of the relative deprivation theory that underlies the methodology and introduces the requirements for scientific valid and reliable measurement. The following section on 'How not to measure child poverty' looks at the limitations of three other highly regarded methodologies:

- the World Bank's 'dollar a day' PPP (purchasing power parity) method
- the Wealth Index method
- Alkire and Foster's Multidimensional Poverty Index method.

The purpose of these critiques is not to revisit 'old ground' and repeat technical criticisms that are already well known. Instead, the section aims to look at the more profound theoretical problems with these prevalent methodologies that are more rarely discussed and understood.

The final section provides a step-by-step worked example from Mexico, showing how multidimensional poverty can be scientifically measured. The chapter concludes with a critique of the 'Bristol Approach' and suggests how it could be improved in future research.

Child poverty measurement methodology

It is not possible to produce valid and reliable measures of anything (for example, speed, mass, evolution or poverty) without a theory and a definition. Validity can only be assessed in relation to a theoretical framework and, without such a framework, all measures of poverty remain merely the opinions of their advocates.

The child poverty measurement methodology of Gordon et al (2003) took Peter Townsend's relative deprivation theory (Townsend, 1979) as its theoretical scientific framework (this is discussed in the next section) and the definition of poverty agreed by the governments of 117 countries at the 1995 World Summit for Social Development in Copenhagen.

Absolute poverty was defined, for policy purposes, as 'a condition characterised by severe deprivation of basic human needs, including food, safe drinking water, sanitation facilities, health, shelter, education and information. It depends not only on income but also on access to social services' (UN, 1995, p 57).

The World Summit definitions of 'absolute' and 'overall' poverty remain to this day the only internationally agreed definitions of poverty. However, one outcome of this work by UNICEF on child poverty was that in December 2006 the United Nations General Assembly's Third Committee, which deals with social, humanitarian and cultural affairs, in its report to the 61st Session of the General Assembly on the promotion and protection of children's rights, adopted the first ever internationally agreed definition of child poverty:

... children living in poverty are deprived of nutrition, water and sanitation facilities, access to basic health-care services, shelter, education, participation and protection, and that while a severe lack of goods and services hurts every human being, it is most threatening and harmful to children, leaving them unable to enjoy their rights, to reach their full potential and to participate as full members of society. (UNGA, 2006, para 46)

UNICEF issued a statement, noting that:

Measuring child poverty can no longer be lumped together with general poverty assessments which often focus solely on income levels, but must take into consideration access to basic social services, especially nutrition, water, sanitation, shelter, education and information. (UNICEF, 2007, p 1)

In order to measure child poverty based on the World Summit for Social Development or UN General Assembly definitions, it is necessary to define the threshold measures of deprivation for each of the component parts of the definition; that is, to measure absolute poverty, definition thresholds *for severe deprivation* of basic human need are required for:

- food
- safe drinking water
- sanitation facilities
- health
- shelter
- education
- information
- access to services.

Relative deprivation theory conceptualises deprivation as a continuum that ranges from no deprivation, through mild, moderate and severe deprivation, to extreme deprivation at the end of the scale (Gordon, 2002). Figure 4.1 illustrates this concept.

Gordon et al (2003) defined 'severe deprivation of basic human need' as those circumstances that are highly likely to have serious adverse consequences for the health, well-being and development of children. Severe deprivations are circumstances that can be causally related to 'poor' developmental outcomes, both long and short term. An idealised taxonomy of deprivation was produced identifying deprivation thresholds

Figure 4.1: Continuum of deprivation

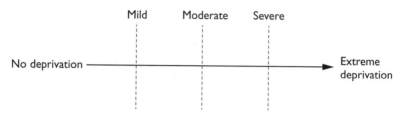

of different levels of severity, and this was subsequently operationalised using widely available data (see, for example, Demographic and Health Survey micro data, Multiple Indicator Cluster Survey micro data, etc). Two such operational threshold levels for each indicator were used in the subsequent Global Study of Child Poverty and Disparities (see Table 4.1) to measure child poverty at different levels of severity.

Developing evidence-based deprivation thresholds for children that were age and gender-specific was a time-consuming process that took several years by an experienced research team. It included a semi-systematic review of the relevant literature to produce an evidence-based *a priori* selection of potential child deprivation indicators, that is, indicators and thresholds which have been shown in previous studies to be good measures of child poverty. Subsequent work can be found in Nandy et al (2005), Pemberton et al (2005, 2007), Nandy and Miranda (2008), Nandy and Gordon (2009) and Nandy (2010).

The purpose of Gordon et al (2003) was to measure children's living conditions that are so severely deprived that they are indicative of absolute poverty. Thus, the deprivation thresholds used represent more severe deprivations than the indicators frequently published by international organisations. For example, 'no schooling' instead of 'non-completion of primary school', 'no sanitation facilities' instead of 'unimproved sanitation facilities', 'no immunisations of any kind' instead of 'incomplete immunisation against common diseases', 'malnutrition measured as anthropometric failure below −3 standard deviations from the reference population median' instead of 'below −2 standard deviations from the reference median', etc. In all cases, a concerted attempt was made to err on the side of caution in defining these indicators of deprivation of basic human need in such severe terms that few would question that these living conditions were unacceptable.

Children who suffer from any severe deprivation of basic human need are very likely to be living in absolute poverty because, in the overwhelming majority of cases, the cause of their severe deprivation is invariably a result of lack of resources/income. However, there may also

Table 4.1: Deprivation thresholds used in UNICEF's Global Study on Child Poverty and Disparities

Deprivation	Thresholds for 'less severe deprivation'	Thresholds for 'severe deprivation'
Shelter	Children living in dwellings with four or more people per room or living in a house with no flooring (ie, a mud or dung floor) or inadequate roofing	Children living in a dwelling with five or more people per room or with no floor material
Sanitation	Children using unimproved sanitation facilities. Unimproved sanitation facilities include: pour flush latrines; covered pit latrines; open pit latrines; and buckets	Children with no access to a toilet facility of any kind
Water	Children using water from an unimproved source such as open wells, open springs or surface water or where it takes 30 minutes or longer to collect water (walk to the water, collect it and return)	Children using surface water such as rivers, ponds, streams or lakes, or where it takes 30 minutes or longer to collect water (walk to the water, collect it and return)
Information	Children (aged 3-17 years) with no access to a radio or television (ie, broadcast media)	Children (aged 3-17 years) with no access to a radio, television, telephone, newspaper or computer (ie, all forms of media)
Food	Children who are more than two standard deviations below the international reference population for stunting (height for age) or wasting (weight for height) or underweight (weight for age)	Children who are more than three standard deviations below the international reference population for stunting (height for age) or wasting (weight for height) or underweight (weight for age). This is also known as severe anthropometric failure
Education	Children (aged 7-17) of school age not currently attending school or who did not complete their primary education	Children (aged 7-17) of school age who have never been to school and who are not currently attending school
Health	Children who have not been immunised by two years of age. If the child has not received eight of the following vaccinations they are defined as deprived: bcg, dpt1, dpt2, dpt3, polio0, polio1, polio2, polio3, measles or did not receive treatment for a recent illness involving an acute respiratory infection or diarrhoea	Children who did not receive immunisation against any diseases or who did not receive treatment for a recent illness involving an acute respiratory infection or diarrhoea

Source: Annex 1: Detailed layout for the statistical tables, Section V. Policy template for country data collection, analysis and reports, *Global Study on Child Poverty and Disparities 2007-2008 guide*

be some children in this situation due to discrimination (for example, girls suffering severe education deprivation) or due to disease (severe malnutrition can be caused by some diseases). For this reason, Gordon et al (2003) assumed that a child is living in absolute poverty *only* if the child suffers from two or more severe deprivations of basic human need as defined in Table 4.1 (second column).

Scientific measurement of child poverty

It is still fashionable among some economists to repeat the old claim that 'For deciding who is poor, prayers are more relevant than calculation, because poverty, like beauty, lies in the eye of the beholder. Poverty is a value judgement; it is not something that one can verify or demonstrate' (Orshansky, 1969, p 37). Mollie Orshansky defended the choices she made when developing the US poverty line by arguing, somewhat illogically, that 'if it is not possible to state unequivocally "how much is enough", it should be possible to assert with confidence how much, on average, is too little' (Orshansky, 1965, p 17). More recently, in discussions about poverty measurement in Europe, it has also been claimed that, since poverty is multidimensional, dynamic and relative, it can never by scientifically measured.

However, poverty is a social fact and all cultures have a concept of poverty (Gordon and Spicker, 1999), which is a difficult finding to explain if poverty were solely in the 'eye of the beholder'. In developing countries, poverty is often a murderous social fact that results in the death of millions of children (Black et al, 2003). The World Health Organization (WHO) has argued that:

> The world's biggest killer and greatest cause of ill health and suffering across the globe is listed almost at the end of the International Classification of Diseases. It is given code Z59.5 – extreme poverty. (WHO, 1995, p 1)

Poverty does not kill children as frequently in rich countries because poverty in countries with functioning welfare states is much less severe than in low-income, developing countries. Nevertheless, poverty still results in premature death even in countries like the UK, where healthcare is free.

Table 4.2 shows that life expectancy at birth for men in the Carlton area of Glasgow in the UK is only 54 years, which is lower than the average life expectancy for men in India (or the Gaza Strip). However, only a few kilometres' walk north-east of Carlton, in the wealthier area of Lenzie, life expectancy for men is 82 years – higher than the average male life expectancy in any country in the world. In a short walk across a city in one of the richest countries in the world, you can travel from

Table 4.2: Male life expectancy in Glasgow and selected countries

Place	Life expectancy at birth
Glasgow (Carlton), Scotland, UK	54
India	62
Philippines	64
Poland	71
Mexico	72
United States	75
Cuba	75
United Kingdom	77
Japan	79
Iceland	79
Glasgow (Lenzie North), Scotland, UK	82

Source: Adapted from WHO (2008)

one area to another where boys have a 28-year difference in their life expectancy; the underlying cause of this difference is poverty, not differences in health-related behaviours (Galobardes et al, 2004, 2008; Davey Smith, 2007; WHO, 2008; Spencer, 2008; Thomas et al, 2010). These deaths are cruel and measurable social facts; they are not in the 'eye of the beholder' and neither is their underlying cause – poverty.

Since poverty has such clear and damaging effects, it should and can be scientifically measured. Poverty may be multidimensional, relative and dynamic, but this does not mean it is impossible to measure – the motion of the planets is also multidimensional, relative and dynamic, but astronomers can predict their positions with a high degree of accuracy and precision. It might be difficult to scientifically measure poverty, but it is far from impossible.

Fortunately, since the work of Orshansky in the 1960s, significant theoretical advances have been made in poverty research. In particular, the research of Peter Townsend resulted in a paradigm shift in poverty measurement methodology. The first paragraph in his seminal work *Poverty in the United Kingdom* is arguably the most important text ever written about poverty. It is now so well known that many researchers and students of social policy can recite it from memory:

> Poverty can be defined objectively and applied consistently only in terms of the concept of relative deprivation....The term is understood objectively rather than subjectively. Individuals, families and groups in the population can be said to be in poverty when they lack the resources to obtain

the types of diet, participate in the activities and have the living conditions and amenities which are customary, or at least widely encouraged or approved, in the society to which they belong. (Townsend, 1979, p 31)

Townsend clearly demonstrated that absolute poverty did not exist as a meaningful concept distinct from relative poverty. Poverty in both rich and poor countries was the same phenomena, and what was termed 'absolute' poverty was in reality just more severe/extreme/deeper poverty. The difference between being 'relatively' and 'absolutely' poor was simply the difference between the 'poor' and the 'poorest'.

Townsend also argued that poverty was not a static phenomenon, but was both dynamic and relative:

> ... poverty is a dynamic, not a static concept.... Our general theory, then, should be that individuals and families whose resources over time fall seriously short of the resources commanded by the average individual or family in the community in which they live, whether that community is a local, national or international one, are in poverty. (Townsend, 1962, pp 219, 225)

According to Townsend, poverty can be defined as having an 'insufficient command of resources over time', and the consequence of a lack of 'resources' is that a 'poor' person/household will eventually become deprived. Thus, poverty is the lack of resources and deprivation is the consequence/outcome of poverty.

Townsend also argued that deprivation, like poverty, is a relative concept:

> Deprivation may be defined as a state of observable and demonstrable disadvantage relative to the local community or the wider society or nation to which an individual, family or group belongs. The idea has come to be applied to conditions (that is, physical, emotional or social states or circumstances) rather than resources and to specific and not only general circumstances, and therefore can be distinguished from the concept of poverty. (Townsend, 1987, p 5)

The two concepts of poverty and deprivation are therefore tightly linked. The concept of deprivation covers the various conditions, independent of income, experienced by people who are poor, while the concept of poverty refers to the lack of income and other resources that makes those conditions inescapable or at least highly likely (Townsend, 1987).

The absolute child poverty measurement methodology of Gordon et al (2003) is based on age and gender-appropriate measures of 'severe deprivation of basic human need'. It does not include measures of low income/inadequate command over resources. This is mainly a result of the lack of good data on income in the Demographic and Health Surveys, Multiple Indicator Cluster Surveys and similar surveys. The Gordon et al (2003) methodology also extends Townsend's (1987) definition of deprivation and measures 'severe deprivation of basic human need' for children relative to globally agreed norms and standards that currently prevail, rather than relative to national or local standards. It should be clear from this discussion that, when identifying child deprivation thresholds to be used for national studies, within a country, then nationally appropriate standards should be used (rather than inappropriate international standards). Similarly, where good national micro data are available on command of resources over time (for example, income and/or expenditure data), these should also be incorporated into the child poverty measure.

Scientific child poverty measurement using both deprivation and low income

A key problem in scientific studies of poverty is how to identify the 'correct' poverty line/threshold (Gordon and Pantazis, 1997). If the line is set too high then children who are not poor will be mistakenly identified as poor. Conversely, if the line is set too low then some children who are poor will not be classified as such. There are many examples of poverty lines that are mainly or wholly arbitrary, for example, the World Bank's US$1 per day PPP poverty line, the European Union's (EU) <60% median equivalised household income 'at risk of poverty' line, etc. It is the difficulty in identifying the correct poverty threshold that has led some commentators to argue that poverty is 'in the eye of the beholder'.

Townsend (1979) argued that, in order to 'objectively' identify the correct poverty line, we require additional information external to income/resources but which varies with income/resources. In the 1968/69 Poverty in the United Kingdom Survey, he developed a deprivation index and produced a scatter plot (Figure 4.2) of deprivation index score against a measure of income. Townsend observed a break

Figure 4.2: Modal deprivation by logarithm of income as a percentage of supplementary benefit (SB) scale rates

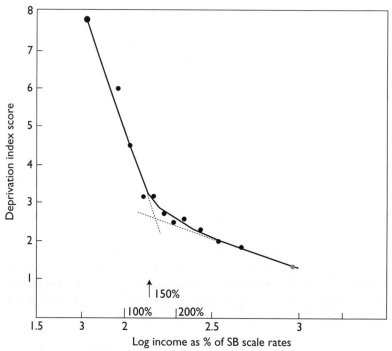

Source: Townsend (1979)

of slope in the graph (that is, the point at which deprivation increases rapidly for a small fall in income – marked 150% in Figure 4.2), and argued that this break point was the optimum position for the poverty line/threshold (Desai and Shah, 1988; Townsend and Gordon, 1993).

There have been considerable advances in computing and statistical methods since Townsend's work in the 1960s and 1970s that allow the identification of the optimal poverty line using multivariate rather than graphical methods. The techniques pioneered by Peter Townsend have been developed and refined by a large number of researchers in many countries over the past 40 years (see, for example, Mack and Lansley, 1985; Desai, 1986; Callan et al, 1993; Halleröd, 1994; Kaijage and Tibaijuka, 1996; Kangas and Ritakallio, 1998; Muffels et al, 2001; Short, 2005; UN Expert Group on Poverty Statistics, 2006; Boarini and d'Ercole, 2006; Whelan and Maitre, 2007; Saunders and Naidoo, 2009). Figure 4.3 illustrates a multidimensional definition of poverty in which the 'poor' are defined as those who suffer from both a low income and a low standard of living (Gordon, 2006). A low standard of living is often measured by using a deprivation index (high deprivation

Figure 4.3: Multidimensional definition of poverty

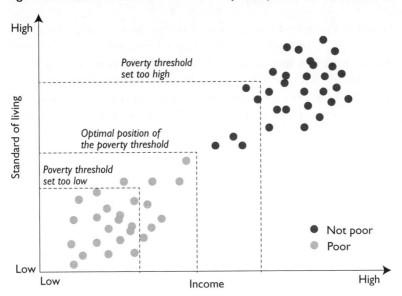

equals a low standard of living) or by consumption expenditure[1] (low consumption expenditure equals a low standard of living). Of these two methods, deprivation indices are more accurate since consumption expenditure is often only measured over a brief period. Deprivation indices are broader measures because they are multidimensional in nature and reflect different aspects of living standards, including personal, physical and mental conditions, local and environmental facilities, social activities and customs.

Figure 4.3 provides an illustration of poverty based on two dimensions, income and standard of living; however, the same principles can be used to separate the 'poor' group from the 'not poor' group in many dimensions. It shows an 'objective' poverty line/threshold that can be defined as the point that maximises the differences *between* the two groups ('poor' and 'not poor') and minimises the differences *within* the two groups ('poor' and 'not poor'). An illustrated step-by-step example of how to do this is discussed later in this chapter. For scientific purposes, broad measures of both income and standard of living are desirable. Standard of living includes both the material and social conditions in which people live and their participation in the economic, social, cultural and political life of the country/society in which they live (Gordon, 2000).

Dynamics of poverty

From the previous discussion, it is clear that those people/households with a high income and a high standard of living are 'not poor' whereas those with a low income and a low standard of living are 'poor' (see Beccaria and Minujin 1988; and Boltvinik, 1992, 1997, for alternative interpretations). However, two other groups of people/households that are 'not poor' can also be identified in a cross-sectional (one point in time) survey.

People/households with a low income but no deprivation. This group is not currently poor but if their income remains low they will become poor – they are currently vulnerable to sinking into poverty. This situation often arises when income falls rapidly (for example, due to job loss), but people manage to maintain their lifestyle, for at least a few months, by drawing on their savings and using the assets accumulated when income was higher. This group is sometimes referred to as vulnerable (Kaztman, 1999) or recently poor (ECLAC/DGEC, 1988; Kaztman, 1996).

People/households with a high income but a low standard of living. This group is currently 'not poor' and if their income remains high their standard of living will rise – they will rise out of poverty. This group is in the opposite situation to the previous group. This situation can arise when the income of someone who is poor suddenly increases (for example, due to getting a job). However, it takes time before they are able to buy the things that they need to increase their standard of living. Income can both rise and fall faster than standard of living. Kaztman has referred to this group as being in inertial poverty (ECLAC/DGEC, 1988).

A cross-sectional 'poverty' survey can provide some limited but useful information on the dynamics of poverty since it is possible not only to identify the 'poor' and the 'not poor' but also those likely to be sinking into poverty (that is, people/households with a low income but a high standard of living) and those escaping from poverty (that is, people/ households with a high income but a low standard of living).

Poverty is, by definition, an extremely unpleasant situation to live in, so it is not surprising that people go to considerable lengths to avoid it and try very hard to escape from poverty once they have sunk into it. Therefore, a cross-sectional survey ought to find that the group of households sinking into poverty was larger than the group escaping from poverty since, when income falls, people will try to delay the descent into poverty but, if the income of a poor person increases, they will quickly try to improve their standard of living. Figure 4.4 illustrates this concept.

Figure 4.4: Dynamics of poverty

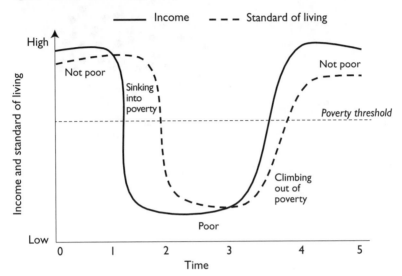

Between time periods 0 and 1 the household has both a high standard of living (dotted line) and a high income (solid line): it is 'not poor'. At time 1, there is a rapid reduction in income (for example, due to job loss, the end of seasonal contract income, divorce or separation, etc); however, the household's standard of living does not fall immediately. It is not until time 2 that the household's standard of living has also fallen below the 'poverty' threshold. Therefore, between time 1 and time 2, the household is 'not poor' but is sinking into poverty (that is, it has a low income but a relatively high standard of living). At time 3, income begins to rise rapidly, although not as fast as it previously fell. This is because rapid income increases usually result from gaining employment but there is often a lag between starting work and getting paid. Standard of living also begins to rise after a brief period as the household spends its way out of poverty. However, this lag means that there is a short period when the household has a high income but a relatively low standard of living. By time 5, the household again has a high income and a high standard of living (Gordon et al, 2000).

On the basis of this discussion, it is possible to update Figure 4.3 to give a more realistic picture of movements into and out of poverty. Figure 4.5 illustrates this (Pantazis et al, 2006, p 39).

Figure 4.5: Revised multidimensional definition of poverty

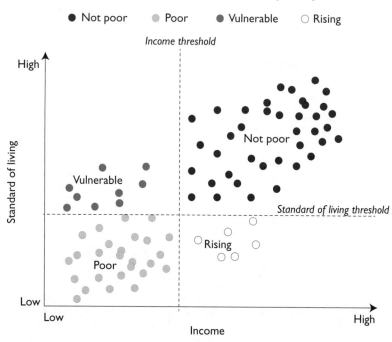

In both industrialised and developing countries, some children live in households which occasionally can suffer from dramatic losses in income due to adverse life events (for example, death of a parent, family breakdown, etc). However, in welfare states, the effective social safety net prevents such households falling too deeply into poverty and higher wages mean that there are fewer families close to the poverty line in the first place, that is, households in rich countries have further to fall before they become 'poor', and the social safety net prevents them from falling too far when disaster strikes. Thus poverty in both rich and poor countries is the same phenomena but poverty in poor countries tends to be both deeper and more prolonged than in rich countries.

The previous sections have examined the scientific theory that underlies the measurement of child poverty used in the UNICEF Global Study on Child Poverty and Disparities. Before providing a worked example on how this can be adapted at a country level, it is important to examine what is wrong with other leading poverty measurement methodologies.

How not to measure child poverty

This section examines three commonly used methods for measuring poverty and argues that each is currently inappropriate for measuring child poverty. The three methods discussed are the World Bank's US$1 a day method, the Wealth Index method and the recently developed Multidimensional Poverty Index method of Alkire and Foster. For a review of other methods see Minujin et al (2006) and Roelen and Gassmann, (2008).

The World Bank's 'dollar a day' method

The World Bank's 'US$1 a day PPP' methodology has been widely used (World Bank, 1990, 1996, 2000; Ravallion et al, 1991, 2008) and is incorporated into the Millennium Development Goals (MDGs). It was not designed to measure child poverty and the World Bank has never attempted to use the methodology for this purpose. There are a large number of critiques of the US$1 a day methodology (Townsend, 1997; Townsend and Gordon, 2002; Kakwani and Son, 2006; Himanshu, 2008; UNDESA, 2010), and interested readers should read the debate between Reddy and Pogge (2010) and Ravallion (2010) recently published in Anand et al (2010). Similarly, there are a range of reasons why the US$1 a day PPP methodology is not suitable for measuring child poverty, and interested readers should see Gordon et al (2003) for a discussion (or Pemberton et al, Chapter 2, this volume). However, the purpose of this discussion is to examine the deeper theoretical reasons why the US$1 a day PPP methodology is unsuitable for measuring child poverty in developing countries even if all the 'technical' problems could be resolved.

A key problem with the World Bank's method is that it adjusts the poverty line using purchasing power parity (PPPs). The international dollar PPP is not a real currency – you cannot buy or hold one – it is a concept. The idea is that, in order to compare the purchasing power of different currencies, a conversion factor (based on the cost of a basket of goods and services) is required. However, rather than use the exchange rate of money bought and sold in the global currency markets, the World Bank and International Monetary Fund (IMF) argue that PPPs should be used as the market exchange rates do not reflect the 'true' value of each currency; that is, they are subject to distortions, even if average monthly or yearly rates are used.

There are a great many criticisms about both the reliability and representivity of PPPs (Rogoff, 1996), but its advocates argue they:

... are the correct converters for translating GDP and its components from own currencies to dollars (the usual numeraire); the alternative measure, exchange rates, obscures the relationship between the quantity aggregates of different countries ... exchange rates systematically understate the purchasing power of the currencies of low-income countries and thus exaggerate the dispersion of national per capita incomes. (Kravis, 1986, p 24)

Conversely, Freeman (2007, p 1435) has argued that this claim is an ideological assertion rather than evidence-based, and that:

We might with equal validity say that PPP "obscures" the underlying monetary reality, "exaggerates" the purchasing power of low-income currencies and "understates" the dispersion of per capita incomes.

This is an interesting argument, particularly as both the IMF and the World Bank were strong supporters of the Washington Consensus and believers in free markets. Free and efficient markets were advocated as they were meant to be able to determine 'correct' prices. Therefore, it is somewhat inconsistent for these organisations to argue that the 'free' money markets are unable to determine the 'true' price of national currencies.

PPP and currency exchange rates produce significantly different results when used to compare the incomes of the poor in different countries. In developing countries, consumer goods tend to be relatively cheaper and capital goods relatively more expensive compared with industrialised countries. The PPP conversion reduces/understates the cost of capital goods compared with market exchange rate conversion (Freeman, 2007).

The differences in the extent and depth of child poverty in rich and poor countries are not just a result of households in rich countries having more money. Children in rich countries also have access to an extensive range of capital goods, for example, schools, hospitals, roads, electricity distribution, water supply infrastructure, sewerage systems, etc. In developing countries, millions of children do not have access to schools, hospitals, safe water, and so on because these capital goods simply do not exist close to where they live. This is important because, by understating the monetary cost of capital goods in developing countries, the PPP conversion, which is an integral part of the US$1 a day poverty methodology, obscures the costs of providing children with the services they need to escape from absolute poverty.

The Wealth Index method

The Wealth or Asset Index is a standard part of recent Demographic and Health Surveys and Multiple Indicator Cluster Survey micro data, and children in households with the lowest asset index scores (for example, bottom 10% or 20%) are sometimes defined as 'poor'; the Wealth Index has also been used to measure disparities among households with children. The method is based on the work of Filmer and Pritchett (1998, 1999, 2001), who used Principal Components Analysis (PCA) to produce a weighted index of household assets. The lack of an adequate theory to underlie the index and the parochial nature of the literature reviewed resulted in not just a 'reinvention of the wheel' but also a 'reinvention of the mistakes made when the wheel was first invented'. To paraphrase George Santayana, it seems that those who cannot learn from history are doomed to repeat it.

The Dutch *Leefsituatie* (Life Situation) Index was developed in 1974 by the Social and Cultural Planning Office (SCP) and subsequently used for resource allocation. It is still in use to this day (Boelhouwer, 2010). Weights were initially derived using PCA but this statistical mistake was quickly corrected and, subsequently, non-linear canonical correlation analyses were used to derive weights (Boelhouwer and Stoop, 1999). Filmer and Pritchett (1998) and the current Asset Index make exactly the same statistical mistake the Dutch corrected over 30 years ago. The problem is that almost all the asset indicators are binary variables (for example, owning a radio – 'yes' or 'no'), whereas it is an assumption of PCA that data are continuous. If this assumption is violated (for example, by including binary variables), then the weights produced (factor loadings) will be incorrect. One technical solution to correct the statistical error of including binary variables in a PCA analysis is to calculate the tetrachoric (or polychoric) correlation coefficients for the binary variables and then use the resulting correlation matrix in the PCA analysis (Kolenikov and Angeles, 2009).

Unfortunately, the Asset Index also makes the even more severe 'area poverty' error by combining a lack of household durables with a lack of community facilities in an atheoretical manner, thereby misclassifying 'rich' households who live in 'poor' rural areas as relatively impoverished.

There is a range of technical problems with the current Wealth Index method, which have been well documented (Falkingham and

Namazie, 2002;Vyas and Kumaranayake, 2006; Howe et al, 2008, 2009). However, the purpose of this discussion is to look at the more profound philosophical problems that are seldom discussed.

Many of the statistical methods that are widely used today were invented in the late 19th century and the first half of the 20th century by a group of accomplished British statisticians. Francis Galton invented regression, Karl Pearson consolidated Galton's work into a general theory of correlation and regression, Charles Spearman and Cyril Burt made significant contributions to both correlation and factor analysis, and Ronald Fisher pioneered analysis of variance (MacKenzie, 1981). All of these statisticians believed in eugenics, a term invented by Francis Galton − literally meaning 'well-born' − to characterise his 'moral philosophy' belief that the human species could be improved by encouraging society's brightest and best to have more children and by reducing the number of children produced by people who were physically or mentally 'deficient' (Kevles, 1985). These white male statisticians were from the upper middle class in England and firmly believed they owed their place at close to the top of the class, 'race' and gender structure of the British Empire to their own innate superiority to virtually everyone else on the planet (Mazumdar, 1992). Many of these statistical techniques, particularly tetrachoric correlation, were invented in order to help scientifically 'prove' these eugenic beliefs (MacKenzie, 1999).

Many of the characteristics that were important to the eugenics arguments about the strength of heredity were binary or categorical, for example, gender, eye colour, etc. However, a correlation coefficient was needed that was directly comparable with those used with continuous variables such as height and weight, so that binary and continuous variables could be compared in the same analysis. Tetrachoric correlation is a complex approximation to a Pearson's Product Moment correlation for binary variables (Pearson, 1901). However, it assumes that there is no such thing as a 'true' binary variable as all binary variables are really cut-offs of an underlying normally distributed continuous variable. Thus, the categories 'dead' or 'alive' were argued to be really measures of a continuous variable 'severity of attack' (MacKenzie, 1999). So, if for the sake of argument, we assume that Brad Pitt and Angelina Jolie are the 'perfect' couple, with Brad Pitt being 100% 'male' and Angelina Jolie being 100% 'female', then everyone else on the planet would rank somewhere on a normally distributed interval scale between 100% male Brad and 100% female Angelina, and the categories 'male' and 'female' would be binary measures of this underlying interval scale.

This idea is, of course, unproveable nonsense which was necessary for the eugenics research agenda (MacKenzie, 1999), but there is no need to make these kinds of assumptions when measuring child poverty or constructing a wealth index. It should also, of course, be remembered that eugenics ideas resulted in mass forcible sterilisation of hundreds of thousands of poor people in Germany, Japan, Sweden and the US, and the mass murder of children with disabilities in Nazi Germany.

It would seem preferable to use non-linear canonical correlation analyses to derive weights for any wealth/asset index designed to measure disparities (or poverty depth) among children rather than using PCA with tetrachoric correlation, which has such problematic statistical assumptions and historical connotations.

Alkire and Foster method (Multidimensional Poverty Index)

Sabina Alkire and James Foster (2007, 2009) have recently developed a method designed to produce a Foster, Geer and Thorbecke Index (Foster et al, 1984, 2010) using child deprivation measures. Alkire and Santos (2010) have produced a Multidimensional Poverty Index consisting of 10 indicators grouped into three domains and based on household micro data from 104 countries. Additionally, Roche (2009) and Alkire and Roche (2010) suggest a 12-step child poverty measurement methodology that builds on the work of Gordon et al (2003). They illustrate this methodology using an example from Bangladesh for children under five years of age and eight deprivation indicators (Roche, 2009).

All this work provides a significant advance in multidimensional poverty measurement, and the mathematical solution for producing a multidimensional Foster, Geer and Thorbecke Index using an intersection approach is an elegant and a welcome advance. Unfortunately, the rest of their child poverty measurement methodology suffers from several serious flaws. In particular, they do not have an explicit definition or theory of poverty. The absence of a definition means that it is impossible to determine the validity of their worked example from Bangladesh. For example, they include absence of vitamin A supplementation and a lack of salt iodisation as indicators of deprivation among children under five, and report that 'deprivation in salt iodisation accounts for 15% of total child poverty in Chittagong, and also has an important contribution to child poverty in Rajshahi (11%), and Dhaka (9%)' (Roche, 2009, p 19). To our knowledge, no previous measure of poverty among children under five has used salt iodisation or vitamin A supplementation as deprivation indicators. These indicators may or may not be valid and reliable measures of poverty among young children, but the authors' 12-step methodology does not provide for tests of the accuracy or precision of either the deprivation indictors or domains. In the absence of any definition of poverty, validity and reliability analyses, the results could be viewed as a collection of things the authors think are 'bad' added together in an essentially arbitrary manner. Of course, the results might correctly identify poor children in Bangladesh; the problem is that there appears to be no way of knowing if this is the case using the 12-step methodology proposed.

Scientific measurement of child poverty requires a methodology that allows the 'best' set of deprivation indicators to be selected and for rejection of inadequate indicators. It should also facilitate the interpretation of meaningful findings from the analyses. For example, Roche (2009) compares the deprivation headcount (H) with the Foster, Geer and Thorbecke modified headcount (M_0) for 12 regions in Bangladesh (see Roche, 2009, Table 6), and argues that 'while the first four positions remain invariant in the ranking according to H and M_0 (column 13), there are important rearrangements in the rankings among the rest of the regions when the headcount ratio is adjusted by the average deprivation among the poor' (Roche, 2009, p 18). He interprets these 'important' differences in rank order to demonstrate that: 'Adjusting the headcount ratio by breadth of deprivation as in the Alkire–Foster approach is clearly a value added to the conventional headcount ratio' (Roche, 2009, p 18).

This interpretation would only be 'correct' if the two rank orders differed significantly rather than due to random variation. We do not have the raw micro data used by Roche (2009) so we can only perform some limited testing of their claim. However, just looking at the rank differences H – M_0 (Roche, 2009, Table 6, column 13) shows:

Rank difference
6 are 0 (six regions have identical ranks on both H and M_0)
4 regions have 1 rank place different
2 regions have 2 rank places different

The Spearman Rho correlation for the 12 Bangladesh regions for H and M_0 is 0.956.

The Sign test for differences in rank between H and M_0 significance is 0.688.

The Wicoxon signed rank test for differences in rank between H and M_0 significance is 0.916.

Both the Kendall's concordance and Friedman's test for differences in rank distribution have a significance of 0.414.

Therefore, none of these non-parametric tests on the ranks of H and M_0 approach statistical significance. There is, therefore, no reason to reject the null hypothesis that the differences in the ranks of H and M_0 for the 12 regions of Bangladesh are due to anything but random fluctuations. It would seem unwise to claim 'value added' for the M_0 measure on the basis of random changes of position in ranked data. This, of course, does not mean that there is no value added in the M_0 measure proposed by Alkire and Foster (2007); however, their example does not provide any *evidence* for added value. In the large majority of situations, as the proportion of children in poverty increases (that is, H, the headcount), so does the depth of child poverty (for example, M_0, adjusted headcount). We know of no two countries or regions that have identical headcount rates of child poverty but where the depth of child poverty differs significantly. Thus, it is possible that there may be little additional value added in the adjusted headcount measure (M_0) proposed by Alkire and Foster (2007, 2009). It is of course possible to measure depth/intensity of child poverty at the household level using the 'Bristol Approach' by simply comparing the aggregated deprivation index score across all children in the household. This methodology has been used in several studies, for example, Gordon et al (2003), Delamonica and Minujin (2007), and Chapter Eleven, this volume, and it is yet to be shown how much added value the Alkire and Foster method provides over this much simpler method.

However, the purpose of this discussion is not to dwell on technical problems with the work of Alkire and Foster but to examine the more profound theoretical issues. They argue that their methodology can measure the breadth, depth and severity of dimensions of child poverty and also that the modified headcount measure can be broken down by dimension to uncover the components of child poverty in different regions or age groups or by gender (Alkire and Roche, 2009). We have argued above that child poverty measurement is not in the 'eye of the beholder' and that relative deprivation theory provides a scientific basis for measuring multidimensional child poverty. Scientific method requires that both deprivation indicators and the dimensions of a multidimensional poverty index need to be tested to demonstrate that they are reliable, valid and additive. Furthermore, a scientific methodology requires the ability to identify and reject deprivation indicators and dimensions which were initially selected for an analysis but which are not shown to be good measure of multidimensional poverty, that is, the methodology must provide for researchers who begin an analyses with different sets of deprivation indicators and dimensions to end up with the same (or very similar) final sets of indicators and dimensions – there is a 'correct'/'best'/'optimal' sub-set of multidimensional child poverty indicators and dimensions of deprivation in any given dataset.

The problem with the Multidimensional Poverty Index method is that there remains uncertainty about the following:

- *How many dimensions there are* – three? (education, health and standard of living) Or six? (food, education, health, dwelling conditions, water and sanitation and standard of living)
- *How these dimensions are related* – that is, are the education and health dimensions orthogonal – at 90° to each other with correlation = 0? Or are these two dimensions correlated, that is, at 45° with correlation = 0.5?
- *The indicators are imperfect* and it is not known how they correlate with each dimension, for example, children not attending school may have a high correlation with the education dimension (for example, 0.8), but since some of these children may not attend school due to ill health, this indicator may also correlate with the health dimension (for example, 0.2).

There are solutions to these problems. For example, the methodology discussed below shows how the validity, reliability and additivity of multidimensional poverty indicators can be measured. Structural Equation Modelling (SEM) or Confirmatory Factor Analysis or Latent Class Models can be used to 'test' the dimensional structure of a multidimensional poverty or standard of living index (Shelvin et al, 2000; Fergusson et al, 2001; Jensen et al, 2002).

It is possible to produce a reliable and valid multidimensional child poverty index without knowing the dimensional structure of the data, for example, the 'correct'/'optimal' number of dimensions. Cronbach's alpha (see below) is a measure of the reliability of an index in both unidimensional and multidimensional space (Cortina, 1993). By aggregating across dimensions to create a single deprivation index, you do not reduce five or six dimensions to one dimension; all that has happened is that indicators have been summed across dimensions, that is, the deprivation index is still multidimensional.

For example, Green et al (1977) generated 10 indicators in five dimensional spaces using Monte Carlo methods. The five dimensions were all orthogonal (uncorrelated) and each indicator loaded 0.45 on two dimensions. No indicator loaded on the same two dimensions – Cronbach's alpha was 0.81 (that is, a highly reliable five-dimensional index).

Most of the theoretical problems concerning the construction of reliable and valid multidimensional poverty and standard of living indices have been extensively discussed (and solved?) over the past 50 years of research in the social policy and standard of living/social indicator literature. It is unfortunate that these extensive literatures appear to have been virtually ignored by many researchers who have attempted to measure child poverty in developing countries.

To conclude this section, there are a range of technical problems with the World Bank's US$1 a day method, the Wealth Index method and the Multidimensional Poverty Index method of Alkire and Foster. However, there are also more profound theoretical issues with these three methods that currently render them as inadequate methodologies for measuring child poverty. The use of PPP in the US$1 a day method obscures the costs of providing children with the services they need to escape from absolute poverty. The current Wealth/Asset Index method requires statistical assumptions about the nature of binary/categorical variables that are untenable and relate to eugenic arguments that could and should be consigned to history. The current Multidimensional Poverty Index method of Alkire and Foster represents a significant advance. However, the fundamental theoretical problem with the Alkire and Foster modified headcount (H) method (M_0) is that although the mathematics are elegant and it has desirable axiomatic properties, this cannot possibly compensate for a methodology which may not produce valid and reliable deprivation indicators and a dimensional structure which may be highly biased.

A worked example from Mexico

This worked example is for both adults and children; however, the same principles can be applied to scientifically measuring child poverty using only child specific deprivation indicators, such as those used by Gordon et al (2003) and in the Global Study on Child Poverty and Disparities (see Table 4.1).

The Mexican legislature ratified unanimously the General Law for Social Development (LGDS) on 20 January 2004. The law requires that poverty must be officially measured multidimensionally. Article 36 of the LGDS requires that the multidimensional poverty measure must include (at least) the following eight dimensions:

- per capita current income
- average gap between compulsory education and actual education at the household level (educational gap)

- access to health services
- access to social security
- dwelling characteristics, space and quality
- access to basic dwelling-related services (water, sewerage, electricity, etc)
- access to food
- level of social cohesion.

An independent parastatal (CONEVAL, www.coneval.gob.mx) was established to develop the best possible scientific methodology for multidimensional poverty measurement, and it consulted both national and international experts to help with this policy research (CONEVAL, 2009). This worked example is based on some initial research for CONEVAL produced by Gordon (2010) using the 2005 ENIGH micro data (the Mexican National Household Expenditure and Income Survey). CONEVAL initially produced a preliminary set of eight indicators as an aid to facilitating a comparison of the results from the different methodologies that have been proposed by all the experts participating in this research:

p_income − per capita current income
p_educatio − educational gap
p_health − access to health services
p_socsec − access to social security
p_dwelling – dwelling quality and space deprivation
p_services – basic service deprivation
p_foodlp2 – access to food
p_cohesion – social cohesion

In the model, the components will be summed to produce a deprivation index; this will be plotted against equivalised household income and an optimal threshold that best separates the 'poor' from the 'not poor' identified using standard statistical methods (that is, maximising the between-group difference and minimising the within-group difference). In order to identify the optimal poverty threshold for income and deprivation, it is first necessary to construct a valid, reliable and additive deprivation index.

Step 1: Creating a 'scientifically' valid deprivation index

In order to construct a valid deprivation index, it is necessary to demonstrate that each component in the index is a valid measure of deprivation. This can be complex; however, since the domains measured by the CONEVAL indicators are considered by the legislature to be important components of multidimensional poverty, this provides *a priori* evidence for 'face validity'. The 'criterion validity' of the deprivation index can be demonstrated by ensuring that the individual components of the index all exhibit statistically significant relative risk ratios with independent indicators or correlates of poverty. There are a limited number of external validators available in the ENIGH dataset; however, it would be expected that each component of a valid index should have a statistically significant correlation with the three measures of poverty developed by the Technical Committee for Poverty Measurement (that is, alimentary/food poverty, capacities/capabilities poverty and patrimony poverty[2]) (Cabrera and Miguel, 2002).

Table 4.3 shows the relative risk ratios (approximately the odds ratios) of being food, capacities and patrimony poor for households that also suffer from each of the eight CONEVAL deprivations. All the risk ratios in Table 4.3 are highly statistically significant (<0.001), and a number of things are also clear from this table. First, those who are food, capacities and patrimony poor also have a 100% chance of suffering from income deprivation (p_income) – their relative risk is effectively infinite (that is, ∞). In fact, the variable p_income is identical to the patrimony poverty variable. Similarly, the p_health variable is also highly correlated with both p_income and all the poverty validation variables (risk ratios of 50.8, 48.2 and almost infinity). Lastly, the social cohesion indicator has statistically significant risk ratios of less than 1, that is, it is inversely correlated with the three poverty measures.

Figures 4.6 and 4.7 show the average equivalised household incomes and expenditures in Mexican pesos by the eight CONEVAL indicators. The incomes and expenditures of those suffering from each deprivation are marked as '1' on each graph. The horizontal line on each graph shows the average equivalised income and expenditure for the

Table 4.3: Relative risk ratios for CONEVAL indicators by poverty measures

CONEVAL deprivation measure	Food poverty	Capacities	Patrimony
p_income	∞	∞	∞
p_health	50.8	48.2	–
p_dwelling	8.7	7.8	6.4
p_foodlp2	8.7	7.7	6.9
p_socsec	8.1	6.1	3.4
p_educatio	6.9	5.9	4.6
p_services	4.6	4.2	3.4
p_cohesion	**0.3**	**0.3**	**0.4**

Figure 4.6: Main effects plot of equivalised household income by CONEVAL indicators

Main effects plot
(data means)
for **OECDINC**

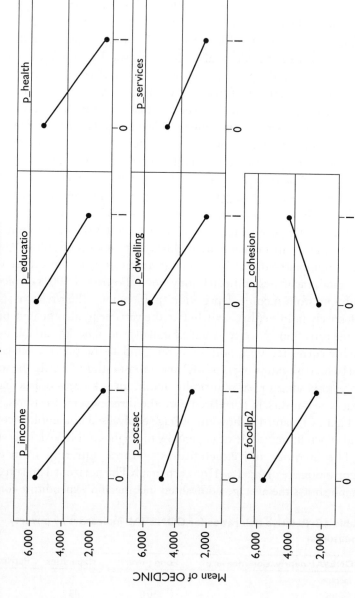

Figure 4.7: Main effects plot of equivalised household expenditure by CONEVAL indicators

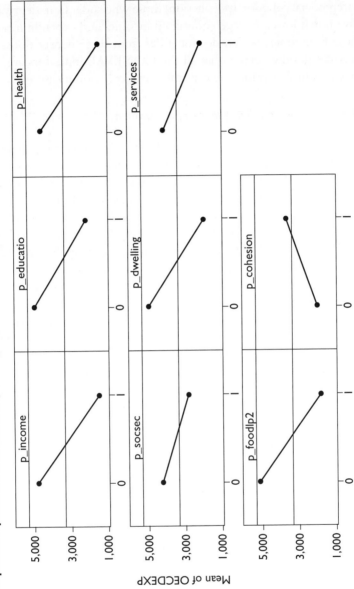

Main effects plot
(data means)
for **OECDEXP**

whole sample. It can be clearly seen that for all CONEVAL indicators except social cohesion (p_cohesion) those who suffer from deprivation have much lower average equivalised incomes and expenditures than those households which do not suffer from these deprivations. This provides good evidence that all the CONEVAL indicators are valid measures of deprivation, except the social cohesion measure.

Step 2: Creating a reliable index of deprivation

After establishing that the individual deprivation index components are all 'scientifically' valid, it is necessary to establish that they also form a reliable scale. A deprivation scale was constructed by simply summing the eight CONEVAL indicator scores (that is, each indicator had a weight of 1). The reliability of an index/scale can be assessed using a classical test theory model by calculating Cronbach's alpha (SPSS reliability) for each deprivation item and removing all items in the index that would increase alpha if the 'item was deleted'. Unreliable items (for example, those that do not decrease alpha) are highlighted in bold in Table 4.4.

The Cronbach's alpha (Cronbach, 1951; Cronbach and Shavelson, 2004) for the eight–item CONEVAL deprivation scale is 0.695, which is slightly less than the recommended minimum of 0.7 (Nunnally, 1981). However, if the social cohesion indicator is removed from the index, then the Cronbach's alpha increases to 0.772, which is a reasonable level of reliability for an index of only seven items.

Step 3: Checking the revised index is additive

The components of any deprivation index should be additive, for example, a person or household with a deprivation score of 3 should be poorer than a person or household with a deprivation score of 2. Some components of the index may not be additive, for example, it is necessary to check that a respondent who is both health service (p_health) and dwelling basic service (p_service) deprived is poorer than a person who is just health service deprived but has basic dwelling services in their home. There is no easy way to do this as the number of possible combinations with an eight-component index is huge (eight factorial), but it is possible to check that any two components are additive by looking at the second order interaction effects in an ANOVA with equivalised income as the dependent variable and all the components of the index as the eight independent variables.

Table 4.4: Reliability analysis of the CONEVAL deprivation indicator index

	Item – total statistics				
	Scale mean if item deleted	Scale variance if item deleted	Corrected item – total correlation	Squared multiple correlation	Cronbach's alpha if item deleted
Per capita current income CONEVAL	3.58	3.162	0.684	0.823	0.591
Educational gap at the household CONEVAL	3.42	3.545	0.427	0.205	0.655
Access to health services CONEVAL	3.63	3.171	0.707	0.830	0.587
Access to social security CONEVAL	3.40	3.730	0.323	0.239	0.680
Dwelling quality and spaces CONEVAL	3.49	3.479	0.463	0.260	0.647
Dwelling basic service access CONEVAL	3.69	3.786	0.344	0.182	0.674
Access to food CONEVAL	3.47	3.577	0.405	0.218	0.661
Social cohesion CONEVAL	**3.15**	**4.903**	**–0.272**	**0.090**	**0.772**

Reliability coefficients

No of cases = 23,174

No of items = 8

Alpha = 0.695

Figure 4.8 shows the second order interaction plots for the eight CONEVAL indicators and OECD (Organisation for Economic Co-operation and Development) equivalised household income. The first graph (top left of Figure 4.8) shows the interaction between the per capita income indicator (p_income) and the educational gap indicator (p_educatio). The vertical scale on each graph is equivalised household income which ranges between 2,000 and 6,000, and the horizontal scale is deprived = 1 or 'not deprived' = 0. There are two lines on the each graph – a solid black line and a fine grey line. The first black dot on the solid line (top left) shows the average equivalised household income of those respondents who were neither income nor educationally deprived. The first grey square on the grey line (on the left, just below the black dot) shows the income of those who are education gap deprived but not per capita income deprived, that is, it is less. The second black dot on the solid line (top right) shows the income of those who are per capita income deprived but who had an acceptable education, and the second grey square on the grey line

Figure 4.8: Second order interaction plots for CONEVAL indicators and OECD equivalised household income

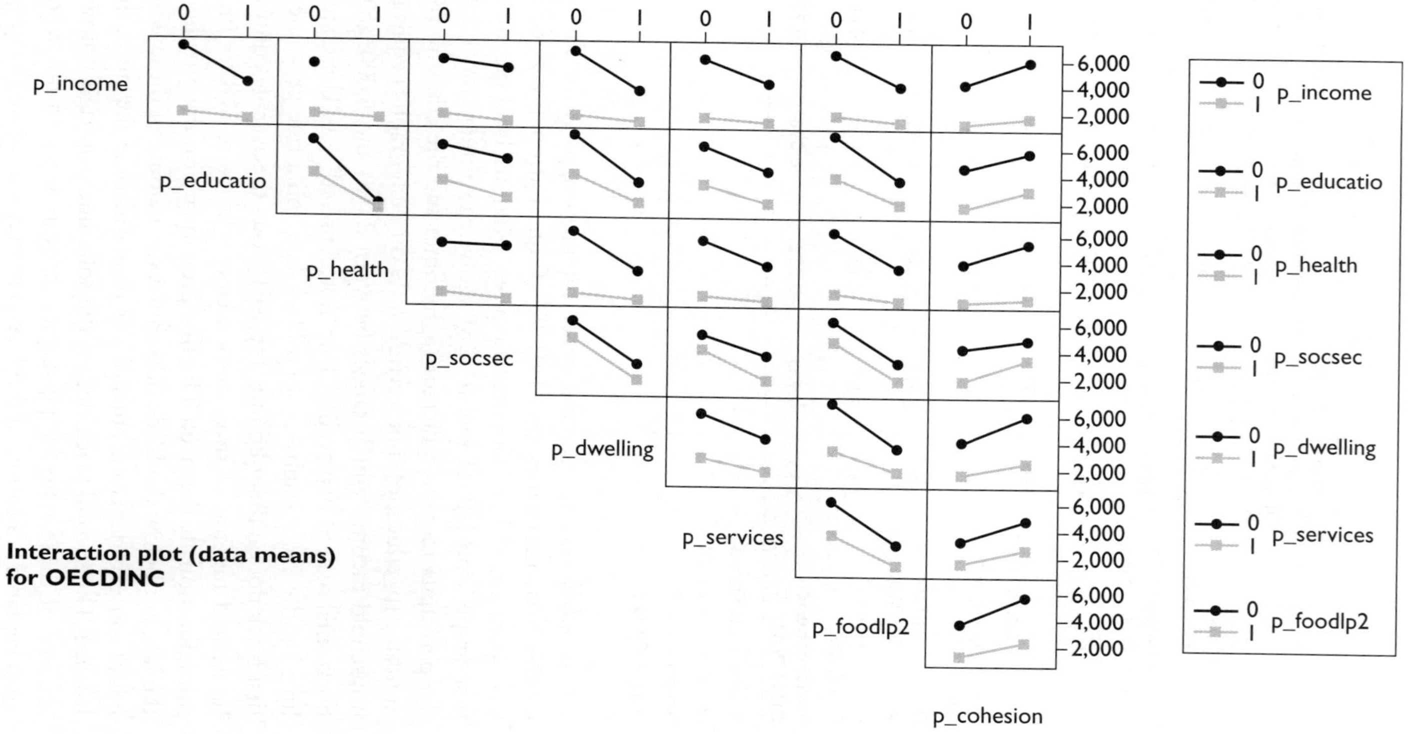

Interaction plot (data means)
for OECDINC

shows the average equivalised household incomes of respondents who are deprived on both indicators (that is, both per capita income and educational gap deprived). Therefore, respondents who are both per capita income and educational gap deprived are likely to be 'poorer' than respondents who are deprived of just one of these items.

Two parallel lines slanting from top left to bottom right indicate that the variables are additive. However, if the lines cross or slope upwards (that is, bottom left to top right) there may be problems; for example, the social cohesion indicator is not additive with any of the other variables.

Figure 4.9 (overleaf) shows the second order interaction plots for the eight CONEVAL indicators and OECD equivalised household expenditure. The results for equivalised expenditure are very similar to those for equivalised income.

Step 4: Producing a valid, reliable and additive deprivation index

It is clear from the results obtained in the previous three steps that the CONEVAL social cohesion indicator is not valid, reliable or additive with the other seven indicators, and so it should be excluded from any deprivation index.

Table 4.5 shows the final reliable, valid and additive deprivation index constructed by summing the scores of the seven CONEVAL deprivation indicators. The index ranges from a score of 0 (no deprivation) to a maximum score of 7 (deprived on all seven indicators).

There are only around 11% of households that have a deprivation score of 0, indicating that almost 90% of Mexican households suffer from one or more CONEVAL deprivations. The average equivalised household incomes and expenditures of the households scoring 0 on

Table 4.5: CONEVAL deprivation index frequencies and average equivalised household incomes and expenditures

Score	Frequency	%	Cumulative %	Average OECDINC	Average OECDEXP
0	2,633	11.4	11.4	8,218	6,916
1	4,307	18.6	29.9	7,389	6,229
2	3,676	15.9	45.8	4,650	3,982
3	2,951	12.7	58.5	3,266	2,679
4	2,493	10.8	69.3	2,181	1,992
5	2,475	10.7	80.0	1,675	1,619
6	2,444	10.5	90.5	1,249	1,310
7	2,195	9.5	100.0	889	874
Total	23,174	100.0		4,090	3,525

Figure 4.9: Second order interaction plots for CONEVAL indicators and OECD equivalised household expenditure

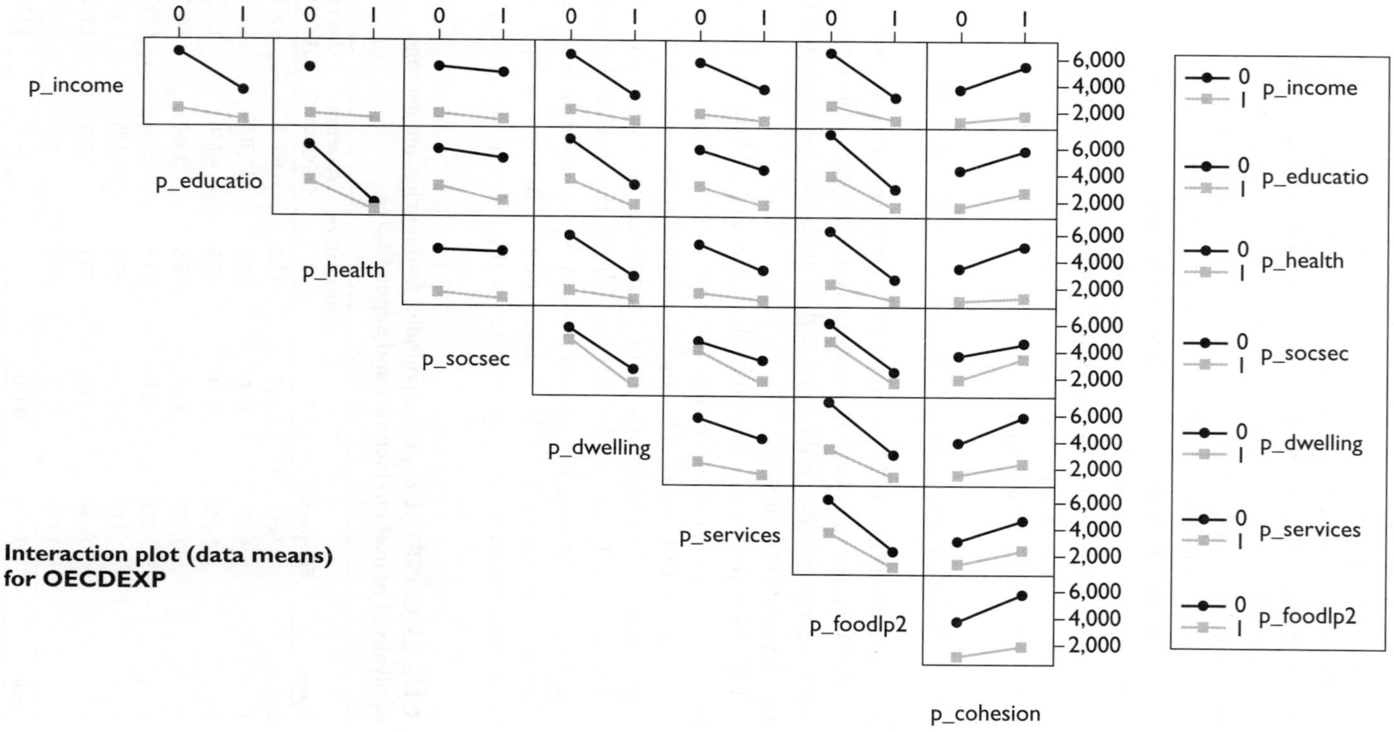

Interaction plot (data means)
for **OECDEXP**

the index are 8,218 and 6,916 respectively. By contrast, the average equivalised household incomes and expenditures of the 9.5% of households scoring 7 on the index (deprived on every CONEVAL dimension) are 889 and 874 – almost an order of magnitude lower than the no deprivation households.

Figure 4.10 shows the average equivalised household incomes for each CONEVAL deprivation index score – income clearly falls with increasing deprivation. There are two breaks of slope on the graph, between a score of 1 or less and 2 or more and also between a score of 4 or more and 3 or less. In order to determine the optimum poverty threshold, it is first necessary to remove any income outliers (the very rich).

Figure 4.11 shows a univariate summary of the OECD equivalised household income variable (unweighted). It is clear that the distribution has a strong right skew (skewness = 5.8) with many 'extremely' high incomes. Since the purpose of this exercise is to identify the poverty threshold rather than study the very wealthy, those with equivalised incomes over 8,000 have been excluded from the modelling exercise below (although the 'rich' are of course added back to calculate the poverty prevalence rate).

Figure 4.10: Average equivalised household income (with 95% Confidence Intervals) by CONEVAL deprivation index score

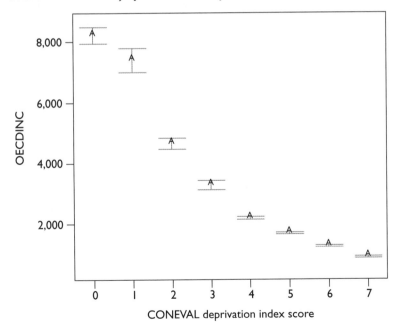

Figure 4.11: Univariate statistical summary of OECD equivalised income variable

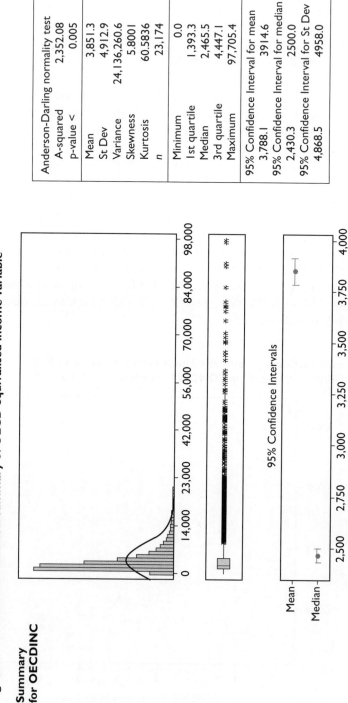

Step 5: Identifying the combined income and deprivation poverty line

The 'objective' combined poverty line can be defined as the division between the 'poor' group and the 'not poor' group that maximises the *between*-group sum of squares and minimises the *within*-group sum of squares. This can be identified using the General Linear Model (in one of its forms, for example, ANOVA, Discriminant Analysis or Logistic Regression), controlling for income, deprivation and household size and composition.

General Linear Models (both ANOVA and Logistic Regression) were used to determine the scientific poverty threshold, for example, the deprivation score that maximises the between-group differences and minimises the within-group differences (sum of squares). These techniques were applied to a succession of groups created by increasing the number of items that respondents were deprived of. Thus, the first analysis was undertaken on groups defined by households lacking no items compared with households lacking one or more items (a deprivation score of 1 or more). Similarly, the second analysis was undertaken on a group comprised of households lacking one or no items against two or more items, and so forth.

The dependent variable in the ANOVA model was net household income and the independent variables were deprivation group (constructed as described above), number of adults in each household and the number of children in each household. With the Logistic Regression models the dependent variable was the deprivation group and the independent variables were net household income, number of adults and number of children. Both the ANOVA and Logistic Regression models yielded the same final result – that a score of 4 or more on the deprivation index was the optimum position for the poverty line. Summary results are shown in Table 4.6.

Table 4.6 shows that the optimum position for the poverty threshold is a deprivation score of 4 or more.

It is hard to identify the exact equivalised income threshold that would constitute the optimal poverty line as the deprivation score contains two indicators (per capita income and access to health services) that are a form of income measure. Therefore, the deprivation and income axes will not be orthogonal and so identifying a 'perfect' ordering is impossible. An additional problem is that the OECD equivalisation scale is probably not optimal for Mexico, and this will add statistical 'noise' to the analysis. For these reasons, no attempt has been made to identify the proportion of people in the 'rising' and 'vulnerable' groups. However, an initial estimate of the equivalised household income poverty threshold

Table 4.6: ANOVA and Logistic Regression models of optimum position for the poverty threshold

Model	F statistic for corrected ANOVA model	Logistic Regression model chi-square
Null model[a]	1,176	
Deprivation score of 1 or more	1,760	2,575
Deprivation score of 2 or more	3,526	6,808
Deprivation score of 3 or more	5,252	11,385
Deprivation score of 4 or more	**5,281**	**13,903**
Deprivation score of 5 or more	4,032	13,597
Deprivation score of 6 or more	2,625	10,762
Deprivation score of 7	1,488	5,954

Note: [a] The null model only contains the number of adults and the number of children in the household as independent variables.

is 2,230. This is the upper bound of the 95% Confidence Interval of the mean incomes of those households scoring 4 on the CONEVAL deprivation index.

If we assume that the 'truly' poor (to use Bjorn Halleröd's 1995 term) in Mexico are those who have incomes below the poverty threshold and also suffer from four or more deprivations, then the poverty prevalence rate using the CONEVAL seven-item deprivation index is approximately 36% of households.

Conclusion

Eradicating child poverty during the 21st century is the greatest policy challenge of the era. If this can be accomplished, millions of children will not die needlessly, and untold suffering will be prevented. Valid and reliable measurement is a prerequisite for effective and efficient evidence-based policy interventions to end child poverty. Without good measurement of child poverty, resources may not be targeted at the groups of children in greatest need, and it will prove impossible to evaluate the cost-effectiveness of anti-poverty policies. This chapter has shown how a scientific theory of poverty measurement can produce valid and reliable estimates of the extent and depth of child poverty. The worked example using data from Mexico demonstrates how statistical criteria can be used to identify a best sub-set of deprivation indicator variables that can be used to identify and reject inadequate indicators in a consistent rather than arbitrary manner. Of equal importance, the methodology can identify 'problems' in the micro data and thereby assist improvements in questionnaire design and data collection.

It is important to understand that the use of the term 'scientific' in this chapter is a claim to 'method' and not a claim to 'truth' (that is, our method must be correct because it is 'scientific') – we are advocating science not scientism.[3] Scientific method is preferable as two researchers who follow the methodology using the same data will produce the same results, even when they begin from different initial starting points. This is unlikely to be true for either the Wealth/Asset Index or the Alkire and Foster (2007) child poverty measurement methodology, as two different researchers might select different sets of deprivation/asset indicators and/or dimensions, and these methods provide no mechanism to determine which one is 'correct'.

There are of course many limitations in the child poverty measurement methodology of Gordon et al (2003). In particular, the normative definition of absolute poverty agreed by 117 governments at the World Summit in Copenhagen, which underlies the methodology, does not include the social needs of children. Children are social beings who in all societies have social roles and obligations to their family and friends. Fulfilling these roles and obligations is an integral part of childhood, and children who are seriously deprived of social interactions become disturbed and fail to thrive. The methodology of Gordon et al (2003) could be improved on by adopting a more comprehensive definition of child poverty that acknowledged children's social needs. Indicators of social deprivation should be incorporated into the poverty measure. An excellent example of how this can be achieved in developing countries can be found in the work of the South African Measures of Child Poverty Project (Barnes, 2009a, 2009b).

Notes

[1] The United Nations (UN) defines household final consumption expenditure as 'the expenditure, including imputed expenditure, incurred by resident households on individual consumption goods and services, including those sold at prices that are not economically significant' (http://unstats.un.org/unsd/snaama/glossresults.asp?gID=31).

[2] Alimentary poverty refers to households with insufficient resources to obtain their basic food and nutritional needs. Capacities poverty refers to those households that are food poor, plus those that cannot cover the necessary expenses for health and education. Patrimony poverty is the third threshold and includes those who are food and capacities poor plus those households that cannot meet basic dwelling, transport and clothing costs (Delgado, 2006).

[3] Scientism is the idea that natural science is the most authoritative/correct world view.

References

Alkire, S. and Foster, J. (2007) *Counting and multidimensional poverty measurement*, Oxford Poverty & Human Development Initiative (OPHI) Working Paper No 7, Oxford: University of Oxford.

Alkire, S. and Foster, J. (2009) 'Counting and multidimensional poverty', in J. von Braun (ed) *The poorest and hungry: Assessment, analysis and actions*, Washington, DC: International Food Policy Research Institute, pp 77-89.

Alkire, S. and Roche, J. (2009) *Beyond headcount: The Alkire-Foster approach to multidimensional child poverty measurement*, Child Poverty Insights, New York: United Nations Children's Fund.

Alkire, S. and Santos, M.E. (2010) *Acute multidimensional poverty: A new index for developing countries*, Oxford Poverty & Human Development Initiative (OPHI) Working Paper No 38, Oxford: University of Oxford.

Anand, S., Segal, P. and Stiglitz, J. (eds) (2010) *Debates on the measurement of global poverty*, Oxford: Oxford University Press.

Barnes, H. (2009a) *Child poverty in South Africa: A socially perceived necessities approach*, Measure of Child Poverty Project Key Report 2, Pretoria: Department of Social Development, Republic of South Africa.

Barnes, H. (2009b) *Children's views of an acceptable standard of living for children in South Africa*, Measures of Child Poverty Project Key Report 3, Pretoria: Department of Social Development, Republic of South Africa.

Beccaria, L. and Minujin, A. (1988) *Métodos alternativos para medir la evolución del tamaño de la pobreza*, Buenos Aires: Instituto Nacional de Estadística y Censos de Argentina.

Black, R. E., Morris, S. S. and Bryce, J. (2003) Where and why are 10 million children dying every year? Lancet, vol 361, pp 2226-34.

Boarini, R. and d'Ercole, M.M. (2006) *Measures of material deprivation in OECD countries*, Working Paper No 37, Paris: Directorate for Employment, Labour and Social Affairs, Organisation for Economic Co-operation and Development.

Boelhouwer, J. (2010) *Wellbeing in the Netherlands. The SCP life situation index since 1974*, The Hague: The Netherlands Institute for Social Research (SCP).

Boelhouwer, J. and Stoop, I. (1999) 'Measuring well-being in the Netherlands. The SCP-index from 1974 to 1997', *Social Indicators Research*, vol 48, pp 51-75.

Boltvinik, J. (1992) *América Latina: El reto de la pobreza, proyecto regional para la superación de la pobreza en América Latina y el Caribe*, Indices de pobreza para los métodos NBI y MIP, Bogotá: United Nations Development Programme.

Boltvinik, J. (1997) *Poverty measurement methods – An overview*, New York: United Nations Development Programme.

Cabrera, A. and Miguel, C. (2002) *Economía Informa*, Número 311, Octubre, Mexico City: Facultad de Economía de la de Universidad Nacional Autónoma de México.

Callan, T., Nolan, B. and Whelan, C. (1993) 'Resources, deprivation and the measurement of poverty', *Journal of Social Policy*, vol 22, no 2, pp 141-72.

CONEVAL (2009) *Metodología para la medición multidimensional de la pobreza en México*, Mexico City: CONEVAL.

Cortina, J. (1993) 'What is coefficient alpha?', *Journal of Applied Psychology*, vol 1, pp 98-104.

Cronbach, L.J. (1951) 'Coefficient alpha and the internal structure of tests', *Psychometrika*, vol 16, no 3, pp 297-334.

Cronbach, L.J. and Shavelson, R.L. (2004) 'My current thoughts on coefficient alpha and successor procedures', *Educational and Psychological Measurement*, vol 64, pp 391-418.

Davey Smith G. (2007) Boyd Orr Lecture. Life-course approaches to inequalities in adult chronic disease risk. Proceeding of the Nutrition Society, vol 66, pp216-236.

Delgado, J.O. (2006) 'The policy of combat to poverty in Mexico, 1982-2005', *Papeles de POBLACIÓN*, vol 47, pp 74-101.

Delamonica, E.E. and Minujin, A. (2007) 'Incidence, depth and severity of children in poverty', *Social Indicators Research*, vol 82, no 2, pp 361-74.

Desai, M. (1986) 'On defining the poverty threshold', in P. Golding (ed) *Excluding the poor*, London: Child Poverty Action Group.

Desai, M. and Shah, A. (1988) 'An econometric approach to the measurement of poverty', *Oxford Economic Papers*, no 40, pp 505-22.

ECLAC (Economic Commission for Latin America and the Caribbean)/Dirección General de Estadística y Censos del Uruguay (DGEC) (1988) *La heterogeneidad de la pobreza: Una aproximación bidimensional* (LC/MVD/R.12/Rev 1), Montevideo.

Falkingham, J. and Namazie, C. (2002) *Measuring health and poverty: A review of approaches to identifying the poor*, London: Department for International Development Health Systems Resource Centre.

Fergusson, D., Hong, B., Horwood, J., Jensen, J. and Travers, P. (2001) *Living standards of older New Zealanders*, Wellington: Ministry of Social Policy.

Filmer, D. and Pritchett, L. (1998) Estimating wealth effects without income or expenditure data – or tears: educational enrolment in India. World Bank Policy Research working paper, No. 1994. Washington DC, World Bank.

Filmer, D. and Pritchett, L.H. (1999) 'The impact of public spending on health: does money matter?', *Social Science & Medicine*, vol 49, pp 1309-23.

Filmer, D. and Pritchett, L.H. (2001) 'Estimating wealth effects without expenditure data – or tears: an application to educational enrollments in states of India', *Demography*, vol 38, no 1, pp 115-32.

Foster, J., Greer, J. and Thorbecke, E. (1984) 'A class of decomposable poverty measures', *Econometrica*, vol 52, pp 761-76.

Foster, J., Greer, J. and Thorbecke, E. (2010) 'The Foster–Greer–Thorbecke (FGT) poverty measures: 25 years later', *Journal of Economic Inequality*, vol 8, no 4, pp 491-524.

Freeman, A. (2007) 'The poverty of statistics and the statistics of poverty', *Third World Quarterly*, vol 30, no 8, pp 1427-48.

Galobardes, B., Lynch, J.W. and Davey Smith, G. (2004) 'Childhood socioeconomic circumstances and cause-specific mortality in adulthood: systematic review and interpretation', *Epidemiological Review*, vol 26, pp 7-21.

Galobardes, B., Lynch, J.W. and Davey Smith, G. (2008) 'Is the association between childhood socioeconomic circumstances and cause-specific mortality established? Update of a systematic review', *Journal of Epidemiology and Community Health*, vol 62, pp 387-90.

Gordon, D. (2000) 'The scientific measurement of poverty: recent theoretical advances', in J. Bradshaw and R. Sainsbury (eds) *Researching poverty*, Aldershot: Ashgate, pp 37-58.

Gordon, D. (2002) 'The international measurement of poverty and anti-poverty policy', in P. Townsend and D. Gordon (eds) *World poverty: New policies to defeat an old enemy*, Bristol: The Policy Press, pp 53-80.

Gordon, D. (2006) 'The concept and measurement of poverty', in C. Pantazis, D. Gordon and R. Levitas (eds) *Poverty and social exclusion in Britain: The Millennium Survey*, Bristol: The Policy Press, pp 29-70.

Gordon, D. (2010) Metodología de Medición Multidimensional de la Pobreza para México a partir del Concepto de Privación Relativa (Methodology for Multidimensional Poverty Measurement in Mexico Using the Concept of Relative Deprivation – in Spanish). In Boltvinik, J., Chakravarty, S., Foster, J. Gordon, D. Hernández Cid, R., Soto de la Rosa, H. and Mora, M. (coord.), Medición Multidimensional de la Pobreza en México México, D.F: El Colegio de México and Consejo de Evaluación de la Política de Desarrollo Social. pp 401-97.

Gordon, D. and Pantazis, C. (eds) (1997) *Breadline Britain in the 1990s*, Aldershot: Ashgate.

Gordon, D. and Spicker, P. (eds) (1999) *The international glossary on poverty*, London: Zed Books.

Gordon, D., Adelman, A., Ashworth, K., Bradshaw, J., Levitas, R., Middleton, S., Pantazis, C., Patsios, D., Payne, S., Townsend, P. and Williams, J. (2000) *Poverty and social exclusion in Britain*, York: Joseph Rowntree Foundation.

Gordon, D., Nandy, S., Pantazis, C., Pemberton, S. and Townsend, P. (2003) *Child poverty in the developing world*, Bristol: The Policy Press.

Green, S.B., Lissitz, R.W. and Mulaik, S.A. (1977) 'Limitations of coefficient alpha as an index of test unidimensionality', *Educational and Psychological Measurement*, vol 37, pp 827-38.

Halleröd, B. (1994) *Poverty in Sweden: A new approach to direct measurement of consensual poverty*, Umeå Studies in Sociology, No 106, Umeå, Sweden: University of Umeå.

Halleröd, B. (1995) 'The truly poor: indirect and direct measurement of consensual poverty in Sweden', *Journal of European Social Policy*, vol 5, no 2, pp 111-29.

Himanshu (2008) 'What are these new poverty estimates and what do they imply?', *Economic and Political Weekly*, vol 43, 25 October, pp 38-43.

Howe, L.D., Hargreaves, J. and Huttly, S. (2008) 'Issues in the construction of wealth indices for the measurement of socio-economic position in low-income countries', *Emerging Themes in Epidemiology*, vol 5, pp 3-17.

Howe, L.D., Hargreaves, J., Gabrysch, S. and Huttly, S. (2009) 'Is the wealth index a proxy for consumption expenditure? A systematic review', *Journal of Epidemiology and Community Health*, vol 63, no 11, pp 871-80.

Jensen, J., Spittal, M., Crichton, S., Sathiyandra, S. and Krishnan, V. (2002) *Direct measurement of living standards: The New Zealand ELSI scale*, Wellington: Ministry of Social Development.

Kaijage, F. and Tibaijuka, A. (1996) *Poverty and social exclusion in Tanzania*, Research Series, No 109, Geneva: International Institute for Labour Studies (IILS).

Kakwani, N. and Son, H. (2006) *New global poverty counts*, International Poverty Centre Working Paper, No 29, Brasília: United Nations Development Programme, International Poverty Centre.

Kangas, O. and Ritakallio, V.M. (1998) 'Different methods – different results? Approaches to multidimensional poverty', in H. Andreß (ed) *Empirical poverty research in a comparative perspective*, Aldershot: Ashgate, pp 167-203.

Kaztman, R. (1996) *Virtues and limitations of census maps for identifying critical deficiencies*, CEPAL Review, No 58 (LC/G.1916-P/I), Santiago, Chile: Economic Commission for Latin America and the Caribbean (ECLAC).

Kaztman, R. (1999) *Activos y estructuras de oportunidades: Estudios sobre las raíces de la vulnerabilidad social en Uruguay* (LC/MVD/R.180), Montevideo, Uruguay: Economic Commission for Latin America and the Caribbean (ECLAC).

Kevles, D.J. (1985) *In the name of eugenics: Genetics and the uses of human heredity*, New York: Alfred A. Knopf.

Kolenikov, S. and Angeles, G. (2009) 'Socioeconomic status measurement with discrete proxy variables: is Principal Component Analysis a reliable answer?', *Review of Income and Wealth*, vol 55, no 1, pp 128-65.

Kravis, I. (1986) 'The three faces of the International Comparison Project', *World Bank Research Observer*, vol 1, no 1, pp 3-26.

Mack, J. and Lansley, S. (1985) *Poor Britain*, London: George Allen & Unwin.

MacKenzie, D. (1981) *Statistics in Britain, 1865-1930: The social construction of scientific knowledge*, Edinburgh: Edinburgh University Press.

MacKenzie, D. (1999) 'Eugenics and the rise of mathematical statistics in Britain', in D. Dorling and S. Simpson (eds) *Statistics in society: The arithmetic of politics*, London, New York, Sydney, Auckland: Arnold, pp 55-61.

Mazumdar, P.M.H. (1992) *Eugenics, human genetics and human failings: The Eugenics Society, its sources and its critics in Britain*, London: Routledge.

Minujin, A., Delamonica, E.E., Davidziuk, A. and Gonzalez, E.D. (2006) 'The definition of child poverty: a discussion of concepts and measurements', *Environment & Urbanization*, vol 18, no 2, pp 481-500.

Muffels, R., Berghman, J. and Dirven, H. (1992) 'A multi-method approach to monitor the evolution of poverty', *Journal of European Social Policy*, vol 2, no 3, pp 193-213.

Muffels, R.J.A. and Fouarge, D.J.A.G. (2001) Social Exclusion and Poverty: Definition, Public Debate and Empirical Evidence in the Netherlands. In D.G. Mayes, J. Berghman and R. Salais (eds) Social Exclusion and European Policy, pp 93-123. Cheltenham (UK)/ Northampton (MA/USA)): Edward Elgar.

Nandy, S. (2010) 'An analysis of changes in child poverty in the developing world at the end of the 20th century', Unpublished PhD Thesis, University of Bristol.

Nandy, S. and Gordon, D. (2009) 'Children living in squalor: shelter, water and sanitation deprivations in developing countries', *Children, Youth and Environments*, vol 19, pp 202-28.

Nandy, S. and Miranda, J. (2008) 'Overlooking undernutrition? Using a composite index of anthropometric failure to assess how underweight misses and misleads the assessment of undernutrition in young children', *Social Science & Medicine*, vol 66, pp 1963-6.

Nandy, S., Irving, M., Gordon, D., Subramanian, S.V. and Davey-Smith, G. (2005) 'Poverty, child undernutrition and morbidity: new evidence from India', *Bulletin of the World Health Organization*, vol 83, pp 210-16.

Nunnally, J.C. (1981) *Psychometric theory*, New Delhi: Tate McGraw-Hill Publishing Company Ltd.

Orshansky, M. (1965) 'Counting the poor: another look at the poverty profile', *Social Security Bulletin*, vol 28, no 1, pp 3-29.

Orshansky, M. (1969) 'How poverty is measured', *Monthly Labor Review*, vol 92, no 2, pp 37-41.

Pantazis, C., Gordon, D. and Levitas, R. (eds) (2006) *Poverty and social exclusion in Britain*, Bristol: The Policy Press.

Pearson, K. (1901) 'Mathematical contributions to the theory of evolution. vii. On the correlation of characters not qualitatively measurable', *Philosophical Transactions of the Royal Society*, Series A 195, pp 1-47.

Pemberton, S.A., Gordon, D., Nandy, S., Pantazis, C. and Townsend, P. (2005) 'The relationship between child poverty and child rights: the role of indicators', in A. Minujin, E.E. Delamonica and M. Komarecki (eds) *Human rights and social policies for children and women*, New York: The New School, pp 47-62.

Pemberton, S.A., Gordon, D., Nandy, S., Pantazis, C. and Townsend, P. (2007) 'Child rights and child poverty: can the international framework of children's rights be used to improve child survival rates?', *PLoS Medicine*, vol 4, pp 1567-70.

Pogge, T. (2010) 'How many poor people should there be? A rejoinder to Ravallion', in S. Anand, P. Segal and J. Stiglitz (eds) *Debates on the measurement of global poverty*, Oxford: Oxford University Press, pp 102-14.

Ravallion, M. (2010) 'Reply to Reddy and Pogge', in S. Anand, P. Segal and J. Stiglitz (eds) *Debates on the measurement of global poverty*, Oxford: Oxford University Press, pp 87-101.

Ravallion, M., Chen, S. and Sangraula, P. (2008) *Dollar a day revisited*, Policy Research Working Paper 4620, Washington, DC: World Bank.

Ravallion, M., Datt, G. and van de Walle, D. (1991) 'Quantifying absolute poverty in the developing world', *Review of Income and Wealth*, vol 37, pp 345-61.

Reddy, S. and Pogge, T. (2010) 'How not to count the poor', in S. Anand, P. Segal and J. Stiglitz (eds) *Debates on the measurement of global poverty*, Oxford: Oxford University Press, pp 42-86.

Roche, J.M. (2009) *Child poverty measurement in Bangladesh: Improving upon existing measures*, Oxford Poverty & Human Development Initiative (OPHI) Working Paper, Oxford: Oxford University.

Roelen, K. and Gassmann, F. (2008) *Measuring child poverty and well-being: A literature review*, Working Paper Series No 2008/WP001, Maastricht: Maastricht Graduate School of Governance.

Rogoff, K. (1996) 'The purchasing power parity puzzle', *Journal of Economic Literature*, vol 34, pp 647-68.

Saunders, P. and Naidoo, Y. (2009) 'Poverty, deprivation and consistent poverty', *The Economic Record*, vol 85, no 271, pp 417-32.

Shelvin, M., Miles, J.N.V., Davies, M.N.O. and Walker, S. (2000) 'Coefficient alpha a useful measure of reliability?', *Personality and Individual Differences*, vol 28, pp 229-37.

Short, K.S. (2005) 'Material and financial hardship and income-based poverty measures in the USA', *Journal of Social Policy*, vol 34, pp 21-38.

Spencer, N. (2008) *Childhood poverty and adult health*, London: End Child Poverty.

Thomas, B., Dorling, D. and Davey Smith, G. (2010) 'Inequalities in premature mortality in Britain: observational study from 1921 to 2007', *British Medical Journal*, vol 341, c3639, doi:10.1136/bmj.c363

Townsend, P. (1962) 'The meaning of poverty', *British Journal of Sociology*, vol 13, no 3, pp 210-27.

Townsend, P. (1979) *Poverty in the United Kingdom*, Harmondsworth: Penguin Books Ltd.

Townsend, P. (1987) 'Deprivation', *Journal of Social Policy*, vol 16, no 2, pp 125-46.

Townsend, P. (1997) 'The poverty line: methodology and international comparisons', in D. Gordon and C. Pantazis (eds) *Breadline Britain in the 1990s*, Aldershot: Ashgate Publishing Ltd, pp 49-69.

Townsend, P. and Gordon, D. (1993) 'What is enough? The definition of a poverty line', in P. Townsend, *The international analysis of poverty*, New York, London, Toronto, Sydney, Tokyo, Singapore: Harvester Wheatsheaf, pp 40-78.

Townsend, P. and Gordon, D. (2002) *World poverty: New policies to defeat an old enemy*, Bristol: The Policy Press.

UN (United Nations) (1995) *The Copenhagen Declaration and Programme of Action*, World Summit for Social Development, 6-12 March, New York: UN.

UNDESA (United Nations Department of Economic and Social Affairs) (2010) *Rethinking poverty: Report on the world social situation 2010*, New York: UN.

UN (United Nations) Expert Group on Poverty Statistics (Rio Group) (2006) *Compendium of best practice in poverty measurement*, Rio de Janeiro and Santiago: Brazilian Institute for Geography and Statistics (IBGE), with the UN Economic Commission for Latin America and the Caribbean (ECLAC).

UNGA (United Nations General Assembly) (2006) *Promotion and protection of the rights of children: Report of the Third Committee*, New York: UN.

UNICEF (2007) U.N. General Assembly adopts powerful definition of child poverty. New York, UNICEF. Available at: www.unicef.org/media/media_38003.html.

Vyas, S. and Kumaranayake, L. (2006) 'Constructing socio-economic status indices: how to use principal components analysis', *Health Policy and Planning*, vol 21, no 6, pp 459-68.

Whelan, C.T. and Maitre, B. (2007) 'Measuring material deprivation with EU-SILC: lessons from the Irish Survey', *European Societies*, vol 9, pp 147-3.

World Bank (1990) *World Development Report 1990: Poverty*, Washington, DC: World Bank.

World Bank (1996) *Poverty assessments: A progress review*, Washington, DC: World Bank.

World Bank (2000) *World Development Report 2000/2001: Attacking poverty*, Oxford: Oxford University Press.

WHO (World Health Organization) (1995) *World Health Report 1995: Bridging the gaps*, Geneva: WHO.

WHO (2008) Commission on Social Determinants of Health, *Final report: Closing the gap in a generation: Health equity through action on the social determinants of health*, Geneva: World Health Organization.

FIVE

Beyond headcount: measures that reflect the breadth and components of child poverty

Sabina Alkire and José Manuel Roche

Introduction

Measures of child poverty undoubtedly influence policies to reduce child poverty. The accuracy, precision and informational content of child poverty measures create value insofar as they enable policy makers, parents and other groups to eliminate the suffering and deprivation of children. Hence debates on measures of child poverty are motivated by a shared objective: creating tools that enable children to enjoy a childhood free from fear and want. This chapter presents a new approach to child poverty measurement, which learns from, and improves on, previous methods.

The Alkire-Foster (2007, 2011) method presented in this chapter seeks to answer the question 'Who is poor?' by considering the intensity of each person's poverty. Once people are identified as poor, the measures aggregate information on poor people's deprivations in a way that can be broken down to see where and how people are poor. The resulting measures go beyond the headcount by taking into account the breadth, depth or severity of dimensions of child poverty. For example, Country A and Country B might both experience 40% child poverty, but in Country A, most children are deprived in three dimensions, whereas in Country B, most children are deprived in six of the same dimensions (these dimensions could include nutrition, water, sanitation, housing and education). Also, policy makers need to know the specific configuration of children's deprivations in their area in order to address poverty adequately. But the headcount ratio cannot be broken down by dimension to uncover the components of child poverty in different regions or age group or by gender. The Alkire-Foster method deals systematically with these issues and can be easily applied to child poverty measurement to enhance the headcount measure. In this chapter we explain how this can be done, and illustrate the case by measuring multidimensional child poverty in Bangladesh using four rounds of the Demographic and Health Survey.

We begin by reviewing the context of composite measures of child poverty. A key partner in dialogue is the 'Bristol Approach' that has contributed substantially to child poverty measurement (Gordon et al, 2003), and their specification of indicators and cut-offs is used insofar as is feasible in the analysis. The subsequent section explains the Alkire-Foster method and the way in which it can enhance existing methodologies by offering a clear specification of the dual cut-off method – a deprivation cut-off and poverty cut-off – by reflecting the intensity of multidimensional poverty, and by enabling the child poverty measure to be broken down by dimension. This is then illustrated with a substantive empirical application in Bangladesh. The final section concludes.

Child poverty and multidimensional measurement

Issues of multidimensionality have received special attention in the recent literature on poverty and inequality. The seminal works of Amartya Sen (1980, 1985, 1992, 1999; see also Foster and Sen, 1997) have systematically critiqued the income and utility focus of neoclassical economics and proposed that well-being be understood as multidimensional and considered in the space of capabilities.[1] Interestingly, while multidimensional studies were – and perhaps still are – relatively scarce in welfare economics, the debate concerning child well-being has predominantly followed a multidimensional perspective (for some reviews, see Minujin et al, 2006; Roelen and Gassmann, 2008).

Recent literature on child poverty follows a rights perspective stimulated by international summits and conventions, including the 1989 United Nations Convention on the Rights of the Child (UNCRC), the 1990 World Summit for Children and the 2002 Declaration 'A world fit for children'.[2] The growing interest in setting goals and targets to monitor progress has stimulated data collection and increased the availability of internationally comparable data. This has been particularly boosted by major international survey projects such as the Multiple Indicator Cluster Surveys and the Demographic and Household Surveys. While richer data frequently provide the opportunity to share more comprehensive or holistic analyses, in practice a large array of indicators may overwhelm or confuse readers. An array also does not provide an overview of progress. Its biggest drawback is that it does not show whether the same children are deprived in multiple dimensions at the same time – yet the multiplicity of deprivations a child experiences directly affects that child's development. Such considerations can be addressed by developing robust indices that summarise multiple dimensions of child poverty in a single measure, and can be used for comparing child poverty across regions and across time. Several existing measures of child poverty were developed to meet this need.

The Bristol Approach adopted by the Global Study (UNICEF, 2007) is one significant effort to provide a methodology for measuring multidimensional child poverty. It was developed by a research team from the Townsend Centre for International Poverty Research at the University of Bristol, and was used to produce the first internationally comparable estimates of child poverty across a large number of developing countries (Gordon et al, 2001, 2003; UNICEF, 2004). Their substantial contribution was to propose a way to align child poverty measurement with the child rights approach and to implement, insofar as data permitted, indicators and cut-offs for child poverty that reflected the definition agreed at the World Summit for Social Development in Copenhagen. This made the final measure arguably suitable for monitoring certain children's rights according to the UNCRC and 'A world fit for children'. At a more practical level, the study is attractive because it used Demographic and Health Survey data and can be replicated with Multiple Indicator Cluster Survey data as shown in the Global Study.

Methodologically, the Bristol Approach belongs to the 'counting' tradition of poverty measures used in Europe and in Basic Needs Approaches (Mack and Lansley, 1985; Erikson, 1993; Nolan and Whelan, 1996; Feres and Mancero, 2001). Like all of the 'counting' approaches to multidimensional poverty measurement, it identifies the poor according to the total number of dimensions in which they are deprived. Then, in common with other counting methodologies, it reports the 'headcount' or percentage of children who have been identified as multidimensionally poor as the final measure. This headcount measure is theoretically relevant, easy and clear to compute, and straightforward to interpret – being analogous to the traditional income headcount ratio. But the headcount provides no incentive for policy makers to prioritise the poorest children of all.

As Delamonica and Minujin (2007) and Alkire and Foster (2007, 2011) observe, the drawback of the headcount is that it does not account for the average intensity of deprivation, much less for depth or severity.[3] The problem is that the headcount ratio remains unchanged when children that are already poor become deprived in an additional dimension, or when their level of deprivation in a particular dimension deteriorates. The traditional FGT measures in income poverty do account for these (see Foster et al, 1984). Imagine two policies that are addressed to 100 children. Policy 'A' focuses on the 30 poorest of poor children while policy 'B' focuses on the 30 poor children that are least poor – that is, those closest to the limit of being non-poor. The headcount ratio would assess the success of each policy only in terms of reducing the number of children who are poor but completely overlook the intensity of poverty among the poor. As a result, policy 'B' could be judged very positively if it lifted, say, 20 children out of poverty merely by reducing the number of children who were close to the poverty threshold. Policy 'A', meanwhile, might be judged to be less successful, even if it significantly alleviated the level of deprivation experienced by all 30 of the poorest children.

Recent breakthroughs in multidimensional poverty methodologies now enable the construction of measures that reward policy makers for addressing the poorest poor, as well as reducing the headcount. This chapter presents and implements one such methodology, which, very simply, uses the average number of deprivations poor children experience – called the 'intensity of poverty' – to supplement the 'incidence of poverty' as captured by the headcount ratio.

The Alkire–Foster method (2007, 2011) combines the intuitive 'counting' approach that has a long history of empirical implementation in multidimensional poverty (Mack and Lansley, 1985; Erikson, 1993; Feres and Mancero, 2001; Gordon et al, 2003) with the literature on axiomatic approaches to multidimensional poverty in welfare economics (see, for example, Chakravarty et al, 1998; Tsui, 2002; Bourguignon and Chakravarty, 2003; Alkire, 2008). It improves existing approaches to multidimensional poverty measurement by creating a measure M_0 that reflects the intensity or breadth of multidimensional poverty when data are ordinal (as data on water, sanitation and housing usually are). When data are cardinal, other M_0 measures can also reflect the depth and severity of multidimensional poverty. As we will see, the Alkire–Foster measures satisfy a series of properties including decomposability that allows the index to be broken down by population subgroup (such as region or ethnicity) and, after identification, by dimension. As we show in the empirical application below, this can help us better understand the dimensions and intensity of poverty, and provides a wealth of data useful for policy makers when planning or assessing interventions. We first explain the method from a theoretical point of view, and then present an empirical illustration from a study of child poverty measurement in Bangladesh.

Alkire-Foster approach to multidimensional poverty measurement

Let us start by explaining briefly the Alkire–Foster method (for a complete formal explanation, see Alkire and Foster, 2007, 2011). The method can be intuitively introduced in 12 steps. The first six steps are common to many multidimensional poverty measures; the remainder are more specific to the Alkire-Foster method.

Step 1: Choose unit of analysis. The unit of analysis is most commonly the individual or the household. In our case, it is the child, so that we can see how each child is doing.

Step 2: Choose dimensions. The choice of dimensions is important yet also more straightforward than is often assumed (see Alkire, 2008). In choosing general categories such as 'health' or 'education', most researchers implicitly draw on five selection methods, either alone or in combination:

- Ongoing deliberative participatory exercises that elicit the values and perspectives of stakeholders. A variation of this method is to use survey data on people's perceived necessities (an example for child poverty is Biggeri et al, 2006).
- A list that has achieved a degree of legitimacy through public consensus, such as the Universal Declaration of Human Rights, the Millennium Development Goals (MDGs), or similar lists at national and local levels. For example, Gordon et al (2003) rely on the consensus agreed in the 1995 World Summit for Social Development in Copenhagen.
- Implicit or explicit assumptions about what people do or should value. At times these are the informed guesses of the researcher; in other situations they are drawn from convention, social or psychological theory or philosophy (as using Nussbaum's list of capabilities by Di Tommaso, 2007).
- Convenience or a convention that is taken to be authoritative or used because these are the only data available that have the required characteristics (for example, available variables in the survey at hand).
- Empirical evidence regarding the core dimensions that are vital for child development; these are often psychological and/or longitudinal studies.

Clearly these processes overlap and are often used in tandem empirically; for example, nearly all exercises need to consider data availability or data issues, and often participation, or at least consensus, is required to give the dimensions public legitimacy.

Step 3: Choose dimensional indicators. Particular indicators are also chosen for their empirical properties, as well as according to their accuracy (using as many indicators as necessary so that analysis can properly guide policy) and to parsimony (using as few indicators as possible to ensure ease of analysis for policy purposes and transparency). For example, indicators must be accurate reflections of each child's own well-being rather than accurate only on average. The purpose of the measure will also shape the indicators: for example, if comparisons are to be made across space and time, then such differences must be interpretable. Statistical properties are often relevant – for example, when possible and reasonable, choosing indicators that are not highly correlated. Note that we will continue to use the word 'dimension' to reflect a particular indicator, so use these terms to some extent interchangeably. Sometimes – as in Alkire and Santos (2010) – it becomes convenient to distinguish these terms.

Step 4: Set and apply deprivation cut-offs. A deprivation cut-off (similar to a poverty line for income) is set for each dimension. This step establishes the first cut-off in the methodology. Every child can then be identified as deprived or non-deprived with respect to each dimension. For example, if the dimension is schooling ('How many years of schooling have you completed?') then for 14-year-olds, '6 years or more' might identify non-deprivation while '1-5 years' might identify deprivation in the domain. Deprivation cut-offs can be tested for robustness, or multiple levels of thresholds can be used to clarify explicitly different categories of the poor (such as poor and extreme poor).

   Having been set, the deprivation cut-offs are applied to the data. This step replaces the child's achievement with their status with respect to each cut-off – for example, in the dimension of health where the indicators are (1) 'having received all vaccinations' and (2) 'vitamin A supplementation', children are identified as being deprived or non-deprived for each indicator. The process is repeated for all indicators for all other dimensions. Table 5.1 provides an example for a group of four children. ND indicates that the child is not deprived (in other words, his or her achievement in that dimension is equal to or higher than the cut-off), and D indicates that the child is deprived (his or her achievement is strictly lower than the cut-off).

Table 5.1: Example, part I

| | Health | | Living standard | | Education | |
| | Measles | | Tenure or | Over-crowded | School | Total |
Children	immunisation	Vitamin A	eviction	housing	attendance	count
Child 1	ND	D	D	ND	D	3
Child 2	ND	ND	ND	D	ND	1
Child 3	ND	D	D	ND	ND	2
Child 4	D	D	D	D	D	5

Step 5: Set and apply weights. Weights must be applied to each dimension. There is some appeal in the use of 'equal weights' due to the easy interpretability of the index. Alternatively, general weights are applied, such that the total weights across all dimensions add up to the number of dimensions. For example, if there are four dimensions, and one dimension is to weight one half, and the others one sixth, then the weights will be $(2, 2/3, 2/3, 2/3)$, because the sum of these four weights is equal to the number of dimensions, namely four. If a person is deprived in a dimension, then their 'D' is now replaced with the weight on that dimension; a 0 is applied for people who are not deprived.

Step 6: Count the number of deprivations for each child. The weighted sum of deprivations for each person is now calculated. This step is demonstrated using equal weights in the last column of Table 5.1.

Step 7: Set the second cut-off (poverty cut-off). Assuming equal weights for simplicity, set a second poverty cut-off, k, which sets the sum of weighted dimensions (in this case, the number of dimensions) in which a child must be deprived in order to be identified as multidimensionally poor. In practice, it may be useful to calculate the measure for several values of k. In the example in Table 5.1, k is set to 3 and the shaded children are identified as poor.

Step 8: Apply cut-off k to obtain the set of poor children and censor all non-poor data. This step is novel and often overlooked. After censoring, the focus is now exclusively on the poor children and the dimensions in which they are deprived. All information on the non-poor children is replaced with zeros. This step is shown in Table 5.2. Recall that by changing the value of k you can see all deprivations or only those of the poorest poor, so the poverty cut-off k is rather like a sliding scale that brings to light different aspects of poverty as it changes.

Table 5.2: Example, part II

Children	Health			Living standard		Education	
	Measles immunisation	Vitamin A		Tenure or eviction	Over-crowded housing	School attendance	Total count
Child 1	0	1		1	0	1	3
Child 2	0	0		0	0	0	0
Child 3	0	0		0	0	0	0
Child 4	1	1		1	1	1	5

Step 9: Calculate the headcount, H. Divide the number of poor children by the total number of children. In our example, when $k = 3$ the headcount is merely the proportion of children who are poor in at least three dimensions. For example, as seen in Tables 5.1 and 5.2, two of the four children were identified as poor, so $H = 2/4 = 50\%$. This is precisely the measure used by the Bristol Approach and it is analogous to the income headcount ratio. The multidimensional headcount is a useful measure, but it does not increase if poor children become more deprived, nor can it be broken down by dimension to analyse how poverty differs among groups. For that reason we augment it by using the information on the intensity of deprivation.

Step 10: Calculate the average intensity, A. A is the average number of (sum of weighted) deprivations a poor child suffers. It is calculated by adding up the proportion of total deprivations each poor child suffers (for example, in Table 5.2, Child 1 suffers three out of five deprivations and Child 4 suffers five out of five) and dividing by the total number of poor children: $A = (3/5 + 5/5)/2 = 4/5$.

Step 11: Calculate the adjusted headcount, M_0. If the data are binary or ordinal, a multidimensional poverty index is measured by the adjusted headcount, M_0, which is simply calculated as $H \times A$.[4] The headcount is multiplied by the 'average' intensity. In our example, $HA = 2/4 \star 4/5 = 2/5$.

Related multidimensional measures: calculate the adjusted poverty gap (M_1) and squared poverty gap (M_2). If the data are cardinal, replace the '1' for each deprived child by their normalised poverty gap (the deprivation cut-off minus their achievement divided by the deprivation cut-off), and calculate the average normalised poverty gap G, which is the sum of the values of the poverty gaps, divided by the number of deprivations (in the case of ordinal data, the poverty gap will always be 1). The adjusted poverty gap M_1 is given by HAG, or the M_0 measure above multiplied by the average poverty gap G. The squared poverty gap M_2 is calculated by squaring each poverty gap individually and replacing G with the average squared normalised poverty gap S, so the measure is HAS. The squared measure reflects inequality among the poor.

Step 12: Decompose by group and break down by dimension. The resulting measures − M_0, M_1 or M_2 can be decomposed by population subgroup (such as region, rural/urban or ethnicity). For example, after constructing M_0 for each subgroup of the sample, we can break M_0 apart to study the contribution of each dimension to overall poverty. To break down by dimension, let A_j be the contribution of dimension j to the average poverty gap A. A_j could be interpreted as the average deprivation share across the poor in dimension j. The dimension–adjusted contribution of dimension j to overall poverty, which we call M_{0j}, is then obtained by multiplying H by A_j for each dimension.

Basic properties of the multidimensional measure M_0

Because cardinal data are often not available, it is likely that the most commonly appropriate measure of child poverty will be M_0. Hence it is quite interesting to note that the adjusted headcount M_0 is particularly useful, for a variety of reasons worth mentioning:

- It can be used to compare different groups in the population, such as children from different regions, ethnic groups or genders.
- It can be broken down into dimensions to reveal to policy makers what dimensions contribute the most to multidimensional poverty in any given region or population group.
- The poverty level increases if one or more children become deprived in an additional dimension, so it is sensitive to the multiplicity of deprivations (or intensity of poverty among the poor).
- It adjusts for the size of the group for which it is being calculated, allowing for meaningful comparisons across different-sized regions or countries.

In this section we have explained the Alkire–Foster method intuitively; we will now move on to illustrate it with a direct application to child poverty measurement based on four periods of Demographic and Health Survey data in Bangladesh.

An illustrative application: indicators of child poverty in Bangladesh

The Alkire–Foster method can be applied to various contexts and purposes. A widely known example is the Multidimensional Poverty Index launched by the United Nations Development Programme (UNDP) in the 2010 *Human Development Report*. The index provides internationally comparable estimates of multidimensional poverty across more than 100 developing countries (Alkire and Santos, 2010; UNDP, 2010).

However, the method can be adapted to other contexts and purposes by adopting different specifications: unit of analysis, choice of dimensions, choice of indicators, dimensional cut-offs, poverty cut-off and weights. There are currently a growing number of applications of multidimensional poverty measurement in academic research (see, for example, Batana, 2008; Santos and Ura, 2008; Alkire and Seth, 2009; Battiston et al, 2009). Interest in policy applications at a national level is also growing fast. A very significant methodology of this type are the official national poverty measures for Mexico (CONEVAL, 2010) and Colombia (Angulo et al. 2011). There have also been applications to other multidimensional measurement problems such as targeting of conditional cash transfers (Azevedo and Robles, 2010) and measuring energy provision (Nussbaumer et al, 2011).

The first adaptation of the Alkire–Foster methodology to child poverty measurement was undertaken by Roche (2009) using Multiple Cluster Indicator Survey data from Bangladesh, while more recent research by Apablaza and Yalonetzky (2011) has applied the method to study child poverty dynamics using the Young Life and Times Survey.[5] The method was also applied to measure trends on child poverty in Egypt as part of the Global Study on Child Poverty and Disparities (El-Laithy and Armanious, 2010). The diversity of applications shows the flexibility of the Alkire–Foster method that can be adapted to multiple contexts and purposes.

We now illustrate the method and different steps in Bangladesh. In this example we use similar specifications to the Bristol Approach in order to show the new insights provided by the Alkire–Foster method to a familiar set of indicators. Clearly all specifications can be adjusted according to the context and purpose of the application. In particular, we show how the Alkire–Foster method provides a fuller understanding of what drives changes in poverty levels over time. We show this by looking at changes in three ways. First we show how poverty has been reduced and whether changes to the incidence or intensity of child poverty have made the biggest contribution to overall reductions. We then look at the performance of each deprivation such as water, shelter and health individually to see where the biggest gains (and losses) have occurred. Finally, we look into regional decompositions to examine subnational variations in child poverty.

Data

Our example is based on the Bangladesh Demographic and Health Survey data from 1997, 2000, 2004 and 2007. This is part of the worldwide Demographic and Health Surveys programme, which is designed to collect data on fertility, family planning and maternal and child health (www.measuredhs.com/). The surveys in Bangladesh are implemented through a collaborative effort of the Bangladesh National Institute of Population Research and Training (NIPORT), Macro International, US, and Mitra & Associates with financial support from the US Agency for International Development (USAID). The international standards and purposes of the Demographic and Health Surveys make them especially well suited to the proposed child poverty measure as they have good quality child-specific indicators to measure health dimensions that are not normally included in living standards household surveys.[6]

The Bangladesh Demographic and Health Survey follows a multistage cluster sampling which is designed to provide separate estimates at the national level for urban and rural areas, and for all six provinces in Bangladesh: Barisal, Chittagong, Dhaka, Khulna, Rajshahi and Sylhet. The survey consists of five questionnaires: (1) a household questionnaire; (2) a questionnaire for individual women aged 10-49; (3) a questionnaire for individual men aged 15-54; (4) a community questionnaire; and (5) a facility questionnaire. The fieldwork activities were implemented during March-August 2007, January-May 2004, November 1999-March 2000 and November 1996-March 1997 respectively. The final sample corresponds to 10,268 households in 2007, 10,053 households in 2004, 10,919 households in 2000 and 9,099 households in 1997. The households and women's response rates are respectively 99.4% and 98.4% in 2007, 99.8 and 98.6% in 2004, 99.3% and 96.9% in 2000 and 99.1% and 97.8% in 1997.

Unit of analysis

As would be expected from a child poverty measure, our estimations use each child as the unit of analysis rather than the household as a whole or an aggregate of all its members. We chose to focus specifically on under-five child poverty, in order to provide policy-relevant information about the incidence and breadth of multidimensional poverty among this particular age group.[7] While poverty can be measured jointly for all age groups in order to provide a general evaluation of child and youth poverty (as in Gordon et al, 2003), age-specific measures allow the identification of areas for particular interventions. Naturally, children's rights and needs are age-specific and social protection should be designed accordingly. The flexibility of the Alkire-Foster method leaves space to adapt the unit of analysis according to the purpose of the measure. The analysis in this chapter takes full advantage of the Bangladesh Demographic and Health Survey design and the broad information regarding the situation of children under five. The values of the indicators of dwelling are ascribed to the children from their household, while all the other indicators are under-five specific.

Indicators, deprivation cut-offs and weights

The extensive review in Minujin et al (2006) and in Roelen and Gassmann (2008) shows the wide spectrum in the choice of dimensions and indicators among the various child poverty measurement exercises. As explained in Chapter Four, these are important choices that are subject to various considerations. For example, the Bristol indicators were chosen for an international measure of child poverty. Therefore, the choice of indicators was justified with respect to international consensus and general agreements reached at world summits.[8] However, a national measure might require indicators and cut-offs that are context-specific in order to orient national public policy and stimulate public debate in that particular country. We do not attempt in this chapter to propose an exhaustive list of dimensions and indicators for Bangladesh,[9] but instead chose a set of indicators and cut-offs that are as close as possible to the Bristol indicators, simply for illustrative purposes. Following that methodology also, the indicators are equally weighted.

Table 5.3 presents the list of six indicators used in this measure and the cut-off values that define deprivations in each particular dimension. Four of the indicators are designed to measure progress in specific MDG targets: nutrition, access to safe drinking water, access to improved sanitation and health (UN, 2003). All indicators were standardised to allow comparability across the four datasets.[10] Only indicators that are relevant to under-five children were selected, so we excluded educational deprivations as these are relevant only to school-age children. We could have good reason to wonder if this is

Table 5.3: Selected indicators and deprivation thresholds

Dimension	Deprivation thresholds
Nutrition	Children who are more than two standard deviations below the international reference population for stunting (height for age) or wasting (weight for height) or are underweight (weight for age). The standardisation follows the algorithms provided by the WHO Child Growth Reference Study (WHO, 2006)
Water	Children using water from an unimproved source such as open wells, open springs or surface water (time to water is not included because this information is not available for the Bangladesh Demographic and Health Survey 1997)
Sanitation	Children using unimproved sanitation facilities such as pit latrine without slab, open pit latrine, bucket toilet and hanging toilet. Surveys were standardised for comparability
Health	Children who have not been immunised by two years of age. A child is deprived if the child has not received eight of the following vaccinations: bcg, dpt1, dpt2, dpt3, polio0, polio1, polio2, polio3, measles or did not receive treatment for a recent illness involving an acute respiratory infection or diarrhoea
Shelter	Children living in a house with no flooring (ie, a mud or dung floor) or inadequate roofing (overcrowding was not taken into account because the Bangladesh Demographic and Health Survey 1997 does not register the number of rooms used for sleeping)
Information	Children with no access to a radio or television (ie, broadcast media). This indicator applies only for children above three years of age

Note: Education deprivation was not included because it is not relevant for under-fives. The indicators from the Bristol study 'Severe Deprivation of Access to Basic Services' was not available for all four Bangladesh Demographic and Health Survey rounds.

an exhaustive list of under-five child poverty indicators and whether it is informative enough for the Bangladesh context. There might be some 'missing dimensions' in this list such as love, care and social relatedness, support for learning and child development, the right to identity, protection against eviction, violence and natural disasters, among others. The list of indicators for a national measure would be adjusted further to suit the context. National poverty measures can also be useful in stimulating the production of more and better data, as was the case in Mexico (CONEVAL, 2010).

Under-five child poverty in Bangladesh (1997-2007)

Incidence of deprivation and adjusted headcount ratio

Let us start by exploring the incidence of deprivation in relation to the indicators (for example, health, water, nutrition, etc) for the most recent year: 2007. Deprivation rates are highest overall for shelter where over 90% of children live in a house with no flooring or inadequate roofing. Shelter is followed by nutrition, sanitation and information (access to broadcast media) where deprivation rates are nearly 60%. The picture is somewhat better for health and water access, with around 20% of children deprived in health and less than 5% lacking access to an improved source of water.

Naturally, however, suffering from only one deprivation is not the same as suffering from multiple deprivations at the same time. If we now examine the intensity of poverty (or 'joint distribution' of deprivations), we find that 10% of children suffer from only one deprivation, nearly 20% are deprived in two dimensions, 30% from three deprivations and 27% from four deprivations. After four deprivations the percentage decreases considerably: those with five or six deprivations experience an 'intensity' of poverty which is significantly high in absolute and relative terms.[11]

As previously explained, Step 7 in the Alkire–Foster method involves defining a 'poverty' cut-off – the number of dimensions children must be deprived of in order to be identified as multidimensionally poor. Table 5.4 presents all possible outcomes depending on the different cut-off values. Column 2 shows the headcount ratio or proportion of children who are considered to be poor according to each poverty cut-off. If the cut-off is set as $k=1$ (children with one or more deprivations), around 96% of children would be identified as poor, which seems to be a high headcount ratio for Bangladesh.[12] If the cut-off is set as $k=2$, the headcount ratio is 86%, and if $k=3$ it is around

Table 5.4: Comparison of multidimensional child poverty for different poverty cut-offs

	1	2	3	4
Poverty cut-off (k)	Multidimensional Child Poverty Index ($M_o = HA$)	Multidimensional headcount (H)	Intensity of deprivation (A)	Average deprivation among the poor
1	0.487	0.964	0.504	3.03
2	0.470	0.864	0.544	3.26
3	0.400	0.655	0.611	3.67
4	0.248	0.351	0.707	4.24
5	0.068	0.081	0.842	5.05
6	0.004	0.004	1.000	6.00

Note: For this example we are considering equal weights but as explained in the methodology, different weights can also be used.

Source: Bangladesh Demographic and Health Survey 2007

66%. The headcount ratio decreases to 8% when the cut-off is set at 5. For our analysis we will consider cut-offs between $k=2$ and $k=4$.

Column 1 presents a figure that can be used as the child poverty index – the *adjusted headcount ratio*. This is the product of the headcount ratio (column 2) and the intensity of deprivation (column 3). The intensity of deprivations (A) is measured according to Step 10 of the methodology. What these figures show is that the average number of deprivations among children who experience at least two deprivations is 3.26 dimensions, and among children who experience at least three dimensions ($k=3$) it is 3.67. M_0 takes into account these variations by adjusting the headcount accordingly.

Changes over time and robustness tests

The choice of poverty cut-off depends, of course, on the purpose of the exercise. For example, if the measure is for targeting purposes, we might decide to set a cut-off that corresponds to the proportion of beneficiaries that can be included in the programme (for example, as determined by budgetary constraints). As we will see, in practice it is recommendable to compute the results for several cut-offs and then assess the most suitable threshold according to the robustness of the conclusions.

Table 5.5 presents the multidimensional poverty figures for Bangladesh for the period 1997 to 2007 (based on a $k=3$ cut-off). It is clear from the results that poverty has decreased. The conclusion is the same if we observe the percentage of children who are poor (H) or the intensity of poverty (A) or the final multidimensional child poverty figure (M_0). For example, the child poverty headcount decreased from

Table 5.5: Changes over time in multidimensional poverty, Bangladesh, 1997-2007

	Multidimensional Child Poverty Index (M_o)	Multidimensional Headcount (H)	Intensity of Poverty (A)
1997	0.555	0.829	0.669
2000	0.495	0.758	0.653
2004	0.485	0.763	0.636
2007	0.400	0.655	0.611
Absolute variation			
1997-2000	−0.060	−0.071	−0.016
2000-04	−0.010	0.005	−0.017
2004-07	−0.085	−0.108	−0.025

Note: The results correspond to a poverty cut-off $k = 3$.

83% in 1997 to around 66% in 2007, and the intensity of poverty from 67% to 61% over the same period.

The question we need to ask is whether the conclusion would be different had we chosen a different cut-off. Figure 5.1 presents a robustness check of how different cut-offs (*k*) change over time. We can see a first order dominance among the curves, which means that no matter which *k* cut-off is considered, multidimensional poverty decreased between 1997 and 2007.[13] As we will see shortly, this robustness check does not always provide such straightforward conclusions, hence the importance of undertaking this analysis.

A crucial question now for policy makers is what has driven the reductions in the child poverty index? Has the percentage of children living in poverty reduced or has the intensity of poverty declined? Table 5.5 shows how much of the reduction in the multidimensional poverty index (M_0) is due to a decrease in the proportion of children who are poor (*H*) and how much is due to a reduction in the intensity of deprivation (*A*). In the first and third period the reduction is observed in both headcount and intensity. In the second period, meanwhile, the small reduction is entirely driven by a decrease in the intensity of poverty, which declined at a similar absolute level as in the first period (−0.017).

So now we want to know which dimensions have driven these changes. Figure 5.2 shows an interesting pattern in the 'censored headcount' – the proportion of children who are simultaneously poor and deprived in a particular dimension. While there is an overall decrease in each dimension over the whole period, deprivations in sanitation, shelter and nutrition actually increased between 2000 and 2004. Interestingly,

Figure 5.1: Robustness check of different cut-off (*k*) in changes in multidimensional poverty over time, Bangladesh, 1997-2004

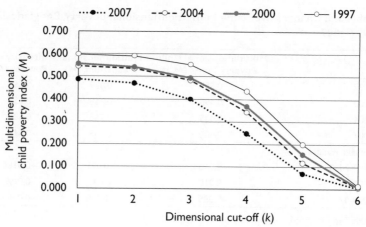

Figure 5.2: Changes over time in censored headcount by indicators, Bangladesh, 1997-2004 (k = 3)

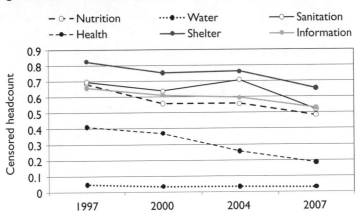

the health dimension shows important improvements over the same period (see the censored headcount and absolute variation Table 5A.2 in Appendix at the end of this chapter). The unique advantage of using this 'censored headcount' approach is that it allows us to unpack the index further and show the factors that drive changes over time using a statistic that is completely mathematically related to the overall index.[14]

Decomposition by subgroup of population

We frequently also want to measure the level of poverty at a regional level, whether for targeting purposes or in order to assess how much a poverty reduction in a region contributes to the overall national change. An important property of the Alkire-Foster method is that the final index can be broken down by population subgroup.

Figure 5.3 shows the changes over time in multidimensional child poverty (M_0) at a provincial level in Bangladesh. While under-five child poverty had been decreasing in the preceding decade, there was a resurgence of poverty in the low-lying coastal regions including Barisal and Chittagong between 2000-04, where the percentage of poor under-five children deprived of improved sanitation facilities, adequate shelter and nutrition actually rose (see Figure 5.4). Strikingly, the region of Barisal was not able to recover as fast as other regions. By 2007 the level of under-five child poverty in Barisal was equivalent to Sylhet – a region from the north east that had much higher poverty than Barisal in 1997. Sylhet is an example of the successes in the eastern part of the country, probably linked to a faster rate of urbanisation (World Bank, 2008). The poor progress in the low-lying coastal regions, meanwhile,

Figure 5.3: Changes over time in multidimensional poverty at a province level, Bangladesh, 1997-2007 (k = 3)

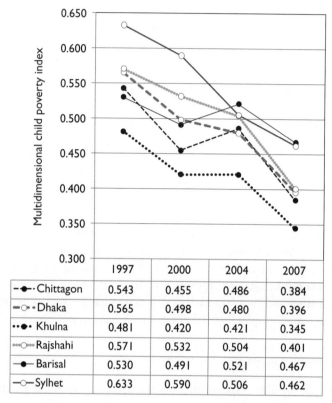

	1997	2000	2004	2007
--●-- Chittagon	0.543	0.455	0.486	0.384
━○━ Dhaka	0.565	0.498	0.480	0.396
••●• Khulna	0.481	0.420	0.421	0.345
⚬⚬○⚬⚬ Rajshahi	0.571	0.532	0.504	0.401
━●━ Barisal	0.530	0.491	0.521	0.467
━○━ Sylhet	0.633	0.590	0.506	0.462

is coherent with findings from research on environmental vulnerability (Azam and Imai, 2009).

We might wonder again about the extent to which the conclusions are sensitive to the choice of cut-off. Figure 5A.1 in the Appendix at the end of this chapter shows robustness checks for different poverty cut-offs in changes in multidimensional poverty over time for all provinces over the period 1997-2007. We can see that the trend is completely robust to changes in poverty cut-off. Provinces such as Dakah, Rajshashi and Sylhet showed improvements over the whole period. Barisal and Chittagong showed improvements in the periods 1997-2000 and 2004-07, but a resurgence of poverty between 2000 and 2004 (robust to $1 \leq k \leq 4$). The Khunla province showed improvements between 1997-2000 and 2004-07, but no statistically significant changes between 2000 and 2004. Similar robustness checks can be performed for ranking comparisons (see Figure 5A.2 in the Appendix to this chapter). We find robust comparisons for Khulna that appears to be

Figure 5.4: Changes over time in the censored headcount by indicator in the provinces of Barisal and Sylhet, 1997–2007 (*k* = 3)

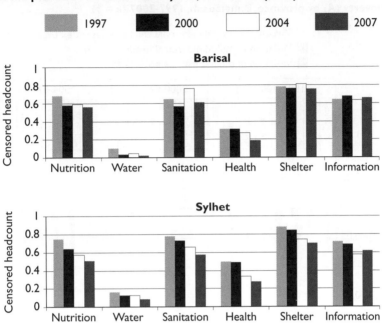

the country's least poor region in all periods (robust to all *k* values). We see, for example, that by 1997 Barisal and Chittagong were the regions with the next lowest multidimensional poverty (robust for 1≤*k*≤4), but that by 2007 Barisal was at the same level as Sylhet (robust for 1≤*k*≤3). As Figure 5A.2 shows, the robustness checks for ranking comparisons is particularly useful – and can be augmented by consideration of standard errors.

What has driven the reduction of child poverty in each province? Figure 5.5 presents the absolute variation in the multidimensional poverty index (M_0), headcount ratio (*H*) and intensity of poverty (*A*) for each province (see Table 5A.1 in the Appendix for detailed figures). We find some very interesting patterns. Khulna reduced overall multidimensional poverty between 1997 and 2000 almost exclusively by decreasing the proportion of poor children (*H*). In contrast Barisal's reduction in multidimensional poverty is driven to a much greater extent by a decrease in the intensity of poverty (*A*). The period 2000-04 is very notable. Dhaka and Rajshashi reduced multidimensional poverty by decreasing the intensity of child poverty (*A*), while Barisal and Chittagong's levels of child poverty actually increased through a rise in the percentage of children who are poor (*H*). The censored headcount in Table 5A.2 (in

Figure 5.5: Absolute variations in the multidimensional child poverty index (M_0), multidimensional headcount (H), and in the intensity of poverty (A) by province. Bangladesh, 1997-2007 ($k = 3$)

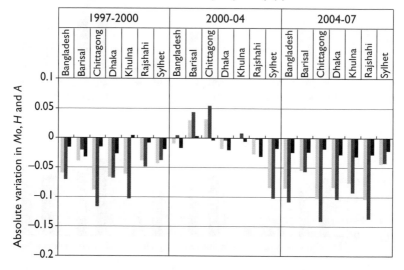

the Appendix) provides information on which dimensions drove these changes in each province – complementing Figure 5.5.

Which province contributes most to overall national poverty? Let's imagine that a child poverty intervention was to be implemented across provinces depending on the level of their need. This would be a function of the size of the region (population share) and the level of multidimensional poverty (H or M_0). Figure 5.6 illustrates how important it is to adjust the poverty headcount ratio (H) by the intensity of poverty (A). A province like Sylhet's contribution to overall poverty is related to its population share, but interestingly the contribution increases even more with M_0 than with H. This is because Sylhet is significantly more poor than other provinces and the intensity of poverty among the poor (A) is also higher. Khulna has the exact opposite pattern. Barisal's contribution by H and M_0 are relatively similar. What these figures show is that if an intervention was going to be implemented to redress child deprivations, it really matters whether we use the headcount ratio (H) or the multidimensional poverty index (M_0). For it is not only the proportion of poor children that matter, but also the intensity of poverty those children experience. This is why M_0 is such a significant tool for policy.

Figure 5.6: Percentage contribution of each province to national population and poverty aggregates, Bangladesh 2007 ($k = 3$)

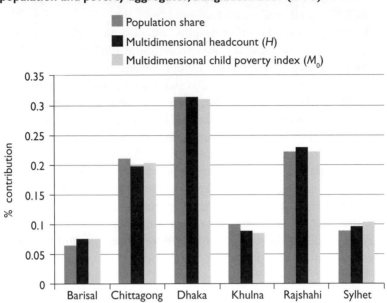

Conclusion

This chapter has explained how a new methodological approach to multidimensional poverty measurement can improve the simple headcount approach to child poverty measurement so that our measures of child poverty reflect the intensity of children's deprivations and also the different contours of poverty in different regions or for different age groups. We have described and applied the Alkire-Foster methodology to demonstrate and assess its potential contribution to multidimensional child poverty measurement.

The results for Bangladesh have shown that the choice of measure does matter, and that measurement has important implications for a range of practical policy applications. The results show that the adjusted headcount ratio M_0 is a significant tool for policy makers as it is likely to produce a different output to the headcount alone, particularly in ranking orders and percentage of contribution to the overall poverty. This is because in contrast to the traditional measures, the adjusted headcount ratio is sensitive to differences in the average deprivations experienced by the poor and – at least in Bangladesh – intensity varies in important ways across regions and over time. Given this, we argue that child poverty should not be assessed only according to the incidence of poverty but also by the intensity of deprivations that batter poor children's lives at the same time. The adjusted headcount ratio M_0 is so useful because it accounts for both.

We have also shown other insights and advantages of the adjusted headcount ratio M_0: that it is easy to compute and interpret, and can be broken down by groups and by dimensions. It also gives rise to a multitude of policy-relevant insights and comparisons. These properties are particularly relevant for targeting and for identifying areas for priority interventions. We also showed how M_0 can be used to analyse changes over time. M_0 can be decomposed by its components to reveal changes that are due to variations in the headcount ratio (H) and those that are attributable to increases or decreases in the intensity of deprivation among the poor. The example of Bangladesh shows that headcount and intensity do not always move together and that any full understanding of changes over time must take these into account.

Finally, a distinct advantage of the Alkire-Foster method is its clear specification of the 'dual cut-off method' – a deprivation cut-off and a poverty cut-off. In many circumstances the cut-off k can seem arbitrary – this might, for example, happen with the poverty measures in the Bristol Approach. The Alkire-Foster method, in contrast, allows us to carry out sensitivity analysis of our results according to different decisions we might take concerning the cut-off k. Naturally, this ability to assess the robustness of the results is useful for making better informed decisions. In addition, the dual cut-off method provides the flexibility to adapt the measure to the specific context, the purpose of the measure and the available or relevant indicators. Should we decide to use the method for targeting, we might decide to select the poverty cut-off according to budgetary considerations.

But of course there are other relevant aspects of the Alkire-Foster method that we did not have the chance to discuss here. For example, we did not explain in detail the possibility of incorporating a system of weights into the adjusted headcount ratio and then assessing the sensitivity of the results given a different weighting structure. Clearly the weight that is attributed to each indicator brings an implicit value judgement with it on the importance of that dimension; while views on weights may vary, the Alkire-Foster method is flexible enough to incorporate general weights. We also did not discuss standard errors, statistical inference, and other basic tools that accompany the method.

Overall, the Alkire-Foster method builds on and improves the counting-based headcount measures of multidimensional child poverty, and in turn it can draw on the significant advances that others are making in identifying the appropriate indicators and thresholds for child poverty measures in different contexts. We hope that this chapter encourages others to explore and critically engage with improved child poverty measures using this methodology, so that more children become free to enjoy a childhood free from fear and want.

Notes

[1] Notice that Sen's approach is more than a simple multidimensional approach to human well-being; it emphasises human agency and the substantial freedoms that people have to achieve valuable beings and doings in life.

[2] The rights-based approach has important linkages with Amartya Sen's human development and capability approach. See Sen (2005); Nussbaum (2003); Fukuda-Parr (2003); Osmani (2005); and Vizard (2005).

[3] Notice that Delamonica and Minujin (2007) use a different terminology. For the remaining of the chapter we follow Alkire and Foster's terminology.

[4] Note that Delamonica and Minujin (2007) were the first to highlight that one of the weakness of the Bristol Approach was not being sensitive to the intensity of poverty which the FGT measure in unidimensional (income/consumption) measures does. They instead propose to measure the average deprivation across the whole population. As will be seen shortly, when $k>1$, focusing on the poor allows computing a final adjusted headcount ratio that satisfies the properties of decomposability and poverty focus. These properties would not be satisfied if we use the average of deprivation across the whole population.

[5] For details on the Young Life study see www.younglives.org.uk/

[6] Note that the Demographic and Health Surveys were also used to compute the Multidimensional Poverty Index (Alkire and Santos, 2010) and child poverty figures in the Global Study (Gordon et al, 2003).

[7] Note that the Multidimensional Poverty Index launched by UNDP identifies all members of the household as equally deprived or poor (Alkire and Santos, 2010). This methodological decision was necessary due to data availability.

[8] In particular the Bristol indicators are based on *the definition of poverty agreed in the* World Summit for Social Development in Copenhagen 1995.

[9] This discussion is covered elsewhere (Alkire, 2008).

[10] This required simplifying indicators. For example, in source of water we do not include distance to water because the information was not available for 1997. Similarly in shelter we did not include an overcrowding index because the variable 'number of rooms used for sleeping' was not included in 1997.

[11] In absolute terms they suffer a high number of total deprivations. On the other hand, this appears to be very uncommon in Bangladesh, and therefore a sign of extreme relative deprivation.

[12] The Bristol study estimates 54% of child poverty in Bangladesh ($k=2$) while 92% in severe deprivation ($k=1$) (Gordon et al, 2003). The figures from the World Bank below US$1.25 PPP a day are around 50% (http://data.worldbank.org/).

[13] Differences might not be statistically significant, but the first order dominance is clear.

[14] The censored headcount is directly computed from the censored matrix that was obtained in Step 7 and represented in Table 5.2. The censored headcount is computed by dividing the total number of children who are poor *and deprived* in each dimension by the total number of children. Children who are deprived but not poor are not included in the numerator. The (weighted) average of the censored headcounts is the overall headcount.

References

Alkire, S. (2008) 'Choosing dimensions: the capability approach and multidimensional poverty', in N. Kakwani and J. Silber (eds) *The many dimensions of poverty*, New York: Palgrave Macmillan, pp 89-119.
Alkire, S. and Foster, J. (2007) *Counting and multidimensional poverty measurement*, Oxford Poverty & Human Development Initiative (OPHI) Working Paper No 7, Oxford: OPHI, University of Oxford.
Alkire, S. and Foster, J. (2011) 'Counting and multidimensional poverty measurement', *Journal of Public Economics*, vol 95, pp 476-87.
Alkire, S. and Santos, M.E. (2010) *Acute multidimensional poverty: A new index for developing countries*, Oxford Poverty & Human Development Initiative (OPHI) Working Paper No 38, Oxford: OPHI, University of Oxford.

Alkire, S. and Seth, S. (2009) *Multidimensional poverty and BPL measures in India: A comparison of methods*, Oxford Poverty & Human Development Initiative (OPHI) Working Paper No 15, Oxford: OPHI, University of Oxford.

Angulo Salazar, R. C., Pardo Pinzón, R., and Díaz Cuervo, Y. (2011). Multidimensional Poverty Index (MPI–Colombia) 1997-2010, *HDCA Conference*, The Hague: The Netherlands.

Apablaza, M. and Yalonetzky, G. (2011) *Measuring the dynamics of multiple deprivations among children: The cases of Andhra Pradesh, Ethiopia, Peru and Vietnam*, Young Life Research in Progress, Oxford: University of Oxford.

Azam, M.S. and Imai, K. (2009) *Vulnerability and poverty in Bangladesh*, Working Paper No 141, Manchester: Chronic Poverty Research Centre, University of Manchester.

Azevedo, V. and Robles, M. (2010) *Multidimensional targeting: Identifying beneficiaries of conditional cash transfer programmes*, Oxford Poverty & Human Development Initiative (OPHI) Working Paper No 20, Oxford: OPHI, University of Oxford.

Batana, Y.M. (2008) Multidimensional measurement of poverty in Sub-Saharan Africa, Oxford Poverty & Human Development Initiative (OPHI) Working Paper No 13, Oxford: OPHI, University of Oxford.

Battiston, D., Cruces, G., Calva, L.F.L., Lugo, M.A. and Santos, M.E. (2009) *Income and beyond: Multidimensional poverty in six Latin American countries*, Oxford Poverty & Human Development Initiative (OPHI) Working Paper No 17, Oxford: OPHI, University of Oxford.

Biggeri, M., Libanora, R., Mariani, S. and Menchini, L. (2006) 'Children conceptualizing their capabilities: results of a survey conducted during the first children's World Congress on Child Labour', *Journal of Human Development*, vol 7, pp 59-83.

Bourguignon, F. and Chakravarty, S.R. (2003) 'The measurement of multidimensional poverty', *Journal of Economic Inequality*, vol 1, pp 25-49.

Chakravarty, S.R., Mukherjee, D. and Renade, R.R. (1998) 'On the family of subgroup and factor decomposable measures of multidimensional poverty', *Research on Economic Inequality*, vol 8, pp. 175-194

CONEVAL (2010) *Methodology for multidimensional poverty measurement in Mexico*, Mexico: Consejo Nacional para la Evaluacion de la Politica Nacional.

Delamonica, E.E. and Minujin, A. (2007) 'Incidence, depth and severity of children in poverty', *Social Indicators Research*, vol 82, pp 361-74.

Di Tommaso, M.L. (2007) 'Children capabilities: a structural equation model for India', *The Journal of Socio-Economics*, vol 36, pp 436-50.

El-Laithy, H. and Armanious, D.M. (2010) *Trends of child poverty and disparities in Egypt: Between 2000 and 2008*, Global Study on Child Poverty and Disparities, Cairo: UNICEF and the Egypt National Child Rights Observatory.

Erikson, R. (1993) 'Descriptions of inequality. The Swedish approach to welfare research', in M. Nussbaum and A. Sen (eds) *The quality of life*, Oxford: Clarendon Press, pp 67-83.

Feres, J.C. and Mancero, X. (2001) *El método de las necesidades básicas insatisfechas (NBI) y sus aplicaciones a América Latina*, Series Estudios Estadísticos y Prospectivos, Santiago de Chile, ECLAC-United Nations.

Foster, J.E. and Sen, A.K. (1997) *On economic inequality: After a quarter century, Annex to the enlarged edition of 'On economic inequality' by A.K. Sen.*, Oxford: Clarendon Press.

Foster, J.E., Greer, J. and Thorbecke, E. (1984) 'A class of decomposable poverty measures', *Econometrica*, vol 52, pp 761-6.

Fukuda-Parr, S. (2003) 'The human development paradigm: operationalizing Sen's ideas on capabilities', *Feminist Economics*, vol 9, p 301.

Gordon, D., Pantazis, C. and Townsend, P. (with A. Minujin, J. Vandemoortele and C. Namizie) (2001) *Child rights and child poverty in developing countries*, Bristol: University of Bristol.

Gordon, D., Nandy, S., Pantazis, C., Pemberton, S. and Townsend, P. (2003) *Child poverty in the developing world*, Bristol: The Policy Press.

Mack, J. and Lansley, S. (1985) *Poor Britain*, London: George Allen & Unwin Ltd.

Minujin, A., Delamonica, E.E., Davidziuk, A. and Gonzalez, E.D. (2006) 'The definition of child poverty: a discussion of concepts and measurements', *Environment & Urbanization*, vol 18, pp 481-500.

Nolan, B. and Whelan, C.T. (1996) *Resources, deprivation and poverty*, Oxford: Oxford University Press.

Nussbaum, M. (2003) 'Capabilities as fundamental entitlements: Sen and social justice', *Feminist Economics*, vol 9, pp 33-59.

Nussbaumer, P., Bazilian, M., Modi, V. and Yumkella, K.K. (2011) *Measuring energy poverty: Focusing on what matters*, Oxford Poverty & Human Development Initiative (OPHI) Working Paper No 42, Oxford: OPHI, University of Oxford.

Osmani, S.R. (2005) 'Poverty and human rights: building on the capability approach', *Journal of Human Development*, vol 6, pp 205-19.

Roche, J.M. (2009) *Child poverty measurement: An assessment of methods and an application to Bangladesh*, Oxford Poverty & Human Development Initiative (OPHI) Research in Progress RP11b, Oxford: University of Oxford.

Roelen, K. and Gassmann, F. (2008) *Measuring child poverty and well-being: A literature review*, Working Paper Series No 2008/WP001, Maastricht: Maastricht Graduate School of Governance.

Santos, M.E. and Ura, K. (2008) *Multidimensional poverty in Bhutan: Estimates and policy implications*, Oxford Poverty & Human Development Initiative (OPHI) Working Paper No 14, Oxford: University of Oxford.

Sen, A.K. (1980) 'Equality of what? (1979 Tanner Lecture at Stanford)', in S. McMurrin (ed) *The Tanner Lectures on human values*, Salt Lake City, UT: University of Utah Press.

Sen, A.K. (1985) 'Well-being, agency and freedom: the Dewey Lectures 1984', *The Journal of Philosophy*, vol 82, pp 169–221.

Sen, A.K. (1992) *Inequality reexamined*, Oxford: Clarendon Press.

Sen, A.K. (1999) *Development as freedom*, New York: Oxford University Press.

Sen, A.K. (2005) 'Human rights and capabilities', *Journal of Human Development*, vol 6, pp 151–66.

Tsui, K. (2002) 'Multidimensional poverty indices', *Social Choice and Welfare*, vol 19, pp 69–93.

UN (United Nations) (2003) *Indicators for monitoring the Millennium Development Goals*, New York: UN.

UNDP (United Nations Development Programme) (2010) *Human Development Report 2010, 20th Anniversary Edition, The real wealth of nations: Pathways to human development*, New York: Palgrave Macmillan.

UNICEF (United Nations Children's Fund) (2004) *The State of the World's Children 2005: Childhood under threat*, New York: UNICEF.

UNICEF (2007) *Global Study on Child Poverty and Disparitities 2007-08: Guide*, New York: Global Policy Section, Division of Policy and Planning, UNICEF.

Vizard, P. (2005) *Poverty and human rights: Sen's 'capability perspective' explored*, Oxford: Oxford University Press.

WHO (World Health Organization) (2006) *WHO child growth standards: Length/height-for-age, weight-for-age, weight-for-length, weight-for-height and body mass index-for-age: Methods and development*, Geneva: Department of Nutrition for Health and Development, WHO.

World Bank (2008) *Poverty assessment for Bangladesh: Creating opportunities and bridging the East-West divide*, Development Series Paper No 26, Dakah: World Bank Office.

Figure 5A.1: Robustness checks of different poverty cut-off (*k*) in changes in multidimensional poverty over time for provinces in Bangladesh, 1997-2007

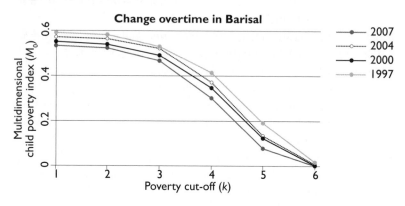

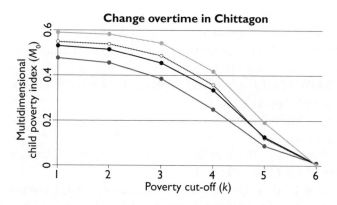

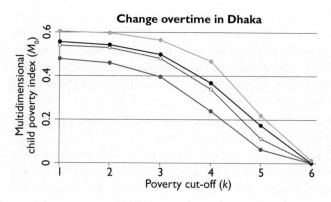

(continued)

Figure 5.A1: Robustness checks of different poverty cut-off (k) in changes in multidimensional poverty over time for provinces in Bangladesh, 1997-2007 (continued)

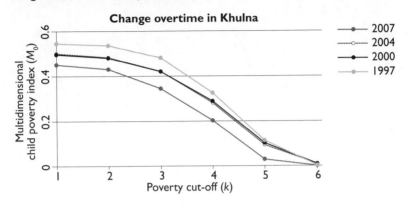

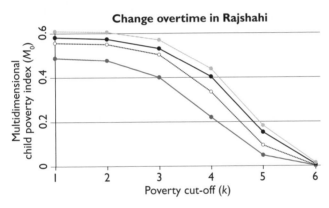

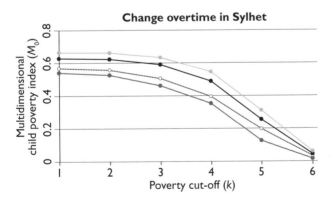

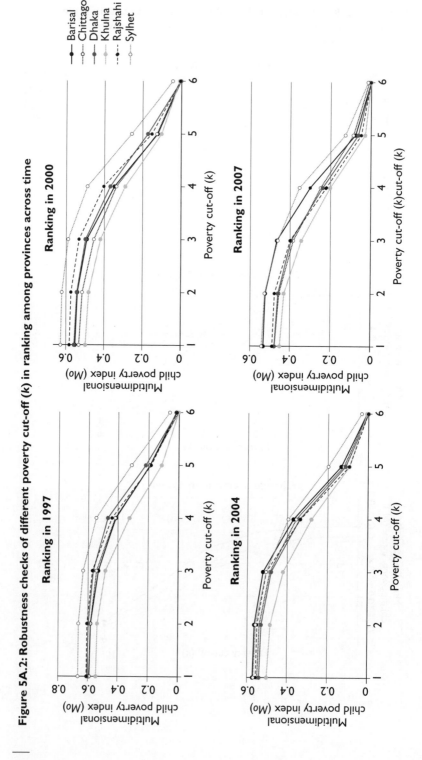

Figure 5A.2: Robustness checks of different poverty cut-off (k) in ranking among provinces across time

Table 5A.1: Changes over time in multidimensional poverty by province, Bangladesh, 1997-2007

	1997	2000	2004	2007	1997-2000	2000-04	2004-07
					Absolute variation		
Multidimensional child poverty index (M₀)							
Bangladesh	0.555	0.495	0.485	0.400	−0.060	−0.010	−0.085
Khulna	0.481	0.420	0.421	0.345	−0.061	0.000	−0.076
Chittagong	0.543	0.455	0.486	0.384	−0.088	0.032	−0.102
Dhaka	0.565	0.498	0.480	0.396	−0.067	−0.019	−0.084
Rajshahi	0.571	0.532	0.504	0.401	−0.039	−0.028	−0.104
Sylhet	0.633	0.590	0.506	0.462	−0.043	−0.084	−0.044
Barisal	0.530	0.491	0.521	0.467	−0.039	0.030	−0.055
Multidimensional headcount (H)							
Bangladesh	0.829	0.758	0.763	0.655	−0.071	0.005	−0.108
Khulna	0.767	0.664	0.672	0.579	−0.103	0.008	−0.092
Chittagong	0.819	0.703	0.757	0.616	−0.117	0.054	−0.141
Dhaka	0.828	0.761	0.757	0.653	−0.068	−0.004	−0.103
Rajshahi	0.864	0.815	0.813	0.676	−0.049	−0.003	−0.137
Sylhet	0.887	0.849	0.748	0.705	−0.038	−0.102	−0.042
Barisal	0.793	0.772	0.816	0.759	−0.020	0.044	−0.057
Intensity of poverty (A)							
Bangladesh	0.669	0.653	0.636	0.611	−0.016	−0.017	−0.025
Khulna	0.628	0.633	0.626	0.595	0.005	−0.007	−0.032
Chittagong	0.663	0.647	0.643	0.624	−0.016	−0.005	−0.018
Dhaka	0.682	0.655	0.634	0.606	−0.027	−0.021	−0.028
Rajshahi	0.661	0.652	0.621	0.593	−0.008	−0.032	−0.028
Sylhet	0.713	0.694	0.676	0.655	−0.019	−0.018	−0.022
Barisal	0.669	0.636	0.639	0.615	−0.033	0.003	−0.024

Note: The results correspond to a poverty cut-off $k = 3$.

Table 5A.2: Censored headcount for each indicator by province, Bangladesh, 1997-2007

	1997	2000	2004	2007	1997-2000	2000-04	2004-07
					Absolute variation		
Bangladesh							
Nutrition	0.684	0.560	0.557	0.485	−0.125	−0.003	−0.072
Water	0.046	0.034	0.033	0.029	−0.012	−0.001	−0.003
Toilet	0.698	0.638	0.708	0.520	−0.060	0.070	−0.188
Health	0.413	0.371	0.255	0.183	−0.041	−0.117	−0.072
Shelter	0.826	0.754	0.761	0.653	−0.073	0.007	−0.108
Information	0.660	0.613	0.595	0.529	−0.047	−0.018	−0.066

(continued)

Table 5A.2: Censored headcount for each indicator by province, Bangladesh, 1997-2007 (continued)

	1997	2000	2004	2007	Absolute variation 1997-2000	Absolute variation 2000-04	Absolute variation 2004-07
Barisal							
Nutrition	0.685	0.581	0.594	0.562	−0.104	0.013	−0.033
Water	0.099	0.033	0.043	0.021	−0.066	0.011	−0.022
Toilet	0.648	0.571	0.764	0.610	−0.077	0.193	−0.154
Health	0.317	0.315	0.273	0.187	−0.002	−0.042	−0.085
Shelter	0.787	0.770	0.816	0.759	−0.017	0.046	−0.057
Information	0.645	0.678	0.638	0.660	0.033	−0.040	0.022
Chittagong							
Nutrition	0.705	0.538	0.572	0.488	−0.167	0.034	−0.084
Water	0.018	0.033	0.041	0.039	0.015	0.008	−0.002
Toilet	0.640	0.565	0.702	0.473	−0.076	0.138	−0.229
Health	0.466	0.318	0.279	0.224	−0.148	−0.040	−0.055
Shelter	0.819	0.696	0.754	0.612	−0.123	0.058	−0.142
Information	0.610	0.579	0.571	0.470	−0.031	−0.008	−0.100
Dahka							
Nutrition	0.676	0.564	0.565	0.484	−0.112	0.001	−0.080
Water	0.032	0.013	0.003	0.009	−0.019	−0.010	0.006
Toilet	0.724	0.661	0.702	0.516	−0.063	0.041	−0.186
Health	0.444	0.412	0.257	0.192	−0.032	−0.155	−0.065
Shelter	0.827	0.752	0.756	0.652	−0.074	0.003	−0.103
Information	0.689	0.588	0.596	0.522	−0.101	0.008	−0.075
Khulna							
Nutrition	0.626	0.479	0.485	0.405	−0.147	0.006	−0.080
Water	0.032	0.054	0.066	0.064	0.022	0.013	−0.003
Toilet	0.590	0.528	0.611	0.475	−0.062	0.083	−0.136
Health	0.287	0.259	0.181	0.100	−0.028	−0.078	−0.081
Shelter	0.764	0.663	0.667	0.579	−0.101	0.004	−0.088
Information	0.590	0.538	0.514	0.444	−0.052	−0.024	−0.070
Rajshahi							
Nutrition	0.681	0.579	0.551	0.488	−0.103	−0.028	−0.063
Water	0.052	0.024	0.010	0.011	−0.029	−0.014	0.001
Toilet	0.768	0.711	0.770	0.541	−0.057	0.059	−0.229
Health	0.370	0.394	0.229	0.129	0.024	−0.166	−0.100
Shelter	0.859	0.815	0.813	0.676	−0.044	−0.003	−0.137
Information	0.692	0.668	0.653	0.558	−0.024	−0.015	−0.095
Sylhet							
Nutrition	0.752	0.646	0.579	0.510	−0.106	−0.067	−0.068
Water	0.165	0.126	0.129	0.085	−0.039	0.004	−0.044
Toilet	0.781	0.735	0.664	0.575	−0.046	−0.071	−0.089
Health	0.497	0.491	0.340	0.278	−0.007	−0.151	−0.062
Shelter	0.881	0.848	0.747	0.702	−0.034	−0.101	−0.044
Information	0.720	0.693	0.576	0.619	−0.027	−0.117	0.043

Note: The results correspond to a poverty cut-off $k = 3$.

SIX

Defining child poverty in South Africa using the socially perceived necessities approach

Helen Barnes and Gemma Wright

Introduction

Since the advent of democracy in 1994, the South African government has committed itself to protecting child rights and reducing child poverty. For example, the Constitution of the Republic of South Africa has a specific section on child rights, the government ratified both the UN Convention on the Rights of the Child (UNCRC) in 1995 and the African Charter on the Rights and Welfare of the Child in 1999, and new legislation, the Children's Act 2005, gives effect to some of the constitutional rights of children. Social assistance remains the main arm of the government's poverty alleviation programme, and the child support grant is the central mechanism for the alleviation of child poverty. This focus on child poverty sits in the context of a broader government commitment to tackle poverty in the country, a constant theme in the government since 1994, including the ongoing War on Poverty Campaign, commissioned by the Presidency and led by the Deputy President.

When considering poverty or child poverty it is helpful to distinguish between concepts, definitions and measurements. *Concepts* are 'the theoretical framework out of which definitions are developed' (Noble et al, 2007a, p 54), *definitions* distinguish the poor from the non-poor and *measurements* are the ways in which the definitions are operationalised, enabling the poor to be identified and counted, and the depth of poverty gauged (Lister, 2004). The focus of this chapter is on the definition process and in particular, the application of the socially perceived necessities approach to the definition of child poverty in South Africa. Several issues arise during the definition process. First, there is the question of who should define poverty: should it be 'experts', the general population, poor people or some combination?

Second, a decision needs to be made about what to include within the definition, in terms of whether to use monetary resources or living standards or some combination. Third, and related to the second issue, a choice has to be made between a uni- or multidimensional approach. Lastly, a poverty threshold needs to be identified.

Children can be said to be in poverty when their standard of living is unacceptably low and this is because of insufficient resources in the households in which they live. Child poverty has been measured in South Africa in relation to monetary resources (see, for example, Barnes, 2009a; Streak et al, 2009), individual indicators of poor living standards (see, for example, Kibel et al, 2010) and multiple deprivation (see, for example, Barnes et al, 2009; Wright et al, 2009). All involved expert definitions, and prior to the study reported here, a general population-derived definition of child poverty had not been explicitly pursued. The socially perceived necessities approach involves 'ordinary' people, including both poor and non-poor individuals, in defining poverty; poverty is treated as an enforced lack (that is, due to insufficient resources) of items that have been identified by the population as essential for an acceptable standard of living;[1] and the focus is explicitly multidimensional. The approach originates from the work of Mack and Lansley (1985; see also Gordon and Pantazis, 1997a, where the original work was extended), and has been applied in many other countries including Australia (see, for example Saunders et al, 2007), Japan (see, for example, Abe, 2006), Sweden (see, for example, Halleröd, 1994) and Vietnam (see, for example, Davies and Smith, 1998). Many of these studies included only a small number of items relating to children, but studies in the UK (see, for example, Adelman et al, 2000; Lloyd, 2006[2]) and by the European Commission (2007) have included a section with a specific focus on children. However, children themselves were not involved in the definition process.

Both adults and children were involved in the definition process described here, which at the time had not been attempted previously (see Bradshaw and Main, 2010, for similar work carried out subsequently in the UK). Adults have a particular insight into children's needs, either as parents or caregivers or simply through their own experience of being a child (see, for example, Hirsch and Smith, 2010). Children, on the other hand, are well informed about their lives and pertinent issues and they have 'their own set of opinions and judgements, which, while not always the same as those of adults, nevertheless have the same moral legitimacy' (Ridge, 2002, p 7). Previous studies comparing adults and children's perspectives on poverty-related issues found distinct differences between the two (Boyden et al, 2003; Harpham et al, 2005; Sixsmith et al, 2007), suggesting that there is justification for eliciting the views of children. However, the point made by Noble et al (2006) is acknowledged: there may be some issues where a child's view is inappropriate, and where an adult (caregiver) perspective may be necessary.[3] Consultation with both adults and children is therefore important to obtain a complete picture of an acceptable standard of living for children.

Until recently, however, the views of children have been largely absent from studies of child poverty, the general preference being for adult perceptions of children's needs (Ridge, 2002). The centrality of children's own perspectives to a study of child poverty is now beginning to grow in prominence, mainly due both to the UNCRC, which states that children have the right to participate in and express their views about decisions affecting them and to freedom to seek, receive and impart information and ideas of all kinds (UN, 1990, Articles 12 and 13), and to the 'new sociology of childhood', which considers the life stage of childhood and emphasises child agency (Ben–Arieh, 2005).[4] These developments have led to numerous investigations of children's experiences and studies of children in their own right. Although children in South Africa were recognised as having made important contributions to the country's social transformations, the predominant view remains one of 'marked disparity in power and status between children and adults', accompanied by 'conservative notions of children's abilities and rightful place in society' (Moses, 2008, pp 331, 336). Nevertheless, some research studies in South Africa have shown the importance of involving children and the insights such an approach can bring (Berry and Guthrie, 2003).

The remainder of this chapter is structured as follows. First, brief details are provided about the methodological approach that was used to derive adult and child definitions of child necessities. Then the findings for both the adult-derived and child-derived definitions are presented and compared. This is followed by a discussion of some of the challenges of using the socially perceived necessities approach to obtain a definition or definitions of child poverty, including those that relate to the involvement of children in the definition process.

Data and methods

The definition element of the socially perceived necessities approach has two main stages: first, constructing a list of possible necessities for an acceptable standard of living; and second, exploring which items are defined as essential by the general population.

In terms of the first stage, a list of items and activities relating to a range of different standards of living for children and a variety of aspects of a child's life was drawn up using a combination of material from focus groups with adults about, inter alia, necessities for children (part of an earlier study – see Noble et al, 2004; Barnes et al, 2007), focus groups with children (described below), previous studies which have used this approach, and inevitably, a degree of researcher judgement. The domains suggested for a model of child poverty in South Africa by Noble et al (2006) were taken as a starting point for considering items across a range of dimensions of deprivation. The eight exemplar domains in the model are material deprivation, human capital deprivation, social capital deprivation, living environment deprivation, health deprivation, physical safety deprivation, adequate care and abuse. As the aim was to be child focused, more general household items were not included. Such items can be found in other household surveys and have been looked at in relation to the adult population (Noble et al, 2007b; Wright, 2008a). Their exclusion from the list does not in any way reduce their importance; the items chosen are simply indicators of an acceptable standard of living and not a definitive list.[5]

Adults' views of an acceptable standard of living for children were derived from a module in the nationally representative South African Social Attitudes Survey (SASAS) 2007 which is run by the Human Sciences Research Council on an annual basis. The sample is based on 2001 Census enumeration areas stratified by province, geographical sub-type and population group.[6] The realised sample for the SASAS 2007 was 3,164 people (adults aged 16 and older).

Adults were asked to say whether it was essential for every parent or caregiver to be able to afford each item or activity on the list for children they care for in order for them to enjoy an acceptable standard of living in South Africa today. There were four options as responses: 'essential' (that is, every child should have), 'desirable' (that is, nice but not essential for every child to have), 'neither' and 'don't know'.

Children's views of an acceptable standard of living were obtained from focus groups with children in schools in the Western Cape and Eastern Cape provinces, as it was not possible to undertake a survey with children for resource reasons. The aim was to include children from a variety of different backgrounds with different experiences of growing up in South Africa. The procedure for selecting schools involved the selection of possible areas based on area type (an urban/rural classification), income level and population group, and then the selection of schools from within these areas. A detailed explanation of the method can be found in Barnes (2009c).

Fifteen large focus groups were conducted in 2007, involving almost 160 children. The aim of these focus groups was mainly to generate lists of items that children[7] need for an acceptable standard of living, for possible inclusion in the final list of items (see Barnes, 2009c, for analysis of the findings). Five of the schools were revisited in 2008 and 13 smaller group discussions were held with some of the children who had participated previously; a total of 44 children participated in these smaller groups, with roughly equal numbers of boys and girls and an age range of 11-16 years. The children were asked for their views – through discussion and debate – on whether the items on the list were necessities or luxuries.

Defining socially perceived necessities

Views of adults

Table 6.1 shows the results from the SASAS module. There were two items that were regarded as essential by over 90% of the population: three meals a day and toiletries to be able to wash every day. Percentages for the other items ranged from less than 10% (an MP3 player/iPod) to just less than 90% (all fees, uniform and equipment required for school).

Deciding on the percentage of the population that must regard the item as essential for it to be classified as a socially perceived necessity is a contentious issue. As Mack and Lansley (1985) remark, any threshold selected is arbitrary, but a straight majority (that is, any item which is defined as essential by 50% or more of respondents) is as good a threshold as any other. In common with many of the studies using a socially perceived necessities approach, a 50% majority is used as the threshold in the following analysis.

Of the 25 items included in the questionnaire, only 11 were regarded as essential by 50% or more of the respondents and can therefore be considered to be the set of socially perceived necessities. Many of these items relate to basic needs, for example, food, hygiene, healthcare, education and clothing, and these are defined as essential by the highest proportion. The 11 items can be mapped onto the domains of the child poverty model mentioned above; the main themes that emerge are material deprivation, human capital deprivation and health deprivation.

Cronbach's coefficient alpha (Cronbach, 1951) is a technique that can be used to test the reliability of the set of socially perceived necessities. The scale reliability coefficient alpha measures the correlation of the set of socially perceived necessities with all other hypothetical sets of items. The square root of the coefficient alpha is the estimated correlation of

Table 6.1: Percentage of adults defining an item as essential

Item	% saying essential
Three meals a day	91.2
Toiletries to be able to wash every day	90.4
All fees, uniform and equipment required for school	88.4
A visit to the doctor when ill and all medicines required	87.9
Clothing sufficient to keep warm and dry	85.1
Shoes for different activities	79.4
Bus/taxi fare or other transport to get to school	74.8
Some new clothes	66.8
Own bed	61.7
Pocket money/allowance for school-aged children	58.9
Story books	50.2
A desk and chair for homework for school-aged children	48.7
Educational toys/games	46.1
A school trip once a term for school-aged children	45.0
Presents at birthdays, Christmas	39.9
Own room for children over 10	39.7
Leisure/sports equipment	33.5
Toys or materials for a hobby	32.7
A computer in the home for school-aged children	32.3
Some fashionable clothes for secondary school-aged children	31.8
A birthday party each year	30.1
Own mobile phone for secondary school-aged children	21.8
A hi-fi/CD player and some tapes/CDs for school-aged children	14.4
A PlayStation/Xbox for school-aged children	12.9
An MP3 player/iPod for secondary school-aged children	9.0

Note: This takes into account the survey weights (ie, it represents the total population aged 16 and over in 2007).

Source: Own analysis of SASAS 2007

the set of items with a set of errorless true scores. For the set of socially perceived necessities the scale reliability coefficient alpha is 0.77 and the square root of the coefficient is 0.88. Nunnally (1981) argues that reliability coefficients of 0.7 or higher are sufficient, and therefore at 0.77, the set of items can be considered reliable.[8]

The validity of the socially perceived necessities approach rests on the assumption that there are not large or systematic differences in the definition of necessities among different groups in society (Gordon and Pantazis, 1997b), because otherwise the definition of a necessity would be the opinion of one group against another (Pantazis et al, 2006). In South Africa, where there are great disparities between social, economic and racial groups, it is particularly important to explore whether there is a common perception about the necessities of life.

Overall there appears to be a common view among adults surveyed in SASAS 2007 of what was required for an acceptable standard of living for children. Table 6.2 summarises the responses of different subgroups. The white population group defined the greatest number of items (17) as essential, including all the 11 socially perceived necessities, while several subgroups defined just 10 items as essential. Story books were the socially perceived necessity that consistently featured in the list of non-essential items. It may be that story books, which are usually written in English rather than Afrikaans or the different African languages, are not an item that is available or meaningful to large sections of the population.

The Spearman's rank correlations between subgroup responses (for example, male compared to female, old compared to young) for all items are generally high – all over 0.9 (and all significant at the 0.001 level) – and there is little disagreement in the items considered essential. However, for certain subgroups, particularly different population

Table 6.2: Summary of subgroup responses

Subgroup	Number of items considered essential by majority (50% threshold)	Number of SPNs (out of total of 11)	Number of items in addition to SPNs
Male	12	11	1
Female	10	10	0
Black African	10	10	0
Coloured[a]	12	9	3
Indian/Asian	12	10	2
White	17	11	6
Young (16 to 24-year-olds)	12	11	1
Old (65 years old and over)	11	11	0
Urban	12	11	1
Rural	10	10	0
Not parent	12	11	1
Parent	10	10	0
No children in household	11	10	1
Children in household	11	11	0
Not poor (self-defined)	14	11	3
Just getting along (self-defined)	10	10	0
Poor (self-defined)	10	10	0

Note: SPN = socially perceived necessity. [a] See footnote 9 for explanation of the term 'coloured'.

Source: Own analysis on SASAS 2007

groups, there are much greater differences of opinion when it comes to looking at the socially perceived necessities only. For example, the responses of black African and coloured respondents correlate 0.76 and the responses of black African and white respondents correlate 0.78 (both significant at the 0.001 level).[9]

There is some evidence to suggest that the experience of poverty leads some people to adjust their desires, expectations and preferences to what is achievable within their limited means (McKay, 2004; Noble et al, 2007b). For all but one item – shoes for different activities – a higher percentage of the non-poor than the poor defined the item as essential. Similarly, a lack of services in rural areas may mean that some rural respondents adjust their views in line with the realities of everyday life (Wright, 2008b). There was a large difference in opinion between urban and rural dwellers for a visit to a doctor (91% compared to 82%, $p<0.001$), which may relate to a lack of services in rural areas. A similar finding for transport to school (78% compared to 68%, $p<0.001$) may be due to a lack of buses/taxis[10] in rural areas.

The above analysis suggests that there is some variation in what people regard as necessary. Previous studies, including Wright (2008b) in South Africa, have shown that when possession of an item is taken into account, the differences between groups are less apparent. This suggests that subgroup differences are not driven by a fundamentally different view of what is an acceptable standard of living. However, the finding on possession is itself a concern in that possession rates of many items are likely to be low in South Africa, which in turn could mean that fewer items are defined as essential. Analysis revealed, however, that the majority of caregivers defined a greater number of items as essential than they actually possessed, suggesting that they aspire to a higher standard of living for their children than they are currently able to provide (Barnes, 2009b).

Views of children

This section considers the contributions from children in the small focus groups about the same set of items that adults were asked about in the SASAS 2007 module. It is important to note that the coloured population is not particularly well represented in the focus groups, and there is also no Indian/Asian representation.[11]

The initial impression from the focus group material was that many children – often the low-income groups, but not always – thought of necessities as those items necessary for mere survival, often basing their judgement on their own experiences. For example, one child stated

'It's a luxury because you can live without a radio and DVDs. All you need is food and water to drink, you can live your life without the rest,' while another remarked (regarding school trips) 'Here we are, alive and well but we've never toured with the school.'

Although the children overall defined a fairly large number of items as essential, they repeatedly stressed that only very basic versions were required. The quantity (for example, 'One or two books is a necessity, but if you have many more then it's starting to become a luxury') and cost (for example, 'It's a necessity, but you don't need that expensive maybe 1,000 rand jacket, you can just get some others that is also as warm as that expensive one') of items were important considerations for the children. Thus the answer to questions about necessities is not always straightforward and cannot necessarily be reduced to a simple binary response. It is not possible to say how children would actually respond when faced with a survey where there is no opportunity to qualify their choices; they may, for example, be more reluctant to define an item as necessary.

A practical justification was given for many items that were defined as necessities, for example, story books ('I think it depends, you know if, if you buy books that has life skills in it, that can help you with your life in the future, but if it's books that don't really mean anything...') and hobbies/toys ('Because your hobby may become a skill later, to earn a living'). The importance of education was also clearly expressed, and items other than school fees, uniform and equipment were justified as necessities in terms of their educational value, or conversely were argued to be luxuries because they might distract a child in school or when studying at home.

At either end of the necessity–luxury spectrum there were various items that were almost unanimously defined as such. These can be seen in the bottom half of Figure 6.1, which is an attempt to bring together the information from SASAS and the small focus groups in order to compare the views of adults and children respectively for all items. Each item is positioned on a scale ranging from necessity to luxury. It is easier to do this for the adult views where the actual percentage responding 'essential' is known. Given that the focus here is on necessities rather than luxuries, the discussion will mainly look at the items generally perceived to be necessities by children and the reasons given for this, particularly where this is at odds with the views of adults.

Six items – three meals a day, toiletries to be able to wash every day, all school fees, uniform and equipment, a visit to the doctor when ill and all medicines required, transport to school, and clothing sufficient to keep warm and dry – were regarded as necessities by most children

Figure 6.1: A comparison of the adult and child views

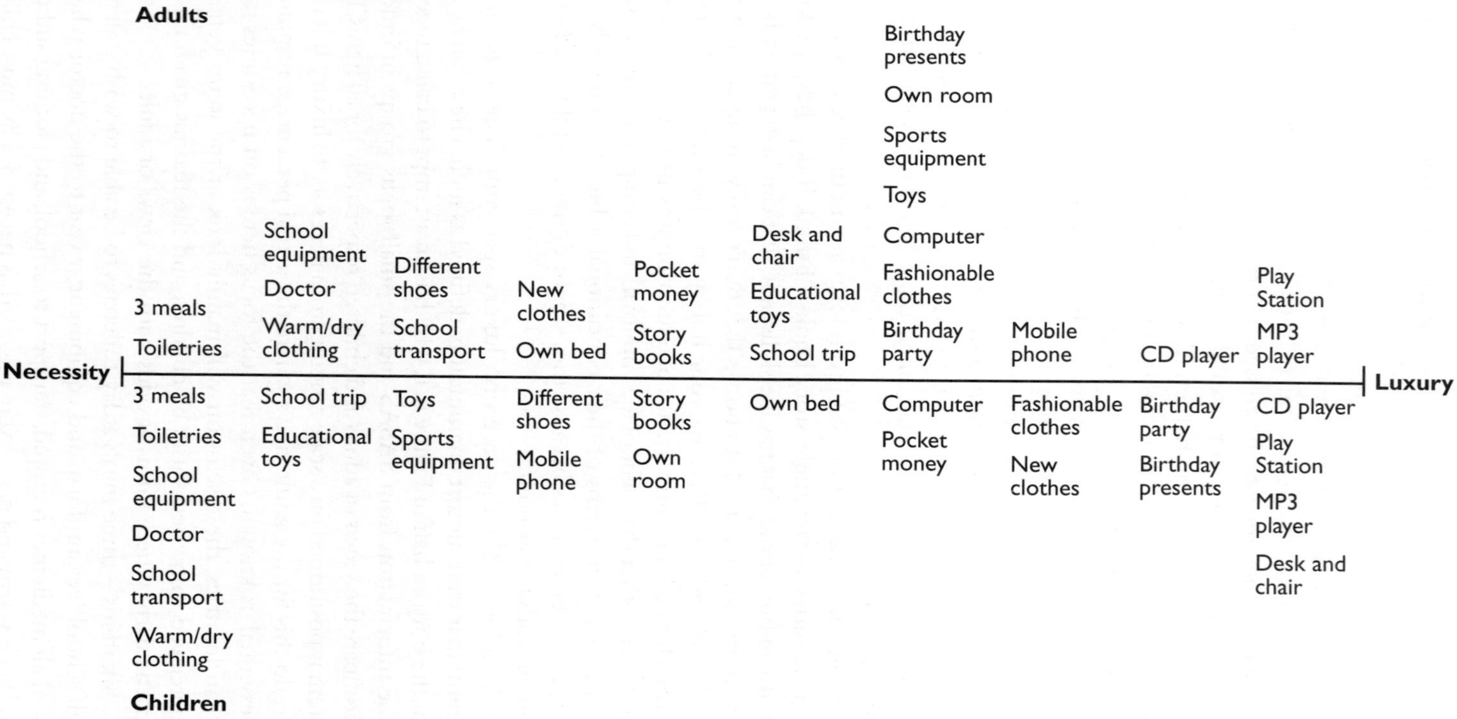

Necessity |———| Luxury

Adults

3 meals				Birthday presents			
Toiletries				Own room			
School equipment			Desk and chair	Sports equipment			Play Station
Doctor	Different shoes	New clothes	Educational toys	Toys			MP3 player
Warm/dry clothing	School transport	Own bed	School trip	Computer	Mobile phone		
		Pocket money		Fashionable clothes		CD player	
		Story books		Birthday party			

Children

3 meals						Birthday party	CD player
Toiletries	School trip	Story books		Computer	Fashionable clothes	Birthday presents	Play Station
School equipment	Educational toys			Pocket money	New clothes		MP3 player
Doctor		Toys		Own bed			Desk and chair
School transport	Sports equipment	Different shoes	Own room				
Warm/dry clothing		Mobile phone					

in the focus groups. With the exception of transport to school, these were all items that adults regarded as particularly important. Other items which were much more favourably regarded by children than adults (and overall seen to be necessities by children but not by adults) include sports or leisure equipment/toys or materials for a hobby,[12] a mobile phone, educational toys and a school trip.

In terms of a school trip, for example, the main reasons given were that it was important to see new places and meet new people: 'It's good to see different places, see where history took place.' School trips were, however, generally regarded as a necessity only if they were an educational experience, as this quote illustrates: 'Once a year, I think it might be necessary once a year, but I mean you've got to learn something from the trip, you can't go for the fun of it.' The main reasons given for a mobile phone being a necessity were to do with safety, for use in emergencies and for communicating with parents. It is interesting to note that children in rural groups talked about using a mobile phone at home, presumably in the absence of a landline, whereas other groups gave examples of needing a mobile phone when they were away from home.

On the other hand, there were items that adults considered necessary but children did not, for example, new clothes and pocket money. Children frequently remarked that as long as clothes were in good condition (that is, not torn and without holes) and clean then it was fine to wear them. However, some children did express the importance of having new clothes in order to present themselves respectably, for example, to go to hospital. With regard to pocket money, a number of focus group participants were concerned that children would buy things they did not need (ranging from sweets to drugs) and therefore it would be better for parents to buy items for them. Conversely, some thought that pocket money was a necessity in case of emergencies and some felt that it could be used to buy food. This comment was made in low-income groups, where children linked pocket money to buying food, rather than just 'treats'.

While the views of the children were very similar to those of adults in many respects, there were important differences. The children gave considered responses and reasoned sensibly, and their views on essential items for children are as valid as those made by adults. There were some differences of opinion within and between focus groups, but overall children had a fairly similar view of what was necessary for children to have an acceptable standard of living.

To conclude the definition process, it is necessary to decide on a poverty threshold that separates the poor from the non-poor. Using the socially perceived necessities approach this means deciding how many of the socially perceived necessities a person must be without to be considered poor, or calculating a weighted summary of lacked items (see, for example, Hallëröd, 1994). This is usually resolved through a statistical process as part of the measurement of poverty and is not discussed further here.

Discussion: challenges

The general challenges of the approach are well rehearsed in the socially perceived necessities literature. The focus of this section is therefore on challenges specific to the South African context (which may have wider relevance) and challenges relating to the involvement of children in the definition process.

A priori, a key challenge of applying the socially perceived necessities approach to South Africa is that the high levels of income poverty and inequality in the country and low levels of possession of items may result in a threshold for an acceptable standard of living being artificially deflated. However, similar to Wright (2008a), this research demonstrates that the socially perceived necessities approach is feasible in such a highly divided and unequal society. South African adults consulted in SASAS have a remarkably common view about what it means to have an acceptable standard of living, and seem to distinguish between what is necessary and what they, and many people like them, currently possess. There is also evidence from the focus groups of generally similar views among children about necessities. A further challenge relating to the structure of South African society is the fact that there are nine official languages. Ensuring that the meanings of, for example, 'necessity', 'essential', 'desirable' and 'luxury' are carried through adequately into each language is therefore important. Although South Africa is a unique country in many ways, similar challenges and considerations may apply to other countries.

In order to accurately derive a child definition and compare to the adult definition it would be necessary to carry out quantitative research with children. A nationally representative survey, perhaps using schools as a means of accessing children, is an important avenue for future research. This is not entirely unproblematic, however, as although school attendance in South Africa is high, those not at school, in many cases the poorest children, will be missed. A survey capturing both the adult and child population together would be ideal, but this is rare in practice. In the survey(s) with adults and children it would be important to consider the inclusion of more general household items, a lack of which can be a serious deprivation. In the South African context particularly, many children lack even the most basic household items, and it is important to capture this deprivation.

Having obtained both an adult and a child definition using quantitative rather than qualitative methods, the question arises as to how the two can be reconciled. Should both definitions be measured and the resultant child poverty rates compared? Should all the items defined as essential by adults and children be included in a single combined definition? Should only the items defined as essential by both adults and children be included? Those in favour of eliciting the views of children usually argue that they should be involved *alongside* rather than *instead of* adults. Thus separate measurements are not required, except to demonstrate the impact the child definition has on the measurement of child poverty. If the views of children differ from those of adults, the degree to which this alters the estimates of poverty derived from an adult definition can be explored. Deciding between the other two options that combine the views of adults and children is not as straightforward. The threshold for an item being classified as a socially perceived necessity was set at 50% or more of the population responding 'essential'. It is debatable whether this should be the survey population (adults and children separately) or the total population (adults and children together).

Although the involvement of children in the definition of an acceptable standard of living is desirable, there are, however, two important issues to consider: adaptive preferences and children's ability to perform the task of defining necessities for *all* children.

Adaptive preferences

There were a number of instances where children were speaking from their own experiences of not having the item in question. Items were defined as non-necessities because children did not have them and their family could not afford them and would probably never be able to afford them. This does not just apply to more expensive items, but also to very basic needs such as food and clothing; for example (referring to new clothes), 'Even if it's torn, I mean what are you going to do, you have to wear it if you don't have an alternative.'

Various studies have shown how children from low-income households avoid asking for items so as not to burden their parents (see, for example, Roker, 1998; Shropshire and Middleton, 1999; Ridge, 2002; van der Hoek, 2005). Ridge, for example, reports how children 'tried to rationalise their inability to have things in different ways: by trying to forget about things they wanted, by keeping quiet about it, by not bothering to ask, and by trying not to care when they could not have things' (Ridge, 2002, p 98). Such behaviours were evident in the child focus groups, for example, 'It's a luxury because it does happen that your family doesn't have the money to meet all those school needs. If you think it's a necessity you'll be bothering your mother and crying, demanding those things and she won't have the money.'

In a review of a number of studies with children in economic disadvantage, Attree (2006) concludes that 'evidence suggests that disadvantage in childhood can lead to the perception that economic and social limitations are 'natural' and normal, thus impacting on children's life expectations' (Attree, 2006, p 61). In general, children from lower income groups (all black African) did appear to be more resigned and accepting of the status quo than their adult counterparts, perhaps feeling more powerless to change the situation, or less aware of how others live. This has implications for the socially perceived necessities approach as there is a risk that children may only define a limited number of items as essential in a survey, and possibly only items which they possess.

Children's ability to define necessities for all children

The ability of children to look beyond their own age group and own experiences when defining child needs is another important (and related) consideration. The activity in the large focus groups showed that some children could produce incredibly detailed shopping lists for children of different ages, particularly babies, perhaps because they had younger or older siblings. However, it was apparent in the small focus groups that some children did have difficulty in deciding on the age when an item became important, and were often unable to look beyond their own age. It may be that children should only be asked to define items relevant to their own age group, or alternatively that the items have to be very general and applicable to all ages.

In summary, it is important to look beyond money metric definitions and measurements to explore the actual living standards of children, identifying as poor those children who have an unacceptable standard of living because their caregivers have insufficient monetary resources. This can be achieved with the socially perceived necessities approach. Although there is a prescribed framework for this approach, the items are driven by the people rather than the researcher, and a poverty threshold set by the population at large is a powerful bargaining tool in the policy arena. There is scope to involve children in a meaningful way in the definition process using this approach, which is not true of many other approaches to the definition and measurement of poverty. There are numerous challenges in the definitional stage of the socially perceived necessities approach, and further considerations at the measurement stage (not discussed here[13]). There are also challenges relating to the involvement of children in this process and combining the adult and child definitions. However, by endeavouring to address each of the challenges explicitly, it would be possible to produce a direct, child-focused, multidimensional and whole population-defined measurement of child poverty.

Acknowledgements

The authors would like to thank the children who participated in the focus groups, the school principals and other members of staff who allowed the research team to visit their schools and carry out focus groups, and the Western and Eastern Cape Education Departments for granting permission to conduct the research in schools. Professor Michael Noble, Director of the Centre for the Analysis of South African Social Policy, is thanked for his oversight of the research project and comments on this chapter. Benjamin Roberts at the Human Sciences Research Council is thanked for including the module for adults about child items within the SASAS 2007. Focus group assistance was provided by Lucie Cluver, Somaya Latief, Naema Latief, Nontobeko Mdudu, Phakama Ntshongwana, Nathi Sohaba and Judith Streak. The research project from which this chapter draws was undertaken for the South African Department of Social Development (DSD) and was funded by the UK Department for International Development (DFID) Southern Africa. An earlier version of this chapter was presented at the Chronic Poverty Research Centre Conference 'Ten Years of War Against Poverty' in September 2010, which drew from reports produced for the DSD.

Notes

[1] The approach does, of course, also involve the researcher, as people's views are obtained within the context of the design of the research project.

[2] This work, from the 1999 Poverty and Social Exclusion Survey, is currently being updated.

[3] Noble et al (2006) also make the point that normative judgements by professionals may be necessary in some instances.

[4] See Ben-Arieh (2005) for further discussion of developments which have contributed to the growth of children's active involvement in the study of their well-being.

[5] There were also various constraints on the size of the module in the survey instrument used (that is, available space in the survey, financial costs and concerns about respondent fatigue).

[6] The standard racial classification used in official statistics, which was generated during the apartheid era, but is still used to measure the dismantling of the apartheid legacy (Klasen, 2000). Statistics South Africa defines 'population group' as follows: 'A group with common characteristics (in terms of descent and history), particularly in relation to how they were (or would have been) classified before the 1994 elections. The following categories are provided in the census: black African, coloured, Indian or Asian, white, other' (Statistics South Africa, 2004, p 12).

[7] Different activities focused on all children, children of different ages, and boys and girls.

[8] If higher thresholds of two thirds (eight items) and three quarters (seven items) of respondents are used, the coefficient alphas are still above 0.7 at 0.73 (square root 0.85) and 0.72 (square root 0.85) respectively.

[9] Du Toit describes 'coloured' as a 'contested, creolized and racialised *cultural* identity; it is commonly used to refer to those who are descended from slaves or indentured Khoi servants' (du Toit, 2004, p 993).

[10] In South Africa minibus taxis are regularly used as an inexpensive form of transport.

[11] This would have been best achieved by undertaking focus groups in KwaZulu-Natal province, which was not possible due to resource constraints.

[12] Sports equipment and toys or materials for a hobby were listed separately, but it became apparent in the child focus groups that sport was often regarded as a hobby and therefore the two items were conflated.

[13] A useful introduction to some of the issues can be found in Bradshaw and Main (2010).

References

Abe, A. (2006) *Empirical analysis of relative deprivation and poverty in Japan*, IPSS Discussion Paper Series No 2005-07, Tokyo: National Institute of Population and Social Security Research.

Adelman, L., Ashworth, K. and Middleton, S. (2000) 'Child poverty in Britain', in D. Gordon, R. Levitas, C. Pantazis, D. Patsios, S. Payne, P. Townsend, L. Adelman, K. Ashworth, S. Middleton, J. Bradshaw and J. Williams (eds) *Poverty and social exclusion in Britain*, York: Joseph Rowntree Foundation, pp 32-42.

Attree, P. (2006) 'The social costs of child poverty: a systematic review of the qualitative evidence', *Children and Society*, vol 20, pp 54-66.

Barnes, H. (2009a) *Child poverty in South Africa: A money metric approach using the Community Survey 2007*, Measures of Child Poverty Project Key Report 1, Pretoria: Department of Social Development.

Barnes, H. (2009b) *Child poverty in South Africa: A socially perceived necessities approach*, Measures of Child Poverty Project Key Report 2, Pretoria: Department of Social Development, Republic of South Africa.

Barnes, H. (2009c) *Children's views of an acceptable standard of living for children in South Africa*, Measures of Child Poverty Project Key Report 3, Pretoria: Department of Social Development.

Barnes, H., Cluver, L. and Wright, G. (2007) *Findings from the Indicators of Poverty and Social Exclusion Project: Children*, Indicators of Poverty and Social Exclusion Project Key Report 5, Pretoria: Department of Social Development.

Barnes, H., Noble, M., Wright, G. and Dawes, A. (2009) 'A geographical profile of child deprivation in South Africa', *Child Indicators Research*, vol 2, no 2, pp 181-99.

Ben-Arieh, A. (2005) 'Where are the children? Children's role in measuring and monitoring their well-being', *Social Indicators Research*, vol 74, no 3, pp 573-96.

Berry, L. and Guthrie, T. (2003) *Rapid assessment: The situation of children in South Africa*, Cape Town: Children's Institute, University of Cape Town.

Boyden, J., Eyber, C., Feeny, T. and Scott, C. (2003) *Voices of children: Experiences and perceptions from Belarus, Bolivia, India, Kenya and Sierra Leone*, Children and Poverty Series Part 2, Richmond, VA: Christian Children's Fund.

Bradshaw, J. and Main, G. (2010) *PSE Measures Review Paper: Children's deprivation items*, Working Paper No 7, Poverty and Social Exclusion in the UK (www.poverty.ac.uk/sites/default/files/WP7.pdf).

Cronbach, L.J. (1951) 'Coefficient alpha and the internal structure of tests', *Psychometrika*, vol 16, no 3, pp 297–334.

Davies, R. and Smith, W. (1998) *The Basic Necessities Survey: The experience of Action Aid Vietnam*, Hanoi: Action Aid Vietnam.

Du Toit, A. (2004) "Social exclusion' discourse and chronic poverty: a South African case study', *Development and Change*, vol 35 no 5, pp 987–1010.

European Commission (2007) *Poverty and exclusion*, Special Eurobarometer 279, Directorate General Employment, Social Affairs and Equal Opportunities, European Commission, http://ec.europa.eu/public_opinion/archives/ebs/ebs_279.pdf

Gordon, D. and Pantazis, C. (eds) (1997a) *Breadline Britain in the 1990s*, Aldershot: Ashgate.

Gordon, D. and Pantazis, C. (1997b) 'The public's perception of necessities and poverty', in D. Gordon and C. Pantazis (eds) *Breadline Britain in the 1990s*, Aldershot: Ashgate, pp 71–96.

Halleröd, B. (1994) *A new approach to the direct consensual measurement of poverty*, SPRC Discussion Paper No 50, Sydney: Social Policy Research Centre, University of New South Wales.

Harpham, T., Thu Hong, N., Thap Long, T. and Tuan, T. (2005) 'Participatory child poverty assessment in rural Vietnam', *Children and Society*, vol 19, pp 27–41.

Hirsch, D. and Smith, N. (2010) *Family values – Parents' views on necessities for families with children*, DWP Research Report No 641, London: Department for Work and Pensions.

Kibel, L., Lake, L., Pendlebury, P. and Smith, C. (eds) (2010) *South African child gauge 2009/2010*, Cape Town: Children's Institute, University of Cape Town.

Klasen, S. (2000) 'Measuring poverty and deprivation in South Africa', *Review of Income and Wealth*, vol 46, no 1, pp 33–58.

Lister, R. (2004) *Poverty*, Cambridge: Polity Press.

Lloyd, E. (2006) 'Children, poverty and social exclusion', in C. Pantazis, D. Gordon and R. Levitas (eds) *Poverty and social exclusion in Britain: The Millennium Survey*, Bristol: The Policy Press, pp 315–46.

McKay, S. (2004) 'Poverty or preference: what do "consensual deprivation indicators" really measure?', *Fiscal Studies*, vol 25, no 2, pp 201–23.

Mack, J. and Lansley, S. (1985) *Poor Britain*, London: Allen & Unwin.

Moses, S. (2008) 'Children and participation in South Africa: an overview', *International Journal of Children's Rights*, vol 16, pp 327–42.

Noble, M., Wright, G. and Cluver, L. (2006) 'Developing a child-focused and multidimensional model of child poverty for South Africa', *Journal of Children and Poverty*, vol 12, no 1, pp 39-53.

Noble, M., Wright, G. and Cluver, L. (2007a) 'Conceptualising, defining and measuring child poverty in South Africa: an argument for a multidimensional approach', in A. Dawes, R. Bray and A. van der Merwe (eds) *Monitoring child well-being: A South African rights-based approach*, Cape Town: HSRC Press, pp 53-71.

Noble, M., Wright, G., Magasela, W. and Ratcliffe, A. (2007b) 'Developing a democratic definition of poverty in South Africa', *Journal of Poverty*, vol 11, no 4, pp 117-41.

Noble, M., Ratcliffe, A., Magasela, W., Wright, G., Mason, D., Zichawo, S. and Chigume, R. (2004) *Preliminary findings from the qualitative stage of the Indicators of Poverty and Social Exclusion Project*, Indicators of Poverty and Social Exclusion Project Key Report 1, Pretoria: Department of Social Development.

Nunnally, J.C. (1981) *Psychometric theory*, New York: Tate McGraw-Hill Publishing Company Ltd.

Pantazis, C., Gordon, D. and Townsend, P. (2006) 'The necessities of life', in C. Pantazis, D. Gordon and R. Levitas (eds) *Poverty and social exclusion in Britain: The Millennium Survey*, Bristol: The Policy Press, pp 89-122.

Ridge, T. (2002) *Childhood poverty and social exclusion from a child's perspective*, Bristol: The Policy Press.

Roker, D. (1998) *Worth more than this: Young people growing up in family poverty*, London: The Children's Society.

Saunders, P., Naidoo, Y. and Griffiths, M. (2007) *Towards new indicators of disadvantage: Deprivation and social exclusion in Australia*, Sydney: Social Policy Research Centre, University of New South Wales.

Shropshire, J. and Middleton, S. (1999) *Small expectations: Learning to be poor?*, York: Joseph Rowntree Foundation.

Sixsmith, J., Nic Gabhainn, S., Fleming, C. and O'Higgins, S. (2007) 'Children's, parents' and teachers' perceptions of child well-being', *Health Education*, vol 107, no 6, pp 511-23.

Statistics South Africa (2004) *Census 2001: Concepts and definitions*, Report No 03-02-26(2001), Pretoria: Statistics South Africa.

Streak, J., Yu, D. and van der Berg, S. (2009) 'Measuring child poverty in South Africa: sensitivity to the choice of equivalence scale and an updated profile', *Social Indicators Research*, vol 94, no 2, pp 183-201.

UN (United Nations) (1990) *Convention on the Rights of the Child* [Adopted and opened for signature, ratification and accession by General Assembly Resolution 44/25 of 20 November 1989, entered into force 2 September 1990].

van der Hoek, T. (2005) *Through children's eyes: An initial study of children's personal experiences of growing up poor in an affluent Netherlands*, Innocenti Working Paper No 2005-06, Florence: UNICEF Innocenti Research Centre.

Wright, G. (2008a) *Findings from the Indicators of Poverty and Social Exclusion Project: A profile of poverty using the socially perceived necessities approach*, Indicators of Poverty and Social Exclusion Project Key Report 7, Pretoria: Department of Social Development.

Wright, G. (2008b) 'Socially perceived necessities in South Africa: is a democratically derived definition of poverty achievable?', DPhil thesis, University of Oxford.

Wright, G., Barnes, H., Noble, M. and Dawes, A. (2009) *The South African Index of Multiple Deprivation for children 2001 at datazone level*, Pretoria: Department of Social Development.

SEVEN

Child well-being in the US: proposal for the development of a 'Tots Index' using the human development conceptual framework

Sarah Burd-Sharps, Patrick Guyer, Ted Lechterman and Kristen Lewis

In my beginning is my end. (T.S. Eliot, *Four quartets*)

Introduction

US society and investments in both the public and private sectors show a concern for young children and their well-being, a concern that has resulted in some very hopeful advances. In health, infant death rates have been declining steadily since the 1940s (Kung et al, 2008), smoking during pregnancy is increasingly rare, and vaccination rates have been rising. In terms of education, there has been a significant increase in both preschool and nursery rates, from nearly half of children in full-day nursery in 1995 to two thirds in 2006 (Land, 2008). In addition to these important signs of progress, there have been a number of innovative local programmes, such as the Olds' Nurse Partnership, the Abecedarian Project and others, that are internationally studied and replicated as 'best practices' to set children on a trajectory of success.

Yet recent international comparisons show us that efforts to support every child to live to his or her full potential are not achieving impressive results for all children. According to the Organisation for Economic Co-operation and Development's (OECD) 2009 publication *Doing better for children*:

- While US average family income for children under 18 is six times higher than the average for the 30 OECD countries, child poverty rates are among the highest, with more than one in five children living in a poor household.

- US incidence of low birth weight children is among the highest of OECD countries; at 8.1%, the rate is nearly double that of Iceland, Finland, Sweden and South Korea.
- The US ranks number 29 out of 30 OECD countries on teen births. Only Mexico has a higher rate.
- The average educational achievement of 15-year-olds compares poorly to other OECD countries on PISA, the international standardised exam (Programme for International Student Assessment) (US students are seventh from the bottom), and the US has larger gaps between good and poor school performers than all but five other OECD countries.

These facts are evidence of massive underperformance in child well-being as compared with other nations, virtually all of which have lower per capita incomes. While the rate of poverty among older people today in the US is about 10%, and 12% among adults aged 18-64, poverty for children under 18 is 19%, and the highest rates of poverty are observed in families with children under the age of three, where more than one in five (22%) live in households below the federal poverty rate (see Table 7.1) (White and Chau, 2009). Looking at change over time, while there has been some movement in child poverty rates over the last decade, we find ourselves in the same place today as we were in 1998, with 19% of children under 18 living in families at or below the federal poverty rate. There was progress in the early part of the 21st century, with a decrease in the child poverty rate to 16% in both 2000 and 2001, but it began to increase steadily after 2001 to its present level of 19% today (Chau, 2009).

The analysis that follows looks closely at the challenges of measuring child well-being in an affluent country context. It assesses existing aggregate measures of child well-being to see if they are adequate for

Table 7.1: 2008 poverty rates in the US by age, showing that the highest rates of poverty are among children under three

Age group	Poverty rate (%)
Under 3	22
Under 18	19
Adults 18-64	12
Elderly 65+	10

Source: White and Chau (2009), using official federal poverty guidelines of the US Department of Health and Human Services

understanding and tracking progress and enabling comparisons among important population groups, such as by subnational geographies or by racial and ethnic background. It explores whether the American Human Development Index (HDI) is a suitable proxy for child well-being in the US, and after concluding that this Index suffers from some critical weaknesses for this purpose, proposes a framework for the development of a 'Tots Index' and the indicators on which it could be based. This proposed index would focus on children under the age of five and offer the possibility of disaggregation to the level of the states and by racial and ethnic background.

American Human Development Index and measuring child well-being

The American Human Development Project, founded in 2006, is an initiative of the non-profit Social Science Research Council. The Project developed a modified American HDI to measure and analyse access to progress and opportunity in the US. It is a composite measure that reflects what most people believe are the basic ingredients of human well-being: a long and healthy life, access to knowledge and a decent standard of living. It is based on the pioneering work of Mahbub ul Haq, Amartya Sen and others who have argued that poverty is more complex than a simple measure of income can capture alone. In seeking to expand the capabilities for people to lead lives that they value, it combines measurements of health, education and income into one easy-to-understand number. This more comprehensive measure broadens the analysis of the interlocking factors that fuel advantage and disadvantage, create opportunities and determine life chances. Because it uses easily understood indicators that are comparable across geographic regions and over time, the Index also allows for a shared frame of reference in which to assess well-being and permits apples-to-apples comparisons from place to place as well as year to year.

The American HDI is the first human development index adapted to an affluent country context. In common with the widely applied global HDI, the American HDI combines the same three powerful components: a long and healthy life, access to knowledge and a decent standard of living, but in some cases it uses different indicators in order to better capture well-being and freedoms in an affluent country context. (For full details on the American HDI, see the methodological notes in Burd-Sharps et al, 2008.)

Given the Project's concern with child well-being in the US and with the patchwork of policies aimed at tackling isolated manifestations of disadvantage and dysfunction in the lives of North America's smallest members of society, we began to explore whether the American HDI was able to capture the distribution of well-being among children, and could be used as a tool to measure progress towards better performance.

Relationships between the Human Development Index and child well-being

The American HDI is primarily a measure of adult well-being. The educational dimension is measured using an indicator of adult educational attainment as well as enrolment for the population ages three to 24, and the standard of living dimension is measured using median personal earnings, an indicator which considers all workers aged 16 and over. That the Index cannot be disaggregated by age group presents one reason to consider supplementary measures of child well-being. However, given the explanatory power of the Human Development Index, it also possible that it already describes enough about child poverty. Investigation reveals some correlations between the American HDI and selected independent indicators of child well-being.

This preliminary analysis (see Table 7.2) shows significant negative relationships between state-level HDI scores and child mortality, child poverty and infant mortality, and a relatively strong positive

Table 7.2: Correlations between the American HDI and selected indicators of child well-being

	HDI	Child mortality	Child poverty	Early education enrolment	Infant mortality	Single-parent household	Uninsured children
HDI	1	−0.628**	−0.646**	0.508**	−0.431**	−0.130	−0.212
Child mortality	−0.628**	1	0.725**	−0.252	0.736**	0.618**	0.240
Child poverty	−0.646**	0.725**	1	−0.122	0.636**	0.708**	0.159
Early education enrolment	0.508**	−0.252	−0.122	1	0.125	0.272	−0.254
Infant mortality	−0.431**	0.736**	0.636**	0.125	1	0.732**	0.008
Single-parent household	−0.130	0.618**	0.708**	0.272	0.732**	1	0.116
Uninsured children	−0.212	0.240	0.159	−0.254	0.008	0.116	1

** Significant to the 0.01 level.

* Significant to the 0.05 level.

Source: US Department of Health and Human Services and US Census Bureau, collected in Burd-Sharps et al (2008), CDC (2006, 2007) and Kids Count (2005a, 2005b, 2005c, 2005d)

relationship between HDI scores and early education enrolment for three- to five-year-olds. There are also strong positive relationships between infant mortality, child poverty and single-parent households, which attest to the interconnections between these health, income and household stability issues.

Since infant and child mortality rates affect life expectancies, on which one third of the HDI score depends, we should not be surprised to see correlations here. Likewise, the child poverty indicator is a function of the income situation of parents, and since median personal earnings are also a part of the HDI, the strong correlation is not surprising.

Recognising the influence of childhood conditions on the components of the HDI, the first American human development report *The measure of America 2008-2009* explicitly addressed several factors that the Index alone obscures. In particular, the report discussed infant mortality and uninsurance, early child education, the impact of the economic recession on child poverty and the relationship between parental incarceration and child well-being (Burd-Sharps et al, 2008).

Shortcomings of the Human Development Index for measuring child well-being

In one sense, however, the need for supplementary explanations to elucidate child well-being belies the utility of the HDI for understanding child poverty. At the same time, while the analyses here show that the Index correlates strongly with other indicators of child well-being such as child mortality and child poverty, these correlations are not one-to-one and the relationships between the HDI and other measures, such as the percentage of children living in single-parent households or lacking health insurance, are insignificant.

Indeed, as discussed above, the American HDI is primarily a measure of adult well-being. We know intuitively that adults and children experience poverty and opportunity differently, and a rich literature attests to the particular salience of child poverty. As predictive as it is, then, the HDI cannot hope to account for the differences in development experiences between adults and children.

At the same time, the HDI manages to accomplish what many measurements of poverty − whether child or adult − fail to do, and that is to conceive of well-being in a multidimensional yet parsimonious way. Ongoing attempts at measuring poverty either extend monetary measurements to children, or use a laundry list of indicators selected to capture as many dimensions of poverty possible in a developing country context.

Why the concern with young children?

In the first *American Human Development Report, The measure of America* (Burd-Sharps et al, 2008), it became clear that a number of the most challenging deficits in well-being in the US are actually symptoms of problems that begin in childhood. The roots of teenage pregnancy, poor school achievement and high school drop-out, behavioural problems, and high rates of juvenile detention and incarceration often trace back to a child's first years of life. But because these symptoms are generally much more visible, they tend to get the attention of society rather than the actual problems: instability, stress or depression in the home environment, inadequate nutrition, lack of access to health insurance, neglect or abuse and other forms of disadvantage that are often passed from generation to generation. Consider the following:

- Recent brain research has confirmed that the human brain has developed to 90% of its potential at age four (Allen and Smith, 2008).
- Deep and persistent poverty in the preschool years is associated with lower rates of high school completion. In 2006, young people aged 16 to 19 from poor families were about three times more likely to be out of school and not working than were their non-poor counterparts (Kutner et al, 2007).
- One in three two-year-olds in the US is not fully immunised (Children's Defense Fund, 2008).
- In contrast to the popular myth, intergenerational mobility in the US is consistently calculated to be the lowest among its peer countries − children born to poor parents are more likely to grow up to be poor in the US than children born to poor parents in the UK, Canada, Germany, Sweden, Finland, Norway or Denmark (Blanden et al, 2005).
- Child poverty takes a heavy economic toll on society through lost productivity of workers, criminal justice costs and inability to compete in the global marketplace. It is estimated it reduces economic output by about 1.3% of gross domestic product (GDP) (Cauthen and Fass, 2008).

Despite the critical importance of young child well-being, in the US, most government involvement does not begin until age five, when the children enrol in nursery. Thus, children under the age of five represent a special demographic, and the ability to measure the extent to which a critical foundation is being effectively constructed requires metrics that are targeted at this specific age group and the special needs and vulnerabilities that they have.

Children under the age of five: a special demographic

All human beings share a set of very basic needs, such as access to water and food, adequate shelter and clothing, and essential services like healthcare and education. These basic needs are well captured by the areas that the American HDI measures. But children aged five and younger have an additional set of needs that are distinct from those of adults and even older children. Satisfying these needs is essential to the development of capabilities required to lead lives of choice and value. Two areas in particular are protection and attachment.

Protection: Young children's need for protection from harm is far greater than that of other age groups for two reasons. First, the youngest children are physically small, comparatively helpless and unable to defend themselves; their immature, still-developing brains and bodies are particularly vulnerable to hazards of all sorts, from lead paint and nutritional deficits to accidents and abuse. Second, evidence from neuroscience is now overwhelming that the interaction of genes and a child's earliest experiences and environments actually shape the architecture of the developing brain. Contrary to popular wisdom, adversity does not make people, particularly children, stronger or more resilient; rather, prolonged exposure to stress creates nervous system and stress hormone reactions that damage the highly plastic brains of the youngest children, increasing their vulnerability and leading to lifelong problems in cognition, emotional regulation, behaviour and physical and mental health (*The Science of Early Childhood Development*, 2007). Adverse events and environments thus do the very young child disproportionate harm in the present and also increase his or her vulnerability to harm in the future. Addressing development impairments through remediation and treatment is less effective and more costly than supporting healthy development in the critical early years.

Attachment: The interaction between genes and environment is mediated through the child's relationships with his or her primary caregivers, typically parents (*The Science of Early Childhood Development*, 2007). For good or for ill, primary relationships shape the child's word, creating the context in which he or she learns about life and copes with its inevitable frustrations and sorrows. In order to thrive and eventually fulfil their human potential, infants and toddlers need a 'secure attachment' with their parent or parents, or another consistent caregiver. Secure attachment develops through positive, consistent interaction with loving, emotionally available caregivers who are attuned to the child and provide appropriate stimulation. It provides a secure base from which a child can explore and learn and to which he or she can return in times of anxiety or distress. Without a secure base, a child's exploratory behaviour is hampered, and the earliest foundations of learning are poorly formed (Karen, 1998). These attachments thus lay the groundwork not just for a child's ability to love and be loved, to trust and be trusted; they also provide the foundation for all future cognitive, linguistic, social, regulatory and moral capabilities. Disruptions in attachment, which can come from a number of factors, from maternal depression to family stress to household dissolution, thus imperil the development of capabilities, the exercise of choice, and the ability to form and maintain healthy relationships.

Attempts to assess the well-being of children under five, therefore, should look at both the basic building blocks of human well-being that apply to everyone – health, access to knowledge and a decent material standard of living – and also those two additional areas that are vital to this age group, namely protection from harm and secure attachment.

Existing methodologies for measuring child well-being in an affluent country context

There currently exist several methodologies for measuring child well-being in an affluent country context. Two examples drawn from the international sphere are the child well-being 'Report Card' series produced by UNICEF's Innocenti Research Centre[1] and the recent report entitled *Doing better for children* by the OECD (Chapple and Richardson, 2009). In addition to these cross-country measures, there are two well-known methodologies used to measure child well-being within the US, the Child Well-Being Index (CWI)[2] developed by Kenneth Land at Duke University and funded by the Foundation for Child Development, and the Kids Count Index developed by The Annie E. Casey Foundation (AECF).[3]

International approaches to measuring child well-being

In addition to annually updated individual indicators of child well-being maintained by organisations such as the United Nations Children's Fund (UNICEF) and the OECD,[4] several attempts have been made to establish international indices of child well-being. These include the work of Heshmati et al (2007) and others in turning data collected by UNICEF into an aggregate index of child well-being, efforts by Bradshaw et al (2007) and others to create a child-centred index for the European Union (EU) countries, and the work of Richardson et al (2008) and others to establish an index for the countries of Central and Eastern Europe (CEE) and the Commonwealth of Independent States (CIS). While these are all excellent contributions to the field, for our purposes here we focus on two especially high-profile child well-being monitoring efforts undertaken by UNICEF and the OECD during this decade.

UNICEF's Innocenti Research Centre published its first 'Report Card' on child well-being in rich countries, *A league table of child poverty in rich nations*, in 2000. The report focused on child poverty, defined both in relative and in absolute terms, as a principal proxy indicator of child well-being. The report concluded that one in every six children in 30 of the world's most affluent countries lived below the poverty line in 2000, as defined by their country of residence. In terms of relative child poverty,[5] the US ranked nearly last, ahead of only Mexico, with over 22% of children living in poverty.

The most recent report from the UNICEF Innocenti Research Centre, released in 2007, incorporated a new innovation, which broadened the exclusive focus in income poverty to account for a variety of other indicators of child well-being. These were grouped broadly into six dimensions: material well-being, health and safety, educational well-being, family and peer relationships, risky behaviours and subjective well-being. The report presented the rankings of OECD countries with significant information in each dimension as well as an overall score for each country. This overall score was not an aggregate of indicator scores per se. Rather, it was an average of how each country ranked across all six dimensions.

Out of 21 countries, the US averaged a rank of only 18 across the six dimensions. The best showing for the US was in the educational well-being dimension, where the country was ranked 12th, and the worst showing was in health and safety, where the US came in last (UNICEF Innocenti Research Centre, 2007).

Picking up where the seventh UNICEF Report Card left off, the OECD's 2009 publication *Doing better for children* also employed a six-dimension approach to evaluating comparative child well-being in OECD countries. Like the UNICEF report, it stopped short of creating an aggregate index and instead simply presented overall findings by listing the rank of each country in each of the dimensions. These dimensions closely mirrored those identified by UNICEF, including material well-being, housing and environment, educational well-being, health and safety, risky behaviours and quality of school life (Chapple and Richardson, 2009, p 27). No OECD country consistently topped the rankings across all six dimensions. However, the US performed poorly in most areas, ranking 23rd out of 30 countries in the material well-being dimension, 25th in educational well-being and 24th in health and safety. The US made its best showing in the housing and environment dimension, where it was placed 12th.

Domestic approaches to measuring child well-being in the US

In the US, official data on child well-being are produced regularly by a variety of federal agencies. The US Census Bureau[6] collects information on family demographics, structure and economic situation, as well as some subjective indicators of neighbourhood safety and community involvement, through its Surveys of Income and Program Participation, Current Population Surveys and American Community Surveys.[7] The National Survey of Children's Health,[8] carried out by the Child and Adolescent Health Measurement Initiative of the US Department of Health and Human Services, collects a variety of indicators on the situation of children and their families, including measures of family structure, neighbourhood safety, family health habits and emotional and mental health. These and other child- and family-centred statistics are compiled by the Federal Interagency Forum on Child and Family Statistics, a centralised data clearing house.[9]

Non-governmental organisations (NGOs) have stepped in to help make existing data on child well-being more accessible and understandable to researchers, advocates, policy makers and the general public. Initiatives such as the Child Trends Data Bank[10] and the AECF Kids Count Data Center[11] are two such examples.

In terms of aggregate indicators of child well-being, two domestic efforts warrant special attention. The first is the CWI, developed by Duke University demographer Kenneth Land and funded by the Foundation for Child Development. The CWI takes 28 indicators into consideration, grouped into six domains of child well-being: family economic well-being, child health, safety and behaviour, education, connectedness to the community, family stability and emotional and spiritual well-being. These are indexed to a base year, and averaged to provide an aggregate index of overall child well-being (Land, 2007). The most recent report concluded that progress on improving the well-being of children and in narrowing disparities between children of different racial and ethnic backgrounds had stalled in the first part of the current decade, and that children's health indicators were actually showing retrogression in recent years. However, the report also found evidence that indicators of child safety and risky behaviour were improving (Land, 2007, p 3). The CWI unfortunately does not disaggregate to the state-level, although separate scores for children by racial and ethnic background are available for 27 of 28 indicators (Land, 2007, p 11).

The second domestic index is the state ranking generated annually by the AECF. In addition to data presentation tools hosted at its Kids Count Data Center, the Foundation has also produced a ranking of all 50 states based on an aggregation of its key indicators annually since 2002. The indicators considered include educational attainment, family economic well-being, family structure, health, and safety measures appropriate for children, adolescents and their families. Standardised scores are obtained, with each component weighted equally, and rankings are based on state-level sums including all key indicators. The resulting AECF rankings are similar to rankings based on the HDI. Indeed there is a strong, positive and significant correlation between the two.[12]

Evaluation of existing approaches

Given the previous discussion of the particular requirements of young children for a safe and consistent home environment, and their relative vulnerability to disease, injury, poor nutrition and neglect, the concern with the above methodologies is that all include indicators which target age groups ranging up to and above 18 years in some cases. Few of the measures utilised in UNICEF Innocenti's research or *Doing better for children* refer to a common age group and most, save for indicators on factors such as immunisation and infant mortality, focus on adolescents and teenagers (UNICEF Innocenti Research Centre, 2007, pp 42-3; Chapple and Richardson, 2009, pp 31-2). In terms of the domestic child well-being indices, some CWI indicators include youth up to 20 years. This is advantageous because it enables the inclusion of indicators of political participation. But it consequently takes the focus off of young children. The educational domain does not look specifically at pre-school or nursery enrolment (Land, 2007, p 17). The AECF data cover similar ground, including some indicators covering children under the age of five (infant mortality, low birth weight babies and preschool/nursery enrolment, for example) and others targeting older children and adolescents.

Disaggregation by geographic location, 'race' and other cleavages is another area in which current measures are lacking. Our own research has laid bare the tremendous gaps in human development between areas of the country and between different groups in the US today. For example, when quantified on our HDI, the level of human development enjoyed by residents in high-human development states such as Connecticut and Massachusetts is vastly different from that in low-human development states such as West Virginia or Mississippi. Comparing the HDI levels of these states with our historical estimates for the nation as a whole, there is almost a 30-year gap in human development between states at the top and bottom of our index (Burd-Sharps et al, 2008, p 32). Large gaps exist between racial and ethnic groups as well. The HDI value for Asian Americans is currently far higher than that of the nation as a whole. However, the human development of African Americans is comparable to that of the entire US in the 1980s. More specifically, almost 20 years of life expectancy separate Asian American women, who on average live the longest, from African American men, who on average live the shortest lives of any demographic in the US (Burd-Sharps et al, 2008, p 39).

In terms of the indices discussed above, the most recent UNICEF 'Report Card' laments the unavailability of indicators disaggregated for gender and age group (UNICEF Innocenti Research Centre, 2007, p 3). Likewise, the authors of *Doing better for children* show that few indicators standardised for international comparison were available disaggregated by all three factors (Chapple and Richardson, 2009, pp 31-2).

At the domestic level, the CWI is limited by its inability to permit disaggregation by state or any other subnational unit. In contrast, and in addition to its key indicators and state rankings, AECF Kids Count has an impressive amount of additional information available by state as well as by county and even by major city in some cases. Some, but not all, indicators are available disaggregated by 'race' and ethnicity, although only at the national level.

In conclusion, none of these measures sufficiently targets our age group of interest, children from birth through age four, or provides as much opportunity for disaggregation by geography or by racial or ethnic background as we would hope to offer a practical tool for understanding, assessing and monitoring progress in child well-being.

What, then, might an index to assess the well-being of very young children look like? Which proxy indicators might best capture the domains of health, access to knowledge, standard of living, protection from harm and attachment?

Proposing the 'Tots Index': a composite measure of young child well-being

The following is an exploration of possible indicators that could be used in the construction of a composite index of well-being for children under the age of five, using the holistic human development conceptual framework. Further work would need to be done to construct a balanced index that is comprehensive without being overly complex and that avoids the inclusion of several indicators that capture the same effect.

Health indicators

The American HDI uses life expectancy at birth as a proxy for health. To zero in on the issues most pertinent to the health of very young children – as opposed to the range of health threats across the life course that are captured in life expectancy – promising indicators include low birth weight, infant mortality and child mortality. All these statistics are available through the US Centers for Disease Control and Prevention.

Infant and child mortality are stark indicators of health. There is significant variation in the US by 'race', place and income level when it comes to deaths among the very young. For instance, the infant death rate in Louisiana in 2007 was 8.9 per 1,000 live births, nearly a third higher than the national average of 6 deaths per 1,000. Louisiana's infant death rate among whites is at the US average, but the rate for African Americans is twice as high, 13.6 deaths per 1,000 live births (Burd-Sharps et al, 2009b).

Low birth weight (weighing less than 2,500 grams, about 5.5 pounds) correlates to impairments in language acquisition and psychological and intellectual development. The well-being and health status of the mother, including her access to healthcare, is strongly associated with low birth weight. The US low birth weight rate is about 8% of newborns, but the variation within the country among regions and racial/ethnic groups is significant. For instance, Mississippi's low birth weight rate is one third higher than the national average, or 12.3%. Further, the rate among African Americans in Alcorn, Prentiss and several adjacent counties in Mississippi is 22.1%, or nearly one in four babies. Among whites in Mississippi, the highest rate is found in Lincoln, Copiah and adjacent counties, with more than one in ten babies put at risk by low birth weight (Burd-Sharps et al, 2009a).

Access to knowledge indicators

The American HDI uses school enrolment and educational degree attainment as its proxies for access to knowledge. For young children, promising indicators include preschool enrolment, child reading or story-telling, and the educational level of the mother.

Intuitively, early childhood enrolment in preschool makes sense as a proxy for the youngest children's access to knowledge. It fits what most people think of as knowledge, that is, something that is learned in the classroom. But the key lessons of early childhood are not learned in classrooms and have little to do with being able to count, recite the alphabet or correctly identify colours or shapes. Rather, the key lessons of early childhood have to do with how to learn, how to think and how to regulate impulses and emotions; these lessons are learned through human interaction with attuned, responsive adults. In addition, measures of preschool enrolment make no assessment as to the nature or quality of the care or education. Childcare and nursery school or preschool are not the same thing, although the lines separating them are blurry and most large surveys do not distinguish among them. Being cared for in the home of a neighbour who did not graduate high school for nine or ten hours each day is a very different experience from attending a nursery school with college-educated teachers and developmentally enriching materials and activities. Both would be categorised as 'early childhood education' in many large surveys. According to this definition, 43% of three-year-olds and 69% of four-year-olds were enrolled in a centre-based early childhood programme in 2005. This indicator is available from the American Community Survey.

Reading to children and telling them stories contributes to their cognitive and linguistic development, and children whose parents read to them do better in school, research shows (Hsin, 2009). The National Survey of Children's Health tracks the percentage of children from birth to age five whose parents read to them, tell them stories or sing to them every day. Data are available by state, disaggregated either by 'race' or by gender. This indicator is a good proxy for early childhood education, but, as we will argue below, it is also one of the few indicators available that could serve as a defensible proxy for attachment. The same survey tracks how many children from birth to age five go on family outings every day, another indicator of the type of stimulation important to the development of cognitive functions.

International and domestic evidence time and again confirm that the best indictor of a child's school success is the educational level of the mother. Given that the vast majority of children under five live with their mothers, and that mothers in the US and most other countries tend to be the primary caretakers of young children, there is a strong case to be made that simply knowing the educational attainment of the mother gives a good indication of her baby or young child's access to knowledge.

A University of Kansas study in the early 1990s found that by age three, the children of more affluent, better-educated mothers had vocabularies twice as large as those of the children of low-income, less educated mothers (Hart and Risley, 1995). More recent studies continue to confirm that educated mothers use a richer vocabulary, engage in longer periods of conversation and encourage child-directed conversation more frequently than less educated, less verbally skilled mothers, and that play and interaction are the pathways through which these mothers transmit verbal skills (Hsin, 2009). College-educated mothers spend more time on childcare, and the activities mothers and children do together are more 'enriching' (that is, they watch less television and spend more time reading and doing art projects) than less educated mothers. Highly educated fathers spend more time playing with, reading to and going on outings with their preschoolers; they also spend more time caring for and playing with their infants than less educated fathers (Bianchi et al, 2004). Adult educational degree attainment is available annually from the American Community Survey.

Standard of living indicators

The American HDI uses median personal earnings as its proxy of a decent standard of living. Children aged five and under have no earnings. Since children live in households with adults, household income is a good proxy for the material standard of living of young children; these data are collected by the American Community Survey every year. Another possible indicator is the employment of parents, a statistic collected annually by the AECF.

Child poverty, the percentage of households with children under five with incomes below the federal poverty line, collected annually by the American Community Survey, is arguably the best indicator for the number of very young children living in extreme poverty, as the poverty line in the US is an absolute, not relative, threshold that is set quite low — about US$20,000 for a family of two adults and two children. Food insecurity, which is tracked by the US Department of Agriculture, gives an indication of how often cash is sufficiently short in a given household that the normal diet is disrupted; this indicator also gets at extreme deprivation. The rate of homelessness among children is a powerful indicator of a child's material well-being.

Knowing familial assets would help round out the picture of the well-being of the youngest children. While income typically covers living expenses, assets act as a cushion in hard times, provide stability in housing and education, and allow for investment in the next generation. Information on assets is not collected as often, as thoroughly, or to the same levels of disaggregation as information on incomes.

Indicators that assess the composition of the household and the educational status of parents also provide important information about children's material standard of living. Children who are born to parents who did not graduate from high school, who are unmarried and who are teenagers, for instance, are extremely likely to be poor.

Prevention of harm indicators

Assessing the degree to which a very young child is protected from harm requires indicators on the child's physical environment, the child's safety from violence at home and the rate of accidents and injuries.

In terms of physical environment, the presence of lead in paint is a known risk factor for young children, associated with cognitive impairments, reduced intelligence, behavioural problems and damage to organs. Although all children living in houses built before 1978, when lead in paint was banned, are at risk, low-income and minority children are four times more likely to be poisoned by contaminated dust and soil generated by lead paint; 16% of low-income children living in older housing are poisoned, compared to about 4% of all children (President's Task Force, 2000).

The Centers for Disease Control and Prevention, Lead Poisoning Prevention Branch compiles state surveillance data for children aged less than 72 months who were tested for lead at least once since 1 January 1997.

The National Survey of Children's Health collects data every four years on child injury, specifically the percentage of children from birth to age five experiencing major injury requiring medical care in the reference year. The Center for Injury Prevention and Control also tracks accidents and injuries, such as drowning, fires and car accidents. There is significant variation among population groups in terms of accidental deaths. For instance, among African American children, American Indian children and Alaskan Native children, the rate of drowning is significantly higher than among white children. African

American, Native American, and very poor young children are more likely to die or be injured in a fire than other children.

In terms of familial violence, very young children (aged three and younger) are the most frequent victims of child fatalities; they die from their caregivers' actions (battering, shaking, drowning, suffocating) and from their failure to act (such as malnutrition or drowning while unsupervised). Most deaths from physical abuse are caused by fathers or other male caregivers, while mothers or female caregivers are responsible for most deaths due to neglect. Child abuse and fatalities are not well counted at present, but the National Child Abuse and Neglect Data System is improving its capacity to track these tragic events by establishing review teams and improving coordination of data collection. The National Child Abuse and Neglect Data System reported an estimated 1,760 child fatalities in 2007 (Child Welfare Information Gateway, 2008). It would also be critical to track non-fatal incidence of child abuse to accurately gauge the well-being of very young children.

Attachment indicators

Attachment, or the existence of a secure, stable and nurturing bond between the very young child and his or her primary caregivers, is not tracked by any large survey instruments. The gold standard for assessing attachment, the so-called 'strange situation' developed by US psychologist Mary Ainsworth, in which the reaction of a toddler to brief separations from and reunifications with his or her mother is assessed in a laboratory situation by trained researchers, cannot feasibly be applied to large groups. Thus proxies for attachment disruptions are the best that can be hoped for.

Indicators that look at changes in the composition of the household or the child's living situation could shed some light on attachment issues. For example, death of a parent, divorce or abandonment, incarceration of a parent, change in the adults living in the house (such as the mother's live-in companion moving out), frequent moves within one year, homelessness – each of these events could signal a disruption in a child's fundamental relationships.

The problem is that most survey instruments do not ask questions about change; rather, they provide snapshots of the situation at the moment the question is asked. There are some exceptions. For instance, every four years, the National Survey of Children's Health asks questions about the number of moves a child has experienced; annually, the

American Community Survey asks about the percentage of children aged one to four who have moved within the year.

There is a need for an indicator that looks specifically at this question of changes in household composition, ideally identifying changes that most directly affect young children. A useful question for a large-scale survey of the well-being of young children would be:

Has one or more primary caretakers of children aged five and younger in this household experienced any of the following:
- Death?
- A debilitating physical or mental illness that affected the adult's ability to interact normally with the child?
- Incarceration for one month or more?
- Hospitalisation for one month or more?
- Absence from the household for one month or more due to other responsibilities, such as employment or caring for a relative?
- Departure from the household due to separation, divorce or abandonment?

In the absence of survey data for these sorts of questions, however, the National Survey of Children's Health indicator on the percentage of children from birth to age five whose parents read to them, tell them stories or sing to them every day provides a good indication of parental attentiveness and responsiveness – appropriately stimulating caregiving – and thus provides a defensible proxy for the existence of a secure attachment between the parent and child.

Conclusion

As the T.S. Elliot quote at the outset implies, decisions and investments in the first years of a child's life play a fundamental role in their life chances. These are years of remarkable opportunity, when the foundation for a productive and fulfilling life can be laid through family and societal investments in health, education and many other areas. On the other hand, children under five are also uniquely vulnerable to a whole host of hazards and deprivations.

There is a strong correlation between human poverty – deprivations including but also going beyond material standard of living – and poor outcomes for children. And deep poverty in the earliest years is particularly damaging in that it sets children on a trajectory of lowered achievement that is difficult to alter at later stages. Disadvantage affects early childhood development in two ways. First, very poor families have insufficient resources to protect their children from adverse environments (among others, neighbourhood violence and environmental hazards like lead paint), and often struggle to provide their children with adequate material goods (nutritious food, books, developmentally appropriate toys), high-quality services (health and education) and investments of time (trips to the library or playground). Second, living in poverty is extremely stressful, and the resulting parental and familial stress adversely affects early childhood development. Stress can lead to parental depression, anxiety and punitive, inconsistent parenting, all of which can disrupt parent–child bonds (Gennetian et al, 2009).

Data currently available in the US are relatively plentiful to help to assess individual factors that contribute to the well-being of children under the age of five, especially when compared with other data-poor countries. Yet much of the assessment and analysis of the situation of small children looks narrowly at family poverty. We have few tools that help to pinpoint on a common scale geographic areas with concentrated disadvantage as well as particularly vulnerable subgroups of young children, looking across a holistic range of child-focused indicators. It is our belief that the development of a 'Tots Index' that is based on the multidimensional human development conceptual framework, could offer such a tool. It could be used to identify particular groups in need and to assess and track the success of policies and programmes over time that aim to bring about better outcomes for particular groups of young children. Ultimately, it could help us as a society to identify and invest in vulnerable groups of young children today, which is a far cheaper and more effective approach than trying to break destructive cycles of teenagers and young adults later.

Notes

[1] UNICEF, Innocenti Report Cards (www.unicef-irc.org/cgi-bin/unicef/series_down.sql?SeriesId=16).

[2] Foundation for Child Development, 'Child Well-Being Index' (http://fcd-us.org/our-work/child-well-being-index-cwi).

[3] Annie E. Casey Foundation, 'Kids Count Data Center' (http://datacenter.kidscount.org/).

[4] UNICEF resources such as Childinfo.org and the annual *State of the World's Children* reports are indispensable sources of data on child well-being. Excellent information is also available through OECD Stat

Extracts (http://stats.oecd.org/Index.aspx?usercontext=sourceoecd) for affluent countries.

[5] Relative poverty was defined as living in households with incomes less than 50% of the national median.

[6] US Census Bureau, *US Census Bureau – Children* (www.census.gov/population/www/socdemo/children.html).

[7] US Census Bureau, *American Community Survey* (http://factfinder.census.gov). Table S0901 is particularly relevant for accessing basic demographic and household poverty data for families with children.

[8] US Department of Health and Human Services Child and Adolescent Health Measurement Initiative, *National Survey of Children's Health* (www.nschdata.org).

[9] Federal Interagency Forum on Child and Family Statistics, *ChildStats. gov* (www.childstats.gov).

[10] www.childtrendsdatabank.org

[11] http://datacenter.kidscount.org/

[12] The correlation coefficient for state rankings based on the HDI for 2005 and the AECF for 2005 was 0.704, significant to the 0.01 level.

References

Allen, G. and Smith, I.D. (2008) *Early intervention: Good parents, great kids, better citizens*, London: The Centre for Social Justice and The Smith Institute (www.smith-institute.org.uk/pdfs/early-intervention.pdf).

Bianchi, S., Cohen, P., Raley, S. and Nomaguchi, K. (2004) 'Inequality in parental investment in child-rearing', in K. Neckerman (ed) *Social inequality*, New York: Russell Sage, pp 189-219.

Blanden, J., Gregg, P. and Machin, S. (2005) *Intergenerational mobility in Europe and North America*, London: Centre for Economic Performance, London School of Economics and Political Science (www.suttontrust.com/reports/IntergenerationalMobility.pdf).

Bradshaw, J., Hoelscher, P. and Richardson, D. (2007) 'An index of child well-being in the European Union', *Social Indicators Research*, vol 80, no 1, pp 133-77.

Burd-Sharps, S., Lewis, K. and Martins, E.B. (2008) *The measure of America: American Human Development Report 2008-2009*, New York: Columbia University Press.

Burd-Sharps, S., Lewis, K. and Martins, E.B. (2009a) *A portrait of Mississippi*, New York: American Human Development Project (www.measureofamerica.org/mississippi).

Burd-Sharps, S., Lewis, K. and Martins, E.B. (2009b) *A portrait of Louisiana*, New York: American Human Development Project (www.measureofamerica.org/louisiana).

Cauthen, N.K. and Fass, S. (2008) *Ten important questions about child poverty and family economic hardship*, New York: National Center for Children in Poverty (www.nccp.org/pages/pdf/page_131.pdf).

CDC (Centers for Disease Control and Prevention) (2006) *Mortality by underlying cause among children: US/state, 1990-2006*, Washington, DC: National Center for Health Statistics, US Department of Health and Human Services (Health Data Interactive, www.cdc.gov/nchs/hdi.htm).

CDC (2007) 'Table 3. Infant mortality rates per 1,000 live births by race and Hispanic origin of mother: United States and each state, Puerto Rico, Virgin Islands, and Guam, 2002-2004 linked files', *National Vital Statistics Reports*, vol 55, no 14, Washington, DC: National Center for Health Statistics, US Department of Health and Human Services (www.cdc.gov/nchs/data/nvsr/nvsr55/nvsr55_14.pdf).

Chapple, S. and Richardson, D. (2009) *Doing better for children*, Paris: Organisation for Economic Co-operation and Development.

Chau, M. (2009) *Low-income children in the United States*, New York: National Center for Children in Poverty (www.nccp.org/publications/pub_907.htm).

Children's Defense Fund (2008) 'Children in the United States' Fact Sheet (www.childrensdefense.org/child-research-data-publications/data/state-data-repository/cits/children-in-the-states-2008-unitedstates.pdf).

Child Welfare Information Gateway (2008) *Child abuse and neglect fatalities: Statistics and interventions*, Washington, DC (www.childwelfare.gov/pubs/factsheets/fatality.cfm).

Gennetian, L.A., Castells, N. and Morris, P. (2009) *Meeting the basic needs of children: Does income matter?*, National Poverty Center Working Paper Series #09-11, Ann Arbor, MI: National Poverty Centre (www.npc.umich.edu/publications/u/working_paper09-11.pdf).

Hart, B. and Risley, T. (1995) *Meaningful differences in the everyday experience of young American children*, Baltimore, MD: Brookes Publishing Company.

Heshmati, A., Tausch, A. and Bajalan, C.S.J. (2007) 'Measurement and analysis of child well-being in middle and high income countries', *European Journal of Comparative Economics*, vol 5, no 2, pp 227-86.

Hsin, A. (2009) 'Parent's time with children: does time matter for children's cognitive achievement?', *Social Indicators Research*, vol 93, no 1, pp 123-6.

Karen, R. (1998) *Becoming attached: First relationships and how they shape our capacity to love*, New York: Oxford University Press.

Kids Count (2005a) *Children in poverty (percent) – 2005*, Baltimore, MD: The Annie E. Casey Foundation (http://datacenter.kidscount.org).

Kids Count (2005b) *Children enrolled in nursery school, preschool or kindergarten by age group (percent) – 2005*, Baltimore, MD: The Annie E. Casey Foundation (http://datacenter.kidscount.org).

Kids Count (2005c) *Children in single-parent families (percent) – 2005*, Baltimore, MD: The Annie E. Casey Foundation (http://datacenter. kidscount.org).

Kids Count (2005d) *Children without health insurance (percent) – 2005*, Baltimore, MD: The Annie E. Casey Foundation (http://datacenter. kidscount.org).

Kung, H.C., Hoyert, D.L., Xu, J. and Murphy, S.L. (2008) 'Deaths: final data for 2005', *National Vital Statistics Reports*, vol 56, no 10 (www.cdc.gov/nchs/data/nvsr/nvsr56/nvsr56_10.pdf).

Kutner, M., Greenberg, E., Jin, Y., Boyle, B., Hsu, Y. and Dunleavy, E. (2007) *Literacy in everyday life: Results From the 2003 National Assessment of Adult Literacy* (NCES 2007-480), Washington, DC: US Department of Education, National Center for Education Statistics.

Land, K.C. (2007) *Child and Youth Well-Being Index, 1975-2005, with projections for 2006*, Durham, NC: Foundation for Child Development (www.fcd-us.org/usr_doc/2007CWIReport-Embargoed.pdf).

Land, K.C. (2008) *2008 special focus report: Trends in infancy/early childhood and middle childhood well-being, 1994-2006*, Foundation for Child Development Child and Youth Well-Being Index (CWI) Project (www.fcd-us.org/usr_doc/EarlyChildhoodWell-BeingReport.pdf).

OECD (Organisation for Economic Co-operation and Development) (2009) *Doing better for children*, Paris: OECD (www.oecd.org/els/ social/childwellbeing).

President's Task Force on Environmental Health Risks and Safety Risks to Children (2000) *Eliminating childhood lead poisoning: A federal strategy targeting lead paint hazards* (www.cdc.gov/nceh/lead/about/ fedstrategy2000.pdf).

Richardson, D., Hoelscher, P. and Bradshaw, J. (2008) 'Child well-being in Central and Eastern European countries and the Commonwealth of Independent States', *Child Indicators Research*, vol 1, no 3, pp 211-50.

The Science of Early Childhood Development (2007) Cambridge: National Scientific Council Center on the Developing Child at Harvard University.

UNICEF (United Nations Children's Fund) Innocenti Research Centre (2000) *A league table of child poverty in rich nations*, Florence: UNICEF.

UNICEF Innocenti Research Centre (2007) *Child poverty in perspective: An overview of child well-being in rich countries*, Report Card No 7, Florence: UNICEF.

White, V.R. and Chau, M. (2009) *Basic facts about low-income children*, New York: National Center for Children in Poverty (www.nccp.org/publications/pub_892.html).

EIGHT

A snapshot of child well-being in transition countries: exploring new methods of monitoring child well-being

Petra Hoelscher, Dominic Richardson and Jonathan Bradshaw[1]

Introduction

Two decades of transition have seen growing diversity across Eastern Europe and Central Asia, both in terms of economic and institutional structures and social developments. Living conditions have changed rapidly during this period, bringing both new opportunities and at the same time greater vulnerabilities for families and children. Economic recovery during the past decade has been hit again by the global economic crisis – many countries in the region belong to the most severely affected countries in the world. While most governments have tried to protect social spending, measures to mitigate the impacts of the crisis are only as good as existing social protection systems. However, these too often prove to be ineffective in reducing child poverty or supporting families with children, not least because cash transfers are too low and too narrowly targeted at the extremely poor to make much of a difference in the lives of poor people. In view of crisis responses, the narrow targeting of cash transfers also reduces the flexibility and responsiveness needed to address new vulnerabilities (Hoelscher et al, 2009).

Rapidly changing living conditions require monitoring systems that are sensitive to qualitative changes in the lives of children. Currently the most important regional monitoring tool is the TransMONEE database, tracking child-related administrative data across Central and Eastern Europe (CEE) and Central Asia (see, for instance, UNICEF, 2009). At country level, on the other hand, much of the monitoring of child well-being has followed the Millennium Development Goal (MDG) indicators which focus mainly on basic health (for example, mortality and immunisation) and education indicators (for example, enrolment in primary education). While these indicators are important, they fail to capture changes in the quality of life of children and their families in transition countries. These countries traditionally have had fairly well developed healthcare and education systems and basic access was often maintained for the majority of the population during the transition period. The bottlenecks are somewhere else: in education, for instance, problems are not so much found in access to primary education but in preschool and secondary education as well as in the declining quality of education. The global economic crisis and beginning recovery period could be a good time to revisit the TransMONEE database and to set a new baseline for child well-being across the region, for tracking developments with a stronger focus on the experiences of children and young people.

This chapter presents the Child Well-Being Index for CEE/Commonwealth of Independent States (CIS) countries to explore new ways of monitoring child well-being across different dimensions of children's lives. The Index gives a snapshot of the state of children in the region, providing insights into patterns of child well-being across countries and exploring what factors could help explain countries' performance. It follows a very pragmatic approach as it relies exclusively on existing data sources but revisits them to make the best of data that is available but often not sufficiently exploited. By giving an overview across a range of dimensions of children's lives, the Index broadens the perspective for improving the situation of children within countries. There are limitations, however. Some data are too old or not child-centred enough. There are data gaps both within some of the dimensions of child well-being and for different age groups of children. And finally, being cross-national, the Index cannot capture disparities within countries.

However, introducing a broader perspective on child well-being can support countries in making the shift towards more child-centred policy analysis and sustainable child monitoring mechanism at country level. This becomes particularly important against the background of the impacts of the global economic crisis on the well-being of children. The concluding part of the chapter therefore discusses strategies and experiences to improve data collection and analysis to build monitoring systems that are sustainable and effective in capturing child well-being in transition countries.

Methods

Child well-being indices organise and report data on child outcomes across different dimensions to compare the situation of children across countries or across regions within countries. Cross-national indices have been developed for OECD and European Union (EU) countries (UNICEF, 2007a, Bradshaw and Richardson, 2009) and most recently for the CEE/CIS region (Richardson et al, 2008). A number of countries are adapting this approach for reporting subnationally on the well-being of children.

Child well-being and deprivation represent different sides of the same coin. From a child rights perspective well-being can be defined as the realisation of children's rights and the fulfilment of the opportunity for every child to be all she or he can be. The degree to which this is achieved can be measured in terms of positive child outcomes, whereas negative outcomes and deprivation point to the denial of children's rights. Against this background child well-being is understood as multidimensional, capturing both children's well-being today and their 'well-becoming', that is, indicators that predict children's future well-being (Ben Arieh, 2008).

The Child Well-Being Index uses already existing data to identify those indicators that best represent a multidimensional, rights-based understanding of child well-being. The actual choice of indicators and dimensions therefore pragmatically depends on data availability and constraints. We have used z scores to summarise indicators into components and components into dimensions. Z scores have the advantage over simple ranking of not only taking account of rank order but also of the degree of dispersion around the group mean. The unit of measurement used is the standard deviation. In other words +1.5 means a country's score is 1.5 times the average deviation from the average. To ease interpretation, the scores for each dimension are presented on a scale with a mean of 100 and a standard deviation of 10. Z scores were calculated for each indicator and then averaged to obtain a score for a component. Then the z scores for the components were averaged to create a dimension average and these were used to produce the overall index rank. However, z scores have an implicit weight – the more dispersed the distribution of a variable, the bigger the difference from the mean and the higher the z scores.[2]

The CEE/CIS Child Well-Being Index includes 54 indicators in 24 components that make up seven dimensions:

- material situation
- housing
- health
- education
- personal and social well-being
- family forms and care
- risk and safety.

The choice of indicators is dependent on the availability of data, but follows three main principles:

1. They should reflect the provisions of the United Nations Convention on the Rights of the Child (UNCRC).
2. As far as possible the child is taken as a unit of analysis.
3. As far as possible data coming from children themselves is used.

Data is taken from administrative sources (TransMONEE and data from international organisations), cross-national household surveys (Multiple Indicator Cluster Surveys) and surveys with children and young people, including Young Voices, Trends in International Mathematical and Science Study (TIMSS) and Progress in International Reading Literacy Study (PIRLS). Survey data has not been available for all countries so there are data gaps in some countries, especially on the qualitative aspects of child well-being. European or OECD surveys, while expanding coverage to the CEE/CIS region, still do not include enough countries to allow for regional comparisons. A full list of indicators and data sources can be found in Appendix 8A.1 at the end of this chapter, and the data for all indicators can be found in Appendix 8A.2.

The following gives a brief overview of the main findings for each of these dimensions.

Child well-being in Central and Eastern Europe/ Commonwealth of Independent States

Material situation

Poverty and deprivation can strongly affect the well-being of children, both directly through the lack of material resources and indirectly through the strain poverty puts on parents' well-being. Poverty is linked to poor child outcomes in health and education, putting children at risk of long-term disadvantage. Impacts on children's personal well-being can be reflected in their subjective well-being, their relationships with peers and family as well as in their risk taking or healthy behaviours (Blanden et al, 2008; Redmond, 2008; for an overview see Bradshaw et al, 2007).

The 'material well-being' dimension includes three components:

• income poverty
• subjective poverty
• deprivation.

Figure 8.1 combines these components into a summary dimension score. Overall, children's material situation is best in Croatia, Bulgaria and Russia, and worst in Moldova and Tajikistan.

Figure 8.1: Children's material well-being

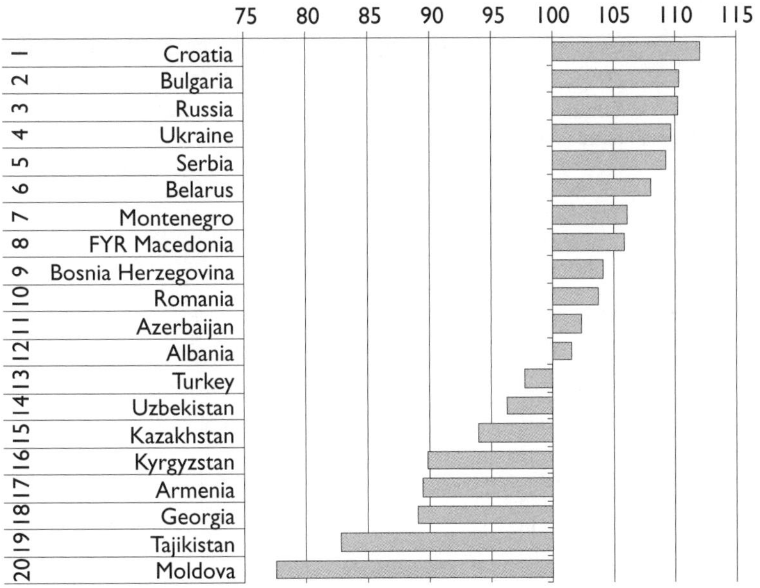

Note: Missing data for Turkmenistan.

Housing

Children's housing situation is another aspect of families' living conditions. Bad or unsafe conditions at home or in the neighbourhood pose a risk to children's health and development. The housing situation of children is difficult to capture, however, and average national values hide substantial disparities within countries, especially between rural and urban areas. The most disadvantaged neighbourhoods may not be captured at all, as they may be informal and not captured by surveys. While overcrowding and safety in the local environment may be a larger problem in cities, access to improved water and sanitation facilities is more difficult in rural areas.

The housing dimension covers three components:

- overcrowding
- safe environment
- access to facilities.

Figure 8.2 shows Croatia, Uzbekistan and Bosnia Herzegovina as performing best on this dimension. Housing conditions are worst for children in Moldova, Romania and Tajikistan.

Figure 8.2: Children's housing conditions

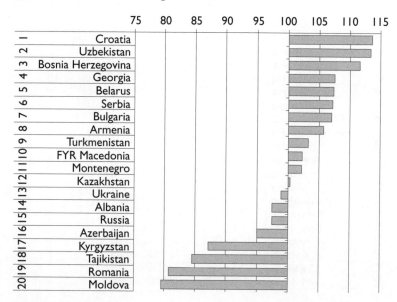

Note: No data for Turkey.

Health

Child health is one of the dimensions of child well-being that is globally best monitored, including across the CEE/CIS region. Traditionally, however, most indicators refer to the health and nutrition status of young children and very little information is available on the health of older children. Likewise in much of the region data is missing on children's own perception of their health and health behaviour.

The child health dimension consists of five components:

- health at birth
- breastfeeding
- immunisation
- nutrition
- other health indicators.

Figure 8.3 combines these components to form the overall health dimension. The best performing countries on this dimension are Croatia, Moldova and FYR Macedonia, whereas Tajikistan and Azerbaijan perform worst.

Figure 8.3: Children's health

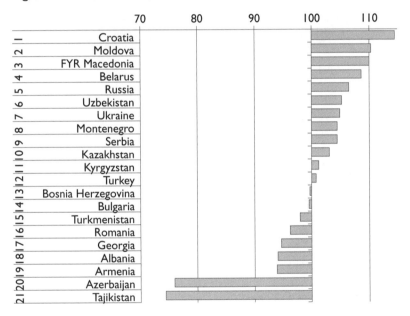

Education

Education is an area where standard indicators of enrolment tend to hide the problems in the education system of many countries in the region. While indicators on access to education and coverage remain high, investments in education are low by international standards and the quality of education is deteriorating. Official enrolment data may not always be reliable because of non-attendance and a tendency in many countries to over-register enrolment in order to maintain existing schools and teaching positions (UNICEF, 2006).

The education dimension includes:

• educational participation
• educational achievement.

Data on children's achievements is included even though the OECD PISA (Programme for International Student Assessment) survey in 2006 only covered nine countries of the region.

As Figure 8.4 shows, Kazakhstan, Belarus and Russia lead the league table on education with Kyrgyzstan, Turkey and Azerbaijan performing worst.

Figure 8.4: Children's education

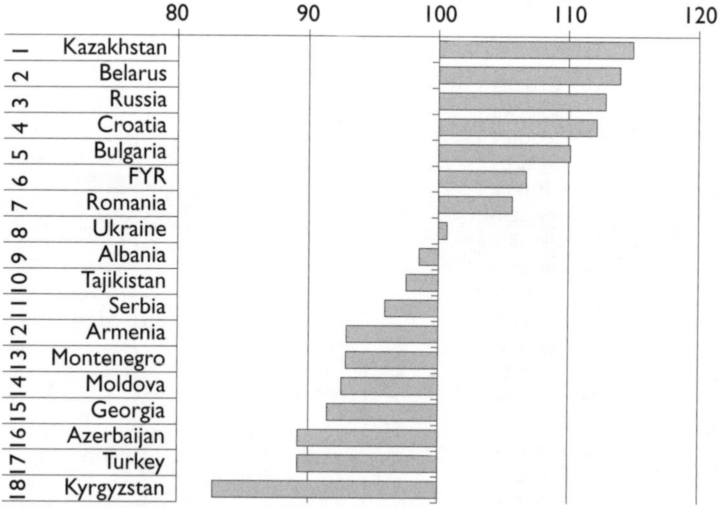

Note: No data for Bosnia Herzegovina, Turkmenistan and Uzbekistan.

Personal and social well-being

Children's subjective well-being and their relationships with friends are crucial for understanding children's present well-being and resilience in dealing with adverse circumstances. Asked about their views of well-being, Irish children see friends next to their family as the most important factor (Hanafin and Brooks, 2005). With growing age, peers become increasingly important, shaping children's values and interests, their sense of belonging and connectedness and therefore their personal well-being. Participation in society is another aspect of children's social live. Engagement with activities outside of the school and home is one way for a child to feel part of the wider community in which they live and learn some of the softer skills they need for their social interactions. Depending on information from children themselves, this dimension is rarely recognised in countries' child monitoring systems across the region.

Against this background we include three components in this dimension with all data drawn from the Young Voices survey.

- engaging with peer group
- social participation
- subjective well-being.

Figure 8.5 shows Croatia and Bosnia Herzegovina as exceptional countries on this scale, far outperforming other countries. At the bottom end of the scale are Albania, Azerbaijan and Moldova.

Figure 8.5: Children's personal and social well-being

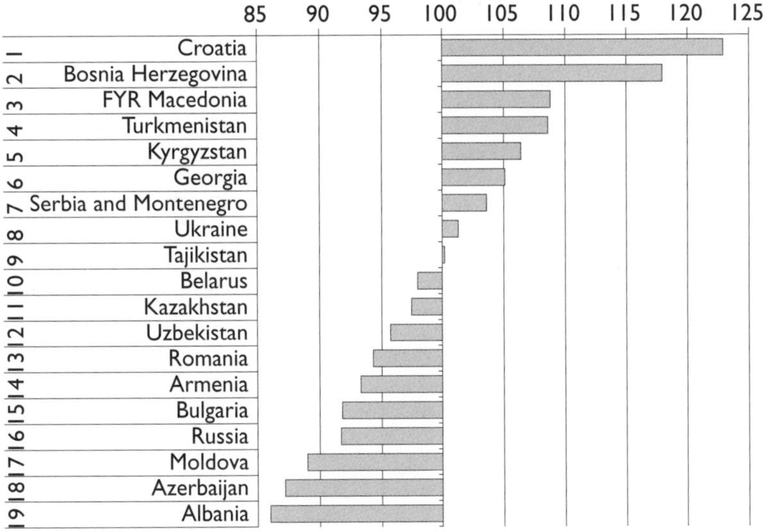

Note: No data for Turkey.

Family forms and care

The quality of family relations belongs to the most important mediating factors for the well-being of children and children's development. Across the CEE/CIS region many children experience disruptions in family life and the separation from one or both of their parents. The institutionalisation of children is still widespread and growing. Migration of one or both parents may leave children in the care of relatives, in institutions or living on their own without parental care. Data on the quality of family relations is, however, still scarce. We use data from the Young Voices survey from 2001 and the 2005 Multiple Indicator Cluster Survey that offers some information on parents' interaction with preschool children and child discipline.

The dimension covers the components:

• family relations
• child discipline
• children in care.

As shown in Figure 8.6, the situation of children in regard to their family situation is best in the states of Former Yugoslavia, including Bosnia Herzegovina, Montenegro and Serbia and worst in Moldova, Ukraine and Georgia.

Figure 8.6: Children's family situations

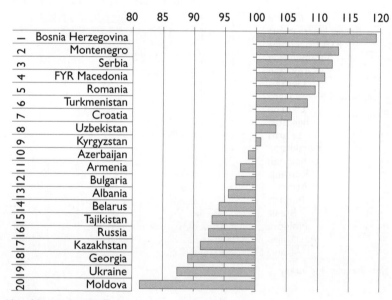

Note: Missing data for Turkey.

Risk and safety

The final dimension is concerned with children's risky behaviour and safety. Risk behaviour is very common among young people, not least as a means of gaining acceptance in their peer group. Young people who do engage in risk behaviour tend to do so in more than one way, for example, they consume alcohol and have unprotected sex. Risk behaviour can also be a response to stress experiences that young people cannot manage successfully and lead to processes of social exclusion that may be difficult to reverse (Klein-Hessling et al, 2005).

This dimension combines indicators from the following components:

• sexual health
• alcohol and drug use
• crime
• child labour
• accidents and suicides.

According to Figure 8.7, the results for this dimension show broad variation, with children and young people in Bosnia Herzegovina, Uzbekistan and Armenia being least engaged in risky behaviour. Russia, Moldova and Bulgaria perform worst.

Figure 8.7: Children's risks and safety

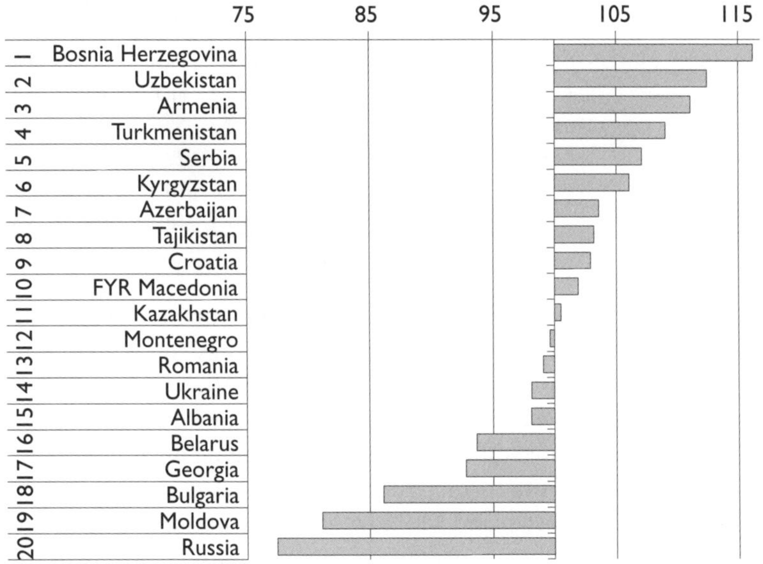

Note: No data for Turkey.

Overall picture of child well-being in Central and Eastern Europe/Commonwealth of Independent States

Table 8.1 is a summary of the findings. Countries are listed in order of their average rank order on the seven dimensions that have been

Table 8.1: Overview of child well-being in Eastern Europe and Central Asia

	Average rank	Material	Housing	Health	Education	Personal and social	Family forms and care	Risk and safety
Croatia	3.4	1	1	1	4	1	7	9
Bosnia Herzegovina	4.8	9	3	13	ND	2	1	1
FYR Macedonia	6.3	8	10	3	6	3	4	10
Serbia	6.6	5	6	9	11	7	3	5
Uzbekistan	7.5	14	2	6	ND	13	8	2
Turkmenistan	7.6	ND	9	15	ND	4	6	4
Belarus	8.3	6	5	4	2	11	14	16
Montenegro	8.6	7	11	8	13	7	2	12
Bulgaria	10.6	2	7	14	5	16	12	18
Ukraine	10.6	4	13	7	8	9	19	14
Kazakhstan	11.1	15	12	10	1	12	17	11
Russia	11.3	3	15	5	3	17	16	20
Kyrgyzstan	11.7	16	17	11	18	5	9	6
Romania	12.0	10	19	16	7	14	5	13
Armenia	12.1	17	8	19	12	15	11	3
Georgia	13.6	18	4	17	15	6	18	17
Turkey	14.0	13	ND	12	17	ND	ND	ND
Azerbaijan	14.1	11	16	20	16	19	10	7
Albania	14.4	12	14	18	9	20	13	15
Tajikistan	14.4	19	18	21	10	10	15	8
Moldova	16.1	20	20	2	14	18	20	19

assessed. The countries have been divided into three groups: white indicates that the country performs in the top third, light grey in the middle third and dark grey in the bottom third. Where countries have insufficient data for single dimensions these are marked as ND, No data.

There are substantial differences in the well-being of children across countries. Many of the former Yugoslav countries perform very well, while Albania, Tajikistan and Moldova are at the bottom of the league table. No country, however, is in the top or bottom third across all dimensions – even Moldova as the country with the lowest score ranks second on child health, reflecting substantial investments and government efforts in this sector. Some country clusters are emerging with one group of countries doing well on the poverty, health and education indicators while having problems in those dimensions that capture more subjective and behavioural indicators, especially family relations and risk behaviour (for example, Russia, Ukraine, Bulgaria,

Belarus). Another group of countries, including Kyrgyzstan, Bosnia and Herzegovina and Turkmenistan, show the opposite pattern.

While the index maps out child well-being across countries, the real challenge is to understand why countries are performing so differently, without following clear regional or political patterns. One obvious hypothesis is that richer countries have higher levels of child well-being than poorer countries because they have more resources to devote to children. Figure 8.8 indeed shows a correlation between overall child well-being and gross domestic product (GDP) per capita, but it is fairly weak and explains only about a third of the variation in child well-being.

Figure 8.8: Overall child well-being and GDP per capita, US$PPP

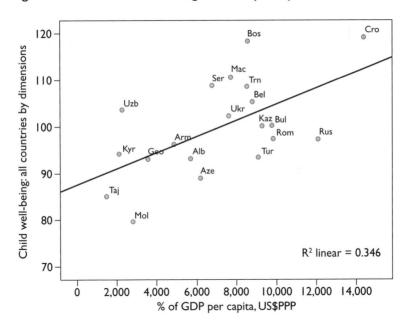

More important than a country's resources is how these resources are spent and how far families and children benefit. There is little comparative data that would allow an assessment of government efforts on behalf of children. However, data on public expenditure on health as a percentage of GDP shows a significant positive correlation with overall child well-being (see Figure 8.9). Investments in services for families and children matter and have an impact on their well-being (Stewart and Huerta, 2006).

Figure 8.9: Overall child well-being and public spending on health, 2002-04

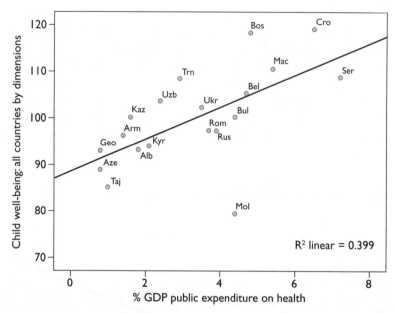

The analysis also explores whether there are single indicators that drive the overall well-being of children in CEE/CIS countries. As Table 8.2 shows, the highest correlations are found with secondary

Table 8.2: Correlations between single indicators and overall child well-being

Indicator	Correlation with overall well-being by dimension
Secondary school enrolment rate (15 countries)	0.67**
Women without comprehensive knowledge of HIV/AIDS prevention (15-19) (16 countries)	−0.64**
Percentage of children living under the US$2.15 poverty line (18 countries)	−0.63**
Adolescent fertility rate (19 countries)	−0.62**
Under-five mortality rate (20 countries)	−0.60**
Percentage of children beaten or insulted as part of punishment (20 countries)	−0.58*
Low birth weight (20 countries)	−0.58*
Infant mortality rate (21 countries)	−0.57*
Prevalence of child malnutrition (moderate and severe) – underweight (% of children under age five) (19 countries)	−0.56*

Note: * $p<0.05$; ** $p<0.01$.

school enrolment rates and for women's comprehensive knowledge of HIV/AIDS prevention. Giving young people a good preparation for a healthy life requires well-functioning social systems that may reflect countries' efforts on behalf of children and young people. Poverty and material deprivation are likewise important factors, followed by a range of health indicators and indicators capturing the subjective well-being of children – violence and safety.

First résumé: Potential and limitations of the Child Well-Being Index

The recognition of the multidimensionality of child well-being represents a shift in perspective for many countries in the region. There is still little collaboration and coordination across sectoral ministries, and each ministry might draw on their own sources of data. At the same time, across the CEE/CIS region, many governments and/or statistical offices have expressed great interest in bringing together child-related data from different dimensions of child well-being and some, like Kyrgyzstan, have already started to implement or explore national child well-being indices that could capture regional disparities. The pragmatic approach behind the index to exploit as fully as possible existing data has proven very effective in drawing attention to previously under-utilised data sources, both on a national and international level.

On the international level, cross-country comparisons of child well-being are becoming increasingly important in OECD and EU countries although any obvious ranking tends to be politically sensitive, especially among the countries at the lower end of the league table (see also European Commission, 2008; OECD, 2009). However, given that no country is performing either in the top or bottom third across all dimensions of child well-being, the role of the Child Well-Being Index is not one of 'naming and shaming' but on the contrary can help to open up space for dialogue and peer support between countries that may share many commonalities but show diverging performance regarding children's well-being.

But there are also limitations. From the perspective of governments the interest of some to develop national child well-being indices already points to one inherent constraint. Cross-national comparisons rely on national-level data that do not easily allow for capturing disparities within countries. At the same time, many of the international child and youth surveys are only representative at national level, with no other similar data sources available in most CEE/CIS countries.

Data gaps, timeliness and quality of data are other major concerns. The CEE/CIS Child Well-Being Index can only be as good as the data available. In regard to data on children's own experiences, the CEE/CIS Child Well-Being Index relies on the Young Voices survey conducted in 2001 – the only survey with children and young people that covers most countries in the region. Other international child and youth surveys such as the Health Behaviour in School-aged Children Survey (HBSC) or PISA are only slowly extending coverage in the region. Data gaps exist for age groups that traditionally have gained little attention (young children beyond health indicators, middle childhood), creating imbalances across some of the dimensions. Finally, much of the internationally reported survey data is not sensitive to children, as the standard poverty, housing and material deprivation indicators used by the international community do not normally include an age break-down for children. The next section discusses how some of these limitations can be addressed.

Ways forward

The CEE/CIS Child Well-Being Index presented in this chapter provides a snapshot of how children are doing across transition countries. The question is how to use this work to move towards more sustainable monitoring mechanisms for the well-being of children in the region, both on a national and international level. Three areas emerge as crucial: the improvement of comparative data covering the region, the strengthening of national data sources and the establishment of stronger linkages with policy analysis.

Improving comparative data

There is still a substantial lack of good quality cross-national data on children and young people's well-being in transition countries that would both enable cross-national comparisons and allow in-depth country analyses of issues such as disparities within countries, the impacts of poverty or the determinants of risk behaviour. Existing European or OECD surveys are slowly spreading into the CEE/CIS region, but it still will take many years for a substantial number of countries to be covered, particularly in the Caucasus and Central Asia. However, surveys such as HBSC or PISA are themed surveys, focusing on young people's health behaviour and educational achievements respectively, with other dimensions of child well-being included as a support or add-on to the main thrust of analysis, making them susceptible to changes or exclusion from one survey round to another.

Against this background there is a case to be made for a new child well-being survey, either conducted at schools or linked to household surveys that could cover countries in Europe, Central Asia and beyond. Such a survey could assess children's perceptions of their material situation, their housing environment, education, subjective well-being, health and health behaviour, family situation and relationships with their peers, risk behaviour and safety.

From another angle the UNICEF TransMONEE database should also be highlighted. TransMONEE was set up in the early 1990s to monitor the situation of children during the transition period. Apart from being a unique source of information on children in CEE/CIS countries based on administrative data, the project has also helped to improve administrative data across the region by working on common definitions of indicators and making data from different countries better comparable. Twenty years after the breakdown of the Soviet Union and at the time of the global economic crisis hitting many transition countries particularly hard, the set-up of the database is being revised to become more responsive to current conditions and data needs.

Strengthening national data sources

At national level much more information on children's well-being is available than is usually expected. The challenge is not so much to create new data sources but to better use and coordinate what is there. For example, Household Budget Surveys and/or Living Standard Measurement Surveys are conducted in most countries, creating a wealth of information on poverty and deprivation, the provision of cash transfers, housing, education and access to healthcare and social services. These surveys have been neutral to children, disaggregating by household structure but not including an analysis with the child as a unit of analysis. Only over the past two years, with support from UNICEF, recent Household Budget Survey and Living Standard Measurement Survey datasets have been re-assessed accordingly, with some national statistical offices planning to mainstream this type of analysis (see, for example, Bradshaw et al, 2008).

At the same time, much administrative and sometimes specialised survey data is collected within government sectors but often not shared or made widely available. The same is true for international organisations and non-governmental organisations (NGOs) where many surveys are conducted but the results are too often not being used beyond the immediate launch and advocacy events. Better coordination of research and sharing of data would go a long way towards more sustainable monitoring at country level.

Last but not least: creating closer links with policy analysis

The Child Well-Being Index, by strengthening a multidimensional perspective on the lives of children, also encourages policy makers to better take into account the impact of policies on children and their families. It is not easy to answer the question why some countries are performing better than others, but it is clear that political priorities and the level of investments in child-related benefits and services are decisive in determining how well children and their families are doing in society. Assessments of the effectiveness of cash transfers and tax and benefit analyses in the region show very little state effort for families with children in the majority of countries. The economic crisis, creating new vulnerabilities and pushing more families into poverty, has exposed the gaps in social protection systems that are not designed to effectively mitigate social risks and prevent and reduce poverty (Hoelscher et al, 2009).

Linking policy analysis to an assessment of child outcomes across different dimensions of well-being highlights the need for integrated and coordinated strategies for combating child poverty and social exclusion. Cash transfers, high quality early childhood education and care, education, healthcare and family-oriented social services as well as activating labour market policies, especially for young people, all have to be part of a comprehensive policy package for families and children.

The Child Well-Being Index not only offers a snapshot but, if repeated as new data becomes available, it can also track changes in countries' performance over time. Complemented by national or cross-national policy assessments and a better understanding of disparities within countries it will be possible to better identify what mix of policies works in what country context to improve current living conditions as well as future life chances of children.

Notes

[1] The views expressed by the authors do not necessarily reflect and cannot be attributed to the United Nations Children's Fund (UNICEF) or Organisation for Economic Co-operation and Development (OECD) and any of its member countries.

[2] For a detailed discussion of methods, see Bradshaw et al (2007).

References

Ben-Arieh, A. (2008) 'The child indicators movement: past, present and future', *Child Indicators Research*, vol 1, pp 3-16.

Blanden, J., Hansen, K. and Machin, S. (2008) *The GDP cost of the lost earning potential of adults who grew up in poverty*, York: Joseph Rowntree Foundation.

Bradshaw, J. and Richardson, D. (2009) 'An index of child well-being in Europe', *Journal of Child Indicators Research*, vol 2, pp 319-51.

Bradshaw, J., Hoelscher, P. and Richardson, D. (2007) *Comparing child well-being in OECD countries: Concepts and methods*, IWP 2006-3, Florence: United Nations Children's Fund.

Bradshaw, J., Chzhen, Y., Gugushvili, D. and Hoelscher, P. (2008) *Child poverty in Georgia*, Background paper to World Bank Poverty Assessment for Georgia. Tblisi: United Nations Children Fund.

Currie, C., Nic Gabhainn, S., Godeau, E., Roberts, C., Smith, R., Currie, D., Pickett, W., Richter, M., Morgan, A. and Barnekow, V. (eds) *Inequalities in young people's health. HBSC international report from the 2005/2006 survey*, Copenhagen: World Health Organization (WHO) Regional Office for Europe.

European Commission (2008) *Child poverty and well-being in the EU. Current status and ways forward*, Brussels: European Commission.

Hanafin, S. and Brooks, A.M. (2005) *The Delphi Technique. A methodology to support the development of a national set of child well-being indicators*, Dublin: The National Children's Office.

HNP (Health, Nutrition and Population) (2008) *Health Nutrition and Population statistics* (http://go.worldbank.org/N2N84RDV00).

Hoelscher, P., Alexander, G. and Scholz, W. (2009) *Preventing and reducing poverty in times of crisis: The role of non-contributory cash transfers*, Background paper for the Ministerial Conference on the social impacts of the economic crisis in Eastern Europe, Turkey and Central Asia, Almaty, Kazakhstan, 7-8 December.

Klein-Hessling, J., Lohaus, A. and Ball, J. (2005) 'Psychological predictors of health related behaviour in children', *Psychology, Health and Medicine*, vol 10, pp 31-43.

OECD (Organisation for Economic Co-operation and Development) (2009) *Doing better for children*, Paris: OECD.

OECD PISA (Programme for International Student Assessment) (2008) *The PISA International Database 2006* (http://pisa2006.acer.edu.au/).

Redmond, G. (2008) *Children's perspectives on economic adversity. A review of the literature*, Innocenti Research Centre Discussion Papers, Florence: Innocenti Research Centre.

Richardson, D., Hoelscher, P. and Bradshaw, J. (2008) 'Child well-being in Central and Eastern Europe and the Commonwealth of Independent States', *Journal of Child Indicators Research*, vol 1, pp 211-50.

Stewart, K. and Huerta, C. (2006) *Reinvesting in children? Policies for the very young in South Eastern Europe and the CIS*, Innocenti Working Paper, IWP 2006-01, Florence: United Nations Children's Fund Innocenti Research Centre.

TransMONEE (2007) *TransMONEE 2007 database*, Florence: United Nations Children's Fund Innocenti Research Centre (www.transmonee.org/).

UIS (2008) UNESCO Institute for Statistics (www.uis.unesco.org/).

UNICEF (United Nations Children's Fund) (2001) *Young Voices Opinion Survey of children and young people in Europe and Central Asia*, Geneva: UNICEF.

UNICEF (2006) *Innocenti Social Monitor 2006. Understanding child poverty in South-Eastern Europe and the Commonwealth of Independent States*, Florence: UNICEF Innocenti Research Centre.

UNICEF (2007a) *Child poverty in perspective. An overview of child well-being in rich countries*, UNICEF Innocenti Report Card 7, Florence: UNICEF Innocenti Research Centre.

UNICEF (2007b) *Education for some more than others? A regional study on education in Central and Eastern Europe and the Commonwealth of Independent States*, Geneva: UNICEF.

UNICEF (2008) *The State of the World's Children 2007*, New York: UNICEF.

UNICEF (2009) *Innocenti Social Monitor 2009. Child well-being at a crossroads: Evolving challenges in Central and Eastern Europe and the Commonwealth of Independent States*, Florence: UNICEF.

UNICEF Statistics (2008) *Child labour* (www.childinfo.org/labour.html/).

WDI (World Development Indicators) (2007) World Development Indicators (http://databank.worldbank.org/ddp/home.do?Step=12&id=4&CNO=2).

WHO (World Health Organization) (2008a) *WHO European health for all database* (http://data.euro.who.int/hfadb/).

WHO (2008b) *WHO mortality data* (www.who.int/healthinfo/statistics/mortality/en/index.html/).

World Bank (2005) *Growth, poverty, and inequality: Eastern Europe and the former Soviet Union*, Washington, DC: World Bank, Annex tables 2 and 4.

Appendix 8A.1: Overview of indicators used in CEE/CIS Child Well-Being Index

Dimension	Component	Indicator	Source
Material situation	Income poverty	Children <16 living under the US$2.15 poverty line (%)	World Bank 2005
	Perception of need (subjective poverty)	% of children who report having no money as something they are worried about	Young Voices
	Deprivation	% of children with four educational possessions (13-15)	TIMSS
		% of children with more than 10 books (13-15)	TIMSS
		MICS 2005: % of children (<60 months) with fewer than three children's books	MICS 2005
Housing and environment	Overcrowding	Overcrowded housing (more than three per room/less than 6m²/person)	WDI
	Environment	Children reporting that the place where they live is rather unsafe or very unsafe to walk around – 2001	Young Voices
	Facilities	Access to improved sanitation facilities	HNP
		Access to improved water sources	HNP
Health	Health at birth	Infant mortality rate (per 1,000 live births)	SOWC
		Share of low weight births	SOWC
	Breastfeeding	% of infants exclusively breastfed at 6 months of age	SOWC
		% of children still breastfed at 20-23 months	SOWC
	Immunisations	DPT 3	HNP
		Polio	HNP
		Measles	SOWC estimate
	Nutrition	Prevalence of stunting	SOWC
		Prevalence of underweight	SOWC
		Prevalence of wasting	SOWC

(continued)

Appendix 8A.1: Overview of indicators used in CEE/CIS Child Well-Being Index (continued)

Dimension	Component	Indicator	Source
Health (continued)	Children's health	Under five mortality rate	SOWC
		% under five(s) with ARI taken to health provider	WHO
		% of under five(s) with diarrhoea receiving oral rehydration and continued feeding	WHO
		% of household consuming iodised salt	SOWC
		Decayed, missing or filled teeth at age 12	WHO Europe
Education	Educational participation	Pre-primary enrolment (net rates) 3-6 years	UNICEF
		Rate of primary school age children out of school	SOWC
		Secondary school net enrolment ratio (% of population of secondary school age)	SOWC
	Educational achievement	Reading literacy, age 9-11	PIRLS
		Science achievements, age 13-15	TIMSS
		Maths achievement, age 13-15	TIMSS
Personal and social well-being	Engaging with the peer group	% of children reporting having a good or very good relationship with a member of their peer group	Young Voices
	Social engagement	Children participating in a local organisation or club	Young Voices
	Subjective well-being	Child's quality of life aspirations in comparison with his/her parents' current life	Young Voices
		Children reporting that they most often feel happy about life in general	Young Voices
Family forms and care	Family relations	% of children living in non-traditional family forms	Young Voices
		HH members engaged in fewer than four activities that promote learning and school readiness (under-fives)	MICS 2005
		Children who report that their opinion is considered when a decision concerning him/her is taken at home	Young Voices
		Children reporting a very good relationship with one or both parents	Young Voices
	Child discipline	Children who report positive responses to good behaviour	Young Voices
		Children who report being beaten or insulted as part of punishment/discipline	Young Voices

(continued)

Dimension	Component	Indicator	Source
Family forms and care (continued)	Children in care	Ratio of children in foster care to children in residential care (per 100,000 population aged 0-17)	TransMONEE
		Rate of children in infant homes	TransMONEE
Risk and safety	Sexual health	Adolescent birth rate (15-19)	HNP
		Sexually transmitted diseases, age 15-19	TransMONEE
		Women without comprehensive knowledge of HIV/AIDS prevention (15-19)	MICS 2005
	Alcohol and drug use	Child reporting that a friend or acquaintance has a tobacco addiction	Young Voices
		Child reporting that a friend or acquaintance has alcohol addiction	Young Voices
		Child reporting that a friend or acquaintance uses illegal drugs or inhalants	Young Voices
	Crime	Registered juvenile crime rate (per 100,000 population aged 14-17)	TransMONEE
		Children reporting having ever been victim of violence	Young Voices
	Child labour	Child labour (5-14)	MICS
	Accidents and suicide	All children accidental and non-accidental death, all under 19 deaths	WHO

Notes:

MICS = Multiple Indicator Cluster Survey

TIMSS = Trends in International Mathematics and Science Study

WDI = World Development Indicator

HNP = Health, Nutrition and Population

SOWC = *The State of the World's Children*

WHO = World Health Organization

PIRLS = Progress in International Reading Literacy Study

ARI = acute respiratory infection

HH = head of household

Appendix 8A.2: Overview of indicators and data

	Material situation					Health						
	Income poverty	Perception of need	Deprivation			Health at birth		Breast feeding		Immunisations		
	Children living under the US$2.15 poverty line (%)	Children who report having no money/their economic situation as something they are mainly worried about	TIMSS: % of children with four educational possessions	TIMSS: % of children with more than 10 books in the home	MICS 2005:% of children (<60 months) with fewer than three children's books	Infant mortality rate (per 1,000 live births)	Share of low weight births (births under 2,500 grams as % of total live births)	% of infants breastfed at three months of age	% of infants breastfed at six months of age	Child immunisation rate, dpt3(% of children 12-23 months)	Polio immunisation rate (% of children under two immunised)	Immunisation, measles (% of children aged 12-23 months)
Albania	30.0	18.8			67.7	15.0	7.0	2.0	20.0	98.0	97.0	97.0
Armenia	54.0	27.8				21.0	8.0	33.0	15.0	87.0	87.0	92.0
Azerbaijan	5.0	10.8	86.7	30.2		73.0	12.0	7.0	16.0	95.0	97.0	96.0
Belarus	3.0	18.5				12.0	4.0	9.0	4.0	99.0	97.0	97.0
Bosnia Herzegovina	6.0	23.0			24.6	13.0	5.0	18.0	10.0	87.0	91.0	90.0
Bulgaria	8.0	11.8	36.4	18.2		12.0	10.0			95.0	96.0	96.0
Croatia		8.8	17.7	25.4		5.0	6.0	23.0		96.0	96.0	96.0
FYR Macedonia	6.0	20.5			51.1	15.0	6.0	37.0	10.0	93.0	92.0	94.0
Georgia	57.0	27.3			27.9	28.0	7.0	18.0	12.0	87.0	88.0	95.0
Kazakhstan	28.0	30.0			33.6	26.0	6.0	17.0	16.0	99.0	99.0	99.0
Kyrgyzstan	80.0	14.0	85.2	31.4	23.8	36.0	5.0	32.0	26.0	92.0	93.0	97.0
Moldova	53.0	44.5				16.0	6.0	46.0	2.0	97.0	98.0	96.0
Montenegro	7.0	16.1	45.9	19.4	23.1	9.0	4.0	19.0	13.0	90.0	90.0	90.0
Romania	21.0	20.0	48.0	16.4		16.0	8.0	16.0		97.0	97.0	95.0
Russia	13.0	16.6	42.1	6.7		14.0	6.0			99.0	99.0	99.0
Serbia	7.0	16.1	31.8	20.1	20.7	7.0	5.0	15.0	8.0	92.0	97.0	88.0
Tajikistan	76.0	29.8			83.0	56.0	10.0	25.0	34.0	86.0	81.0	87.0
Turkey	29.0		62.5	22.8		24.0		21.0	24.0	90.0	90.0	98.0
Turkmenistan		20.5			58.0	45.0	4.0	11.0	37.0	98.0	98.0	99.0
Ukraine	2.0	16.6			3.4	20.0	4.0	6.0	11.0	98.0	99.0	98.0
Uzbekistan	50.0	19.5			57.5	38.0	5.0	26.0	38.0	95.0	94.0	95.0

Appendix 8A.2: Overview of indicators and data (continued)

	Health								Education		
	Nutrition				Children's health				Educational participation		
	Prevalence of child malnutrition (moderate and severe) – stunted (% of children under five)	Prevalence of child malnutrition (moderate and severe) – underweight (% of children under five)	Prevalence of child malnutrition (moderate and severe) – wasting (% of children under five)	% of households consuming iodised salt (STWC)	Under-five mortality rates	% of under-fives with ARI taken to health provider	% of under-fives with diarrhoea receiving oral rehydration and continued feeding	Decayed, missing or filled teeth at age 12 (DMFT-12 index)	Pre-primary enrolments (net rates, % of population aged 3-6)	Rate of primary school-age children out of school	Secondary school net enrolment ratio (% of population of secondary school age)
Albania	22.0	8.0	7.0	62.0	17.0	38.0	50.3	3.0	51.3	6.4	74.0
Armenia	13.0	4.0	5.0	97.0	24.0	11.0	48.0		31.8	13.7	84.5
Azerbaijan	13.0	7.0	2.0	26.0	88.0		40.0		20.9	14.6	77.5
Belarus	3.0	1.0	1.0	55.0	13.0	67.0	54.2	2.7	73.4	10.1	88.5
Bosnia Herzegovina	7.0	2.0	3.0	62.0	15.0	73.0	52.5	4.8	6.2		
Bulgaria				100.0	14.0			4.4	73.7	5.5	88.0
Croatia	1.0	1.0	1.0	90.0	6.0			3.5	49.3	7.0	85.0
FYR Macedonia	9.0	2.0	2.0	94.0	17.0	74.0		3.0	32.5	2.8	82.0
Georgia	12.0	3.0	2.0	91.0	32.0		36.5		33.8	12.7	81.0
Kazakhstan	13.0	4.0	4.0	92.0	29.0	32.0	48.0		18.4	1.2	91.5
Kyrgyzstan	14.0	3.0	4.0	76.0	41.0	45.0	22.3		11.1	6.4	80.5
Moldova	8.0	4.0	4.0	60.0	19.0		52.0	1.3	67.2	14.8	76.0
Montenegro	5.0	3.0	3.0	71.0	10.0	57.0	64.3	3.3	29.7		
Romania	10.0	3.0	2.0	74.0	18.0			7.3	73.8	5.2	80.5
Russia	13.0	3.0	4.0	35.0	16.0			3.7	69.6	7.5	
Serbia	6.0	2.0	3.0	73.0	8.0	57.0	71.0	3.3	29.7		
Tajikistan	27.0		7.0	46.0	68.0	41.0	22.1		6.9	2.5	79.5
Turkey	12.0	4.0	1.0	64.0	26.0		19.0	2.5		9.8	66.5
Turkmenistan	15.0	11.0	6.0	87.0	51.0	50.0	25.2		21.8		
Ukraine	3.0	1.0	0.0	18.0	24.0				54.8	9.4	79.5
Uzbekistan	15.0	5.0	3.0	53.0	43.0	56.0	28.1	0.9	21.3		

Appendix 8A.2: Overview of indicators and data (continued)

	Education			Personal and social well-being				Family forms and care			
	Educational achievement			Engaging with peer group	Social engage-ment	Subjective well-being		Family relations			
	PISA Reading literacy, 2006 – age 15	PISA Science literacy, 2006 – age 15	PISA Mathematics literacy, 2006 – age 15	% of children reporting having a good or very good relationship with a member of their peer group – (ages 9 to 17), Young Voices, 2001	Child participates in an local organisation or club (includes sport, music, literature, science and politics)	Child's perception of their future quality of life in the future in comparison with his/ her parents' current life (better or much better)	% of children reporting that they most often feel happy about their life in general (ages 9 to 17), Young Voices, 2001	Proportion of children living in non-traditional family forms (with siblings only, grandparents, sole parents and other)	HH members engaged in fewer than four activities that promote learning and school readiness (under-fives)	Consideration of the child's opinion when a decision concerning him/ her is taken at home, cross-tabulation	Proportion of children reporting a very good relationship with one or both parents
Albania				88.3	11.5	89.0	46.0	5.0	32.0	36.9	75.5
Armenia				91.8	23.3	64.3	62.3	10.5		49.8	84.8
Azerbaijan	353.0	382.0	476.0	89.5	13.3	66.8	68.8	10.2		75.2	81.8
Belarus				88.0	29.0	72.8	69.8	18.8	15.9	59.6	63.3
Bosnia Herzegovina				98.3	33.5	81.5	71.0	12.0	24.4	51.0	82.0
Bulgaria	402.0	434.0	413.0	92.5	19.0	67.5	59.0	11.8		58.8	71.3
Croatia	477.0	493.0	467.0	98.3	42.5	75.8	75.8	12.0		57.8	75.5
FYR Macedonia				94.3	31.0	72.3	75.0	5.5	14.8	59.4	83.8
Georgia				94.8	25.3	84.3	58.0	12.3	16.0	45.0	76.3
Kazakhstan				89.8	27.5	68.5	69.5	20.0	19.0	44.3	56.0
Kyrgyzstan	285.0	322.0	311.0	88.3	27.8	81.3	86.5	19.0	29.0	68.5	66.3
Moldova				87.8	34.5	68.3	38.0	19.8		42.8	59.3
Montenegro	392.0	412.0	399.0	93.5	19.6	90.1	61.9	10.0	11.1	58.3	81.0
Romania	396.0	418.0	415.0	94.5	11.8	74.8	63.8	16.5		60.7	74.0
Russia	440.0	479.0	476.0	83.6	29.8	68.0	72.5	27.1		60.1	51.9
Serbia	401.0	436.0	435.0	93.5	19.6	90.1	61.9	10.0	15.6	58.3	81.0
Tajikistan				89.5	27.3	75.0	71.3	14.5	40.3	49.0	75.5
Turkey	447.0	424.0	424.0								
Turkmenistan				89.8	28.0	95.3	69.7	12.5	20.5	45.8	70.3
Ukraine				91.0	27.8	74.9	67.9	22.3		62.4	58.0
Uzbekistan				86.0	22.5	81.3	73.0	9.5	28.7	45.0	68.5

Appendix 8A.2: Overview of indicators and data (continued)

| | Family forms and care | | | | Housing and environment | | | | Risk and safety | | |
| | Child discipline | | Children in care | | Over-crowd-ing | Environ-ment | Facilities | | Sexual health | | |
	Children who report positive responses to good behaviour (congrats, hugs, rewards), Young voices 2001	Proportion of children who report being beaten or insulted as part of punishment/discipline, Young Voices 2001	Ratio of children in foster care to children in residential care (per 100,000 population aged 0-17)	Rate of children in infant homes (per 100,000 population aged 0-3)	Average proportion of overcrowded housing (more than three per room or less than 6m²/person)	Children reporting that the place where they live is rather unsafe or very unsafe to walk around, 2001	Access to improved sanitation facilities, total (% of population)	Access to an improved water source, total (% of population)	Adolescent fertility rate (births per 1,000 women aged 15-19)	Sexually transmitted diseases in population aged 15-19 (newly registered cases of syphilis and gonorrhoea per 100,000 relevant population)	Women without comprehensive knowledge of HIV/AIDS prevention (aged 15-19)
Albania	84.0	25.5		66.9	11.9	31.5	91.0	96.0	16.4		95.3
Armenia	68.0	16.3		52.2		13.8	83.0	92.0	29.2	19.4	93.0
Azerbaijan		20.3	0.3	31.7		14.5	54.0	77.0	30.0	13.3	98.0
Belarus	77.8	2.0	0.6	354.1	3.7	18.8	84.0	100.0	25.2	167.6	70.8
Bosnia Herzegovina	88.3	3.8	2.4	54.7	4.9	11.5	95.0	97.0	22.0		36.2
Bulgaria	80.8	5.5	0.2			19.0	99.0	99.0	41.8		
Croatia	79.8	6.0	0.8	75.2		11.0	100.0	100.0	14.2	1.6	
FYR Macedonia	81.8	10.8	1.3	108.3	15.3	13.5			22.2	1.2	76.6
Georgia	76.5	13.8	0.2		9.0	10.5	94.0	82.0	30.9	54.2	66.8
Kazakhstan	79.3	2.5		231.9	9.3	19.5	72.0	86.0	27.8	47.8	77.6
Kyrgyzstan	85.0	8.8	0.3	62.5	25.9	24.0	59.0	77.0	31.7	50.1	79.7
Moldova	76.5	13.3	0.4	247.4		43.8	68.0	92.0	29.7	213.9	81.0
Montenegro	84.9	10.4	1.4	66.8	18.4	14.5	87.0	93.0	23.5		70.2
Romania	80.3	8.5	1.6			23.5		57.0	33.0	68.5	
Russia	88.8	3.9	1.0	358.1		27.4	87.0	97.0	28.6	231.7	
Serbia	84.9	10.4	1.4	66.8	7.2	14.5	87.0	93.0	23.5		57.7
Tajikistan	82.3	16.5	0.3	25.4	40.5	8.0	51.0	59.0	28.4	10.2	97.7
Turkey									37.9		
Turkmenistan	82.3	2.8		49.2	10.1	5.5	62.0	72.0	16.1	75.2	91
Ukraine	66.8	4.3	1.4	318.1	2.8	19.1	96.0	96.0	28.0	113.7	64.2
Uzbekistan	82.0	5.0	0.8	34.1	17.1	8.0	67.0	82.0	34.5	40.9	64.7

Appendix 8A.2: Overview of indicators and data (continued)

| | Risk and safety | | | | | | |
| | Alcohol and drug use | | | Crime | | Accidents and suicide | |
	Child has friends or acquaintances of their age having had an addiction to harmful or illegal substances TOBACCO, Young Voices 2001	Proportion of children with friends/acquaintances of the child's age having had addiction to harmful or illegal substances ALCOHOL, Young Voices 2001	Child has friends or acquaintances of their age using inhalants or illegal drugs, Young Voices 2001	Registered juvenile crime rate (per 100,000 population aged 14-17)	Child having ever been victim of any type of violence, Young Voices 2001	Child labour (5-14 years), 1999-2004	All child accidental deaths: all under 19 deaths per 100,000 children
Albania	37.3	9.3	3.0	273.4	11.2	12.0	20.0
Armenia	23.3	5.0	0.3	199.5	8.8		4.4
Azerbaijan	26.8	15.0	0.5	70.2	4.3	11.0	10.7
Belarus	54.0	18.8	3.5	1508.3	3.8	5.1	28.8
Bosnia Herzegovina	18.8	6.0	2.3	255.2	5.5	5.3	15.9
Bulgaria	34.5	12.7	5.0	2772.4	11.8		18.0
Croatia	29.5	10.0	9.8	1216.8	5.3		30.3
FYR Macedonia	31.0	8.0	5.5	1856.0	8.8	5.7	13.0
Georgia	51.0		5.8	632.9	3.8	18.4	10.5
Kazakhstan	33.8	8.5	3.5	274.9	8.3	2.2	41.9
Kyrgyzstan	24.8	9.0	1.3	691.4	7.8	3.6	14.0
Moldova	38.5	17.3	1.8	186.2	17.8		45.0
Montenegro	30.5	6.5	6.5	948.1	7.6	9.9	
Romania	19.0	6.0	2.3	1445.7	12.0	1.0	32.7
Russia	48.6	15.5	4.6	1739.8	6.5		51.2
Serbia	30.5	6.5	6.5	632.9	7.6	4.4	
Tajikistan	29.0	9.0	1.8	62.4	10.5	10.0	5.4
Turkey						5.0	
Turkmenistan	29.8	13.5	2.5	29.6	3.5		16.1
Ukraine	42.4	10.9	2.4	974.5	7.1	7.3	25.7
Uzbekistan	28.9	6.0	0.8	100.3	5.3	2.0	10.4

Notes:

TIMSS = Trends in International Mathematics and Science Study

MICS = Multiple Indicator Cluster Survey

ARI = acute respiratory infection

DMFT = decayed, missing or filled teeth at age 12

PISA = Programme for International Student Assessment

HH = head of household

SOWC = State of the World's Children report

Enhancing the fight against child poverty in the European Union: a benchmarking exercise

Isabelle Maquet-Engsted

The fight against child poverty: a European Union priority

Out of the 17% of Europeans at risk of poverty, 20 million are children. In most countries of the European Union (EU) children are at greater risk of poverty than adults, and this situation has not improved since 2000. In March 2006, member states were asked by EU heads of state and governments 'to take necessary measures to rapidly and significantly reduce child poverty, giving all children equal opportunities, regardless of their social background' (European Council presidency conclusions March 2006). In response, member states chose tackling child poverty as the focus theme for 2007 in the context of the EU social inclusion strategy, a framework for policy cooperation between countries.

Social policy in the EU remains the responsibility of member states. EU cooperation in the fight against poverty therefore rests on regular reporting, peer pressure and mutual learning (see Box 9.1). In the absence of any binding mechanism, a large part of the effectiveness of the method lies in the capacity to analyse thoroughly the situation of each country in an international context. It is also crucial to be able to assess whether the policy priorities and corresponding policy tools identified at national level are appropriate to meet the commonly agreed objectives. Mutual learning – one of the key features of EU policy coordination – becomes easier when countries can compare their respective strengths and weaknesses on the basis of a common framework.

In 2007, member states conducted a benchmarking exercise (based on widely available indicators) that promoted a common understanding of the determinants of child poverty in each country. This work helped identify common challenges and explain why considerable differences

Box 9.1: The Open Method of Coordination (OMC) in the field of social protection and social inclusion

In the context of the OMC, social policy remains under the competency of member states. In order to coordinate their action, member states agree on common goals (for example, making a decisive impact on the eradication of poverty) (a full description of the agreed common objectives is available at http://ec.europa.eu/employment_social/spsi/docs/social_inclusion/2006/objectives_en.pdf) and on common indicators used to monitor progress and compare best practices. Member states translate the common goals into their own strategic objectives, and regularly report on the policies they put in place to reach these objectives. The National Strategy Reports are analysed and assessed at EU level, and common policy conclusions drawn from this analysis are jointly adopted by the European Commission and member states in the yearly *Joint report on social protection and social inclusion*. The EU also runs an action programme to support mutual learning through a variety of instruments: financing of EU stakeholder networks, peer reviews on specific policy issues, independent experts network, round table, EU meeting of people experiencing poverty, transnational and awareness-raising projects, studies, data collection....

Action at European level has increased political awareness of poverty and exclusion and placed the fight against poverty higher on national political agendas. It encouraged member states to critically examine their policies. It highlighted how countries perform well in certain areas, spurring on other member states to perform better. It also created a better basis for policy making by involving a range of actors such as non-governmental organisations (NGOs), social partners, local and regional authorities and those working with people in poverty. The method also allowed the creation of a clear consensus about a number of common key priorities in the fight against poverty and social exclusion: child poverty, truly inclusive labour markets, decent housing for all, etc....

In the absence of any binding mechanism, a large part of the effectiveness of the method lies in the capacity to analyse thoroughly the situation of member states in an international context. It is also crucial to be able to assess whether the policy priorities and corresponding policy tools they have identified at national level are appropriate to meet the commonly agreed objectives. This analytical capacity rests on the commonly agreed indicators that member states have identified through a collective and consensual process to reflect their situation vis-à-vis the common objectives. In order to ensure the transparency and legitimacy of the assessment, the EU's analytical capacity also needs a common and agreed framework on how to use and interpret the common EU indicators.

remain across member states in the situation regarding children. Ultimately, the findings were meant to increase the knowledge base informing governments in their use of the main policy instruments at their disposal: labour market policies that support parental employment and tax and benefit systems that support children and families both financially and through the provision of key services (for example, childcare).

These findings were published in the final report, *Child poverty and well-being in the EU: Current status and way forward*, adopted by the Social Protection Committee (SPC) in January 2008 (European Commission, 2008a). In this report, member states also adopted 15 recommendations to better monitor and assess child poverty and well-being in the context of EU and national policy making. They committed to developing the EU and national analytical capacity to fully reflect the multidimensional nature of child poverty and well-being (including material deprivation, education, health, etc).

Anti-poverty measures have a long history in the member states, but child poverty took longer to emerge as a priority. Some member states had a pioneering approach; in others the issue lacked recognition. EU cooperation was instrumental in promoting a strategic vision that is now shared by all. But did the 2007 benchmarking exercise help in promoting the fight against child poverty on the national political agendas? The analysis of the new round of strategic plans for social inclusion (received in September 2008) showed that a significant number of member states have strengthened or adapted their original strategy to align it with the findings of the exercise.

This chapter presents a summary of the original benchmarking exercise, reviews it in the light of more recent data and reflects on possible next steps to keep the momentum and maintain the fight against child poverty high on the political agenda.

Child poverty and its main determinants: a framework for European Union benchmarking

The need to significantly reduce child poverty and social exclusion has become even more acute in the last decade in the light of a number of stubborn facts. In most EU countries children are at greater 'risk of poverty' than the overall population. The persistence of high and sometimes increasing levels of child poverty in the richest group of countries in the world has been commented on by the United Nations Children's Fund (UNICEF), among others (UNICEF, 2005, 2007). Children growing up in poverty and social exclusion are less likely than their better-off peers to do well in school, enjoy good health and stay out of dealings with the criminal justice system. Child poverty and social exclusion also have damaging effects on the future life opportunities of children, and on their future capacity to contribute to tomorrow's society.

While most EU member states recognise these facts and are launching or have policies in place to address child poverty and social exclusion, these policies are still at very different stages of implementation, and considerable differences in outcomes remain. The aim of the following analysis is to understand better the reasons behind such differences.

This chapter focuses on *relative income poverty* since it remains a key aspect of children's living conditions for which the current EU social indicators and statistics are abundant (European Commission, 2009c).[1] Experiencing income poverty is one of those life circumstances most likely to have a direct or indirect negative impact on the well-being of children (educational outcome, health, housing conditions, quality of environment, etc) and on children's future life opportunities. The focus on relative income poverty is also politically relevant to support member states in their use of the main policy instruments they have at their disposal to support families: labour market policies that support parental employment and tax and benefit systems that support children and families both financially and through the provision of key services (for example, childcare).

Twenty million children are living under the poverty threshold in the European Union

In 2008, 20 million children were living under the poverty threshold in the EU-27,[2] meaning that 20% of children were at risk of poverty, against 17% for the total population (see Figure 9.1). In most EU countries children are at greater risk of poverty than the rest of the population, except in Denmark (where 10% of children live below the poverty threshold against 12% for the overall population), in Finland (12% against 14%), Cyprus (14% against 16%) and in Estonia (17% against 19%). In Germany and Slovenia the child poverty rate is equivalent to that of the overall population. In almost half of the EU countries, the risk of poverty for children is 20% or above, reaching 25% or more in Italy, Latvia, Bulgaria and Romania.

The severity of poverty, as measured by the at-risk-of-poverty gap,[3] helps in assessing how poor the poor children are. Again the picture is very contrasted across the EU. In one fourth of countries (Bulgaria, Greece, Spain, Latvia, Lithuania, Portugal and Romania), the median equivalised income of poor children is 26% to 40% lower than the national poverty threshold. In contrast, the intensity of child poverty is 16% or less in France, Cyprus, Luxembourg, the Netherlands, Austria,

Figure 9.1: At-risk-of-poverty rates in the EU (%), total and children, EU-27, 2008

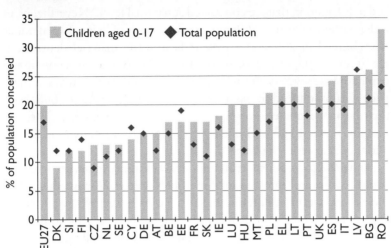

Note: Refer to the 'List of country abbreviations' in the Appendix at the end of this chapter.

Source: Eurostat – EU-SILC (2008); income year 2007; except for UK (income year 2008) and for Ireland (moving income reference period 2007-08)

Slovenia and Finland. It is in the countries with the highest child poverty rates that the intensity of poverty is most severe.

The standards of living of 'poor' children vary greatly across the EU, as illustrated by the poverty thresholds expressed in purchasing power standards (PPS). In 12 of the 15 'old' member states (EU-15), the monthly disposable income under which a family with two adults and two children is considered at risk of poverty varies from €PPS-1,500 to €PPS-2,000, while it ranges from €PPS-300 to €PPS-800 per month in 8 of the 12 'new' member states (EU-12). The income of poor households with children is therefore likely to be four times higher in the three richest EU countries than in the three poorest.

These poverty thresholds help in complementing the picture of poverty provided by the at-risk-of-poverty rate, which in the context of EU political cooperation remains defined in relation to national median income. As seen in Figure 9.1, countries with very different gross domestic product (GDP) per capita can have similar at-risk-of-poverty rates, thus providing a counter-intuitive picture of child poverty in Europe. Many stakeholders have, for instance, questioned the value of an indicator rating child poverty at 23% in the UK (one of the richest European nations) against 17% in Slovakia (one of the eight EU member states with a GDP per capita below 75% of the EU average).

This definition of poverty, agreed at high political level,[4] corresponds to the need to evaluate the impact of social policies, such as employment and redistribution that are conducted at national level.[5] Nevertheless, in order better to illustrate differences in standards of living, EU member states agreed in 2009 on a new indicator, the material deprivation rate (Guio, 2009). It is defined as a headcount of people whose living conditions are severely affected by a lack of resources. For instance, these people cannot afford to pay their rent, mortgage or utility bills, keep their home adequately warm, face unexpected expenses, eat meat or proteins regularly, go on holiday, or cannot afford to buy a television, a fridge, a car or a telephone.[6]

Figure 9.2 presents the material deprivation rate together with the at-risk-of-poverty rate and its threshold. While on average in the EU the percentage of children living in materially deprived households is the same (20%) as the percentage of children living in households at-risk-of-poverty, the ranking of countries is very different, and the variability of the material deprivation rate is much higher but similar to the variability of the poverty threshold. With a few exceptions (Estonia, the Czech Republic, Italy and Cyprus), material deprivation rates are high where the poverty threshold is low, and vice versa.

This material deprivation rate refers to children living in households with serious economic constraints. It therefore remains a measure reflecting solely material conditions, and not other aspects of deprivation that can have an adverse impact on children's well-being and development.

Despite the lack of internationally comparable income data over long-term trends,[7] national data shows that in most EU countries child poverty either remained stable or tended to increase between the mid-1990s and the mid-2000s. Signs of decrease were observed in Austria, Hungary and Spain, and it is only in the UK that child poverty significantly decreased since early 2000, as a result of their integrated anti-child poverty strategy. The Organisation for Economic Co-operation and Development (OECD) also reports that in most EU countries, the difference between the poverty rate of children and of the overall population increased in the late 1990s and early 2000s. The only countries where the gap was reduced were Spain, Ireland, Hungary, Austria and the UK.

Since the EU benchmarking exercise was conducted (2007), first trend data has become available from the EU harmonised data source EU-SILC covering the survey years 2005-08.[8] A very first analysis of these recent trends is presented later in this chapter.

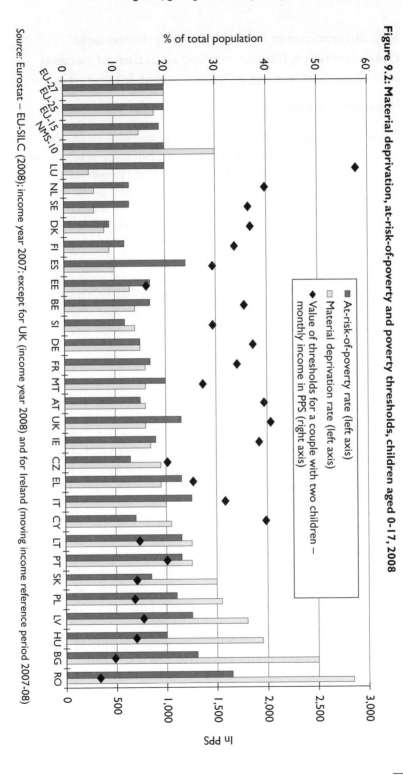

Figure 9.2: Material deprivation, at-risk-of-poverty and poverty thresholds, children aged 0-17, 2008

% of total population

Legend:
- At-risk-of-poverty rate (left axis)
- Material deprivation rate (left axis)
- Value of thresholds for a couple with two children – monthly income in PPS (right axis)

In PPS

Source: Eurostat – EU-SILC (2008); income year 2007; except for UK (income year 2008) and for Ireland (moving income reference period 2007-08)

Key determinants of child poverty: household characteristics, labour market situation of parents and the effectiveness of government intervention

Household characteristics

Among the factors influencing the income situation of children, the size, composition and characteristics (age, educational level of parents) of the household they live in play an important role. Household structures evolve on the basis of the way individuals choose to organise their lives. This happens in the context of specific cultural, social and demographic trends, where economic conditions play an important role.[9]

In the EU in 2006,[10] children whose *parents were below the age of 30* had much higher risk of poverty than those living with older parents: 27% when the mother was under 30, as against 19% when she was between 30 and 39 and 16% when she was between 40 and 49. This is mainly due to the fact that young parents who are at the start of their career tend to earn less than older parents and are more often unemployed.

The *educational level of parents* is another key determinant of children's current and future situation since it has an impact both on the current labour market and income situation of the parents and on the children's own chances to do well at school.[11] In the EU, most children are raised with at least one of their parents having fulfilled secondary education. The parents' education profile of poor children differs significantly from their peers, since for more than 30% of poor children, none of the parents reached a secondary level of education (against 16% for all children), and only 16% of them had a parent with higher education (against 32% for all children).

In the EU in 2007, half of poor children live in the two types of households that are most at risk of poverty: 22% live in *lone-parent households* and 27% in *large families*. However, the extent to which children – and especially those growing up in lone-parent households and large families – experience greater risks of poverty both depends on their characteristics (age, education level of parents, etc), and on the labour market situation of the parents (joblessness, in-work poverty, etc). This can in turn be influenced by the availability of adequate support through access to enabling services such as childcare, measures of reconciliation of work and family life and in-work income support (see Box 9.2).

Box 9.2: Children living in lone-parent households and in large families

In 2007, 11% of children in the EU lived in a *lone-parent household*, their numbers have increased in most countries, and their share ranges between 17% and 21% in Denmark, Ireland, Sweden and the UK. On average, their risk of poverty is almost twice as high as for children as a whole (37% against 20%), and their parent is more often low skilled. However, the risk of poverty of children living in lone-parent households varies greatly across the EU, from 17% in Denmark to 40% or more in the Baltic States, the Czech Republic, Ireland, Luxembourg and the UK. These differences in poverty risks depend on a number of factors: the age and education level of the parent and their labour market situation.

The main causes leading to lone parenthood (out-of-wedlock birth, separation) also play an important role and vary across countries. In the UK and Ireland, lone parents are more often young, low-skilled unmarried mothers who gave birth out of wedlock. In the Nordic countries, Germany and the Netherlands, they are more often divorced or separated, older and more likely to be employed.

Twenty-one per cent of children lived in *large families* (with three children or more) and faced a risk of poverty of 25% on average in the EU. The shares of children living in large families were lowest in Southern countries (15% or less in Greece, Spain, Italy and Portugal) and in the Czech Republic, the Baltic States and Slovenia (14% to 18%) where they faced the highest risks of poverty (30% or more, except in the Czech Republic, Estonia and Slovenia). By contrast, the number of children in large families is highest in the Nordic countries (26% to 32%) and in Ireland and Benelux (31% to 33%), where they faced the lowest risks of poverty (9% to 15% in the Nordic countries and 21% to 22% in the Benelux), and where their parents more often had a higher level of education.

Labour market situation of parents

The labour market situation of parents is a key determinant of the conditions in which children live and develop. Earnings from work are naturally the main source of income for parents in their prime age, and joblessness represents the main risk of poverty for households with children. However, in-work poverty remains an important cause of low income among families. The capacity of parents to draw an adequate income from work depends on the level of earnings and on how much the adults in the household work (one or two earners working full time or part time, and to what extent they work continuously throughout the year). The capacity of parents to participate in the labour market depends both on active labour market policies that support parental employment (and especially mothers' employment) and the availability and on the affordability of enabling services (for example, childcare).

The presence of children in the household mainly has an impact on the mother's labour force participation. In 2008, in the EU as a whole, the *employment rate of mothers* aged between 20 and 49 with children was lower than those of the same age who did not have children (68.4%, against 78.5%). Such a large gap can be observed in most EU countries and reaches 15 percentage points or more in the Czech Republic, Ireland, Lithuania, Hungary, Malta and the UK. However, in a number of countries, mothers and women without children had similar employment rates (Latvia, Portugal and Finland). Furthermore, in Denmark, Lithuania and Slovenia the gap was in favour of mothers whose employment rate was 3 to 7 percentage points higher than that of women without children. This suggests that very different settings prevail across countries in the way labour market and tax and benefit systems (including enabling services such as childcare) support or do not support mothers' employment.

Living in a household where no one works was likely to significantly affect both children's current living conditions and the conditions in which they developed by lack of an appropriate role model. In 2008, 9.2% of EU children lived in jobless households, with this proportion ranging from less than 4% in Slovenia, Denmark, Greece, Luxembourg and Cyprus to more than 14% in Hungary and the UK (see Figure 9.3). In the EU as a whole and in most EU countries, the situation has not significantly improved since 2000, despite the general improvements in EU labour markets during the period before the economic crisis.

The indicator of children living in jobless households is calculated on the basis of the EU Labour Force Survey (LFS). In this context, a household is considered 'jobless' if none of the adults aged 18-59, and not studying, was in employment in the four weeks preceding the date of the interview. Unfortunately, poverty rates cannot be calculated on the basis of the LFS; we therefore need to approximate the situation of these jobless households in the EU-SILC survey. The 2009 study by Tàrki and Applica conducted on behalf of the European Commission explores different possibilities (Tàrki and Applica, 2009). They found that the poverty rate of children living in households not working at all over the whole year or working very little (work intensity[12] below 0.33) reached 63% and concerned approximately 11% of children.

Joblessness mainly affects lone-parent households that face particular difficulties in reconciling work and family life. In 2007, half of children living in a jobless household lived in a lone-parent household, 40% lived

Figure 9.3: Children and adults (aged 18-59, not students) living in jobless households, EU-27, 2008

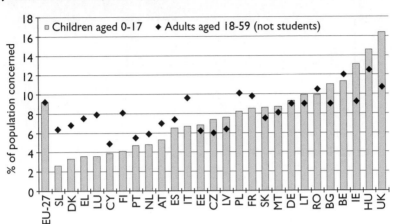

Source: Eurostat – Labour Force Survey

in a two-adult household and 10% in a household with three adults or more. However, this pattern varies significantly across countries.

Should both parents work, and how much? Not all children whose parents are at work are protected from the risk of poverty. In 2007, 11% of children living in households with at least one parent at work were living under the poverty threshold (see Figure 9.4). This rate ranged from 7% or less in Belgium, the Czech Republic, Denmark, Germany, Ireland and Slovenia to 16% or more in Greece, Spain, Italy, Luxembourg and Poland. In-work poverty may result from recurrent unemployment or unstable jobs, involuntary part-time work, low wages or from a particular household structure with, for example, only one working-age adult and two or more dependants (both children and other dependants). A detailed analysis of the determinants of in-work poverty is available in Tàrki and Applica (2009).

In most EU countries, single-earner families (whether couples or lone parents) are more and more exposed to the risk of poverty. Increasingly, households with children need to rely on two earners to ward off the risk of poverty. In the EU, the two breadwinners model prevails for 50% of children living with both parents. This rate reaches 60% or more in Denmark, Cyprus, Slovenia, Slovakia and Sweden and is lowest (ranging from 30% in Malta to 40-45% in Germany, Ireland, Italy, Luxembourg, Hungary and Austria).

When both parents are working, children face a risk of poverty of 5% on average, against 24% of children with only one of their two parents at work (and working full time). The risk of poverty of children in

Figure 9.4: At-risk-of-poverty rates of children living in households at work, EU-25, 2007

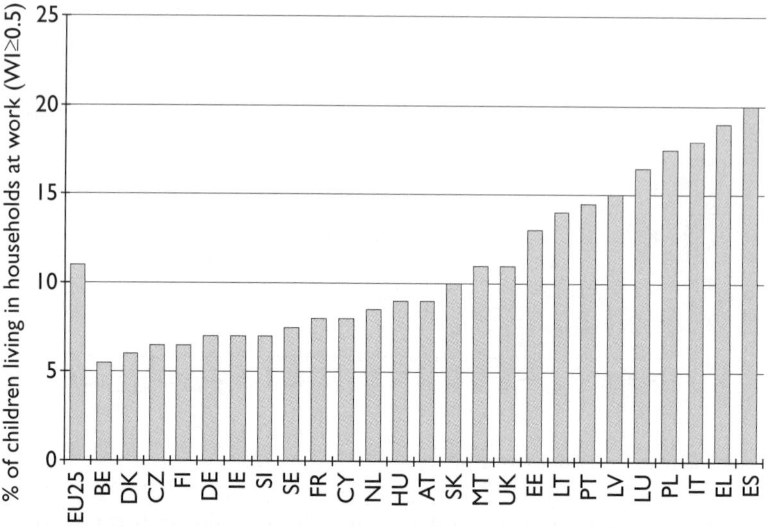

Source: EU-SILC (2007) – income year 2006 (income year 2007 for Ireland and the UK). Calculation by Tàrki and Applica (2009)

single-earner families ranges from around 10–12% in Germany, Ireland and Finland to 27% or more in Greece, Spain, Italy, Lithuania, Latvia, Poland, Portugal, Slovenia and the UK.

On average in the EU, having one parent *working part time* doesn't increase the risk of poverty for children who live with both parents. However, this average hides a much contrasted picture across the EU. In a number of countries, the risk of poverty of children with one parent working full time and the other working part time is equally low (the Czech Republic, Denmark, Germany, Estonia, Ireland, France, Italy, Cyprus, Luxembourg, Austria, Sweden and the UK) or even lower (Belgium and the Netherlands) than those whose parents both work full time. In these countries, part-time work may be seen as an element of work–life balance for two-earner families. On the contrary, in Greece, Lithuania, Latvia, Hungary, Poland and Portugal, the risk of poverty of children with one of their parents working part time ranges from 19% to 30% and is two to four times higher than the risk of poverty of children with both parents working full time. The impact of part-time work on the household's income depends on the level of skills, the number of hours worked and the availability and affordability of childcare and other support services available to families (for a more detailed analysis of the evolution and impact of part-time work on poverty, see European Commission, 2009b).

Children of lone parents face a relatively low risk of poverty of 15% (against 19% for all children) if their parent works full time. This risk falls between 4% and 14% in Belgium, Germany, Denmark, Ireland, France, the Netherlands, Finland, Sweden and the UK, but it is only in the Nordic countries and France that the majority of children living with a lone parent have their parent working full time. This illustrates that the higher risks of poverty faced by children of lone parents depend to a great extent on the ability of lone parents to access and retain quality jobs as well as on the availability of quality enabling services, in particular quality childcare.

Government intervention

Assessing the impact of government intervention on child poverty is a complex task since a broad range of government policies influences the actual living standards of households with children. Using a broad definition, tax and benefit systems can redistribute income towards families by different means, such as providing a minimum income level for those without paid employment (unemployment benefits, social assistance, disability allowances) or supplementing the income of all households with children whether they are in employment or not. The income of families can also be influenced by minimum wages policies. Also crucially, child poverty is influenced by a number of policy choices in the area of education (free schooling at an early age, length of the school day), health (access to free services for children), housing and childcare services, etc.

Across the EU, the countries with the lowest child poverty rates are clearly those who spend most on social benefits (excluding pensions[13]), with the notable exception of Cyprus and, to a lesser extent, Slovenia. This partly reflects a wealth effect that is observed among EU countries whereby the richest countries are those that can afford the highest levels of social protection and redistribution. However, differences in the starting positions of households before receipt of benefits, as well as in the design and overall effectiveness of the tax and benefit systems, mean that countries with similar levels of wealth and social spending as a percentage of GDP experience widely differing levels of child poverty.

On average in the EU social transfers other than pensions reduce the risk of poverty for children by 40%, which is a higher impact than for the overall population (33%) (see Figure 9.5). This is true in most EU countries, except in Bulgaria, the Czech Republic, Greece,

Figure 9.5: Impact of social transfers (excluding pensions) on poverty risk for children and for the overall population (in % of the poverty risk before all social transfers), EU-27, 2008

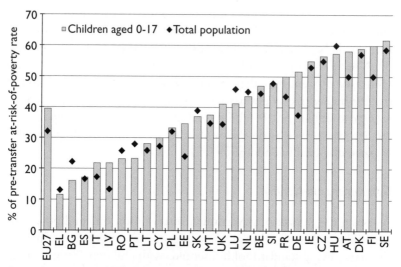

Source: Eurostat – EU-SILC (2008); income year 2007; except for UK (income year 2008) and for Ireland (moving income reference period 2007-08)

Luxembourg, the Netherlands, Portugal, Romania and Slovakia, where it is slightly smaller. In the Nordic countries, the Czech Republic, Germany, Ireland, France, Hungary and Austria, social transfers (other than pensions) reduce the at-risk-of-poverty for children by 50% or more. In Bulgaria, Greece and Spain, this reduction is less than 20%.

Benefits specifically targeted at children have the strongest impact and reduce child poverty by 28% on average. The countries in which total benefits have the biggest impact on child poverty are also those in which family benefits have the strongest impact in reducing child poverty. In 2007, in Germany, Ireland, France, Luxembourg, the Netherlands, Austria and Finland, family benefits reduced the risk of poverty of children by one third or more. In these countries, the differences in final child poverty outcomes are partly due to the very different levels of market income poverty. Market income poverty depends *inter alia* on the incidence of joblessness and in-work poverty in these countries. A detailed analysis of the impact of transfers on the risk of poverty for children is available in Tàrki and Applica (2009). This also analyses the relative impacts of universal benefits allocated to all children versus benefits targeted at specific children (for example, in poor or lone-parent families).

Among the tools to support families, the provision of affordable *childcare* can play an important role to improve the labour market and financial situation of families. Again, situations differ greatly across the EU, especially for young children under the age of two depending on the availability of childcare and on the parental leave arrangements. Can parents afford to work? In its 2007 edition of *Benefits and wages* (chapter 4), the OECD shows that for low wage earners, childcare costs significantly add to the effective tax burden on gross earnings both for a second earner and a lone parent taking up work. The extra burden for lone parents moving into low wages is lowest in the Nordic countries, Belgium, Germany, France, Hungary and the Netherlands and highest in Ireland, Slovakia and the UK.

The diagnosis

Table 9.1 (a) and (b) summarises the main findings of the analysis of the main determinants of the risk of child poverty presented in the original report (based on 2006 EU-SILC data, and updated with 2008 data). In the first column, countries are assessed according to their relative performance in child poverty outcomes, into six levels from +++ (countries with the highest performance) to − − − (countries with the lowest performance). In the next three columns, countries are assessed according to their relative performance (also using a six levels scale) with regard to the three main factors influencing child poverty risk, namely: children living in *jobless households*, children living in households at risk of *in-work poverty* and the *low impact of social transfers* on the risk of child poverty. Countries are then grouped according to the main challenge they face (where they have most − [negative] scores).

The detailed analysis of Table 9.1 (a) and (b) confirms that child poverty outcomes result from complex interactions between joblessness, in-work poverty and the impact of transfers, and that the countries achieving the best outcomes are those that are performing well on all fronts, notably by combining strategies aimed at facilitating access to employment and enabling services (childcare, etc) with income support.

With only four countries changing grouping over time (underlined and in italics), the framework shows a certain level of stability; however, some details of the analysis point to the limitations of a system only based on relative performance, as discussed below.

- *Group A* gathers countries that reach relatively *good child poverty outcomes by performing well on all three fronts.* They combine relatively good labour market performance of parents (low levels of joblessness

Table 9.1: (a) Relative outcomes of countries related to child poverty risk and main determinants of child poverty risk, EU-SILC 2006

		Child poverty risk outcomes	Joblessness: children living in jobless households	In-work poverty: children living in households confronted with in-work poverty	Impact of social transfers (cash benefits excluding pensions) on child poverty
Group A	AT	+	+	++	++
	CY	+++	+	+++	+
	DK	+++	+	+++	++
	FI	+++	++	+++	+++
	NL	+	+	+	+
	SE	+	(++)	++	++
	SI	++	+++	+++	++
Group B	BE	+	--	+++	+
	CZ	-	--	+	+
	DE	++	--	+++	+++
	EE	--	--	+	-
	FR	++	-	++	++
	IE	-	---	+	+
	SK	-	---	+	+
Group C	HU	---	---	-	+
	MT	-	--	--	-
	UK	--	---	--	+
Group D	EL	--	+++	--	---
	ES	---	+	---	---
	IT	---	++	---	--
	LT	---	+	--	--
	LU	--	+++	--	+
	LV	---	-	--	--
	PL	---	-	--	--
	PT	--	+	--	--

Source: SPC report on child poverty and well-being – data updated to 2006; Luxembourg excluded from analysis

and of in-work poverty among households with children) with relatively high and effective social transfers. Nordic countries achieve these goals despite high shares of children living in lone-parent households. They seem to succeed in so doing notably by supporting adequate labour market participation of parents in these families through childcare provision and a wide range of measures of reconciliation of work and family life. While the impact of social transfers on child poverty is relatively low in Cyprus, children in

Table 9.1: (b) Relative outcomes of countries related to child poverty risk and main determinants of child poverty risk, EU-SILC 2008

		Update			
		Child poverty risk outcomes	Joblessness: children living in jobless households	In-work poverty: children living in households confronted with in-work poverty	Impact of social transfers (cash benefits excluding pensions) on child poverty
Group A	AT	++	++	+	+++
	CY	+++	++	++	-
	DK	+++	+++	+++	+++
	FR	++	+	++	++
	FI	+++	+++	+++	+++
	NL	+++	++	+	+
	SE	++	(++)	++	++
	SI	+++	+++	++	++
Group B	BE	++	--	+++	++
	CZ	+	-	+++	++
	DE	+++	-	++	+++
	HU	≈	=	±	++
	IE	+	---	++	++
	SK	---	-	+	-
Group C	*EE*	±	≈	=	±
	LT	=	=	=	≈
	MT	+	-	-	-
	UK	+	---	-	+
Group D	EL	--	+++	---	---
	ES	---	++	---	---
	IT	---	++	---	--
	LU	-	+++	---	+
	LV	-	+	--	--
	PL	--	+	---	-
	PT	---	++	--	--

Note: Countries that changed groupings between 2006 and 2008 appear underlined and in italics.

Source: SPC report on child poverty and well-being – data updated to 2008; Luxembourg excluded from analysis

this country have so far been protected against the risk of poverty by strong family structures dominated by two-adult families and complex households in which most working-age adults are at work. In the Netherlands, while children in part benefit from the low levels of inequality in the country and from a relatively good integration of parents in the labour market, child poverty outcomes may be further improved by addressing the intensity of poverty and improving the impact of social transfers (which is lower than for other countries in this group). Since 2006, France has moved from Group B to Group A, notably by slightly improving the relative situation of children in jobless households. However, the position of this country in this group is uncertain, since the child poverty rate in France has increased over the last three years. This may point to the limitation of a benchmarking exercise based too much on a relative assessment.

- *Group B* gathers countries that achieve relatively good to below average poverty outcomes. The main matter of concern in these countries is the *high numbers of children living in jobless households.* At the same time, children living in families at work experience lower levels of poverty than in other EU countries. In most of these countries, around half of the children in jobless households live with a lone parent. Among these six countries, Belgium and Germany seem to be more successful at limiting the risks of poverty for children than the others through relatively high and effective social transfers. The interaction between the design of these benefits, the availability and affordability of childcare and the labour market participation of parents deserves further analysis.[14] Policies aimed at enhancing access to quality jobs for those parents furthest away from the labour market may contribute to reducing child poverty in these countries. Since 2006, Hungary has moved from Group C to Group B, notably by improving the impact of social transfers and significantly reducing in-work poverty.

- *Group C* gathers countries that record average or just below average child poverty outcomes, despite *a combination of high levels of joblessness and in-work poverty among parents.* In the UK, joblessness mainly concerns lone parents, while in Malta it concerns mainly couples with children. The main factors of in-work poverty are low work intensity in Malta (very few two-earner families) and the UK (incidence of part-time work). In this group of countries, the UK partly alleviates very high risks of pre-transfer poverty among children through relatively effective social benefits. In Malta, despite the relatively poor integration of their parents in the labour market, children benefit from low pre-transfer risk of poverty, probably as a result of family structures that so far remain protective. In these countries, different policy mixes may be needed to give access to quality jobs to parents living in jobless households, to enhance the labour market participation of second earners and to adequately support the incomes of parents at work. Since 2006, Estonia has moved from Group B to Group C, notably because in-work poverty increased. However, the effectiveness of social transfers has increased significantly, which is likely to explain the significant improvement of child poverty outcomes. This points to the need for further analysis, including of the policy reforms, to understand the mechanisms at stake in this country (see below). Lithuania has moved from group D to C, thanks to a significant improvement of the impact of social transfers, accompanied, however, by a strong increase in the percentage of children living in jobless households.

• *Group D* gathers countries recording relatively high levels of child poverty. While they have low shares of children living in jobless households, they experience *very high levels of in-work poverty among families*. The main factors of in-work poverty in these countries are the low work intensity (the number of two-earner families are among the lowest in Spain, Greece, Italy, Luxembourg and Poland) combined (or not) with low in-work incomes (the poverty rates of two-breadwinner households are among the highest in Spain, Greece, Portugal and Poland). In these countries (apart from Luxembourg), *the level and effectiveness of social spending are among the lowest in the EU*. The analysis indicates that in these countries family structures and intergenerational solidarity continue to play a role in alleviating the risk of poverty for the most vulnerable children. Living in multigenerational households and/or relying on inter-household transfers, whether in cash or in kind, may partly compensate for the lack of governmental support for the parents in the most vulnerable situations. These countries may need to adopt comprehensive strategies aimed at better supporting families' income, both in and out of work, and at facilitating access to quality jobs, especially for second earners.

What happened since 2007 and the way forward

Was the EU benchmarking exercise used in policy making?

At European Union level

An agreed analytical framework relying on common indicators increases the transparency and legitimacy of a diagnosis at EU level. This framework allows us to highlight not just the relative outcomes of each country, but also to identify the main causes of child poverty in each country. Knowledge of the main determinants of child poverty allows us to deduce in which areas action is needed and to define the policy priorities. An example of the application of the framework can be found in the 2008 *Joint report on social protection and social inclusion* (European Commission, 2008b). The analysis was complemented by a jointly agreed assessment of the policies in place in member states, and resulted in the issuing of key policy messages by all EU ministers. The framework was also used in the supporting document to the 2009 *Joint report on social protection and social inclusion* (European Commission, 2009a) to assess the new round of national strategies for social inclusion for 2008-10. It provided a reference to evaluate whether countries had identified the right priorities for intervention in their fight against poverty.

For instance, the supporting document analysed the measures taken or foreseen in *Group B* countries (Belgium, the Czech Republic, Germany, France, Estonia, Ireland and Bulgaria) for which the main challenge was to bring down the high number of children living in jobless households and to help parents stay durably on the labour market. In most of these countries, measures were envisaged to make work pay for parents while adequately supporting their income. Measures included tax rebates for low-income families (Belgium, the Czech Republic and Estonia) and activation measures targeted at parents (Belgium, Bulgaria and the Czech Republic). Ireland was planning to substantially increase child income support and to structure the payments to remove employment disincentives. Ireland also decided to look at increasing the low take-up of in-work supplement for low-income families. In France, the newly introduced RSA (Revenue de Solidarité Active, an income support scheme designed to support individuals through their transition back to work) will take account of the size and composition of the household. Most of the countries in this group had substantial plans to improve the availability and affordability of childcare to help parents back into work.

Another example is provided by the analysis of the measures announced by *Group D* countries (Spain, Greece, Italy, Lithuania, Latvia, Poland and Portugal) in which comprehensive strategies were most needed to address high levels of in-work poverty and a relatively low effectiveness of social transfers. In most of these countries, governments intended to take or reinforce measures to significantly increase income support to families and facilitate the labour market participation of parents, especially of the second earner. Latvia, Lithuania, Poland and Portugal in particular have enhanced income support to families through a wide range of measures including enhancing the level and coverage of family benefits. In Lithuania and Poland child poverty has decreased significantly (see the following section on recent trends), but not in the two other countries. Significant efforts to develop affordable childcare provision are notable in Hungary, Italy, Lithuania, Luxembourg, Poland and Portugal in order to encourage the labour market participation of the second earner, and thus address in-work poverty linked to low work intensity in the household.

At national level

A common analytical framework can help policy makers at national level because it allows benchmarking of the performance of each country against that of countries sharing the same challenges. It also allows a better appreciation of the true magnitude of those challenges and in some instances to pinpoint emerging trends. Mutual learning – one of the key features of the Open Method of Coordination (OMC) – becomes easier when countries are able to compare their respective strengths and weaknesses on the basis of a common framework. A number of national administrations have indicated that they have used the EU framework in the preparation of their national strategies for social protection and social inclusion.

Recent trends

The SPC report on child poverty and child well-being noted that once reliable trend data become available from EU-SILC, a dynamic dimension will have to be added to the proposed diagnosis. As the 2008 EU-SILC data was released in December 2009, recent trend data are becoming available covering four survey years, from 2005 to 2008. This section presents these first trends for a selection of countries together with a very preliminary analysis.

Between 2003-2008, child poverty *increased* in five EU countries. It increased from relatively low levels in Germany, France and Sweden. Further analysis is needed to understand the causes of this increase, but Table 9.2 points to a significant reduction in the effectiveness of social transfers in reducing child poverty in all three countries, and an increase in in-work poverty in Sweden. Child poverty also increased in Greece and Latvia from already high levels. In Greece, in-work poverty increased further and the effectiveness of social transfers remained at the lowest level in the EU. In Latvia, the effectiveness of transfers decreased.

On the contrary, child poverty *decreased* in the Czech Republic, Estonia, Ireland, Lithuania and Poland. In all five countries, the

Table 9.2: Change between 2005 and 2008 in percentage points

	Poverty rate	Poverty gap	Jobless households	In-work poverty	Impact of transfers
EU25	⇔	⇘	⇘	⇔	↘
EU15	⇔	⇘			↘
NMS10	↘	↘			↗
BE	⇔	⇔	↘	↘	⇔
CZ	↘	⇗	⇘	↘	↗
DK	⇔	⇔	↘	⇔	⇔
DE	↗	⇗	↘	⇔	↘
EE	↘	↘	↘	⇔	↗
IE	↘	⇘	⇗	↘	↗
EL	↗	⇗	⇘	↗	⇔
ES	⇔	⇘	⇗	⇔	⇔
FR	↗	⇔	⇔	⇔	↘
IT	⇔	↘	⇗	⇔	⇔
CY	⇔	⇘	⇔	⇔	↘
LV	↗	⇘	⇔	⇔	↘
LT	↘	⇘	↗	↘	↗
LU	⇔	⇔	⇗	⇔	↘
HU	⇔	⇘	⇗	↘	↗
MT	⇗	⇔	⇔	↘	⇔
NL	⇘	↘	↘	↘	↘
AT	⇔	⇗	⇘	↘	⇔
PL	↘	↘	↘	↘	↗
PT	⇔	⇘	⇔	↘	⇔
SI	⇔	⇔	⇘	⇔	↘
SK	⇘	⇔	↘	↘	⇔
FI	⇗	↗	↘	⇔	↘
SE	↗	⇔		↗	↘
UK	⇔	⇘	⇔	↘	↘

Source: Eurostat based on tables in annex

Reading note concerning the evolution of the key variables between 2005 and 2008

Poverty rate and poverty gap	↘	Strong decrease by 3 percentage points or more
	⇘	Moderate decrease by 2 percentage points
	⇔	Stagnation between +1 and −1
	⇗	Moderate increase by 2 percentage points
	↗	Strong increase by more than 3 percentage points or more
Jobless households	↘	Strong decrease by more than 1.5 percentage points
	⇘	Moderate decrease between 0.5 and 1.5 percentage points
	⇔	Stagnation between +0.5 and −0.5
	⇗	Moderate increase between 0.5 and 1.5 percentage points
	↗	Strong increase by more than 1.5 percentage points
In-work poverty	↘	Strong decrease compared to EU average
	⇔	Stagnation or change equivalent to EU average
	↗	Strong increase compared to EU average
Impact of transfers	↘	Strong decrease by 2 percentage points or more
	⇔	Stagnation between −2 and +2 percentage points
	↗	Strong increase by 2 percentage points or more

effectiveness of social transfers increased by 9 percentage points in the Czech Republic, 2 in Estonia, 12 in Ireland, 7 in Lithuania and 8 in Poland against a decrease of −5 percentage points on average in the EU. The percentage of children in jobless households was reduced in the Czech Republic and Poland and in-work poverty dropped in all five countries.

This first insight into recent trends calls for further analysis, especially of the reforms that were implemented in the countries reviewed. The Tàrki and Applica study (2009) reviews the latest policy developments in 11 EU countries and contains interesting elements that could support this analysis. For instance, it notes that Estonia and Poland implemented new child allowances between 2005 and 2008.

The analysis of trends in child relative poverty might also be influenced by the evolution of other groups of the population. The selection of trends presented in Figure 9.6 shows, for instance, that in some countries, the strong increase in older people at-risk-of-poverty rates may have contributed to driving down child poverty rates. This happened in particular in countries that experienced strong economic growth in the years before the economic crisis, accompanied by a strong increase in wages. Where pensions were not indexed to wages, at-risk-of-poverty rates for older people strongly increased, thus enhancing the relative decrease of child poverty (refer to the Baltic States in Figure 9.6). This illustrates the limitations of an assessment of poverty solely based on a relative definition of poverty.

As mentioned earlier, in 2009 the EU agreed on a new indicator of material deprivation, which reflects more directly the living conditions of Europeans and is based on a common EU definition. The series of diagrams below, in Figure 9.6, presents for a selection of countries at-risk-of-poverty and material deprivation rates for the main age groups: children, the working-age population and older people. At EU level, there is no evolution of the risk of poverty over time, and a slight improvement of material deprivation rates, mainly due to the strong improvements observed in the new member states (NMS-10),[15] from 45% for children in 2005 to 30% in 2008. The material deprivation rate seems to capture the overall improvements in living conditions of the new member states, as they experienced strong growth in the years before the crisis.

The old (EU–15) and new (NMS–10) member states also differ in terms of the relative position of children; in the EU–15, children have poverty rates above average but below the poverty rates of older people. In the NMS–10, children also have above average poverty rates, but experience much higher risk of poverty than the population of older people.

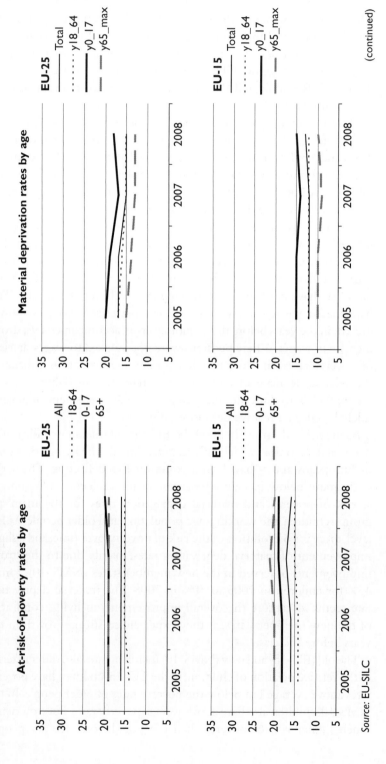

Figure 9.6: Recent trends in at-risk-of-poverty rates and material deprivation rates, 2005-08, EU-SILC

Material deprivation rates by age

At-risk-of-poverty rates by age

(continued)

Source: EU-SILC

Figure 9.6: Recent trends in at-risk-of-poverty rates and material deprivation rates, 2005-08, EU-SILC (continued)

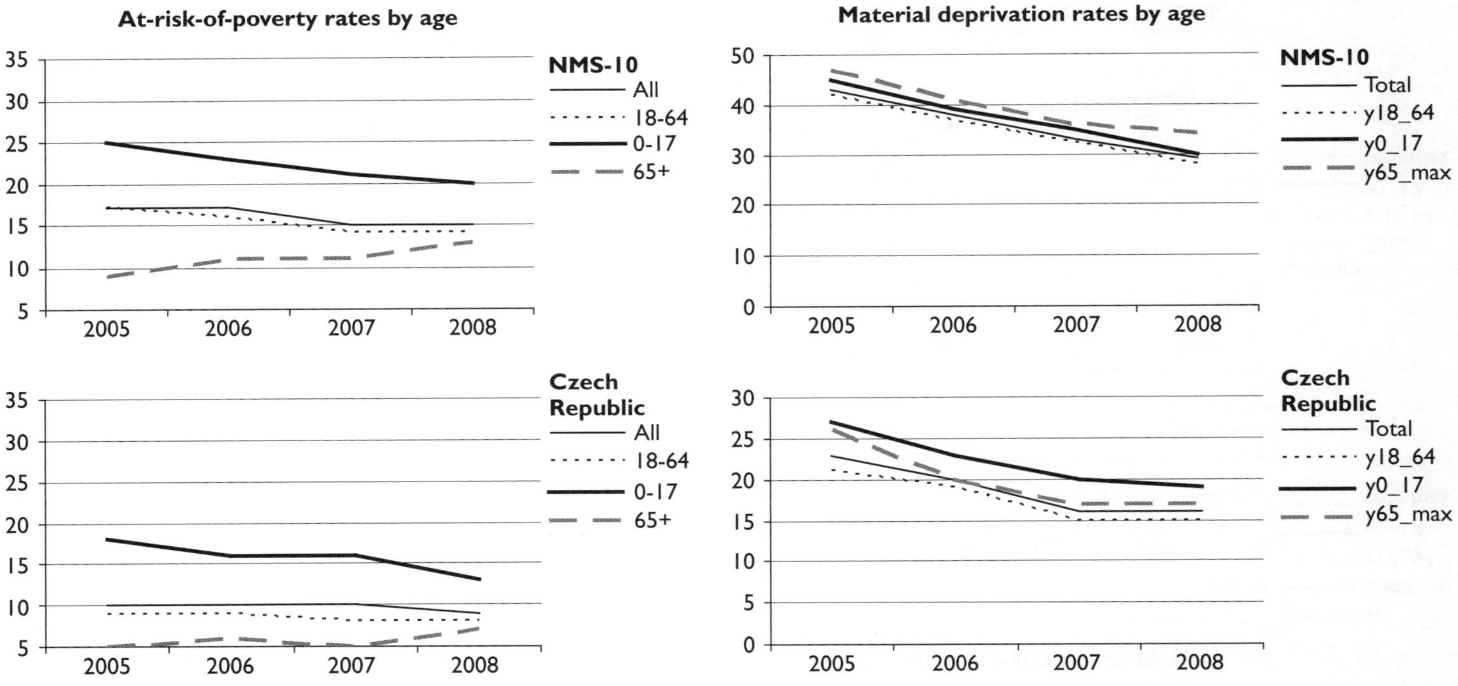

At-risk-of-poverty rates by age

Material deprivation rates by age

Source: EU-SILC

(continued)

231

Figure 9.6: Recent trends in at-risk-of-poverty rates and material deprivation rates, 2005-08, EU-SILC (continued)

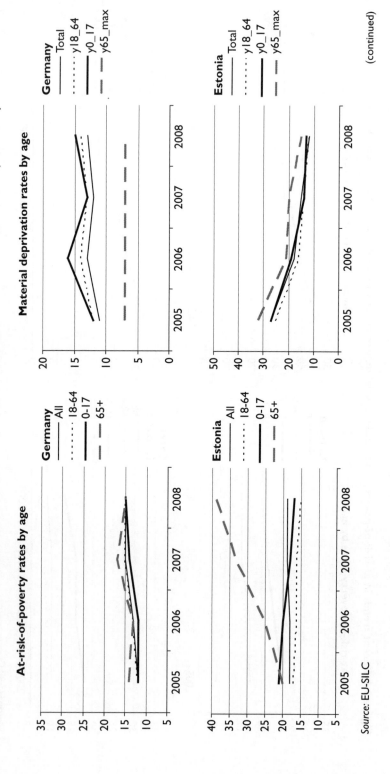

(continued)

Source: EU-SILC

Figure 9.6: Recent trends in at-risk-of-poverty rates and material deprivation rates, 2005-08, EU-SILC (continued)

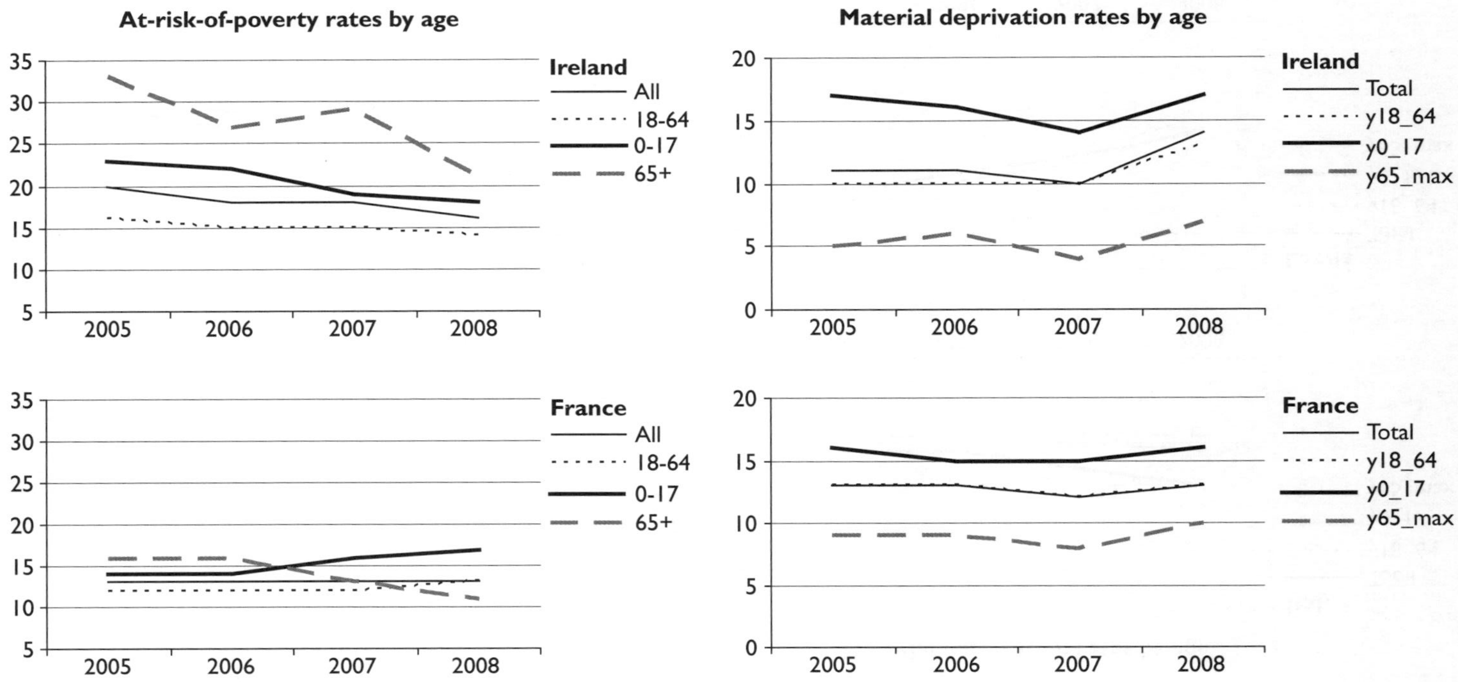

Material deprivation rates by age

At-risk-of-poverty rates by age

Ireland
— Total
····· y18_64
— y0_17
– – y65_max

France
— Total
····· y18_64
— y0_17
– – y65_max

Ireland
— All
····· 18-64
— 0-17
– – 65+

France
— All
····· 18-64
— 0-17
– – 65+

(continued)

Source: EU-SILC

Figure 9.6: Recent trends in at-risk-of-poverty rates and material deprivation rates, 2005-08, EU-SILC (continued)

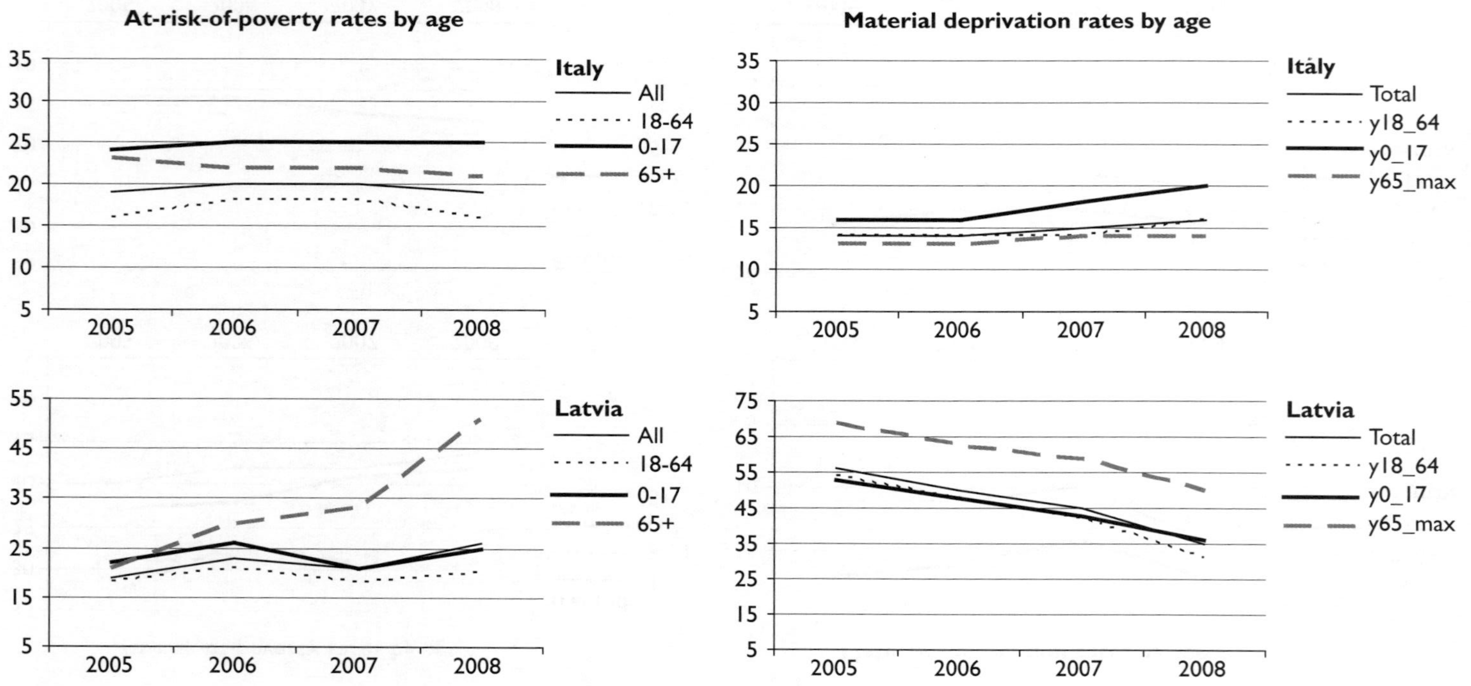

At-risk-of-poverty rates by age

Material deprivation rates by age

(continued)

Source: EU-SILC

Figure 9.6: Recent trends in at-risk-of-poverty rates and material deprivation rates, 2005-08, EU-SILC (continued)

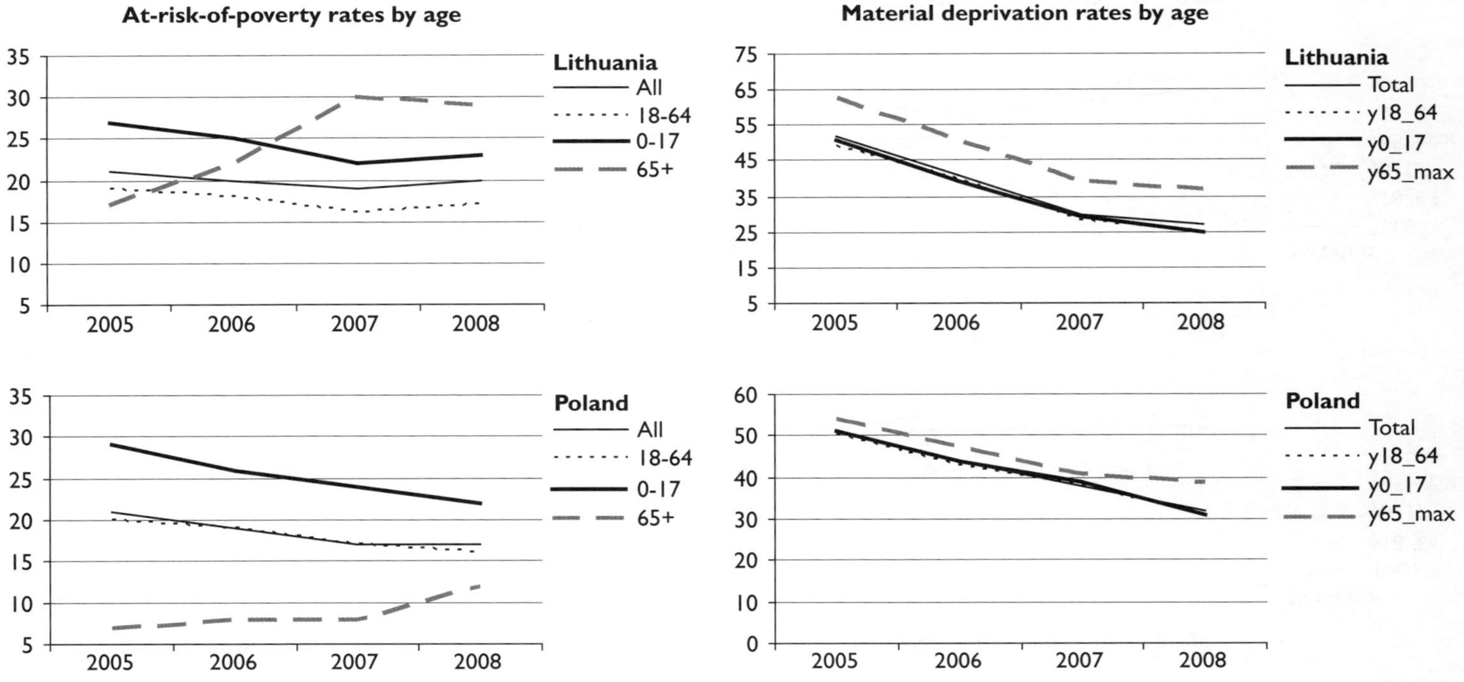

At-risk-of-poverty rates by age

Material deprivation rates by age

(continued)

Source: EU-SILC

Figure 9.6: Recent trends in at-risk-of-poverty rates and material deprivation rates, 2005-08, EU-SILC (continued)

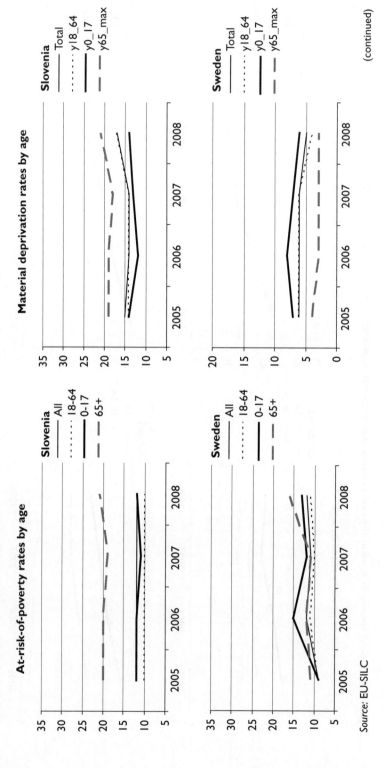

(continued)

Source: EU-SILC

Figure 9.6: Recent trends in at-risk-of-poverty rates and material deprivation rates, 2005-08, EU-SILC (continued)

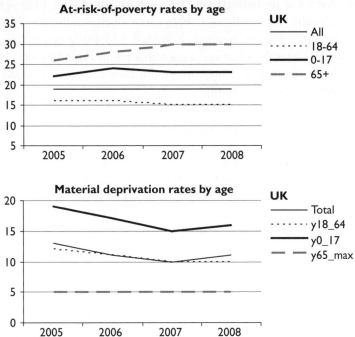

Source: EU-SILC

This partly reflects the age orientation of social protection in these countries where pensions used to appear relatively generous compared to weak support to families with children (see European Commission, 2008c). In most NMS-10, the relative situation of older people has worsened in recent years. However, in nearly all NMS-10, material deprivation rates have significantly improved overall and for all age groups. Slovenia is a notable exception, having a pattern very similar to most EU-15 countries, both in terms of relative poverty and material deprivation rates.

Among the old EU-15 member states, child poverty has increased in Germany, for children and for all other age groups. Ireland is the only country to have reduced relative poverty for all age groups between 2005 and 2008, even though the material deprivation rates seemed to increase again in 2008, perhaps reflecting the first impacts of the economic crisis.

More analysis is needed to draw firm conclusions from these preliminary trends, which is beyond what the timing and context of this chapter allows. However, the fact that for the first time, this information is available for 30 European countries in a comparable way and covering two key and complementary dimensions of hardship is of great value in itself. Beyond the analysis that will be done in the context of the EU institutions, these data will enrich the possibilities of many governments, many stakeholders and many researchers to understand better the situation of poor children in a rich Europe. There is no doubt that it will contribute significantly to better knowledge-based policy making in Europe.

Further investments in the knowledge base

Since the adoption of the report on *Child poverty and child well-being* in January 2008, the European Commission has continued to invest in the knowledge base needed to underpin policies to fight child poverty and to promote child well-being in the EU. The following lists briefly the different activities conducted in line with the main recommendations of the report.

A new study

On 26 November 2009, a seminar on child poverty and well-being presented the results of a study financed and carried out jointly by two European research institutes, Tàrki and Applica, on behalf of the European Commission. The study's main aims were threefold: to update and test the benchmarking exercise with the most recent data, to link it to a detailed analysis of policy measures existing in a selection of countries and to reflect on a list of indicators to better monitor child well-being at EU level. This chapter draws heavily on the analysis contained in this study, to be published early in January.

Statistical developments

In the field of statistics, the European Statistical System has agreed on a list of material deprivation items to be tested in the 2009 EU-SILC module on material deprivation. It includes 21 child-specific items that should allow us to develop a specific child deprivation indicator to better reflect key dimensions of children's lives, including nutrition, access to healthcare, education and social relations that have an impact on children's well-being and well-becoming. The data became available early in 2011 for 30 EU-SILC countries, including all 27 EU countries.

Basic needs for all household children
- New (not second-hand) clothes
- Two pairs of properly-fitting shoes (including a pair of all-weather shoes)
- Fresh fruit and vegetables once a day
- Three meals a day
- One meal with meat, chicken or fish (or vegetarian equivalent) per day

Educational or leisure needs for all household children
- Go on holiday at least one week a year
- Books at home suitable for their age
- Outdoor leisure equipment (bicycle, roller skates, etc)
- Indoor games (educational baby toys, building blocks, board games, computer games, etc)
- Regular leisure activity (swimming, playing an instrument, youth organisations, etc)
- Celebrations on special occasions (birthdays, name days, religious events, etc)
- Invite friends round to play and eat from time to time
- Participate in school trips and school events that cost money
- Suitable place to study or do homework
- Outdoor space in the neighbourhood where children can play safely

Medical needs for all household children
- Unmet need for consulting a doctor or specialist
- Main reason for unmet need for consulting a doctor or specialist
- Unmet need for consulting a dentist
- Main reason for unmet need for consulting a dentist
- Unmet need for buying medicine/medical equipment
- Main reason for unmet need for buying medicine/medical equipment

The European Commission has engaged in a joint effort with the OECD and UNICEF for the development of indicators of child well-being. An international consultation took place at the OECD on 25-27 May 2009, and the OECD has published a comprehensive report on child well-being (OECD, 2009). In 2010, the OECD, in cooperation with the European Commission (including its statistical office, Eurostat), made an assessment of existing international databases to evaluate their comparability and reliability, to be discussed at the second expert consultation on 2-3 November 2011. This will provide the necessary reassurance to EU governments.

New indicators of child well-being

The Indicators Sub-Group (ISG) of the SPC is the body in charge of developing indicators to support policy coordination at EU level. Based on the thorough proposals put forward by the Tàrki and Applica study, the ISG will select a number of indicators of child well-being to be included in the overall list of social inclusion indicators. Member states will also identify a list of core indicators best suited for a detailed examination of child well-being, beyond child poverty, once the EU decides to reiterate the 2007-08 in-depth review.

Monitoring of the social impact of the economic crisis

Finally, it is worth mentioning that the European Commission and the member states have engaged early on (at the end of 2008) in the joint monitoring of the social impact of the current global economic crisis. The latest report, published in December 2010 (Council of the European Union, 2010), reviews the latest economic and social trends in the EU and lists the policy interventions that member states have taken in response to the crisis, including labour market measures, measures to support people's income (for example, strengthening unemployment and social assistance benefits) and measures to support mortgage holders from repossessions. Many of these measures concerned or were targeted at families with children. Analysing the impact of the crisis on children goes beyond the scope of this chapter. However, in the coming year, as the Commission reflects on ways to strengthen further the political commitment against child poverty at EU level, it will have to take account of the impact of the recession on child policies, especially in a context of a greater constraint on public finances.

Notes

[1] For updated figures related to all EU indicators, see the Eurostat website (http://epp.eurostat.ec.europa.eu/portal/page/portal/employment_social_policy_equality/omc_social_inclusion_and_social_protection/overarching).

[2] EU averages (for example, EU-15, EU-25, EU-27) provided in this report are calculated as a population-weighted average of the available national values.

[3] The poverty gap measures the distance between the median equivalised income of people living below the poverty threshold and the value of that poverty threshold; it is expressed as a percentage of the threshold.

[4] The EU Council of Ministers in 1975 defined the poor as 'individuals or families whose resources are so small as to exclude them from the minimal acceptable way of life of the member state where they live'. (European Council conclusions 1975)

[5] For a discussion of poverty rates and related EU indicators, see Maquet-Ensted and Stanton (2010).

[6] The indicator measures the percentage of the population that cannot afford at least three of the nine items quoted above.

[7] Due to the transition from the European Community Household Panel (ECHP) to the EU Statistics on Income and Living Standards (EU-SILC), EU-SILC results should not be compared to ECHP data.

[8] Eurostat released the 2008 data in December 2009.

[9] The prevalence of different household structures in a country, and especially those that are exposed to the greatest risks of poverty (for example, lone-parent households), can depend on the availability of affordable housing (which influences the ability to afford living independently), access to the labour market (and thus to earnings from work), the design of tax and benefit systems (for example, individualised or not), and in particular the level and conditionality of social transfers (in cash or in kind).

[10] By lack of direct access to micro-data, some detailed calculations based on 2006 EU-SILC data from the EU report on child poverty and exclusion could not be updated in the 2009 version of the chapter.

[11] See the chapter of the EU report on child poverty and well-being (European Commission, 2008a) analysing the results of the EU-SILC 2005 module on the intergenerational transmission of disadvantage.

[12] The work intensity of a household is defined here as the amount of work performed by all working-age adults in the household during one year in relation to the total potential amount of work these adults would perform if they were all working full time, and over 12 months of the year. A household with two working-age adults would have a work intensity of 1 if both adults worked full time over the whole year; 0.5 if only one worked and worked full time over the whole year; 0.5 again if both adults worked half time over the whole year, etc. This new

definition differs from the EU agreed definition, since it takes account of the incidence of part-time work. See Tàrki and Applica (2009).

[13] In the analysis presented here pensions are considered part of the 'original' income.

[14] See 'make work pay' analysis including childcare costs components in the 2007 edition of *Benefits and wages,* OECD (2007) and Tàrki and Applica (2009).

[15] Bulgaria and Romania are not included.

References

European Commission (2008a) *Child poverty and well-being in the EU: Current status and way forward,* Luxembourg: Office for Official Publications of the European Communities.

European Commission (2008b) *Joint report on social protection and social inclusion 2008,* Luxembourg: Office for Official Publications of the European Communities.

European Commission (2008c) *Social protection and social inclusion 2008: EU indicators,* Luxembourg: Office for Official Publications of the European Communities.

European Commission (2009a) *Joint report on social protection and social inclusion 2009,* Luxembourg: Office for Official Publications of the European Communities.

European Commission (2009b) *Jobs, growth and social progress: A contribution to the evaluation of the social dimension of the Lisbon Strategy,* Report from the Social Protection Committee adopted in September 2009, Brussels: European Commission.

European Commission (2009c) *Portfolio of indicators for the monitoring of the European Strategy for Social Protection and Social Inclusion, 2009 update,* Brussels: European Commission.

Council of the European Union N°16905/10 (2010) *2010 update of the joint assessment by the Social Protection Committee and the European Commission of the social impact of the economic crisis and of policy responses, Full report.* http://register.consilium.europa.eu/pdf/en/10/st16/st16905.en10.pdf

Guio, A.C. (2009) *What can be learned from deprivation indicators in Europe?,* Eurostat Methodologies and Working Paper 40, Luxembourg: Eurostat.

Maquet-Engsted, I. and Stanton, D. (2010) 'Income indicators for the EU's social inclusion strategy', in Kenneth A. Couch and Douglas J. Besharov (eds), *Counting the poor: New thinking about European poverty measures and lessons for the U.S.*, New York: Oxford University Press.

OECD (Organisation for Economic Co-operation and Development) (2007) *Benefits and wages 2007*, Paris: OECD (www.oecd.org/doc ument/33/0,3746,en_2649_34637_39619553_1_1_1_1,00.html).

OECD (2009) *Doing better for children*, Paris: OECD Publishing.

Tàrki and Applica (2009) *Child poverty and child well-being in the European Union*, Brussels: European Commission.

UNICEF (United Nations Children's Fund) (2005) *Child poverty in rich countries*, Innocenti Report Card No 6, Florence: Innocenti Research Centre.

UNICEF (2007) *Child poverty in perspective:An overview of child well-being in rich countries*, Innocenti Report Card No 7, Florence: Innocenti Research Centre.

Appendix: List of country abbreviations

EU-27   European Union, 27 member states
EU-25   European Union, 25 member states before 1 January 2007 enlargement
AT   Austria
BE   Belgium
BG   Bulgaria
CY   Cyprus
CZ   Czech Republic
DE   Germany
DK   Denmark
EE   Estonia
EL   Greece
ES   Spain
FI   Finland
FR   France
HU   Hungary
IE   Ireland
IT   Italy
LT   Lithuania
LU   Luxembourg
LV   Latvia
MT   Malta
NL   the Netherlands

PL   Poland
PT   Portugal
RO   Romania
SE   Sweden
SI   Slovenia
SK   Slovakia
UK   United Kingdom

Assessing child well-being in developing countries: making policies work for children

Shirley Gatenio Gabel and Sheila B. Kamerman

Child development and child well-being are major concerns in many countries, both developed and developing, and are the subject of ongoing concern at the United Nations Children's Fund (UNICEF) as well as the European Union (EU) and the Organisation of Economic Co-operation and Development (OECD). These concerns have led to a search for policies affecting child and family well-being designed to reduce or alleviate child poverty, deprivation, vulnerability and the risk factors that can trigger a lifelong cycle of disadvantage.

The lack of systematic and comparative data on policies affecting children in developing countries and related outcome measures has repeatedly been noted as an obstacle in the further development of policies to promote child well-being (UNICEF, 1998, 2008; Kamerman and Gatenio Gabel, 2007; Save the Children UK, 2008). A prior effort focused on the OECD countries (Kamerman et al, 2003).

This chapter focuses primarily on developing countries and summarises the availability of data on both policies and outcomes measuring child well-being. We begin with a brief discussion of the history, definition and purposes of childhood social indicators in the US and internationally. Following this we present a preliminary child policy paradigm for developing countries. We use this paradigm to organise our explorations of global databases on child policies and policy outcomes. We then assess the strengths and weaknesses of available data for comparative analysis of child policies and outcomes. Finally we conclude with a brief description of current challenges and future needs for international indicators of child-conditioned policies and outcomes.

The purpose of this overall effort is to better understand the well-being of children in developing countries and the effects of social policies in these countries on reducing income poverty and improving child well-being.

The interest in children's well-being indicators stems, in part, from a movement towards accountability-based public policy that required more accurate measures of the conditions children face and the outcomes of various programmes designed to address those conditions (Ben-Arieh and Frones, 2007). Rapid changes in family life also prompted an increased demand from child development professionals, social scientists and the public for a better picture of children's well-being. Ben-Arieh and Frones further argue (2007) that in addition to the growing policy demands for accountability, the growth in what has become the child indicators movement can be attributed to the emergence of new normative and conceptual theories as well as methodological advancements. The normative concepts of children's rights (for example, acting in the best interests of the child), the sociological conceptualisation of childhood as an independent stage (Qvortrup, 1994) and ecological theories of child development have contributed to the evolution of the child indicators. Similarly, the three methodological issues that facilitated the popularity of child indicators were the emerging importance of the subjective perspective; the child as the unit of observation; and the expanded use of administrative data and the growing variety of data sources.

During the 1970s there was a sustained effort in the US to develop a comprehensive system of social indicator measures, including child and family indicators. At the forefront of this effort was the Social Science Research Council's Center for Coordination of Research on Social Indicators. The primary purpose of the Center was to show the potential for indicators to increase understanding of the dynamics of social change (Watts and Hernandez, 1982). The devolution of social programmes in the US and simultaneous reduction in the funding of social science research beginning in the 1980s are believed to have sustained interest in social indicators. Beginning in the 1970s in the US, despite the lack of government support, private foundations (Carnegie Foundation, Charles Stewart Mott, Foundation for Child Development, The Annie E. Casey Foundation) funded the work of organisations such as Child Trends, and individuals such as Nicholas Zill, Trude Lash, Alfred J. Kahn, Sheila B. Kamerman and Kristin Moore.

In the early 1990s, interest in indicators measuring child well-being increased exponentially. The Annie E. Casey Foundation initiated the annual publication of *Kids Count*, a national statistical portrait of children in the US. Soon after, Kids Count reports were published in each of the states. Several organisations such as Child Trends, the Institute for Research and Poverty, the National Institute for Child and Health Development, the Office of the Assistant Secretary for Planning and Evaluation, the Administration for Children and Families in the US Department of Health and Human Services, the Board at the National Academy of Sciences, Chapin Hall at the University of Chicago, University of California at Berkeley and the Joint Center on Poverty at Chicago/Northwestern, among others, took a leadership role in promoting the use and development of childhood indicators.

As a result of their efforts, the Office of the Assistant Secretary for Planning and Evaluation annually publishes *Trends in the well-being of America's children and youth*. In addition, a Federal Interagency Forum on Children and Family Statistics was founded in 1994 to better coordinate, collaborate and integrate federal data collection efforts among 22 federal government agencies on children's well-being (www.childstats.gov). Since 1998, the Forum has published *America's children: Key national indicators of well-being,* which summarises trends in child well-being.

During the 1990s, interest in child indicators in the US grew at the state level as well. An increasing number of states became interested in social indicators as basic tools of governance, and initiated the systematic use and monitoring of social indicators (for example, individual state Kids Count).

The interest in tracking child well-being has likewise grown among other industrialised countries. The formation of the European Union (EU) motivated the increased attention to harmonising social and economic indicators across member countries and for surveying the public policies of member countries. There has been a major effort in industrialised countries to develop statistical surveys and to generate indicators that represent the multifaceted dimensions of social and child well-being. Beginning in 1981, the OECD published its annual report on *Society at a glance*, providing child well-being indicators beginning at the turn of the century, followed by the establishment of a Family Database in 2006. The online Family Database was created in response to the strong interest in cross-national indicators on the situation of children and families in OECD countries. The database includes indicators on child and family well-being as well as indicators of child and family policies in OECD countries.

Across the globe, interest is growing in developing social indicators on child well-being. UNICEF's *State of the World's Children* report, first published in 1980, is a world-renowned source. The UN Convention on the Rights of the Child (UNCRC) provides a normative framework for understanding children's well-being. Its articles support non-discriminatory practices (Article 2), promote the best interest of the child (Article 3), holistically conceptualise the multidimensional civic, political, social, economic and cultural rights of children (Article 6), and acknowledge the view of the child to be heard and considered with regard to decisions affecting them (Article 12) (Bradshaw, 2006).

The effects of the UNCRC in ushering childhood indicators was most profound in the developing world but also had an effect among industrialised countries as well. The UNICEF Innocenti Research Centre publishes a Report Card on the well-being of children in rich countries. Recognising that well-being was more than income, Jonathan Bradshaw, together with UNICEF's Innocenti Research Centre, recently developed a composite index of child well-being in industrialised countries based on seven dimensions of child well-being: material well-being, health and safety, education, peer and family relationships, subjective well-being, and behaviour and risk (Bradshaw et al, 2007; UNICEF, 2007).

Among developing countries, efforts have been made to record progress or the lack of regularly collected data. Since 1980, UNICEF's annual *State of the World's Children* report summarises the living conditions and challenges confronting children around the world using available statistics and research. It is a benchmark of childhood indicators and a measure of the effectiveness of policy initiatives that have been implemented. Available statistics are reported annually on infant and child mortality, life expectancy, average income, school enrollment, nutrition; health such as immunisations and availability of medication; HIV/AIDS; demographic and economic indicators; the status of women; child protection; and the rate of progress. Save the Children UK recently introduced the Child Development Index (Save the Children UK, 2008). The index spans across over 140 developed and developing countries and is a multidimensional tool to monitor and compare the well-being of children. It is made up of three indicators of three areas of child well-being: health (as measured by the under-five mortality rate); nutrition (the percentage of under-fives who are moderately or severely underweight); and education (measured as the percentage of primary school-age children who are not enrolled in school). This index is periodically collected.

UNICEF's current Global Study on Child Poverty and Disparities intends to find context-specific evidence to assess policy responsiveness to outcomes related to child poverty by conducting analyses of disparities in nutrition, health, education and child and social protection in over 40 developing countries. This study should yield comparable information on policies affecting children and their effectiveness (UNICEF, 2007).

The UNCRC has not only set a normative standard across the globe but it has resulted in a change in how policy making is made within many countries. The UNCRC and the subsequent increased multi-source funding for child-related services and benefits particularly in developing countries has opened the nexus of policy making from within largely segregated nation states to an increasingly globalised policy-making environment. A new child-centred focus on a normative framework of childhood as a period of nurturance, opportunity and protection has emerged in an effort to create and carry out the UNCRC.

From this emerged a research-related community that spurned new conceptualisations of child-related social issues and policy interventions, and expanded the number of actors influencing policy making and knowledge of child-related policies beyond national borders (see Figure 10.1). This international community of child policy experts (who were largely from industrialised countries) allowed for new ideas to circulate from societies to governments as well as from country to country. Haas refers to this as an 'epistemic community', that is, a network of knowledge-based experts or groups with an authoritative claim to policy-relevant knowledge within the domain of their expertise (Haas, 1992). Members of an epistemic community hold a common set of causal beliefs and share notions of validity based on

Figure 10.1: Epistemic community for child policies in developing countries

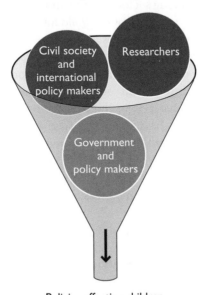

Policies affecting children

internally defined criteria for evaluation, common policy projects and shared normative commitments. An epistemic community enhances the role of research across national borders by providing conceptual frameworks and technical assistance for country responses to social issues to policy makers. The danger, of course, is that the ideology and knowledge of an epistemic community can dominate and dismiss locally based understanding and responses to social issues.

The epistemic community on child policies spurned increased research into the lives of children across the globe and with this has come the need for regularly collected, reliable and comparative indicators of children's lives. These indicators are used to both assess the situation of children and for comparative assessments, as well as to evaluate the impact of policies on children's lives. Since policy making for children is increasingly transnational, the relevance of comparative research has not only increased but has widened.

The increasingly transnational nature of policy making has led to increased donor interventions as well, and with this a need to monitor and evaluate the effects of such interventions. Donors are increasingly concerned with interventions that have medium- and long-term impacts and in adopting systematic approaches through the promotion of policy reforms, the development of physical and institutional capacity and increased effectiveness of programmes. These outcomes are achieved sometimes by targeting programmes to specific population groups (Gnanathurai, 2002). To accomplish this, donors are interested in refining and sharpening socioeconomic indicators directly related to the goals of the interventions that can yield information on the success and failures of previous experiences. Today's discourse on child policies has also shifted from a singular focus on children and basic services to a broader concern with children and macroeconomic policies.

As knowledge about child policies has increasingly become transnational, so has advocacy on child-related issues. The proliferation of translational advocacy has provided alternative sources of information on child-related issues and has helped to reframe issues and transmit new knowledge. The power of information has reinforced calls for evidence-based policies and for reliable social indicators to be used both in research and as outcome measures for policy initiatives.

Definitions and purpose

R.A. Bauer was among the first to use the term 'social indicators'. In his book of the same title, he defines social indicators as the 'statistics, statistical series, and all other forms of evidence ... that enable us to assess where we stand and are going with respect to our values and goals' (Bauer, 1966, p 1). Recently, Corbett defined an indicator 'as a measure of some phenomenon or attribute that taps something of importance to society' (Corbett, 2008, page 334). Those social indicators that are specific to children and highlight the situation and living conditions of children are called childhood social indicators. These are quantitative measures of child well-being.

Moore and Brown note that these statistical markers can be used to: (1) track trends and patterns, and to identify areas of concern as well as positive outcomes; (2) monitor how well we are doing by tracking outcomes that may or may not require policy intervention of some kind; (3) set goals that reflect societal values and establish quantifiable thresholds to be met within specific time periods; (4) increase accountability for policies and programmes; and finally (5) inform practices in a given community or programme (Moore and Brown, 2003).

Policies are often pluralistic in purpose and additionally carry unintended consequences. Corbett defines *outcomes* as the 'numerical measures of behaviours or events that are generally believed to be as a result of a policy or program of interest. Outcomes typically are positive and relate to goals that the program or policy hopes to achieve. Some actual outcomes may be unanticipated, negative, or undesired' (2008, p 339). Outcome data are unlikely to be collected as part of experimental design methods, and although causality is often suggested, it is not always plausible to conclude that policies or reforms have shaped outcome variables. The range in outcomes may or may not be attributed to design, implementation or administrative differences but can also be affected by the differences in outcome measurements.

According to Ben-Arieh (2008), the childhood social indicator field is clearly growing. Between 2000 and 2005 twice as many *State of the World's Children* reports were published than in the entire decade of the 1980s (Ben-Arieh, 2006). Ben-Arieh suggests that while this movement may be peaking in the West, the growth is likely to continue in non-Western and non-English-speaking countries, where publication of national state of the child reports is relatively new.

Our interest in this chapter was to explore the existence of indicators available to capture policy initiatives related to children across countries and to simultaneously assess the availability of data and its regularity on outcome measures related to child policies. Most of the existing data sources focus on indicators of children's well-being, and we argue here that increased knowledge is also needed on the existence of social policies affecting children and their families.

A preliminary paradigm for child policies and outcomes in developing countries

Drawing on the literature (Miringoff et al, 1999; Gaynor and Watson, 2007; Gran, 2007; Hagerty and Land, 2007; Land et al, 2007; European Commission, 2008; UNICEF, 2008) on indicators of child policies and on child well-being, we highlighted five dimensions as being particularly critical: health, family economic well-being, education, child welfare and children's rights. For each of these dimensions, we developed measures of child-conditioned policies and related child outcomes. The choice of these indicators was influenced by the availability and comparative usefulness of this data. For example, indicators of family composition, housing and family work schedules in developing countries, while being important, was difficult to locate during our preliminary search and was not included. We carried out internet-based and literature-based searches for databases on social indicators and child well-being, as well as social policy databases. The databases including indicators of child policies and outcomes used in our preliminary paradigm is listed in Table 10.1.

Findings

In the last two decades there has been tremendous growth in the development and use of social indicators measuring the well-being of children. The *State of the World's Children* report, once a pioneering document, is now a staple for those interested in measuring the well-being of children across nations. Likewise, in industrialised countries, the Innocenti Research Centre's Report Card series focuses on the well-being of children in industrialised countries. Each Report Card includes a league table ranking OECD countries according to their record on the subject under discussion. The Report Cards are published every six months and are used to advocate for policy changes affecting children in every country (UNICEF Innocenti Research Centre, 2008). The adoption of the Millennium Development Goals (MDGs) and the need to use indicators to measure progress in the implementation of the MDGs has fuelled further interest, creating comparative policy and outcome measures that are particularly scarce in developing countries. Most recently, the UNICEF Global Study of Child Poverty and Disparities promises to provide new data on the existence of child policies and outcomes in over 50 countries.

Our survey of global policies and related outcome measures affecting children revealed expected and unexpected findings. Most apparent

Table 10.1: A paradigm for child policies and outcomes in developing countries

Policies	Outcomes
Health	
Immunisation programme	Infant mortality rate
Nutrition programmes	Low birth weight
Healthcare services	Child mortality rate
Programmes for children affected by	Maternal health
HIV/AIDS	Malnutrition
Birth registration	Obesity
Family economic well-being	
Family allowances	Child poverty rate
Conditional cash transfers	Deprivations assessment
Other child-conditioned cash transfers	
Tax benefits	
Maternal/parental leaves and benefits	
Birth grants	
Education	
Early childhood education and care	% of preschool-aged children enrolled in early
programmes	childhood education and care programmes
Compulsory primary education	% of school-aged children enrolled in primary
	education
	% of school related costs that are borne by
	parents
Child protection	
Out-of-home care	% of children living in institutions
Institutional vs community care	Rate of childhood injuries
Programmes for street children	Violence against children
Home-based services	
Child rights (statutory)	
Civil	% of children in labour force
Freedom to practice religion	% of children performing hazardous work
Freedom from imprisonment with adults	% of children imprisoned
Social	% of children enrolled in school
Right to education	% of registered births
Right to healthcare	
Economic	
Freedom from hazardous work	
Freedom from economic exploitation	

are the gaps in data regarding child-conditioned policies beyond the industrialised countries. This was anticipated, but what was surprising was the potential for filling these gaps. In the areas of health, education and child protection there is potential for developing a global, child-conditioned policy database from existing data, drawn largely from country reports and/or other primary sources, yet the frequency of the data collection is irregular. In most countries data is available on child immunisations and immunisation schedules, disease, malnutrition, HIV/AIDS policies and services. The majority of the data to be used for child policy indicators is not collected annually so it is more likely that reports could only be generated periodically rather than annually.

Spending on education programmes for and the enrolment of pre-primary and primary age school children is documented in a number of sources. This information is often available by gender and is collected more frequently and regularly. Information on mandatory school age, and on parental fees and costs, is less accessible.

With regard to the area of family economic well-being, the findings are mixed. There is considerable data on policies affecting the well-being of children and families in industrialised and near industrialised countries. The primary databases are OECD and MISSOC I and II (Mutual Information System on Social Protection) (which extends into Central and Eastern European countries) (see the Appendix at the end of this chapter). The Social Security Worldwide Database does have information regarding child/family allowances, maternal and parental leaves and grants and birth grants for 170 countries, but it does not have data on newer policy regimes or on social assistance programmes that also affect the well-being of children. There was no international database identified thus far that included comparative information on conditional cash transfers; this information would need to come directly from national reports.

Like economic well-being, data for policies reflecting children's rights needs to be retrieved from country reports available from the International Labour Organization (ILO), UN Educational, Scientific and Cultural Organisation (UNESCO) and the Child Rights Information Network (CRIN). This is the area that would have the least information available from an aggregated database covering multiple countries.

Data to measure changes in policy outcomes is more available for almost all of the indicators. For child-conditioned health policy outcomes, the World Health Organization (WHO), World Development Indicators (WDI), the Global Fund and the UN Joint Programme for HIV/AIDS (UNAIDS) are the main sources of information, supplemented by data from the Demographic and Health Survey, OECD, Multiple Indicator Cluster Survey and the UN Development Programme (UNDP). For policy outcomes of family economic well-being, no database includes measurements of poverty rates for families with children. Several data sources compiled global child poverty rates (such as the OECD Family Database, WDI, UNDP Human Development Report Statistics), although the definitions of child poverty varied across datasets. Information on global education policy outcomes are well established. Policy outcomes for child protection appears to be available from several sources although the extent and depth of this information across countries needs to be explored further.

Discussion

The growth in international child indicators is unprecedented and continuing. Unlike earlier indicators of child well-being that focused on child survival and negative outcomes, today's indicators of child well-being have broadened to include positive outcomes and on 'well-becoming' (indicators en route to well-being) (Ben-Arieh and Frones, 2007). Although this is a global trend, developing countries continue to be more likely to focus on indicators on survival, while industrialised countries are increasingly inclusive of more positive indicators. Current indicators of child well-being are also more likely to be based on the child as the unit of analysis and to include the child's perspective, not just adult views of what is important. Child well-being indicators are also more likely to be based on and driven by the UNCRC.

A search for global child indicators going back at least 20 years shows that regional, national and local reporting was significantly less regular and less likely to have occurred on local and regional levels. This trend is far more prominent among industrialised countries, but increasingly relevant to developing countries. Among industrialised countries, there are multiple sources of policy information that are lacking across developing countries.

Across all child-conditioned policies and outcomes, the comparability of the data needs to be explored in more depth. As noted by a recent Innocenti report, 'Cross-country surveys on children can become more readily complementary if there is greater synchronicity in contextual variables between the different datasets and efforts to reach younger children, while many household surveys can become more suited to child research (and policy development) with some additions and modifications made to existing modules' (UNICEF Innocenti Research Centre, 2008).

To strengthen the global compatibility of data on children's policies and outcomes from nationally representative survey datasets, there should be further exploration of existing micro survey instruments in both developing and industrialised countries. To ensure reliability of measures monitoring child well-being, multiple sources should be pursued including administrative data derived from vital registration systems, household surveys, censuses and specialised child surveys. This will allow for a more comprehensive analysis of well-being and potentially stimulate national and international debates and policy responses that are in the best interests of children.

In this regard, it is important not only to search for country-specific policy statements and laws that effect children, but also measures that monitor the implementation and enforcement of the policies and laws. The UNCRC is a good example of this. Of the 192 countries that have adapted the UNCRC, most countries are far from realising its full implementation (CRIN). The implementation and monitoring of MDGs is a good example of how policy implementation can be done. If we can identify and understand the legal, social, financial and other obstacles preventing the full implementation of policies, we are more likely to design ways and means to overcome these obstacles.

There remain many measures of child well-being that have not been developed globally or are in early stages. For example, indicators of childhood trauma, children's mental health and the social exclusion of children in developing countries are only recently being explored. Compared to surveys on late childhood, there is also relatively little survey and time series data on early childhood (under the age of six).

Numerous efforts are currently underway to develop composite indicators of child well-being at all geographic levels (local, national and international). Included should be an index of child policy-oriented efforts and outcomes, which we hope to further explore.

At a time when there is interest in developing international indicators of policies affecting children and their well-being, it is important that we do not squander the opportunities presented. Increasingly, there is a higher expectation of accountability from all types of funders and policy makers, whether it be government or private or otherwise. It is important for decision makers to understand the unique features of policy instruments and the environments in which they work most effectively. Indicators of child-conditioned policies and outcomes need contextual information about the socioeconomic and political environment of children to assess their potential and effectiveness. Our measures of policies and policy outcomes are critical in relaying information to policy makers and in developing these indicators that we remind ourselves of the multiple purposes they may serve. As Corbett reminds us, 'Just because something can be measured does not mean it would be a good social indicator' (Corbett, 2008, p 341).

We end with a list of the characteristics of good social indicators that was originally constructed by Kristin Moore, the former director of Child Trends (1997), and since modified by Corbett (2008):

- Indicators should assess well-being across a broad array of outcomes, behaviour and processes.
- Indicators should be clear and comprehensible.

- Indicators should be both positive and negative.
- Indicators should have a common interpretation across different groups and subgroups, jurisdictions and over time.
- Indicators should be forward-looking and predictive.
- Indicators should be subject to rigorous methods. The population covered should be complete or very high, and data collection methods should be of high quality and consistent over time.
- Indicators should have depth, breadth and duration.
- Indicators should be developed at different geographic levels and cover populations of interest.
- Selected indicators should be cost-efficient and feasible.
- Indicators should be reflective of broader social goals.

References

Bauer, R.A. (1966) *Social indicators*, Cambridge, MA: The MIT Press.

Ben-Arieh, A. (2006) 'Is the study of the "*State of our children*" changing? Revisiting after five years', *Children and Youth Service Review*, vol 28/7, pp 799-811.

Ben-Arieh, A. (2008) 'The child indicators movement: past, present and future', *Child Indicators Research Journal*, 1, 3-16.

Ben-Arieh, A. and Frones, I. (2007) 'Indicators of children's well being: theory, types and usage', *Social Indicators Research*, vol 83, no 1, pp 1-4.

Bradshaw, J. (2006) 'A rights based multi-dimensional understanding of child well-being in the EU', Tools for Measuring the Well-being of Children, Proceedings of the Seminar held in Rome, 20 March, MedChild Paper No 4, Genoa: MedChild Institute, pp 41-9.

Bradshaw, J., Hoelscher, P. and Richardson, D. (2007) 'An index of child well-being in the European Union', *Social Indicators Research*, vol 80, no 1, pp 133-77.

Corbett, T.J. (2008) 'Social indicators as a policy tool: welfare reform as a case study', in B. Brown (ed) *Key Indicators of child and youth well-being: Completing the picture*, New York: Lawrence Erlbaum Associates.

European Commission (2008) *Child poverty and well-being in the EU: Current status and way forward*, Luxembourg: Office for Official Publications of the European Communities.

Gaynor, C. and Watson, S. (2007) *Evaluating DFID's policy on tackling social exclusion: Baseline, framework and indicators*, Evaluation Working Paper 22, London: DFID.

Gnanathurai, V.N. (2002) 'Building statistical capacities for improving the measurement and monitoring of development and aid effectiveness in ADB's developing member countries', Paper presented at the Asian

Development Bank Roundtable on Better Measuring, Monitoring and Managing for Development Results, Washington, DC.

Gran, B. (2007) 'Do children's rights improve children's welfare?', Paper presented at the 2007 Annual Meeting of the ISA Research Committee 19 on Poverty, Social Welfare and Social Policy, University of Florence, 6 September 6.

Haas, P. (1992) 'Knowledge, power, and international policy coordination', *International Organization*, vol 46, no 1, Winter, pp 1-35.

Hagerty, M.R. and Land, K.C. (2007) 'Constructing summary indices of quality of life: a model for the effect of heterogeneous importance weights', *Sociological Methods and Research*, vol 35, May, pp 455-96.

Kamerman, S. B. and Gatenio Gabel, S. (2007). Social protection for children in low and middle–income countries in Asia. *Malaysian Journal of Human Rights*, vol. 1, July.

Kamerman, S. B., Neuman, M., Waldfogel, J. and Brooks-Gunn, J. (2003). Social policies, family types and child outcomes in selected OECD countries. Working paper. Paris: OECD.

Land, K.C., Lamb, V.L., Meadows, S.O. and Taylor, A. (2007) 'Measuring trends in child well-being: an evidence-based approach', *Social Indicators Research*, vol 80, pp 105-32.

Miringoff, M.L., Miringoff, M.-L. and Opdycke, S. (1999) *The social health of the nation: How America is really doing*, New York: Oxford University Press.

Moore, K. (1997) 'Criteria for indicators of child well-being', in R. Hauser, B. Brown and W. Hauser (eds) *Indicators of children's well-being*, New York: Russell Sage Foundation, pp 36-44.

Moore, K. and Brown, B. with H. Scarupa (2003) *The uses (and misuses) of social indicators: Implications for public policy*, Washington, DC: Child Trends Research Brief, 2003-01.

Qvortrup, J. (1994) 'Childhood matters: an introduction', in J. Qvortrup et al (eds) *Childhood matters: Social theory, practice and politics*, Brookfield, VT: Avebury, pp 1-24.

Save the Children UK (2008) *The Child Development Index: Holding governments to account for children's well-being*, London: Save the Children.

UNICEF (United Nations Children's Fund) (1998) *Indicators for global monitoring of child rights*, Summary Report, New York: Division of Evaluation, Policy and Planning.

UNICEF Innocenti Research Centre (2008) *Child poverty in perspective: An overview of child well-being in rich countries*, Innocenti Report Card No 7, Florence: UNICEF.

UNICEF (2007) *Global Study on Child Poverty and Disparities 2007-2008 Guide*, New York: UNICEF.

Watts, H.W. and Hernandez, D.J. (eds) (1982) *Child and family indicators: A report with recommendations*, New York: Social Service Research Council.

Table 10A.1: Databases

OECD Family Database	www.oecd.org/els/social/family/database
MISSOC I and II	http://ec.europa.eu/social/main. jsp?catId=815&langId=en http://ec.europa.eu/employment_social/social_ protection/missceec_en.htm
Social Security Worldwide	www.issa.int/Observatory/Country-Profiles
World Development Indicators (WDI)	http://data.worldbank.org/data-catalog/world-development-indicators
Luxembourg Income Study (LIS)	www.lisproject.org/
Statistical Information and Monitoring Programme on Child Labour (SIMPOC)	www.ilo.org/ipec/ChildlabourstatisticsSIMPOC/ lang--en/
Human Development Report	http://hdr.undp.org/en/statistics/data/
World Education Indicators (WEI)	www.uis.unesco.org/
OECD Education Database	www.oecd.org/document/54/0,3746, en_2649_37455_38082166_1_1_1_37455,00.html
International Society for Prevention of Child Abuse and Neglect (ISPCAN)	www.ispcan.org/resource/resmgr/world.../world_ persp_2008_-_final.pdf
Multiple Indicator Cluster Survey	www.unicef.org/statistics/index_24302.html
Demographic and Health Survey	www.measuredhs.com/

PART 3

Multidimensional child poverty in Tanzania: analysis of situation, changes and sensitivity of thresholds[1]

Alberto Minujin and Enrique Delamonica

Introduction

Traditionally, since before independence, Tanzania has been an egalitarian society.[2] However, economic stagnation, the debt crisis of the 1980s and the ensuing adjustment policies period have proved detrimental to equity. The economic recovery enjoyed by Tanzania in the last few years has not resulted in a significant reduction of income poverty nationwide.[3]

While there has been progress in some social indicators (for example, child malnutrition, education, under-five mortality), progress has been unconscionably slow for many dimensions of well-being. These observations call for a deeper analysis of the characteristics of poverty and disparities, moving beyond income poverty and income distribution. Thus, this chapter approaches the issue from the perspective of child poverty and its characteristics. Using a multidimensional approach, the analysis is centred on the depth and severity of child poverty and on the changes between 1999 and 2004/05.

The chapter begins with a presentation of the methodology to analyse child poverty. This is followed by an analysis of the extent of child poverty in 2004/05 and its various dimensions and characteristics, including depth and severity. Changes in child poverty between 1999 and 2004/05 are then explored before presenting sensitivity analyses, including the exploration of alternative thresholds to determine child poverty. Finally, some preliminary conclusions are offered.

Methodological considerations

Poverty measurement

The different approaches to poverty measurement can be roughly classified in two groups: simple (unidimensional) measures and multidimensional ones.[4] The monetary approach is the typical unidimensional approach and it is the most widely used by analysts and development agencies (Boltvinik, 1998). This approach relies on the level of income (or consumption) of households (or individuals) to measure poverty and to identify who counts as 'poor'.[5] Once the percentage of the population whose income falls short of the poverty line[6] is established, the depth and the severity of poverty can be measured.

The unidimensional, monetary approach to the poverty line, however, suffers from several shortcomings. These include, among others, the fact that despite the best efforts to establish a set of goods and services that constitute the poverty line in a scientific way, there is always a level of arbitrariness in setting the value or threshold of the poverty line. In addition, the composition of the 'consumption basket' often varies within regions of a country (for example, the food, shelter and clothing requirements in a tropical coast area are different from those in a dry and high altitude plateau), and reconciling these differences with a consistently applicable poverty threshold is often very complex. Finally, there may be important sources of welfare that are not traded in the market and thus establishing monetary value is problematic. Even if families have the money to 'purchase' these items, they often cannot since the goods may not be available.

In contrast to the money metric approach, the typical multidimensional approach to poverty, usually referred to as 'basic needs', directly assesses the household or individual's actual conditions in a select group of material deprivations (ILO, 1976; Streeten et al, 1981; Streeten, 1984; Beccaria and Minujin, 1988). It is important to highlight that the list of basic needs should not be very extensive, since it becomes difficult to handle, interpret and correlate with other problems. Also, in order to assess poverty, the deprivation should be of goods and services, not of other (undoubtedly important) aspects of life in which individuals could be deprived (for example, happiness, love, family ties or voting rights). Finally, material deprivations can be measured directly. As a result, families or individuals could enjoy them even if their income is below the poverty line (for example, if the state provides the services, as in the case of free schooling or healthcare).

Besides being conceptually clearer and measuring directly the satisfaction of needs and not the hypothetical capacity to purchase items with which to satisfy them, this approach is less demanding. It is also based firmly on international agreements such as the World Summit for Social Development held in Copenhagen in 1995. The information and recall (by interviewees) requirements are substantially less than in the monetary approach. A variant of this approach was used to estimate child poverty in Tanzania and is discussed in this chapter.

The utilisation of a rights deprivation/basic needs approach raises some issues about the possibility of finding different estimates of child poverty depending on the definitions of the thresholds which determine if a child is classified as deprived (the basic need being unsatisfied) or not. Thus, in a later section, sensitivity analysis is carried out to explore what happens with the estimate of child poverty when different thresholds are used. Basically two possibilities exist: the estimates do or do not change much. In the former case, we have a robust measure of child poverty. In the latter, the situation may imply the estimate is not very solid and quite arbitrary. This assumes that the question being asked is 'which is the right and which is the wrong estimate?' This, however, is the wrong question to ask.

In the monetary approach, of course, changing the poverty line yields a different estimate (for example, indigence, extreme poverty or poverty). This does not invalidate the approach. Rather it requires carefully asking the question about what these different measures mean. If the estimates vary significantly, it means that large parts of the population have incomes that are concentrated near the values of these poverty lines. Similarly, if changing the thresholds to determine deprivation when estimating child poverty results in different estimates, it means that many children are living very close to the level of deprivation. By changing the threshold of various dimensions of poverty the analysis may yield further information regarding who and where poor children with various degrees of deprivation are, and this evidence can be useful for policy makers.

Methodology used for estimating child poverty in Tanzania

The approach used here is a variant of the basic needs approach to poverty measurement. Unless otherwise stated, child poverty refers to a deprivations-based measurement in the rest of the chapter. This is a widely accepted methodology in the study of poverty in general, which has also been successfully applied in the first ever measurement of child poverty in developing countries (Gordon et al, 2003). This approach has been used by UNICEF in its Global Study of Child Poverty and Disparity (see Chapter Twenty-one of this volume).

Several reasons could be found for this choice (Vandemoortele, 2000; Feeny and Boyden, 2003; Minujin, 2005). First, an income-based estimate of child poverty would basically rely on assuming that children actually receive a fair share of the household income. This approach would face intractable issues of deciding how to establish or measure such a share.[7] From a practical point of view it would require breaking down household expenditures by each household member, a daunting – if not impossible – task. This could at best only be an indirect approach to child poverty. It would not measure whether children actually receive that share.

Second, increases in household income that could be perceived as reducing child poverty could actually be detrimental to child well-being. The typical case here is the occurrence of child labour. Sending a young child out to work may well increase the family income, and thus reduce child poverty (measured through the income approach), but it would be a violation of the child's rights and reduce his/her well-being.

Furthermore, the monetary approach neglects to note that children's well-being also depends on non-market-based goods. Access to basic services and a safe environment for play is generally more dependent on the level of public provision than on household income. Thus, individual families cannot purchase these goods for their children, even if they have sufficient income.

Lastly, a more comprehensive picture of child poverty is arrived at if a set of carefully selected indicators of material deprivation is measured for each child separately. Then, for each individual child, these various dimensions of deprivation are combined to provide a holistic view of child poverty. This results in a direct measure of the actual situation of children.

Households (or the children therein) are considered living in poverty depending on insufficient access to each of seven elements representing various rights of children: health, education, shelter, water, sanitation, nutrition and information (see Appendix 1 on the definitions and Appendix 2 on method at the end of this chapter).

When dealing with the measurement of deprivation, it is necessary to define: (a) thresholds for the indicators, that is, the cut-off point or level of an indicator below which the child is considered deprived, and (b) the number of indicators that determine deprivation.

For a given indicator, the degree or intensity of its satisfaction will result in whether a child is classified as not enjoying this good or right. For instance, in education, lack of schooling could be determined by fewer than two years of attendance in a formal school, or fewer than four years, or not having completed primary schooling, or not having completed secondary level. Thus, a (relatively arbitrary) threshold needs to be established in order to measure poverty. In other words, there is a continuum from no deprivation to extreme deprivation (absolute absence). Gordon et al (2003) used very strict measures of severe deprivation for each of the seven indicators as their intent was to err on the side of caution. Using such strict and restrictive thresholds to reflect severe deprivation prevents a critique based on the argument that the ensuing estimates of the number of children living in poverty is inflated.

Nevertheless, thresholds could be adapted to a country's characteristics and conditions and also range from extreme deprivation to moderate (see, for example, UNICEF Mozambique, 2006). In order to maintain comparability with other countries, the thresholds used to assess child poverty in Tanzania are described in Appendix 1, although to test the sensitivity of the indicators and the approach, some alternative thresholds were explored, not least to make the measures more relevant to the Tanzanian context.

Second, given that seven indicators are used simultaneously, it is necessary to establish how many deprivations will result in a child being considered 'poor'. Given that UNICEF, based on the idea that rights are indivisible, considers deprivations of any basic needs to be violations of children's rights, we consider the experience of deprivation of one basic need as sufficient to classify a child as poor.[8,9] Note, however, that it is always possible to analyse the different number of deprivations experienced by children when examining the depth and severity of their poverty.[10]

Child poverty

What is the situation of child poverty in Tanzania?

A first step is to provide a comprehensive yet simple 'picture' of child poverty in Tanzania by incorporating various dimensions of the social conditions in which children grow up and develop. Table 11.1 shows the proportion of children suffering one or more severe deprivations in Tanzania in 2004/05, according to the deprivations measure

Table 11.1: Child poverty in Tanzania, 2004/05 (% of children)

Tanzania	87.8
All rural	96.0
All urban	57.7
Dar es Salaam	41.3
Mainland	87.8
Zanzibar	62.8

Source: Own calculations based on Democratic and Health Survey 2004/05 data

described in the previous section. The information, extracted from the Demographic and Health Survey, is also disaggregated for urban and rural residence as well as between Zanzibar and the Mainland.[11]

Two conclusions clearly emerge from this table. First, *the level of child poverty is very high, over 80%.* With a population of about 46 million, of which children are roughly half, this figure results in around 22 million poor children.[12] Second, *child poverty is primarily a rural problem.* In Tanzania, most families and children (about 75%) live in rural areas.

It is interesting to contrast these results with income poverty estimates. According to the *Poverty and Human Development Report* (UNDP and GoT, 2005), in 2000, the incidence of income poverty was about 36 per cent.[13] This is considerably less than the estimates of child poverty presented in Table 11.1. This attests to the need to measure child poverty directly. Moreover, measuring child poverty directly is less data demanding and, consequently, can be measured more regularly than monetary poverty, thereby improving monitoring.

The approach described in the previous section indicates that the total level of child poverty can also be disaggregated along each of the seven dimensions and geographically. Figure 11.1 shows separately the level of severe deprivation in each dimension of child poverty. The public policy areas (for example, water) are highlighted where most progress is needed. For instance, children in Tanzania do better than the rest of Sub-Saharan African children in terms of nutrition, health and education, but fare worse in terms of access to information. Nevertheless, the total incidence of child poverty is similar to the rest of Sub-Saharan Africa but below the rest of developing countries.

Figure 11.1: Child deprivation in each of the seven dimensions of child poverty, 2004/05

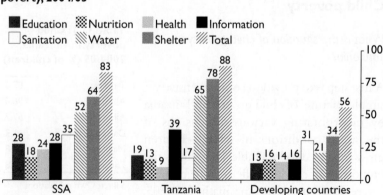

Source: Own calculations based on Demographic and Health Survey 2004/05 data

Figure 11.1 also shows the wide range of differences across the various dimensions of child poverty. While 'only' 8.8 per cent of children in Tanzania are health deprived, shelter deprivation affects almost 80% of them. While it is obvious that the overall results (87.8% of children are considered poor) are strongly influenced by shelter deprivation, the relatively low numbers for health and nutrition deprivation should not be a source of comfort. They refer, as explained in the previous section, to very severe levels of deprivation.

It is important to know how estimates of child poverty would change if a more moderate definition of deprivation were used. Two examples of what is usually called sensitivity analysis can help underscore this point. For instance, severe health deprivation is defined as children having no immunisations whatsoever. This is clearly a very stringent threshold. It could be relaxed by saying that if children have three doses of DPT (diphtheria, pertussis and tetanus), they should be considered 'only' moderately deprived. Similarly, if they have received all but one vaccine, they could be considered mildly deprived, and if they have all of their prescribed immunisations, they are not deprived at all. In this case, health deprivation would jump from 8.8% to 14.1% (moderate deprivation), almost double the level of severe deprivation.

Similarly, nutrition deprivation refers to three standard deviations from the international norm. The usually reported figures refer to moderate malnutrition, which entails 'only' two standard deviations from the international norm. In this case, nutrition deprivation would be 37.7% instead of 13.2%. Nevertheless, social infrastructure (that is, shelter and water) deprivation would still be the main sources of child poverty in Tanzania. This type of sensitivity analysis is carried out further later in this chapter.

Depth and severity of child poverty

While the discussion so far has concentrated on the percentage of children suffering from at least one deprivation, which is conceptually similar to the idea of a poverty headcount, it is well known that this measure does not capture the depth of poverty. In other words, from the perspective of the child's well-being, suffering from one deprivation is not the same as suffering from three or four of them (Alkire and Foster, 2007; Delamonica and Minujin, 2007). Table 11.2 shows the distribution of children suffering only one, only two, only three, or four and more deprivations. On average children suffer just above two deprivations. However, in urban Tanzania the average is one, while in rural areas children suffer on average 2.5 deprivations.

Table 11.2: Depth of child poverty (one, two, three or four and more deprivations), by place of residence, 2004/05

| | Mainland and Zanzibar by urban/rural residence | | | | | | | | |
| | Mainland | | | | | | Zanzibar | | |
	Total	Total	Urban Dar es Salaam	Other	Urban	Rural	Total	Urban	Rural
No severe deprivation	12.2	11.5	41.6	58.7	35.7	3.4	37.2	65.2	26.0
At least one severe deprivation	*87.8*	*87.8*	*58.4*	*41.3*	*64.3*	*96.6*	*62.8*	*34.8*	*74.0*
One severe deprivation	17.0	16.7	29.2	27.1	29.9	13.4	24.8	24.7	24.9
Two severe deprivations	30.6	31.0	18.7	12.0	21.0	34.2	18.8	6.8	23.6
Three severe deprivations	27.2	27.6	8.4	2.2	10.5	32.7	13.3	2.5	17.6
Four or more severe deprivations	13.0	13.2	2.1	0.0	2.9	16.2	5.9	0.8	7.9
Total	100	100	100	100	100	100	100	100	100
Average number of deprivations experienced	2.1	2.1	1.0	0.6	1.2	2.5	1.2	0.5	1.6

Source: Own calculations based on Democratic and Health Survey 2004/05 data

The differences in the depth of poverty are quite startling. For instance, in Mainland rural Tanzania almost half the children suffer at least three deprivations (32.7% suffer three and 16.2% suffer four or more) while in Mainland urban areas the corresponding estimate is just above 10%. In Mainland rural areas, more than 80% of the children suffer at least two deprivations, compared to only 10% of urban children in Zanzibar. Children in rural Zanzibar are nearly four times more likely to suffer at least four deprivations than their counterparts in Mainland urban areas (7.9% versus 2.1%).

In the last row, data on the average number of deprivations experienced is presented. These are calculated in the following way: using data from the first column, we see that 17% of children in Tanzania experience one deprivation, resulting in a 'score' of 17 (that is, 17×1). Thirty-one per cent of the children suffer two deprivations, making a score of 61.2 deprivations (that is, 30.7×2), 27.2% of the children suffer three deprivations which counts as 81.6 deprivations (27.2×3), and 13% of the children suffer four or more deprivations representing 52 deprivations (13×4). Adding all these scores together results in a total deprivation score of 211.8. Divided by 100 (that is, all children) means the average number of deprivations experienced by children in Tanzania is 2.1 deprivations. So, while 87.8% of the children in Tanzania suffer at least one deprivation (see Table 11.1), on average children are estimated to experience two deprivations. In Mainland rural areas, however, the average is 2.5 deprivations, five times higher the average of urban Zanzibar (0.5 deprivations).

In addition to being able to examine the depth of poverty, the approach followed here can also be used to assess the severity of poverty, which is mainly a comparative measure. It shows the situation of children experiencing the most deprivations, that is, how poor the poorest children actually are. This can be done by taking the average number of deprivations and calculating how far children fall below this average using the standard deviation (see Table 11.3).

Table 11.3: Severity of child poverty, by place of residence, 2004/05

	Depth of child poverty (average no of deprived children)	Standard Deviation	Severity of child poverty (average plus Standard Deviation)
Mainland	2.1	1.1	3.2
Mainland urban	1.0	1.1	2.1
Dar es Salaam	0.6	0.9	1.5
Other urban	1.2	1.2	2.4
Mainland rural	2.5	1.1	3.6
Zanzibar	1.2	1.0	2.2
Zanzibar urban	0.5	0.8	1.3
Zanzibar rural	1.6	1.3	2.9
Total	2.1	1.3	3.4

Source: Own calculations based on Democratic and Health Survey 2004/05 data

The first column of Table 11.3 reproduces the last row of Table 11.2, that is, the depth of poverty (the average number of deprivations per child). The second column shows the variation around the average (measured by the standard deviation). In the third column, the average and the standard deviation are added together to produce the measure of the severity of child poverty (Delamonica and Minujin, 2007[14]). Thus, given the standard deviation of 1.3 on top of the average number of deprivations being 2.1, *roughly one out of six children suffer more than 3.4 deprivations in Tanzania* (last column, bottom row of Table 11.3). It is not surprising to observe that Mainland rural is the area with the highest severity as the average number of deprivations is the highest but also, the percentage of children suffering more than four deprivations is the highest (16.2%, see Table 11.2). Figure 11.2 shows the geographic distribution of severity.

Figure 11.2: Severity of child poverty: % of children suffering four or more deprivations

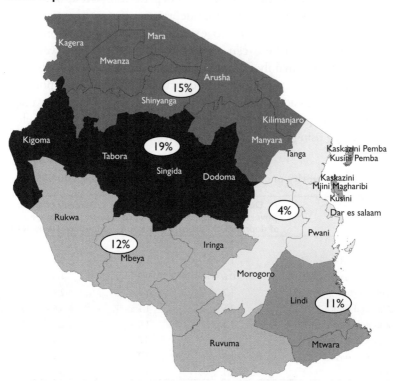

Source: Own calculations based on Demographic and Health Survey 2004/05 data

Child poverty and its characteristics

In this section we concentrate on poor children and some of their demographic characteristics. We therefore analyse the differences in child poverty between urban and rural settings, geographic zones and socioeconomic status.

Table 11.4 shows the situation of children in terms of each of the dimensions of child poverty, further disaggregating the rural and urban information. The wide variation in deprivation by indicator can be observed. Moreover, the difference within each indicator can also be explored. For instance, children in Mainland rural Tanzania are twice as likely as children in Mainland urban to be malnourished.

Analysing deprivations in each zone (Table 11.5) shows that the gaps are very wide for some dimensions (for example, water deprivation stands at 13.5% in Zanzibar and 73% in the South). Nevertheless, for other indicators, the differences are much smaller (for example,

Table 11.4: Distribution of child deprivation by geographic location, 2004/05

	Main geographic location rural vs urban (2004/05)						
	Mainland					Zanzibar	
	Total	Urban	Dar es Salaam	Other Urban	Rural	Urban	Rural
Nutrition	13.2	7.7	3.1	9.3	14.8	5.7	8.3
Health	8.8	4.2	5.1	3.9	9.8	9.0	11.7
Shelter	77.9	36.2	13.6	44.1	90.3	15.8	55.8
Water	63.3	32.2	20.6	36.3	73.4	6.4	16.4
Sanitation facilities	15.0	2.8	1.0	3.8	17.7	5.1	42.4
Information	38.3	20.1	17.5	21.0	44.1	9.7	20.6
Education	18.8	7.3	4.4	8.3	2.1	8.2	22.6

Source: Own calculations based on Democratic and Health Survey 2004/05 data

Table 11.5: Distribution of child deprivation by mainland zones and Zanzibar, 2004/05

	Mainland zones							
	Total	East	South	South Highland	Lake	North	Central	Zanzibar
Nutrition	13.2	9.2	18.1	14.8	12.1	10.9	17.7	7.5
Health	8.8	4.1	5.3	9.4	9.8	9.2	10.7	11.0
Shelter	77.9	57.4	91.7	78.0	85.5	70.4	89.3	44.3
Water	63.3	48.8	73.2	66.1	72.1	59.3	67.7	13.5
Sanitation facilities	15.0	3.9	5.9	10.0	22.1	16.3	17.5	31.7
Information	38.3	29.2	45.5	44.4	35.7	37.2	46.9	17.5
Education	18.8	10.8	20.9	21.5	18.7	12.7	26.9	18.4

Source: Own calculations based on Democratic and Health Survey 2004/05 data

education deprivation ranges from 10.8% in the East to 26% in the Central zone). Also, as discussed earlier, shelter and water are the dimensions in which children are most deprived. This is particularly the case in the South, Lake and Central zones where more than 80% of the children suffer from shelter deprivation and at least two thirds of the children suffer water deprivation.

Child poverty can be analysed according to household and child characteristics, that is, households were classified into quintiles based on their physical assets and not on their current monetary income. Wealth, then, is determined by the types of materials used to construct the house, the presence in the household of amenities like electricity or a refrigerator, and other assets like a bicycle. All these assets are combined into an index that ranges from 1 to −1. This index is quite independent of the measure of child poverty, except for the overlap of availability of water and sanitation (Filmer and Pritchett, 1998a, 1998b; Gwatkin et al 1999; Minujin and Delamonica, 2003). It is not surprising that all children in the bottom 40% of the wealth distribution[15] suffer at least one deprivation (Table 11.6). It is striking, however, that the incidence of child poverty is almost 40% among the children in the richest quintile and over 90% in the second highest quintile.[16]

The depth of poverty is substantially higher among children living in the poorest 20% of the households than among children from the 20% wealthiest families. The former suffer from on average over three deprivations while the latter suffer less than one (Table 11.7).

There are no gender differences picked up by these data, whether the analysis centres on the gender of the child or the gender of the head of the household. This is to be expected as shelter, water, sanitation and information are measured at the household level. It is interesting to point out that even for the dimensions which are measured at the individual child level (health, education and nutrition) there are no gender differences either.

Table 11.6: Distribution of child deprivation by household wealth, 2004/05

	Poorest	Poorer	Middle	Richer	Richest
At least one deprivation	100.0	100.0	100.0	93.3	38.9
Nutrition	18.1	16.0	14.4	11.1	4.0
Health	13.1	8.7	10.3	6.4	3.7
Shelter	100.0	100.0	99.4	72.7	7.1
Water	80.0	75.8	72.4	58.5	23.8
Sanitation facilities	40.5	13.1	12.5	5.4	0.7
Information	82.2	34.7	39.8	22.3	8.2
Education	35.3	26.6	17.7	9.3	4.8

Source: Own calculations based on Democratic and Health Survey 2004/05 data

Table 11.7: Depth of child poverty by wealth quintile

	Poorest	Poorer	Middle	Richer	Richest
No severe deprivation				6.7	61.1
One severe deprivation	0.7	8.6	12.8	33.2	32.2
Two severe deprivation	13.5	44.4	42.2	44.5	6.0
Three severe deprivation	47.4	36.4	33.9	13.4	0.6
Four or more severe deprivation	38.4	10.6	11.1	2.2	
Average	3.2	2.5	2.4	1.7	0.5

Source: Own calculations based on Democratic and Health Survey 2004/05 data

Child poverty changes between 1999 and 2004/05

The existence of a Demographic and Health Survey for 1999 provides a baseline against which to contrast the results based on the 2004/05 Demographic and Health Survey. Combining the two sets of results, changes since the introduction of policies associated with the Poverty Reduction Strategy Paper (PRSP) of 2000 can be scrutinised. However, care needs to be taken in order not to be confused by changes that are due to the comparison of two different surveys, as each survey consists of a stratified random sample. Both a small increase in a dimension of child deprivation or a small reduction in another dimension could be interpreted as a negative or a positive trend, whereas the numbers are merely two different point estimates of the same underlying value. In other words, it is possible that the actual deprivation suffered by children is the same (for example, 20%) yet, using two different samples to estimate deprivation, slightly different (but not statistically different) estimates can result (for example, 19% and 22%).[17] Thus, in each case, the margins of error of the estimates need to be considered in order to test if an observed change is statistically significant.

Moreover, the change also has to be meaningful. It could be that the estimate of child deprivation is reduced by 1 percentage point and the change is statistically significant. However, a mere 1 percentage point reduction in five years (especially given the high level of economic and population growth) should not be a source of great satisfaction.

Table 11.8 shows what changes occurred in Tanzania between 1999 and 2004/05. There was a *reduction in child poverty of 7 percentage points, from 94.6 per cent to 87.8 per cent.*[18] There are various ways to find out if this is a statistically significant difference. One is to check if each component, or at least some dimensions, of child poverty was reduced. As it is shown below, this is the case. Thus, *the reduction in child poverty is*

Table 11.8: Child poverty trends, 1999-2004/05

Mainland and Zanzibar	DHS 1999	DHS 2004/05	Change
Severely deprived (1+)	*94.6*	*87.8*	Decrease
Water deprived	68.7	63.3	Decrease
Sanitation deprived	13.2	15.0	*Increase*
Shelter deprived	83.2	77.9	Decrease
Information deprived	35.7	38.3	*Increase*
Health deprived	5.3	8.8	*Increase*
Nutrition deprived	18.0	13.2	Decrease
Education deprived	35.5	18.8	Decrease

Source: Own calculations based on Democratic and Health Survey 1999 and 2004/05 data

statistically significant. Nevertheless, given the rapid economic expansion during the period 1999–2004, a more drastic reduction in child poverty could have been observed.

In Table 11.8 it can be observed that *the major reductions in child deprivation occurred in education and nutrition*.[19] The percentage of children severely deprived dropped from 18.2% to 13.2% (see also Minujin and Delamonica, 2008). There seem to be three dimensions (sanitation, information and health) where there was some retrogression, with increases between 1999 and 2004/05. This, however, is probably not the case, as the changes are small and are not statistically significant. Unfortunately, the same can be said of water and shelter deprivation, where the reductions are not statistically significant.

Table 11.9 shows that 94.6% of the children suffered at least one of the seven deprivations in 1999. The average number of deprivations experienced declined from 2.4 to 2.1 at the national level between 1999 and 2004/05. It also declined from about one third to one half across the board.

Table 11.9: Depth of child poverty by place of residence, 1999

| | Mainland and Zanzibar by rural vs urban (1999) | | | | |
| | | Mainland | | Zanzibar | |
	Total	Urban	Rural	Urban	Rural
No severe deprivation	5.4	22.4	1.1	32.5	5.9
One severe deprivation	9.6	25.4	5.3	39.7	15.6
Two severe deprivations	18.3	22.4	17.2	17.5	22.1
Three or more severe deprivations	66.7	29.8	76.4	10.4	56.5
Total	100.0	100.0	100.0	100.0	100.0
Average	2.4	1.6	2.7	1.0	2.3

Source: Own calculations based on Democratic and Health Survey 1999 data

As can be observed in Figure 11.3, the situation of the poorest of the poor children did show some improvement, given that three or more deprivations were suffered by two thirds of the children in 1999; by 2004/05 the figure had fallen to 'only' 40 per cent of children. This is particularly the case for Mainland rural children, where the drop was from 76.4% in 1999 to 48.8% in 2004/05. Thus, while the incidence of child poverty is roughly the same (98.9% in 1999 and 96.6% in 2004/05) and the average number of deprivations (depth) did not change much (that is, from 2.7 to 2.5), there has been a major improvement in some aspects of child deprivation affecting the most deprived children.

Figure 11.3: Changes in number of deprivations (1999-2004/05)

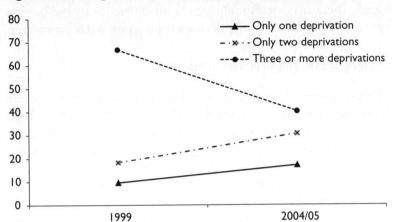

Source: Own calculations based on Demographic and Health Survey 1999 and 2004/05 data

Sensitivity analysis: adapting the thresholds to the Tanzania context

As mentioned earlier, it is important to analyse the sensitivity of the child poverty estimates. This can be done by altering the thresholds that determine whether or not deprivation experience is severe. This is similar to adapting the thresholds to determine deprivation to the national context.

Access to water

UNICEF's Global Study uses a slightly different definition of 'access' to water than the one used above to estimate child poverty in Tanzania. The difference, however, is not large. It involves modifying the time required to fetch water from 15 to 30 minutes. Using this wider threshold to make an estimate of severe water deprivation and child poverty is useful as a check on the robustness of the results presented above.

The results are not surprising. While using 15 minutes results in slightly over 60% of the children being severely deprived of water, changing the cut-off point to 30 minutes reduces the incidence of water deprivation to 57.3%. In other words, only an additional 5% of children are counted as water deprived.

In terms of the impact on the total incidence of child poverty (that is, when the new water deprivation measured is combined with all the other deprivations), the change is almost imperceptible. Child poverty, using the revised water deprivation indicator, falls to 87.1% from 87.8%. Clearly there is no statistically significant difference to the poverty estimates when 15 or 30 minutes are used to assess water deprivation.

Changing shelter and sanitation thresholds

The possibility of using different thresholds to determine severe deprivation has been mentioned. In this section two such attempts are presented, in order to advance the discussion about finding the most appropriate measure of child poverty for Tanzania. In particular, changes were made in the cut-off criteria for shelter (which seems to have 'too high' a level of severe deprivation) and in sanitation (which seems to have 'too low' a level of severe deprivation).

For shelter, in addition to overcrowding and the quality of the floor material, the quality of the roof and the walls were considered.[20] This resulted in a reduction of shelter deprivation from 77.9% to 28.6%.

While this different estimate is considerably lower, it does not have much of an impact on the total child poverty estimate (81.2% instead of 87.7% with the original definition of shelter deprivation). This is due to the fact that many of the children who suffer from shelter deprivation (under the original definition, that is, almost four out of five children) also suffer from another deprivation. Thus, not considering them shelter deprived does not mean that they are still not considered poor due to some other deprivation. However, the depth of poverty is affected, as can be observed in Table 11.10.

For sanitation, the opposite was done in the sense that a looser threshold was needed in order to increase the level of incidence. Given that water deprivation is over 60%, sanitation deprivation at less than 20% does not seem very realistic. Thus, the threshold was expanded

Table 11.10: Incidence and depth of child poverty with alternative threshold for shelter, 2004/05

	Alternative thresholds			Difference with original threshold (see Table 11.2)		
	Total	Mainland	Zanzibar	Total	Mainland	Zanzibar
No deprivation	18.8	18.0	43.7	6.6	6.5	−13.5
At least one deprivation	81.2	82.0	56.3	−6.6	−6.5	−6.5
Only one deprivation	30.6	30.7	26.3	13.6	14.0	1.5
Only two deprivations	27.2	27.5	16.7	−3.4	−3.5	−2.1
Only three deprivations	15.3	15.5	9.4	−11.9	−12.1	−3.9
Four or more deprivations	8.2	8.3	4.0	−4.8	−4.9	−1.9

Source: Own calculations based on Democratic and Health Survey 2004/05 data

to include a traditional pit toilet as part of the elements that would constitute severe deprivation.[21] In this case, the incidence of severe deprivation increased dramatically, from less than 20% to over 90%.

However, the impact on the overall level of child poverty is not as strong. Of course, child poverty cannot be less than the level of sanitation deprivation. However, it is not much higher, as all the children who were counted as poor before because of their severe deprivation in other dimensions also suffer from the revised deprivation in sanitation, although the depth does increase under the new definition of sanitation severity (Table 11.11).

Table 11.11: Incidence and depth of child poverty with alternative threshold for sanitation, 2004/05

	Alternative thresholds			Difference with original threshold (see table 11-2)		
	Total	**Mainland**	**Zanzibar**	**Total**	**Mainland**	**Zanzibar**
No deprivation	3.8	3.5	11.4	−8.4	−8.0	−45.8
At least one deprivation	96.2	96.5	88.6	8.4	8.0	25.8
Only one deprivation	10.2	9.5	32.9	−6.8	−7.2	8.1
Only two deprivations	16.9	16.5	29.4	−13.6	−14.5	10.6
Only three deprivations	34.3	34.8	19.1	7.1	7.2	5.8
Four or more deprivations	34.8	35.7	7.2	21.8	20.5	1.3

Source: Own calculations based on Democratic and Health Survey 2004/05 data

Conclusion: child poverty in Tanzania, an intolerable but hopeful story

The results presented and analysed in this chapter show with clarity that the vast majority of children suffer from one or more severe deprivations in Tanzania. This is especially critical in rural areas where children are greatly affected by poverty. Simultaneously, children are the major resource that Tanzania has for moving ahead.

Two dimensions of deprivation are particularly acute: shelter and drinking water. Both have strong negative effects on child well-being and survival as well as on their chances to contribute to society with all their potential when they become adults. Lack of safe drinking water contributes to the spread of illnesses and malnutrition that create a vicious circle which affects negatively the child's chances in life. Living in an overcrowded household and low-quality housing also contribute in negative ways to children's development and self-esteem.

The analysis of the overall changes in child poverty between 1999 and 2004/05 shows a small change. As discussed, this was driven by progress in education and nutrition, in particular in Mainland rural areas.

However, the analysis of changes in the different dimensions gives a great deal of hope. Basic education, one area to which the government has given particular priority and invested through budgetary efforts, shows remarkable progress. The percentage of children suffering from severe education deprivation had a remarkable reduction from 34.9% in 1999 to 18.8% in 2004/05. This result gives even more hope because of the well-known synergetic effect of education on other aspects of well-being.

The other important dimension that shows a statistically significant reduction is related to undernutrition, which declined from 18.2% to 13.2%. No significant differences in gender were observed, as discussed.

Moreover, there is an observed reduction in the depth of poverty (that is, the percentage of children who suffer multiple deprivations). It is significant both for the whole country as well as for urban and rural areas. This welcome effect is most probably due to the expansion of education and the reduction in nutrition deprivation among children who, unfortunately, still suffer from other deprivations.

The sensitivity analysis was carried out by modifying the threshold for water, sanitation and shelter. It showed, on the one hand, that it is important to adapt the deprivation thresholds to the situation and culture in the country. On the other hand, the percentage of child deprivation did not change significantly. This means that the estimation of child deprivation is robust

In these results there are important lessons to be learned. This evidence should give indications on how to pursue effective policies that could improve the situation of children, especially girls, not only in education and nutrition but in the other dimensions as well.

Notes

[1] This chapter is based on a report prepared by a team led by Alberto Minujin and Enrique Delamonica for the United Nations Children's Fund (UNICEF) Country Office in Tanzania. The team members were Louisa Lippi, Ana Ferreira, Anna Williams, Kerem Sengun, Pablo Gutierrez and Eduardo Molina. We are very grateful for the analytical and substantive support received from Mikala Lauridsen, Edith Mbatia, Dorothy Mwanyika and Carol Watson of the UNICEF Tanzania Office and the members of the Global Study Secretariat Dr Francis Sichona, Aldegunda Komba, D. Ruhiye and Julius Kivelia. The report was particularly strengthened by comments received during a workshop held in January 2008 in Dar es Salaam.

[2] These trends had, five years after independence, resulted in the adoption of the Arusha Declaration which says that allocations should be made so as to use 'all the resources of this country towards the elimination of poverty, ignorance and disease' to ensure the well-being of all citizens.

[3] However, there is insufficient data on income poverty trends due to the need to engage in costly and time-consuming surveys to measure income poverty; there is more on this point and the advantages of monitoring progress through child poverty reduction later in this chapter.

[4] Another common classification is between relative and absolute poverty. Both can be based on a single or various dimensions.

[5] An example of this approach is the US$1 a day measure proposed by the World Bank. According to this measure, about half of the children in developing countries would be struggling to survive with less than US$1 a day (Vandemoortele, 2000, and Reddy and Pogge, 2003, present valid criticisms of the US$1 a day measure).

[6] Also known as the incidence of poverty or the level (in percentages) of poverty. It answers the question 'How many poor are there?'

[7] This is different from the debate on adult equivalent scales; see, among others, McClements (1977) or Gordon and Pantazis (1997).

[8] In other words, a minimum threshold is determined for seven basic needs for children. Children are considered severely deprived when the minimum is not reached for any of the indicators of basic needs. See, *inter alia*, ILO (1976), Wratten (1995), OHCHR (2002) and Ruggeri et al (2003).

[9] This is not exactly the terminology used by Gordon et al (2003). They distinguish between the households and children living in conditions where at least one deprivation is present (which they call 'severe deprivation') and where at least two deprivations are present (which they call 'absolute poverty').

[10] For more discussion of this point see Chapter Five in this book, and Delamonica and Minujin (2007).

[11] The two-stage cluster sample consisted of about 10,000 households (roughly 2,000 from Zanzibar, 2,000 from the Urban Mainland, and 6,000 from Rural Mainland).

[12] While the percentage of children under 18 years old in Mainland rural areas is 58%, it is 51% in Mainland urban areas. In Zanzibar this proportion is 56%.

[13] It is interesting to note that, even with a higher poverty line, the incidence of income poverty would still be estimated at less than 60% (UNDP and GoT, 2005, Appendix B, p 114). This is the monetary poverty estimate closest in time to our child poverty calculation.

[14] Alkire and Foster (2007) present a different set of steps to calculate depth and severity but the approaches are fundamentally the same.

[15] However, this approach has other limitations, as mentioned in Chapter Four, this volume.

[16] This is quite striking as there is some overlap in the dimensions of poverty and the estimation of the wealth index. For instance, both include shelter characteristics and access to water and sanitation. However, as the methodological tools are different, there is no risk of spurious association.

[17] Consequently, there is no increase, from 19% to 22%. Rather we have two different estimates of the same value (of about 20%).

[18] This is in terms of incidence. The reduction is more significant in the depth of poverty (see later).

[19] A test of differences (t-test) was used to find out if the observed changes were statistically significant or not. As each indicator was tested separately and their standard deviations are different, the absolute difference reported in the table may be misleading as a rule of thumb to specify which differences are significant. So, although the magnitude of the change in shelter seems larger than in education, given the margins of error, the former is not statistically significant while the latter is significant.

[20] The categories that were used were quality of the walls (the household was considered deprived if the walls were made of poles, mud or grass) and the roof (the household was considered deprived if the roof was made of grass, leaves or mud).

[21] This was not decided in a completely arbitrary way. It is based on the way the questions and answers are coded in the Demographic and Health Survey of Tanzania. Basically, including the pit latrine is moving up to the next level of quality in the Demographic and Health Survey.

[22] Although, they could attend pre-primary and nursery schooling, these elements were not considered in the definition of poverty.

References

Alkire, S. and Foster, J. (2007) *Counting and multidimensional poverty measurement*, Oxford Poverty & Human Development Initiative (OPHI) Working Paper No 7, Oxford: University of Oxford (www.ophi.org.uk/pubs/OPHI_WP7-5.pdf).

Beccaria, L. and Minujin, A. (1988) *Metodos alternativos para medir la evolucion del tamaño de la pobreza*, Buenos Aires: Instituto Nacional de Estadística y Censos de Argentina (National Institute of Statistics and Census).

Boltvinik, J. (1998) *Poverty measurement methods – An overview*, SEPED Series on Poverty Reduction, New York: United Nations Development Programme (www.undp.org/poverty/publications/pov_red/ Poverty_Measurement_Methods.pdf).

Delamonica, E.E. and Minujin, A. (2007) 'Incidence, depth and severity of children living in poverty', *Social indicators Research*, vol 82, pp 361-74.

Feeny, T. and Boyden, J. (2003) *Children and poverty: A review of contemporary literature and thought on children and poverty*, Children and Poverty Series, Part I, Richmond, VA: Christian Children's Fund.

Filmer, D. and Pritchett, L. (1998a) *Estimating wealth effects without expenditure data – or tears: An application to educational enrollments in states of India*, World Bank Working Paper, Washington, DC: World Bank.

Filmer, D. and Pritchett, L. (1998b) *Education attainment of the poor (and rich): DHS evidence from around the globe*, World Bank Working Paper, Washington, DC: World Bank.

Gordon, D. and Pantazis, C. (1997) *Breadline Britain in the 1990s*, Aldershot: Ashgate.

Gordon, D., Nandy, S., Pantazis, C., Pemberton, S. and Townsend, P. (2003) *Child poverty in the developing world*, Bristol: The Policy Press.

Gwatkin, D.R., Rustein, S., Johnson, K., Pande, R. and Wagstaff, A. (1999) *Socio-economic differences in health, nutrition, and population: Country notes*, Washington, DC: World Bank.

ILO (International Labour Organization) (1976) *Employment, growth and basic needs: A one-world problem*, Geneva: ILO.

McClements, L.D. (1977) 'Equivalence scales for children', *Journal of Public Economics*, vol 8, issue 2, pp 191-210.

Minujin, A. (2005) 'Constructing a definition and measurements of children living in poverty', Global Policy Section contribution to Innocenti Research Centre meeting on Child Poverty in Central and Eastern Europe/Commonwealth of Independent States, 24 January, Florence, Italy.

Minujin, A. and Delamonica, E.E. (2003) 'Mind the gap! Widening child mortality disparities', *Journal of Human Development*, vol 4, issue 3, November, pp 397–418.

Minujin, A. and Delamonica, E.E. (2008) *Report on child poverty and disparity in Tanzania*, Report to UNICEF Country Office, Dar es Salaam, Tanzania, UNICEF Tanzania.

OHCHR (Office of the High Commissioner for Human Rights) (2002) *Draft guidelines on a human rights approach to poverty reduction strategies* (prepared by P. Hunt, M. Nowak and S. Osmani for OHCHR), Geneva: OHCHR.

Reddy, S. and Pogge, T. (2003) *Unknown: The extent, distribution and trend of global income poverty*, Mimeo (www.socialanalysis.org).

Ruggeri, C., Saith, R. and Stewart, F. (2003) *Everyone agrees we need poverty reduction, but not what this means: Does it matter?*, Helsinki: WIDER.

Streeten, P. (1984) 'Basic needs: some unsettled questions', *World Development*, vol 12, issue 9, pp 973–8.

Streeten, P., Burki, S.J., ul Haq, M., Hicks, N. and Stewart, F. (1981) *First things first: Meeting basic human needs in developing countries*, Oxford: Oxford University Press.

UNDP (United Nations Development Programme) and Government of Tanzania (2005) *Poverty and Human Development Report*, Dar es Salaam, Tanzania: UNDP.

UNICEF (United Nations Children's Fund) Mozambique (2006) *Child poverty and disparity in Mozambique*, Mozambique: UNICEF Mozambique.

Vandemoortele, J. (2000) *Absorbing social shocks*, UNICEF Working Paper, New York: United Nations Children's Fund.

Wratten, E. (1995) 'Conceptualizing urban poverty', *Environment & Urbanization*, vol 7, issue 1, pp 11–38.

Appendix 1

Severe education deprivation – children aged between 7 and 18 who had never been to school and were not currently attending school (for example, no professional education of any kind).

Severe water deprivation – children who only had access to surface water (for example, rivers) for drinking or who lived in households where the nearest source of water was more than 15 minutes away (for example, indicators of severe deprivation of water quality or quantity).

Severe shelter deprivation – children in dwellings with more than five people per room (severe overcrowding) or with no flooring material (for example, a mud floor).

Severe deprivation of sanitation facilities – children who had no access to a toilet of any kind in the vicinity of their dwelling (for example, no private or communal toilets or latrines).

Severe information deprivation – children aged between 3 and 18 living in a household with no access to radio, television, telephone or newspapers.

Severe health deprivation – children who either had not been immunised against any diseases or young children who had a recent illness involving diarrhoea and had not received any medical advice or treatment.

Severe nutrition deprivation – children whose heights and weights for their age were more than -3 standard deviations below the median of the international reference population, that is, severe anthropometric failure.

Appendix 2

A particular problem emerges when using a variant of the basic needs approach applied to children under the age of 18, as not all dimensions are defined for the same age group. For instance, attending school can only be measured for children over five or six years old. Similarly, the undernutrition questions are only asked of children under five.

This is addressed in the following simplified example (Table 11A.1), comprising 10 children (labelled A through J). Only three areas of deprivation are listed, to make the example as simple as possible. In this example, children labelled A through E are under age 5 and children labelled F through J are over five years old. Thus, nutrition deprivation is only measured among the first group and education deprivation is only measured in the latter group. This explains the empty cells in the first two rows – these indicators are not measured for those children.

Table 11A.1: Sample analysis of child poverty based on age specific deprivation

Access to:	A	B	C	D	E	F	G	H	I	J	%
Nutrition (0-5 years old)	✓	✓	NO	✓	✓						20
Education (7-17 years old)						✓	NO	✓	NO	✓	40
Shelter (0-17 years old)	✓	NO	✓	✓	NO	✓	NO	✓	✓	✓	30
Deprived?	OK	POOR	POOR	OK	POOR	OK	POOR	OK	POOR	OK	50

It should be noticed that as shelter applies to all children, all 10 have an input in the last to previous row.

For each child, whether they are deprived (NO) or enjoy that right (✓) is listed in the corresponding column. Thus, it can be seen that child A suffers no deprivations. Consequently, child A is not considered poor (the big 'OK' in the last row). However, child B is deprived of shelter. Thus, child B is considered poor (POOR) in the last row. However, the deprivations are estimated *only* for the relevant age group (that is, children under five are not asked about being in school).

Measuring horizontally, one of the five children is nutrition deprived. This corresponds to the 'incidence' of undernutrition being 20%. The same applies through the other rows. Thus, shelter deprivation is around a third and education deprivation is 40%.

An assessment along the corresponding column is made as to whether the child has all their basic needs satisfied or not. The corresponding level of incidence is 50%, which is neither the sum nor the average of the single deprivations. This method looks at the integrated set of indicators (rights) for each child. It is an holistic approach. Moreover, it purposefully avoids overestimating (actually it underestimates) the extent of child poverty, as explained above, in order to be cautious in the assessment of child poverty.

TWELVE

A multidimensional profile of child poverty in Congo Brazzaville

Geranda Notten, Chris de Neubourg, Bethuel Makosso and Alain Beltran Mpoue

Introduction[1]

The Republic of Congo is a central African oil exporting country with a population of 3.5 million inhabitants, of which 46% are children. Armed conflict in the 1990s caused a strong deterioration of social and economic living conditions – the Human Development Index plunged from 0.54 in 1985 to 0.45 in 1999 (UNDP, 2005). Since peace agreements in 2002, conditions have gradually improved, but the economy and government revenues of this lower middle-income country are heavily reliant on oil exports, and it is a net importer of goods including basic foodstuffs (IMF, 2007). Unemployment is high and one in every two Congolese lives in monetary poverty (Ministère du Plan, 2006). To determine pro-poor development strategies and priorities, Congo, like many other developing countries, started the process of formulating a Poverty Reduction Strategy Paper (PRSP). In addition to consolidating peace and promoting economic growth, the Congolese PRSP draft also specifies objectives such as improving access to basic social services (health and education) and improving the social environment such as water and sanitation, housing, employment and social protection (Comité National de Lutte contre la Pauvreté, 2008). In March 2008, a final draft of the PRSP was submitted to the World Bank and the International Monetary Fund (IMF), whose approval was also needed to obtain debt relief through the Heavily Indebted Poor Country initiative (HIPC).

Like any policy-making process, formulating a PRSP requires information about the economy, the population as well as government finances and services; a poverty analysis is a key component of such a situational analysis. In developing countries such poverty analyses are

287

typically based on a traditional, monetary concept of poverty that is measured by comparing households' expenses to an absolute poverty line using nationally representative survey data. However, poverty is inherently a multidimensional concept – sometimes even people with sufficient financial resources are unable to achieve satisfactory levels of well-being in other dimensions (Bourguignon and Chakravarty, 2003). This is particularly true for children, who comprise such a large part of developing countries' populations, and whose well-being in dimensions such as education, nutrition and health also affects their future well-becoming as adults. Against the background of PRSP processes in developing countries, this chapter uses the Republic of Congo as a case study to explore one way of better using the available information in household survey data to have an improved and more representative poverty diagnostic.

From an academic perspective we also want to show that a multidimensional approach to poverty has more uses than summarising poverty in a single index or for comparing deprivation rates between dimensions. Following a multidimensional approach to poverty, this chapter further uses information on the prevalence of multiple deprivations at the level of the child to analyse to what extent children suffering from multiple deprivations have different characteristics and problems than children suffering from only one deprivation or none at all. We thereby focus on children of school-going age and deprivation patterns in the dimensions of financial resources, education and work. The resulting poverty profile helps identify commonalities and differences between subgroups of vulnerable children among a larger and much more heterogeneous group of deprived children. A better profile, in turn, gives more direction for subsequent in-depth problem analyses and policy-making processes, including that of allocating scarce budget shares to specific sectors and policy goals.

This chapter first describes the conceptual framework, data and definitions of the welfare indicators used in each dimension of well-being. This is followed by a presentation of the poverty rates in each dimension and the degree to which children simultaneously suffer from several deprivations. Subsequently, the multidimensional poverty profile of children in the age group 6 to 17 in the dimensions of education and money is explored. The last section concludes by putting the findings from the multidimensional poverty profile into a policy context.

Methodology: concepts, indicators and data

The analysis in this chapter focuses on a particular insight that the authors gained while conducting a much broader multidimensional poverty study on behalf of UNICEF in the Republic of Congo. For reasons of space restrictions and clarity of communication, this section only briefly sketches our approach to measuring multidimensional poverty in Congo, and explains the three dimensions of well-being in more detail. For more information the reader is referred to the original report (Notten et al, 2008) and a working paper (Notten, 2008).

Poverty, or deprivation, is defined as the lack of access to resources and services that are needed to satisfy basic needs. We thereby largely follow the deprivation approach as set out by Townsend (1979) and, for children, Gordon et al (2003a, 2003b). The UN Convention on the Rights of the Child (UNCRC) (1989)[2] is another source of inspiration because children's and adults' needs differ in important respects and children's current well-being and future well-becoming is largely determined by other agents than the child (parents, family, community, state). The inclusion of well-being dimensions and welfare indicators is constrained by available data. We use the nationally representative Congolese household survey (Enquête Congolaise auprès des Ménages, ECOM). This survey was conducted in 2005 and includes information on household expenditures and living conditions as well as child-specific information on a range of issues including health, education and work. We selected eight dimensions of well-being (money, education, nutrition, health, work, water and sanitation, housing and integration) and in each of these dimensions we defined one or a set of welfare indicators that are relevant in Congolese society and a deprivation threshold. Table A1 in the Appendix at the end of this chapter provides a summary of all dimensions.

In the monetary dimension, adult equivalent expenditures are used as an indicator for the level of financial resources of the household. A child is considered poor when the adult equivalent expenditures of the household the child lives in are below the national poverty line. The poverty line is based on the monetary value of a minimum calorie intake including an allowance for non-food expenditures. Its annual value is 306,400 CFA (Congolese francs) or approximately US$629 (US$1.72 a day). Household expenditures are adjusted for household-specific demographics using the equivalence scales of the Food and Agriculture Organization (Ministère du Plan, 2006).

In the education dimension, the focus is on children aged 6 to 17. In Congo the mandatory age for enrolment in primary education is six. Although school enrolment is not mandatory for children aged 16 and 17, this age group is included given the importance of completing secondary education for children's future well-being. A child is considered deprived in their access to education if they are not going to school, or alternatively, their progress in the educational system is more than two years delayed according to age. Therefore, the education deprivation indicator captures non-enrolment, late enrolment as well as slow progress through the educational system (that is, repeating classes and/or interruptions).

The work dimension captures the prevalence of child labour for children aged from 10 to 14: a child in this age group is deprived when they have any remunerative activity outside the household. The deprivation threshold is inspired by the labour convention of the International Labour Organization (1973),[3] which states that the age of 15 is the minimum age at which a person should be allowed to work. This study employs a rather narrow definition of child labour, one that is likely to underestimate the prevalence of child labour. The reason is that even though the Congolese survey includes information about whether children worked in the household, a family business or on the families' land, it does not include information that is needed to determine whether these children have too much responsibilities in accordance with their age (that is, information about the type of work and the number of hours worked). Unfortunately, information about remunerative activities of children is only available for children as of the age of 10.

Patterns of deprivation within and across dimensions

With the exception of monetary poverty, deprivation in the other dimensions is measured using ordinal data. This study focuses on the so-called headcount poverty measure that simply reflects the number of poor children measured as a percentage of the total child population (Alkire and Foster, 2008). Although methods that construct more advanced aggregate poverty measures using ordinal data exist, this research does not aggregate deprivation across dimensions by means of constructing a multidimensional poverty index. We depart from the view that each of the dimensions reflects an intrinsic part of child well-being and being deprived in one of those dimensions is already relevant and worrisome by itself. Further, this study aims to exploit the information on cumulative deprivations not by means of aggregation but by studying the degree to which deprivations overlap at the level of the child. The rationale being that different combinations of deprivation potentially require different policy responses. And even though poverty diagnostics represent only a first step towards problem analysis and subsequent policy making, identifying large patterns of heterogeneity early can only be beneficial in determining next steps. We discuss the patterns of deprivation starting with a one-dimensional perspective followed by bi- and multidimensional perspectives.

The incidence of child deprivation in each of the dimensions is reported in Table 12.1. The magnitude of deprivation is very high in nearly every dimension: by far, the highest child deprivation rates can be found in the dimensions of housing (62%), water and sanitation (70%), monetary poverty (54%) and education (53%), affecting more than half of Congolese children in each dimension. Nevertheless, child deprivation rates in nutrition (44%), health (44%) and integration (34%) are still considerable, while the incidence of child labour is lowest, affecting 6% of the children in the age group from 10 to 14.

In the dimensions where adult and child deprivation are measured using the same indicator, Table 12.1 also reports the deprivation rates for the population as a whole. Typically, children are more likely to be deprived in most dimensions. With the exception of deprivation in health, the higher incidence of child deprivation in comparison to the overall population is entirely explained by the fact that all deprivation indicators are measured at the household level and that children are disproportionately more likely to live in deprived households than adults.

In Notten (2008; 2009) one-dimensional poverty profiles have indicated that certain household characteristics are associated with a

Table 12.1: Incidence of deprivation in % of children and individuals

Dimension	Incidence (%)	
	Children	Population
Money	53.7	50.1
Education (only children aged 6 to 17)	52.5[a]	–
Work (only children aged 10 to 14)	5.6[b]	–
Nutrition[c]	43.7	42.9
Health	44.0	44.5
Water and sanitation	69.9	67.5
Housing	61.6	58.7
Integration	33.8	32.1
Population share	46.2	100

Note: [a] Incidence boys 53.7% and girls 51.2%. [b] Incidence boys 4.9% and girls 6.3%. [c] Includes only 38% of the individuals in the sample (only those people who have been ill in the four weeks before the survey).

Source: Estimates based on ECOM 2005

higher poverty risk in general – in particular, households living in rural and semi-urban areas, single-parent households and households with an elderly household head are more likely to be poor in most of the dimensions (results not reported here). However, this pattern is not the rule. The studies also show that there is some evidence of heterogeneity in poverty risk characteristics across dimensions of well-being. This not only warns against the use of a one-dimensional poverty profile (such as monetary poverty) as a proxy for poverty risk in other dimensions, but it also provides a rationale for constructing poverty profiles in an alternative way, by means of comparing the profiles of single and multiple deprived groups.

Given the high levels of deprivation in each dimension, to what extent do children suffer from a combination of deprivations at the same time? Table 12.2 reports the percentage of children who are simultaneously suffering from a given combination of two deprivations. In line with the high deprivation rates in housing and water and sanitation, the largest double deprivation is in a combination of these two dimensions, affecting 54% of all Congolese children. Double deprivation rates are also high for combinations between previously mentioned dimensions and that of money and education, with more than 30% of the children simultaneously suffering from a bi-combination of deprivations in these four dimensions.

Table 12.2: Double deprivations in % of children (risk ratio in brackets)

	Money	Education	Work	Nutrition	Health	Water and sanitation	Housing
Money	–						
Education	32 (1.14)	–					
Work	4 (1.33)	5 (1.70)	–				
Nutrition	27 (1.15)	25 (1.09)	2 (0.82)	–			
Health	26 (1.10)	28 (1.21)	3 (1.22)	26 (1.35)	–		
Water and sanitation	42 (1.12)	40 (1.09)	5 (1.28)	33 (1.08)	34 (1.11)	–	
Housing	37 (1.12)	37 (1.14)	5 (1.45)	31 (1.15)	31 (1.14)	54 (1.25)	–
Integration	24 (1.32)	20 (1.13)	2 (1.06)	19 (1.29)	18 (1.21)	28 (1.19)	26 (1.25)

Note: All children (weighted) except for the dimensions education (only includes children aged from 6 to 17) and work (only includes children aged from 10 to 14). The risk ratio is calculated by dividing the actual probability of double deprivation by that of the expected probability of deprivation. For instance the money–education risk ratio: $0.32/(0.537*0.525 = 1.14)$.

Source: Estimates based on ECOM 2005

The risk ratios displayed in brackets in Table 12.2 further reveal that, across the board, there is a positive relation between the probability of being deprived in one dimension and another. A risk ratio higher than 1 indicates that there are more double deprivations than one would expect if the risk of deprivation in one dimension would be independent of the risk of deprivation in the other dimension. For instance, the risk ratio of 1.14 between education and money indicates that 14% more children (aged 6 to 17) are double deprived in those dimensions than expected. Table 12.3 looks at all four possible combinations of deprivation: in addition to 32% of double deprived children, 20% of the children are education deprived but not money deprived and 23% of the children are money deprived but not education deprived. Only a quarter of the children are not deprived on these two dimensions. The risk ratios for non-deprived and double deprived are above 1, while those for the single deprivations are below 1. One could interpret the risk ratios from Tables 12.2 and 12.3 as consistent with the existence of a multidimensional poverty trap in which deprivation is 'contagious' across dimensions. This view, however, needs to be qualified as the single deprivation groups represent a large part of the child population.

Table 12.3: Close up: education and money in % of children (risk ratio in brackets)

		Education	
	Deprived	**Yes**	**No**
Money	Yes	32 (1.14)	23 (0.90)
	No	20 (0.82)	25 (1.14)

Note: All children (weighted) aged from 6 to 17. The risk ratio is calculated by dividing the actual probability of double deprivation by that of the expected probability of deprivation. For instance the money–education risk ratio: $0.32/(0.537*0.525 = 1.14)$.
Source: Estimates based on ECOM 2005

The aim of this chapter is to explore to what extent these groups of deprived children differ from one another. With eight dimensions of well-being there are many different groups of children one could potentially compare. Here we explore differences between children in the dimensions of money, education and work. One reason is that in a 'traditional' monetary poverty profile a child focus is often missing. Decompositions are usually made with respect to the level of education and the employment status of the head of the household; they generally show an increased monetary poverty risk for low levels of education and unemployment. Combining child-specific deprivation indicators for education and work with the traditional (household level) monetary poverty indicator allows us to explore the degree to which (a lack of) household's monetary resources can be associated with a child's well-being in the education and work dimensions. Further, while child deprivation rates in the work dimension are rather low, the risk ratios in Table 12.2 suggest that there are strong linkages with the money (1.33) and education (1.70) dimensions. Finally, investigating the characteristics of these groups also stimulates thinking about the potential cross-cutting effects of policies in sectors such as social protection, education and child protection.

The Venn diagram in Figure 12.1 explores the patterns of deprivation combining the money, education and work dimensions. Due to data limitations we can only map the overlap patterns for work deprivation with other dimensions for children aged 10 to 14. Nevertheless, Figure 12.1 is revealing: every child deprived in work is also deprived in at least one of the other two dimensions. Thus, even though child labour is not widespread in the Republic of Congo, it is strongly associated with deprivations in education and money dimensions.

Is the overlap between deprivations in these three dimensions equally large for adolescents in the age group of 15 to 17? International and

Figure 12.1: Deprivations in dimensions money (A), education (B) and work (C), in % of children aged 10-14

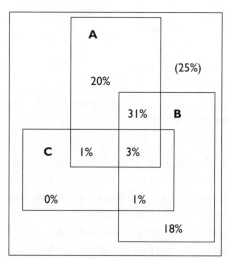

Notes: A = deprived in money, B = deprived in education, C = deprived in work (age 10-14: child labour).
Source: Estimates based on ECOM 2005

national legislation allows children in this age group to be engaged in remunerative activities, but even though there is no legal impediment for this group to work, having a job may easily conflict with the legal obligation to go school (up to the age of 17 in the Republic of Congo) or with the right to education of children, as expressed in the UNCRC. Figure 12.2 looks only at the adolescents aged 15 to 17 who are active in the labour market. They comprise 27% of children in that age group. Instead of using the child labour definition now we use an adult definition of deprivation in work: an adolescent is deprived in labour if they are unemployed or underemployed. Adolescents are underemployed if they have been working fewer than 35 hours in the past week and have been looking for ways to get additional income from work at the same time. By far most of the adolescents who are active on the labour market, whether deprived of work or working, are also deprived in the money and/or education dimension. Only 2% of work-deprived adolescents and 2% of the working adolescents are not deprived in education and money dimensions: although being active on the labour market for adolescents in this age group is not in violation with the rights of children in a narrow sense, it is strongly associated with simultaneous deprivation in money and education.

Figure 12.2: Deprivations in dimensions money (A), education (B) and work (C), in % of children aged 15-17

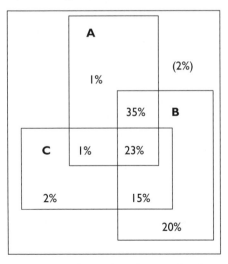

Notes: A = deprived in money, B = deprived in education, C = deprived in work (age 15-17: unemployed or underemployed).
Source: Estimates based on ECOM 2005

Poverty profile

Poverty diagnostics not only report the incidence of poverty (that is, how many people or children are poor) but they typically also explore information about which population groups are more likely to be poor (that is, which personal characteristics are associated with an increased/ decreased risk of poverty) and to what degree poverty is associated with other contextual factors that could potentially explain the causes and consequences of poverty. This type of analysis, also known as a poverty profile, is exploratory (as opposed to causal) and uses mainly descriptive statistics and is often complemented with descriptive multivariate regression techniques. Poverty profiles help identify vulnerable groups in society and may also point to areas where policy could potentially play a role to improve the situation. It is important to stress that to better understand the causal mechanisms underlying poverty for these groups and the potential impact of policy changes, a more in-depth analysis would be needed.

In a one-dimensional context, a poverty profile involves the comparison of poor population groups to the non-poor population. In a multidimensional poverty analysis where there is, for each individual, information on multiple dimensions, there are potentially many other reference groups that can be included in the comparison. In this study we investigate whether children who are simultaneously deprived in education and money have different characteristics than single or non-deprived children in their age group. Our comparison thus involves four reference groups: double deprived, deprived in money but not education, deprived in education but not in money and not deprived. Such information is relevant for policy makers because it is *a priori* not clear whether this double deprived group needs special attention or if the problems of this group could be equally well addressed with policy interventions that are aimed at reducing deprivation in one dimension such as social protection (for example, cash transfers to poor households) and education policy (such as policies aimed at free primary education, more teachers or curriculum improvement).

Table 12.4 compares the incidence of deprivation of specific subpopulations of children to the overall incidence in the child population for a range of characteristics such as region, gender and family composition. The two region-oriented decompositions reveal an interesting pattern: children living in rural and semi-urban households are more likely to be doubly deprived with incidence rates of respectively 11 and 8 percentage points above the average of 32%. While children from the two major urban areas are most likely not to

Table 12.4: Children aged 6-17: profile for deprivation in money and education

	Population share (%)	Double deprived	Money deprived	Education deprived	Not deprived
Incidence of deprivations (%)	100	32.3	22.7	20.0	24.8
By characteristic of child	Population share (%)	Deviation from population incidence (in percentage points)			
By settlement area					
Rural	43.2	11.4	−2.3	0.6	−9.4
Urban	56.8	−8.7	1.8	−0.1	7.2
By strata					
Brazzaville	27.0	−7.2	10.1	−5.4	2.6
Pointe Noire	23.7	−13.0	−6.6	5.4	14.4
Other urban communities	6.2	1.6	−2.2	1.6	−0.8
Semi urban	7.8	8.2	−1.2	−1.8	−5.1
Rural	35.4	12.1	−2.6	1.2	−10.4
By household size					
1-3 people	5.3	−8	−10.1	10.6	7.7
4-6 people	39.5	−4.8	−1.2	2.3	3.9
7-9 people	37.7	3.1	0.1	−1.2	−1.8
>9 people	17.5	6.4	5.7	−4.6	−7.3
By household type					
Single caretaker	7.5	0.5	−1.9	4	−2.4
Children and 2 adults	33.0	−4.9	−2.3	2.5	4.9
Children and >2 adults	30.1	−1.3	0.8	−1.6	2.2
Triple generations	28.4	6.7	2.4	−1.4	−7.5
Other types	1.0	5.4	−2.5	−3.1	0.3
By gender of head of household					
Male	78.8	−0.5	−0.9	0.9	0.6
Female	21.2	1.6	3.4	−2.5	−2.3
By age of head of household					
<35 years	13.4	2.0	−2.0	2.4	−2.2
35-45 years	35.4	−3.4	−0.3	−0.7	4.6
46-54 years	25.3	−2.9	−1.3	1.3	3
55 and above	25.8	6.5	2.8	−0.9	−8.2
By gender of child					
Boys	50.3	1.4	−0.5	0	−0.7
Girls	49.7	−1.4	0.5	0.4	0.7
By age of child					
6-11 years	50.7	−10.2	9.9	−6.6	7.1
12-14 years	25.8	7.0	−6.1	2.5	−3.2
15-17 years	23.5	14.3	−14.6	12.3	−11.7

Source: Estimates based on ECOM 2005

be deprived at all, the single deprivation column shows that children in Brazzaville are more likely to live in monetary poor households (10 percentage points above average while incidence in Point Noire is 7 points below average) and children in Pointe Noire are more likely to be deprived in education (5 percentage points above average while incidence in Brazzaville is 5 points below average). One message that could be distilled from this picture is that rural areas ought to be prioritised when it comes to the regional allocation of national budgets regarding existing, new or scaled-up programmes that address deprivation in these dimensions.

The differences in incidence rates for household characteristics related to the composition and the head of the household are smaller. Extended family households are at higher risk of double deprivation and of deprivation in these dimensions in general. A similar pattern holds for households with an elderly head of the household and larger households (it is likely that these three subgroups largely overlap, however). The decomposition according to the gender of the household head suggests that children living in female-headed households are more likely to be single deprived in money and less likely in education, but it may well be that these modest differences would not or only marginally pass a statistical significance test.

There are no large differences between boys and girls but there is some variation according to age groups: children in the age group 15-17 are most at risk of double deprivation (14 percentage points above average) and of deprivation in education (12 percentage points above average). Children in the age group 6 to 11 are more likely to live in monetary poor households (10 percentage points). Since we used two complementary thresholds for defining deprivation in education (not going to school, too slow progress in school) we explore this further in Table 12.5 that decomposes the type of educational deprivation by age and gender. Of all children who are deprived in education, 13% do not go to school and 87% are two or more years behind in class given the normal age at which children are supposed to attend this class. This is an interesting finding, especially in relation to the enrolment-based indicators that are typically used to monitor progress, for instance, with respect to the second Millennium Development Goal (MDG).[4] Slow progress through the school system is the main problem in the Republic of Congo while non-enrolment is predominantly a problem for children in the age group of 15 to 17 (25%). In Notten and Buligescu (2008), evidence is presented that slow progress can be linked to late enrolment into primary education (30% on average, 34% of all pupils in primary public schools) and high repetition rates (20%

Table 12.5: Type of deprivation in education by age and gender

	All education deprived children	Double deprived		Education deprived	
		Boys	**Girls**	**Boys**	**Girls**
Does not go to school	12.8	13.9	10.9		
Age: 6-11 years	4.9	6.1	3.6	4.3	5.5
Age: 12-14 years	7.8	7.9	8.8	7.1	6.9
Age: 15-17 years	24.6	26.9	29.6	16.8	21.6
Slow progress	87.2	86.1	89.1		
Age: 6-11 years	95.1	93.9	96.4	95.7	94.5
Age: 12-14 years	92.2	92.1	91.2	92.9	93.1
Age: 15-17 years	75.4	73.1	70.4	83.2	78.4

Note: Only includes children in the age group 6 to 17 years deprived in education.
Source: Estimates based on ECOM 2005

on average, 27% of all pupils in primary public schools), but the data do not allow further distinguishing between both problems. There are some differences according to gender but they are rather modest: girls aged 15 to 17 are more likely not to be enrolled while slow progress affects more boys of the same age group. Finally, while there is not much difference between double and single deprived children for younger age groups, non-enrolment coincides much more frequently with monetary poverty for the oldest age group.

In addition to the information for constructing the education deprivation indicator, the child education section in the living standards component of the survey also includes information on perceptions of parents, motivation and distance to school facilities. Using the same reference groups, we exploit this information to get a better understanding of the context underlying this pattern of educational deprivation and the potential role of monetary poverty as an explanatory factor for deprivation in education (Table 12.6).

It is clear that the overall perception of parents about their children's schools is highly unfavourable. For instance, 42% of the parents of non-deprived children confirm that the lack of books is a problem at their child's school; complaints about the lack of teachers and too large class sizes are also frequently mentioned. The decomposition further shows that the school situation of children who are deprived in either or both of the money and education dimensions is even worse, with the highest prevalence of complaints by parents of double deprived children. Congolese parents are not satisfied with the quality of education that their children receive.

Further, parents of children who are not going to school have been asked for what reason their child is not enrolled. The most prevalent

Table 12.6: Educational context underlying patterns of deprivation

	Double deprived	Money deprived	Education deprived	Not deprived
Insufficiencies of the school[a]				
Satisfied	21.6	26.9	24.8	36.0
Lack of books	50.2	47.4	48.2	42.4
Mediocre teachers	15.2	12.9	12.2	11.0
Lack of teachers	38.9	30.5	27.2	20.4
Building in bad shape	26.5	21.5	15.8	13.2
Teachers are often absent	17.0	16.0	17.4	13.8
Classes too large	24.0	26.1	29.3	22.6
Reason for not going to school[a]				
Too young	26.8	–	30.9	–
Too old/has finished school	9.3	–	12.7	–
Too far	1.5	–	3.2	–
Lack of means/too expensive	63.9	–	52.5	–
Works	4.3	–	2.8	–
Useless/no interest	38.9	–	35.4	–
Illness/pregnancy	19.7	–	20.8	–
Failed exam	9.0	–	11.3	–
Is married	0.3	–	1.1	–
Other reason	19.5	–	24.6	–
Paid non regulatory school fees				
Yes	14.7	16.7	12.7	13.0
Walking distance to school				
Primary: more than 30 minutes	11.7	7.4	5.7	4.8
Secondary: more than 30 minutes	43.1	32.3	27.3	19.3

Note: [a] More than one affirmative answer possible. Includes children in the age group 6 to 17 years.

Source: Estimates based on ECOM 2005

answer is that going to school is too expensive or that there were no (financial) means available for going to school (64% of the parents of double deprived children and 53% of education deprived), indicating that the costs of education affects demand for schooling. Note also that the parents of these children are somewhat more likely to report that they had to pay non-regulatory school fees. However, the prevalence of other non-financial motivations for non-enrolment also point towards social or cultural reasons for not going to school (that is, being too young or too old). Whether it is due to a discrepancy between the skills needed for the labour market and those taught at school, the difficulty of finding a job in the first place or simply a reflection of the low quality of teaching, the high incidence of the response category 'useless/lack of interest' is disconcerting and merits further research. The distance to primary or secondary school is seldom used as an explanation for not going to school, despite the fact that deprived children are more likely to live further away from school than the non-deprived children; in that respect it seems that the key problem in the Congolese education system is more one of quality schooling rather than one of too few schools.

Similar decompositions for children aged 10 to 14 further suggest that child labour is essentially a rural phenomenon, affecting 12% of the rural children but only 0.7% of the urban children (Notten et al, 2008; results not shown here). Further, the perceptions of parents whose children perform paid work are even more negative in comparison to the parents of education and monetary deprived children. Combining these two pieces of information, these scores are suggestive of considerable inequalities in the quality of schools between rural and urban areas.

Conclusion

While the analysis in this chapter does not provide conclusive evidence about the transmission mechanisms between monetary poverty and deprivation in other dimensions of well-being, and it cannot prescribe specific policies, it provides an innovative and child-relevant perspective on the situation of multidimensional poverty in the Republic of Congo. It furthermore explores the cumulative patterns of deprivation in the money, education and work dimensions, and analyses the degree to which children suffering from multiple deprivations are different from single or non-deprived children. While the data to do so are often available, traditional poverty analyses in less developed countries do not reveal this picture.

Some of the key findings of this approach are that a disproportionate share of Congolese children in the age group 6 to 17 is simultaneously deprived in money and education (one in every three children). From a political perspective this is a non-negligible group. Within the context of formulating Poverty Reduction Strategies, the analysis also provides information that is relevant for translating broad strategies and goals into actual policies, budget allocations and synergies in policy making between corresponding policy sectors. In the case of the Republic of Congo, for instance, it is important to realise that the principal type of deprivation in education arises because children are progressing too slowly through the education system. This, in combination with the analysis of parents' perceptions about the problems of their children's school, suggests that there are shortcomings in terms of the supply of quality education. The higher drop-out rates of adolescents seems, in part, also related to these supply-side problems in the sense that a poor quality of education increases the opportunity costs of going to school. However, drop-out rates are also associated with the actual costs of schooling and the lack of resources at the household level. The latter is an indication that monetary reasons are a motivation for reduced demand for schooling. There are further some clues that non-enrolment in education is in part also related to social or cultural motivations. While the contextual analysis shows that the problems associated with children's well-being in terms of education are pervasive (that is, they also affect many children who are not deprived in education), it is clear that double deprived children are disproportionately affected by these problems.

According to the state budget, most of the investment funds reserved for basic education are destined for building new and upgrading old school facilities (Ministère du Plan et de L'Aménagement du Territoire, 2008). The analysis in this chapter suggests that a successful implementation of the PRSP not only requires action in terms of the physical upgrading of existing education infrastructure, but that efforts to improve the quality of education and to address the problems on the demand side for education should not be neglected (Comité National de Lutte contre la Pauvreté, 2008; Notten and Buligescu, 2008). This is relevant for all Congolese children of school-going age but is of particular importance for children involved in remunerative activities. The three-dimensional analysis has further identified two groups with a set of specific problems that may better be addressed through more narrowly targeted policy initiatives; the analysis suggests that child labour is still a relevant issue in rural areas while adolescent labour market participation is associated with dropping out of school and/or financial strain.

Notes

[1] This chapter benefits from previous research efforts described in the report *La pauvreté multidimensionnelle des enfants et des femmes en République du Congo* (April 2008) that was commissioned and financed by the United Nations Children's Fund (UNICEF) Congo Brazzaville. We thank the *Ministère du Plan, de l'Aménagement du Territoire et de l'Intégration Économique* for providing access to the 2005 household budget survey (ECOM, 2005).

[2] See the UN Treaty Collection (treaties.un.org/Pages/ViewDetails.aspx?src=TREATY&mtdsg_no=IV-11&chapter=4&lang=en).

[3] C138 Minimum Age Convention, 1973 (www.ilo.org/ilolex/cgi-lex/convde.pl?C138).

[4] See, for instance, the MDG website (www.undp.org/mdg/goal2.shtml).

References

Alkire, S. and Foster, J. (2008) *Counting and multidimensional poverty measurement*, Oxford Poverty & Human Development Indicator (OPHI) Working Paper Series, No 7, Oxford: OPHI, University of Oxford.

Bourguignon, F. and Chakravarty, S.R. (2003) 'The measurement of multidimensional poverty', *Journal of Economic Inequality*, vol 1, pp 25-49.

Comité National de Lutte contre la Pauvreté (2008) *Document final de Stratégie de Réduction de la Pauvreté* [*Final document of the Poverty Reduction Stategy*], March, Brazzaville: Ministere du Plan et de L'Amenagement du Territoire.

ECOM (Enquête Congolaise auprès des Ménages) (2005) *Enquête Congolaise auprès des ménages* [*Congolese Household Survey*], Brazzaville: Centre National de la Statistique et des Études Économique, CD-ROM.

Gordon, D., Nandy, S., Pantazis, C., Pemberton, S. and Townsend, P. (2003a) *The distribution of child poverty in the developing world*, Bristol: Centre for International Poverty Research, University of Bristol.

Gordon, D., Nandy, S., Pantazis, C., Pemberton, S. and Townsend, P. (2003b) *Child poverty in the developing world*, Bristol: The Policy Press.

IMF (International Monetary Fund) (2007) *Republic of Congo: Statistical appendix*, IMF country report No 07/207, Washington, DC: IMF.

Ministère du Plan et de L'Aménagement du Territoire (2008) *Budget de l'Etat, Volet investissement exercise 2008* [*State Budget, 2008 investment sheet*], Annexe a la loi de finances No 5-2008 du 15 Février 2008 pour l'Année 2008, Brazzaville: Ministere du Plan et de L'Amenagement du Territoire.

Ministère du Plan, de l'Aménagement du Territoire et de l'Intégration Économique (2006) *Profil de la Pauvreté au Congo en 2005: Rapport d'analyse* [*Poverty profile in Congo in 2005: Analytical report*], Brazzaville: Centre National de la Statistique et des Études Économique, April (www.cnsee.org/Donnees/Enquete/PDF/Ecom.pdf).

Notten, G. (2008) *Multidimensional poverty in the Republic of Congo: Being poor simultaneously in many ways*, BWPI Working Paper Series, Working Paper No 65, Manchester: Brooks World Poverty Institute (www.manchester.ac.uk/bwpi).

Notten, G. (2009) 'Is monetary poverty a suitable proxy for deprivation in the physical environment?', *Children, Youth and Environments*, vol 19, no 2, pp 20-35.

Notten, G. and Buligescu, B. (2008) *Policy options to reduce child poverty and improve access to education and health care in the Republic of Congo: Cost and impact simulations*, October, Brazzaville: United Nations Children's Fund Congo Brazzaville.

Notten, G., Makosso, B. and Mpoue, A. (April 2008) *La pauvreté multidimensionnelle des enfants et des femmes en République du Congo* [*Multidimensional poverty of children and women in the Republic of Congo*], Final report, Brazzaville: United Nations Children's Fund Congo, April (www.unicef.org/wcaro/wcaro_congo_poverty-resized.pdf).

Townsend, P. (1979) *Poverty in the United Kingdom: A survey of household resources and standards of living*, London: Penguin Books.

UNDP (United Nations Development Fund) (2005) *Rapport national sur les objectifs du millenaire pour le développement* [*National report on the Millennium Development Objectives*], Brazzaville: UNDP.

Table 12A.1: Overview of deprivation indicators and thresholds

Dimensions	Measurement	Welfare indicator	Threshold
Money	Household level[a]	Per equivalent adult expenditures	Expenditures below the national poverty line
Education	Individual level (age 6-17)	Enrolment and progress in school (grade versus age)	When a child does not go to school or has a delay of two or more grades
Work	Individual level (age 10-14)	Child labour	When a child works outside the household for wages
	Individual level (age 15-17)	Unemployment or underemployment	An adolescent is un(der) employed if they do not have a job (worked fewer than 35 hours in the past week) and searched for ways to get additional income from work
Nutrition	Household level	Did the household experience problems to satisfy its needs in terms of food?	Deprived when the answer is 'often' or 'always'
Health	Individual level	Use of health services in case of illness	Deprived when health services were not consulted
Water and sanitation	Household level	Distance to nearest source of drinking water, type of water source, type of toilet, mode of evacuation of waste water	Deprivation relative to a non-deprived reference household by means of multivariate methods (method: multiple correspondence analysis and cluster analysis)
Housing	Household level	Material walls, material floor, electricity, main energy source for cooking, number of people per room	
Integration	Household level	Distance to public transport, ownership of radio, television, telephone, means of transport (bicycle, car, boat, motorcycle)	

Note: [a] Although many indicators have been measured at a household level, all poverty rates are calculated counting individuals, not households.

THIRTEEN

Multidimensional child poverty in Vietnam

Keetie Roelen and Franziska Gassmann[1]

Introduction

The development and use of child poverty approaches has received increasing attention over the last decade resulting from the widespread acknowledgement that children deserve a child-focused perspective in the development and poverty reduction process worldwide (see, for example, Gordon et al, 2003; Minujin et al, 2005). This increased acknowledgement can be attributed to a number of reasons (see Gordon et al, 2003; Waddington, 2004; Minujin et al, 2005). The dependence on parents, household and community for the distribution of basic needs puts children at a higher risk of poverty and makes their situation less transparent (White et al, 2003). Moreover, poverty often manifests itself as a vicious circle, causing children to be trapped in poverty from birth onwards (Corak, 2006a), and children have different basic needs than adults (Waddington, 2004). Child-focused poverty approaches are crucial to account for these issues and to provide detailed information at the level of the individual child. A generally accepted definition and measurement method of child poverty is an important tool for both academics and policy makers. It provides an opportunity to gain insight into the poverty status of children but also gives the possibility to formulate and monitor sound poverty reduction objectives, strategies and policies (see, for example, Ben-Arieh, 2000; Corak, 2006b).

Since the Doi Moi (renovation) reform policies came into place in the late 1980s, Vietnam has experienced a period of outstanding economic growth, accompanied by a large reduction in poverty. Central planning was replaced by free market-oriented economic policies, inducing great changes in the agricultural sector, private business and employment development, foreign trade and social sector policies, creating business and entrepreneurial opportunities for Vietnamese people as well as for foreigners. The reforms proved to be greatly beneficial for Vietnam's economic performance, with average economic growth rates of 6.9%

from 1988 to 1994 and 7.4% from 1994 to 2000 (Glewwe, 2004). Furthermore, monetary poverty was also substantially reduced, from 58% in 1993 to 19.5% in 2004 (VASS, 2006). These poverty figures can be further disaggregated for various demographic groups and are often presented by region, gender and ethnicity. However, representation per age group is less common and, as a consequence, little is known about the state of child poverty in Vietnam. This chapter therefore presents a detailed multidimensional child poverty analysis, using a country-specific and child-focused approach.

The remainder of the chapter is structured as follows: first, we look at the child poverty approach for Vietnam in more detail. Second, the data and methodology are put forward. An extensive empirical analysis follows, providing insights into the multidimensional aspects of child poverty in Vietnam. Finally, we draw a number of conclusions.

Multidimensional child poverty in Vietnam from a country-specific and child-focused perspective

A careful assessment of current advances in child poverty measurement indicates that many have followed a similar process in their construction process, taking the same steps in a mostly similar sequence (Roelen et al, 2009). However, it also becomes apparent that many of these steps are taken in an implicit rather than explicit manner. Consequently, there is a lack of distinction between the different elements of the child poverty approach (Noble et al, 2006), and its underlying construct is not transparent (Ruggeri Laderchi et al, 2003). As a result, child poverty approaches are misinterpreted and misunderstood. Different scholars have emphasised the importance of having a clear understanding of the underlying rationale and concept of a poverty approach to be able to adequately and appropriately use it (see, for example, Ravallion, 1994; Ruggeri Laderchi et al, 2003; Vandivere and McPhee, 2008) and the lack thereof in many poverty debates (Noble et al 2006). Roelen et al (2009) established a generic construction process from the analysis of child poverty approaches to illustrate and clarify the steps taken in the development of child poverty approaches. These steps include the identification of the rationale and purpose of the approach, the formulation of its concept, the selection of domains and indicators and finally, the establishment of poverty measures. The development of the multidimensional child poverty approach for Vietnam has carefully followed this process to ensure that choices at each step are made in an explicit manner to avoid misunderstandings and misinterpretation (Roelen et al, 2009).

The identified rationale and purpose of the child poverty approach for Vietnam is two-fold, and the result of extensive discussions and deliberations with policy makers (including line ministries, United Nations [UN] agencies and other international organisations). On the one hand, the approach should serve as a policy advocacy tool, and on the other hand, it should provide detailed information about child poverty to act as a policy input or monitoring tool. This two-fold purpose requires a versatile approach that is able to provide intuitive output understandable for the lay public as well as information at different levels of disaggregation to serve as detailed policy input. The formulation of the approach's conceptual framework then followed after a careful assessment of current advances in child poverty measurement and discussions with partners and counterparts. A first consideration in the conceptual framework was the monetary versus multidimensional focus, a division commonly made within the area of poverty measurement. Against the backdrop of a number of conceptual and technical drawbacks of the money metric poverty approach, it was deemed more suitable to develop a multidimensional approach for the measurement of child poverty in Vietnam, including other aspects than income considered to more adequately reflect the state of poverty (see Roelen et al, 2010). Moreover, we chose to focus on an outcome rather than opportunity-based approach for two reasons. First, opportunities are very hard to define and observe, making it difficult to operationalise opportunity-based approaches such as Sen's capability approach (Alkire, 2008). Second, the degree to which instruments can be transformed into outcomes is dependent on different factors, one being age (Sen, 1999; Wagle, 2002). Children might not have the power to fully utilise their opportunity set as they are dependent on their direct environment, including parents, family and community, for the transformation of opportunities into positive outcomes (White et al, 2003). The approach proposed here is child-specific, ensuring that the actual situation of that child is considered without making assumptions about the distribution of resources within the household (White et al, 2003). The notion of a child-specific approach, however, does not prevent the use of household-level indicators as certain issues are only measured at the household level (Gordon et al, 2003). Finally, the proposed approach was tailored to fit the social and cultural context of Vietnam, only including issues deemed to adequately reflect child poverty. Along the lines of the consistency versus specificity trade-off (Thorbecke, 2008), we chose to be specific at the national level to facilitate consistent intra-country comparisons.

By definition, a multidimensional poverty approach is comprised of a set of domains, reflecting different aspects that are considered to constitute poverty. Indicators are chosen to provide a comprehensive representation of the development within the respective domains. An elaborate discussion on the choice of domains and indicators is important as it is subject to value judgements that should be made as explicit as possible, and firmly grounded in the academic and policy arena (Alkire, 2008). Alkire (2008) and Biggeri (2007) identified various mechanisms for the selection of domains for multidimensional poverty measurement purposes. These selection mechanisms include the assessment of available data, expert opinions or assumptions, public consensus, participatory assessments and empirical evidence about people's values with respect to poverty and well-being (Biggeri, 2007; Alkire, 2008). As all these mechanisms have advantages and disadvantages and alone do not suffice as a valid selection method (Alkire, 2008), a combination of mechanisms was used for the purposes of this child poverty approach. The method of assumptions and expert opinion inspired a first set of domains and indicators, complemented by those identified on the basis of public consensus. Next, participatory processes were employed to account for the views of stakeholders and key informants, thereby ensuring the incorporation of the Vietnamese context. A final selection mechanism at work during the identification process for domains was the assessment of existing data. The interviews with key informants, an in-depth assessment of available data and consistency check with the conceptual framework provided a reduced and final feasible list of seven domains and twelve indicators (see Table 13.1; see also Roelen et al, 2009).

Data and methodology

Multiple Indicator Cluster Survey 2006

The data used for the calculation of multidimensional child poverty in Vietnam was the Multiple Indicator Cluster Survey from 2006. The Vietnam Survey is based on the standardised Multiple Indicator Cluster Survey as technically supported by the UN Children's Fund (UNICEF). The first and second round was conducted in 1995 and 2000, while the third round was completed in 2006. The survey contained a range of questions especially focused on education, health, reproductive health and HIV/AIDS, and was separated into questionnaires for households, women of reproductive age and children under five. Regions were identified as the main sampling domains and the sample was selected

Table 13.1: Indicators of the Vietnam child poverty approach

Domain	Indicators
1. Education poverty	% of children not enrolled at the appropriate level
	% of children not having completed primary school
2. Health poverty	% of children not fully immunised
3. Shelter poverty	% of children living in dwellings without electricity
	% of children living in dwellings without proper roofing
	% of children living in dwellings without proper flooring
4. Water and sanitation poverty	% of children living in dwellings without hygienic sanitation
	% of children living in dwellings without safe drinking water
5. Child work	% of children working
6. Leisure poverty	% of children not having toys
	% of children not having at least one book
7. Social inclusion and protection poverty	% of children not having their birth registered

in two stages, based on enumeration areas from the census (GSO, 2007). The sample consisted of a total number of 8,356 households with 36,573 individuals, out of which 10,874 were children up to 16 years of age.

Household surveys such as the Multiple Indicator Cluster Survey provide micro-data at the level of the individual child, allowing for the decomposition of all deprivations by the individual child. A number of limitations are also inherent to the use of the Multiple Indicator Cluster Survey. A first limitation is that the micro-data was not collected for all children of all age groups. While information on health was only collected for children up to five years of age, educational information was only collected for children aged five and upwards. Hence, the total number and types of deprivations that a child suffers theoretically depends on the age category.[2] A second limitation is that data on nutrition was not available at the time of writing. This is a considerable drawback as nutritional indicators are important aspects of a multidimensional measurement of child poverty. Third, the sampling method of the Survey (and other household surveys in Vietnam) caused a substantial group in the society to be omitted from the sample and subsequent data. The sample was constructed on the basis of the official lists of registered households in communes and urban wards in Vietnam that have lived in the enumeration area for at least six months

(Pincus and Sender, 2006). This implies that households or individuals that had recently migrated were not included in the sampling frame (Edmonds and Turk, 2004). Furthermore, due to the strict household registration system, or *ho khau* system, many households and individuals did not satisfy the necessary criteria to newly register and thus stay unregistered (Pincus and Sender, 2006). The omission of this group in society is not only important because of its suspected significant size, but even more so because of the denial of social and public services they experienced due to their status. The structural exclusion of this group from the data will most likely present us with underestimations for child poverty in Vietnam.

Methodology

The methodology to aggregate the indicator and domain-level information builds on previous work by Atkinson (2003), Gordon et al (2003) and Alkire and Foster (2008).

The first level of aggregation entails the aggregation from the indicator to domain level. Domain poverty is constituted by not meeting the poverty line for at least one of the indicators within that domain. At the next level of aggregation, poverty in at least one domain constitutes poverty in terms of the union approach, and poverty in all domains constitutes poverty along the definition of the intersection approach (Atkinson, 2003). While the intersection approach is generally considered to be too constricting, excluding too many children from the definition of poverty, the union approach is widely thought to be too inclusive and to lead to overestimations of poverty (Alkire and Foster, 2008). The multidimensional poverty line of our approach was based on a dual cut-off identification strategy (Alkire and Foster, 2008), implying that a child is identified as poor when he/she is vulnerable in at least two domains. The dual cut-off identification strategy is an alternative measure, satisfying a number of important properties such as decomposability, symmetry and dimensional monotonicity (Alkire and Foster, 2008), and was previously used in the global child poverty study by Gordon et al (2003). We opted for an equal weighting strategy in the aggregation of indicator and domain poverty rates. Existing (child) poverty approaches have opted for different schemes, some applying equal weighting (see, for example, Land et al, 2001; Gordon et al, 2003; Bradshaw et al, 2006), while others have used statistical inference methods such as Principal Components Analysis (PCA) (see, for example, Tanton et al, 2006) or stated Preference Methods (see, for example, de Kruijk and Rutten, 2007; Watson et al, 2008). The choices for these methods are inspired by practical and feasibility considerations, conceptual motivations and technical reasons but remain subject to debate and value judgements. In the case of Vietnam, conceptual considerations have not resulted in compelling reasons to assign greater weight to certain domains over others.

For comparative purposes and in order to evaluate the use of the dual cut-off identification strategy, we produced poverty incidence rates using poverty in one domain (union approach) as well as two domains (dual cut-off identification strategy). Poverty outcomes on the basis of the union approach are referred to as *child deprivation* while outcomes based on the dual cut-off identification strategy are referred to as *child poverty*.

A detailed picture of child poverty in Vietnam

An analysis of the child poverty rates at the indicator and domain level provides detailed insight into issues more or less stringent for different demographic groups. Indicator and domain poverty rates disaggregated by gender, area, region, ethnicity and age group are presented in Table 13.2.

The results suggest that the most pressing areas of poverty are leisure, sanitation and health. Almost 70% of all children are deprived in the leisure domain, almost half of all children do not use proper water and sanitation facilities and one out of three children is vulnerable with respect to health. The highest indicator poverty rates can also be found within these domains. Almost two thirds of children up to age five do not have a children's book or picture book, and 41% of all children live in a dwelling without a hygienic sanitation facility. Moreover, one out of three children aged two to four have not received the full package of vaccinations. Indicators with lower, but still considerable, poverty rates include availability of toys, child work and type of flooring in the dwelling in which the child resides, which range between 20% and 30%. Furthermore, almost one out of five children aged 5-15 are not enrolled at the appropriate level of schooling for their age. Primary school completion, electricity and proper roofing in the child's dwelling, safe drinking water and birth registration are indicators with the lowest overall poverty rates, ranging from 4% to 13%.

Demographic decomposition of these figures displays large disparities for some groups, which can also differ from indicator to indicator. Across the board, there is no sign of gender inequality. All indicators display fairly equal poverty rates for boys and girls. Decomposition by area, however, points towards a large urban—rural divide in Vietnam.

Table 13.2: Indicator and domain poverty rates for children in Vietnam

Domain poverty rate	Education poverty		Health poverty	Shelter poverty			Water and sanitation poverty		Child work	Leisure poverty		Social inclusion and protection poverty
	18.7	31.4	24.6	44.1	23.7	69.1						12.4
	Enrolment poverty rate (% children not enrolled)	Completion poverty rate (% children not having completed primary school)	Immunisation poverty rate (% children not fully immunised)	Electricity poverty rate (% children in dwellings without electricity)	Roofing poverty rate (% children in dwellings without proper roofing)	Flooring poverty rate (% children in dwellings without proper flooring)	Sanitation poverty rate (% children in dwellings without hygienic sanitation)	Drinking water poverty rate (% children in dwellings without safe drinking water)	Child work rate (% children working)	Toy poverty rate (% children not having toys)	Book poverty rate (% children not having at least one book)	Birth registration poverty rate (% children not having birth registration)
Total	18.38	9.11	31.37	4.02	9.01	21.95	41.10	12.56	23.67	29.32	65.63	12.37
Gender												
Male	18.93	9.54	31.61	4.27	9.18	22.57	41.62	12.29	22.97	27.87	64.35	12.75
Female	17.79	8.66	31.14	3.76	8.82	21.30	40.54	12.85	24.39	30.90	67.02	11.95
	***	***	***	***	***	***	***	***	***	***	***	***
Area												
Urban	12.27	5.12	20.16	0.65	2.22	6.75	13.06	3.26	10.40	10.71	40.41	5.73
Rural	19.99	10.19	34.86	4.95	10.87	26.13	48.79	15.11	27.19	35.08	73.43	14.42
	***	***	***	***	***	***	***	***	***	***	***	***
Region												
Red River Delta	12.65	2.45	16.94	0.00	1.04	4.74	13.41	1.26	23.25	13.97	50.79	2.22
North East	20.67	14.39	52.78	13.59	25.64	51.46	51.55	19.34	33.24	62.02	78.05	17.42
North West	33.57	20.28	58.90	28.09	18.82	69.49	74.63	30.96	40.69	41.58	74.73	24.73
North Central Coast	13.08	4.87	33.01	0.28	5.76	12.70	35.74	8.47	30.01	44.76	73.02	12.70
South Central Coast	16.67	7.79	23.35	1.06	3.18	8.71	40.76	11.29	18.63	21.79	55.71	13.21

(continued)

	Education poverty		Health poverty	Shelter poverty			Water and sanitation poverty		Child work	Leisure poverty		Social inclusion and protection poverty
Domain poverty rate	Enrolment poverty rate (% children not enrolled)	Completion poverty rate (% children not having completed primary school)	Immunisation poverty rate (% children not fully immunised)	Electricity poverty rate (% children in dwellings without electricity)	Roofing poverty rate (% children in dwellings without proper roofing)	Flooring poverty rate (% children in dwellings without proper flooring)	Sanitation poverty rate (% children in dwellings without hygienic sanitation)	Drinking water poverty rate (% children in dwellings without safe drinking water)	Child work rate (% children working)	Toy poverty rate (% children not having toys)	Book poverty rate (% children not having at least one book)	Birth registration poverty rate (% children not having birth registration)
	18.7	31.4	24.6	44.1	23.7	69.1						12.4
Region (continued)												
Central Highlands	22.30	17.49	42.59	6.57	2.90	18.24	57.01	18.02	14.81	40.27	71.81	21.70
South East	20.37	8.98	21.29	1.75	1.35	6.85	26.45	7.17	15.54	18.75	55.36	4.17
Mekong River Delta	23.23	13.73	32.29	3.18	17.86	38.99	69.17	23.41	20.88	18.98	75.30	19.88
Ethnicity	***	***	***	***	***	***	***	***	***	***	***	***
Kinh/Chinese	16.33	6.9	25.51	1.03	5.22	13.77	33.79	8.98	21.24	20.74	61.65	8.44
Other	28.76	21.11	58.53	18.84	27.74	62.41	77.25	30.28	35.81	69.35	84.29	30.62
Age groups	***	***		***	***	***			***			
0-2	na	na	32.60	4.46	9.41	22.89	43.59	12.42	na	31.99	70.87	14.92
3-4	na	na	30.71	4.55	9.06	24.49	45.47	13.67	na	25.18	57.48	8.38
5	17.65	na	na	5.10	10.05	25.74	45.45	13.64	1.01	na	na	na
6-10	6.87	na	na	4.68	10.43	23.51	41.77	13.01	11.69	na	na	na
11-14	17.49	9.86	na	3.26	7.54	19.09	38.16	11.73	38.19	na	na	na
15	59.64	6.37	na	2.64	8.32	20.56	37.76	12.47	na	na	na	na

Note: ***<0.001, significance level chi-squared group equality of means.
Source: Authors' calculations from Multiple Indicator Cluster Survey 2006

Although significant, the rates and their urban—rural differences are fairly modest with respect to the educational and social protection indicators. However, large disparities can be observed, especially when considering the water and sanitation and shelter domains. Poverty incidence in terms of these indicators is four to seven times higher in rural areas than it is in urban areas. Regional results also display considerable differences with respect to indicator poverty rates. The Red River Delta region holds the smallest percentage of vulnerable children in terms of all indicators, except for child labour. The northern mountainous North West and North East regions are always among the regions with the highest proportion of vulnerable children followed by the Mekong River Delta and Central Highlands regions. Nevertheless, the regional rankings of poverty rates differ from indicator to indicator, especially among the middle rankings. The North Central Coast region, for example, ranks second best with respect to the educational indicators while it has the second largest poverty rate when considering the leisure domain. Finally, interpretation of age group results is less straightforward as not all indicators are observed for all children. Nevertheless, the results indicate, in line with intuition, that older children are more vulnerable with respect to net enrolment while a larger proportion of younger children suffer poverty in terms of leisure and social protection and inclusion.

The detailed information at the indicator and domain level is consequently further aggregated to arrive at composite poverty indicators: the child deprivation rate and child poverty rate. Child deprivation is constituted by deprivation in at least one domain along the lines of the union approach. By the same token, the dual cut-off identification strategy implies that child poverty is based on deprivation in at least two domains. Estimates for the two different rates are presented in Table 13.3.

Overall child deprivation amounts to 67%, while one third of all children are identified as poor. The patterns for both child deprivation and child poverty in terms of different demographic groups are generally similar to those observed for individual indicators. There is no significant difference in poverty incidence for boys and girls. Furthermore, poverty incidence is much higher in rural areas than it is in urban areas, regardless of the poverty definition used. Rural child deprivation is 74% compared to 39% in urban areas. The relative disparity is even greater in terms of child poverty, with respective rates of 12% and 43%. Regional figures point towards the North West and North East regions as bad performers while the Red River Delta and South East regions hold the lowest poverty rates. Child poverty has

Table 13.3: Child deprivation and child poverty in Vietnam

	Child deprivation rate (one-domain poverty line)	Child poverty rate (two-domain poverty line)
Total	66.97	36.65
Male	66.39	36.86
Female	67.58	35.42
	***	***
Urban	38.80	12.04
Rural	74.70	43.40
	***	***
Red River Delta	47.63	11.26
North East	80.20	58.76
North West	93.09	77.65
North Central Coast	68.49	30.95
South Central Coast	60.61	28.79
Central Highlands	74.21	40.53
South East	55.14	22.63
Mekong River Delta	83.20	59.95
	***	***
Kinh/Chinese	61.51	28.27
Other ethnicity	93.96	78.09
0-2	82.98	51.12
3-4	76.50	52.04
5	60.52	28.08
6-10	56.21	27.30
11-14	65.38	35.05
15	73.59	36.14

Note: ***<0.001, significance level chi-squared group equality of means.

Source: Authors' calculations from Multiple Indicator Cluster Survey 2006

an incidence rate of 11% in the Red River Delta, while this amounts to 78% in the North West region. Previous studies have also identified these large spatial differences relating to monetary indicators (see, for example, Minot, 2000; Minot and Baulch, 2004; Nguyen et al, 2007). With respect to age groups, the authors observe high rates of poverty for the youngest children, in age brackets 0-2 and 3-4, and the oldest children of age 15. These results, however, only present a partial picture, as not all indicators are observable for all children.

The figures in Table 13.3 indicate that child deprivation is almost twice as high as child poverty, basing poverty measurement on the union approach compared to the dual cut-off identification strategy. The high headcount rate for child deprivation confirms the previously identified inclusive nature of the method, suggesting that it suffers a large inclusion error and does not discriminate well between poor and non-poor children. This finding underlines the conceptual reasoning to employ child poverty as the most preferred method. A sensitivity test by plotting child poverty rates against various cut-off points/poverty lines for children living in different regions indicates that poverty rankings only change when using cut-off points higher than two domains, illustrating the robustness of the approach.

Overlap of domain poverty

A more detailed picture of child poverty in Vietnam and the most common combinations of domain poverty can be obtained by considering the overlap of domain poverty. An insight into these combinations of domain poverty might provide important input into the policy formulation and design process when effectively aiming to reduce child poverty in multiple dimensions. The poverty incidence rates in Table 13.4 represent the proportion of children considered poor in both domains as a share of all children for whom both domains can be observed. For example, 6.7% of all children aged 5-15 are deprived with respect to both education and shelter. Correlation coefficients for the corresponding combinations and their levels of significance are also reported in Table 13.4.

The most prevalent combinations of deprivation inevitably include domains with the highest poverty rates. The combined deprivation of leisure and water and sanitation is most prevalent, with an incidence rate of 40% for children aged 0-4. In other words, 4 out of 10 children in Vietnam aged 0-4 suffer deprivation with respect to leisure as well as water and sanitation. Shelter and health poverty in combination with leisure poverty is suffered by, respectively, 23% of the different age groups. The domains referring to housing conditions are most strongly associated with a correlation coefficient of 0.435. Despite high incidence rates, the correlation coefficients do not display a high degree of correlation between domain deprivations. These low coefficients are largely due to taking the whole child population in Vietnam as a reference group. The poverty incidence rate is 37%, meaning that 63% of all children do not suffer deprivation in a combination of at least two domains. The inclusion of non-poor children in the reference group weakens the overall correlation coefficients.

Table 13.4: Multiple poverty and correlation matrix

	Education	Health	Shelter	Water and sanitation	Labour	Leisure	Social inclusion and protection
Education	5-15, n=8,167 18.7%	x	5-15, n=8,167 6.7% 0.1626*	5-15, n=8,167 10.9% 0.1654*	5-15, n=8,167 4.7% 0.1309*	x	x
Health		2-4, n=1,627 31.3%	2-4, n=1,627 12.8% 0.2745*	2-4, n=1,627 19.2% 0.2209*	x	2-4, n=1,627 23.2% 0.2084*	2-4, n=1,627 4.2% 0.2029*
Shelter			0-15, n=10,874 24.6%	0-15, n=10,874 20.4% 0.4351*	0-15, n=10,874 7.1% 0.1167*	0-4, n=2,707 22.8% 0.2574*	0-4, n=2,707 6.7% 0.2730*
Water and sanitation				0-15, n=10,874 44.1%	5-14, n=7,228 12.1% 0.1043*	0-4, n=2,707 39.5% 0.3232*	0-4, n=2,707 9.4% 0.2660*
Labour					5-14, n=7,228 23.7%	x	x
Leisure						0-4, n=2,707 69.1%	0-4, n=2,707 11.5% 0.2257*
Social inclusion and protection							0-4, n=2,707 12.4%

Notes: x indicates that no overlap could be observed due to non-corresponding age groups, *<0.01, significance level Phi correlation coefficient.

Source: Authors' calculations from Multiple Indicator Cluster Survey 2006

Conclusion

In this chapter, we have taken a multidimensional and child-specific approach for the measurement of child poverty in Vietnam. This approach has provided conceptual as well as empirical outcomes that add value to the debate on child poverty measurement in the academic and policy arena. In conceptual terms, the use of a child poverty approach that is multidimensional in nature combined with an outcome, child-specific and country-specific focus comprises the study's contribution. Empirical outcomes include an investigation into the use of different poverty lines, a detailed multidimensional child poverty analysis for Vietnam and an analysis of the overlap and correlation of domain poverty.

Conceptually, this chapter has explored the use of a country-specific approach to capture child poverty in a multidimensional matter. It has illustrated the process of development and the inherent choices and decisions that were made to construct a sound and solid approach. Such choices include the formulation of the rationale and purpose of the approach, the establishment of its conceptual framework and selection of domains and indicators. Furthermore, the chapter has explored the use of two aggregation methods, namely the union and dual cut-off identification strategy.

Empirical findings highlight a number of relevant issues. The detailed child poverty profile on the basis of indicator and domain poverty rates point towards water and sanitation, leisure and shelter as the most pressing areas for children in Vietnam. Domain poverty is lowest with respect to education. Demographic decomposition of poverty estimates do not display any signs of gender inequality but do suggest a large urban–rural divide and regional disparities in terms of poverty incidence at indicator and domain level. The direction of regional disparities might differ, depending on the indicator or domain under consideration. The aggregated estimates suggest that the use of either a union or dual cut-off identification strategy has far-reaching implications for the outcomes for children in Vietnam. Child deprivation, based on the union approach, is estimated at 67% of the total child population in Vietnam while child poverty, based on the dual cut-off identification strategy, captures 32% of all children. Incidence rates based on the dual cut-off identification strategy are found to be a more robust and representative measure of child poverty. Analysis of combined domain vulnerabilities and overlap of deprivations indicate that poverty referring to shelter and water and sanitation are most closely related.

Considering the chapter's conceptual and empirical outcomes, we consider the multidimensional child poverty approach for Vietnam to be an important tool for policy making and academic research. It fills a knowledge gap in Vietnam and sets an example for the development of other country-specific child poverty approaches. It provides detailed information that is decomposable at different levels of analysis, allowing for detailed policy design and evaluation. Further research should explore the causes and determinants of child poverty at the indicator, domain and aggregate level, and the relation between poverty in various domains in more detail.

Notes

[1] Part of this study is based on a research project commissioned by UNICEF Vietnam in cooperation with the Ministry of Labor, Invalids and Social Welfare and the General Statistical Office.

[2] For example, seven indicators are observable for children in the age bracket 6-10 while nine indicators are observable for those in the age bracket 3-4. Hence, the latter group by definition has more chance of being captured by the poverty measure.

References

Alkire, S. (2008) 'Choosing dimensions: the capability approach and multidimensional poverty', in N. Kakwani and J. Silber (eds) *The many dimensions of poverty*, New York: Palgrave Macmillan, pp 89-119.

Alkire, S. and Foster, J. (2008) *Counting and multidimensional poverty measurement*, Oxford Poverty & Human Development Initiative (OPHI) Working Paper 7, Oxford: OPHI, University of Oxford.

Atkinson, A.B. (2003) 'Multidimensional deprivation: contrasting social welfare and counting approaches', *Journal of Economic Inequality*, vol 1, pp 51-65.

Ben-Arieh, A. (2000) 'Beyond welfare: measuring and monitoring the state of children − new trends and domains', *Social Indicators Research*, vol 52, pp 235-57.

Biggeri, M. (2007) *Choosing dimensions in the case of children's wellbeing*, Number 7, Maitreyee, Boston, MA: Human Development and Capability Association. (www.capabilityapproach.com/pubs/Maitreyee7_February_07.pdf)

Bradshaw, J., Hoelscher, P. and Richardson, D. (2006) 'An index of child well-being in the European Union', *Social Indicators Research*, vol 80, no 1, pp 133-77.

Corak, M. (2006a) *Do poor children become poor adults? Lessons from a cross-country comparison of generational earnings mobility*, Bonn: Institute for the Study of Labor (IZA).

Corak, M. (2006b) 'Principles and practicalities for measuring child poverty', *International Social Security Review*, vol 59, no 2, pp 3-132.

De Kruijk, H. and Rutten, M. (2007) *Weighting dimensions of poverty based on people's priorities: Constructing a composite poverty index for the Maldives*, Q-Squared Working Paper No 35, Toronto: Q-Squared, University of Toronto.

Edmonds, E. and Turk, C. (2004) 'Child labor in transition in Vietnam', in P. Glewwe, N. Agrawal and D. Dollar (eds) *Economic growth, poverty and household welfare in Vietnam*, Washington DC: World Bank, pp 505-50.

Glewwe, P. (2004) 'An overview of economic growth and household welfare in Vietnam in the 1990s', in P. Glewwe, N. Agrawal and D. Dollar (eds) *Economic growth, poverty and household welfare in Vietnam*, Washington, DC: World Bank, pp 1-26.

Gordon, D., Nandy, S., Pantazis, C., Pemberton, S. and Townsend, P. (2003) *Child poverty in the developing world*, Bristol: The Policy Press.

GSO (General Statistical Office) (2007) *Findings from the Vietnam Multiple Indicator Cluster Survey 2006*, Hanoi: GSO, Vietnam Committee for Population Family and Children and UNICEF.

Land, K., Lamb, V. and Mustillo, S. (2001) 'Child and youth well-being in the United States, 1975-1998: some findings from a new index', *Social Indicators Research*, vol 56, pp 241-320.

Minot, N. (2000) 'Generating disaggregated poverty maps: an application to Vietnam', *World Development*, vol 28, no 2, pp 319-31.

Minot, N. and Baulch, B. (2004) 'The spatial distribution of poverty in Vietnam and the potential for targeting', in P. Glewwe, N. Agrawal and D. Dollar (eds) *Economic growth, poverty and household welfare in Vietnam*, Washington, DC: World Bank, pp 229-72.

Minujin, A., Delamonica, E.E., Gonzalez, E. and Davidziuk, A. (2005) 'Children living in poverty: a review of child poverty definitions, measurements and policies', UNICEF Conference on Children and Poverty: Global Context, Local Solutions, New York: UNICEF, The New School.

Nguyen, B., Albrecht, J., Vroman, S. and Westbrook, D. (2007) 'A quantile regression decomposition of urban–rural inequality in Vietnam', *Journal of Development Economics*, vol 83, pp 466-90.

Noble, M., Wright, G. and Cluver, L. (2006) 'Developing a child-focused and multidimensional model of child poverty for South Africa', *Journal of Children and Poverty*, vol 12, no 1, pp 39-53.

Pincus, J. and Sender, J. (2006) *Quantifying poverty in Vietnam*, Hanoi: UNDP, School of Oriental and African Studies.

Ravallion, M. (1994) *Poverty comparisons*, Langhorne, PA: Harwood Academic Publishers.

Roelen, K., Gassmann, F. and de Neubourg, C. (2009) 'The importance of choice and definition for the measurement of child poverty – the case of Vietnam', *Child Indicators Research*, vol 2, no 3, pp 245-63.

Roelen, K., Gassmann, F and de Neubourg, C. (2010) Child Poverty in Vietnam – providing insights using a country-specific and multidimensional model, *Social Indicators Research*, 98, no 1, 129.

Ruggeri Laderchi, C., Saith, R. and Steward, F. (2003) 'Does it matter that we do not agree on the definition of poverty? A comparison of four approaches', *Oxford Development Studies*, vol 31, no 3, pp 243-74.

Sen, A. (1999) *Development as freedom*, Oxford: Oxford University Press.

Tanton, R., Harding, A., Daly, A., Mcnamara, J. and Yap, M. (2006) 'Children at risk of social exclusion. Methodology and overview', International Geographic Union Conference, Brisbane, 3-7 July.

Thorbecke, E. (2008) 'Multidimensional poverty: conceptual and measurement issues', in N. Kakwani and J. Silber (eds) *The many dimensions of poverty*, New York: Palgrave Macmillan. pp 3-19.

Vandivere, S. and McPhee, C. (2008) 'Methods for tabulating indices of child well-being and context: an illustration and comparison of performance in 13 American states', *Child Indicators Research*, vol 1, no 3, pp 251-90.

VASS (Vietnamese Academy of Social Sciences) (2006) *Vietnam poverty update report: Poverty and poverty reduction in Vietnam 1993-2004*, Hanoi: VASS.

Waddington, H. (2004) *Linking economic policy to childhood poverty: A review of the evidence on growth, trade reform and macroeconomic policy*, Childhood Poverty Research and Policy Centre (CHIP) Report, London: CHIP.

Wagle, U. (2002) 'Rethinking poverty: definition and measurement', *International Social Science Journal*, vol 54, no 171, pp 155-65.

Watson, V., Sutton, M., Dibben, C. and Ryan, M. (2008) *Deriving weights for the Index of Multiple Deprivation based on societal preferences: The application of a discrete choice experiment*, Oxford Poverty & Human Development Initiative (OPHI) Working Paper 23, Oxford: OPHI, University of Oxford.

White, H., Leavy, J. and Masters, A. (2003) 'Comparative perspectives on child poverty: a review of poverty measures', *Journal of Human Development*, vol 4, no 3, pp 379-96.

FOURTEEN

Multidimensional child deprivation in Iran

Sepideh Yousefzadeh Faal Deghati, Andrés Mideros Mora and Chris de Neubourg

Introduction

In recent decades there has been worldwide acknowledgement that children's well-being should be analysed in a multidimensional way (Gordon et al, 2003a,b; Minujin et al, 2005; Redmond, 2008; Roelen, 2010). Subsequently, various methodologies have evolved over time concerning the definition and measurement of various aspects of deprivation (Nussbaum, 1992; Sen, 1993; Robeyns, 2006; Alkire and Foster 2008). Therefore, a wide range of literature has been produced on the status of deprived children in various developing and developed countries (Wagstaff and Watanabe, 1999; UNICEF Innocenti Research Centre, 2000; Land et al, 2001; Gordon et al, 2003a,b; Notten and Roelen, 2010). Meanwhile, poverty scholars are increasingly highlighting the importance of contextualising deprivation analyses within the sociopolitical realities that surround communities (Wagstaff and Watanabe, 1999; Gassmann, 2000; Rogers, 2003; Belloni and Carriero, 2008; Jones, 2009; Wells, 2009; Bourdillion et al, 2010). Similarly, the context in which children's deprivations are studied is important. Despite commonalities among this age cohort, there are socioeconomic and political particularities in different societies that affect children's lives and their transition to adulthood. These particularities shape children's being and social identity in multicultural societies (Matthews and Limb, 1999; Qvortrup, 1999; de Moura, 2001; Monteith and McLaughlin, 2005).

As a multi-ethnic and multicultural society, Iran is not unusual in exposing children of various regions to diverse socioeconomic political and cultural realities (Atabaki, 2005; Hosseinbor, 2009; Khorshidi et al, 2010). However, for decades, scholars have predominantly focused on political disparities while studies on minorities' socioeconomic conditions are scarce. Similarly, there are few disaggregated data on children's well-being from different ethnic groups in Iran. This chapter aims to analyse children's multidimensional deprivation and to examine differences between regions in Iran in 2009. The analysis aims to explore who are the most deprived children and how inequalities in children's deprivation can be distinguished on regional grounds. The data used in this study are drawn from the latest national income and expenditure survey conducted by the Statistical Centre of Iran in 2009).

Contextual analysis

In the past three decades, Iran has gone through many changes in sociopolitical, cultural and economic conditions. It is important to investigate some of these changes in order to contextualise the findings of this chapter.

Economy

With approximately US$330 billion gross domestic product (GDP) in 2009, Iran has the second largest economy in the Middle East and North Africa (after Saudi Arabia), and is categorised as a lower middle-income country (World Bank, 2010). Economic instability and fragility have blighted the country since the 1979 revolution. In 1977, two years before the revolution, Iran was experiencing its highest economic growth, with the real GDP per capita growing 6.6% per year (Abrahamian, 1980; Salehi-Isfahani, 2006). The economic growth was mainly a result of an improved oil export and as such, subject to fluctuation in the international market. On the other hand, a small elite controlled the oil revenue with little regard for fair income distribution. Therefore, the sharp rise in income did not translate directly into the living standards of the average Iranian household (Salehi-Esfahani and Pesaran, 2008). The Islamic revolution in 1979 was partly a consequence of these inequalities. After the revolution, GDP per capita declined continuously due to various reasons: the eight years of devastating war with Iraq (1980-88), oil price collapse, emigration of skilled professionals and international sanctions imposed on the country. By the end of the war (1988), GDP per capita was half its previous level of 1977 (Salehi-Isfahani, 2006). After the Iran–Iraq war, the country was left with over a million casualties and US$650 billion in damage (Ehsani, 1994); in many ways reconstruction was an overwhelming task. The government started to decrease its control over the market, oil revenue started to recover and at the same time private investments were initiated. Nevertheless, the country was not able to set a long-term industrialisation strategy or to mobilise internal resources required for economic transformation (Ehsani, 1994).[1] As such during the 1990s, GDP per capita continued to react to various economic and political instabilities. To date, economic instability remains a major challenge for the government. Both the World Bank and the International Monetary Fund (IMF) reported GDP per capita annual growth as 7% in 2007-08, and 2-2.5% in 2008-09. In this chapter, child deprivation is analysed for 2009.

Childhood

Within the childhood discourse, some contextual specifications also need to be acknowledged. First is the age of end of childhood. The Iranian Constitution, civil and penal codes are all prepared in the light of a particular interpretation of *Sharia law*[2] (Yousefzadeh, 2010). Consequently, there are implications for children at various levels, especially for girls. For instance, the age of criminal responsibility is 8 years and 9 months for girls and 14 years and 7 months for boys;[3] the minimum age for marriage is 13 for girls and 15 for boys, and so on. As such, from a legal perspective, children's transition to adulthood happens at a very young age in Iran. Second is the cultural diversity among children. Iran is populated by diverse ethnic and linguistic groups that are mainly concentrated in certain geographic areas (Aghajanian, 1983). There is no official data on the population of ethnic and religious minorities in Iran; however, different sources refer to more than 40% of the population as minority ethnic groups in the country (Akhbari and Zolfeghari, 2009; Kheiltash et al, 2009; Khorshidi et al, 2010). Over time, ethnic groups in Iran have experienced various times of political unrest (Atabaki, 2005). For instance, Arabs and Kurds were in the frontline cities in the war with Iraq (1980-88). The civil conflicts after the 1979 revolution affected Kurdistan and southern cities of West Azerbaijan differently and more severely than other provinces. Meanwhile, for decades some of these regions have been among the more deprived areas of the country. Although this chapter only focuses on a snapshot from 2009, it is acknowledged that deprivation is carried over from past decades in some provinces inhabited by minority ethnic groups, particularly Sistan and Baluchistan (Aghajanian, 1983; Chillar, 2005). Third is the overall socioeconomic development of the country. Being a lower middle-income country, Iran has been able to improve its basic health and education indicators (World Bank, 2007). Although disparities still exist (both in terms of gender and geography), the overall trend has improved, especially since the 1990s.[4] Therefore, child rights issues in contemporary Iran are not that much about basic education or vaccination coverage, but about other evolving issues related to modernisation. For instance, in 2009, immunisation coverage for all vaccines was 99%, and the primary school attendance ratio between 2005 and 2009 was 91% for girls and 94% for boys (UNICEF, 2011). However, the modernisation process and subsequent rapid urbanisation have contributed to evolving urban social inequalities. Some of those social inequalities directly affected children in the poor neighbourhoods of large cities as well as suburban areas, street children and child labour (Assadi, 2011). Nevertheless, due to a lack of data, we were not able to examine these important dimensions. As such, it is important to note that multidimensional child deprivation in Iran, as portrayed in this chapter, does not capture all child rights issues in contemporary Iran, including child abuse, street children, prostitution, execution of minors and juvenile delinquency.

Methodology and conceptual framework

Some United Nations (UN) exclusive summits and events have provided specific insights into poverty and child poverty in particular.[5] The UN General Assembly in 2007 provided a multidimensional definition of children's deprivation, using a rights-based approach. In this chapter, in order to define child deprivation dimensions and indicators, the UN Convention on the Rights of the Child (UNCRC) is used as the reference in this study for a number of reasons:[6]

- The Convention applies a holistic approach in defining children's rights and brings together the socioeconomic, cultural, civil and political rights of the child. Therefore, using the UNCRC as the point of entry assists this research to consider different dimensions of children's well-being. It must be noted, however, that not every dimension is examined in this research because of a lack of available data.

- Applying the UNCRC also makes it possible to view the child and childhood from a social construct perspective. Under its different articles, it deconstructs the concept of the child as the girl child, at-risk children, refugees and minority groups, etc. It also deconstructs children's different roles and rights (the right to freedom of expression, freedom of association, etc). Therefore using the Convention as a guide could lead this research to take into account the diversity and particularity of the child, interactions with his/her surroundings and the setting of childhood (Kjorholt, 2004).

• In an ideal world, children, child rights practitioners, policy makers and other duty bearers should work together to define the various dimensions of child deprivation, and in turn, ensure the objectivity of the indicators. A number of studies have applied such an approach in defining different dimensions of child deprivation (Feeny and Boyden, 2003; Harpham et al, 2005; Sixsmith et al, 2007; Barnes and Wright, 2009). However, this research did not have the luxury to engage children and child rights stakeholders in defining deprivation dimensions. Therefore, using the Convention as a guide also helps in avoiding subjective judgements in choosing the dimensions.

It must be noted that the Convention itself has been criticised by various scholars for its universalist approach and for imposing Western standards (Bentley, 2002; Arts, 2010).[7] However, the drafting process of the UNCRC was participatory, and delegates of different countries debated and negotiated areas of their concern. Eventually, the Convention set the minimum non-negotiable rights, and some more controversial areas were left flexible in order to accommodate more diversity (see, for example, Article 1 and the definition of the child) (Arts, 2010). The Iranian delegate also participated actively in that process (Afshin-Jam and Danesh, 2009) and eventually Iran ratified the Convention in 1994 with a general reservation: 'The Government of the Islamic Republic of Iran reserves the right not to apply any provisions or articles of the Convention that are incompatible with Islamic Laws and the international legislation in effect.'[8]

One of the areas affected largely by the negotiating process of drafting the UNCRC was the defining age for the end of childhood. The Convention's Article 1 defines children as 'every human being below the age of eighteen years unless under the law applicable to the child, majority is attained earlier'. Meanwhile, the Iranian legal system defines the age of end of childhood as nine lunar years for girls and fifteen lunar years for boys (Article 1210 of the Civil Code) (Yousefzadeh, 2010). Applying the Convention's Article 1 may not help in defining the age threshold of the indicators of this research as it leaves it flexible to the domestically applicable laws. Nevertheless, when it comes to *some* important indicators (minimum age of marriage, minimum age for work), the Convention refers to other international instruments[9] with specific thresholds.[10]

While the Convention is treated as a guide for this research, it is also important to define the methodology for applying the Convention to the research. This research applied the 3 P's approach in categorising dimensions of poverty: *provision, protection and participation* (Cantwell, 1993; Penn, 1999; Lurie, 2003/04). The various categories do not compete with each other and were not considered as distinct definitions. The aim was rather to formulate the articles for easier examination of the applications of those rights, while acknowledging the essential interdependence of the three categories. Under *provision* are grouped children's rights to material and non-material resources that are essential for their full development (money, love, power, opportunity, knowledge, self-esteem, etc). Also, the importance of including all children, particularly from marginalised groups, is elaborated under various articles. Under *protection* are categorised children's rights to be protected from exploitation, neglect and abuse. Similarly, the right to access the proper means of information as well as an enabling environment to *participation* are explained under a number of articles.

Accordingly, child deprivation in this chapter is discussed under six dimensions, seven indicators and three main categories (the 3 P's). The study focused on outcome indicators, with the level of analysis focusing on the individual child. Nevertheless, for some indicators the data was only available or relevant at the household level. Data was accessed through the Statistical Centre of Iran and is available to the local independent researchers. The Statistical Centre of Iran conducts an income and expenditure study on an annual basis of sample households in both rural and urban areas (36,868 households in the 2009 survey). The samples are representative at the national level. The income and expenditure surveys have been running since 1963, but the computerised version is only available from 1984 onwards. The government collects the data for macroeconomic analysis. It is carefully designed and considerably detailed (Salehi-Isfahani, 2007). It has a wide geographic coverage and includes large samples. The sampling consists of two stages, stratified at rural and urban and province levels. The latest census is referred to in order to select sample blocs and households on a random basis (five blocs and five households from each bloc). In each level – rural, urban and province – the number of blocs is the total number of observation divided by five (Farzin, 2008). Apart from information in income and expenditure, there are also questions on general characteristics of the household members, some of which is used in this research. In this chapter we use the latest available data, that is, 2009.[11] In defining indicators, a three-level division was applied (deprived, moderately deprived, not deprived) as opposed to a binary approach. The continuum range of deprivation has already been introduced by other scholars within the child poverty discourse (Gordon et al, 2003a). The reason to apply a deprivation continuum approach in this chapter is that the binary approach separates different groups of children in an absolute term. For instance, a child is either enrolled in school at the right age, or is not. As such, those children who attend school, but who are older than their cohort, are equated with those children who are not enrolled at all. In this particular example, very different reasons could contribute to the child's status of not going to school or repeating grades. Therefore, and in order to avoid unjustified dichotomies in this study, we decided to define indicators of deprivation at three levels.

In order to measure the multidimensional poverty rate in this study, a dual cut-off identification strategy was applied (Gordon et al, 2003a; Alkire and Foster, 2008). As such, children who were deprived from at least two dimensions were identified as deprived. Moderately deprived children were identified as being moderately deprived in two or more dimensions or deprived in one dimension. Deprivation was measured for each dimension using the indicators and thresholds described in Table 14.1. The thresholds were defined to establish three mutually exclusive deprivation levels (deprived, moderately deprived, not deprived), and to avoid deprivation level overlapping. We used two groups of indicators: the first group was used for education, child labour and child marriage dimensions and measured for each child; the second group was measured at the household level and was used for housing, water and sanitation, and information dimensions. The first group of indicators was measured for the whole population and disaggregated by gender and area (urban and rural). In addition, both groups were presented by province and household type. The correlation between education deprivation and child labour was analysed in detail and discussed by age cohort.

Rationale behind the choices for the indicators in the Iranian context

Education

The education system in Iran consists of three levels: five years of primary school, three years of secondary school (junior high school) and three years of high school. Primary school starts when children complete their sixth birthday. However, those children who are born after August have to enrol with the next year's cohort. As such, as this

Table 14.1: Indicators for children's multidimensional poverty in Iran

	Dimension	Indicator	Not deprived	Moderately deprived	Deprived	Age group
Provision	Education	School enrolment	% of children attending primary or secondary school – age matches the grade	% of children attending primary or secondary school – age does not match the grade	% of children not attending primary or secondary school	6-17
	Housing	No of people per room	% of children living in households with two people or less per room	% of children living in households with three people per room	% of children living in households with more than three people per room	0-17
		House materials	% of children living in houses with metal skeleton	% of children living in concrete houses	% of children living in houses made with brick, stone, wood or mud	0-17
	Water and sanitation	Access to safe drinking water and sanitation	% of children living in households with access to safe drinking water and bathroom	% of children living in households with access to safe drinking water but no bathroom	% of children living in households with no access to safe drinking water	0-17
Protection	Child labour	Working status of children	% of children not working (neither paid job nor household care)	% of children: 15-17 who are in paid job and study, 7-17 children who do household chores and study, and children who seek job and study	% of children: under 15 children who are in paid job, children who seek job and do not study, children who do the household chores and do not study, children who seek job and do not study, and children who are in paid job and do not study	0-17
	Child marriage	Marital status of children	% of children who are not married and have no children	% of children who are married	% of children who are married and have children	9-17
Participation	Information	Access to means of information	% of children living in households with access to radio, television, computer and internet	% of children living in households with access to radio or television; and computer or internet	% of children living in households with no access to radio, television, computer and internet	0-17

study also shows, some children start the first year of primary school at the age of six and some at the age of seven. In light of the fact that each grade has a different code, the relevant code was considered to identify the children's grade in each cohort.

Both primary and secondary school enrolments were examined in this study. The Iranian Constitution elaborates the right to education under Article 30, 'the right of the people'. Article 30 defines the government's duty to provide free education, not only for primary school but also for secondary education. There is also the Education Act 1974, which spells out the government's duty in providing *free* and *compulsory* education for *all* up to the end of secondary school (junior high school). As such, the Act sets the standard lower than what is stated within the Constitution. Article 30 of the Iranian Constitution also focuses on education for all and is therefore introducing a non-discriminatory principle in providing education to children. On the other hand, the Constitution's Article 13 focuses on *recognised* minorities and their religious performances within the limits of the law. Accordingly, Zoroastrians, Jews and Christians are the only recognised minority religions. There is no reference to other religious minorities and their right to education. For instance, Bahahi children cannot attend public schools unless they declare themselves as Muslims and deny their own religion. Similarly, refugee and migrant children may only benefit from public school if they have official documents. Hence, in practical terms, the non-discriminatory principle, as defined in the Iranian Constitution, is not applied for children's education. The UNCRC, on the other hand, spells out a child's right to education in different articles. Article 28 stresses compulsory and free primary education for all, and elaborates on equal opportunity and progressive realisation of a child's right to education. Under the Convention, a state's duty to ensure access to secondary education is second in priority after primary education. In fact, while states are called on to ensure free and compulsory primary education for all children, they are *encouraged* to provide different forms of secondary education and to offer financial assistance in *case of need*. The unequal stress on primary and secondary education in the Convention does not imply unequal usefulness. Rather, it means that providing free and accessible compulsory secondary education may not be possible for a number of countries. Therefore, they should focus on free and obligatory primary education for all as the first step.[12] Iran has progressively improved primary school enrolment (Millennium Development Goal 2006); therefore, secondary education is also examined in this study.

Net enrolment in each schooling year is an indicator for the proportion of children who are not deprived. Also, children who are younger than the matching age for each grade are categorised as not deprived. Children who are enrolled in school, but their age does not match their grade (older), are categorised as moderately deprived. Deprived children are the age cohort not enrolled in school at all. Other relevant education indicators (for example, quality of education) were not analysed in this chapter due to lack of information.

Housing

Under this dimension, two indicators were examined, both contextually specific and domestically designed: the safety of homes and number of people per room. In the past decades, Iran has been affected by strong earthquakes, causing devastating casualties (1972, more than 5,000 dead; 1978, over 25,000 dead; 1990, more than 40,000 dead; and in 2005 over 25,000 dead) (Amirabadi et al, 2007). Expert opinions concerning the number of dead and injured are primarily concerned with the strength of the houses, their frame and structure and materials used in the building (Amirabadi et al, 2007). Accordingly, the Statistical Centre of Iran has conducted a series of studies to measure the strength of homes in different parts of the country. 'Strong homes' are defined as shelters with a metal or concrete structure (Amirabadi et al, 2007). Accordingly, in this study, children living in houses with either concrete or metal structures were categorised as not deprived; those who lived in houses with metal or stone in the material (but not the structure) were categorised as moderately deprived; and those living in houses with mud or wooden materials were categorised as deprived. As for the second indicator, that is, number of people per room, the domestic standards define the appropriate density as two people or less per room (Kazemipoor, 2004). Accordingly, children living in houses with up to two people per room were categorised as not deprived; three people per room were defined as moderately[13] deprived; and more than three people per room were categorised as deprived. Eventually, one composite indicator was used: children deprived in at least one indicator were deprived; children who were not deprived in any of the indicators were not deprived; and the rest were categorised as 'moderately deprived'.

Water and sanitation

There is no specific reference to water or sanitation in the Iranian Constitution. In the UNCRC, access to safe drinking water is mentioned under the child's right to the highest standard of health services, that is, Article 24. Access to safe drinking water and a bathroom were the two indicators under this dimension. Ideally, sanitation should be analysed (WHO and UNICEF, 2004) as opposed to having a bathroom. Nevertheless, the questionnaire used in this study did not include any question on sanitation. Therefore, owning a bathroom was extrapolated to mean sanitation. No access to drinking water was categorised as deprived under this research – regardless of access to a bathroom. Access to water but no bathroom was categorised as moderately deprived. And access to both water and bathroom indicates non-deprivation.

Child labour

In the Iranian Constitution, there is no specific reference to child labour. However, in the Labour Law there are several articles discussing children. Article 79 of the Iranian Labour Law prohibits employing individuals of below 15 years of age.[14] In addition, according to Article 84, in case of hazardous jobs for the health or moral character of the trainees and youth, the minimum age is defined as 18. The UNCRC refers to child labour in Article 32 specifically as well as Article 39. The articles do not introduce a specific minimum age. However, the *Implementation handbook for the Convention* calls for defining the minimum age based on other international instruments, particularly International Labour Organization (ILO) No 138 (the Minimum Age Convention 1973).

In order to define the threshold for the child/adolescent's work, the context and social class needs to be taken into account (Zimmer-Gembeck and Mortimer, 2006). For instance, in many developed countries, adolescents may choose to work in order to have independence from their family, or use their income for other purposes, for example, travelling. However, in developing countries, neither the deprived families nor their children seem to have other choices but to send their children to work when they need extra income for the household. In other words, children have to contribute to the family's income; they do not choose to work. In addition, their parents cannot trade off the immediate benefit from their children's work with long-term educational achievements. In fact, a family's social class and economic resources are the key factors in sending their children to work (Newman, 1999; Blustein et al, 2000). Consequently, children's work and education are often in direct competition (Shanahan et al, 2002). One other consideration about adolescent labour is that often their work (for both girls and boys) is examined within the paid market. Therefore, if the work involves producing goods for self-consumption or household chores, it is not considered as *work*. As it is predominantly girls who are involved with household chores, the work also means acquiring gender roles (Cunningham, 2001; Leaper and Friedman, 2007). In this study and in the context of Iran, non-deprivation means no engagement in income-earning jobs. Additionally, a child's education was considered a key factor in defining the threshold. Finally, doing household chores was also treated as *work*. As such, the threshold was defined as follows:

Deprived:
• Children under 15 who are working
• Children under 17 doing household chores, *and not studying*
• Children under 17, working or seeking a job *and not studying*

Moderately deprived:
• Children under 17, seeking job and study
• Children under 17, doing household chores, and studying
• Children over 15, working and studying

Not deprived:
• Children, under 18, not working

Child marriage

According to Article 1041 of the Iranian Civil Code, the minimum age for marriage is 13 for girls and 15 for boys. As for the UNCRC, a specific minimum age is not set for marriage. However, the *Implementation handbook of the Convention* refers to Article 2 in order to apply a non-discriminatory approach to set the minimum age for boys and girls. It also refers to the Convention on the Consent to Marriage[15] as well as the general recommendation of the Committee on the Elimination of Discrimination against Women (CEDAW).[16] In this study, age 18 was considered to define the threshold for marriage indicator. The threshold was set as 18 mainly in order to ensure children's rights to education, health and development. Nevertheless, in Iran specifically there are also reasons related to age of legal responsibilities for financial matters. Article 1210 of the Iranian Civil Code defines the age of maturity as 9 for girls and 15 for boys. However, the Article has a note that conditions financial responsibility to full legal capacity,[17] and the age for full legal capacity is not elaborated further. This note also refers to boys, that is, age 15 is also not considered the age of full legal capacity. Therefore, married children may not be given required legal financial responsibilities. In practical terms, they are not considered *matured*. Accordingly, indicators are defined as: children who are married and are already parents, categorised as deprived; children who are married as moderately deprived;[18] and those who are not married by the age of 17 as not deprived.

Access to means of information

Increasingly, children use the media in its different forms in their daily lives. In Iran, too, although television and radio continue to dominate the role of providing information, the internet and computers are increasingly available to both children and adults. Even in some of the most deprived regions of Iran, internet cafes provide children and adolescents with the opportunity to access some of the latest technology and means of information.[19] Access to means of information and media sources are codified in the Iranian Constitution as well as the UNCRC. Both sources refer to responsibilities of the state to improve public awareness through the media (Article 3 of the Iranian Constitution and Article 17 of the UNCRC). The right of minority ethnic groups to use their own language in the press and media at the regional level is spelled out in Article 15 of the Iranian Constitution. Similarly, Article 17(d) of the UNCRC refers to the particular linguistic needs of minority groups. The dataset, however, enables us to analyse access exclusively. However, we acknowledge the importance of examining the quality and nature of the media products. It is also crucial to analyse how much time is spent watching television or what kinds of programmes are being watched. What kinds of programmes are produced for different social groups? How do various social groups differ in their use of diverse forms of media? How are computers or the internet used? And so on (Vandewater et al, 2006; Dooly, 2010; Rideout et al, 2010). Due to lack of qualifying information, this study only examined *access* to television and radio, computers and the internet. In light of the fact that qualifying information on access was not available in the questionnaire, possession of the means (television, radio, etc) was examined as the proxy measure. Computers and the internet were examined partially because they could have educational value. But equally important was exposure to independent news through them (as opposed to what the state media was providing). Meanwhile writing 'blogs' is another form of access to information. Blog writing has been an important area of exposure to information, particularly for adolescent girls. It allows them to raise and share social issues that concern them in an anonymous manner (Shekarloo, 2004; Yousefzadeh and Sherkaloo, 2010). Access to all means is an indicator of non-deprivation. Partial access (either of the means) shows moderate deprivation, and no access to any of the means indicates deprivation.

Data analysis

As mentioned earlier, the research examines data from the 2009 national survey on households' income and expenditure. The overall sample included 36,868 households and 150,647 people from all 30 provinces in the country and was nationally representative. It represents a population of 76 million. Out of this number, 22 million (46,613 observations) were children (0–17), that is, 29%, 48.5% girls and 51.5% boys. About 66.6% of the children of the sample lived in rural areas and 33.4% of the children were living in urban areas. The survey sample was weighted at the household level. The dataset has frequently been used for poverty estimations,[20] and scholars refer to the fact that the large samples that cover wide geographic areas allow for estimates of average expenditures (Farzin, 2008). Demographic results (see Table 14.2) are comparable with the UN population prospects (UN, 2009), especially for the child population.

Table 14.2: Demographic stratification comparison (2009)

	Survey (weighted)	UN – population prospects
Total population (000s)	75,999	74,196
Children (0-17) (000s)	22,064	22,221
Children (% of total population)	29.0	29.9
Male children (% of total males)	29.7	30.2
Female children (% of total females)	28.3	29.7
Boys (% of total children)	51.5	51.3
Girls (% of total children)	48.5	48.7

Table 14.3 presents the proportion of children under all three levels, that is, deprived, moderately deprived and not deprived, as a share of all children for whom the indicator can be applied. At the country level, the dimensions with higher deprived ratios are housing (30.5%), education (9.4%), child labour (7.6%) and water and sanitation (3.4%), followed by information (1.5%) and child marriage (0.5%). The moderately deprived ratios are higher for information (92.9%), housing (55.3%), education (11.3%) and water and sanitation (7.8%), followed by child labour (3.3%) and child marriage (2.1%). The order does not change by gender or by area (urban/rural). Deprivation is respectively higher for girls and rural areas than for boys and urban areas.

As shown in Table 14.3, the most pressing issues for the 'deprived' groups are housing and education in rural areas. Some 44% of rural children live in houses where either there are more than three people

Table 14.3: Dimensional deprivation incidence rate (%)

	Level	Education	Housing	Water and sanitation	Child labour	Child marriage	Information
		Provi-sion	**Protec-tion**	**Partici-pation**			
Total	**Deprived**	**9.4**	**30.5**	**3.4**	**7.6**	**0.5**	**1.5**
	Moderately deprived	**11.3**	**55.3**	**7.8**	**3.3**	**2.1**	**92.9**
	Not deprived	**79.3**	**14.2**	**88.8**	**89.1**	**95.4**	**5.6**
Female	Deprived	10.3	–	–	8.3	0.9	–
	Moderately deprived	10.0	–	–	3.2	3.5	–
	Not deprived	79.7	–	–	88.5	95.6	–
Male	Deprived	8.5	–	–	6.8	0.0	–
	Moderately deprived	12.6	–	–	3.5	0.7	–
	Not deprived	78.9	–	–	89.7	99.3	–
Rural	Deprived	14.8	43.8	9.2	12.9	0.5	3.3
	Moderately deprived	12.8	52.0	18.4	4.8	2.6	95.5
	Not deprived	72.4	4.2	72.5	82.3	97.9	1.2
Urban	Deprived	6.7	23.8	0.6	4.9	0.4	0.6
	Moderately deprived	10.6	56.9	2.5	2.6	1.8	91.6
	Not deprived	82.7	19.3	96.9	92.5	97.8	7.8
Provinces							
Sistan and Baluchistan	Deprived	21.3	62.6	19.1	14.6	1.0	10.5
West Azerbaijan	Deprived	16.5	28.1	3.7	14.9	1.0	0.6
Qazvin	Deprived	6.3	41.7	0.1	4.4	1.2	0.5
Kerman	Deprived	9.6	41.1	13.2	6.3	0.4	2.8
Khorazan Razavi	Deprived	12.2	39.5	1.5	9.8	1.2	0.9
Hormozgan	Deprived	9.5	29.5	11.4	6.9	0.5	4.1
Zanjan	Deprived	8.4	43.2	1.4	7.9	0.5	0.1
Kurdistan	Deprived	11.1	27.5	1.7	8.4	0.8	0.1

(or more) per room or the house does not meet national safety standards. Further examination of housing indicators, at the national level, suggests that under the number of people per room indicator, 26% are deprived (more than three people) and about 21% are moderately deprived (more than two but up to three people). Also, under the safety indicator, 9% of the children are deprived and 70% are moderately deprived. The safety of the house and materials used in the structure is a major challenge; that is, most children are moderately deprived. The deprivation rate under the number of people per room is significantly higher in rural areas (34.5% rural, 21.3% urban). Similarly, house safety is more of a rural issue for deprived groups (19.1% deprivation in rural and 4.0% deprivation in urban areas). Moderately deprived groups, however, are equally bad in both rural and urban areas (73.7% rural, 68.0% urban) under house safety. As such, safety of the rural buildings could explain the casualty of the earthquakes in the rural areas.

Table 14.4 shows that 3.5% of children between the ages of 6 and 11 are deprived of an education, that is, they are not enrolled in a school at all. UNICEF's *State of the World's Children 2010*[21] indicates net primary school rates at 91% for boys and 100% for girls between 2003 and 2008 (UNICEF, 2010). Neither the overall enrolment ratio (net) nor disparities between boys and girls at the primary school level in UNICEF's report is consistent with our findings in this study. Also, UNICEF's report does not show the breakdown for urban/rural areas. The UN Educational, Scientific and Cultural Organization's (UNESCO) statistics, however, show 96% net enrolment in primary school for girls and 100% for boys in 2008 (UNESCO, 2008). Finally, the Iranian government's second report (in collaboration with the UN) for the Millennium Development Goals (MDGs) indicates more than a 98% enrolment rate overall for primary schools in 2005 and does not provide a breakdown for boys and girls (Government of Iran, 2006). Deprivation among children of secondary school age (12-14) is higher compared to the primary school cohort. Our study indicates that some 12% of all 12- to 14-year-old children were deprived and 19% moderately deprived. UNICEF's 2010 report indicates 21% deprivation among boys and 25% deprivation among girls. Neither UNESCO nor the second MDG report provide information on secondary school enrolment rates. In our study, the deprivation rate for the high school cohort was not included under the education indicator. However, it is important to note that education deprivation increases by age (see Table 14.4). Similarly, child labour is more frequent among older children. As for moderate education deprivation, children aged 12-14 outnumber other age cohorts. Moreover, below the age of 14,

Table 14.4: Education deprivation rate, disaggregated by age cohorts (%)

	Deprivation level	**6-11**	**12-14**	**15-17**
Education	Deprived	3.5	11.8	15.6
	Moderately deprived	9.6	18.7	7.9
	Not deprived	86.9	69.5	76.5
Labour	Deprived	1.1	9.2	15.2
	Moderately deprived	0.0	0.1	10.7
	Not deprived	98.9	90.7	74.1

moderate deprivation is higher than deprivation. Thus it is more likely that children continue their education while working when they are in primary or secondary school. However, working children who are older than 14 are more likely to drop out of school.

Our analysis (see Table 14.3) shows that deprivation from access to safe drinking water and sanitation is highest in Sistan and Baluchistan, Kerman and Hormozgan respectively (19.1%, 13.2%, 11.4%). The latest official report indicating access to water and sanitation in 2002 by UNICEF and the World Health Organization (WHO) suggests that in 2002, 4% of the urban population and 31% of the rural population did not have access to sources of safe drinking water in their houses. Similarly, 14% of the urban population and 22% of the rural families did not have access to sanitation (UNICEF and WHO, 2004).

Breakdown of the rural/urban data suggests that the critical issues for moderately deprived children are information and housing, both for rural and urban areas. Some 95.5% of rural children have limited access to means of information. In addition, 68.0% of the children in urban areas live in houses with moderately safe materials used in the structure. As for child labour, 12.9% of rural children are deprived, that is, they are either under 15 years old and already working, or they are between 15 and 17 years old and are engaged in income-earning jobs or household chores and *do not attend school*. As for gender differences with regards to child labour, girls outnumber boys (8.3% versus 6.8%). The higher rate is partially due to household chores performed by young girls. It is important to note that in our analysis household chores were counted as deprivation only if the child was not attending school. As such, the working status of the child affects girls more proportionately than boys. As for marriage, married children, who are already parents, make up less than 1%. However, 4.4% of girls are married under the age of 17, most of them between 15 and 17.

Regional disparities, gender inequality and the rural/urban divide exist under all indicators. The highest education deprivation rates exist among rural girls in Sistan and Baluchistan (26.2% girls, 16.8% boys), West Azerbaijan (20.1% girls, 12.5% boys) and Kurdistan (14.9% girls, 7.7% boys). Similarly, child labour has the highest gender disparity in West Azerbaijan (18.9% girls, 10.5% boys), Sistan and Baluchistan (18.6% girls, 11.1% boys), Hamedan (12.8% girls, 10.3% boys), North Korasan (11.8% girls, 9.1% boys), Golestan (12.8% girls, 9.0% boys), Kurdistan (10.1% girls, 7.1% boys) and East Azerbaijan (11.8% girls, 6.8% boys).

Sistan and Baluchistan has the highest level of deprivation in four dimensions (education, housing, water and sanitation and information), and the second one in two dimensions (labour and marriage). West Azerbaijan (labour, education and marriage), Qazvin (marriage and housing), Kerman (housing, water and sanitation and information), Khorazan Razavi (education, labour and marriage), Hormozgan (water and sanitation and information), Hamedan (education and labour) and Golestan (education and labour) have high deprivation rates[22] under two or more dimensions. Zanjan (housing), Kurdistan (marriage), Khuzestan (information), Qom (housing), South Korazan (water and sanitation), North Korazan (labour) and Ardebil (marriage) have high deprivation rates in one dimension. It is important to note that most of the above-mentioned disparity provinces (see Table 14.2) host minority ethnic groups. Therefore, child deprivation is more likely to affect areas with minority ethnic groups, particularly Sistan and Baluchistan and West Azerbaijan.

Examining correlations between different dimensions suggests that a high correlation exists between education and labour (0.76). Other important correlations are between housing and water and sanitation (0.27), child marriage and labour (0.23), and information with housing (0.22). Figure 14.1 shows the correlation between child labour and education across different provinces. Sistan and Baluchistan and West Azerbaijan have the highest rate of working children who are not enrolled in school. Kurdistan and East Azerbaijan are in the middle, while Tehran is among the provinces with the lowest percentage of working children who do not attend school. It must be mentioned, however, that street children selling flowers, newspapers, and so on are

Figure 14.1: Correlation between education and child labour, disaggregated by province

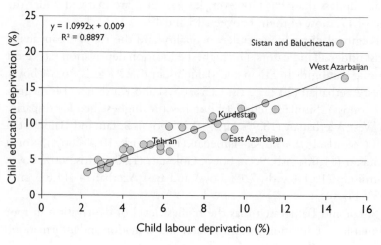

observed more frequently in Tehran and its suburbs. As such, it is more likely for working children not attending school at the provincial level to work either at home or in factories or workshops.

Closer examination of the family system data suggests higher deprivation rates under housing, labour and child marriage in polygamous families (see Table 14.5), and under education in single-headed, extended and polygamous families. On the other hand, there is a lower deprivation rate among children living with both parents in nuclear families, except for child marriage and housing, which are lower for single-headed families. Also, Table 14.5 suggests that working children are more likely to drop out of school in polygamous families. However, the ratio of working children who still attend school is higher in single-headed families. As such, children in polygamous and single-headed families are more likely to fall within deprived and moderately deprived groups. Further qualifying information is, of course, required to examine the causality between family system and dynamics with regard to children's multidimensional well-being. Although this analysis does not suggest a causality relationship, the correlation is observed.

Disaggregated data on single-headed families shows higher deprivation rates in male-headed families under all dimensions, except for child marriage. The most pressing areas are education and labour. Fourteen per cent of children in female-headed families are deprived

Table 14.5: Deprivation rate, disaggregated by household type (%)

Dimensions	Deprivation level	Single-headed nuclear	Both parents nuclear	Both parents extended	Single-headed extended	Poly-gamous
Education	Deprived	15.3	8.0	16.8	19.4	19.3
	Moderately deprived	12.9	11.1	11.9	15.7	11.0
	Not deprived	71.8	80.9	71.3	64.8	69.7
Housing	Deprived	26.5	30.0	35.0	28.3	46.9
	Moderately deprived	61.4	54.4	59.3	64.9	47.9
	Not deprived	12.1	15.6	5.7	6.8	5.2
Child labour	Deprived	13.1	6.3	14.2	14.0	15.1
	Moderately deprived	3.9	3.0	5.7	9.0	4.1
	Not deprived	83.0	90.7	80.1	77.0	80.8
Child marriage	Deprived	0.0	0.5	0.5	0.0	0.9
	Moderately deprived	1.1	1.5	6.8	5.5	1.8
	Not deprived	98.9	98.0	92.7	94.5	97.3

from education compared to 23.2% of children in male-headed families. Similarly, while 12.7% of children in female-headed families are deprived under labour, in male-headed families 15.7% of children are deprived (see Table 14.6).

Table 14.6: Deprivation rate in single-headed households, disaggregated by gender (%)

Dimension	Female-headed households	Male-headed households
Education	14.0	23.2
Housing	24.8	37.2
Water and sanitation	4.0	8.1
Child labour	12.7	15.7
Child marriage	1.1	0.0
Information	3.7	11.3

A comparison between the deprived and moderately deprived ratio in different provinces (see Table 14.7) indicates that the ranking of the provinces is not consistent in rural and urban areas. As expected, rural areas have higher deprivation rates than urban areas. While the disparities between deprived rural and urban children are significantly large, inequalities under moderately deprived children are relatively small. As for gender differences, deprived girls outnumber boys, whereas moderate deprivation is almost the same for girls and boys. As discussed earlier, the gender difference could partially be explained within differences in the labour and education dimensions. Provinces with a higher rank in child deprivation also have higher disparities between rural and urban areas. Overall deprivation at country level is not representative of the situation of deprived children in Sistan and Baluchistan, Kerman, South Khorasan and West Azerbaijan. It is also important to note that while dimensional deprivation rates suggest higher deprivation in provinces with minority ethnic groups, the overall deprivation ratio masks large ethnic disparities. Overall child deprivation is highest in polygamous and single-headed families respectively.

The moderately deprived rate (75.3%) significantly outnumbers the deprived rate (8.6%). Figure 14.2 shows the multidimensional deprivation rate in both rural (dotted line) and urban areas. Ranking in rural and urban areas is different for moderate deprivation. Also, provinces with a higher deprivation rate have lower moderate deprivations.

Overall, about 75% of children are moderately deprived on a national level, and there are clear disparities between rural and urban

Table 14.7: Child multidimensional deprivation and moderate deprivation rate (%)

Province	Rural deprivation	Urban deprivation	Rural moderate deprivation	Urban moderate deprivation
Zanjan	13.4	2	86.5	86.1
Yazd	9.8	3	88	90.2
West Azerbaijan	20.6	5.3	75.6	82
Tehran	8.2	3.4	83.5	63
South Khorasan	20.8	4.4	79.2	85.2
Sistan Baluchistan	43.7	16.5	56.2	8?.7
Semnan	3.9	1.4	95.2	87.7
Qom	15.6	4.2	81.4	81.8
Qazvin	8.6	3.1	89.3	77.1
Noth Khorasan	15.4	5.9	82.5	79.3
Mazandaran	3	2.9	81.1	60.9
Markazi	8.1	0.6	88.8	86.7
Lorestan	14.4	1.4	79.2	80.4
Kurdistan	14.6	2.9	82.3	75.7
Kohgiluyeh Boyerahmad	5.3	0.6	90.8	65.9
Khuzestan	14.7	6.6	84.3	78.5
Khorasan Razavi	13.7	5.9	85.3	78.6
Kermanshah	14.1	1.5	85.4	94.1
Kerman	26.5	6.6	67.9	71
Ilam	9.1	1.6	87.6	84
Hormozgan	16.6	4.7	80.1	69.2
Hamedan	15.6	5.7	83.2	82.3
Golestan	15.6	4	80.6	75.3
Gilan	9.7	2.2	81.5	67.6
Fars	7.5	3.9	88.5	85.4
Esfahan	12.6	6	78	63.4
East Azerbaijan	17.5	2.1	74.5	58.5
Chaharmahal Bakhtiari	8	1.5	89.2	86.1
Bushehr	6.7	2.7	83.9	73.1
Ardebil	18.2	2.2	73	77.6
Country	**16.6**	**4.6**	**79.1**	**73.4**
Female	9.0		75.6	
Male	8.2		75.0	
0-5	3.2		80.1	
6-11	5.4		77.9	
12-14	12.6		73.7	
15-17	16.9		66.7	
Single-headed nuclear	15.3		73.0	
Both parents nuclear	7.5		74.7	
Both parents extended	12.9		81.0	
Single-headed extended	11.0		80.4	
Polygamous	24.4		71.2	

Table 14.8: Child multidimensional moderate deprivation rate (%)

Province	Rural	Urban	Province	Rural	Urban
Semnan	95.2	87.7	South Khorasan	79.2	85.2
Kohgiluyeh Boyerahmad	90.8	65.9	Lorestan	79.2	80.4
Qazvin	89.3	77.1	Esfahan	78.0	63.4
Chaharmahal Bakhtiari	89.2	86.1	West Azerbaijan	75.6	82.0
Markazi	88.8	86.7	East Azerbaijan	74.5	58.5
Fars	88.5	85.4	Ardebil	73.0	77.6
Yazd	88.0	90.2	Kerman	67.9	71.0
Ilam	87.6	84.0	Sistan Baluchistan	56.2	80.7
Zanjan	86.5	86.1	Country	75.3	
Kermanshah	85.4	94.1		79.1	73.4
Khorasan Razavi	85.3	78.6			
Khuzestan	84.3	78.5	Female	75.6	
Bushehr	83.9	73.1	Male	75.0	
Tehran	83.5	63.0	0-5	80.1	
Hamedan	83.2	82.3	6-11	77.9	
Noth Khorasan	82.5	79.3	12-14	73.7	
Kurdistan	82.3	75.7	15-17	66.7	
Gilan	81.5	67.6	Single-headed nuclear	73.0	
Qom	81.4	81.8	Both parents nuclear	74.7	
Mazandaran	81.1	60.9	Both parents extended	81.0	
Golestan	80.6	75.3	Single-headed extended	80.4	
Hormozgan	80.1	69.2	Polygamous	71.2	

Figure 14.2: Comparing children's multidimensional deprivation and moderate deprivation rate (%)

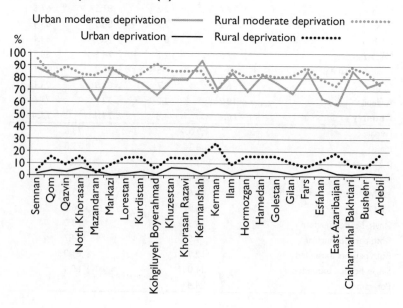

areas. Therefore, while decentralised strategies are needed to alleviate pockets of deprivation, different levels of policies are required to address systemic moderate deprivation in Iran. Information and housing are the two key indicators contributing to moderate deprivation. Excluding 'information' from the multidimensional calculations suggests a much smaller moderate deprivation at the country level, that is, 16.4%. Although we calculate the difference in deprivation ratios excluding the dimension of 'information' (that is, 7.6%), we do not recommend such an approach. As mentioned earlier, the government sponsors the media and there is no independent channel to access neutral information for adults and children alike. Therefore, it is important for children to be able to access independent sources of information. Access to computers and the internet is therefore becoming increasingly important.

As for non-deprived groups, only 16.1% of children are not deprived at the national level.

Conclusion

In this chapter, a multidimensional child poverty approach was applied for Iran using data from the 2009 national level income and expenditure survey. We have argued that the contextual specification of the country should be considered when defining deprivation indicators and conducting analysis. Six dimensions were examined related to education, shelter, water and sanitation, child labour, child marriage and information, under the three broad categories of rights, that is, provision, protection and participation (the 3 P's approach).

The availability of data has limited a comprehensive analysis, and some aspects of the 3 P's approach are missing. As such, it must be highlighted that important areas in the context of Iran such as nutrition, child abuse, juvenile delinquency and execution of minors, freedom of thought, expression and association have therefore not been analysed in this chapter. We acknowledge the importance of these areas, particularly in the contemporary situation, where state-sponsored acts are limiting children's enjoyment of certain rights (Yousefzadeh, 2010). Nevertheless, further information is needed in order to be able to elaborate further on such areas. A clear conclusion of this chapter is that girls living in rural areas are significantly worse off than their male counterparts in the same regions and than their female peers in urban areas. The underlying determinants deserve to be investigated more thoroughly and this is one of the areas where future research will be focused. We have also analysed the situation of moderately deprived children. It is crucial to analyse the status of moderately deprived and deprived children as their vulnerabilities could lead to weaker capabilities and problems in their transition to adulthood. In addition, duty bearers (both the state and families) need different resources and policies to remove barriers in moderate deprivation status compared to deprived situations. For instance, while barriers for school attendance are removed for deprived children, further steps are required to enable the children to adapt their educational needs. The analysis has also shown that children in particular regions are in more vulnerable situations compared to their peers in other regions. These regions are characterised by a large number of children from minority ethnic groups. Their status needs further exploration and deeper analysis to identify their specific needs and vulnerabilities.

Notes

[1] Ehsani (1994) refers to Ayatollah Khomeini's death, lack of clear vision to transform social and economic orders based on an Islamic model, and lack of homogeneity of the ruling clerics as some of the contributing factors in Iran lacking a long-term industrialisation strategy.

[2] *Sharia law* refers to the Islamic law defined by the Qur'an. It must be noted, however, that there are many different interpretations of the Qur'an within the Muslim world based on different doctrines. Consequently, the concept of *Sharia law* is rather vague and often reflects contradicting implications in different Islamic societies. Definition of the *Sharia law* and the way it is currently mainstreamed in Iranian legislation may not be considered as the only or the 'Shiite' interpretation of the Qur'an. Like most other religious sects, in Shiite Islam too, there are different interpretations. After the revolution, although different scholars with diverse doctrines were engaged in initial stages of Constitutional revision, gradually, progressive thinkers were excluded and marginalised extensively (Vahdat, 2003; Shaditalab, 2005). The progressive scholars believe in 'dynamic jurisprudence', a doctrine that focuses on the notion of time and place in interpreting *Sharia law* (Najafinejad et al, 2010; Künkler et al, 2007). The Late Grand Ayatollah Montazeri, Ayatollah Mojtahed-Shabestari, Late Grand Ayatollah Shariatmadari and Grand Ayatollah Sanei are some of the scholars with progressive views.

[3] Based on the age of puberty.

[4] We are also working on multidimensional child poverty analysis in Iran from 1984 to 2009.

[5] For instance, the World Summit for Social Development in Copenhagen in 1995 and the UN General Assembly in 2007.

[6] It is important to mention that the UNCRC embraces other important international commitments and standards such as the Millennium Development Goals (MDGs) or 'A World Fit For Children', with defined indicators that the Iranian government is committed to achieve.

[7] Articles related to the freedom of religion, adoption, alternative care, etc are some of these areas.

[8] Mehrpoor (2007), a former member of the Iranian Guardian Council, spells out the specific areas of concern regarding the UNCRC: Article 12(1) respect for views of the child; 13(2) freedom of expression; 14(1),(3) freedom of thoughts; 15(2) freedom of association; 16(1) right to privacy; and 29(d-1) the preparation of the child for a responsible life in a free society. These areas highlighted by the Iranian government are crucially important for reviewing the situation of children in contemporary Iran. Although these areas are largely overlooked and require examination, this chapter cannot focus on them due to lack of data.

[9] Committee on the Elimination of Discrimination Against Women (CEDAW) or C138 Minimum Age Convention, 1973.

[10] However, for areas like criminal responsibility, the age of end of childhood remains a crucial challenge.

[11] This chapter is part of a PhD thesis analysing multidimensional child poverty in Iran from 1984 to 2009. The original research includes some other dimensions (including household income, exposure to violence, mobility, social exclusion and communication) among other dimensions that are discussed in this chapter. In light of the fact that the data still need further cleaning and administrative work, those dimensions could not be analysed in this chapter.

[12] *Implementation handbook for the Convention on the Rights of the Child* (2007).

[13] Some international studies on shelter deprivation categorise three people per room as moderately deprived (Gordon et al, 2003a,b).

[14] However, there are two exceptions to applying a minimum age to working children: individuals covered by the Civil Servants Act or other special employment laws and regulations; and workers in family workshops whose work is performed exclusively by the employer and

his spouse and blood relatives of first degree are not be governed by the provisions of this Law.

[15] Which set 15 as the minimum age for marriage for both boys and girls.

[16] That proposes 18 as the minimum age for marriage.

[17] '... the properties which had belonged to a minor who has now reached the age of majority may be given to him only if it has been proved that he has full legal capacity.'

[18] In fact, children who were married before 18 should be categorised as deprived and those who were married and parents as severely deprived. However, in order to keep consistency in defining indicators, we did not choose this option.

[19] Observed by one of the authors in Chabahar (Sistan and Baluchistan province) in an internet cafe at a shopping mall with young girls and boys using computers, visiting different websites. It is not possible to generalise the mentioned observation to all provinces and rural areas in Iran. Nevertheless, as the information in this study will also show, access has been improving throughout the country.

[20] Salehi–Isfahani (2006, 2007and Farzin (2008). It must be mentioned, however, that Salehi–Isfahani estimates the weights himself using the census data.

[21] *The State of the World's Children* is an annual report prepared by UNICEF in collaboration with governments' specialised ministries. As such, the data presented in those reports reflect government studies and their results for most parts.

[22] More than one standard deviation over the median.

References

Abrahamian, E. (1980) 'Structural causes of the Iranian Revolution', *MERIP Reports*, vol 87, pp 21-6.

Afshin-Jam, N. and Danesh, T. (2009) *From cradle to coffin: A report on child executions in Iran*, London: The Foreign Policy Centre.

Aghajanian, A. (1983) 'Ethnic inequalities in Iran: an overview', *International Journal of Middle Eastern Studies*, vol 15, no 2, pp 211-24.

Akhbari, M. and Zolfeghari, H. (2009) 'A geopolitical analysis of ethnicity in Iran, with an emphasis on challenges and opportunities', *Geopolitics Quarterly*, vol 5, no 3, pp 45-69.

Alkire, S. and Foster, J. (2008) *Counting and multidimensional poverty measurement*, Oxford Poverty & Human Development Initiative (OPHI) Working Paper No 7, Oxford: OPHI, University of Oxford.

Amirabadi, M., Seif, A. and Honari, H. (2007) *Shakheshaye maskan-e amn ba estefadeh az natayej-e sarshomari sal-e 1385.* (Indicators for safe shelter, using the result of 2006 national census, Tehran, Statistical Centre of Iran).

Arts, K. (2010) 'Coming of age in a world of diversity? An assessment of the UN Convention on the Rights of the Child', Paper presented at the Inaugural lecture delivered on 18 November, The Hague.

Assadi, L. (2011) *Khoshoonat alayh-e dokhtar bacheha va eghdamat va ta'ahodat-e beinolmelali-e dolat-e Iran.* (Violence against the girl child, and Iranian governments international accountabilities and interventions (website: http://www.rahana.org/archives/37114).

Atabaki, T. (2005) 'Ethnic diversity and territorial integrity of Iran: domestic harmony and regional challenges', *Iranian Studies*, vol 38, no 1, pp 23-44.

Barnes, H. and Wright, G. (2009) *Defining child poverty in South Africa using the socially perceived necessities approach*, Oxford: Centre for the Analysis of South African Social Policy, Department of Social Policy and Social Work, University of Oxford.

Belloni, M.C. and Carriero, R. (2008) 'Childhood: a homogenous generational group?', *Comparative Social Research*, vol 25, pp 293-326.

Bentley, K.A. (2002) *Can there be any universal children's rights? Some considerations concerning relativity and enforcement*, San Marcos, Texas State University.

Blustein, D.L., Juntunen, C.L. and Worthington, R.L. (2000) 'The school-to-work transition: adjustment challenges in the forgotten half', in S.D. Brown and R.W. Lent (eds) *Handbook of counseling in the forgotten half*, New York: Wiley. pp 311-323

Bourdillion, M., Levison, D., Myers, W. and White, B. (2010) 'Children, work and education in communist revolution and post-communist transition', in M. Bourdillion, D. Levison, W. Myers and B. White (eds) *Rights and wrongs of children's work*, New Brunswick, NJ: Rutgers University Press, pp 75-87.

Cantwell, N. (1993) *Monitoring the Convention through the Idea of the '3Ps'*, Vienna: Eurosocial.

Chillar, N.A. (2005) *Ab'ad-e goonagoon-e faghr dar Iran.* Different dimensions of poverty, Tehran, Central Bank of Iran.

Cunningham, M. (2001) 'Parental influences on the gendered division of housework', *American Sociological Association*, vol 66, no 2, pp 184-203.

de Moura, S.L. (2001) 'The social construction of street children', *British Journal of Social Work*, vol 32, no 3, pp 353-67.

Dooly, M. (2010) *Empowering language minorities through technology: Which way to go?*, Barcelona: Autonomous University of Barcelona, Spain.

Ehsani, K. (1994) *Tilt but don't spill: Iran's development and reconstruction dilemma*, Middle East Report, 191, November-December (http://www.merip.org/).

Farzin, A. (2008) *Development policy, economic adjustment and welfare in Iran*, London: University of Westminster.

Feeny, T. and Boyden, J. (2003) *Children and poverty – Shaping a response to poverty: A conceptual responding to children living in poverty*, Richmond, VA: Christian Children's Fund.

Gassmann, F. (2000) 'On the verge of poverty: welfare and economic transition in Latvia', Unpublished book, Maastricht: Maastricht University.

Gordon, D., Nandy, S., Pantazis, C., Pemberton, S. and Townsend, P. (2003a) *The distribution of child poverty in the developing world*, Bristol: University of Bristol.

Gordon, D., Nandy, S., Pantazis, C., Pemberton, S. and Townsend, P. (2003b) *Child poverty in the developing world*, Bristol: The Policy Press.

Government of Iran and President's Deputy for Strategic Planning and Control (2006) *The second Millennium Development Goals report of the Islamic Republic of Iran*, Tehran: President's Deputy for Strategic Planning and Control, Deputy for Social Affairs in cooperation with United Nations in the Islamic Republic of Iran.

Harpham, T., Houng, N.T., Long, T.T. and Tuan, T. (2005) 'Participatory child poverty assessment in rural Vietnam', *Children & Society*, vol 19, pp 27-41.

Hosseinbor, M.O. (2009) 'Dominant collective identity in multicultural society of Iran', Unpublished Working Paper presented at the 3rd Global Conference on Multiculturalism, Conflict and Belonging, 25 September, Mansfield College, Oxford.

Jones, G. (2009) 'What is youth?', in G. Jones (ed) *Youth*, Cambridge: Polity Press, pp 1-29.

Kazemipoor, S. (2004) *Mabani-e jamiat-shenasi*, Tehran: Markaz motale'at va pazhoheshaye jamiati Asia va Oghianousieh. Principles of demography, Tehran, Center for Asia and Pacific studies and researches.

Kheilatash, O., Rust, Val D. (2009) 'Inequalities in Iranian education: representations of gender, socioeconomic status, ethnic diversity, and religious diversity in school textbooks and curricula', *Inequality in Education*, pp 392-416.

Khorshidi, M., Fee, L.Y. and Soltani, F. (2010) 'Ethnic secessionism in Iran: accusation or fact', *Journal of Politics and Law*, vol 3, pp 269-76.

Kjorholt, A.T. (2004) 'Childhood as a social and symbolic space: discourses on children as social participants in society', Unpublished PhD thesis, Norwegian University of Science and Technology, NTNU, Trondheim.

Künkler, M., Stepan, A. and Somos, A. (2007) 'Democratic voices in the world's religions: Islam', Unpublished Working Paper, New York: Columbia University.

Land, K.C., Lamb, V.L. and Mustillo, S.K. (2001) 'Child and youth well-being in the United States', *Social Indicators Research*, vol 56, no 3, pp 241-318.

Leaper, C. and Friedman, C.K. (2007) 'The socialization of gender', in J.E. Grusec and P.D. Hastings (eds) *Handbook of socialization: Theory and research*, New York: Guilford Press, pp 561-87.

Lurie, J. (2003-04) 'The tension between protection and participation – general theory and consequences as related to rights of children, including working children', *IUC Journal of Social Work*, no 7 (www.bemidjistate.edu/academics/publications/social_work_journal/issue07/articles/Tension.htm).

Matthews, H. and Limb, M. (1999) 'Defining an agenda for the geography of children: review and prospect', *Progress in Human Geography*, vol 23, no 1, pp 61-90.

Mehrpoor, H. (2007) 'Barkhi keshvarha amadegi-e lazem jahat-e ejraei shodan-e convansion-ha ra nadarand', *ISNA News Agency*. Some states do not have the necessary preparedness to implement Conventions, Tehran, ISNA News Agency.

Minujin, A., Delamonica, E.E. and Davidziuk, A. (2005) 'Children living in poverty: a review of child poverty definitions, measurements and policies', Paper presented at the UNICEF Conference on Children and Poverty: Global Context, Local Solutions, New York: The New School, 25-27 April.

Monteith, M. and McLaughlin, E. (2005) 'Child poverty and social exclusion in Northern Ireland', Unpublished Working Paper, Belfast: Equality & Social Inclusion in Ireland, Queen's University Belfast.

Najafinejad, A., Ahmad, Z.B. and Jawan, U.A. (2010) 'Human rights in Iranian juridical approach', *Cross-Cultural Communication*, vol 6, no 3, pp 10-17.

Newman, K.S. (1999) *No shame in my game: The working poor in the inner city*, New York: Russell Sage Foundation and Vintage Books.

Notten, G. and Roelen, K. (2010) *Multidimensional child poverty in the European Union: Puzzling with the few pieces that the EU-SILC provides*, BWPI Working Paper 135, Brighton: Institute of Development Studies, University of Sussex.

Nussbaum, M. (1992) 'Human functioning and social justice: in defence of Aristotelian essentialism', *Political Theory*, vol 20, no 2, pp 202-46.

Penn, H. (1999) *The rights of young children*, London: Institute of Education, London University.

Qvortrup, J. (1999) 'Childhood and social macrostructures, childhood exclusion by default', Unpublished Working Paper, Odense: Odense University.

Redmond, G. (2008) 'Child poverty and child rights: edging towards a definition', *Children and Poverty*, vol 14, no 1, pp 63-82.

Rideout, V.J., Foehr, U.G. and Roberts, D.F. (2010) *Media in the lives of 8-to 18-year-olds*, Kaiser Family Foundation Study, Menlo Park, CA: Kaiser Family Foundation.

Robeyns, I. (2006) 'The capability approach in practice', *The Journal of Political Philosophy*, vol 14, no 3, pp 351-76.

Roelen, K. (2010) *False positives or hidden dimensions*, Maastricht: Maastricht University.

Rogers, W. (2003) 'Gendered childhood', in M. Woodhead and H. Montgomery (eds) *Understanding childhood*, Hoboken, NJ: John Wiley & Sons Ltd in association with the Open Library, United Kingdom, pp 193-212.

Salehi-Esfahani, H. and Pesaran, M.H. (2008) 'Iranian economy in the twentieth century: a global perspective', Paper presented at the Iran and Iranian Studies in the 20th Century, University of Toronto, 19-20 October.

Salehi-Isfahani, D. (2006) 'Revolution and redistribution in Iran: poverty and inequality 25 years later', Paper presented at the Third Annual World Bank Conference on Inequality, Washington, DC, 5-6 June.

Salehi-Isfahani, D. (2007) 'Poverty, inequality, and populist politics in Iran', Unpublished Working Paper. Virginia Polytechnic Institute and State University, Department of Economics.

Sen, A. (ed) (1993) *Capability and well-being*, Oxford: Oxford University Press.

Shaditalab, J. (2005) 'Islamization and gender in Iran: is the glass half full or half empty?', *Signs: Journal of Women in Culture and Society*, vol 32, no 1, pp 14-21.

Shanahan, M.J., Mortimer, J.T. and Krüger, H. (2002) 'Adolescence and adult work in the twenty-first century', *Journal of Research on Adolescence*, vol 12, pp 99-120.

Shekarloo, M. (2004) 'Cyberspace as subversive space for women? Women's websites and weblogs in Iran', Presented at Woodrow Wilson International Center for Scholars, New York.

Sixsmith, J., Gabhainn, S.N., Fleming, C. and Higgins, S.O. (2007) 'Children's, parents' and teachers' perceptions of child well-being', *Health Education*, vol 107, no 6, p 29.

UN (United Nations) (2009) *World population prospects: The 2008 revision*, New York: Department of Economics and Social Affairs, Population Division, UN.

UNESCO (United Nations Educational, Scientific and Cultural Organization) UIS (Institute for Statistics) (2008) *UIS statistics in brief* (http://stats.uis.unesco.org/unesco/TableViewer/document. aspx?ReportId=121&IF_Language=eng&BR_Country=3640).

UNICEF (United Nations Children's Fund) (2010) *The State of the World's Children: Special edition celebrating 20 years of the Convention on the Rights of the Child*, New York: UNICEF.

UNICEF (2011) *The State of the World's Children 2011: Adolescence, an age of opportunity*, New York: UNICEF.

UNICEF and WHO (World Health Organization) (2004) *Meeting the MDG drinking water and sanitation target: A mid-term assessment of progress*, New York and Geneva: UNICEF and WHO.

UNICEF Innocenti Research Centre (2000) *Child poverty in rich nations*, Florence: UNICEF Innocenti Research Centre.

Vahdat, F. (2003) 'Post-revolutionary Islamic discourses on modernity in Iran: expansion and contradiction of human subjectivity', *Journal of Middle Eastern Studies*, vol 35, pp 599-631.

Vandewater, E.A., Bickham, D.S. and Lee, J.H. (2006) 'Time well spent? Relating television use to children's free-time activities', *Pediatrics*, no 117, pp 181-91.

Wagstaff, A. and Watanabe, N. (1999) *Socioeconomic inequalities in child malnutrition in the developing world*, World Bank Working Paper No 2434, Washington, DC: World Bank.

Wells, K. (2009) 'Race, class and gender', in K. Wells, *Childhood in global perspective*, Cambridge: Polity Press, p 220.

WHO (World Health Organization) and UNICEF (United Nations Children's Fund) (2004) *Core questions on drinking water and sanitation for household surveys*, Geneva and New York: WHO and UNICEF.

World Bank (2007) *Islamic Republic of Iran – Health sector review*, Washington, DC: World Bank Group.

World Bank (2010) 'Country Brief', Washington, DC: World Bank (http://web.worldbank.org/WBSITE/EXTERNAL/COUNTRIES/MENAEXT/IRANEXTN/0,,menuPK:312966~pagePK:141132~piPK:141107~theSitePK:312943,00.html).

Yousefzadeh, S. (2010) 'The socioeconomic, legal and political development in Iran, 1979-2010. A child focused analysis', Unpublished Working Paper, Maastricht: Maastricht Graduate School of Governance.

Yousefzadeh, S. and Shekarloo, M. (2010) 'Adolescent girls in Iran: becoming a citizen of the Islamic State at the intersection of gender and youth', Paper presented at the United Nations Children's Fund (UNICEF) and Graduate Programme in International Affairs (GPIA) International Conference 2010: Adolescent Girls − Cornerstone of Society: Building Evidence and Policies for Inclusive Societies, 26-28 April, New York: The New School.

Zimmer-Gembeck, M.J. and Mortimer, J.T. (2006) 'Adolescent work, vocational development, and education', *Review of Education Research*, vol 76, no 4, pp 537-66.

FIFTEEN

Multidimensional child poverty in Haiti[1]

David Gordon, Audrey Lenoel and Shailen Nandy

Introduction

Haiti has long been a beacon of hope for the poor and oppressed peoples of the world. It was the first and only country to have a successful slave-led revolution that resulted in independence from a colonial power. The Haitian Revolution of Independence between 1791 and 1804 has been described by many eloquent authors (see, for example, James, 1938; Dupuy, 1989). At the time of the revolution, Haiti was one of the most productive and wealthiest countries on the planet. Since gaining its independence, however, the Republic of Haiti has been plagued by a history of poverty, political unrest and natural disasters (Farmer, 2003). The devastating earthquake of 12 January 2010 struck a country that was already one of the poorest and least developed in the world. This chapter uses data on child poverty and deprivation created using the 'Bristol Approach' (see Chapter Four, this volume) to show that, in the years before the earthquake, hardly any progress had been made in reducing poverty and deprivation among children in Haiti. The work represents the first ever study of child poverty in the country, and its findings were disheartening, since it was hoped that the benefits of lifting international sanctions on Haiti would be manifested most apparently in positive outcomes for children.

Despite the severe impact of poverty in Haiti, the number of studies on this issue is still limited. The results should be directly relevant to policy makers as methods used are based on internationally agreed standards and definitions of poverty and deprivation.

Overview of child poverty in Haiti

Haiti is one of the poorest and least developed countries in the world,[2] and the poorest nation of the Americas. Already afflicted by endemic poverty and extreme socioeconomic disparities, the country experienced a near apocalyptic event when it was struck by a massive earthquake on 12 January 2010. The catastrophe undoubtedly heightened the vulnerability of children, many of who had already been living in dire poverty.

The earthquake

At 4.53pm, on 12 January 2010, Haiti was hit by a magnitude 7.0 earthquake. Aftershocks of magnitude 5.9 and 5.5 followed, which also caused immense structural damage and loss of life. The earthquake's epicentre was 17km south west of the capital Port-au-Prince, and the Government of Haiti website[3] records that 97,000 buildings were destroyed and 188,000 seriously damaged. Over 220,000 people are estimated to have died, with more than 300,000 injured (UNOCHA, 2011a). In January 2011, over one million people remained displaced as a result of the earthquake, over a third of who (380,000) were children (UNOCHA, 2011a; UNICEF, 2011).

The UN Office for the Coordination of Humanitarian Affairs (UNOCHA) reported that over 1.3 million people, in about 260,000 households, were in need of assistance and shelter. By the end of March 2010, approximately two thirds had received some emergency help, mainly the provision of tarpaulins (UNOCHA, 2010). Approximately half a million children, and 200,000 pregnant or lactating women, were estimated to have been affected by the earthquake and to be at risk of malnutrition, and comprehensive child protection and needs assessments had not yet been completed by March 2010 (UNOCHA, 2010). Close to 5,000 schools were affected by the earthquake, causing the entire education system to shut down, not least because the Ministry of Education itself collapsed (UNICEF, 2011). While affecting all Haitians, the earthquake heightened the vulnerability of women and girls, and their risks of experiencing gender-based violence, especially when faced with the dangers of crowded and precarious living conditions in displacement camps. Following the earthquake, Haiti reported the highest levels of rape and sexual assault since 2006, as well as a rise in domestic violence and commercial sexual exploitation of children (UNICEF, 2011). With families and entire communities displaced, the Haiti government[4] estimated that around 511,000 people had moved out of the capital Port-au-Prince to other areas (see Figure 15.1).

Conditions worsened in late 2010, with the emergence of cholera and its rapid spread throughout the country's 10 departments. Over 2,500 people died and more than 100,000 fell sick (UNICEF, 2011). In January 2011, UNICEF grimly observed that 'cholera is now adding

Figure 15.1: Population displaced from Port-au-Prince as a result of the earthquake

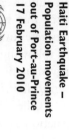

Haiti Earthquake –
Population movements
out of Port-au-Prince
17 February 2010

Source: www.reliefweb.int/

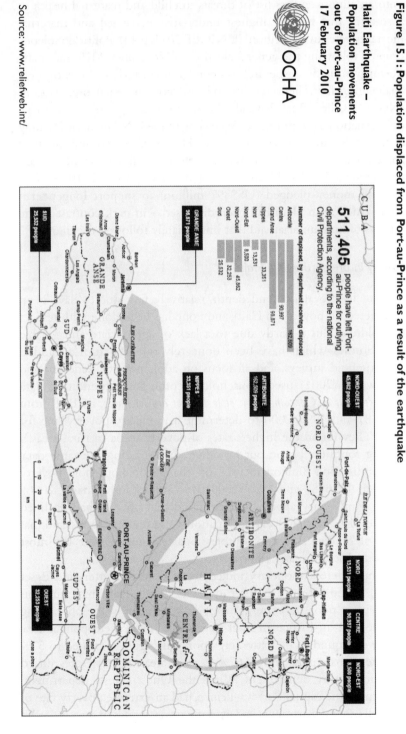

onto an almost endless list of threats to child and maternal health in a country that has the highest under-five, neo-natal and maternal mortality rates in the region' (UNICEF, 2011, p 14). Political violence erupted following the general election of November 2010, and made the provision of desperately needed humanitarian aid extremely challenging for relief agencies and non-governmental organisations (NGOs). Relief efforts have also been hamstrung by an apparent lack of international commitment. According to the UN Financial Tracking Service,[5] the humanitarian appeal for Haiti received commitments of approximately US$700 million by March 2010 – about half the amount requested by the UN (UNICEF, 2011, p 7). By October 2010, less than half the money pledged (US$897 million) to support longer-term reconstruction in Haiti had been disbursed – in stark contrast to the inflows of humanitarian aid that immediately followed the disaster.[6]

Poverty in pre-earthquake Haiti

Despite its prevalence and depth, relatively few studies have been conducted on poverty in Haiti, and none has been done with respect to children. This is partly due to a lack of appropriate and reliable data. Studies which have been done rely on data from a handful of household surveys, and all focus on adult poverty. Pedersen and Lockwood (2001) used household income and expenditure data (*Enquêtes sur la Consommation et le Budget des Ménages*, ECBM) from 1986/87 and 1999/2000 to determine a monetary poverty line for Haiti. They found the highest rates of poverty to be in rural areas, a finding routinely borne out by other studies. Using the same data, Boccanfuso and Siméon focused on changes in household poverty between 1986/87 and 1999/2000 (Boccanfuso and Siméon, 2006). Using a monetary approach, they found that poverty had declined between 1987 and 2000, at both national and regional levels, and that place of residence and socioprofessional categories were the most important determinants of poverty.

Using different monetary indicators of poverty, Sletten and Egset (2004) found more than three quarters of the Haitian population were either 'poor' or 'extremely poor',[7] with most of the poor living outside Port-au-Prince, in rural areas. In the main metropolitan area, 23% were found to be extremely poor. This figure increased to 57% in other urban areas, and to 67% in rural areas. Poverty rates varied considerably by department. While the Ouest (West) department, containing the capital Port-au-Prince, had an extreme poverty rate of 34%, all other departments had extreme poverty rates of over 60%; the highest rates were found in the North East and North West. Households with relatives living abroad, or who were receiving remittances from abroad, had lower rates of extreme poverty and, unsurprisingly, there was a strong inverse relationship between education level of the main provider and incidence of extreme poverty (70% extreme poverty among households where the main provider had no education, compared to only 7% poverty when the main provider had received a higher education).

A different approach was taken by Jadotte, who derived indigence and poverty lines based on the cost of basic needs in Haiti using data from the 2001 Haiti Living Conditions Survey (ECVH-2001) (Jadotte, 2006). Using thresholds of HTG (Haitian Gourdes) 4,846 for an indigence line, and HTG 6,439 for a poverty line, the study found two thirds of people living below the indigence line, and three quarters living below the poverty line. The study also examined the inequality in income distribution in Haiti (the first such study to do so), and found an extremely high Gini coefficient of 0.65, one of the highest in the world. Nearly 70% of national income went to the top 20%, while the bottom 20% received less than 1.5%. Once again, the relationship between education level and poverty was clear-cut (sharply inverse), as was the contribution of remittances from abroad in reducing poverty (especially among female-headed households). Place of residence was also important, with households living outside the metropolitan area (or outside the West department) at much greater risk of poverty and indigence.

None of the economic studies mentioned above focused on children, or used them as the unit of analysis. There are, however, a number of studies that have assessed the impact of insecurity and international sanctions on children's health, education and well-being. Gibbons and Garfield (1999) and Reid et al (2007) both looked at the impacts of the three-year long international embargo (October 1991 to October 1994) imposed on Haiti following a military coup that ousted democratically elected President Jean-Bertrand Aristide. Each found that the sanctions had had grave and protracted effects on the most vulnerable sections of Haitian society, that is, women and children.

In a comparative study of child survival interventions around the world, Victora et al (2005) showed how children in the poorest groups were the least likely to receive the complete set of appropriate interventions (for example, immunisations, access to safe water, maternal healthcare etc) (see Figure 15.2).

They found that children in Haiti were the least likely to receive six or more interventions deemed important for child survival. Only children in Cambodia fared more poorly. Haiti was characterised as

Figure 15.2: Percentage of children receiving six or more child-survival interventions, by socioeconomic group and country

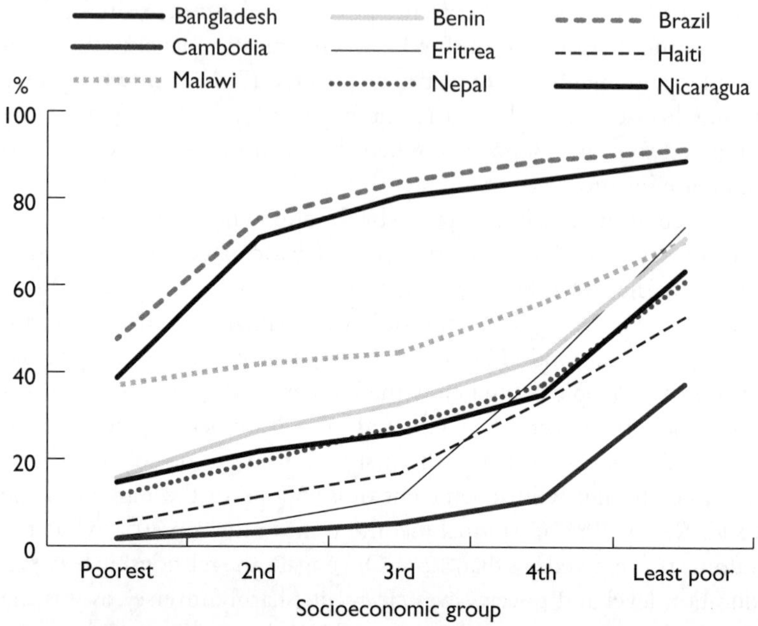

Source: Victora et al (2005)

having low coverage of child survival interventions and high levels of inequality between socioeconomic groups.

Deprivation and absolute poverty of children in Haiti, 2000-05

Child poverty in Haiti was assessed using the methods and indicators developed by Gordon et al (2003), now referred to as the 'Bristol Approach' (see Chapter Four, this volume). Indicators were developed which operationalised the internationally agreed definition of absolute poverty within the context of the child rights framework of the UN Convention on the Rights of the Child (UNCRC). Estimates of child poverty and deprivation for Haiti were made using the 2000 and 2005 rounds of the Haiti Demographic and Health Surveys (also referred to as Enquête Mortalité, Morbidité et Utilisation des Services, EMMUS). Three Demographic and Health Surveys have been conducted in Haiti – in 1994/95, 2000 and 2005. A fourth is currently underway (2011). This chapter uses data from the 2000 and 2005/06 surveys (EMMUS III and IV). Full details of the surveys can be found in reports prepared by the Haitian Institute for Childhood (Institut Haïtien de l'Enfance, IHE), in collaboration with the Haitian Institute for Statistics and Computing (Insitut Haïtien de Statistique et d'Informatique, IHSI) (Cayemittes et al, 2001, 2007). The reports present details of the sampling methods. Interviews for the 2000 Demographic and Health Survey took place between February and July 2000 and those for the 2005/06 between October 2005 and June 2006. EMMUS III included interviews with 9,595 households, 10,159 women aged 15 to 49 and 3,171 men aged 15 to 59, while EMMUS IV involved interviews with 9,998 households, 10,757 women and 4,958 men of the same age categories as in 2000. Both surveys followed a stratified cluster sampling design. In 2000, 19 strata were defined: the nine regional departments of Haiti (split by urban and rural) and the metropolitan area of Port-au-Prince. At the first level of stratification, 317 clusters were selected from a list of numbered sections from the Multiple Survey Master Sample (EMEM) put in place by IHSI based on the General Census of the Population and Housing for 1982 (Cayemittes et al, 2001). In 2005, the availability of recent national census data allowed 21 strata to be defined: the 10 regional departments of Haiti split by urban and rural and the metropolitan area of Port-au-Prince. At the first level of stratification, 339 clusters were selected from a list of numbered sections from the EMEM put in place by IHSI based on the General Census of the Population and Housing for 2003 (Cayemittes et al, 2007). EMMUS/Demographic and Health Survey data on all children under 18 were selected and post-stratification population weights were calculated using the UN Population Division (UNPOP) median population estimates and applied to four age and gender groups (0-4, 5-9, 10-14, 15-17 for boys and girls).

Child poverty and deprivation in Haiti

This section presents results for 2005. The section following presents data for both 2000 and 2005, to show whether or not there were any reductions in deprivation and child poverty in Haiti, and also whether any changes were statistically significant.

Deprivation among children in Haiti in 2005

Figure 15.3 shows estimates of severe deprivation and absolute poverty among children in Haiti in 2005. More than 4 in 10 children (43%, or 1.62 million) lived in absolute poverty, with seven out of ten children (70%, or 2.66 million) experiencing severe deprivation of at least one basic need.

Figure 15.3: Deprivation and absolute poverty among children, Haiti, 2005

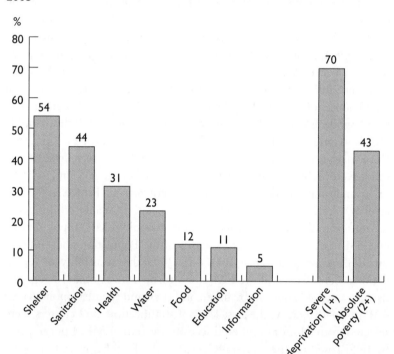

More than half of all children (54%, 2.1 million) in Haiti were severely shelter deprived. This means that they were living in homes with mud floors, or in severely overcrowded conditions, with more than five people per room. This prevalence of shelter deprivation in pre-earthquake Haiti is important to note as it is this kind of poorly built housing that suffers great damage in earthquakes and resulted in many poor adults and children being killed or injured. More than four out of ten children (44%, 1.7 million) were severely sanitation deprived, living in homes where there were no toilet facilities whatsoever. About one in five children (23%, or 861,000 children) were severely water deprived, drinking from unsafe open water sources (for example, ponds, dams) or having to walk such a long way to water that it was not possible to carry enough to maintain good health (a 30-minute round trip). Around one third of all children (31%, 1.2 million) were severely health deprived. They had not received immunisations against any diseases or medical treatment when suffering from a serious illness; over 100,000 young children under five were so severely food deprived and malnourished that, if they survived, their health would have been permanently affected. A quarter of a million children (that is, 11%, or one in nine) between the ages of 7 and 18 had never been to school, and were identified as being severely education deprived. Five per cent of children aged 3 to 18 were severely information deprived and had no source of information about the outside world in their homes, that is, no access to a radio, television, computer, telephone or newspapers. These levels of deprivation are some of the highest seen in the Americas, and on a par with poor countries in Sub-Saharan Africa and South Asia (see Chapter Seventeen, this volume). The impacts of such deprivation are well known, and the earthquake of January 2010 will undoubtedly mean that thousands more Haitian children will be experiencing very severe deprivations of their basic needs. Analyses of the next round of EMMUS/Demographic and Health Survey data (2011) are likely to paint a very depressing portrait of childhood in Haiti.

Patterning of deprivation and poverty among children in Haiti in 2005

All previous research on poverty and inequality in Haiti (see above) has identified large and widespread disparities in outcomes and opportunities, and the same is true regarding child poverty and deprivation. Table 15.1 shows how the prevalence of severe deprivation

Table 15.1: Prevalence (%) of severe deprivation and absolute poverty among children, Haiti, 2005

	Severe deprivation (1+)	Absolute poverty (2+)
Haiti	70	43
Location		
Capital city	37	8
Small city	54	25
Town	54	20
Countryside	86	61
Region/department		
Centre	89	69
Grand Anse + Nippes	86	61
South East	81	49
Artibonite	79	53
North	76	51
North West	73	49
North East	72	41
South	71	42
Metropolitan areas/west	52	22

(continued)

Table 15.1: Prevalence (%) of severe deprivation and absolute poverty among children, Haiti, 2005 (continued)

	Severe deprivation (1+)	Absolute poverty (2+)
Occupational social class		
Agriculture self-employed	91	70
Unskilled manual	73	41
Sales	72	42
Household domestic	66	40
Skilled manual	52	29
Professional, technical, managerial	46	18
Highest education of women in household		
No education	92	70
Primary	79	49
Secondary	45	15
Higher	14	1
Adults of working age in home		
No	81	55
At least one adult of working age in house	70	42
Household size		
<3 members	57	31
3-4 members	61	37
5-6 members	73	43
7+ members	72	45
Sex of head of household		
Male	74	47
Female	66	38
Household standard of living quintile		
Poorest	99	91
Poorer	91	62
Middle	77	32
Richer	47	12
Richest	23	3

(that is, of one or more deprivations) and absolute poverty (that is, two or more deprivations) among children was patterned in Haiti in 2005.

As one might expect, the prevalence of absolute poverty and severe deprivation were lower in urban areas, especially in the capital city (Port-au-Prince), where 8% of children lived in absolute poverty; the highest prevalence was among children living in the countryside (61%). Intra-urban disparities, however, are known to be considerable, so it is likely the depth of poverty experienced by children in slum or shanty-town areas of Port-au-Prince is considerable.

Regional disparities were also clear. In 2005, prior to the earthquake, the department containing Port-au-Prince had the lowest rate of absolute poverty (22%). It is certain that following the earthquake, poverty rates will have increased significantly. In 2005, the highest rates of poverty were found in Centre (69%) and Grande Anse and Nippes (61%) departments. Three departments (the North East, South and West) had poverty rates below the national average (43%).

A lack of government or private investment in basic infrastructure partly explains why regions are deprived or poor. Structural factors, however, also provide an explanation. The types of jobs people do (if employed), and their remuneration, are linked to their levels of education and also to their access to available work. Occupation has traditionally been used as an indicator of 'social' or 'occupational' class, and those households in the higher class categories (that is, professional, technical and managerial; clerical; services, etc) are less likely to be poor. Those in lower class categories, including agricultural and unskilled manual workers, tend to be in the lowest paid jobs, and so are more likely to be poor. Well-paid jobs in poor countries tend to be concentrated in urban areas, and particularly in the capital. The EMMUS/Demographic and Health Survey asked eligible women (aged 15 to 49) in each household about their occupation and the occupation of their partner. Household social class in this analysis is based on the highest class group of anyone within the household. As expected, there is a clear relationship between social class, severe deprivation and child poverty, with prevalence rates highest for children of unskilled manual and agricultural workers and the self-employed (70%), nearly twice the national average.

Concern is frequently expressed about the vulnerability of certain types of household, with particular attention paid to households headed by women. While some research suggests female-headed households in some parts of the world are more likely to be poor, others contest this (for example, Chant, 2003). Based on 2005 data for Haiti, it appears rates of absolute poverty were lower among households headed by women (38%) than by men (47%). We do not contest the greater vulnerability of children and women in female-headed households to potential threats of sexual and other violence from outsiders, as was documented both before and after the 2010 earthquake.

Research shows that large families are more likely to be poor than smaller families. Households in Haiti were divided into four groups: those with fewer than three members, those with three or four members, those with five or six members and those with seven or more members. From the 2005 data, it appears that there is some ambiguous evidence for a gradient associated with increasing household size. That said, what might be a more important determinant of poverty is the number of children rather than the number of household members per se. The presence of adults of prime working age (that is, between the ages of 18 and 54) in a household can act as a protective factor against poverty in countries that do not have comprehensive pension or welfare provisions. Children in households where there was an adult of working age were less likely to be poor or experience severe deprivation than children in households where there were no adults of working age.

As expected, there was a clear inverse relationship between the level of education and poverty. The highest level of education of women were aggregated to household level and applied to the analysis. Children in households where women had not received any formal education were highly likely to be poor or severely deprived. In households where a female member had received a higher education (that is, post-secondary), almost no children experienced absolute poverty, with only a small proportion experiencing one or more severe deprivations.

The EMMUS/Demographic and Health Surveys include a wealth index that can be used to assess inequalities between groups in society. The index is based on household ownership of different assets and access to certain public services. The Demographic and Health Survey wealth index is based on a statistical methodology of dubious validity (see Chapter Four, this volume, for more details) so, while the results should be interpreted with caution, it is used here as one measure of the extent of disparity and inequality in Haiti. Almost all children in households in the poorest wealth quintile in 2005 lived in absolute poverty and experienced severe deprivation. Conversely, almost no children in the richest quintile were poor, although nearly one quarter did experience one or more severe deprivations.

Changes in child poverty and deprivation in Haiti, 2000-05

The previous section detailed the extent of severe deprivation and absolute poverty among children in Haiti in 2005. The methods, data and indicators used mean reliable comparisons over time are possible, and this section shows how the extent of child poverty and severe deprivation changed between 2000 and 2005.

The EMMUS/Demographic and Health Surveys are complex samples, and estimates need to reflect the effects of sample clustering and stratification (Kish and Frankel, 1974; Kneipp and Yarandi, 2002). This involves adjusting (widening) the size of Confidence Intervals appropriately. When Confidence Intervals overlap, differences in means are not statistically significant; when there is no overlap, differences are significant. Ignoring the complex sample design of surveys like the Demographic and Health Survey runs the risk of producing biased estimates. Inferences based on such analyses could be misleading, as observed differences between groups may simply be a result of random sampling variation between the two surveys. This in turn could affect policy design and implementation, for example, the targeting of extra or withdrawal of resources to particular regions or groups.

Figure 15.4 shows the changes in absolute poverty and severe deprivation in Haiti between 2000 and 2005. While it appears that the mean prevalence of absolute poverty fell slightly, from 46% to 43%, the fall is not statistically significant, as the 95% Confidence Intervals for both estimates overlap. On this basis, it is unfortunately the case that neither absolute poverty, nor severe deprivation, among children in Haiti declined between 2000 and 2005.

Figure 15.4: Changes in absolute poverty (2+) and severe deprivation (1+) among children in Haiti, 2000 and 2005 (with 95% Confidence Intervals)

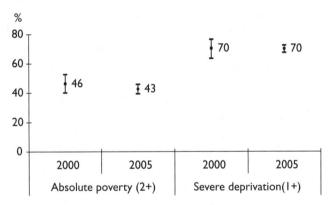

Comparing geographic differences over the five years is interesting. While absolute poverty was much more prevalent in rural areas/countryside, and lower in urban areas, it is *urban areas* which saw increases in child poverty between 2000 and 2005. Figure 15.5 shows large increases in child poverty in the capital, Port-au-Prince, and other small cities, and small apparent decreases in child poverty in towns and the countryside. However, given that in each instance 95% Confidence Intervals overlap, we cannot say if these changes are statistically significant. Other research (Boccanfuso and Siméon, 2006) identified a similar aggravation of poverty in the capital city over the

Figure 15.5: Changes in absolute poverty among children, by place of residence, Haiti, 2000 and 2005 (with 95% Confidence Intervals)

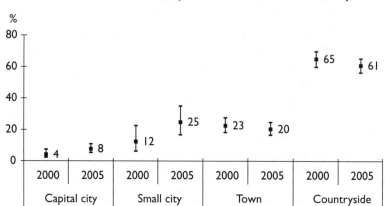

period 1986/87 and 1999-2000 that lends support to our findings. It is clear that there is no evidence that poverty among children in Haiti fell between 2000 and 2005.

Figure 15.6 shows changes in the levels of absolute poverty in each department, between 2000 and 2005. Two departments, Centre and Grande Anse, saw increases in absolute poverty between 2000 and 2005, from 55% to 69% and from 59% to 61% respectively, although given overlaps in Confidence Intervals, the changes were not statistically significant. Apparently large decreases in child poverty were seen in the North, North West, South, South East and North East, with relatively smaller decreases seen in the Metropolitan area/West department, although once again, none was statistically significant.

Figure 15.7 shows what changes occurred in the extent and prevalence of each of the seven main deprivations. There were apparent increases in the prevalence of shelter, sanitation and food deprivation, and decreases in health, information and education deprivation, although many of these were not statistically significant. There do appear to have been small (and statistically significant) reductions in the proportions of children suffering from health and information deprivation.

Conclusion

Children and youth represent 43% of the population of Haiti but 100% of its future. It is not in anyone's interest for seven out of ten Haitian children to suffer the harms caused by severe deprivation and for more than four in ten to grow up in the squalid conditions of absolute poverty. Ending absolute child poverty should not just be a policy priority; it

Figure 15.6: Changes in absolute poverty among children by department, Haiti, 2000 and 2005 (with 95% Confidence Intervals)

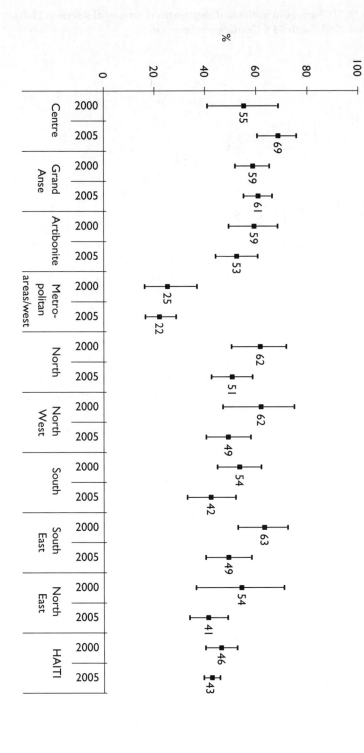

Figure 15.7: Changes in individual deprivations among children in Haiti, 2000 and 2005 (with 95% Confidence Intervals)

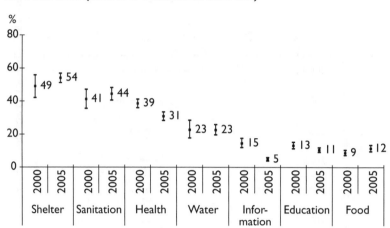

should be *the* policy priority. The urgency of the situation cannot be over-emphasised. Policies that will reduce poverty in 20 or 30 years are of no use to today's children. Their childhoods will be just a distant and painful memory by the time these policies have had an effect and the long-term damage of child poverty will have already been done.

Neoclassical economic theory has a simple and elegant explanation for both poverty and wealth. Wealth is a result of work, waiting and economic efficiency; poverty is a result of the absence of productivity and the inability or unwillingness to work and wait (Clark, 2002). Child poverty (and wealth) are entirely absent from this theory – children are not economically productive, they should not work and they cannot wait. Children do make an appearance in neoclassical economic theory in discussions of human capital. Investment in children's health, nutrition and education is needed so that they can grow up to become productive adult workers in the future. Children's current needs, agency and economic rights are invariably entirely absent from such discussion.

The absence of any useful economic theory of child poverty is not a result of the complex nature of this subject. In fact, the economics of child poverty are very simple and are entirely concerned with redistribution – where sufficient resources are redistributed from adults to children there is no child poverty; where insufficient resources are redistributed from adults to children, child poverty is inevitable (Gordon, 2008).

Macroeconomic adjustment and restructuring policies are designed to promote future economic growth as a means of reducing poverty.

Typical adjustment policy packages include controlling inflation, reductions in government expenditure (at least in the short term), privatisation and increased openness to international trade. The results are almost an invariable increase in poverty in the short term but, if the policies are successful, poverty may fall in the medium or long term. Policies that increase poverty today in the hope of reducing poverty in the future are highly problematic from the perspective of the child. They may condemn the children of today to a childhood of abject poverty in the hope that the children of tomorrow may lead better lives. The morality of adjustment policies is therefore highly dubious from a child rights perspective.

The results presented here indicate the need for some key policies to alleviate the worst effects of severe child poverty and deprivation. In particular, there are severe problems of physical capital deprivation among children in rural areas of Haiti. Policies are needed to improve squalid housing and to provide safe sanitation and drinking water facilities. A third of all children in Haiti suffer from severe health deprivation; therefore, continued efforts are needed to improve vaccination rates and access to good quality healthcare, particularly in rural areas.

A key problem faced by children living in absolute poverty and their families is a severe lack of economic resources (for example, money). One lesson that can be drawn from the experiences of industrialised countries in reducing child poverty is that, after public infrastructure investment (in housing, sanitation and water), the most effective anti-poverty policy for children is the establishment of a child or family social security benefit (Gordon et al, 2003; Townsend, 2009). All 'rich' countries with low rates of child poverty have some kind of universal child or family benefit paid in cash or in kind. Universal child benefits are easy and cheap to administer and do not require complex administrative machinery. These benefits are effective, cost–efficient and extremely popular (and therefore politically sustainable). A global universal child benefit of the equivalent of US$1 a day per child would eradicate child poverty as measured by the World Bank. However, in the absence of international funding for a universal child benefit, it would need to be introduced in stages in Haiti. For example, for children under a given age, say 10 years, or five years or infants under two (Townsend, 2008). A scheme could be phased in and precedents in Nepal,[8] parts of Latin America, and, in South Africa, such as the Child Support Grant (Case et al, 2003), could be copied and extended. UNICEF and other international organisations (such as the International Labour

Organization, ILO) should campaign for a legal right to child benefit under Articles 25 and 27 of the UNCRC (Gordon et al, 2003).

In the past, both national and international policy makers have not given sufficient consideration to the needs of children and the impacts of even successful policies on their vulnerable lives. For example, in September 1991, the democratically elected President Jean-Bertrand Aristide was overthrown by a military coup d'état. In response, the Organisation of American States (OAS) and, subsequently, the UN, imposed economic and other sanctions, which eventually led in October 1994 to a multinational peacekeeping force removing the military junta and helping to restore democracy. This could therefore be considered to be a successful policy intervention that supported political and civil rights in Haiti. However, the policy was not so successful from the perspective of the children of Haiti (Gibbons and Garfield, 1999). Elizabeth Gibbons (head of the UNICEF Office in Port-au-Prince at that time) records that as a result of the international sanctions:

> Unemployment increased by half (from 50 percent in 1990 to 75 percent in 1994), agricultural output declined by 20 percent, prices for basic foodstuffs increased more than 100 percent while annual per capita income declined 30 percent, bottoming out at $250. Child malnutrition doubled and thousands of children perished in a measles epidemic; maternal mortality increased by 29 percent; school enrolment dropped by a third; the number of street children doubled, and some 100,000 children were placed in domestic service to live as little more than slaves. (Gibbons, 1999 p 95)

Gibbons subsequently posed the important question:

> Which is worse – death from deliberate torture and violence or death from the deliberate withholding of a measles vaccine? Which is more immoral? (p 111)

Fortunately, Haitian and international policy makers today are not faced with such a dilemma. The children of Haiti can be spared from the horrors of growing up in absolute poverty if simple policies are adopted and funded to improve housing conditions, access to safe water and sanitation facilities and to education, health services and social security. No Haitian child needs to have their health and development permanently impaired by severe malnutrition, and all children can be provided with essential information about the outside world. The costs of implementing the policies required to end absolute child poverty are relatively low and the long-term benefits for society as a whole are huge. No scientific innovations are needed before absolute child poverty can be eradicated. What is needed is political will.

Notes

[1] This chapter is based on work funded by the United Nations Children's Fund (UNICEF) Haiti. We would like to thank Donatien Tameko, Adriano Gonzalez-Regueral, Daniel Badillo, Bertrand Njanja-Fassu, Christian Skoog, Gaudeamus Mbabazi, Elizabeth Augustin, Aldine Parisot and Elizabeth Gibbons for their help, advice and support.

[2] It ranked 149th out of 162 countries in the 2009 Human Development Index.

[3] http://unocha.org/cap/appeals/revision-flash-appeal-haiti-2010

[4] http://unocha.org/cap/appeals/revision-flash-appeal-haiti-2010

[5] http://fts.unocha.org/pageloader.aspx?page=emerg-emergency CountryDetails&cc=hti&yr=2010

[6] By December 2011, over half a million people had become sick from cholera, more than 280,000 people had been hospitalised and almost 7,000 people had died from this terrible disease (MSPP, 2011). Unfortunately, the number of organisations working on water and sanitation in Haiti is now falling, and a survey in November 2011 found that the the number of functional hand-washing stations in displaced persons camps is dwindling. Only 6% are equipped with hand-washing stations and soap and water in sufficient quantities (UNOCHA, 2011b).

[7] Sletten and Egset defined 'poor' as living on <US$2 a day and 'extremely poor' as living on <US$1 a day.

[8] https://sites.google.com/site/globalstudy2/nophotos-StirbuMariana-Socialprotect.ppt

References

Boccanfuso D. and A. Siméon (2006) *Dynamique de la pauvreté en Haïti et ses déterminants*, GREDI Working Paper, 06-15, Sherbrooke University.

Case, A., Hosegood, V. and Lund, F. (2003) *The reach of the South African Child Support Grant: Evidence from KwaZulu-Natal*, CSDS Working Paper No 38 (www.sarpn.org.za/documents/d0000582/P538_Child_Support_KZN.pdf). Durban: University of KwaZulu Natal.

Cayemittes, M., Placide, M.F., Barrère, B., Mariko, S. and Sévère, B. (2001) *Enquête Mortalité, Morbidité et Utilisation des Services, Haïti 2000*, Calverton, MD: Ministère de la Santé Publique et de la Population, Institut Haïtien de l'Enfance et ORC Macro.

Cayemittes, M., Placide, M.F., Mariko, S., Barrère, B., Sévère, B. and Alexandre, C. (2007) *Enquête Mortalité, Morbidité et Utilisation des Services, Haïti, 2005-2006*, Calverton, MD: Ministère de la Santé Publique et de la Population, Institut Haïtien de l'Enfance et Macro International Inc.

Chant, S. (2003) *Female household headship and the feminisation of poverty: Facts, fictions and forward strategies*, London: London School of Economics and Political Science (http://eprints.lse.ac.uk/574/1/femaleHouseholdHeadship.pdf).

Clark, C.M.A. (2002) 'Wealth and poverty: on the social creation of scarcity', *Journal of Economic Issues*, vol 36, no 2, pp 415-21.

Dupuy, A. (1989) *Haiti in the world economy: Class, race, and underdevelopment since 1700*, London: Westview Press.

Farmer, P. (2003) *The uses of Haiti*, Monroe, ME: Common Courage Press.

Gibbons, E. (1999) *Sanctions in Haiti: Human rights and democracy under assault*, The Washington Papers, Washington, DC: Center for Strategic and International Studies.

Gibbons, E. and Garfield, R. (1999) 'The impact of economic sanctions on health and human rights in Haiti, 1991-1994', *American Journal of Public Health*, vol 89, no 10, pp 1499-504.

Gordon, D. (2008) 'Children, policy and social justice', in G. Craig, T. Burchardt and D. Gordon (eds) *Social justice and public policy: Seeking fairness in diverse societies*, Bristol: The Policy Press, pp 157-80.

Gordon, D., Nandy, S., Pantazis, C., Pemberton, S. and Townsend, P. (2003) *Child poverty in the developing world*, Bristol: The Policy Press.

Jadotte, E. (2006) *Income distribution and poverty in the Republic of Haiti*, PMMA Working Papers 2006-13, Barcelona, Universitat Autonoma de Barcelona (http://portal.pep-net.org/documents/download/id/13564).

James, C.L.R. (1938) *The black Jacobins: Toussaint l'Ouverture and the San Domingo Revolution*, London: Secker Warburg.

Kish, L. and Frankel, M.R. (1974) 'Inference from complex samples', *Journal of the Royal Statistical Society. Series B (Methodological)*, vol 36, pp 1-37.

Kneipp, S.M. and Yarandi, H.N. (2002) 'Complex sampling designs and statistical issues in secondary analysis', *Western Journal of Nursing Research*, vol 24, pp 552-66.

MSPP (Ministère de la Santé Publique et de la Population) (2011) Rapports journaliers du MSPP sur l'évolution du choléra en Haiti, 18 December(www.mspp.gouv.ht/site/download.php?file=downloads/Rapport%20journalier%20MSPP%20du%2018%20decembre%202011.pdf).

Pedersen, J. and Lockwood, K. (2001) *Determination of a poverty line for Haiti*, Oslo: FAFO Institute of Applied Studies.

Reid, B.C., Psoter, W. et al (2007) 'The effect of an international embargo on malnutrition and childhood mortality in rural Haiti', *International Journal of Health Services*, vol 37, no 3, pp 501-13.

Sletten, P. and Egset, W. (2004) *Poverty in Haiti*, Fafo Paper 2004:31, Oslo: Fafo (www.fafo.no/pub/rapp/755/755.pdf).

Townsend, P. (2008) *The abolition of child poverty and the right to social security: A possible UN model for child benefit?*, London: London School of Economics and Political Science.

Townsend, P. (2009) *Building decent societies. Rethinking the role of social security in state building*, London: Palgrave.

UNICEF (2011) *Children in Haiti: One year after — The long road from relief to recovery*, New York: UNICEF.

UNOCHA (United Nations Office for the Coordination of Humanitarian Affairs) (2010) Haiti *earthquake situation report, Number 29, 15 March 2010*, New York: UNOCHA (http://www.crid.or.cr/crid/terremoto_haiti/OCHA_no29_15marzo.pdf).

UNOCHA (2011a) *Haiti — One year later, 18 January 2011*, New York: UNOCHA (www.unocha.org/issues-in-depth/haiti-one-year-later).

UNOCHA (2011b) *Humanitarian bulletin (19 November -19 December 2011)*, New York: UNOCHA (http://reliefweb.int/sites/reliefweb.int/files/resources/Full_Report_3147.pdf).

Victora, C.G., Fenn, B., Bryce, J. and Kirkwood, B.R. (2005) 'Co-coverage of preventive interventions and implications for child-survival strategies: evidence from national surveys', *The Lancet*, vol 366, pp 1460-6.

SIXTEEN

Child poverty in Latin America: multiple deprivation and monetary measures combined

Ernesto Espíndola Advis and María Nieves Rico

Introduction

According to estimates, close to 13% of Latin America's population lived in households with incomes insufficient to meet food needs in 2008, and poverty and inequality were afflicting a large portion (33%) of the population. The percentage of people living in extreme poverty would have grown as a result of the recent international financial crisis, and the number would have reached three million (ECLAC, 2009). The region's income distribution inequality is the most regressive in the world, and has improved little over the last 20 years.

Not all people experience poverty in the same way, are equally vulnerable to it or have the same potential for overcoming it. A significant fraction of the region's children and adolescents face adversities that not only have direct impacts during this phase of their life cycle, but lead to repercussions over the course of their future lives, as well as being transmitted to subsequent generations. The children and adolescents most affected are those who are trapped in situations of insufficient income and who are deprived of their rights to survival, shelter, education, health and nutrition, among other things.

Although many studies have examined poverty, most fail to recognise the specific nature of the poverty affecting children and adolescents. Understanding child poverty requires a multidimensional approach that takes account of both material deprivation (poor or lacking public goods and services directly relevant to children) and family income levels that are insufficient to satisfy the general gamut of needs.

Children and adolescents are of particular concern for a variety of reasons. They are 'over-represented' in the poor population (Minujin et al, 2006), they are more dependent and less autonomous in the family context, and they are more vulnerable to the consequences of poverty and inequality. Better knowledge of the determinants and experience of poverty in childhood and adolescence can help to design effective public policy that addresses child poverty and breaks the intergenerational cycle, as well as to evaluate the impact that programmes and projects in the countries have on the breadth and depth of the problem.

This chapter describes the implementation and principal results of a study of child poverty conducted jointly in 2008-09 by the Economic Commission for Latin America and the Caribbean (ECLAC) and the Regional Office of the United Nations Children's Fund (UNICEF TACRO). In addition to providing a more or less customary analysis of the characteristics of child poverty and its multiple dimensions, the study was designed to establish a regional baseline for future replication of the study (ECLAC/UNICEF TACRO, 2010).

One of the special features of this study is its combination of a multiple deprivation approach, based on the methodology developed by the University of Bristol in a study conducted in 2003, but with some further innovations, and the monetary approach. The present study drew on available living conditions surveys in the region, selecting surveys that provided relatively adequate information for both methodologies. However, the absence of anthropometric measurements for constructing child malnutrition indicators meant that it was necessary to use additional data from the UNICEF Multiple Indicator Cluster Surveys and Demographic and Health Surveys. This strategy made it possible to construct models to estimate the probability of malnutrition. Then those models were applied in more traditional household surveys, thus incorporating this essential dimension in estimating child poverty in the region.

Conceptual approach: the notion of child poverty

The term 'poverty' has differing connotations, and major semantic differences are sometimes involved. Spicker (Gordon and Spicker, 1999) identifies 11 ways of construing and interpreting poverty – in terms of needs, standard of living, resource insufficiency, problems of basic security, lack of entitlements, multiple deprivations, exclusion, inequality, class, dependency and unacceptable types or levels of suffering (Gordon and Spicker, 1999; Feres and Mancero, 2001).

In speaking of poverty, many authors and institutions emphasise 'quality of life'. Altimir (1979), for example, defines poverty as a situational syndrome characterised by under-consumption, malnutrition, precarious housing, low educational levels, poor health conditions, unstable insertion in the production system, attitudes of discouragement and disrespect for the rule of law, low levels of participation in mechanisms of social integration, and perhaps adherence to a value system somewhat different from that of the rest of society.

The UN Development Programme (UNDP) (1997) defines poverty as a situation that makes it impossible for people to lead a tolerable life, distinguishing between income poverty and human poverty. Income poverty is a one-dimensional deprivation, and is used as a definition when only this type of poverty is considered of interest, or when other types of deprivation are thought to be reducible to this as a common denominator. Human poverty, on the other hand, involves deprivation on various dimensions: long healthy life, knowledge, decent standard of living and participation. The concept of human poverty includes income as an important – but not the sole – element in human deprivation.

Thus, although some dimensions of welfare can be satisfied with goods and services available in the marketplace, others require goods that income cannot buy, such as public and private goods made available by government subsidy. The supply of public goods (public recreation spaces, for example) does not diminish with individual consumption. Rather, they remain available for collective consumption. The relevant private goods include social services such as education, healthcare, environmental sanitation and housing, services that tend to be totally or partially subsidised. Most of these constitute private goods from which people may be excluded by price. Examples are curative healthcare, potable water, residential housing, and so on.

Public provision of social services is part of the state's redistributive action. This usually involves covering basic needs and contributing to the formation of human capital. Thus, these services play a role in overcoming poverty and providing more equal opportunities. To a greater or lesser extent, their presence represents a process of de-mercantilisation through which societies guarantee certain goods and services as social entitlements, choosing to address them as non–market issues (Esping-Andersen, 1990).

Some essential aspects of welfare depend on access to non-economic goods and services, for instance, freedom of thought, belief, membership and assembly, and the right to elect and be elected, which have long been recognised as fundamental human rights. However, it is the economic aspects of welfare that are traditionally considered measures of poverty, and that involve access to goods and services that have opportunity costs. Ways of conceptualising, understanding and measuring poverty depend significantly on how welfare is thought of – what it is considered to consist of, and how it is achieved. Examples of different conceptual approaches are the utilitarian, John Rawls's theory of justice as impartiality and Amartya Sen's concept of functions, capacities and entitlements (Larrañaga, 2007).

Although there is not today a single approach by which child poverty is defined and measured, most studies and organisations regard it as a multidimensional phenomenon, and recognise that understanding what happens to children living in poverty requires a comprehension of the social context of poverty and inequality in which they live, since they are clearly not isolated actors.

The State of the World's Children 2005 report states that children living in poverty are those who 'experience deprivation of the material, spiritual and emotional resources needed to survive, develop and thrive, leaving them unable to enjoy their rights, achieve their full potential or participate as full and equal members of society' (UNICEF, 2005, p 18).

This approach to child poverty emphasises the multidimensional nature of the phenomenon, but as Minujin (2005) underlines, other factors are also central to the definition: not only material deprivation, but access to basic services, and other factors related to the discrimination and exclusion that affects children and adolescents' psychosocial development. These matters go beyond the strictly monetary view based on goods tradeable in the marketplace, which dominates many studies of poverty.

In addition to broadening the analysis of income poverty, most current definitions make an explicit connection between child poverty and the violation of their human rights. This generates a rights–based approach that is useful not only in research but also in policy making. The rights–based approach is considered a conceptual framework, as well as a framework for action, that should be used both in dealing with poverty and in addressing development issues (Abramovich, 2006). UNICEF proposes a perspective that includes the deprivation of rights as an approach that can help reduce the scourge of child poverty.

The choice of conceptual approach of course affects the indicators chosen for measurement, as well as the children and adolescents identified as poor, the scope of their poverty and their specific unmet needs. UNICEF (2004) believes that the concept of child poverty, along with estimates of its scope, can be constructed on the basis of ability to exercise specific economic and social rights, of which failure to fulfil can mean lack of access to potable water, sanitation services, medical services, information and education, with the consequences that these problems entail, including premature death, hunger and malnutrition.

Measuring child poverty: the methodological approaches used in this study

The ECLAC/UNICEF TACRO study followed two major methodological traditions of poverty measurement. The first is the direct method. The version of this most commonly used in the region is based on the assessment of unmet basic needs (UBNs). The present study used the Bristol approach (see Chapter Four), but adapted it to measure different levels of children's deprivation. The second tradition is indirect measurement, in which absolute poverty is measured in terms of per capita household income.

The multiple deprivations approach

One of the important large-scale efforts to measure child poverty in the framework of a rights approach was conducted by UNICEF with researchers from the University of Bristol and the London School of Economics and Political Science. This was considered to be the first scientific estimation of child poverty in the developing world (Rio Group on Poverty Statistics, 2007). The Bristol approach listed a basket of goods and services that it deemed essential for children's welfare, and defined various deprivation thresholds (Gordon et al, 2003). The set of indicators used was based on the principle that children have basic rights on various dimensions: adequate nutrition, potable water, decent sanitary services, health services, housing, education and information (Minujin et al, 2006).

The Bristol study used a concept of deprivation that included a continuum ranging from none to extreme, and provided operational definitions for placement on this scale. Another notable aspect of the study was its argument that since children's needs differ in degree and type from those of adults, the unit of analysis should be the child, not (as is traditional) the household. This is the case, the study argues, even though the needs of adults and children may overlap in certain dimensions, making it difficult to separate the experience of a family or household's children from the experience of its adults. However, analysis from a children's perspective paves the way for policy interventions designed to produce specific impacts different from the impacts targeted for adults.

The Bristol study used Demographic and Health Surveys and Multiple Indicator Cluster Surveys. Unfortunately, despite the recent availability of new surveys of this type, their regional coverage in Latin America is low. In order to incorporate income measurements simultaneously, therefore, household surveys available for 18 of the region's countries were used. Nevertheless, the Demographic and Health Surveys and Multiple Indicator Cluster Surveys were used as a reference to estimate levels of child malnutrition, as will become clear later. To make estimates of child poverty, the present study had to define indicators that could be measured by data available from existing household surveys.[1]

The deprivation thresholds used in the 2003 Bristol study represented only the most severe levels of child deprivation. The present study adopted the earlier criterion, but in addition, thresholds were defined so as to distinguish situations of moderate deprivation in which needs that go unmet can affect children's welfare and development. Table 16.1 shows the dimensions that represent the basic needs that must be met for children's proper development, the indicators that correspond to these dimensions and that were available through the instruments mentioned earlier, and the thresholds that define moderate and severe deprivation.

Table 16.1: Definition of indicators; thresholds of severe and moderate deprivation for children

Levels of deprivation Dimensions and indicators of deprivation	Moderate (not excluding severe)	Severe	Unit of analysis for which indicator is measured and applied	Article of the UNCRC that is violated
Nutrition[a] **Weight to age ratio** **Height (length) to age ratio**	(Global chronic malnutrition) Moderate/severe Underweight or moderately/severely low height (length) for age: less than −2 standard deviations from reference curve	Severe underweight or low height/ weight for age: less than −3 standard deviations from reference curve	Person: children 0-4 years old	24(2)(c) Health
Water and sanitation (1) **Access to potable water, by:** **Origin** **Supply** **Access time (if data available)**	a) Origin: drilled or dug well, natural sources b) Water supply outside of house and beyond land parcel (public cisterns, water trucks, etc)	(a) Unsafe water source: natural sources (rivers, springs) (b) If indicator of access time is available, 15 minutes or more	Housing: children and adolescents 0-17 years old	24(2)(e) Health

(continued)

Table 16.1: Definition of indicators; thresholds of severe and moderate deprivation for children (continued)

Levels of deprivation — Dimensions and indicators of deprivation	Moderate (not excluding severe)	Severe	Unit of analysis for which indicator is measured and applied	Article of the UNCRC that is violated
Water and sanitation (2) **Connection to sewer system (elimination of excreta)**	No sewer connection (eg, outhouses), or access outside of house or beyond land parcel	No sewer service (eg, direct channelling to river)	Housing: children and adolescents 0-17 years old	24(2)(c) Health
Housing **Number of people per bedroom/ room** **Floor material** **Wall material** **Roofing material**	Crowding: three or more people per bedroom/room (excluding bathroom and kitchen), dirt floor[b], unsafe building materials (walls or roof of mud or other similar materials)	Crowding: five or more people per bedroom/room; temporary housing (tents, etc), walls or roof built with waste materials	Housing: children and adolescents 0-17 years old	27(3) Standard of living
Education **School attendance and number of years of school completed**	Children and adolescents who have attended school but dropped out before completing secondary school	Children and adolescents who have never attended school	Person: children aged 7 or 8 to 17	28(1)(a)/(b) Education
Information **Access to electricity; possession of radio, television or telephone**	Housing unit without electricity, telephone (landline or mobile), or radio/television (at least two of these elements lacking)	Housing unit without access to electricity, telephone (landline or mobile), radio/ television (all lacking)	Household: children and adolescents 0-17 years old	13/17 Information

Notes: It is important to stress that the situations defined are situations of deprivation. Therefore, the deprivation thresholds are implicitly defined as welfare superior to the specified level.

[a] These indicators were obtained from the Demographic and Health Survey and Multiple Indicator Cluster Survey. A set of models was developed to estimate the probability of malnutrition using binary logistical regressions, and the models were then applied to the household survey data.

[b] Unlike the Bristol study, which considered a dirt floor to be an instance of severe deprivation, dirt flooring was defined as only a moderate deprivation in the present study.

Applying the rights-based perspective, the study considered each type of deprivation as a poverty indicator that *a priori* violates or fails to satisfy at least one right. Of course, a child may be affected by parents' decisions, discrimination in the community or health problems (problems due to malnutrition in this case, which, although not associated with insufficient resources or lack of access to basic social services, in themselves represent a failure to ensure basic rights). By ratifying the United Nations Convention on the Rights of the Child (UNCRC), states obligate themselves to satisfy all of children's rights to the full extent possible given available resources. This includes covering healthcare costs that are difficult for households to cover, and providing safeguards against discrimination, among other obligations. Measuring poverty in the framework of a rights approach thus means considering children poor if any of their rights – be it but one – are not fulfilled. Under the general unmet basic rights approach, a 'co-realisation' criterion applies, that is, the indicators are considered to be perfect proxies, and households or people suffering from at least one deprivation are poor (Rio Group on Poverty Statistics, 2007). For the same reason, national thresholds were constructed without urban–rural differentiation (although access to basic services is more difficult in rural areas due to high investment costs), since the rights apply in any context.[2]

Thus, the process of identifying poor children consisted of determining the number of dimensions on which the children to whom the data referred suffered from deprivation. To distinguish those in severe poverty, the study counted the number of dimensions on which severe deprivations were present. Those affected by at least one severe deprivation were considered to be living in severe poverty. A similar procedure was used to identify children in moderate poverty (at least one moderate deprivation putting a child in this category).

Monetary or income approach

Of the indirect measures of welfare frequently used by all of the region's countries to measure inequality and poverty, ECLAC promotes the method based on the cost of a basic needs basket, which measures households' current income[3] and its reflection at the individual (per capita) level, without applying measures of equivalence. This requires determining the cost of a *minimum food basket* constructed on the basis of the monetary value of the foods that are part of the observed consumption pattern of a reference group, which suffice to satisfy minimum energy needs for a moderate level of activity. The procedure makes it possible to determine a first monetary threshold, under which the household and its members are considered to be living in extreme poverty or indigence (the indigence line).

ECLAC currently constructs a real—normative food poverty line that represents the cost of a basket based on certain normative nutritional guidelines that reflect a population's consumption habits and the market prices available to it. The process of constructing the line includes a number of steps which include determining energy requirements, selecting a reference group whose average is taken as the nutritional threshold and determining the content and value of the food basket (Rio Group on Poverty Statistics, 2007).

The cost of the *basket of goods needed to satisfy basic non-food needs* (clothing, housing, transportation, communication, etc), the composition of which is based on observing the above-mentioned reference group, is determined by using the inverse of the Engel coefficient or fixed Orshanksy multiplier, which is twice the value of the food basket. A second monetary threshold is thus established, under which households and their members are considered poor (the poverty line).

As in the case of the multiple deprivation method, three categories of children were defined based on these two thresholds, the category in which a child fell depending on his or her households' potential capacity to satisfy the child's basic needs through market purchases. Per capita income was examined in relation to the indigence and poverty lines, designating those with insufficient levels of welfare as indigents or non-indigent poor, as opposed to non-poor.

Both multiple deprivation methods and monetary methods have their respective aggregation indexes that are shown in the Appendix at the end of this chapter.

The data: household surveys, Demographic and Health Surveys and Multiple Indicator Cluster Surveys

As Table 16.2 shows, household surveys are conducted primarily by national statistics institutes, except in the Dominican Republic, where they are conducted by the Central Bank, and Chile, where they are conducted by the Ministry of Planning and Cooperation (MIDEPLAN). Their principal objectives are to obtain information from representative population samples regarding the population's demographic, educational, housing, occupational and income characteristics. In some countries, the surveys also cover elements such as migration, access to healthcare systems and additional dimensions

Table 16.2: Household surveys used to measure child poverty in Latin America

Country	Year	Name	Coverage	Executing agency
Bolivia, Plurinational State of	2007	Encuesta Continua de Hogares	National	Instituto Nacional de Estadística (INE)
Brazil	2007	Pesquisa Nacional por Amostra de Domicilios	National	Fundaçao Instituto Brasileiro de Geografia e Estatistica (IBGE)
Chile	2006	Encuesta de Calidad de Vida de los Hogares (CASEN)	National	Ministerio de Planificación Nacional (MIDEPLAN)
Colombia	2008	Gran Encuesta Integrada de Hogares	National	Departamento Administrativo Nacional de Estadística (DANE)
Costa Rica	2007	Encuesta de Hogares de Propósitos Múltiples	National	Instituto Nacional de Estadística y Censos (INEC)
Dominican Republic	2007	Encuesta Nacional de Fuerza de Trabajo	National	Banco Central de la República Dominicana
Ecuador	2007	Encuesta de Empleo, Desempleo y Subempleo en el Área Urbana y Rural	National	Instituto Nacional de Estadística y Censos (INEC)
El Salvador	2004	Encuesta de Hogares de Propósitos Múltiples	National	Dirección General de Estadística y Censos (DIGESTYC)
Guatemala	2006	Encuesta Nacional sobre Empleo e Ingresos	National	Instituto Nacional de Estadística (INE)
Honduras	2007	Encuesta Permanente de Hogares de Propósitos Múltiples	National	Instituto Nacional de Estadística (INE)
Mexico	2006	Encuesta Nacional de Ingresos y Gastos de los Hogares	National	Instituto Nacional de Estadística, Geografía e Informática (INEGI)
Nicaragua	2005	Encuesta Nacional de Hogares Sobre la Medición de Niveles de Vida	National	Instituto Nacional de Estadísticas y Censos (INEC)
Panama	2003	Encuesta de condiciones de vida[a]	National	Ministerio de Economía y Finanzas y Programa de Naciones Unidas para el Desarrollo (PNUD)
Paraguay	2007	Encuesta Permanente de Hogares	National	Dirección General de Estadística, Encuestas y Censos (DGEEC)
Peru	2008	Encuesta Nacional de Hogares – Condiciones de Vida y Pobreza	National	Instituto Nacional de Estadística e Informática (INEI)

(continued)

Table 16.2: Household surveys used to measure child poverty in Latin America (continued)

Country	Year	Name	Coverage	Executing agency
Bolivarian Republic of Venezuela	2007	Encuesta de Hogares por Muestreo	National	Oficina Central de Estadística e Informática (OCEI)
Argentina	2006	Encuesta Permanente de Hogares	31 urban clusters	Instituto Nacional de Estadística y Censos (INDEC)
Uruguay	2007	Encuesta Continua de Hogares	Urban	Instituto Nacional de Estadística (INE)

Note: [a] Living Standard Measurement Surveys programme.

Source: Economic Commission for Latin America and the Caribbean (ECLAC), household survey database

of living conditions. The information obtained makes it possible to generate estimates of populations' and households' social and economic living conditions by estimating their monetary or UBNs, crowding, education, and so on.

The Demographic and Health Surveys are conducted by the US Agency for International Development (USAID). The MEASURE Demographic and Health Survey + programme is implemented by ORC Macro, based in the state of Maryland (US). The objective is to obtain information from the population/households on reproductive health, nutrition, coverage of health services, infant mortality, vaccination rates and prevalence/incidence of certain pathologies in children aged 5-9. The Demographic and Health Surveys are conducted with representative samples for each country's national, urban and rural populations.

The Multiple Indicator Cluster Surveys are part of a UNICEF programme designed to help countries obtain information on their populations' nutritional state, infant mortality and children's health, environment, water and sanitation conditions, the security and durability of housing tenancy, the protection of children, child labour, child discipline, early marriage and polygamy, feminine genital mutilation, domestic violence, discipline, HIV and orphans and other vulnerable children. Multiple Indicator Cluster Surveys are conducted by sampling representative clusters of the population and households at the national level. They have been carried out every five years since 1995.

Both the Demographic and Health Survey and Multiple Indicator Cluster Survey were used to develop a group of statistical models to estimate the probability of being malnourished (among children under five) when using household surveys (see the Appendix at the end of this chapter, and the list of surveys used in Table 16.3).

Table 16.3: Demographic and Health Surveys and Multiple Indicator Cluster Surveys examined by the present study

Country	Year	Coverage	Phase
Demographic and Health Surveys			
Bolivia, Plurinational State of	2003	National	4
Brazil	1996	National	
Colombia	2005	National	4
Dominican Republic	2007	National	4
Ecuador	1987	National	
El Salvador	1985	National	
Guatemala	1999	National	
Haiti	2005/06	National	
Honduras	2005	National	4
Mexico	1987	National	
Nicaragua	2001	National	
Paraguay	1990	National	
Peru	2008	National	4
Multiple Indicator Cluster Surveys			
Bolivia, Plurinational State of	2000	National	2
Belize	2006	National	3
Cuba	2006	National	3
Dominican Republic	2000	National	2
Jamaica	2005	National	3
Suriname	2000	National	2
Trinidad and Tobago	2000	National	2
Venezuela, Bolivarian Republic of	2000	National	2

Note: Although the phase 3 Multiple Indicator Cluster Survey in Guyana, Suriname and Trinidad and Tobago have been carried out, the results were not available at the time of the study.

Sources: www.measuredhs.com and www.childinfo.org

Principal results

The principal findings regarding the magnitude and depth of extreme and total child poverty in the region's different countries are presented in this section. The proportion and number of children affected by household income insufficiency are also shown (indigence and non-indigent poverty by income). The cross of the two estimates is provided as well.

Child poverty in Latin America: the assessment

One out of five children in Latin America is extremely poor.[4] *Thus, over 32 million children in the region are affected.* Around 2007, 17.9% of the region's children under 18 were living in extreme poverty, summing somewhat over 32 million in all in 18 countries (see Table 16.4). These children were severely affected by one or more extreme deprivations consisting of precarious housing, household lack of access to potable water or sanitation services, severe chronic or global malnutrition (or both), lack of access to educational systems (children who had never attended school) or lack of access to communication and information systems (including lack of electricity in the home).

The realities of children's lives vary enormously from country to country, however. In the countries with the most child poverty (Bolivia, El Salvador, Guatemala, Honduras, Nicaragua and Peru) approximately 41% of children were extremely poor; in intermediate

Table 16.4: Latin America (18 countries): children in extreme and total poverty (% and 000s of children)

| | | Poor children 0-17 years of age | | | | | |
| | | Extreme child poverty | | | Total child poverty[a] | | |
Country	Year	%	000s	Gap with respect to extreme poverty threshold[a]	%	000s	Gap with respect to total poverty threshold[a]
Bolivia, Plurinational State of	2007	48.6	2,040	−14	77.2	3,241	−16
Guatemala	2006	47.2	2,979	−13	79.7	5,030	−14
Nicaragua	2005	42.4	941	−12	78.5	1,740	−14
El Salvador	2004	39.0	1,071	−12	86.8	2,384	−10
Peru	2008	38.0	4,104	−11	73.4	7,916	−15
Honduras	2007	29.2	1,033	−11	67.9	2,405	−13
Panama	2003	26.9	311	−12	51.1	590	−13
Ecuador	2007	20.4	1,070	−12	50.4	2,639	−13
Venezuela, Bolivarian Republic of	2007	16.4	1,632	−11	35.7	3,557	−11
Colombia	2008	15.6	2,410	−10	38.5	5,952	−12
Brazil	2007	14.6	8,554	−11	38.8	22,713	−10
Paraguay	2007	13.7	345	−9	56.5	1,426	−12
Mexico	2006	11.0	4,301	−10	40.4	15,844	−10
Argentina(urban areas)	2006	10.0	730	−9	28.7	2,097	−8
Dominican Republic	2007	7.7	269	−9	49.3	1,725	−9
Uruguay	2007	6.2	58	−9	23.9	225	−8
Chile	2006	6.1	290	−9	23.2	1,097	−10
Costa Rica	2007	4.4	64	−9	20.5	298	−9
Latin America	**2007**	**17.9**	**32,201**	**−11**	**45.0**	**80,879**	**−11**

Note: [a] Includes children in extreme poverty.

Source: ECLAC, based on special tabulations of data from national household surveys

countries (Brazil, Colombia, Dominican Republic, Ecuador, Mexico, Panama and Paraguay) the figure was slightly less than 14%; and in the countries with the lowest levels of child poverty, only 8% of children were so placed. Fifty-three per cent of the region's extremely poor children were in Brazil (8.5 million), Mexico (4.3 million) and Peru (4.1 million). The relatively high numbers in Brazil and Mexico are to be expected, given the size of their populations and their stage of demographic transition. However, the percentage of extremely poor children was only 14.6% in Brazil and 11% in Mexico, while the percentage in Peru was around 38%.

The depth of extreme poverty tends to be greatest precisely where there is a higher percentage of extremely poor children. High levels of extreme child poverty are associated not only with more or less widespread deprivation of some rights, but in many cases with multiple extreme deprivations present simultaneously for a large percentage of children. Although the existence of a single extreme deprivation in itself is very serious in terms of a child's development, the presence of a 'syndrome' of multiple deprivations signals a certain loss of opportunity to develop personal potentials, and leads to the intergenerational reproduction of poverty (for more statistical information about the depth of extreme and total poverty, see ECLAC/UNICEF TACRO, 2010).

Nearly one half of the region's children are either moderately or extremely poor. Poverty affects 80.9 million individuals under the age of 18 in the region. While, in most of the countries, the number of children subject to severe deprivations is not small, this population tends to be circumscribed, principally consisting of children of native peoples in rural areas or marginal urban areas. Moderate deprivation, on the other hand, affects broader and more diverse populations. Thus, in Latin America, 45% of children are subject to at least moderate, and in some cases, severe, deprivation. Thus, 81 million children in the region are affected, with the largest numbers residing in Brazil (22.7 million), Mexico (15.8 million) and Peru (7.9 million).

Despite these general regional realities, *the level of child poverty varies greatly from country to country*, ranging from one to four children out of five. In countries such as Bolivia, El Salvador, Guatemala, Honduras and Peru, over two thirds of children are poor, while in countries such as Chile, Costa Rica and Uruguay, fewer than one out of four are severely or moderately deprived of one or more basic rights.

Thus, among the countries whose children are most affected by various moderate or severe deprivations (where over two thirds of poor children are in this situation), child poverty affects 76% of children (22.7 million). In countries with intermediate levels of child poverty (where over one third and less than two thirds of poor children are poor), an average of 40%, or nearly 50.9 million children, are subject to such deprivations.[5] In countries where children's basic rights are more fully met, on the other hand, somewhat fewer than 26% of children are in poverty (approximately 3.7 million).

Figures for several countries where extreme child poverty is extremely low nevertheless heavily increase total poverty because of the widespread presence of moderate deprivations, principally in the areas of housing, potable water and sanitation. Cases in point are the Dominican Republic, where the number of poor children is six times the number of extremely poor, Costa Rica, where this factor is five, and Paraguay, where it is four. In other countries, the factor is lower either because of high levels of extreme poverty or because a significant number of poor children are subject to extreme deprivations (for example, Bolivia, Guatemala and Nicaragua).

In contrast to the case of extreme poverty, the total poverty depth or gap does not reveal a pattern clearly associated with the phenomenon's incidence. In other words, observed levels of total poverty in the countries are not clearly related to the incidence of moderate or severe deprivations affecting children. This indicates that in most of the countries there is a large proportion of children who are only affected by one moderate deprivation.

One out of three extremely poor children in the region has at least one basic right seriously violated, and one out of two poor children is deprived in terms of only one need. At the regional level, 29.4% of the over 32 million extremely poor children suffer from more than one severe deprivation, and only slightly over 8% from three or more such deprivations. This explains the fact that the measures of depth (gap as measured in distance from the threshold) of extreme poverty in Latin America are not as high as might be expected: 22.7 million children are affected by only one extreme deprivation. As regards total child poverty, 53% of the 80.9 million children are affected by a single moderate or severe deprivation (slightly over 43 million children), and only one out of five poor children are deprived in three or more dimensions of their welfare (see Figure 16.1). However, it is important to recognise the heterogeneity of the situations of child poverty in the region's different countries, as well as different capacities to fund public policies with major coverage for children.

Among the countries with least child poverty, at least 1% of children are deprived of at least two or more basic needs (12% of extremely poor children), and the number of children with three or more severe deprivations is minimal. Three out of four poor children suffer only

Figure 16.1: Latin America (18 countries): poor and extremely poor children according to number of deprivations (in cumulative percentages)

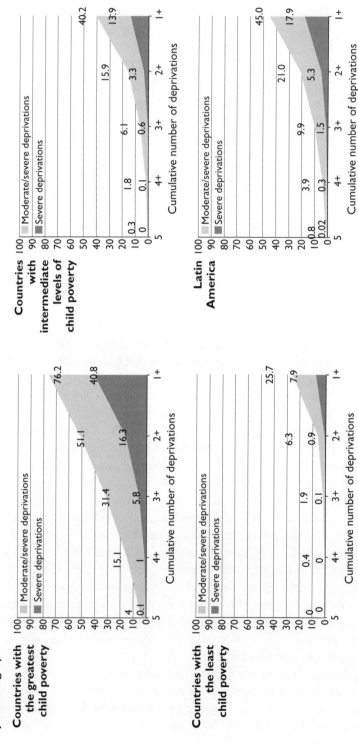

Source: ECLAC, based on special tabulations of data from national household surveys

one moderate or severe deprivation, and only 7% suffer three or more deprivations. In those countries where between 35% and 60% of children are poor, one out of four extremely poor children suffer from two or more deprivations (3.3% of all children), while 1 out of 20 lives in deeper extreme poverty (three or more deprivations), over 800,000 children finding themselves in this very high risk situation. Nearly 40% of children in extreme or moderate poverty, however, suffer from two or more deprivations, and nearly 6% of all children are affected by three or more deprivations (7.6 million children). Finally, one group of countries is highly affected by poverty in general, and by child poverty in particular. In these countries, where 41% of children are extremely poor, 40% of these suffer from two or more deprivations (4.9 million children), and 14% from three or more (approximately 1.7 million). As to total poverty, 51% of the children are affected by more than one deprivation, which represents nearly 67% of poor children, and 31% by three or more deprivations (41% of poor children).

In rural areas, three out of four children live in poverty, while in urban areas only one out of three is in this situation. But the great population concentration in urban areas implies that the number of urban poor children is 0.9 million more than the number of poor rural children. Around 123 million children live in the region's urban areas, while approximately 53 million live in rural areas. In the former, slightly over 9% of children are extremely poor, while in the latter the figure is nearly 39%. Meanwhile, 32% of urban children live in severe or moderate poverty, a situation that contrasts sharply with the 76% figure in rural areas.

Nevertheless, there is a great concentration of children in urban areas due to successive waves of migration from the countryside, generally motivated by lack of jobs, low incomes or the search for better access to various services, such as education and health. For this reason, *of the nearly 90 million poor children, those living in urban zones represent 51%,* that is, there are 40.9 million urban poor children versus 40 million rural (see Figure 16.2).

Despite the above, the situation is the reverse for extreme child poverty. The high incidence of extreme poverty in rural areas means that the absolute number of extremely poor children in rural areas is 20.4 million, which is 8.5 million more than the number of extremely poor children in urban areas (see Table 16.5). *The probability of a rural child being extremely poor is four times higher than that of an urban child.* This is principally due to the scarcity of social services and the long distances that both children and adults must sometimes travel for services, especially healthcare and education. In addition, it is more difficult to provide potable water, basic sanitation and electricity in

Figure 16.2: Latin America (18 countries): incidence of poverty and extreme poverty among children according to ethnic origin and geographical area,[b] and depth of same[c] (%)

Incidence of child poverty

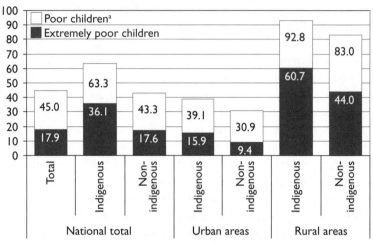

Poverty gap

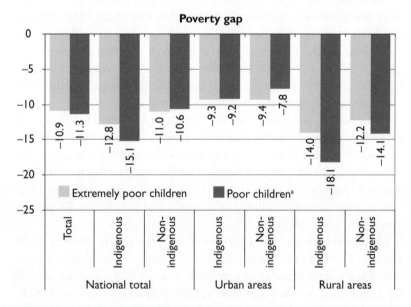

Notes:
[a] Includes extremely poor children.
[b] The distinction by ethnic origin is available for eight countries (Plurinational State of Bolivia, Brazil, Chile, Ecuador, Guatemala, Nicaragua, Panama and Paraguay). The overall total is for the 18 countries.
[c] Depth figures are gaps, which were calculated only among poor children (not entire child population).
Source: ECLAC, based on special tabulations of data from national household surveys

Table 16.5: Latin America (18 countries): incidence of child poverty and extreme child poverty by type of geographical area (% and 000s of children)

Country	Year	Extreme child poverty				Total child poverty [a]			
		Urban areas		Rural areas		Urban areas		Rural areas	
		Inci-dence	000s	Inci-dence	000s	Inci-dence	000s	Inci-dence	000s
Bolivia, Pluranational State of	2007	30.2	784	78.3	1,256	63.6	1,650	99.2	1,591
Guatemala	2006	26.8	721	62.4	2,258	61.6	1,659	93.2	3,370
Nicaragua	2005	22.4	253	63	688	62.8	707	94.6	1,033
El Salvador	2004	19.7	295	62.2	776	84.3	1,262	89.9	1,122
Venezuela, Bolivarian Republic of [b]	2007	16.4	1,632	–	–	35.7	3,558	–	–
Panama	2003	13.9	88	42.6	223	35.8	226	69.6	364
Peru	2008	13.9	873	71.9	3,231	56.4	3,551	97.1	4,366
Honduras	2007	12.7	183	40.4	850	51.9	745	78.9	1,660
Argentina (urban areas)	2006	10.0	730	–	–	28.7	2,097	–	–
Ecuador	2007	9.1	297	39.3	773	32.4	1,060	80.3	1,579
Brazil	2007	8.1	3,842	41.4	4,712	28.4	13,398	81.9	9,317
Paraguay	2007	8.0	108	20.2	238	36.3	490	79.8	936
Colombia	2008	7.0	776	37.3	1,634	25.9	2,870	70.4	3,082
Dominican Republic	2007	5.9	130	10.8	139	36.5	807	71.4	918
Uruguay	2007	5.9	52	10.5	6	22.1	195	50.3	30
Mexico	2006	4.1	931	20.7	3,371	25.4	5,830	61.4	10,014
Chile	2006	3.2	132	25.9	158	16.4	675	69.3	422
Costa Rica	2007	1.8	14	7.4	50	10.5	81	31.9	217
Latin America [c]	**2007**	**9.3**	**11,839**	**38.8**	**20,361**	**32.1**	**40,860**	**76.2**	**40,022**

[a] Includes children in extreme poverty.
[b] The figures for the Bolivarian Republic of Venezuela represent national totals.
[c] The absolute totals may not coincide with the other tables because of rounding.
Source: ECLAC, based on special tabulations of data from national household surveys

rural areas, because the population is so dispersed. Another significant factor is the use of inadequate materials for housing construction. This is aggravated by the higher costs of construction (due to the need to transport material over large distances), repair and replacement in rural areas. Yet another factor is the inadequacy of household incomes to self-finance services and housing investment, and the low level of investment in road and productive infrastructure that is typical in the region's rural areas. Therefore, not only are levels of poverty and extreme poverty among children greater in rural areas, but the depth of their poverty is also greater: rural children tend to be deprived simultaneously in terms of various needs that correspond to basic rights.

Children of indigenous and African-Caribbean groups are much more affected by poverty than others, one out of three of these children living in extreme poverty, and two out of three in poverty. The situation is worse in rural areas, where 9 out of 10 children are poor, and 6 out of 10 extremely poor. In countries whose measurement methods identify children's ethnic origins, the greater exclusion of members of native peoples and African-Caribbean individuals is evident. In general terms, extreme child poverty in these groups is double that seen among other children (36.1% versus 17.6%). Poor children of indigenous or African-Caribbean origin have an incidence of moderate or severe poverty higher than that of other groups by around 20 percentage points, and 63.3% of these children are so affected.

Although a superficial reading tends to attribute indigenous poverty to the fact that these people inhabit rural areas (although this is not the case for children of African descent), which are normally poorer than urban areas, data on the levels of extreme and moderate deprivation by ethnic origin and place of residence show that *in all areas, ethnic origin is associated with unsatisfied children's rights.*[6] Moreover, *the depth of poverty and extreme poverty among children of indigenous and African-Caribbean origin is greater than in the other groups*, although these differences are less pronounced in urban areas. This shows that (in rural areas primarily) children of indigenous origin more frequently than their non-indigenous peers have more than one of their rights violated or unsatisfied.

Other interesting findings have to do with the association of various characteristics of the household and its adult members with child poverty. For example, *family structure and stage of life cycle, and, most important, the number of children in a household, are associated with child poverty.* In the first place, and in contrast to what occurs with income poverty, it is not in the nuclear family that child poverty is most prevalent. Rather, it is slightly higher among extended, and especially compound, families.[7] Moreover, as family size stabilises, there is an increase in poverty, which diminishes as the children leave the home.

Child poverty is strongly associated with low levels of educational capital, and with low maternal educational levels in particular. It is also associated with informal labour insertion on the part of the head of household. According to the evidence obtained in this study, there is a strong relation between maternal educational level and the incidence of extreme and non-extreme child poverty. The percentage of extremely poor children for women who have no schooling or completed only some years of primary school is 34%, while it is 13.1% among mothers who have complete primary school, 4.8% for mothers who have completed secondary school and under 2% for mothers who have a tertiary education. In the case of total child poverty, suffice to mention that a child's probability of being poor is nearly seven times higher when the child's mother has not completed primary school than when the mother has completed college, and 3.3 times greater than when the mother has finished secondary school. In addition, *the children of mothers with less education suffer a greater depth of poverty and extreme poverty*, that is, they more frequently suffer from more than one deprivation. This is even more pronounced in the case of poor children (moderate and severe). Educational capital tends to be related with type of labour insertion. Thus, *the probability that a child will be poor or extremely poor increases significantly if the head of household works in the informal sector of the economy, and the depth of child poverty in this case tends to be greater.*

The above points to a serious problem characteristic of the region's labour markets, and which reinforces the vicious circle reproducing poverty and inequality: *it is the poorest who tend to work in the informal sector, which is generally associated with low educational level. And it is precisely those in the informal sector who have least access to social protections, particularly in health, although they are precisely the ones most in need of this.* Moreover, the very fact of informality implies the absence of records of the individuals, their characteristics and their households, making it even more difficult to locate them, and hence impeding the possibility of providing assistance.

Children belonging to poor households as measured by per capita income

As regards poverty measured monetarily, *it is children who are most affected by lack of household income. There are more children than adults, proportionally, in this situation, and they are poorer than adults.* The basic reason for this is that the probability of being poor increases with household size, especially if the household is dominated numerically by members who depend on the income generated by others – principally inactive older adults and, in particular, children.[8] An additional factor in the case of young children (and older adults) is the additional needs for care and protection that in most cases lead to at least one member of the family being dedicated exclusively to this task, further reducing the household's income-generating capacity.

In addition, *nearly one half of children live in households with incomes that put them under the poverty line, and small children are especially affected*. In Latin America in around 2007, there were in the order of 84.5 million children living in poor households, of whom 33.6 million were members of indigent households. Proportionally speaking, 47% of children belonged to poor households and 18.7% to indigent households. The countries in which this situation is particularly severe are Honduras, Nicaragua, Paraguay, Bolivia and Guatemala, where over 60% of children are poor and 35% indigent. On the other end of the spectrum are Chile, Costa Rica, Uruguay and Venezuela, where fewer than 40% of children live in poor households, although in the latter two countries over 10% of children live in households with per capita income insufficient to cover their food needs (see Figure 16.3).

Over one half of the people living in indigent households are children. According to the last measurements available, while children under the age of 18 constituted 48.4% of all poor, they represented 52.8% of the members of indigent households, where incomes, even if dedicated exclusively to food, would not satisfy the food needs of all their members.

Despite the seriousness of extreme income insufficiency, especially for the youngest children, a significant number of children live in households with incomes that could potentially satisfy their food needs, but not all of their basic needs (children in non-indigent poverty).[9] Nearly 51 million children in the region live in this situation. Although this is not the most serious situation, it usually entails a series of postponements that affect the development of children's abilities and competencies, reproducing the chain of poverty and inequality.

The double face of child poverty: lack of resources and multiple deprivations

Already towards the end of the 1980s in Latin America there were a number of attempts to integrate monetary and non-monetary methodologies (see ECLAC/DGEC, 1988). These approaches did not regard income insufficiency as a dimension additional to those relating to material deprivation, but defined the former as a potential way of satisfying needs, or an entry factor, and the latter as the result or consequences of insufficient income or inequitable distribution of income within households (see, for example, Townsend, 1979).

Measuring welfare and poverty according to income is insufficient to reflect all the deprivations that may have a negative impact on children's development. However, measuring poverty monetarily also provides valuable information for describing the children's situation, as well as for making public policy decisions. In addition, although at first glance income poverty and child poverty as measured by deprivations are highly correlated (and the correlation is even greater where total poverty in relation to extreme poverty is concerned), these associations are not so clear at the individual (or household) level. For this reason,

Figure 16.3: Latin America (18 countries): children belonging to income-poor and indigent households[a], incidence and gaps[b] (%)

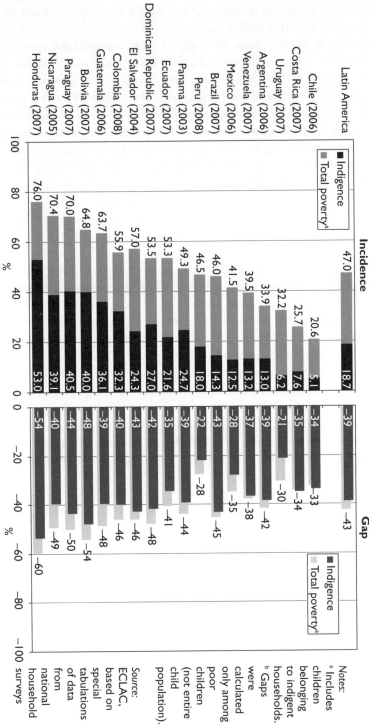

Notes:
[a] Includes children belonging to indigent households.
[b] Gaps were calculated only among poor children (not entire child population).

Source: ECLAC, based on special tabulations of data from national household surveys

it was also necessary to examine the children's situation from the perspective of both methodologies.

Children in extreme poverty. Although it may be supposed that reversing some of the extreme deprivations that affect children can restore a normal course of development, the gravity of the deprivations and their persistence over time often have permanent impacts. This is true of malnutrition, lack of a healthful environment, failure to attend school and dropping out of school. It is also possible that extreme deprivations affecting children can be overcome both through direct intervention – health services and nutrition, potable water, sanitation, and so on – and indirect interventions that increase household income (through the labour market, or via monetary transfers). However, *extreme income insufficiencies are not always accompanied by severe deprivation, and severe deprivations are not always associated with income insufficiencies*:

- only around 43% of all extremely poor children (17.9%, or over 32 million) belong to households whose incomes are potentially insufficient to satisfy food needs;
- 18.4 million children suffer extreme deprivations of their rights despite the fact that their households' incomes are not under the value of the minimum food basket;
- 10.6% of all children (19 million) belong to households whose incomes define them as indigent, without suffering extreme lacks;
- In all, *28.9%, or 52.1 million, of the region's children live in extreme poverty, are affected by serious income insufficiencies, or are subject to both*;
- at one extreme, many more children in Colombia, the Dominican Republic, Honduras and Paraguay are in situations of indigence than in extreme poverty;
- at the other extreme, the number of children suffering one or more severe deprivations in countries such as Bolivia, El Salvador, Guatemala and Peru is much greater than the proportion belonging to indigent households.

Since many of the current interventions to address poverty use the family as the basic beneficiary unit, it is safe to say that there are approximately 4.1 million households in the region with children who simultaneously suffer from severe violation of their rights and from grave income insufficiencies (traditionally denominated *chronic poverty*). In 8.3 million households, the problem is not essentially monetary, which points to a degree of *inertia* at work in the serious failure to meet children's basic needs. This may be due to inequitable distribution of resources within the home, to the fact that per capita income is barely above the indigence line, or to the instability of income. Finally, although children in 6.8 million households do not have access to resources with the potential to meet their needs, their rights are not severely violated. (Since the extreme insufficiency of monetary resources in this case does not lead to severe deprivations, this situation is called *recent* poverty.)

Poor children. Total child poverty, which includes both severe and moderate deprivation, is a general expression of social exclusion, and at the same time the mechanism by which poverty reproduces itself. Although children in moderate poverty do not suffer severely bad living conditions, their future opportunities do suffer because of poor nutrition, poor academic performance, their dropping out of school, their involvement in child labour, lack of expectations and discrimination because of being and seeming poor. These factors not only represent problems in terms of their rights in the present, but will very probably leave them in the lower strata of the social scale, where they will reproduce as adults the precariousness of their welfare as children, in turn affecting future generations.

Unlike extreme child poverty, total poverty in the region as measured by extent of deprivation is more closely related to income insufficiency. This is in part because extremely poor families tend more frequently to develop survival strategies that involve community solidarity and social assistance from civil society and government, which allow them to some extent to avoid severe deprivations despite the fact that they cannot count on minimum incomes, or even on sufficient income for adequate food. In not extremely poor families, attention tends to be placed on autonomous generation of income, and therefore real satisfaction of needs does not always receive the attention it deserves. Moreover, in these strata there are more people participating in the labour market, which, among other things, makes it necessary for them to dedicate a greater proportion of resources to clothing and transportation, and limits the development of relationships of solidarity with the rest of the community.

Overall in Latin America:

- 29.2% of children suffer from moderate or grave deprivation, and in addition their families do not have sufficient incomes to satisfy their basic needs. This situation affects around 52.5 million children in some 19.2 million households;
- 15.8% of the region's children – 28.3 million – suffer moderate or severe deprivations despite the fact that their families – 15.9 million – have incomes that are potentially sufficient to prevent

these deprivations. It should be noted that unlike the stratum
described earlier, where the ratio of children per household is 2.7,
these households have an average of 1.8 children, which partially
explains the greater availability of income here;

- 17.8% of children do not suffer from deprivations that violate their
  rights as children, but do belong to households with insufficient
  incomes. Some 32 million children in 12.5 million households are
  in this situation. The average number of children per household
  here is 2.6, reducing per capita household income;

- in all, 62.7% of children are affected by one or another form of
  poverty, that is, are in households with insufficient income or suffer
  from some deprivation. In the order of 113 million children in the
  region live with levels of social exclusion that affect their welfare,

Table 16.6: Latin America (18 countries): child poverty and children in households with insufficient incomes (monetary method) (in millions and %)

Extreme poverty

Method of measuring poverty		Extreme child poverty (multiple deprivation)					
		Extremely poor children		Children not extremely poor		Subtotal	
		Millions	%	Millions	%	Millions	%
Monetary indigence of households	Children in income indigence	14	7.7	20	11.0	34	18.7
(examined in children)	Non-indigent children	18	10.2	128	71.1	146	81.3
Subtotal		32	17.9	148	82.1	180	100.0

Total poverty[a]

Method of measuring poverty		Child poverty (multiple deprivation)					
		Poor children		Non-poor children		Subtotal	
		Millions	%	Millions	%	Millions	%
Monetary poverty of households	Children in income poverty	53	29.2	32	17.8	85	47.0
(examined in children)	Non-poor children	28	15.8	67	37.3	95	53.0
Subtotal		81	45.0	99	55.0	180	100.0

[a] Includes extremely poor children and those belonging to indigent households.

Source: ECLAC, based on special tabulations from national households surveys

and suffer or potentially suffer from failure to meet their basic rights (see Table 16.6).

Conclusion and recommendations

As this chapter makes clear, child poverty is extensive in Latin America, although there are significant differences between countries. Among children, the many faces of poverty (deprivations in terms of nutrition, housing and access to potable water and sanitation services, education, information and household income) have permanent negative impacts that mark them for the rest of their lives, and to a great extent lead to the reproduction of poverty.

Fighting child poverty is not only a moral imperative and a sign of respect for their basic rights. Child poverty and its dangerous consequences affect not only individuals but also societies as a whole, damaging the basis of sustainable long-term economic and social development.

Although space limitations here do not allow for specific sectoral recommendations in areas such as food, health, housing, education, and so on, some general conclusions and recommendations can be stated:

• In the countries with the least child poverty, which are those that have high per capita GDP in the regional context and have a greater capacity to fund public policy to protect children, fighting child poverty requires more than a large volume of resources. Making large advances in reducing child poverty calls for *political will, comprehensive programmes and well-targeted instruments.*

• In the region's medium-income countries, addressing child poverty requires mobilising a significant set of resources, and possibly *redesigning anti-poverty policies to orient them more decisively to children,* since the population affected is large, and there are great possibilities for the problem to reproduce itself.

• In the countries with the most child poverty – the majority of which are in Central America and the Andean region – the depth of child poverty is greater, and hence reducing it requires tremendous resources to fund action in different areas (health and nutrition, education, information access, housing, sanitation, and so on). The limitations of current government revenues, as well as the urgency of intervention, call for the *use of multilateral funding mechanisms and for mobilising international cooperation.*

- It is possible to overcome extreme child poverty with actions not necessarily designed to *improve household income*, but there is a need to redesign public anti-poverty policy that aims to *create jobs* or that focuses on monetary transfers, so as to establish *effective conditions on interventions that ensure that the interest of children is emphasised*, that is, so that the primary beneficiaries of the resources spent are in fact individuals under the age of 18.

- Sectoral interventions should be designed with a comprehensive view of the phenomenon of poverty. In this connection, it is important to be aware that interventions aiming to improve children's quality of life in many cases must be designed so as to improve the quality of life of the entire family. It is also essential to recognise that *mere sectoral intervention, although it can reduce deprivation in particular areas of deprivation, does not necessarily ensure that all of children's basic rights will be met, and that in the culture of poverty children's rights also suffer from the fact that anti-poverty measures are in many cases not designed with all of their rights in mind.* Exploitation and physical and psychological violence are cases in point. Therefore, comprehensive action to reduce child poverty not only means coordinated action by the state through different sectoral policies and programmes, but also requires that interventions address psychosocial issues, in particular focusing on the need to ensure that a culture of recognition and respect for children's rights is developed.

- Rethinking sectoral policy, and especially anti-poverty policy, is a pressing matter, both because of the magnitude of the phenomenon and its urgency. Breaking the cycle of reproduction of poverty and inequality requires decisive and well-planned action *oriented to target populations where positive impacts are obtainable.* This calls not only for improving social management (in terms of the *design, monitoring and evaluation of policies and programmes,* and the implementation of appropriate instruments), but for developing comprehensive visions that take account of the multifaceted nature of the problem of child poverty, that is, are not designed simply to improve incomes or education – and of its consequences. Public policy must not only address current poverty, but also *build systems of social promotion and protection that compensate for its consequences* (poor health, low educational levels and poor self-esteem, informal labour, low incomes, etc) and thus mitigate the effects of these factors that facilitate the reproduction or resurgence of poverty.

Notes

[1] The adaptation of the indicators included making them compatible with the 2000-round population and housing censuses available for 19 of the region's countries used to locate the geographical concentrations of child poverty, and to conduct detailed assessment of poverty experienced by African-Caribbean children and adolescents or belonging to indigenous peoples.

[2] The application of this principle is another element that distinguishes the present study from the Bristol study, which defined children subject to two or more simultaneous deprivations as poor, using variance analysis and logistical regression models to determine the optimal position of the poverty threshold – which was determined to be at the level of two deprivations (Gordon et al, 2000; Rio Group on Poverty Statistics, 2007). The ECLAC/UNICEF TACRO study followed the Latin American tradition of measuring poverty by the UBN method (the 'co-realisation' criterion mentioned above), which also avoided methodological problems resulting from the distinction between severe and moderate deprivation thresholds. However, the non-differentiation of urban and rural thresholds is an important difference from the traditional use of the UBN method in the region.

[3] ECLAC corrects the data because wage earners', independent workers' and retirees' answers to some income questions are lacking, and because it is important to minimise probable bias due to understatement of income. This operation involved comparing income figures in the survey with those resulting from an estimate of the household income and expense account of the System of National Accounts (SNA) made in response to the recommendations of the Canberra Group (Canberra Group, 2001).

[4] Situations that imply at least one severely under-satisfied need give rise to the category 'extreme child poverty'. The use of the term 'extreme poverty' follows the UBN tradition, and does not refer to the presence of extreme deprivations such as those reflected in Table 16.1, which cannot be measured in surveys, but to grave or severe deprivations. Moderate failure to meet any of the relevant rights creates a situation of moderate child poverty. The term 'child poverty' reflects measurements of both levels of deprivation, in a procedure similar to interpretation based on the income method.

[5] This group includes Brazil and Mexico, whose populations are much larger than those of the region's other countries.

[6] This is beyond the fact that the cosmologies of some indigenous cultures do not include a set of notions regarding children's rights (in particular, the principle of the child's best interest) that are proper to Western society.

[7] This is due in part to the fact that the formation of nuclear families often depends on families moving to new residences (new locales), which, if the family's economic capacity makes such autonomy possible, may be better equipped than their original housing. On the other hand, strategies of continuing to live with parents, or arrangements in which households include people who are not blood relations – which are helpful in putting together the resources needed to cover basic needs – generally involved older housing that is frequently precarious and does not provide proper access to basic water and sanitation services.

[8] One of the criticisms of the monetary method used by ECLAC is that it takes account neither of economies of scale within households (expenses that do not increase in proportion to the number of members) nor of 'adult equivalency' in consumption, that is, the fact that other members (such as children) consume less than adults.

[9] According to various studies, households whose per capita incomes are over the indigence line (or food poverty line) but under the total poverty line dedicate their incomes primarily to purchasing the food needed for survival, secondly to the purchase of basic non-food goods, and finally to basic food commodities. This may affect nutrition levels, and the composition of children's diets in particular (Feres and Mancero, 2001).

References

Abramovich, V. (2006) 'La articulación de acciones legales y políticas en la demanda de derechos sociales', in A. Yamin (ed) *Los derechos económicos, sociales y culturales en América Latina. Del invento a la herramienta*, Plaza y Valdés/IDRC. Ottawa: IRDC.

Alkire, S. and Foster, J. (2008) *Counting and multidimensional poverty measurement*, Oxford Poverty & Human Development Initiative (OPHI) Working Paper No 7, December 2007 [revised May 2008], Oxford: OPHI, University of Oxford.

Altimir, O. (1979), *La dimensión de la Pobreza en América Latina*, Cuadernos de la CEPAL, no 27, Santiago: United Nations.

Boltvinik, J. (1992) *Índices de pobreza para los métodos NBI y MIP*, América Latina: el reto de la pobreza, Beccaria et al (comps.), Bogotá: UNDP.

Bourguignon, F. and Chakravarty, S. (2003) The measurement of multidimensional poverty, *Journal of Economic Inequality*, vol. 1, no 1, April.

Canberra Group (2001) *Final report and recommendations*, Ottawa: Canberra Group.

Cerioli, A. and Zani, S. (1990) *A fuzzy approach to the measurement of poverty*, in *Income and Wealth Distribution, Inequality and Poverty*, Studies in Contemporary Economics, Dagum, C. and Zenga, M. (eds.), Berlín, Springer Verlag.

Deutsch, J. and Silber, J. (2005) *Measuring multidimensional poverty: An empirical comparison of various approaches*, Review of Income and Wealth, Series 51, no 1, Tel Aviv: Bar-Ilan University.

ECLAC (Economic Commission for Latin America and the Caribbean) (2009) *Social panorama of Latin America 2009*, LC/G.2423-P/E, Santiago: ECLAC, November.

ECLAC/DGEC (Dirección General de Estadística y Censos) (1988) *La heterogeneidad de la pobreza: Una aproximación bidimensional*, LC/MVD/R.12/Rev.1., Montevideo: ECLAC/DGEC

ECLAC/UNICEF TACRO (The Americas and the Caribbean Regional Office) (2010) *Pobreza infantil en América Latina y el Caribe*, LC/R.2168, Santiago: ECLAC, December.

Esping-Andersen, G. (1990) *Three worlds of welfare capitalism*, Cambridge: Polity Press.

Feres, J.C. and Mancero, X. (2001) *El método de las necesidades básicas insatisfechas (NBI) y sus aplicaciones en América Latina*, Estudios estadísticos y prospectivos series, no 7, Santiago: ECLAC, February.

Foster, J., Greer, J. and Thorbecke, E. (1984) *A class of decomposable poverty measures*, Econometrica, vol. 52, no 3, May.

Gordon, D. and Spicker, P. (1999) *The international glossary on poverty*, London: Zed Books.

Gordon, D. et al (2000) *Poverty and social exclusion in Britain*, York: Joseph Rowntree Foundation.

Gordon, D. et al (2003) *Child Poverty in the Developing World*, The Policy Press, Bristol, United Kingdom.

Klasen, S. (2000) *Measuring poverty and deprivation in South Africa*, Review of Income and Wealth, vol. 46, no 1.

Larrañaga, O. (2007) *La medición de la pobreza en dimensiones distintas al ingreso*, Estudios estadísticos y prospectivos series, no 58, Santiago: ECLAC, October.

Minujin, A. (2005) 'Constructing a definition and measurements of children living in poverty', in Group on Poverty Statistics contribution to Innocenti Research Centre meeting on Child Poverty in Central and Eastern Europe/Commonwealth of Independent States, Florence, January.

Minujin, A. and Delamonica, E. (2005) *Incidence, depth and severity of children in poverty*, Working Paper, Division of Policy and Planning, New York, UNICEF.

Minujin, A., Delamónica, E. and Davidziuk, A. (2006) *Pobreza infantil. Conceptos, medición y recomendaciones de políticas públicas*, Cuaderno de Ciencias Sociales, no 140, Costa Rica: FLACSO.

Rio Group on Poverty Statistics (2007) *Compendium of best practices in poverty measurement*, Group on Poverty Statistics, Santiago: ECLAC.

Towsend, P. (1979) *Poverty in the United Kingdom*, London: Allen Lane and Penguin.

UNDP (United Nations Development Programme) (1997) *Human Development Report 1997* (http://hdr.undp.org/en/reports/global/hdr1997/chapters/).

UNICEF (United Nations Children's Fund) (2004) *PRSPs and children: Child poverty, disparity and budgets*, CD PRSPs Resource Package, New York: UNICEF

UNICEF (2005) *The State of the World's Children 2005: Childhood under threat*, New York: UNICEF.

Methodological appendix:
Aggregation indexes for multidimensional approach and monetary approach, and models to estimate the probability of malnutrition among children under five

The aggregation index used for the multidimensional approach

The aggregation index used for measuring child poverty under the multidimensional approach corresponds to a family of indices presented by Bourguignon and Charkravarty (2003) that is similar to the one developed by Foster, Greer and Thorbecke (1984) for income measurement. It meets the axiomatic principles of Sen and others (focus, monotonicity in subgroups, transfer axioms, etc). A similar family of indexes was developed by Alkire and Foster (2008), which can be extended from the 'union approach' (where an individual is considered poor if deprived in one or more needs, compatible with a rights–based approach) to the 'intersection approach' (an individual is considered as poor only when he/she has all deprivations), including different cut-offs by number of deprivations (often two or more).

The current approach to poverty analysis considers indicators as a 'fuzzy set' (Rio Group on Poverty Statistics, 2007), and the particular approach is the 'totally fuzzy approach' (TFA) initially developed by Cerioli and Zani (1990) for dichotomous, polychotomous and continuous variables (see also Deutsch and Silber, 2005).

The general formula is:

$$P_\alpha^\theta(X;z) = \frac{1}{n}\sum_{i\in S_j}\left(\sum_{j=1}^m a_j \cdot MAX\left[1-\frac{x_{ij}}{z_j};0\right]^\theta\right)^{\alpha/\theta} = \frac{1}{n}\sum_{i\in S_j}\left(\sum_{j=1}^m a_j\left(S_j^i\left(1-\frac{x_{ij}}{z_j}\right)\right)^\theta\right)^{\alpha/\theta}$$

where:

n is the number of individuals (or households), m is the number of attributes of the individual (or household) i, x_{ij} is the attribute j of each individual (or household) i, z_j is the deprivation threshold for attribute j, S_j^i is the function of the indicator, such that $S_j^i = 1$ if $i \in S_j$ (there is deprivation with respect to indicator j), and $S_j = 0$ in any other case $(x_{ij} \geq z_j)$,

while the one-dimensional expression

$$\sum_{i\in S}\left(1-\frac{x_i}{z}\right)$$

is equivalent to

$$\sum_{i=1}^q\left(1-\frac{x_i}{z}\right)$$

where: q is the number of individuals (or households) suffering deprivation with respect to the indicator (as with the Foster-Green-Thorbecke or family of indices), α is a positive parameter, such that $\alpha = 0$ makes it possible to calculate the count index – otherwise it is an indicator of 'aversion to inequality', where $\alpha = 1$ represents the poverty or 'depth' of multidimensional poverty, and higher values give greater weight to those in situations of greater deprivation (as with the

Foster-Green-Thorbecke indices), a_j is the weighting factor for attribute j, and θ is the parameter describing the substitution elasticity between the gaps of various attributes, each of which is measured by the expression $1 - \frac{x_{ij}}{z_j}$.

Nutritional deficit cannot reasonably be equated with access to education or other indicators, but determining its substitution elasticity would be a subject for another type of study, and would require identifying substitution elasticity factors for each pair of indicators. This in turn would require designing a much more complex specification for the index (Bourguignon and Chakravarty, 2003). Therefore, the present study assumed the parameter $\theta = 1$, already implicit in measures of depth based on counting deprivations.

The need to distinguish between situations of extreme and total poverty based on moderate poverty thresholds made it necessary to make the measures of depth and severity of poverty more complex, despite the attractiveness of measuring these parameters by counting the number of deprivations, giving equal weight to each (for examples, see Klasen, 2000, and Minujin and Delamonica, 2005). Here, a variant system was used to weight deprivations. Various studies have done this, attributing a certain relative weight to the different deprivations. An example is the UK study by Peter Townsend (Townsend, 1979). However, it requires applying the previously mentioned principle of co-realisation as well as criteria of perfect substitution ($\theta = 1$).

Finally, it should be noted that the index presented earlier requires constructing indicator values that assume, at least in theory, that a continuum of distances from the deprivation norm or threshold exists, and that they have the same range of variation. This resembles Boltvinik's proposal (Boltvinik, 1992). In the present study, the values are as follows. Threshold (no deprivation) = 3; moderate deprivation = 2 (two thirds of distance to threshold); severe deprivation = 1 (one third of distance to threshold); while 0 represents a theoretical state of extreme deprivation (starvation, no access to water or housing, etc). The severe deprivation threshold = 2 (and severe deprivation is present at one half of the threshold). The problems of this approach include the fact that most indicators used to measure deprivation are ordinal. Although the degree to which needs are satisfied can be conceived as continuous, the scalar values assigned to these indicators as a measure of distance – with the corresponding homologisation required – are arbitrary.

In practical terms, based on the previously discussed assumptions, the basic family of indices would be as follows:

Headcount index ($\alpha = 0$; $\theta = 1$):

$$H = \frac{1}{n}\sum_{i \in S_j}\left(\sum_{j=1}^{m} a_j S_j^i \left(1 - \frac{x_{ij}}{z_j}\right)\right)^0 = \frac{1}{n}\sum_{i=1}^{q}\left(\sum_{j=1}^{m} a_j S_j^i \left(1 - \frac{x_{ij}}{z_j}\right)\right)^0 = \frac{q}{n}$$

Depth index (poverty gap: $\alpha = 1$):

$$PG = \frac{1}{n}\sum_{i=1}^{q}\left(\sum_{j=1}^{m} a_j S_j^i \left(1 - \frac{x_{ij}}{z_j}\right)\right)$$

where

$$a_j = \frac{w_j}{\sum_{j=1}^{m} w_j}, \quad w_j = 1 - \frac{q_j}{n}, \text{ and } q_j = \sum_{i=1}^{n} S_j^i$$

Severity index (equivalent to Foster-Green-Thorbecke$_2$), when $\alpha = 2$:

$$SI = \frac{1}{n}\sum_{i=1}^{q}\left(\sum_{j=1}^{m} a_j S_j^i \left(1 - \frac{x_{ij}}{z_j}\right)\right)^2$$

The aggregation index used for the monetary approach

This aggregation index corresponds to the well-known family of parametric indices proposed by Foster, Greer and Thorbecke (1984), which are given by the following expression:

$$FGT_\alpha = \frac{1}{n}\sum_{i=1}^{q}\left(\frac{z - y_i}{z}\right)^\alpha$$

where n represents the size of the population, q is the number of people with incomes under the poverty or indigence line (z), and the parameter $\alpha > 0$ assigns different degrees of importance to the distance between the incomes (y) of each poor or indigent individual and the poverty or indigence line.

When $\alpha = 0$, the above expression corresponds to the headcount index (H), which reflects the number of persons with incomes under the poverty or indigence line:

$$H = \frac{q}{n}$$

When $\alpha = 1$, the procedure produces an indicator of the relative deficit of the income of the poor with respect to the poverty or indigence line. This is known as the poverty gap or indigence gap,

$$HG = \frac{1}{n}\sum_{i=1}^{q}\left(\frac{z - y_i}{z}\right) = H \cdot I$$

$$I = \frac{z - \bar{y}}{z}$$

where I is the 'proportion of the income gap', defined as $I = \frac{z - \bar{y}}{z}$ $(z - \bar{y}/z)$ and z represents the poverty line, while $\bar{y}$ is the average income of the poor population.

Finally, when $\alpha = 2$, the procedure produces an indicator that also reflects the degree of disparity in the income distribution of the poor or indigent. This indicator measures the distance between the poverty or indigence line and individual income, but squares the distance to give more relative weight to those who are far from overcoming poverty or indigence:

$$FGT_2 = \frac{1}{n}\sum_{i=1}^{q}\left(\frac{z - y_i}{z}\right)^2$$

The model used for estimating the probability of malnutrition

The objective of developing a set of models to estimate the probability of malnutrition among children under five based on instruments that include anthropometric measurements was to apply the models to household surveys, and thus be able to include this indicator in measuring child poverty according to the multiple deprivations method, subsequently crossing the results with the monetary approach.

More specifically, models were developed to calculate the probability of global chronic malnutrition, both at severe levels (less than -3 standard deviations) and moderate/severe levels (less than -2 standard deviations) in children between the ages of 0 and 59 months, based on the Demographic and Health Survey and Multiple Indicator Cluster Survey.

First, a set of variables used in the previously mentioned surveys was studied. These can be thought of as proximate determinants of the various anthropometric indicators of malnutrition (for example, birth weight, exclusive and complementary breastfeeding, episodes of diarrhoea, level of haemoglobin in the blood, among others). Although the models optimally should include these variables, the study opted in practice for a set of factors that, although pertinent, exclude the variables indicated earlier. This decision resulted from the need to use variables (and units of measurement) that were replicable in household surveys.

Unfortunately, not all the available Multiple Indicator Cluster Surveys for the region include anthropometric measurements, and the numbers of children in the samples were not large enough to make reasonably strong multiple logistical regression models feasible. Therefore, the decision was made to work primarily with Demographic and Health Survey data, which were already available for more countries, had sample sizes sufficient to make calculations with more complex models, and without exception included anthropometric measurements for children under five. In addition, their anthropometric measurements were standardised in accord with the new World Health Organization (WHO) growth curves, which published new international child growth curves for infants and children under five beginning in April 2006. The new curves provide information on ideal growth. For the first time, they show that under optimal conditions children born in different world regions have the potential to grow and develop to similar heights and weights (see www.who.int/childgrowth).

The modelling work covered global malnutrition (weight to age ratio) and chronic malnutrition (height to age ratio). These variables are expressed in Z scores based on the WHO growth curves (where Z is a standardised normal variable with $\bar{x} = 0$ and $s = 1$).

To calculate the probability of malnutrition, the study used regression models for binary response variables. In these models, an individual's Y response can have only two values: either 1 (the child is malnourished) or 0 (not malnourished). Let be the explanatory variables; we seek to calculate the probability (p) that an individual is malnourished given the presence of the k explanatory variables, that is, $p = P(Y = 1/x_1, x_2, x_3, \ldots x_k)$, through the logistical regression model. The linear form of the logistical regression model is:

$$logit\left(p\right) = \ln\left(\frac{p}{(1-p)}\right) = \alpha + \beta_1 x_1 + \beta_2 x_2 + \beta_3 x_3 + \ldots + \beta_k x_k$$

and

$$p = \frac{1}{1 + e^{-(\alpha + \beta_1 x_1 + \beta_2 x_2 + \beta_3 x_3 + ... + \beta_k x_k)}}$$

where α and $\beta_1, \beta_2, ... \beta_k$ are the parameters of the regression.

Construction of the response variables. For each malnutrition indicator (global and chronic) there are two cut-off points – less than −3 SD and less than −2 SD – which means that there are four response variables (and four models) to be constructed for each country.

Since the percentage of severely malnourished in most of the countries' global malnutrition indicators averages 1%, the sample available to the study would have been very small. The decision was therefore made to consider moderate and severe malnourished as a single group so as to obtain a larger sample. The predictive quality of the individual models in relation to the general model (moderate/severe) did not suffer. In addition, the severe malnutrition models made it possible to use different (and better) predictive variables than were possible in the general model. The percentage of severe malnourished in the chronic malnutrition model is around 10%, which minimised the problem.

The predictive variables used. The predictive variables used in the model were classified in two groups: categorical variables (factors) and continuous variables. In general, the categorical variables were availability of potable water, availability of sanitation services, availability of fuel for cooking, mother's education, mother's current working/non-working status, type of sibling (older, younger, twin), number of bedrooms, whether husband lives in the household and ethnic group. The continuous variables (or those treated as such) were mother's age, children's ages (0-4) and number of children under five in the household. Finally, some stratification variables were used to estimate the models' error levels. They included place of residence (region or department) and type of residence (urban/rural).

Computer calculation. The SURVEYLOGISTIC procedure of the SAS statistical package was used to calculate the logistical regression models. This incorporates the design of complex samples, including designs of stratified samples, by clusters and with different expansion factors, as used in the Demographic and Health Survey and Multiple Indicator Cluster Survey.

To assess the model's predictive capacity, an index of correlations between the estimated probabilities and the observed responses (Somers' D) was used. Thus:

$$\text{Somers' } D = \frac{(n_c - n_d)}{t}$$

where n_c = the number of concordant pairs, n_d = the number of discordant pairs, and t = the total number of pairs. A pair of observations with different ordered responses is concordant if the observation with the lower order of response has a lower estimated average score than the observation with the higher order of response. If the observation with the lower order of response has an estimated average score greater than the observation with the higher order response, then the pair is discordant. If the pair is neither concordant nor discordant, then it is considered tied.

The score of the estimated average of an observation is the sum of the ordered values minus 1, weighted according to the estimated probability of the particular observation. The score of the estimated average is equal to $\sum_{i=1}^{k+1}(i-1)p_i$, where $k+1$ is the number of levels of response, and p_i is the estimated probability of the i-th ordered response.

As a criticism of the models used, it may be pointed out that the probability of not being malnourished (severely or moderately-severely) for each malnutrition indicator includes children of normal weight, overweight children and obese children. Hence the reference group with which the group of malnourished is compared is very broad. Being obese is perhaps as dangerous as being malnourished. There are some common risk factors (among those measured), and therefore the individual models cannot optimally discriminate between the malnourished and others.

Procedure for estimating the probability of malnutrition from household surveys. After obtaining the optimal models with different combinations of the variables initially selected, a pairing of these variables with those from the household surveys was carried out, so that the categorical variables would be transformed into binary alternatives (0,1) and the continuous variables would have equal, or at least assimilable, units of measurement. Based on this, each model of the probability of being malnourished was reconstructed with its own regressors. The children between the ages of 0 and 4 were ordered according to their estimated probability of being malnourished (lower to higher), and the threshold was established (to define who had a high probability of being malnourished) when the expanded cumulative number of children reached the estimated value based on official international sources (WHO, Millennium Development Goals website and the World Bank).

Finally, the reasonableness of each of the estimates was validated by conducting a crossing with variables exogenous to the model – income-related ones in particular (incidence of indigence and poverty by monetary measures, and household per capita income deciles).

SEVENTEEN

Changes in child poverty and deprivation in Sub-Saharan Africa and South Asia at the end of the 20th century

Shailen Nandy

Introduction

The importance of examining and researching child poverty as a distinct topic is now widely acknowledged (UNICEF, 2004, 2007) and reflected by the United Nations (UN) General Assembly's adoption of an international definition of child poverty in 2006 (UNGA, 2006). The financial and economic crisis which swept across the world in 2008/09 has had and will continue to have serious implications for the lives of children and their families, not least because of rising food prices, widespread unemployment and cuts in government expenditure and social service provision (Mendoza, 2009). The UN Children's Fund (UNICEF) Global Study on Child Poverty and Disparities[1] conducted in over 50 countries could not be more timely or appropriate. By examining national policies and collating statistical and other relevant data it emphasises how and why services and programmes for children are of paramount importance. Such programmes require protecting and, in difficult times, expanding (Townsend, 2002, 2008).

The Global Study has produced some excellent country studies on child poverty, many of which have used what has come to be known as the 'Bristol Approach' (Minujin et al, 2006; Roelen and Gassmann, 2008), assessing child poverty using indicators of deprivation of basic needs (Gordon et al, 2003).[2] Some countries (for example, Egypt and Senegal) have combined data on both deprivation and household income (UNICEF – Senegal, 2009; UNICEF – Egypt, 2010) to show that (a) estimates of child poverty vary according to the choice of indicator; (b) that when child poverty is seen in terms of deprivation, its prevalence is revealed to be greater than monetary indicators suggest;

and (c) that there are important overlaps between different deprivations which can have quite detrimental impacts on children's lives and even their very survival (Notten, 2008). The fact that such studies are being carried out, and the findings presented to governments, shows a growing commitment by researchers, activists and policy makers to investigating and tackling child poverty in its own right. Most studies of child poverty have, until recently, been conducted in rich and transition economies, although UNICEF has now shifted the focus onto children in the rest of the world by arguing forcefully that poverty reduction policies, if they are to have an impact, need to begin with children (UNICEF, 2000).

Debates over global trends and changes in monetary poverty are often heated, with different parties contesting the nature, magnitude and directions of change (Kanbur, 2001; Reddy and Pogge, 2002; Sala-i-Martin, 2002; Vandemoortele, 2002; Milanovic, 2005; Chen and Ravallion, 2008; Reddy, 2008). As far as child poverty in the developing world is concerned, data on which to judge changes over time are seriously lacking. There is no lack of information on different aspects and dimensions of poverty (for example, education, child mortality, child labour, and so on) but reliable and representative regional and global estimates of child poverty *per se* are extremely rare (MacPherson, 1987; Gordon et al, 2003; Plan International, 2005). It is the aim of this chapter to show how patterns of child poverty in Sub-Saharan Africa and South Asia changed at the end of the 20th century. The fortunes of these two regions are important for any global estimates of child poverty, accounting as they do for most of the world's poorest children. While snapshots of the extent of poverty are important, of equal interest and value is evidence on how things are changing – has child poverty improved or worsened in these regions? Until now, the data required to answer such a simple question have not been available.

Briefly, the 'Bristol Approach' operationalised a number of indicators to reflect the 1995 World Summit for Social Development's internationally accepted definition of absolute poverty as 'a condition characterised by severe deprivation of basic human needs, including food, safe drinking water, sanitation facilities, health, shelter, education and information. It depends not only on income but also on access to social services' (UN, 1995). These indicators can be used singly or in combination to reflect the extent of individual or multiple deprivations; children experiencing multiple deprivations are considered to be living in absolute poverty (Townsend and Gordon, 2002; Gordon et al, 2003).

This chapter sets out how estimates of child poverty and deprivation for South Asia and Sub-Saharan Africa were made. It presents results for Sub-Saharan Africa, first showing changes in child poverty and deprivation in urban and rural areas. It also examines gender differences in health, education and food deprivation. The same analyses are then provided for South Asia. A discussion of the changes in both regions and the possible reasons behind them follows, with conclusions drawn at the end.

Estimating child poverty in Sub-Saharan Africa and South Asia

The 'Bristol Approach' to estimating child poverty has been peer reviewed by the UN Expert Group on Poverty Statistics and cited as an example of best practice of poverty research (Rio Group, 2006). The regional estimates presented here follow the Bristol Approach, adopting its indicators and thresholds, and are part of a wider piece of research looking at changes in child poverty across the developing world between 1995 and 2000.

Data and sample details

All estimates presented are based on individual level, nationally represented household survey data. The data come from national Demographic and Health Surveys (Vaessen, 1996) and UNICEF's Multiple Indicator Cluster Surveys (UNICEF, 1999). Given the nature of these surveys, with similar sampling methodologies and questionnaires, it is possible to create indicators that are directly comparable between countries and regions. Thus a child deprived of, say, sanitation or shelter in one region is assessed in exactly the same way as a child is in another region. Estimates are centred on two reference years, 1995 and 2000. Table 17.1 shows the number of states in each region, the number of states with survey data in each round (Round 1 refers to 1995, Round 2 to 2000), the total child population (that is, under 18 years) of the states with survey data and thus the proportion

Table 17.1: Regional details

Region	Total number of states in region	Round 1 (1995)			Round 2 (2000)		
		Number of states with data	Child population covered (000s)	% child population repre-sented	Number of states with data	Child population covered (000s)	% child population repre-sented
Southern Asia	9	3	506,861	89	3	479,738	80
Sub-Saharan Africa	47	19	180,620	59	38	330,444	97

of the region's children covered by either a Demographic and Health Survey or Multiple Indicator Cluster Survey. In 1995, survey data were available in countries that accounted for nearly 90% of children in South Asia and 60% of children in Sub-Saharan Africa. In 2000, these proportions changed, so that 80% of children in South Asia and 97% of children in Sub-Saharan Africa were covered.

Table 17.2 shows the regional sample size, the regional child population and the resulting sampling fraction for each round. For 1995, the samples for South Asia and Sub-Saharan Africa included data on over 274,000 children and 335,000 children respectively. In 2000, data on many more countries in Sub-Saharan Africa (38, rather than 19 in 1995) were available, resulting in a much larger sample for Sub-Saharan Africa, of over 810,000 children. As a result of such large samples, the regional sampling fractions are extremely low: in 1995, one in every 2,066 children in South Asia and one in 911 children in Sub-Saharan Africa were represented. In 2000, the sampling fraction for Sub-Saharan Africa improved so that one in every 422 children was represented.

Table 17.2: Regional populations, sample sizes and sampling fractions

	Round 1 – 1995			Round 2 – 2000		
Region	Sample size	Population 0-17 years (000s)	Sampling fraction (1 child in...)	Sample size	Population 0-17 years (000s)	Sampling fraction (1 child in...)
Southern Asia	274,368	566,833	2,066	263,975	597,477	2,263
Sub-Saharan Africa	335,341	305,543	911	810,949	342,371	422

Table 17.3 shows the overall changes in child populations in the two regions between 1995 and 2000, as well as the changes in urban and rural areas. These data are important for many reasons as they indicate how fast changes have to be simply to outpace population growth. The extremely rapid rate of child population growth in urban Sub-Saharan Africa, at around 20%, means reductions in poverty will need to be considerable for there to be a net decrease in the numbers of children affected. In the analyses that follow, estimates of the change in prevalence and the numbers of children affected are presented. As will be seen, it is possible that while the prevalence of a particular deprivation falls, the number of children deprived actually increases (for example, water deprivation in Sub-Saharan Africa).

Table 17.3: Percentage change in child population, 1995-2000

Region	Urban	Rural	Overall
Sub-Saharan Africa	19.6	8.8	12.1
Southern Asia	9.8	3.7	5.4

Source: Urban–rural population distributions taken from UN DESA (2008, Table A.2)

Child poverty and deprivation in Sub-Saharan Africa, 1995-2000

Most studies of global poverty show that Sub-Saharan Africa not only has the highest rates of poverty, but also that the numbers of people living in poverty increased during the 1990s (World Bank, 2000; Sala-i-Martin, 2002; Chen and Ravallion, 2004). As already noted, these studies are not without their critics (Reddy and Pogge, 2002; Townsend and Gordon, 2002; Wade, 2004), but what is not contested is the fact that Sub-Saharan Africa performs poorly across a range of measures, including infant, child and maternal mortality, school enrolment, and general access to basic services.

Sadly, the same negative assessment applies with regard to child poverty, as assessed using a deprivations approach. Sub-Saharan Africa experienced statistically significant increases in the proportion and number of children living in absolute poverty between 1995 and 2000 (see Table 17.4). In the year 2000, over 200 million (59%) children across the continent were severely deprived of two or more basic needs, and could be said to be living in absolute poverty. While the relative increase in the prevalence of absolute poverty among children was around 5%, once population growth is taken into account, the increase in numbers of poor children (in percentage terms) was around 18%.

Table 17.4 also provides estimates of the proportions and numbers of children in Sub-Saharan Africa affected by individual deprivations. In no instance was there an improvement or a decline in the extent of deprivation between 1995 and 2000. The most prevalent deprivation, affecting the greatest number of children, was for shelter, with around 65% of children affected in 2000. These 222 million children were living in either extremely overcrowded conditions, or in dwellings built with poor quality materials. Over a third of children in the region were either water (40%), health (37%), or sanitation (34%) deprived in 2000.

There were no statistically significant decreases for any of the seven deprivations. In fact, there were statistically significant *increases* in the prevalence of five deprivations (information, sanitation, health, shelter and food) and, given high population growth, statistically significant

Table 17.4: Severe deprivation and absolute poverty among children, Sub-Saharan Africa, 1995-2000 (with 95% Confidence Intervals (CIs))

	Round 1 (1995) % of children (95% CI)	Round 2 (2000) % of children (95% CI)	% change
Shelter	**57.9** (56.4-59.4)	**64.8** (64.1-65.6)	+12
Water	**41.1** (39.2-42.9)	**39.6** (38.5-40.8)	
Health	**33.4** (32.4-34.4)	**37.4** (36.7-38.1)	+12
Sanitation	**29.6** (28.1-31.1)	**33.8** (32.8-34.7)	+14
Education	**28.8** (27.5-30.1)	**29.8** (29.1-30.5)	
Information	**22.4** (21.7-23.1)	**26.4** (26.0-26.9)	+18
Food	**20.7** (19.9-21.4)	**22.4** (21.8-23.0)	+8
Severe deprivation	**79.4** (78.4-80.3)	**80.7** (80.0-81.3)	
Absolute poverty	**56.3** (55.0-57.6)	**59.4** (58.6-60.2)	+5
	Number of children (000s)	**Number of children (000s)**	% change
Shelter	**176,976** (172,323-181,629)	**221,960** (219,483-224,437)	+25
Water	**125,497** (119,921-131,073)	**135,722** (131,840-139,604)	+8
Sanitation	**90,473** (85,805-95,140)	**115,590** (112,346-118,833)	+28
Information	**68,568** (66,446-70,691)	**90,400** (88,859-91,941)	+32
Education	**48,636** (46,385-50,886)	**57,231** (55,864-58,598)	+18
Health	**25,661** (24,870-26,453)	**34,007** (33,346-34,667)	+33
Food	**15,962** (15,397-16,526)	**20,362** (19,799-20,924)	+28
Severe deprivation	**242,453** (239,550-245,357)	**276,137** (273,839-278,434)	+14
Absolute poverty	**172,094** (168,146-176,041)	**203,306** (200,500-206,112)	+18

Note: % change reported when statistically significant; health and food data refer to children under five; education data refer to children 7-18.

increases in the numbers of children affected. The lower half of Table 17.4 shows that there were increases of more than 30% in the numbers of children health and information deprived, and increases of 25% or more in the numbers of children sanitation, shelter or food deprived. The pattern of deprivations appears not to have changed. In 1995, the most prevalent deprivations were for shelter, water and health. In 2000, the pattern remained the same, but with even larger numbers of children affected.

Deprivation and poverty among urban and rural children

One fact on which most poverty studies agree is that poverty tends to be most prevalent in rural areas. This is not to downplay the deep and significant poverty visible in informal urban settlements, shanty towns and slums that now characterise many major cities in the developing world. The distribution of child poverty in Sub-Saharan Africa follows a similar pattern, with rural areas faring poorly. However, the picture is mixed when one considers how things are changing. Rural urban disparities can increase in a number of ways, not all of which are necessarily bad. This issue is discussed in more detail below, but suffice to say here that increases in the ratio of rural to urban deprivation often mask quite interesting processes.

Tables 17.5 and 17.6 present data on changes in absolute poverty and severe deprivation among urban and rural children in Sub-Saharan Africa. Looking first at changes among urban children, there are increases in deprivation for almost all basic needs, and statistically significant increases in the proportions of urban children living in absolute poverty and severe deprivation of 57% and 18% respectively. When urban population growth is taken into account, there was almost

Table 17.5: Severe deprivation and absolute poverty among urban children, Sub-Saharan Africa, 1995 and 2000 (with 95% Confidence Intervals (CIs))

	Round 1 (1995)	Round 2 (2000)	
	% urban children deprived	% urban children deprived	% change
Shelter	28.1 (26.5-29.6)	37.3 (36.2-38.3)	+33
Health	19.0 (17.5-20.4)	28.1 (26.9-29.3)	+48
Education	15.9 (14.4-17.5)	14.2 (13.3-15.1)	
Food	12.8 (11.6-13.9)	15.8 (14.8-16.7)	+23
Water	10.3 (8.9-11.7)	15.9 (14.4-17.3)	+54
Information	7.5 (6.8-8.3)	14.0 (13.3-14.6)	+86
Sanitation	7.0 (4.4-9.7)	10.3 (9.4-11.2)	+47
Severe deprivation	46.3 (44.4-48.3)	54.7 (53.4-56.0)	+18
Absolute poverty	16.9 (15.4-18.3)	26.6 (25.5-27.7)	+57
	Number of urban children (000s)	Number of urban children (000s)	% change
Shelter	21,909 (20,695-23,123)	36,489 (35,460-37,518)	+67
Water	8,047 (6,932-9,162)	15,532 (14,090-16,974)	+93
Education	6,606 (5,960-7,252)	8,008 (7,477-8,538)	+21
Information	5,864 (5,293-6,436)	13,685 (13,049-14,320)	+133
Sanitation	5,497 (3,405-7,588)	10,066 (9,213-10,920)	+83
Health	3,058 (2,827-3,289)	6,947 (6,644-7,250)	+127
Food	2,195 (1,998-2,392)	3,901 (3,658-4,144)	+78
Severe deprivation	36,143 (34,659-37,630)	53,532 (52,274-54,790)	+48
Absolute poverty	13,170 (12,039-14,302)	26,027 (24,933-27,122)	+98

Note: % change reported when statistically significant; health and food data refer to children under five; education data refer to children aged 7-18.

a doubling in the number of urban children in Sub-Saharan Africa living in absolute poverty between 1995 and 2000.

The largest increase in percentage terms was for information deprivation (86%), but perhaps equally worrying were the increases in water (54%), health (48%), sanitation (47%) and shelter (33%) deprivation, all of which have very real implications for the lives of children. In 2000, over 36 million urban children in the region were shelter deprived (a 67% increase in terms of numbers), around seven million urban children under five years old were health deprived (more than double the number in 1995), and four million urban children were severely food deprived (more than 75% the number in 1995). The only apparent improvement was for education, but even this change was not statistically significant. Again, given urban population growth, there was a statistically significant *increase* of 21% in the number of urban children education deprived between 1995 and 2000.

Table 17.6 presents data to show that the picture for rural children in Sub-Saharan Africa was equally bleak. There were statistically significant increases in the prevalence of all deprivations except water. The most heartening thing one might say about the prevalence of rural child poverty is that it did not worsen (it certainly did not improve), although when population growth is taken into account, there were around 12% more rural children living in poverty in 2000 than in 1995.

The most prevalent deprivation was for shelter, with 76% of rural children (that is, 185 million) deprived in 2000. Around half of all rural children in Sub-Saharan Africa were water deprived, either using unsafe sources of water or with water sources located a long distance from their homes. The largest increase was for sanitation deprivation (16% in terms of the proportion of children deprived, and 24% in terms of numbers of children). Information, education, shelter and health deprivation all saw increases of over 10% in terms of proportions of children affected, with increases of 20% or more in terms of numbers for information, health, shelter and food deprivation. While large, these increases in deprivation are on a lesser scale than those experienced by urban children in the region. Such data provide important signposts about the future of child poverty in Sub-Saharan Africa, emphasising to policy makers the scale and nature of interventions required and where they should be made.

The data in Tables 17.5 and 17.6 can be used to assess changes in disparities between urban and rural children. Taking the simple ratio of the prevalence of rural deprivation to that of urban deprivation, we can compare how things change over time (see Figure 17.1). In 1995, the ratio of absolute poverty between rural and urban children was

Table 17.6: Severe deprivation and absolute poverty among rural children, Sub-Saharan Africa, 1995 and 2000 (with 95% Confidence Intervals (CIs))

	Round 1 (1995) % rural children deprived	Round 2 (2000) % rural children deprived	% change
Shelter	**68.1** (66.2-70.1)	**75.9** (74.9-76.8)	**+11**
Water	**51.6** (49.2-54.0)	**49.2** (47.7-50.6)	
Sanitation	**37.3** (35.5-39.2)	**43.2** (41.9-44.4)	**+16**
Health	**37.2** (36.0-38.5)	**40.9** (40.0-41.8)	**+10**
Education	**33.0** (31.3-34.7)	**36.2** (35.3-37.2)	**+10**
Information	**27.6** (26.7-28.5)	**31.4** (30.8-31.9)	**+14**
Food	**22.9** (22.0-23.8)	**24.9** (24.1-25.6)	**+8**
Severe deprivation	**90.7** (89.6-91.8)	**91.0** (90.3-91.8)	
Absolute poverty	**69.8** (68.2-71.5)	**72.5** (71.4-73.6)	
	Number of rural children (000s)	Number of rural children (000s)	% change
Shelter	**155,067** (150,575-159,559)	**185,471** (183,218-187,725)	**+20**
Water	**117,450** (111,987-122,914)	**120,190** (116,586-123,795)	
Sanitation	**84,976** (80,803-89,148)	**105,523** (102,394-108,653)	**+24**
Information	**62,704** (60,660-64,748)	**76,716** (75,312-78,119)	**+22**
Education	**42,030** (39,874-44,185)	**49,223** (47,963-50,484)	**+17**
Health	**22,604** (21,847-23,361)	**27,060** (26,472-27,647)	**+20**
Food	**13,767** (13,238-14,296)	**16,461** (15,953-16,968)	**+20**
Severe deprivation	**206,310** (203,815-208,805)	**222,605** (220,682-224,528)	**+8**
Absolute poverty	**158,923** (155,141-162,705)	**177,278** (174,695-179,862)	**+12**

Note: % change reported when statistically significant; health and food data refer to children under five; education data refer to children 7-18.

about 4; by 2000 the ratio had fallen to just under 3. There were similar declines for all deprivations except education, which rose slightly.

These declines suggest disparities between urban and rural children lessened between 1995 and 2000, but as noted above, disparities can change for a number of reasons, some of which are clearly undesirable. In the case of Sub-Saharan Africa, the reductions in disparities appear to be driven not by more rapid improvements for rural children, but rather by conditions for urban children deteriorating faster.

Gender disparities

The nature of the Demographic and Health Surveys and Multiple Indicator Cluster Surveys means individual level comparisons of certain

Figure 17.1: Rural–urban ratios of deprivation, Sub-Saharan Africa, 1995 and 2000

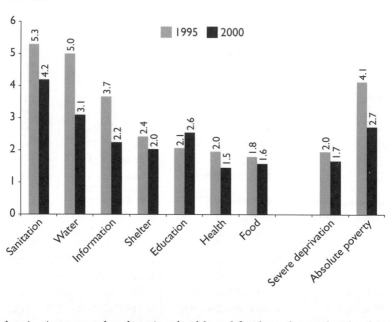

deprivations, namely education, health and food, can be made. The data provide evidence about the extent of gender differences with regards to deprivation, and allow for assessments of whether or not conditions improve or worsen at similar rates for boys than girls.

Table 17.7 shows that roughly equal proportions of boys and girls in Sub-Saharan Africa are health and food deprived, around a third and a fifth respectively. What differences there are between the two are not statistically significant since the 95% Confidence Intervals overlap. Significant differences, however, are apparent for education deprivation, with girls around 20% more likely to be deprived than boys in both 1995 and 2000.

While the increase in the proportion of boys and girls education deprived was not statistically significant, the rise in numbers of children deprived was, with around 18% more boys and girls deprived. There were statistically significant increases in the proportions of boys and girls health deprived, and also in the numbers affected. While the increase in the proportion of children food deprived was not statistically significant, the increase in terms of numbers deprived was significant.

Other studies and indicators of child well-being, such as the Save the Children's Child Development Index (CDI), show that in the same period (that is, between 1990/94 and 1995/99) children in Sub-Saharan Africa fared worse than all other regions (Save the Children UK, 2008).

Table 17.7: Education, food and health deprivation by gender, Sub-Saharan Africa, 1995 and 2000 (with 95% Confidence Intervals (CIs))

	Round 1 (1995)	Round 2 (2000)	% change
	% boys deprived	% boys deprived	
Health	34.0 (32.7-35.2)	37.5 (36.6-38.3)	+10
Education	25.9 (24.6-27.2)	26.8 (26.1-27.5)	
Food	21.6 (20.7-22.5)	23.2 (22.5-23.9)	
	Number of boys (000s)	Number of boys (000s)	% change
Education	22,017 (20,926-23,109)	25,876 (25,219-26,534)	+18
Health	13,054 (12,586-13,522)	17,185 (16,792-17,578)	+32
Food	8,350 (8,008-8,691)	10,632 (10,315-10,948)	+27
	% of girls deprived	% of girls deprived	% change
Health	32.6 (31.4-33.9)	37.1 (36.2-38.0)	+14
Education	31.9 (30.3-33.4)	33.0 (32.1-33.9)	
Food	19.6 (18.5-20.8)	21.5 (20.7-22.3)	
	Number of girls (000s)	Number of girls (000s)	% change
Education	26,696 (25,396-27,997)	31,558 (30,725-32,392)	+18
Health	12,532 (12,058-13,007)	16,728 (16,306-17,150)	+33
Food	7,586 (7,128-8,044)	9,698 (9,340-10,056)	+28

Note: % change reported when statistically significant; health and food data refer to children under five; education data refer to children 7-18.

Between the middle and end of the 1990s, the CDI improved in Latin America and the Caribbean by 40%, 20% in East Asia, 18% in South Asia and 16% in the Middle East and North Africa. In comparison, the improvement for Sub-Saharan Africa was less than 6% (Save the Children UK, 2008, p 8), a fraction of what was achieved in other regions of the developing world.

Child poverty and deprivation in South Asia, 1995-2000

The lack of improvement in Sub-Saharan Africa stands in stark contrast to the changes that occurred in South Asia, whose data are presented in Table 17.8. While Sub-Saharan Africa witnessed a 5% increase in the proportion of children living in absolute poverty, South Asia saw a decrease of 22%. This meant a fall in the number of children living in absolute poverty in the region of 18%, a reduction of around 63 million children.

The most prevalent deprivation in South Asia in 2000 was for sanitation, with 60% of children (360 million) lacking any form of

Table 17.8: Severe deprivation and absolute poverty among children, Southern Asia, 1995-2000 (with 95% Confidence Intervals (CIs))

	Round 1 (1995)	Round 2 (2000)	%
	% of children (95% CI)	% of children (95% CI)	change
Sanitation	**64.4** (63.5-65.2)	**60.3** (59.4-61.2)	−6
Shelter	**58.0** (57.1-58.9)	**47.8** (47.0-48.6)	−18
Health	**38.5** (37.7-39.2)	**25.5** (24.8-26.1)	−34
Food	**36.3** (35.5-37.2)	**27.5** (26.8-28.2)	−24
Information	**32.6** (32.0-33.3)	**17.3** (16.9-17.8)	−47
Education	**27.5** (26.8-28.2)	**16.0** (15.6-16.4)	−42
Water	**9.5** (8.9-10.2)	**6.7** (6.3-7.0)	−30
Severe deprivation	**83.4** (82.8-84.0)	**77.7** (77.1-78.3)	−7
Absolute poverty	**62.1** (61.4-62.9)	**48.5** (47.7-49.3)	−22

	Numbers (000s)	Numbers (000s)	% change
Sanitation	**364,836** (359,995-369,676)	**360,410** (355,089-365,731)	
Shelter	**328,566** (323,501-333,631)	**285,569** (280,752-290,387)	−13
Information	**185,011** (181,202-188,819)	**103,644** (101,008-106,280)	−44
Education	**90,333** (88,013-92,652)	**57,077** (55,575-58,578)	−37
Water	**53,924** (50,289-57,559)	**39,821** (37,540-42,102)	−26
Health	**44,288** (43,424-45,152)	**24,059** (23,414-24,705)	**−46**
Food	**41,811** (40,851-42,771)	**25,996** (25,327-26,666)	**−38**
Severe deprivation	**472,623** (469,298-475,948)	**464,265** (460,773-467,756)	
Absolute poverty	**352,241** (347,846-356,635)	**289,702** (284,787-294,617)	**−18**

Note: % change reported when statistically significant; health and food data refer to children under five; education data refer to children 7-18.

sanitation in or around the home. This figure does not include those children with access to unimproved forms of sanitation (for example, pit latrines, communal toilets, etc) and it could be argued that this figure underestimates the true degree of need. Just under half of all children in the region were shelter deprived (286 million). In percentage terms, the greatest reductions in South Asia were for in 2000 information, education and health deprivation (47%, 42% and 34% respectively). Deprivation of food and shelter also reduced, by 24% and 18% respectively. The least change occurred for sanitation deprivation (6%), where there was no statistically significant decrease in the number of children deprived. To have six out of ten children in the region lacking access to even basic sanitation is shocking, given the known links between poor sanitation, child health and survival.

Urban and rural areas

Tables 17.9 and 17.10 present results of changes among urban and rural children in South Asia. Among urban children there were impressive reductions in absolute poverty and severe deprivation, both in terms of numbers of children and the proportions affected. Between 1995 and 2000, the proportion of children in poverty fell by more than a third, from 25% to 17%. This represents a reduction of nearly 11 million urban children living in absolute poverty. The 26 million urban children living in poverty in South Asia was roughly equal to the number for urban children in Sub-Saharan Africa.

The largest improvements among urban children were for information, education and health deprivation, with decreases in the proportions affected of 49%, 44% and 35% respectively. There was an

Table 17.9: Severe deprivation and absolute poverty among urban children, Southern Asia, 1995 and 2000 (with 95% Confidence Intervals (CIs))

	Round 1 (1995)	Round 2 (2000)	
	% urban children deprived	% urban children deprived	% change
Shelter	**33.2** (31.5-34.9)	**24.3** (22.4-26.2)	**−27**
Food	**27.9** (26.1-29.6)	**20.2** (18.9-21.5)	**−28**
Health	**24.5** (23.2-25.8)	**15.8** (14.9-16.7)	**−35**
Sanitation	**22.2** (20.1-24.2)	**20.4** (18.1-22.6)	
Education	**13.6** (12.6-14.7)	**7.6** (6.7-8.5)	**−44**
Information	**13.4** (12.6-14.3)	**6.8** (5.9-7.8)	**−49**
Water	**3.6** (3.0-4.1)	**2.8** (2.3-3.2)	
Severe deprivation	**51.4** (49.5-53.3)	**42.3** (40.4-44.2)	**−18**
Absolute poverty	**25.2** (23.6-26.9)	**16.5** (14.7-18.4)	**−35**
	Number of urban children (000s)	Number of urban children (000s)	% change
Shelter	**47,808** (45,352-50,265)	**37,558** (34,645-40,472)	**−21**
Sanitation	**31,900** (28,904-34,895)	**31,449** (27,956-34,943)	
Information	**19,363** (18,110-20,616)	**10,584** (9,128-12,039)	**−45**
Education	**11,090** (10,232-11,947)	**6,428** (5,654-7,202)	**−42**
Food	**7,337** (6,885-7,789)	**3,976** (3,717-4,236)	**−46**
Health	**6,451** (6,116-6,785)	**3,116** (2,940-3,292)	**−52**
Water	**5,117** (4,313-5,921)	**4,255** (3,549-4,960)	
Severe deprivation	**73,956** (71,231-76,682)	**65,368** (62,474-68,262)	**−12**
Absolute poverty	**36,329** (33,929-38,728)	**25,511** (22,665-28,357)	**−30**

Note: % change reported when statistically significant; health and food data refer to children under five; education data refer to children 7-18.

encouraging improvement in shelter deprivation, with a reduction from 33% in 1995 to 24% in 2000, but this still meant 38 million urban children in the region were shelter deprived. While these improvements are encouraging, the lack of progress with regards water and sanitation deprivation is obviously a concern.

There were also improvements for rural children in the region. Table 17.10 shows prevalence rates for all deprivations fell and that absolute poverty fell by 20% in terms of the proportion of children, and by 16% in terms of numbers of children. This meant there were around 52 million fewer rural children living in poverty in South Asia in 2000 than there were in 1995. This change is tempered somewhat by the fact that severe deprivation did not change much (that is, a 4% reduction in prevalence).

Table 17.10: Severe deprivation and absolute poverty among rural children, Southern Asia, 1995 and 2000 (with 95% Confidence Intervals (CIs))

	Round 1 (1995)	Round 2 (2000)	% change
	% rural children deprived	% rural children deprived	% change
Sanitation	78.7 (77.8-79.6)	74.3 (73.4-75.2)	−6
Shelter	66.4 (65.3-67.4)	56.0 (55.1-56.9)	−16
Health	42.7 (41.8-43.6)	28.0 (27.2-28.8)	−34
Information	39.2 (38.3-40.0)	21.0 (20.5-21.5)	−46
Food	38.9 (37.9-39.8)	29.4 (28.6-30.3)	−24
Education	32.1 (31.2-32.9)	18.7 (18.2-19.1)	−42
Water	11.5 (10.7-12.4)	8.0 (7.5-8.5)	−30
Severe deprivation	94.3 (93.8-94.7)	90.1 (89.6-90.5)	−4
Absolute poverty	74.7 (73.8-75.6)	59.6 (58.7-60.5)	−20
	Number of rural children (000s)	Number of rural children (000s)	% change
Sanitation	332,936 (329,134-336,738)	328,961 (324,948-332,974)	
Shelter	280,758 (276,328-285,187)	248,011 (244,174-251,848)	−12
Information	165,648 (162,052-169,244)	93,060 (90,862-95,257)	−44
Education	79,243 (77,088-81,398)	50,649 (49,362-51,935)	−36
Water	48,807 (45,262-52,351)	35,566 (33,397-37,735)	−27
Health	37,837 (37,040-38,634)	20,943 (20,322-21,565)	−45
Food	34,475 (33,628-35,321)	22,020 (21,402-22,637)	−36
Severe deprivation	398,666 (396,761-400,571)	398,897 (396,944-400,850)	
Absolute poverty	315,912 (312,230-319,594)	264,192 (260,184-268,199)	−16

Note: % change reported when statistically significant; health and food data refer to children under five; education data refer to children aged 7-18.

Despite progress in the region, around three quarters of all rural children (329 million) in South Asia lacked access to any form of sanitation. Over half (56%, 248 million) were deprived of basic shelter and three out of ten rural children under five (22 million) were severely food deprived. Around one in four rural children under five (21 million) were severely health deprived.

The different rates of progress for urban and rural children in South Asia have implications for rural urban disparities. As noted earlier, disparities can reduce for different reasons, but they can also increase. In the case of South Asia, the more rapid improvements among urban children meant that rural–urban disparities in the region *worsened* between 1995 and 2000 (see Figure 17.2). The implications of such changes for policy makers should alert them to the nature of change and for the need to increase attention and resources on improving conditions for rural children, given both the greater prevalence of deprivation and slower rate of improvement.

Figure 17.2: Rural–urban ratios of deprivation, Southern Asia, 1995 and 2000

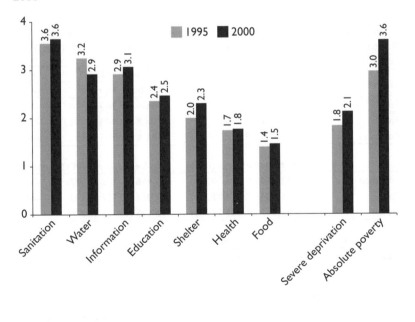

Gender disparities

Female disadvantage across a range of outcomes is known to be particularly acute in South Asia. Evidence for this comes from a large body of research, including a study that used Demographic and

Health Survey data on over 40 developing countries (Smith, 2000). It found, that compared to Sub–Saharan Africa, Latin America and the Caribbean, and the Near East and North Africa, the difference in years of education between men and women was greatest in South Asia, age at marriage of girls was lowest, male births were most preferred, and the difference in vaccination scores between boys and girls was greatest. Other measures, such as the Gender–related Development Index (GDI), also show female disadvantage to be high among countries in South Asia (UNDP, 1995). Do data on child deprivations support the case that female disadvantage is particularly acute in South Asia?

Table 17.11 shows the prevalence rates and estimated numbers of boys and girls experiencing education, food and health deprivation in South Asia in 1995 and 2000. There is no statistically significant difference in the proportions of boys and girls severely food deprived in 1995, but this is not the case in 2000, where a slightly higher proportion of girls are food deprived. One reason for this could be due to the different rates of improvement, with food deprivation reducing faster for boys than for girls (that is, decreases of 27% and 19% respectively).

Table 17.11: Education, food and health deprivation by gender, Southern Asia, 1995 and 2000 (with 95% Confidence Intervals (CIs))

	Round 1 (1995)	Round 2 (2000)	% change
	% boys deprived	% boys deprived	
Food	36.6 (35.2-37.9)	26.6 (25.7-27.5)	−27
Health	36.3 (35.0-37.5)	24.8 (23.9-25.6)	−32
Education	19.4 (18.6-20.3)	11.5 (11.0-11.9)	−41
	Number of boys (000s)	Number of boys (000s)	% change
Education	32,810 (31,384-34,236)	20,956 (20,135-21,777)	−36
Food	21,524 (20,728-22,321)	13,014 (12,587-13,442)	−40
Health	21,345 (20,582-22,108)	12,125 (11,715-12,536)	−43
	% of girls deprived	% of girls deprived	% change
Health	40.8 (39.6-42.1)	26.5 (25.6-27.3)	−35
Education	35.7 (34.8-36.6)	20.6 (19.7-21.4)	−42
Food	35.6 (34.2-36.9)	28.7 (27.9-29.6)	−19
	Number of girls (000s)	Number of girls (000s)	% change
Education	57,037 (55,592-58,482)	35,682 (34,185-37,180)	−37
Health	22,938 (22,224-23,652)	12,050 (11,669-12,432)	−47
Food	19,970 (19,196-20,745)	13,090 (12,693-13,487)	−34

Note: % change reported when statistically significant; health and food data refer to children under five; education data refer to children aged 7-18.

Girls were also disadvantaged with regards to health and education deprivation, in both 1995 and 2000. In 2000 girls were around 80% more likely than boys to have never been to school, and thus to be educationally deprived. While around one in eight boys (21 million) in 2000 was education deprived, the figure for girls was one in five (around 36 million). Girls accounted for more than 60% of all educationally deprived children in the region. The results for South Asia confirm the existence of female disadvantages in food, health and education deprivation in 2000, and thus support the findings of other studies (Chen et al, 1981; Sen, 1984; Das Gupta, 1987). However, they also show that while improvements have occurred for both boys and girls, they need to occur faster for girls if gender disparities are to be reduced. Parity has almost been achieved with regards to food and health deprivation, but it remains to be seen how long it will take to achieve parity in education.

Comparing regional profiles

Having shown the extent and nature of deprivation and poverty among children in Sub-Saharan Africa and South Asia, it is perhaps worth comparing them to see if there are any important differences or similarities. Such information can inform policy makers and governments, as well as non-governmental organisations (NGOs) working to reduce child poverty.

Figure 17.3 shows the prevalence rates for each of the seven deprivations in these regions for the year 2000. Deprivation rates are higher in Sub-Saharan Africa than in South Asia for all basic needs except sanitation. Such a finding should be an embarrassment to the governments of South Asia and to India in particular, since it alone accounts for much of the region's deprivation. Note again that the indicator used to identify deprivation was extremely restrictive, selecting only those households that lacked *any* form of sanitation. If people in the relatively poorer countries of Sub-Saharan Africa are able to build and use even basic forms of sanitation, like pit latrines, there is no reason why the same cannot be done in South Asia.

The extent of sanitation deprivation in South Asia is surprising, especially since it appears that water deprivation is relatively low (7%). Water and sanitation programmes often go together, and one might well ask why progress in reducing sanitation deprivation has not been concurrent with water? In Sub-Saharan Africa, by contrast, it is water deprivation that is more pressing, along with shelter deprivation. Given these most basic of needs remained unmet at the end of the 20th

Figure 17.3: Patterns of deprivation among children, Sub-Saharan Africa and South Asia, 2000

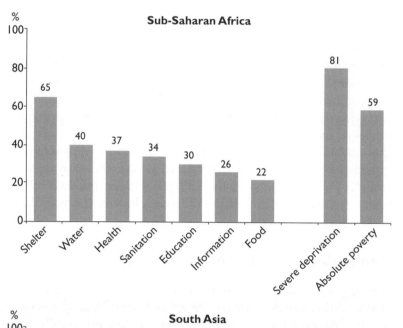

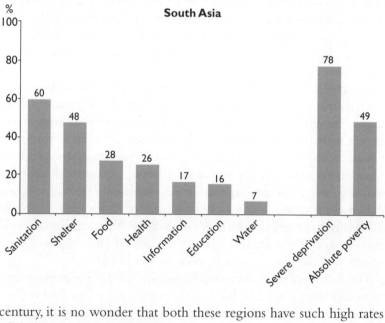

century, it is no wonder that both these regions have such high rates of child mortality and morbidity.

Figure 17.3 may also provide some evidence of the so-called 'Asian Enigma' (Ramalingaswami et al, 1996), which observes that rates of malnutrition are higher among children in South Asia than in

Sub-Saharan Africa, despite the fact that poverty is more widespread in Africa. Some of the reasons (many of which interact with each other) identified for this situation include the social status of women, low birth weights of children, poor feeding and hygiene practices (evidenced here by the higher prevalence of sanitation deprivation in South Asia), and a lack of access to healthcare (Gillespie and Haddad, 2003).

The data presented in this chapter have shown how extensive deprivation was at the end of the 20th century in Sub-Saharan Africa and South Asia. In all likelihood, the numbers presented provide an underestimate of the numbers of children whose most basic needs (and thus their fundamental economic, social and human rights) remain unmet. Of particular concern should be shelter deprivation. Not only is it one of the most prevalent deprivations affecting children, it is also not one that forms an important part of the international Millennium Development Goals (MDGs). Only one target of one goal (Goal 7 'To ensure environmental sustainability') refers to shelter and that too only indirectly. Its aim is 'By 2020, to have achieved a significant improvement in the lives of at least 100 million slum dwellers.' A footnote in the handbook on the MDGs states:

> The actual proportion of people living in slums is measured by a proxy, represented by the urban population living in households with at least one of the four characteristics: (a) lack of access to improved water supply; (b) lack of access to improved sanitation; (c) overcrowding (3 or more persons per room); and (d) dwellings made of non-durable material. (UN Statistics Division, 2006)

In doing so it confirms that rural households, living in very similar conditions, form no part of the target or goal, and so effectively remain invisible in international statistics of shelter deprivation (Nandy and Gordon, 2009).

Discussion

Table 17.3 showed that the child populations of Sub-Saharan Africa and South Asia grew by around 12% and 5% respectively between 1995 and 2000. Rapid population growth in countries where governments often lack the resources and capacity to meet people's basic needs means that what improvements are made are frequently undermined. The implications of population growth for the numbers of deprived children are set out in Table 17.12. It shows, for both regions, the

Table 17.12: Changes in the prevalence and numbers of children deprived, Sub-Saharan Africa and South Africa, 1995-2000

Deprivation	Sub-Saharan Africa			South Asia		
	% change in prevalence	% change in numbers of children deprived	Absolute change in numbers of children deprived (000s)	% change in prevalence	% change in numbers of children deprived	Absolute change in numbers of children deprived (000s)
Shelter	+12	+25	+44,984	−18	−13	−42,997
Water	ns	+8	+10,225	−30	−26	−14,103
Health	+12	+33	+8,346	−34	−46	−20,229
Sanitation	+14	+28	+25,117	−6	ns	−4,426
Education	ns	+18	+8,595	−42	−37	−33,256
Information	+18	+32	+21,832	−47	−44	−81,367
Food	+8	+28	+4,400	−24	−38	−15,815
Severe deprivation	ns	+14	+33,684	−7	−2	−8,358
Absolute poverty	+5	+18	+31,212	−22	−18	−62,539

Note: ns = change not statistically significant.

change (in percentage terms) of both the prevalence and number of children deprived of basic needs, as well as those experiencing severe deprivation (that is, one or more deprivations) and absolute poverty (that is, two or more deprivations).

The prevalence of absolute poverty among children in Sub-Saharan Africa increased by 5%, from 56% in 1995 to 59% in 2000. However, once population growth is taken into account, the percentage increase in real terms of the *numbers* of children affected is much more striking, at around 18%. This increase represents an additional 31 million children living in absolute poverty. If one considers changes in individual deprivations, then between 1995 and 2000, the number of children in Sub-Saharan Africa severely deprived of shelter *increased* by 45 million, and there were an additional 22 and 25 million children or information sanitation deprived. In stark contrast, in South Asia a 5% increase in the child population respectively combined with a 22% reduction in the prevalence of absolute poverty, resulted in a fall of around 18% in the number of children affected, around 63 million children. The largest reductions (in terms of numbers of children deprived) were for information (81 million fewer children) and shelter (43 million fewer children). However, the most prevalent deprivation affecting the greatest number of children in South Asia, sanitation deprivation, saw the least improvement; however, even this meant around four million fewer children were sanitation deprived.

Rapid population growth of course only partly explains why child well-being in Sub-Saharan Africa failed to improve as it did in other regions. History provides examples of countries managing to develop their economies and to tackle poverty in times of high population growth, not least the UK during the Industrial Revolution (Chang, 2003, 2008). If we are to understand why conditions worsened for children in Sub-Saharan Africa and improved in South Asia, we need to consider the much more important structural causes and determinants of poverty and social development.

Many developing countries adopted structural adjustment policies (SAPs) in the 1980s and 1990s following the economic shocks of oil price rises in the 1970s and an increase in indebtedness during the 1980s (George, 1988). With access to private sources of lending and capital restricted, developing country governments had few options but to turn to multilateral lenders and international financial institutions (IFIs) such as the World Bank and International Monetary Fund (IMF) (Todaro, 1994). Loans from IFIs came with conditionalities whose main aim was to reduce budget deficits by stabilising and adjusting national economies (Sobhan, 1991). The term 'adjustment' dramatically underplays the turbulent nature and degree of change that ensued in many countries, particularly in Sub-Saharan Africa (Adepoju, 1993; Logie and Woodroffe, 1993; Stromquist, 1993; Walton and Seddon, 1994; Donkor, 2002). The social impact of adjustment on children in particular is well documented, not least in UNICEF's major report *Adjustment with a human face* (Cornia et al, 1987). With IFI loan conditions requiring reductions in public expenditure, it was inevitable that per capita spending on basic services, such as healthcare and education, reduced (Jespersen, 1992). The introduction of cost recovery mechanisms, like user fees, meant children from poor households were frequently withdrawn from school and often took up paid employment instead (Anyinam, 1989). The impacts of these and other structural changes rippled out across Sub-Saharan Africa over the following decade, and perhaps explain in part why child poverty and deprivation did not decrease at the end of the 20th century (Mehrotra, 2006).

SAPs dictated the nature and pace of social and economic development of many countries throughout the 1990s. The neoliberal ideological basis underpinning most SAPs required (among other things) a reduction in the role of the state and the opening of economies to the 'free' market (Chang, 2003). These changes, however, were precisely what industrialised countries (and those developing countries which had made progress during the 1960s and 1970s) had avoided in their own paths to economic development. Research on different 'high fliers', that is, developing countries which achieved high human development outcomes despite similar resource constraints, by UNICEF (Mehrotra and Jolly, 1997; Mehrotra, 2004), identified key commonalities: a strong role for the government in managing the economy; an emphasis on state-provided primary level services, particularly healthcare and education; ensuring proper nutrition and the proliferation of basic services, such as housing, water and sanitation; and the deliberate avoidance of policies of 'trickle down' and a reliance on economic growth alone to bring about poverty reduction.

A number of other structural factors undermined progress in Sub-Saharan Africa during the 1990s, not least real *reductions* in overseas development assistance (ODA) to the region throughout most of the 1990s, as shown in Figure 17.4 (OECD, 2010). Violent conflict and political instability during the 1990s clearly affected many countries in Sub-Saharan Africa, resulting in over four million refugees and internally displaced people at the end of the decade (UNHCR, 2000). Environmental pressures, such as widespread flooding in Ethiopia in 1994 and in Mozambique in 1999, prolonged droughts in the Sahel region, in the Horn of Africa and in southern Africa, and other hazards associated with climate change affected people's lives and livelihoods, contributing to the displacement of millions around the continent (Mulugeta et al, 2007). Such forces have driven rural to urban migration, adding to the millions of people living in informal settlements in urban areas (UNCHS, 1996), whose basic needs are not being met by governments. These pressures and changes explain in part the patterns of change in child poverty in Sub-Saharan Africa, and the deteriorating conditions for urban children in particular.

Figure 17.4: Trends in total net ODA to Sub-Saharan Africa and South Asia across the 1990s

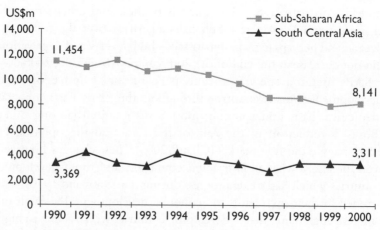

Source: OECD ODA database (http://stats.oecd.org)

While the data on child poverty in Sub-Saharan Africa tell a story similar to that of most other poverty indicators, the picture with regards changes in South Asia is less clear. Estimates of poverty for South Asia will clearly rely on data from India since it is by far the largest and most populous country in the region. While India experienced impressive rates of economic growth during the 1990s, with an annual growth in gross domestic product (GDP) of around 6% across the decade (the World Bank, 2000), what is uncertain is whether or not there was a concurrent fall in poverty. Due to methodological changes in the way in which poverty is measured in India, some have argued that '... official figures (implying a decline from 36 per cent to 26 per cent in the all-India headcount ratio between 1993-94 and 1999-2000) are, strictly speaking, invalid' (Deaton and Dreze, 2002, p 3745). As such confusion persists as to whether or not monetary poverty fell in India and thus the region. Studies have also demonstrated that there were significant increases in inequality, especially between urban and rural areas, in India during the 1990s (Topalova, 2008), and data on changes in other indicators present a mixed picture with regards the pace and direction of change compared to what was achieved in the 1980s (for example, slower increases in rural wages and declines in infant mortality, but faster declines in illiteracy and fertility) (Deaton and Dreze, 2002). The data presented in this chapter suggest real progress was achieved in reducing child poverty and deprivation across the region during the 1990s, but also that rural–urban disparities did increase, due to faster improvements in urban areas (see Figure 17.2). Given the nature of the survey data used and the consistency of the Bristol Approach, one can be confident that the information presented on changes in child poverty and deprivation in both regions is valid and reliable.

Conclusion

The aims of this chapter were to present regional assessments of child poverty and deprivation in Sub-Saharan Africa and South Asia, and to show how things had changed at the end of the 20th century. The prevalence of deprivation for all basic needs among children in Sub-Saharan Africa either remained the same or increased between 1995 and 2000. Combined with rapid population growth, there were actually *more* children deprived of basic needs and living in absolute poverty at the end of the century than in 1995, a damning indictment of international efforts aimed at reducing poverty. Particularly concerning are the lack of progress in reducing poverty among rural children and the much more evident increase of deprivation and poverty among urban children. These changes occurred in a decade when development assistance to the region fell consistently (see Figure 17.4). The contrasting fortunes of South Asia have been highlighted, with significant reductions observed for all deprivations. However, more rapid improvements in urban areas meant an increase in rural–urban disparities, a finding confirmed by other studies of poverty in the region.

The merits of the 'Bristol Approach' to assessing child poverty using indicators of severe deprivation of basic needs are widely recognised. In time, as policy makers increasingly agree that poverty is more than simply a lack of income and financial resources requiring indicators which reflect its complex and multidimensional nature (UNDESA, 2009), indicators reflecting severe deprivation among both adults and children can be developed and used to track changes in poverty over time, and, more importantly, to shape and determine policies to improve people's lives around the world.

Notes

[1] www.unicef.org/socialpolicy/index_45357.html

[2] See Chapter Four, this volume, for further details on the methodology.

References

Adepoju, A. (ed) (1993) *The impact of structural adjustment on the population of Africa*, London: James Currey Ltd.

Anyinam, C.A. (1989) 'The social costs of the International Monetary Fund's adjustment programs for poverty: the case of health care development in Ghana', *International Journal of Health Services*, vol 19, pp 531-47.

Chang, H.-J. (2003) *Kicking away the ladder: Policies and institutions for economic development in historical perspective*, London: Anthem Press.

Chang, H.-J. (2008) *Bad Samaritans – The guilty secrets of rich nations and the threat to global prosperity*, London: Random House Business Books.

Chen, L.C., Huq, E. and de Souza, S. (1981) 'Sex bias in the family allocation of health care in Bangladesh', *Population and Development Review*, vol 7, pp 55-70.

Chen, S. and Ravallion, M. (2004) *How have the world's poorest fared since the early 1980s?*, World Bank Policy Research Working Paper, Washington, DC: World Bank.

Chen, S. and Ravallion, M. (2008) *The developing world is poorer than we thought, but no less successful in the fight against poverty*, Washington, DC: World Bank.

Cornia, G.A., Jolly, R. and Stewart, F. (1987) *Adjustment with a human face: Protecting the vulnerable and promoting growth*, Oxford: Oxford University Press.

Das Gupta, M. (1987) 'Selective discrimination against female children in Rural Punjab, India', *Population and Development Review*, vol 13, pp 77-100.

Deaton, A. and Dreze, J. (2002) 'Poverty and inequality in India: a re-examination', *Economic and Political Weekly*, 7 September, pp 3729-48.

Donkor, K. (2002) 'Structural adjustment and mass poverty in Ghana', in P. Townsend and D. Gordon (eds) *World poverty: New policies to defeat an old enemy*, Bristol: The Policy Press, pp 197-232.

George, S. (1988) *A fate worse than debt*, London: Penguin Books.

Gillespie, S. and Haddad, L. (2003) *The double burden of malnutrition in Asia – Causes, consequences, and solutions*, New Delhi: Sage Publications.

Gordon, D., Nandy, S., Pantazis, C., Pemberton, S.A. and Townsend, P. (2003) *Child poverty in the developing world*, Bristol: The Policy Press.

Jespersen, E. (1992) 'External shocks, adjustment policies and economic and social performance', in G.A. Cornia, R. van der Hoeven and T. Mkandawire (eds) *Africa's recovery in the 1990s: From stagnation and adjustment to human development*, New York: St Martin's Press, pp 9-50.

Kanbur, R. (2001) 'Economic policy, distribution and poverty: the nature of disagreements', *World Development*, vol 29, pp 1083-94.

Logie, D.E. and Woodroffe, J. (1993) 'Structural adjustment: the wrong prescription for Africa?', *British Medical Journal*, vol 307, pp 41-4.

MacPherson, S. (1987) *Five hundred million children: Poverty and child welfare in the third world*, Hemel Hempstead: Wheatsheaf Books.

Mehrotra, S. (2004) *Improving child wellbeing in developing countries: What do we know? What can be done?*, Childhood Poverty Research and Policy Centre (CHIP) Report No 9, London: CHIP, Chronic Poverty Research Centre, Save the Children and the Department for International Development.

Mehrotra, S. (2006) 'Child poverty', in D. Clark (ed) *The Elgar companion to development studies*, Cheltenham: Elgar.

Mehrotra, S. and Jolly, R. (1997) *Development with a human face: Experiences in social achievement and economic growth*, Oxford: Clarendon Press.

Mendoza, R. (2009) *Aggregate shocks, poor households and children: Transmission channels and policy responses*, New York: United Nations Children's Fund.

Milanovic, B. (2005) *Worlds apart: Measuring international and global inequality*, Princeton, NJ: Princeton University Press.

Minujin, A., Delamonica, E.E., Davidziuk, A. and Gonzalez, E.D. (2006) 'The definition of child poverty: a discussion of concepts and measurements', *Environment & Urbanization*, vol 18, pp 481-500.

Mulugeta, G., Ayonghe, S., Daby, D., Dube, O.P., Gudyanga, F., Lucio, F. and Durrheim, R. (2007) *Natural and human-induced hazards and disasters in Sub-Saharan Africa*, Pretoria: International Council for Science (ICSU) Regional Office for Africa.

Nandy, S. and Gordon, D. (2009) 'Children living in squalor: shelter, water and sanitation deprivations in developing countries', *Children, Youth and Environments*, vol 19, pp 202-28.

Notten, G. (2008) *Multidimensional poverty in the Republic of Congo: Being poor simultaneously in many ways*, Manchester" Brooks World Poverty Institute, University of Manchester.

OECD (Organisation for Economic Co-operation and Development) (2010) *Development aid at a glance − Statistics by region − 2 Africa*, Paris: OECD.

Plan International (2005) *Growing up in Asia*, Bangkok: Plan International.

Ramalingaswami, V., Jonsson, U. and Rohde, J. (1996) 'Commentary: the Asian enigma', in P. Adamson (ed) *The Progress of Nations 1996*, New York: United Nations Children's Fund.

Reddy, S. (2008) 'Counting the poor', *Americas Quarterly*, Spring, pp 37-41.

Reddy, S. and Pogge, T. (2002) *How not to count the poor*, New York: Columbia University.

Rio Group (2006) *Compendium of best practices in poverty measurement*, Rio de Janeiro: Expert Group on Poverty Statistics, IBGE.

Roelen, K. and Gassmann, F. (2008) *Measuring child poverty and well-being: A literature review*, Maastricht: Maastricht University.

Sala-i-Martin, X. (2002) *The world distribution of income (estimated from individual country distributions)*, National Bureau of Economic Research (NBER) Working Paper No 8933, Cambridge, MA: NBER.

Save the Children UK (2008) *The Child Development Index: Holding governments to account for children's wellbeing*, London: Save the Children Fund.

Sen, A.K. (1984) 'Family and food: sex bias in poverty', in A.K. Sen (ed) *Resources, values, and development*, Cambridge, MA: Harvard University Press, pp 346-68.

Smith, L. (2000) *Women's status and its effect on child undernutrition: A pooled analysis using 40 DHS data sets*, Washington, DC: International Food Policy Research Institute.

Sobhan, R. (ed) (1991) *Structural adjustment policies in the third world: Design and experience*, Dhaka: University Press Ltd.

Stromquist, N. (1993) 'The impact of structural adjustment programmes in Africa and Latin America', in C. Heward and S. Bunwaree (eds) *Gender, education and development – Beyond access and empowerment*, London: Zed Books, pp 17-32.

Todaro, M.P. (1994) *Economic development*, New York: Longman.

Topalova, P. (2008) *India: Is the rising tide lifting all boats?*, IMF Working Papers, Washington, DC: International Monetary Fund.

Townsend, P. (2002) *The restoration of 'universalism' – The rise and fall of Keynesian influence on social development policies*, Geneva: United Nations Research Institute for Social Development (UNRISD).

Townsend, P. (2008) *The abolition of child poverty and the right to social security: A possible UN model for child benefit?*, London: London School of Economics and Political Science.

Townsend, P. and Gordon, D. (2002) *World poverty: New policies to defeat an old enemy*, Bristol: The Policy Press.

UN (United Nations) (1995) *The Copenhagen Declaration and programme of action*, World Summit for Social Development, 6-12 March, New York: UN.

UNCHS (United Nations Centre for Human Settlements) (1996) *An urbanising world: Global report on human settlements*, Oxford: Oxford University Press.

UNDESA (United Nations Department of Economic and Social Affairs) (2008), *World urbanization prospects – the 2007 revision*, New York: United Nations.

UNDESA (2009) *Rethinking poverty – Report on the world social situation 2010*, New York: United Nations.

UNDP (United Nations Development Programme) (1995) *Human Development Report 1995: Gender and human development*, New York: Oxford University Press.

UNGA (United Nations General Assembly) (2006) *Promotion and protection of the rights of children, Report of the Third Committee*, New York: UN.

UNHCR (United Nations High Commissioner for Refugees) (2000) *Refugees and others of concern to UNHCR – 2000 statistical overview*, Geneva: UNHCR.

UNICEF (United Nations Children's Fund) (1999) *Evaluation of Multiple Indicator Cluster Surveys*, New York: UNICEF.

UNICEF (2000) *Poverty reduction begins with children*, New York: UNICEF.

UNICEF (2004) *The State of the World's Children 2005: Childhood under threat*, New York: UNICEF.

UNICEF (2007) *UN General Assembly adopts powerful definition of child poverty*, New York: UNICEF (www.unicef.org/media/media_38003. html).

UNICEF – Egypt (2010) *Child poverty and disparities in Egypt – Building the social infrastructure for Egypt's future*, Global Study on Child Poverty and Disparities, Cairo: UNICEF – Egypt.

UNICEF – Senegal (2009) *Rapport national Sénégal – Etude mondiale sur la pauvreté et les disparités chez les enfants au Sénégal*, Dakar: UNICEF – Senegal.

UN Statistics Division (2006) *Millennium Development Goals indicators*, New York: UN Statistics Division (http://mdgs.un.org/unsd/mdg/ Host.aspx?Content=Indicators/OfficialList.htm).

Vaessen, M. (1996) 'The potential of the Demographic and Health Surveys (DHS) for the evaluation and monitoring of maternal and child health indicators', in M. Khlat (ed) *Demographic evaluation of health programmes – Proceedings of a seminar in Paris*, Paris: Committee for International Cooperation in National Research in Demography and the United Nations Population Fund.

Vandemoortele, J. (2002) 'Are we really reducing global poverty?', in P. Townsend and D. Gordon (eds) *World poverty: New policies to defeat an old enemy*, Bristol: The Policy Press, pp 377-400.

Wade, R. (2004) 'Is globalization reducing poverty and inequality?', *World Development*, vol 32, pp 567-89.

Walton, J. and Seddon, D. (1994) *Free markets and food riots: The politics of global adjustment*, Oxford: Blackwell Publishers.

World Bank (2000) *World Development Report 2000/2001 – Attacking poverty*, Oxford: Oxford University Press.

PART 4

EIGHTEEN

Utopia calling: eradicating child poverty in the United Kingdom and beyond

Ruth Levitas

2009 marked the 20th anniversary of the United Nations Convention on the Rights of the Child (UNCRC) (UNICEF, 2009). It marked the 10th anniversary of former Prime Minister Tony Blair's pledge to eradicate child poverty in the UK by 2020 and to halve it by 2010. And 2010 was also the European year of combating poverty and social exclusion. That the European Union (EU) designated a specific year for this indicates the subordination of its social goals to the economic goals of continued growth: the latter are ongoing and dominant, and thus do not need a particular year for their promotion. This chapter considers the principles on which society would have to be organised to ensure the genuine eradication, rather than merely alleviation, of child poverty. It focuses primarily on the UK, but the framework has general relevance. It broadens out into a global perspective on the kind of society that would secure the rights of children to economic and social security and the 'development of the child's personality, talents and mental and physical abilities to their fullest potential' (UNICEF, 2007, p 10).

2009 also marked the centenary of Eleanor Rathbone's election to Liverpool City Council, and the 80th anniversary of her election to Parliament, aged 56, as an Independent member for the now abolished Combined English Universities constituency: until 1948 alumni of Bristol, Durham, Leeds, Liverpool, Manchester, Reading and Sheffield Universities received a second vote by virtue of their graduate status. Rathbone began campaigning for some form of family allowance in 1917, and in 1924 published the first edition of *The disinherited family* (Rathbone, 1986 [1924]). She argued that the principle of paying men a 'family wage' sufficient to support two parents and their children was impractical and uneconomic, and did not keep working-class families out of poverty. In order to provide adequately for the support of wives and children, wages would have to be set much higher, but they would then be unnecessarily inflated for those men who were as yet unmarried and/or childless, who had fewer children than the norm (presumed to be three) and for those whose children were no longer dependent, as well as inadequate for those whose families were larger than average. The solution was to divert part of the overall wage bill to family allowances, either at the level of individual industries or direct from the state. These allowances should be paid to mothers both as the most effective means of ensuring the money would in fact be spent on necessities for children, who were properly the concern of the whole community, and as recompense for the unpaid work undertaken by mothers in looking after their children and husbands: 'The man in getting his wages is paid, not for his own work alone, but for the work of his wife as child-bearer, nurse and housekeeper' (Rathbone, cited in Pedersen, 2004, p 108). From the outset, there were differences between those who supported the financial recognition of women's work in the home, and those who thought this would undermine women's claims to equal pay and opportunities in employment. These arguments were to surface again around the 'Wages for Housework' campaign in the 1980s, which many socialist and equal rights feminists then saw as risking the ghettoisation of women within the home. The difference was summed up in two postcards circulating around 1980 – one a picture of domestic chaos with the legend 'I thought the best way to show you what I do all day was not to do it' and the other 'A house does not need a wife any more than it needs a husband.' In the 1930s, Rathbone became known as the 'Member for Refugees'. She supported the legitimately elected Republican government against the Nationalist insurgency in the Spanish Civil War. She was an early opponent of appeasement and supported the causes of Spanish Republican refugees after Franco's victory and of refugees, dissidents and Jews from Czechoslovakia, Germany and Austria in pre-war and war-torn Europe – especially refugee children. And then, just a year before she died in 1946 at the age of 73, at the inception of the postwar welfare state, the first Family Allowances were paid – albeit at a lower level than needed and without a separate element for mothers themselves.

Rathbone's biographer, Susan Pedersen, says that in the 1920s family allowances were 'seen as an issue for cranks and utopians' (Pedersen, 2004, p 201). And indeed in 1930, just a year after she became an MP, Rathbone gave a radio broadcast entitled 'Utopia calling'. That utopia was a world free from child poverty to be founded on the payment of family allowances to mothers. She was writing at a time of deep recession, rising unemployment and extensive, widening hardship – a recession to which the post-2008 economic crisis is frequently compared. Rathbone drew attention to the economic stimulus created by putting money into the pockets of the poorest households where it would be spent on the immediate needs of growing children: 'picture to yourself what an increased demand there would be for cotton frocks and woollen jerseys, for boots and coal, from all the happy beneficiaries of family allowances. Would that make no difference to the depressed industries?' (Rathbone, 1930, p 7). It is clear that Rathbone herself was not using the term 'utopia' in its colloquial sense of 'perfect but impossible', nor with its later connotations of a totalitarian blueprint. Rather, she was imagining society as a totality, but a totality extrapolated from the first principle of the absence of child poverty. Notably, although she was not committed to the ideal of equality, she said that in her utopia there would not only be no very poor people but no very rich people either. And though certainly no Marxist, like Marx she was unwilling to predict the needs and wants of future generations. Thus she concluded that if family allowances were provided 'so that each child might have a fair start in life, the children would themselves build for us Utopia' (Rathbone, 1930, p 7). In this sense, utopia is an image of the good society aspired to, the imputed goal of policy initiatives.

If Rathbone's utopia is underdeveloped, it nevertheless indicates a different approach to social policy from that which is now prevalent. Social policy, whether in academic or government circles, generally takes an approach that is piecemeal and pragmatic, attempting to solve evident current problems. It is stuck in the present, with the future appearing only as an extrapolation of present trends. Genuine attempts at 'joined-up thinking' which look across the social and economic system as a whole, identify the causes of 'social problems', envisage in a holistic manner the society we are trying to build, and consider what might be necessary to achieve that, are rare (Levitas, 2001).

2009 was also just three years after the centenary of an essay by H.G. Wells, 'The so-called science of sociology', in which he argued for utopia as a *method* of thinking about society: 'the creation of utopias – and their exhaustive criticism – is the proper and distinctive method of sociology' (Wells, 1914, p 204), and it is this idea of utopia as a method that I am seeking to develop (Levitas, 2005, 2007) and to apply here to the issue of eradicating child poverty. The utopian method is intrinsically holistic, and expressed at the concrete level of social institutions and processes. But it allows an element of ethical and institutional separation from the present. As the French sociologist Andre Gorz put it, 'it is the function of utopias ... to provide us with the distance from the existing state of affairs which allows us to judge what we *are* doing in the light of what we *could* or *should* do' (Gorz,

1999, p 113). It has both an archaeological and an architectural mode. The archaeological mode excavates the idea of the good society implicit in political positions, or buried in the barrage of political rhetoric and policy proposals with which we are constantly bombarded. The architectural mode develops scenarios for the future. In both cases this is an aid rather than an impediment to the democratic process. There is also a third mode, the ontological mode, which addresses the question of what kinds of *people* particular societies develop and encourage. What is understood as human flourishing, what capabilities are valued, encouraged and genuinely enabled by specific social arrangements?

Utopia as archaeology: the limitations of current proposals

The abolition of child poverty is a goal that, at least notionally, has cross-party support in the UK. The meanings that might attach to this, the overall shape of society that this new era implies and the policy changes necessary to arrive there are less often spelt out. The 2010 Child Poverty Act, passed just before Labour lost power in May 2010, gives a range of measures of child poverty, all of which are required to be met. This was intended to forestall a future government deciding to change the measure and use only what is now called an 'absolute' measure – the number of children in households with less than 60% of median income at a fixed point in time (here 2010). Nevertheless, because an 'absolute' measure is one of the four included, there is a risk of the emphasis shifting in this direction, although such a measure does also enable us to check whether things are getting worse in absolute terms. The other indicators listed in the Act are the headline measure of the number of children living in relative low-income poverty, meaning in households with less than 60% of current median income; those in households experiencing low income and material deprivation; and those suffering persistent poverty. The United Nations Children's Fund (UNICEF) UK raised concerns that the definition of a child for the purposes of the Act does not include all those under the age of 18 (which is the definition in the UNCRC), but only those under 16, or otherwise eligible for Child Benefit by virtue of being in full-time education. Given differential educational participation rates, this already discriminates against poorer children. And the notion of 'eradication' is limited, since on the headline indicator it is defined as no more than 10% of all children being below 60% current median income, and no more than 5% falling below any other measure. So we could have a situation where one in ten children suffer relative income poverty, and one in twenty are worse off in absolute terms in 2020 than in 2010, and a substantial number of 16- and 17-year-olds are excluded from the figures entirely, but child poverty is deemed to no longer exist.

Of course, this would still be a major advance on the situation where, according to the Households Below Average Earnings (HBAI) figures, in 2009/10 around 28% of all children in the UK – or 3.8 million children – lived in households with incomes below 60% median after housing costs (AHC), and 18% lived in households below 60% of the median income for 1998/99 (DWP, 2011). There are gender and ethnic disadvantages. In 2009/10 nearly half of all children in lone-parent households (overwhelmingly headed by women) were below the 60% median income level AHC, and three quarters of those where the parent was not in paid work. The risks of poverty were higher for all minority ethnic groups and almost two thirds of children in households headed by someone of Pakistani or Bangladeshi origin lived in households below 60% median income (HBAI 2011). In 2007, the UK came bottom of 21 OECD (Organisation for Economic Co-operation and Development) countries ranked in terms of child well-being (UNICEF, 2007). Although levels of child poverty fell under the Labour administration, it was evident as we approached 2010 that the target of halving child poverty from its 1999 level would not be achieved without major additional investment, estimated at between £3 billion and £4 billion.

A fundamental problem lay in the overall view Labour adopted since the mid-1990s about the working of society as a whole, its insistence that work is the best route out of poverty, and indeed its identification of social inclusion with participation in paid labour. This was consistently coupled with an overblown attachment to supply-side solutions, so that the 'problem' was defined as the lack of qualifications and motivation of the poor, low levels of employability and limited earning potential. These supply-side approaches were repeated in the 2008 government document *Ending child poverty: Everybody's business* (HM Treasury, 2008). Early years interventions were adopted principally in the belief that they would foster better educational outcomes and thus social mobility. Notwithstanding the minimum wage and the complex system of tax credits, it remains the case that work does not lift families out of poverty, and is especially unlikely to do so for lone-parent households. Labour's policy response to this was to increase the pressure on parents to work. The principal goal of the 2009 Welfare Reform Act was to force greater labour market participation by tightening the conditions for receipt of benefits, and widening and deepening the sanctions for non-compliance. It was largely based on a report by Paul Gregg called

Realising potential: A vision for personalised conditionality and support (Gregg, 2008). Behind this lies an image of society as a meritocracy, in which the provision of a floor below which only a few are allowed to fall will lead to greater social mobility and especially to an improvement in the quality of employment and its financial rewards as a direct result of the better education and skills of young people coming on to the labour market. The neoliberal model of society consistently neglects the time needed for the unpaid work which holds society together, and its economic value, such that those outside the labour market are consistently described as economically inactive and increasingly simply as 'inactive'. Concerns about community cohesion, social capital, parenting and the promotion of voluntary work accompany ever-increasing upward pressure on labour force participation rates.

Approaches to child poverty and child well-being are wider than this, but fail to challenge the basic framework. An example of this is the 2009 conference by the Child Poverty Unit (CPU) and the Institute for Public Policy Research (IPPR), organised to address the policies needed to achieve a poverty-free childhood, and to consider what 2020 might then look like (Cooke et al, 2009). It was a multifaceted approach. But despite the aim of 'a stretching, yet achievable, vision for 2020', the CPU report implicitly assumes that poverty and disadvantage will remain. The short time scale perhaps makes this inevitable, but it is also trapped in the assumptions of a meritocratic, market-based model.

The CPU report opens with the admirable goal, attributed to Paul Gregg, of achieving a society 'where your life chances are not related to your childhood family circumstances' (Cooke et al, 2009, p 2). The 10 areas identified by Gregg as the main policy areas for development all focus on family and school interventions, implicitly locating the problem with the poor. They begin with intensive family support, and free childcare for children from poor families. Seven of the 10 points focus on primary and secondary education, including extra payments to schools for taking deprived/special educational needs (SEN) children and higher pay for teachers working in these more challenging environments; and proper targeting of additional resources already going to local authorities on the poorer children for whom they are intended (a point also raised by the Child Poverty Action Group, CPAG [2009]). Concern is also expressed about peer mix: 'concentrations of SEN children with behavioural and learning difficulties – and probably higher levels of deprivation – impact on other children' (Cooke et al, 2009. p 3). Gregg's only suggestion of directly raising the resources of families is to extend paid maternity (or parental) leave to a year, and to give a payment which can be used either for income or childcare between the ages of one and two.

Another key contributor, Graeme Cooke, argues that the benefit system is too complex and still 'insufficiently oriented to work' (Cooke et al, 2009, p 5). While insisting that increasing the number of couple families with two earners and the number of hours that lone parents work is important in reducing child poverty, Cooke does address demand-side issues such as low pay, the quality of work and gender inequity in the labour market: 'More effective and appropriate work preparation activities and job placement needs to be complemented by greater attention on [sic] the nature of the low wage labour market' including 'employment rights, gender and part-time pay gaps, flexible working opportunities' (Cooke et al, 2009, p 65). He notes too that future employment trends do not point to the decline of low-end jobs, but if anything, to an extension of those labour market positions including personal services that are characterised by low pay. No policies are proposed to counter this process. Donald Hirsch argues that 'unless other aspects of the 2020 scenario are favourable (in particular parental employment and earnings), ending child poverty is likely to prove unaffordable'; 'Eliminating child poverty by raising benefits and tax credits, on its own, is too expensive. The Joseph Rowntree Foundation and the Institute for Fiscal Studies estimated in 2006 that it would cost in the order of £30 billion a year more in transfers in 2020 ... to end child poverty' (Cooke et al, 2009, p 52). Some families, says Hirsch, especially those with an adult or child with a disability in the household, will continue to need support, and the financial support system for non-working families needs to lift them over the poverty line, and to be uprated at a level between prices and earnings, in a way which retains adequacy without reducing work incentives. Better opportunities and support mechanisms (including childcare) are more likely to bring about the necessary changes in participation in paid work than increasing conditionality of benefits. Anne Power broadened the agenda, raising the need for affordable, energy-efficient housing, child-friendly spaces, and the quality of the physical and social environment.

Despite the very strong emphasis on supply-side measures and work first, there is a clear recognition of broader issues and inequities. The discussion emphasised the central importance of Child Benefit. But delegates thought that 'true simplification of the benefits system was unlikely to be either workable or affordable', just as Gregg argued that although income inequalities have 'a causal effect on children's development', 'reductions in income inequality can never plausibly be large enough to offer more than a supporting role in equalising social gradients in the development of children'. Hence his emphasis on direct interventions in the home and school (Cooke et al, 2009, p 21). A 2008 Joseph Rowntree Foundation report, *What is needed to end child poverty in 2020*, also reiterates this point and the claim that only if working and earning patterns for parents change substantially would it be possible to eradicate child poverty at a 'conceivable level of public spending' (Hirsch, 2008, p 3). However, another report (Hirsch, 2009) argues that allowing child poverty to continue costs about £25 billion a year. *What is needed to end child poverty in 2020* says that more of the same will not be enough. What will suffice is 'only a different kind of world', one 'in which many more families were well integrated into the labour market and the government felt able to support those who remained outside work at above the poverty line. This different world would require new attitudes from all parties involved – government, employers and families on low incomes' (Hirsch, 2008, p 9). The potentially more critical assessment of what is necessary is persistently undercut by the question of what is deemed possible, plausible or affordable.

There are two key points about these arguments. One is that despite strongly critical undercurrents, the vision of the eradication of child poverty is essentially minimalist. It involves raising the standard of living of poor children to a floor well below the median for all children. The focus remains on the poor, rather than on society as a whole, even where moderate rises in taxation of the rich are proposed in order to effect this. It thus sustains the legitimacy of relative poverty, albeit less deep poverty. And it feeds public sympathy with David Cameron's argument that the focus must be on the poor relative to the middle rather than the poor relative to the rich (Cameron, 2009). The second point is that what is necessary is constantly trimmed to what seems possible. And the third is the assumption, even in the context of both economic and ecological crises, that 'possible' policy responses in terms of the social organisation of production and distribution, or means of livelihood and ways of life, entail restoring 'business as usual' as quickly as possible.

The pragmatism of this is understandable. But the more critical elements are subordinated in part because of Labour's truce on inequality, first noted by Peter Townsend in 1959:

> During the last ten years the general image of the Labour Party as presented to the public seems to have undergone a subtle but significant change. The party now seems to be characterised by a diminished attachment to moral and social principle and by a correspondingly greater concern with piecemeal social reform, at least in social policy. Its

leaders today rejoice in the impressions that they are honest, practical men of restraint dealing with the immediate realities of life.... Among the reasons for this shift in political character a future historian might well pick out for special attention the fading of interest in the subject of inequality. The main political parties and trade unions, together with economists and sociologists, appear to have called a truce over inequality. (Townsend, 1959, p 381)

It is important to stress the weaknesses of Labour's approach to the reduction of child poverty, despite the gains made, in order to see how the policy of the incoming Conservative-led coalition government from 2010 extended the same way of thinking about the poor. In a piece of inclusive window-dressing, the Labour MP Frank Field was invited to advise the government on the causes and elimination of poverty. But Field had long been convinced that the problem was not resources but poor parenting which resulted in the intergenerational transmission of poverty. Thus his 2010 report emphasised early years intervention and was called '*The foundation years: preventing poor children becoming poor adults*' (Field, 2010). Early in 2011, the government produced a revised child poverty strategy (DWP/DfE 2011). The focus here is again on making work pay and early intervention, with the quality of parenting, and with social mobility rather than reductions in overall inequality, although it does also propose a single Universal Benefit to be gradually introduced in future years rather than the current patchwork of benefits. Moreover, the wide range of benefit cuts, reductions in uprating against inflation, and tighter eligibility conditions imposed as part of the austerity measures in 2010 and 2011 meant that the burden of the economic crisis was disproportionately carried by those least able to afford it. One of those cuts was the effective means testing of Child Benefit, no longer to be paid to households including a higher-rate tax payer. Households with two earners just below the threshold continue to receive Child Benefit, while those with a single high earner just over that level will lose theirs. Not only is this measure manifestly unjust. It removes universality from this benefit, which has always been part of its strength and its economic efficiency: and it redistributes financial power from women to men. Because it affects only higher earners, it has little immediate effect on the income distribution below the median, and little immediate impact on the numbers of children in poverty.

The same cannot be said of Coalition policy as a whole. In October 2011, the Institute for Fiscal Studies modelled the outcome in terms of the probable numbers of children in poverty through to 2020, the date by which child poverty should, under current legislation, be effectively abolished. The inadequate gains of the last decade will go into reverse, and child poverty, both relative and absolute, will rise. Absolute poverty will rise further and faster than relative poverty, as living standards fall for most people except the very rich and median household income is expected to fall by 7% by 2013. The rate of relative child poverty calculated BHC is predicted to rise from 19.7% in 2009 to 24.4% in 2020, representing an additional 700,000 children. The rate of absolute poverty, those worse off than in 2010, is predicted to rise from 19.3% to 23.1% – an additional 900,000 children.[1] The predictions are shocking, but even more shocking is the conclusion of the IFS report, which suggests abandoning the targets of the Child Poverty Act as unrealistic:

> Although this project did not assess what policies would be required in order for child poverty to be eradicated, it is impossible to see how relative child poverty could fall by so much in the next 10 years without changes to the labour market and welfare policy, and an increase in the amount of redistribution performed by the tax and benefit system, both to an extent never-before seen in the UK. IFS researchers have always argued that the targets set in the Child Poverty Act were extremely challenging, and the findings here confirm that view. It now seems almost incredible that the targets could be met, yet the government confirmed its commitment to them earlier this year in its first Child Poverty Strategy, and remains legally-bound to hit them. We suggest that the government consider whether it would be more productive to set itself realistic targets for child poverty and provide concrete suggestions for how they might be hit... (Brewer et al, 2011, p 3)

Utopia as architecture: a wider view

If the consequence of realism is, as the IFS suggest, abandoning the project of eliminating child poverty, it behoves us to be more radical and to ask what would be necessary 'to create a society where your life chances are not related to your childhood family circumstances'? We do need to be more imaginative, more visionary, more holistic – yes, more utopian – in our thinking about policies to deliver social justice for children, and indeed for the adults who care for them. We need to develop the submerged recognition in current work of what is necessary. And the first element of this must be a radical reduction in inequality, a point on which the CPAG manifesto (CPAG, 2009) is unequivocal. Its 10-point agenda calls for steps to protect jobs; mend the safety net; move away from means tests towards universal benefits and more progressive taxation; remove barriers to work; stop in-work poverty; evolve a child-first strategy for childcare, focused on children's needs, not on the priority of parental employment; end the classroom divide, increasing per pupil spending and reducing extra school costs; improving public services; ensure that the poor do not pay more in taxes and for services; and ensure decent and affordable homes for all through a programme of social housing (CPAG, 2009, pp 6-7). The manifesto consistently argues that the eradication of poverty requires the reduction of inequality. It notes the tension – or even contradiction – between the Labour government's commitment to eradicating child poverty, and its continuing extremely relaxed attitude to the fortunes of the very rich. Yet despite this, the CPAG manifesto is also caught in the dilemma of prescribing immediate and plausible policies.

A vision of a world genuinely free of child poverty needs to ask fundamental questions about the distribution and definition of the social product. Indeed, it needs to go further and to reveal, critique and reconstitute the institutions and processes that generate poverty and inequality, rather than simply devising strategies for their alleviation.

At its core are six key principles:

- promoting equality;
- revaluing care, and thinking in terms of the total social organisation of labour;
- rethinking what counts as production and wealth;
- universal child benefit and a guaranteed basic income or citizen's income;
- making sustainability central;
- prioritising human flourishing and well-being.

Promoting equality

Addressing inequality is fundamental. As Townsend consistently argued in relation to both national and global inequities, the problem of poverty is one part of the problem of inequality and the process of social exclusion is one part of the process of social polarisation. Social polarisation entails not just an inequitable distribution of resources, but of power, and is maintained by global social and economic institutions and processes controlled by the rich. It is worth reminding ourselves just how much inequality widened in the UK in the 30 years from 1979, and roughly how it compares with earlier distributions. Inequality is greater than before the 1939-45 war. In 2007/08 the richest 10% took

Table 18.1: Percentage shares of total net income received by individuals in different deciles of the income distribution in the UK from 1938/39 to 2007

	1938/39	1972/73	1979	1990/91	1996/97	2002/03	2007/08
Top 10%	34.6}	21.4	21	27	28.5	29.0	30.8)
Second 10%	12.7}56.9	14.3	14	16	14.7	14.9	14.8)57.4
Third 10%	9.6}	12.3	12	12	12.5	12.0	11.8)
Fourth 10%	]	10.8	11	10	10.5	10.2	10.1
Fifth 10%	] 27.7	9.6	10	10	9.0	8.8	8.6
Sixth 10%	]	8.4	8	7	7.7	7.5	7.4
Seventh 10%	]	7.3	7	7	6.2	6.4	6.2
Eighth 10%	}	6.3}	7}	5}	5.0}	5.2}	5.0)
Ninth 10%	}15.4	5.3}15.9	6}17	4}11	3.9}10.9	4.1}11	3.9)10.3
Bottom 10%	}	4.3}	4}	2)	2.0}	1.9}	1.4)

Source: 1938/39 and 1972/73: Royal Commission in Income and Wealth; 1979, 1990/91 Joseph Rowntree Foundation 1995; 1996/97 onwards, HBAI. The 1938/39 and 1972/73 figures are not strictly comparable with the later series, and are merely indicative. The figures from 1979 are calculated AHC.

over 30% of national household income, and the poorest 30% shared about 10%. Much of the gain at the top end has been concentrated in the top 1% (Brewer et al, 2007). In 1979, the richest 10% had average household incomes roughly five times those of the poorest 10%; 30 years later, their average household income was 22 times those of the poorest 10%. And this is without considering the even greater disparities in the distribution of wealth, which also widened in that 30 year period, and where the gains are also concentrated in the top 1%. Child poverty also started to rise in the late 1970s as inequality began to widen dramatically. Reducing the share of the top 10% to its 1979 level would liberate a full 10% of national household income each year. These 10 percentage points would be more than enough to raise the shares of the lowest three deciles to 6% each, and give the lowest 30% a larger share of national household income than hitherto recorded.

Rathbone said that she had been reliably informed that redistribution would not generate enough money to lift families out of poverty. Yet this is plainly now untrue, at least as poverty is currently defined. Indeed, although it is difficult to estimate the actual sum generated by the level of redistribution suggested here, estimates on the basis of different sets of official statistics suggest that it is of the order of £56 billion to £90 billion – considerably more than the amount described by Hirsch as inconceivable.[2] In any case, what is conceivable in terms of public intervention now needs revision, in the light of the vast sums of public money poured into bailing out the financial sector: it is a matter of political priorities.

Social gradients in health (for children and adults) are linked to the widening disparity in incomes, while inequality itself has a negative impact on health and well-being, and on mortality rates, across the whole social spectrum (Wilkinson and Pickett, 2009). But since 1997, the Labour government declared itself interested in redistributing opportunity rather than incomes. The reliance on education is partly because of the supply-side orientation of current thinking, and partly because of a desire to promote social mobility. Similarly, equalities legislation in the EU and the UK is concerned only with removing discrimination on the grounds of gender, ethnicity, religion, age, disability and sexual orientation (and notably not income or class). Removing discrimination in the labour market would help to close the gender gap in pay and reduce the disadvantage of children in lone-parent families and from minority ethnic groups. But the relative disadvantage of children in these households would be more effectively addressed by reducing inequality overall, rather than relying simply on removing discriminatory practices, however necessary this may be. Rather than equalising chances of ending up in disadvantaged positions, the goal should be abolishing the structural positions of deprivation into which the poor are currently more likely to be delivered.

The concern with social mobility is itself partly the result of the long-standing truce on inequality, and is blind to one vital element. Upward mobility through the education system was possible for a postwar generation partly through free university education, but largely through a major change in the occupational structure. Here too, if the next generation of parents are to have jobs that keep them and their families out of poverty, badly paying, 'low-end' jobs need to disappear, and there are no policies to ensure that this happens. With or without such a change, upward mobility on a substantial scale is possible only if accompanied by downward mobility of those who currently dominate professional and better-paid occupations. Evidence shows that the closure of professions such as medicine and law has increased rather than decreased. And this comes as no surprise when you consider the inequitable distribution of education spending. In 2006, the UK contributed a smaller proportion of total spending on educational institutions at primary, secondary and post-secondary non-tertiary levels than almost any other OECD country, at 75% − a notable drop since 2000. Only Korea and Chile also contributed less than 80%. This means that 25% of UK education expenditure comes from private, mainly household, sources. And while some of this may be a shift towards household contributions to schools across the board, most of it is on private education – and thus on the 7% of children educated in the private sector. The UK also had among the highest fees at university level (OECD, 2009) even before the Coalition axed most support for university teaching, resulting in fee increases to £9000 a year. If the total spending on education were spread evenly across all children, there would be both greater equality and more resources for poorer children. Creating 'a society where your life chances are not related to your childhood family circumstances' means tackling privilege as well as poverty.

Revaluing care

Buried in the CPU document is a suggestion that perhaps parents need to be recognised as carers. There is some recognition of caring responsibilities for adults through the benefits system, although Carer's Allowance is set at a derisory level. Parenting, however, is not recognised as care in this sense. Much personal care of adults and children takes place on an unpaid basis outside the labour market, but care provided on a paid basis makes up part of those personal services identified by Cooke as characterised by low pay. Revaluing care both morally and economically would have an impact on poverty levels generally, and on levels of child poverty. First, a recognition that looking after children is a legitimate and valuable social contribution would lessen the current pressure on lone parents in particular to move into paid work and would also imply raising current levels of benefit above the poverty line to provide an adequate standard of living. Second, rates of pay for paid carers need to improve. This would make it more likely that parents in paid work would be able to earn enough to avoid poverty. And for this to happen, more jobs need to be kept within, or moved back into, the public sector to ensure decent pay and conditions, rather than being contracted out to the private sector. This of course is quite the opposite of what is happening under Coalition policy.

Revaluing care requires that we rethink what we understand by work. Critique of the centrality of paid work is already present in every feminist recognition of women's unpaid work outside the labour market. It is already signalled in social policy by the development of ideas around an 'ethic of care'. But perhaps the most useful concept here is Miriam Glucksmann's 'Total Social Organisation of Labour' (TSOL) that entails looking at work both within and outside the market that is necessary to the maintenance and reproduction of human livelihoods (Glucksmann, 1995). Thinking in terms of the TSOL points up the absurdity of counting childcare as work when it is carried out within the market by a registered childminder but not when it is carried out by the child's mother who needs to be forced off benefit and into work, but more importantly reveals the amount of unpaid work on which we all depend.

Rethinking production and wealth

In turn, this means rethinking the language of benefits, transfer incomes and (re)distribution and, crucially, denaturalising the distribution of resources that emerges from the market. In this context it becomes impossible to presume that marketised work is inherently superior or more deserving of reward, or even that it is in any meaningful sense worth what is paid for it. High wages and salaries, and City bonuses, are not determined simply by supply and demand, but frequently, as has recently been so clearly demonstrated, by the power of certain groups to reward themselves. Conversely, it is not inevitable and natural but a matter of social policy that 80% of children living in households with no one in paid work are in poverty. In this and other ways we need to rethink what counts as production and wealth as well as the means of its distribution. The 19th-century critic John Ruskin coined the term 'illth' as opposed to wealth for much that was produced in Victorian Britain. Most of us could not claim to have, in William Morris's formulation, 'nothing in our houses that we do not know to be useful or believe to be beautiful' (Morris, 1992 [1882], p 77) – either because we are relatively rich and simply have too much stuff, or because we are relatively poor and have to make do with what we can afford. Ruskin and Morris's objection was not simply to mass production per se, but to the fact that much of what was produced for mass markets is both functionally and aesthetically poor in quality, produced for its exchange value and profit, not its usefulness.

This is not just a matter of revaluing objects, with all the class-bound issues of taste entailed. It is also a matter of what literally 'counts' in the assessment of wealth, specifically in the calculation of gross domestic product (GDP), and thus 'growth' or at the moment 'shrinkage' in the economy. GDP is a most peculiar measure, which assumes the value of goods, services and labour to be their market value. Again, childcare outside the market contributes nothing to GDP, but the same activity inside the market does. Environmental disasters such as oil spillages also lead to increased GDP, as the activity generated in clearing up generally passes through the market. Globally, much of women's work is outside the market, especially in developing countries. We need both a different system of intrinsic valuing of forms of work and activity, and better forms of social measurement. The New Economics Foundation has pioneered these, including the Index of Sustainable Economic Welfare and its successors.

Citizen's Income and Child Benefit

There is already a strong lobby to retain universal Child Benefit and to increase its value in real terms. In one of his last lectures, Townsend (2009) suggested that the most effective way of getting closer to the target for 2010 would be an immediate doubling of universal Child Benefit relative to average earnings, and that this would immediately lift 300,000 children and their families out of poverty. The fundamental claim is that children as citizens have the right to be provided for and to develop their full potential, and the emphasis on universal benefits is that this is both the most effective and the cheapest way of ensuring help goes to those who need it, especially when coupled with progressive taxation. Yet children cannot be lifted out of poverty unless their parents are, and they cannot look forward to a life free from poverty unless that is guaranteed to adults as well as children – and especially so that their children in turn can be guaranteed a poverty-free life. There is a strong argument to extend the principle of Child Benefit into a Citizen's Income or Basic Income Guarantee. The 1994 Commission on Social Justice discussed a Participation Income that would depend on 'approved' activity such as involvement in some form of education, work, or caring (1994). The financial crisis draws into sharp focus the need to find some less punitive way of supporting working-age populations in an era of rapidly rising unemployment, and of reducing the complexity and bureaucratic costs of existing benefit systems. But the rights of children also point in this direction. While low levels of such income may be entirely compatible with capitalist labour markets, higher levels probably are not. In 1999, Gorz was arguing for a Basic Income that was neither a minimum income that permits mere subsistence, nor a participation income. For Gorz, such an income must be both unconditional and adequate for a decent existence in the society in question. Only on this basis, he argued, could there be effective validation of, and adequate recompense for, caring, voluntary, and non-market activities.

Making sustainability central

We also need to widen the perspective to future generations, which in turn means leaving a habitable planet. That suggests we will all need to live differently. There are questions about whether an economy based on the pursuit of profit and oriented to constant growth is actually compatible with resource constraints – including constraints of water, land and raw materials, as well as the limited ability to absorb carbon emissions. It is salutary to remember that London has an ecological footprint 125 times its own size. This means that the amount of land required to sustain it is 125 times the area of the city, and almost the same size as the total productive land area of Britain. If everyone in the world used resources at this rate, we would need three planets instead of one. If we all used resources at the rate of the US, we would need five planets. Reducing resource use needs to be accompanied by the kind of redistribution suggested earlier, for otherwise we will simply allow the rich to buy their way out of restraint, and penalise the poor.

Human flourishing

The UNCRC requires 'the development of the child's personality, talents and mental and physical abilities to their fullest potential' (UNICEF, 2007, p 10). This is a much larger ambition than creating 'a society where your life chances are not related to your childhood family circumstances' (Cooke et al, 2009, p 2). It means the encouragement in children of what Roberto Unger calls a 'prophetic identity' – thinking about themselves in terms of what they might become, rather than where they are currently socially situated (Unger, 2007). And it means providing the context and resources for this development. But education always reflects the values of the social context in defining which talents and abilities are recognised and socially valued. The commitment to developing capabilities as a necessary part of personal and social development has of course been promoted by Amartya Sen. In Sen's work the framework of the market is still largely taken for granted so that valued capabilities remain defined by market value. This limitation is the reason why Gorz argued that the development of human capacities needs to be freed from the obsession with marketable skills, and reoriented to pleasurable and useful human creativity. He says:

> It has to be recognised that neither the right to an income,
> nor full citizenship, nor everyone's sense of identity and

> self-fulfilment can any longer be centred on and depend
> on occupying a job. And society has to be changed to take
> account of this. (Gorz, 1999, p 54)

This signals not simply a shift in attitudes at a cognitive level, but in modes of identification in which 'work' – in the sense of paid work, or work that you are given to do – can no longer be central to individual life projects.

> But this central problem will only be confronted ... if
> "work" ... loses its centrality in everyone's minds, thinking
> and imagination. And this is what all the established powers
> and dominant forces are working to prevent.... The place
> of work in everyone's imagination and self-image and in
> his/her vision of a possible future is the central issue in
> a profoundly political conflict, a struggle for power. Any
> transformation of society ... requires the capacity to think
> differently, or quite simply to formulate what everyone is
> feeling. (Gorz, 1999, p 54)

Of course, this does not mean the disappearance of socially necessary labour and human creativity. The point is to create space for the redirection of human energies towards real human needs. But this is possible only in a society in which the distribution of the social product and the organisation of work are not effected through the wage relation. It presages the revival of civil society, a space that is neither the private world of the family nor the privatised world of market relations. This raises questions about the built environment. Sustainable, energy-efficient and affordable housing, as well as schools and hospitals, are fundamental bases of material and social well-being for people of all ages. So, too, is the extension and physical character of public spaces. Enabling children to further their own development and exercise their right to social participation in public space entails a quite different approach to education. A qualitative shift from fomenting anxiety with recurrent testing towards building on children's curiosity is needed – and one which will counter the current terrifying statistics that fewer than 20% of children aged 11, 13 and 15 in the UK like school a lot; 35% report being bullied in the last two months; and fewer than 45% find their peers kind and helpful (UNICEF, 2007). The learning experience of children, inside and outside school, needs to be far richer in drama and music, both of which are also forms of social education.

More inclusive *social* relations cannot be determined by economic arrangements. Nevertheless, equality and security, a revaluing of care and a different kind of economy and education would make possible a world where neither children nor parents – nor anyone else – lacks the resources for social participation that others take for granted. And, as Marx and Rathbone recognised, what may then result is something to be decided by generation after generation of children free from poverty who might, as Rathbone hoped, build a better world.

Beyond the nation state

The utopian method is an approach implicitly endorsed by Peter Townsend, when he argued that 'Vision is the counterpart of analysis' and pointed to the need to interrelate ideas into an image of what society might be like. Townsend observed that:

> William Morris ends his *News from Nowhere* with his vision of a future society – "the fully-developed new society" as he called it. "If others can see it as I have seen it then it may be called a vision rather than a dream." After dreaming his dream that "mastery has turned into fellowship" he recognised the reality that "while you live you will see all around you people engaged in making others live lives which are not their own". (Townsend, 1993, p 16)

Townsend also indicated what would be necessary for a society without poverty, both on a national and a global scale. Thus, in *Poverty in the United Kingdom*, he argued that an effective assault on poverty would include the abolition of excessive wealth and income; a more equitable income structure and some breakdown of the distinction between earners and dependants; the abolition of unemployment, reorganisation of employment and the reorganisation of community service (Townsend, 1979). In 2002 he located the causes of social polarisation on an international scale in defective structural adjustment policies, the concentration of hierarchical power, privatisation and the shortcomings of targeting and safety nets. He called for a more integrated critique of the processes generating poverty, social exclusion and social polarisation, and for the introduction and legal enforcement of 'measures for international taxation, regulation of transnational corporations and international agencies, reform of representation at the UN, and new guarantees of human rights, including minimal standards of income' (Townsend, 2002, p 19). He went on to argue for the necessity of an international welfare state:

> New legal and political institutions for social good in a global economy have to be built. A start would come with new international company and taxation law, combined with the modernisation and strengthening of social insurance and more imaginative planning and investment in basic services, such as health and education.... (Townsend, 2002, p 19)

Although this chapter has focused on the UK, the abolition of child poverty is a global issue. Many of the issues raised here, not least the problems of rising inequality, the undervaluing of women's work and ecological sustainability apply on a global scale. Our six principles are even more challenging on an international scale than within an affluent nation state, although the barriers in terms of the dominance of global capital are identical.

Just as inequality within the UK has been rising over the last few decades, so too have international inequalities. In 1960, the average income of the world's richest 20% was 30 times the average income of the poorest 20%. By 1997 it was 74 times as large (UNDP, 1999, p 36). Inequalities have continued to widen (UNDP, 2009a, p 35). Globally, in the first few years of the 21st century, the richest 50 individuals had a combined income greater than that of the poorest 416 million (UNDP, 2005, p 4). The poorest 40% of the world's population shared 5% of global income, while the top 10% took 54% of the total (Martens, 2005). Income differences between countries account for about 70% of global income inequality (UNDP, 2006, p vi), and these disparities are reflected in huge discrepancies in life expectancy and access to education. Such inequalities impede economic growth and development assessed by both the conventional measure of GDP and the more complex measures of human development favoured by the UN (UNDP 2009b). They exacerbate the differential impact of climate change. They create migration pressures even before the impact of global warming on the habitability of parts of the world, leading to forced migrations, is taken into account. The effects on children are stark: in 2007, 9.2 million children under the age of five died, the majority in Africa and Asia; 148 million children were underweight for their age; and 101 million children of primary school age were not in school, with girls less likely than boys to be so (UNICEF, 2008, p 23). Reducing these inequalities is essential to reducing let alone eradicating child poverty.

The severity of our ecological predicament is beginning to be recognised, as climate change is already affecting livelihoods through the melting, flooding or dehydration and desertification of habitats. At the same time, the need to reduce carbon emissions raises questions over the impact of development. Ultimately, security against poverty requires universal provision for children and adults – that is, some form of child benefit, and some form of citizen's income. Of course there are all sorts of difficulties to be resolved here, not least the question of who is defined as a citizen and where. Here, Rathbone's commitment to the welfare of refugee children suggests that residency should entitle children to have their needs met, rather than nationality. And universal provision of course means not only the right to an adequate income, but the universal right to service provision – of water, sanitation, health services and education. The probable increase in forced migrations that will result from global warming only intensifies these questions.

The challenges of redistribution, development and sustainability necessitate a global rethink of what counts as production and wealth. A small start on this has been made by the UN 'Human Development Indicators', which include the development of human capital, health status and educational provision as well as conventional market measures of GDP. But this does not go nearly far enough. In 1988 – the year before the UNCRC – Marilyn Waring argued for a new feminist economics (Waring, 1988) that would properly value women's work. Especially in developing countries, where a larger proportion of women's productive work remains outside the market, their work is undervalued and uncounted – and therefore their access to power and resources is limited. Waring's perspective, like Glucksmann's, demands that non-market work, whether productive or reproductive, is recognised and accorded greater 'value' and reward. This again means valuing the work of care, for children and adults, and ensuring through universal provision an equitable standard of living. Through all these demands runs the need to prioritise human flourishing and well-being and the need to understand in the widest possible way what might be entailed in 'the development of the child's personality, talents and mental and physical abilities to their fullest potential' (UNICEF, 2007, p 10).

In 2001, I concluded an article in *Critical Social Policy* thus:

> The utopian method serves to highlight the limitations
> of current policy and the framework within which future
> plans are constructed and constrained. It provides us with a
> space in which to consider the means by which collective
> provision can be made against the risks not only of poverty,

illness and ageing, but the hazards of environmental degradation which threaten the ecological viability of our current systems of social organisations. In so doing, it provides a measure of the inhumanity of those systems, and the inadequacy of all current conceptions of social policy. It is, in fact, the necessary starting point for a critical social policy. (Levitas, 2001, p 464)

I see no reason to change that judgement, whether thinking at a national or a global level. I would add only that it is also the necessary starting point for social justice in the future, and the real eradication of child poverty.

Acknowledgements

The approach of Utopia as Method taken here draws on work supported by a Leverhulme Trust Research Fellowship between 2010-12. The substantive content draws on preparatory work for the 2011 Poverty and Social Exclusion Survey, funded by ESRC Large Grant RES-060-25-0052. Both sources of support are gratefully acknowledged.

Notes

[1] The measures in the Chancellor's 2011 Autumn Statement added a further 100,000 to these figures.

[2] HBAI figures for 2007/08 give the mean household income before housing costs (BHC) as £487 per week, or £25,324 per year and after housing costs (AHC) as £415 per week or £21,580 per year. The grossed up population number used in the HBAI is 59.9 million. The average household size is around 2.3, which suggests a total number of around 26 million households, and thus 2.6 million in the top 10%. The monetary value of the additional 10 percentage points of AHC income is therefore £56 million, 10 percentage points of BHC income would be £65 billion – although the rise in share of BHC income over the period is slightly less than 10 percentage points. Neither estimate will be a precisely correct measure. The incomes of the top 10% are themselves estimates, and all the incomes used in the HBAI are equivalised for household composition. National Accounts (ONS, 2009, p 37) give the total household income for 2008 as £890 billion, and hence one tenth as £89 billion. The ROI (Redistribution of Income analysis) gives a mean household income for 2006/07 of £27,370 (Jones 2008) which, using the same household figures as above, generates a figure of

£71 billion. Income is defined slightly differently in different sources. The distributive pattern shown in the ROI analysis is closer to the BHC distribution of the HBAI than to the AHC measure.

References

Brewer, M., Browne, J. and Joyce, R. (2011) *Child and working-age poverty from 2010 to 2020*, London: Institute for Fiscal Studies.

Brewer, M., Sibieta, L. and Wren-Lewis, L. (2007) *Racing away? Income inequality and the evolution of high incomes*, IFS Briefing Note 76, London: Institute for Fiscal Studies.

Cameron, D. (2009) 'The Big Society', Hugo Young Memorial Lecture, 10 November (www.conservatives.com/News/speeches/2009/11/David_Cameron_The_Big_Society.aspx).

Commission on Social Justice (1994) *Social justice: Strategies for social renewal*, London: Vintage.

Cooke, G., Gregg, P., Hirsch, D., Jones, N. and Power, A. (2009) *Ending child poverty: 'Thinking 2020'*, Department for Work and Pensions (DWP) Working Paper 56, London: DWP/The Stationery Office.

CPAG (Child Poverty Action Group) (2009) *Ending child poverty: A manifesto for success*, London: CPAG.

DWP (Department for Work and Pensions) (2009) *Households Below Average Incomes: An analysis of the income distribution 1994/5 to 2007/8*, London: DWP.

DWP (Department for Work and Pensions) (2011) *Households Below Average Incomes: An analysis of the income distribution 1994/5 to 2009/10*, London: DWP.

DWP/DfE (Department for Work and Pensions and Department for Education) (2011) *A new approach to child poverty: Tackling the causes of disadvantage and transforming families' lives*, London: DWP and DfE, Cm8061.

Field, F. (2010) *The foundation years: preventing poor children becoming poor adults. The report of the independent review of poverty and life chances* London: Cabinet Office.

Glucksmann, M. (1995) 'Why "work"? Gender and the "Total Social Organization of Labour"', *Gender Work and Organization*, vol 2, no 2, pp 63-75.

Gorz, A. (1999) *Reclaiming work: Beyond the wage-based society*, Cambridge: Polity Press.

Gregg, P. (2008) *Realising potential: A vision for personalised conditionality and support*, London: Department for Work and Pensions/The Stationery Office.

Hirsch, D. (2008) *What is needed to end child poverty in 2020?*, York: Joseph Rowntree Foundation.

Hirsch, D. (2009) *Ending child poverty in a changing economy*, York: Joseph Rowntree Foundation.

HM Treasury (2008) *Ending child poverty: Everybody's business*, London: The Stationery Office.

Jones, F (2008) 'The effects of taxes and benefits on household income, 2006/7', *Economic and Labour Market Review*, Vol 2, no. 7, July, pp 37-47, A1-27, London: Office of National Statistics.

Levitas, R. (2001) 'Against work: a utopian incursion into social policy', *Critical Social Policy*, vol 21, no 4, pp 449-65.

Levitas, R. (2005) 'The Imaginary Reconstitution of Society: Why sociologists and others should take utopia more seriously', Inaugural Professorial Lecture, University of Bristol (http://www.bris.ac.uk/spais/files/inaugural.pdf)

Levitas, R. (2007) 'The Imaginary Reconstitution of Society: Utopia as method', in R. Baccolini and T. Moylan (eds) *Utopia, method, vision*, Berne and Oxford: Peter Lang, pp 47-68.

Martens, J. (2005) *A compendium of inequality: The Human Development Report 2005*, FES Briefing Paper, Berlin: Friedrich Ebert Stiftung.

Morris, W. (1992 [1882]) 'The beauty of life', in *Hopes and fears for art*, in *The collected works of William Morris, Volume XXII*, London: Routledge/Thoemmes Press.

OECD (Organisation for Economic Co-operation and Development) (2009) *Education at a Glance 2009: OECD indicators*, Paris: OECD.

ONS (Office for National Statistics) (2009) *United Kingdom National Accounts: The Blue Book*, London: Palgrave Macmillan.

Pedersen, S. (2004) *Eleanor Rathbone and the politics of conscience*, Cambridge: Cambridge University Press.

Rathbone, E. (1930) 'Utopia calling! A plea for family allowances', From an address broadcast by Miss Eleanor Rathbone, MP, from Northern Stations on 11 February, Family Endowment Society.

Rathbone, E. (1986 [1924]) *The disinherited family*, Bristol: Falling Wall Press.

Townsend, P. (1959) 'The truce on inequality', *New Statesman*, 26 September, pp 381-2.

Townsend, P. (1979) *Poverty in the United Kingdom: A survey of household resources and standards of living*, Harmondsworth: Penguin.

Townsend, P. (1993) 'Closing remarks at a celebration to mark a retirement from the University of Bristol', Excerpted in *Peter Townsend 1928-2009*, Bristol: The Policy Press, p 16.

Townsend, P. (2002) 'Poverty, social exclusion and social polarisation: the need to construct an international welfare state', in P. Townsend and D. Gordon (eds) *World poverty: New policies to defeat an old enemy*, Bristol: The Policy Press, pp 3-24.

Townsend, P. (2009) *1909-2009: Beatrice Webb and the future of the welfare state*, London: Fabian Society (www.fabians.org.uk/events/speeches/peter-townsend-lecture-text).

UNDP (United Nations Development Programme) (1999) *Human Development Report 1999*, New York: UN.

UNDP (2005) *Human Development Report 2005*, New York: UN.

UNDP (2006) *World Economic and Social Survey 2006*, New York: UN.

UNDP (2009a) *Human Development Report 2009*, New York: UN.

UNDP (2009b) *World Economic and Social Survey 2009*, New York: UN.

Unger, R. (2007) *The self awakened: Pragmatism unbound*, Cambridge, MA: Harvard University Press.

UNICEF (United Nations Children's Fund) (2007) *Child poverty in perspective: An overview of child well-being in rich countries*, Report Card No 7, Florence: UNICEF Innocenti Research Centre.

UNICEF (2008) *The State of the World's Children 2009: Maternal and newborn health*, New York: UNICEF.

UNICEF (2009) *The State of the World's Children: Celebrating 20 years of the Convention on the Rights of the Child*, New York: UNICEF.

Waring, M. (1988) *If women counted: A new feminist economics*, London: Macmillan.

Wells, H.G. (1914) 'The so-called science of sociology', in *An Englishman looks at the world*, London: Cassell & Co, pp 102-206.

Wilkinson, R. and Pickett, K. (2009) *The spirit level: Why more equal societies almost always do better*, London: Allen Lane.

NINETEEN

Continuity and change in poor children's lives: evidence from Young Lives

Jo Boyden, Abby Hardgrove and Caroline Knowles

Introduction

In this chapter our aim is to provide an overview of Young Lives and of its emergent findings. Young Lives is a longitudinal study of childhood poverty in four developing countries – Ethiopia, India (Andhra Pradesh), Peru and Vietnam – which was set up in 2001 with two principle aims: to improve understanding of the *causes* and *consequences* of childhood poverty and to inform the development and implementation of future policies and practices that will *reduce* childhood poverty.[1] The study countries were chosen to reflect a wide range of cultural, economic, geographical, political and social conditions, the intent being to explore similar challenges in diverse contexts. The challenges include high debt burden, post-conflict reconstruction (except in India) and volatile environmental conditions with recurring drought and flooding in many areas. As it happens, all four countries have experienced consistent economic growth since Young Lives was established. However, as we know from developed contexts, economic growth does not equate to the eradication of poverty. There are persistently high levels of social and economic inequality in India and Peru, and this is also an emerging concern in Vietnam, associated with rapid levels of growth in recent years. What this means is that Young Lives is able to study transforming economies in which poverty has become entrenched. In contrast, poverty levels remain high throughout Ethiopia, even with recent growth, and levels of inequality are less marked. This contrast offers an opportunity to consider causes for continuity and change in poverty situations for Young Lives children.

Young Lives encompasses research, communications and policy influencing elements in each of the study countries and we are keen to contextualise our analysis and to evaluate the importance of different policy approaches for children, although this chapter concentrates on the research. The chapter begins by outlining the Young Lives research design and conceptual and analytical framework and then turns to a discussion of some of the key findings to date, and concludes by considering some of the more significant policy messages emerging from our work.

Design of Young Lives research

Young Lives is tracking 12,000 children, their families and communities across the four study countries. In each country, there are 2,000 children who were born in 2000–01 and 1,000 born in 1994–95, with roughly equal numbers of boys and girls in both cohorts. The sample is pro-poor and highly clustered. Sites are purposively sampled, with 20 sites per country selected to reflect national diversity, highlighting rural/urban, livelihood, ethnic and other distinctions. Households with children in the right age group were randomly sampled within sites.

We have planned five survey rounds in total, with the first in 2002 and the last in 2015. Qualitative research involving a mix of collective and individual methods is being administered with a sub-sample of children and adults in a total of four rounds. The survey instruments comprise a set of core questions which cover topics such as the dynamics of household poverty, risk and uncertainty, intra-household resource allocation, children's service access, their development and well-being. In addition, a set of country-specific questions concern policies and programmes in each country that are of particular significance for childhood poverty. All core data are archived with the UK Data Archive so as to be available to current and future researchers internationally.[2]

Conceptual and analytical framework

It seems useful to begin the overview of the analytical and conceptual framework by articulating the ways in which Young Lives understands the core concepts of 'poverty', 'childhood' and 'intergenerational poverty transmission'.

Poverty

Young Lives is concerned with household and child poverty and its effects on children's well-being. It has adopted a multidimensional view in which income and material insufficiency is one aspect among others. Our definition of poverty is relative because children's well-being and life chances are inextricably linked to prevailing social norms. Our conceptualisation emphasises that poverty is a complex, dynamic phenomenon subject to both contextual specificity and multiple, interacting contributory factors. Thus, a number of variables must be used to provide the most comprehensive picture of poverty experience. Foremost among these are expenditure, levels of access to material assets of various kinds, to good quality services and to social resources, preventative and/or protective buffers, together with susceptibility to economic shocks, risk and uncertainty, and to power imbalances and violations.

Childhood

Children are recognised as different from adults in all human societies. Because they have less social power and their development involves specific vulnerabilities to various kinds of deprivations, often with a lasting effect, they are generally more susceptible to poverty than adults (Dawes and Donald, 2005; Grantham-McGregor et al, 2007; Victora et al, 2008). Researchers have underscored the loss of 'developmental potential' in children who experience poverty and other adversities (Grantham-McGregor et al, 2007; Engle, 2009).

While we give due emphasis to these universal features of childhood, we recognise the inseparability of 'young lives' from the settings, systems of relationship and cultural processes within which their well-being, learning and development is embedded. It is in these specific contexts that childhoods are socially constructed and regulated according to socioeconomic and cultural processes (Bronfenbrenner, 1979; Rogoff, 2003). Hence, we acknowledge that how childhood is understood and experienced varies widely across cultures, as well as by social group. Personal and social distinctions (notably linked to gender, ethnicity, religion and birth order) find expression in all aspects of children's lives, in schooling, work and informal interactions *among* children and *between* children and adults (Nieuwenhuys, 1994). The transition from childhood to adulthood is also highly variable and may occur at menarche, marriage, parenthood and/or the assumption of paid work, all of which are affected by gender. To add to this complexity, different thresholds may apply to different activities, as when the minimum age of marriage is at variance with the age of criminal culpability. Young Lives research aims to encapsulate both the universal and context-specific aspects of childhoods lived in poverty.

Intergenerational poverty transmission

We have chosen to use 'transmission' to express the conveyance of poverty from one generation to another.

The multidimensional conceptualisation of poverty we use necessitates a multidimensional view of intergenerational poverty transmission. Previous theoretical and empirical work has examined a number of causes and consequences including the role of monetary deprivation (Rodgers, 1995; Mayer and Lopoo, 2005), family structure (Rodgers and Rodgers, 1993; Corcoran and Chaudry, 1997), educational achievement (Rodgers and Rodgers, 1993; Corcoran and Chaudry, 1997; Rose and Dyer, 2008), cultures of poverty (Wilson, 1987; Pepper, 2000) and correlated disadvantages (Corcoran, 1995). Each of these lines of enquiry has merit and we incorporate elements of each as well as extending them to a more multifaceted approach that is useful within our research contexts.[3]

We consider poverty to be transmitted through the interaction of systems over the course of time. We operationalise our multidimensional conceptualisation of poverty through the language of capitals (human, financial, social and cultural) (Moore, 2001). Poverty as an outcome is not transmitted and the process is not inevitable. Rather, the financial and non-financial assets, qualities and characteristics are conveyed and culminate in transmission of poverty (Walters, 2007).

Analytical framework

The employment of complex and multidimensional concepts in the study of childhood poverty requires an analytical framework that encompasses many components. The framework integrates the child outcomes of poverty, the means by which poverty shapes children's transitions and trajectories through childhood, the life course and intergenerational dynamics of poverty and the impact of public policies and programmes designed to protect and enable children.

Young Lives draws on ecological systems theory (Bronfenbrenner, 1979) and life course theory (Elder, 1994) in analysing the causes and outcomes of poverty. We understand poverty as a product of multiple, interwoven and interacting processes. We also recognise that the effects of poverty are not always obvious or directly connected to a certain cause but may be influenced by a range of mediating and moderating factors which are also central to the analysis. Thus, Young Lives research investigates an extensive array of issues pertaining to children's well-being and development. These include individual, household, community, environmental and political. While we track individual children, emphasis is also given to differences between children in different social categories, which involves examination of patterns of inequality, discrimination and exclusion at community and national levels, as well as intra-household power dynamics and differences. Intra-household issues are considered through analysis of decisions about resource allocation, service access, protection, caregiving and time use.

One of the key defining features of Young Lives is its holistic approach to childhood. We examine children's physical and psychosocial well-being and development, their cognitive competencies, their experiences, roles, responsibilities, personal understandings, values and aspirations, together with their material circumstances. This involves gathering data on children's school readiness and achievement, their diet, height and weight, their subjective rating of their health and well-being, service utilisation, sense of inclusion, aspirations for the future and other aspects of their lives. The survey instruments pose a number of questions directly to the children that allow us to measure their perceptions, feelings and attitudes reflecting characteristics such as self-esteem, aspirations and respect, the qualitative research exploring these issues in greater depth. This is helping us to form a fuller and dynamic picture of the children's lives and how they change over time. The cumulative consequences of childhood poverty can be conceptualised as *life course poverty transmission*, in which the focus is on factors that inhibit children's development, with impacts for their adult years. The patterns and mechanisms of intergenerational poverty transmission are traced through investigation of the circumstances of caregivers and households in which Young Lives children live, alongside the study of two generations of children. We are, or will be, able to document change over three generations – parents and other caregivers, Young Lives children and the future children of Young Lives children.

In keeping with the conceptualisation of childhood poverty as a multidimensional phenomenon, a holistic view of policy is employed. General macroeconomic, social sector development and poverty reduction policies are scrutinised together with policies that focus explicitly on children. Policy monitoring and analysis are employed in a two-way process. On the one hand, empirical findings on childhood poverty from Young Lives sites are assessed for their policy implications. On the other, specific policies and programmes are examined in terms of their consequences for children living in poverty, particularly Young Lives children. Such investigation takes place at the international, national and subnational levels. The former two provide a broad contextualisation for Young Lives research and analysis.

An important element of this policy focus concerns the role of school and education policies in Young Lives countries and research sites. Initially, Young Lives research was centred on household-based surveys and qualitative research. With the second wave of data, it became very evident that education plays an essential and powerful role in shaping the lives of the children we study. Therefore, we plan in future to incorporate data collection on the quality of schools available to Young Lives children. This will provide vital evidence about school systems, which helps us to contextualise our results concerning children's school readiness, enrolment, attendance and/or drop-out and educational performance.

Key findings and trends

Within the broad Young Lives conceptual framework we have developed three overlapping areas of study. The first of these concerns the dynamics of poverty and uncertainty as they affect family decisions, with attention to the means by which households become trapped in or escape poverty and the impact of social protection measures and other forms of support. The second examines children's learning through formal (school) and informal processes, their changing responsibilities and related time use and readiness for school and work at different points in their lives. The third addresses how poverty affects children's physical and psychosocial well-being and examines the major sources of risk, vulnerability and resilience in their lives, as well as how family, peer and other relationships influence their well-being. There is also an emergent interest in intergenerational dimensions of poverty that arises out of our attention to the mechanisms through which poverty is perpetuated.[4] In this section we outline some key findings with respect to each of these research foci, drawing on the first two rounds of survey and qualitative data.

Poverty dynamics, risk and social protection

Risk, resilience and uncertainty are crucial themes for Young Lives. Household poverty is a risk in and of itself. But poverty is also a risk for other adversities, including environmental hazard, extreme susceptibility to market forces and poor quality, limited or no services. Poor households often endure multiple risks and seldom have access to preventive or mitigating buffers, leading to high levels of uncertainty. Recurring misfortune and uncertainty may in turn result in rejection of innovative livelihoods strategies that show promise for climbing out of poverty. Thus, risk and uncertainty are not simply correlates of poverty, but an important cause of poverty persistence and poverty traps in their own right (Dercon, 2005, p 1). Hence, our investigation of poverty dynamics focuses on the interaction of risk, uncertainty and material deprivation with consideration also of the role of household livelihood strategies, social resources and social protection measures in poverty prevention and alleviation.

Young Lives is able to report some positive trends with respect to the living standards of our households between 2002 and 2006, the dates of Rounds 1 and 2 of the survey. All of our research countries experienced macroeconomic growth during this period. In each case this translated into overall reduction in headcount poverty, even in Ethiopia, the poorest country in the study. This has also meant increases in infrastructure and service access, especially in urban areas. However, micro-level processes of growth can be very volatile and many Young Lives households remain in a precarious condition, even in the context of growth. With the current global economic crisis there is real potential that households climbing the ladder could fall back into poverty through unemployment, price increases and other economic shocks, of which there are many. The effects of multiple interacting adversities are most evident in rural areas of Ethiopia where high levels of poverty and risk arise from a mix of fragile ecologies, absolute shortages, ill health and death in humans and animals (Dercon, 2004).

Very often, household susceptibility to risk is due to entrenched structural inequalities (Hart, 2008). Young Lives has very clear evidence that, even in times of national economic growth, overall decreases in poverty do not necessarily diminish disparities. High inequality can be seen in a range of indicators. It can be seen in Peru, for example, in the substantial gap in stunting rates between urban and rural children from the first months of life. By the time they reached 18 months of age, the stunting rate in rural areas was three times that in urban areas (looking at the younger cohort in Round 1, 2002). In Andhra Pradesh caste and ethnic differences are particularly important markers of inequality, such that 18% of scheduled tribe children in the older cohort (aged 12) and 29.2% of scheduled tribe children in the younger group (aged 4.5 to 5.5 years) live in absolute poverty,[5] as compared to a state average of 11.2% (Galab et al, 2008). Not only is inequality high, with much higher absolute poverty in the countryside, but we also have evidence of it intensifying across our sample, with consumption levels rising more quickly in urban than rural areas between 2002 and 2006.

In recent decades social protection measures have been promoted as an efficient and cost-effective means of reducing poverty among the most vulnerable populations. Most recently several actors, including the UK Department for International Development (DFID), have jointly called for social protection to be child sensitive and have begun to build the evidence base of what this may mean in practice (DFID et al, 2009). Young Lives research has observed a number of social protection programmes that influence child welfare in India, Peru and Ethiopia (Singh, 2008; Uppal, 2009; Cueto et al, 2009b; Woldehanna, 2009). Effective social protection strategies for children involve a combination of action to support incomes and livelihoods, actions to promote human development, and action on the root causes of vulnerability. Young Lives is interested in the effects of these social protection programmes on children's experiences of poverty.

Woldehanna (2009) examined the effects of the Productive Safety Net Programme (PSNP) in Ethiopia on children's time use between work and schooling. The PSNP is designed to reduce the vulnerability of poor people to drought, and as such, it should protect children against the risks associated with poverty and shocks. In this study, Woldehanna concludes that the PSNP has been instrumental in improving child well-being by reducing time spent on working, childcare and household chores and increasing girls' time spent studying. However, the associated Public Work Programme (PWP) is not effective enough to increase the highest grade completed, or time children spend on studying at home, and actually increased the time children spend working (probably because of labour displacement within the household). Although the PWP increased the amount of time both girls and boys spent on paid work, it reduced the amount of time girls spent on childcare and household chores. The net effect is that the total hours children devoted to work were reduced. The PWP also increased the time girls spent on studying.

Similarly, Singh (2008) has analysed some effects of the Midday Meals Scheme in Andhra Pradesh, India. The implications for nutrition and cognition are significant. Children who participate in the scheme show a greater gain in cognitive achievement scores than would have otherwise been the case. The protective effects of the scheme were particularly pronounced where the household had experienced drought (partly because of policy design) showing the potential to mitigate risk. Equally important, the midday meal can function as a nutritional 'safety net', which helps to protect children from the negative consequences of food insecurity and supports development and learning.

Research by Vennam and Crivello (2009) on the impact of the current global financial crisis in India documents children's perspectives on the way programmes and services in their communities mediate their experiences of recent change. Children identified both negative and positive changes in their households and communities. They described how financial crisis has an impact on their time use, for example, balancing school and work, as well as how they experience the various programmes aimed to protect them and their households. Some of these programmes are highlighted here, namely, the National Rural Employment Guarantee Scheme (NREGS), the 'Arogyasree' health insurance scheme and the Public Distribution System (PDS). Children not only provided critical commentary on how economic and political changes have an impact on their lives, they also discussed how children and their families cope with change (for example, by eating less or working more) and what communities and governments should do to better protect different groups of children in these contexts.

What we are seeing is that programmatic interventions can have a significant influence on children's experience of poverty and reduce the effects of shocks. The influence is not always straightforward, however. Intended outcomes are not always achieved, and there may be other, unanticipated consequences, positive, or negative. At the same time, emergent findings on the PSNP in Ethiopia cause concern that the thresholds for eligibility may be too low, leaving many families on the edge of crisis.

Well-being

Young Lives research on the changing impacts of various forms of deprivation and misfortune on children traces the effects across different domains of their development and with regard to their sense of well-being.[6] It has long been established that poverty poses a major threat to children's survival and physical health, especially in early childhood. Improved services and awareness have led to significant reductions in infant and child mortality and morbidity in many parts of the world in recent decades. Nevertheless, poverty remains an important cause and consequence of poor health in many populations, creating a vicious cycle that many poor households find difficult if not impossible to break. Poor children are more prone to the effects of diseases and malnutrition (Pollitt, 1994; Walker et al, 2007). They also have a higher risk of injury due to their insecure work and living environments (WHO/UNICEF, 2000).

The early months and years of life are widely recognised as a crucial period of human development in which negative experiences and/or deprivation, particularly in regards to nutrition, may incur long-term outcomes (Tanner and Finn-Stevenson, 2002; Grantham-McGregor et al, 2007). Stunting (low height for age) is an indicator of long-term child malnutrition and poor health. It occurs mainly in the first three years of life. Young Lives provides new evidence for the well-established and robust link between early child nutrition and the intellectual development of children. We find strong associations between poor nutrition in the first months of life and cognitive development scores at around age five in Peru and Vietnam (adjusted for different child, household and community characteristics) (Le Thuc, 2009; Sanchez, 2009). For example, Le Thuc (2009) has examined the consequences of stunting (based on height-for-age z-score at age 6 to 18 months) on children's cognitive achievement at 4.5 to 5.5 years. The study found that the height-for-age z-score has a positive impact on cognitive achievement at age five. Further, the effects of parental education have strong statistical significance. This suggests that some of the disadvantages in socioeconomic status are being transmitted across generations by influencing the cognitive capacity of young children.

These findings support the importance of early child nutrition, not just for children's immediate physical well-being, but also their long-term cognitive development. We recognise that, in general, nutrition interventions are most effective in early childhood. However, an evaluation of the government's Midday Meal Scheme in our study sites in India suggests that such interventions can help to protect older children in poverty in a number of ways, including to improve cognitive abilities at school (Singh, 2008). This reflects the positive effects of neural plasticity (Tanner and Finn-Stevenson, 2002), and supports the significance of nutritional interventions beyond the first five years of life. The longitudinal nature of Young Lives will allow us to investigate mid- and long-term effects on child malnutrition on cognitive development and in how far this might translate into reduced school performances, educational achievement and economic productivity in adult life.

Our research also shows some associations between child malnutrition and psychosocial well-being such as self-esteem and self-respect. Dercon and Krishnan (2009) explored the relationship between material poverty and the psychosocial competencies of (older cohort) children across the four Young Lives study countries. They found that measures of self-efficacy, sense of inclusion, self-esteem and educational aspirations all correlate with indicators of material well-being of the family in which they are growing up. They argue that psychosocial competencies are important life skills that may affect children as adults and shape their future socioeconomic status. Controlling for household economic status and community characteristics, they provide evidence that malnourished children (in terms of height for age) tend to aspire to less education in Ethiopia and Vietnam, and show an increased sense of shame and low self-esteem in Peru and Vietnam.

With changing lifestyles and diets in some developing countries, particularly in urban areas, new child nutrition problems are beginning to emerge (Popkin, 2001; Shetty, 2002; Popkin and Gordon-Larsen, 2004). Rapidly rising rates of obesity are a major health concern in Peru, where 55.4% of all mothers in our sample were overweight. Maternal overweight is associated with household wealth, urban residence and mothers' occupation. Prevalence of overweight in children is also increasing and we expect higher levels in the older cohort in Round 3 data. Co-existing maternal overweight and child undernutrition affects households in Ethiopia, India and Vietnam, but is especially prevalent in Peru (VanderKloet, 2008; Barnett, 2010).

While absolute material lack is a major factor in children's well-being, cultural values and practices can also have a significant impact. This can be particularly apparent in the differential treatment of children within households in accordance with their gender, birth order and household sibling composition. In the context of a study of childhood poverty, this may mean that some children in a household fair less well than others. In some cases, certain children are 'sacrificed' to promote the well-being of their siblings, as when girls are placed in work in order to help provide the means for their brothers to attend school. What we are seeing is that there is less of a gender gap, in general, than we might have expected (see Filmer, 2000), although there are some significant gender disparities in nutrition and education. In general, boys seem to have the advantage over girls in education. For example, in Peru, fewer girls than boys were enrolled in pre-school, giving boys the advantage in learning and making the transition to school (Ames et al, 2009). In India, while almost equal numbers of boys and girls enrol in school, girls, especially in rural areas, are more likely to drop out, even by the age of 12 (Himaz, 2009a). However, there are some areas where boys do not fare so well. In Peru, 60% of 12-year-old children are older than they should be for their class, either because they started school late, or because they were kept back for poor achievement (Escobal et al, 2008). This applies particularly to boys.

Young Lives research has identified several other influences on children's sense of well-being. Material deprivation and cultural values are important factors, but there is also a vital relational element. Urban children, who are generally better off in terms of material goods, have lower levels of well-being than rural children (see Round 2 survey reports). Since differentials in household economic status are far higher in urban than rural areas, this suggests that relative rather than absolute poverty may be a more important influence on children's sense of well-being. There are also important intergenerational aspects to well-being. In all countries, children say they feel better about themselves if parents are educated (Dercon and Krishnan, 2009). Relationships within their families and communities – being cared for and caring for others – are important to children. Research into the effects of being orphaned in Ethiopia shows that the death of a father between the ages of 8 and 12 reduces a child's sense of optimism (Himaz, 2009b). The death of a mother during this same age range corresponds with significant reduction in educational performance. Children who do not have adequate nutrition also feel shame and a lack of self-esteem and self-respect (Dercon, 2008).

Risk and resilience in children

Within our research on well-being, Young Lives explores children's responses to household economic shocks and other forms of risk, focusing in particular on patterns of risk, protective mechanisms and individual and collective responses. The rationale for this enquiry is threefold: the susceptibility of poor children to multiple risks; the evidence that while children who experience multiple risks are liable to be overwhelmed psychologically (Garbarino, 1999), some remain remarkably resilient (Rutter, 2001); and the importance of identifying sources of resilience, coping and support in children. Our attention to risk centres on circumstances that may *predispose* children and their families to adversity, as well as threats to well-being that *result from* experiences of adversity. We refer to resilience broadly as 'the phenomenon of doing well in the face of adversity' (Patterson, 2002, p 350). We recognise that 'resilience' as a construct can pose theoretical and methodological challenges (Luthar, Cicchetti and Becker, 2000; Boyden and Cooper, 2007). However, we have chosen to use the term to refer to our interest in the child protection strategies and resources brought to bear in difficult situations by children, their families and communities. We seek to understand how these may serve as protective processes, as well as how social protection and child protection schemes contribute to household and child outcomes.

We have argued that risk in children is not merely a matter of chance, but influenced by social and cultural values and practices that result in differential treatment and levels of exposure of distinct groups, with boys and girls experiencing different kinds and degrees of risk, for example. However, we have found that gendered patterns of adversity are not always as might be expected, as in the finding that in India stunting is more common among boys than girls, particularly in the younger cohort. This trend most likely reflects biological differences between the sexes and contrasts with extensive evidence that in India girls are highly disadvantaged as compared to boys. Political economy also plays a crucial role in the distribution of risk, with some groups systematically oppressed or marginalised within societies through powerful structural forces (Hart, 2008). Nair (2009) has examined the risks related to caste membership and how these have an impact on the cognitive development of young children in Andhra Pradesh, India. The study shows significant evidence of a disparity in cognitive skill development by caste. Castes were differentiated by lower parental education and lower household socioeconomic status, suggesting an intergenerational mechanism of transmission of outcomes.

Young Lives is concerned to identify specific childhood risks and their effects. Emergent evidence suggests that many boys and girls contend with significant violence at home and in school, and further investigation is needed so as to better understand which children are affected by which practices and with what consequences. A significant percentage of Young Lives children work, and it needs to be established whether or not they confront workplace hazards. A large number face family separation, whether through migration, mortality or the breakdown of relationships. By 2006, one in five of the children in our Ethiopian sample had experienced the death of one or both parents. We found that these children face specific risks according to the age at which their parent died, and the gender of the surviving parent (Himaz, 2009b). Our research thus far suggests that losing a mother between the ages of 8 and 12 reduces school enrolment and educational achievement, and increases drop-out. Children who have lost a parent gain fewer skills and qualifications, with potential impacts on what they can do in the future (Camfield et al, 2009).

However, despite powerful evidence of detrimental outcomes for children due to exposure to adversity, Young Lives does not find all effects harmful. Our research highlights the complex interplay of risk and protective factors in the lives of boys and girls. It shows that adversity and risk have different meanings in different cultures and for different actors, such that in some situations and under some circumstances assumed risks can be protective and may even foster specific competencies in young people. So, although much evidence does suggest that adversity has a negative effect on children, further research in this area could usefully explore where this is not the case in order to develop a more nuanced, multi-actor view of these processes.

For example, Boyden (2009) examines the prevalence of reported household adversities among the older cohort of children in Ethiopia, as well as their role in responding to them. As indicated, this is a context of high adult morbidity and mortality, frequent environmental catastrophes in rural areas, poverty and other household hardships. But she finds less evidence of negative effects in children than might be expected given their high levels of exposure. One of the ways children manage difficulties is by working.[7] Children's work helps mitigate household risk, has the added effect of fostering children's sense of responsibility and belonging, and can strengthen intergenerational ties. This is an important insight to note, as there is a large body of literature suggesting that child work is an undesirable and negative experience for children and adversely affects their schooling (Allais and Hagemann, 2008; Ranjan, 2009). However, it is important to recognise that even while children's work strengthens family ties and builds pro-social skills in children, some young people are also weighed down by the burden of their responsibilities. This is especially the case when adults are too dependent on them, when they are involved in tasks that they dislike, or when work commitments harm their schooling. Where there is no choice, children's work can also be a source of shame, such as when it conflicts with traditional gender roles.

These are but a few of the risks to specific adversities we are seeing in our Young Lives sample. We have only just begun to explore children's resilient capabilities to adapt and respond to such difficulties. Future rounds of data will give us a better sense of the consequences of adversities and children's abilities to overcome them.

Children's learning in context

This line of enquiry involves exploration of the changing effects of poverty on children's learning and adaptation. Young Lives recognises that children's learning and adaptation are complex processes involving individual and environmental, biological and social influences. To this end, we analyse how poverty affects children's home lives, their schooling, work and recreation, and how in turn these contexts shape their competencies, aspirations and life trajectories.

Our key finding so far in this area has to do with the centrality of school education to children's lives. In recent decades, schooling has become one of the most crucial defining features of modern childhood throughout the world, with unprecedented increases in school access in developing countries at the pre-school and primary levels. This has been largely associated with the push to expand access in line with the Education for All agenda, and the Millennium Development Goal (MDG) 2 on universal primary education. We have observed high levels of overall enrolment among Young Lives children at both pre-school and primary school levels. The majority of younger children in Ethiopia (52%), India (86%), Peru (81%) and Vietnam (89%) are enrolled in pre-school (Round 2 survey data, 2006).[8] However, there are stark inequalities in enrolment at both pre- and primary school. Urban children are more likely to attend school than those who live in rural areas, often because there are no nurseries in the countryside (Woldehanna et al, 2008a; Ames et al, 2009; Woodhead, 2009). We also find that attendance at school improves when children have educated mothers (Woodhead, 2009). In Vietnam we observed that minority ethnic children are less likely to attend school than other children (Truong, 2009). In Peru, indigenous children show high enrolment rates, although they are far more likely to drop out or repeat a grade than their Spanish-speaking peers (Cueto et al, 2009a). We have also observed that shocks such as parental death, illness and drought interrupt children's education in all countries (Himaz, 2009b).

Of course, school enrolment does not equate with attendance. And attendance does not guarantee quality of experience. We are finding stark evidence of the ways in which low attendance and/or systems' deficiencies undermine the outcomes of schooling, as reflected in grade repetition, achievement and other indicators. For example, in Ethiopia 94% of children in the older cohort were enrolled in school during Round 2 of the survey, though 39% could not read a basic sentence such as 'The sun is hot' (Woodhead et al, 2009).

In order for its relevance, utility and outcomes to be fully appreciated, schooling needs to be examined within its social context, and in the light of the United Nations Convention on the Rights of the Child (UNCRC), and demand for education to be directed at development to the fullest potential of the child (Article 29). We find that despite the evident challenges and some very discouraging literacy rates, children and their parents are overwhelmingly positive about school education and have high expectations for educational participation and achievement (Crivello, 2009; Tafere and Camfield, 2009). This reflects a widely held belief in the power of schooling to improve living and working conditions for children (Harper et al, 2003; Rose and Dyer, 2008). In Ethiopia and Peru schooling is regarded by Young Lives children and caregivers as the most important means by which the young can lift themselves and their families out of poverty, breaking enduring cycles of hardship (Crivello, 2009; Crivello and Boyden, 2011). In Peru, school is perceived as essential to 'becoming somebody'

(Crivello, 2009). The belief is that through education children will get better jobs and be able to support their parents in the future. Children say that they want to stay on until secondary school and even university. This reflects an intergenerational appreciation and commitment to education.

In terms of investment in schooling, there is evidence of gender disparity. In Ethiopia, India and Vietnam, parents spend more on their sons than their daughters for school-related expenses in both the younger and the older cohorts (Himaz, 2009a; Vennam et al, 2009). In India, parents are more likely to send boys to private schools that they believe will provide better quality education in English, which is perceived as providing advantages in the labour market (Vennam et al, 2009). However, once families have decided to educate a child beyond the upper primary level, there is no expenditure bias and an equal proportion of boys and girls are sent to private schools (Himaz, 2009a). It is difficult to disentangle the underlying attitudes or policies that lead to these differences. However, Young Lives has observed that many parents, especially mothers, have very positive attitudes towards their daughters' education, particularly at primary school. If their mothers have been to school, girls are more likely to be sent as well. Whether these high expectations can be realistically fulfilled remains to be seen. There is a risk of diminishing returns to education, in both the quality received and the ability to achieve better jobs in the future.

Already, schooling presents some challenges. Crivello (2009) notes that children's participation in school provides new spheres of influence and exposure to different cultural ideals. This has created some intergenerational tension as children have embraced a less traditional style of dress, for example. Parents express ambivalence, desiring their children to receive the benefits of a school education, and yet being reluctant to see their children preferring non-traditional cultural practices and ideas. School attendance also poses major challenges for children who have family responsibilities, including those who care for younger siblings, sick or incapacitated adults (Boyden, 2009). In many parts of the world family life is underpinned by powerful intergenerational ties in which all members of the household contribute actively to its maintenance according to their physical and mental ability. Boys and girls normally play a role in keeping with their evolving developmental capacities, the gendered division of labour within the household, the birth order and composition of the sibling group, and other factors. In this context, children's work can be crucial to household survival as well as a source of respect and pride (Bolin, 2006). As such, work is not necessarily regarded as a risk for the young and is more often thought of as essential to their moral and social learning and an important complement to school education (Crivello and Boyden, 2011). Young Lives children have expressed concerns about balancing the competing demands of school and work (Boyden, 2009). The challenge of balancing school and work is a theme we expect to see more of in our subsequent rounds of data collection.

Most of the Young Lives children who work are involved in unpaid domestic or farm activities that enable parents and other caregivers to focus on paid or more complex tasks. Some are in paid employment, however. Occasionally the young are assigned to specific occupations, as in certain rural areas of Andhra Pradesh, where the belief that children's (especially girls') involvement results in a good crop has been one of the factors encouraging seasonal child work in cotton pollination and related tasks (Morrow and Vennam, 2009). The size of the cotton plants is also an important factor for engaging children. Children are the 'right height' to hold the plants and do the crossing, whereas adults have to bend down. Nevertheless, there are concerns about low wages received by children in this and other sectors of the economy. And some children are involved in work that makes too much demand on them or is hazardous. Young Lives expects to be focusing a lot more on this topic with future rounds of data.

Intergenerational transmission of poverty

One of the principle aims of studying childhood poverty is to understand its place in perpetuating disadvantage throughout the life cycle and across generations. Hence our developing focus on the mechanisms of intergenerational transmission of poverty. While we continue to collect data, and while Young Lives children are still in the process of growing up, we cannot draw definitive conclusions about transmission. However, we can increasingly identify contributing factors, and consider other possible influences in future rounds of data collection.

Household capital

Many of the resources and opportunities available to poor children are determined by the environments in which they live. We refer to these as 'environmental capital'. Environmental capital denotes the assets, qualities, characteristics, vulnerabilities and hazards that come with living in a particular ecological context (rural, urban, coastal, mountainous, etc) (Moore, 2001).

As we have seen, living in an urban rather than a rural environment provides better access to services and more opportunities for education. Urban areas usually offer closer proximity to school (Woldehanna et al, 2008b; Ames et al, 2009). The contrast between access to education in rural and urban areas is clearly manifested in Ethiopia, where household wealth has a positive, statistically significant influence on enrolment among rural children (Woldehanna et al, 2009) but not among the urban sample. Woldehanna et al attribute the difference to the proximity of schools for most urban households—an environmental asset not available to rural children. This indicates that poorer urban children (at least in Ethiopia) are more likely to access and benefit from educational enrolment than their rural counterparts. If inequalities in education persist in this manner, we are likely to see a greater degree of poverty transmission within rural households.

Monetary assets (including debt) and material wealth (for example, land, livestock, dowries or inheritance), expressed as 'financial/material capital' (Moore, 2001; Walters, 2007), are clearly linked to education opportunity (Ames et al, 2009; Woldehanna et al, 2009), and to the timing of children's transitions to school, work and marriage (Tafere and Camfield, 2009). For instance, bride wealth often prompts marriage at particular times as a way of household financial planning.

Types of material wealth seem to have an important role to play as well. In Ethiopia, Woldehanna et al (2009) observe that wealth in livestock often requires time-consuming efforts from children and reduces their ability to attend and participate at school. This is a useful distinction to consider in rural households, where wealth in cattle versus wealth in another form may explain the difference between children's educational enrolment and participation. In other words, the types of wealth and livelihoods into which children are born and reared may significantly restrict their ability to break out of poverty cycles, because of the daily commitment required of them to survive.

We are seeing the importance of 'human capital' in very clear ways within Young Lives. Human capital refers to the assets housed within a particular individual or group of persons, such as educational attainment, skills, credentials or capacity for particular kinds of labour. Strong connections between parent/caregiver education levels are seen in encouragement and efforts towards early childhood education in Andhra Pradesh and Peru (Woodhead, 2009). More substantially, children's health (Moestue and Huttly, 2008; Le Thuc, 2009) and subjective well-being (Dercon and Krishnan, 2009; Ko and Xing, 2009) are significantly associated with parents' and caregivers' education levels. This supports the vital importance of school education for the health, well-being and quality of children's lives, both now and in the future. The more children who are educated now, the greater likelihood that their children will also be educated, offering future generations better opportunities to break free from situations of chronic poverty – that is, so long as schooling continues to facilitate good employment in adults.

We are finding that 'social capital' is strongly connected to children's health status. Social capital refers to the real and potential resources that flow from relationships and connections with others (Adler and Kwon, 2002). De Silva and Harpham (2007) note that feelings of trust and social cohesion, along with individual, supportive relationships, are significantly linked to better child nutritional status in all four Young Lives countries. Being part of a community with more educated adults is significantly associated with better child nutrition and height for age in Andhra Pradesh (Moestue et al, 2007). Community literacy rates are positively associated with less stunting and underweight children in Vietnam (Moestue and Huttly, 2008). This underscores the importance of education, relationships and community networks for children's positive growth and development.

What we see here is an indication of *what* Young Lives households are transmitting from one generation to another. These associations raise the important question – *how* are these household capitals being conveyed to children? In other words, what *processes* facilitate, enable or impede the transmission we are already observing?

Intra-household factors

One way in which transmission takes place is within the interactions, dynamics, decisions and other such processes that take place within the household. These intra-household level factors influence the roles and responsibilities of members, as well as resource allocation among members. We find several intra-household factors are significant to a preliminary understanding of poverty transmission.

When looking at the household level, we need to start by assessing the influence of household composition on child outcomes. One of the clearest ways we see the influence of household composition is in educational enrolment. Woldehanna et al (2009) identify a noticeable pattern among large households with high numbers of children. The more children there are, and the more total members, the greater the likelihood that children will not be enrolled. They conclude that poor households cannot afford to educate all of the children in their care. This points to the significance of size and dependency ratios (that is, the ratio of dependent members to working/contributing members)

(Bird, 2007) for later outcomes among children from larger families. Being reared in larger households may be one of the primary ways in which children's opportunities are restricted, and the poverty cycle is continued.

The values, intentions and perceptions of caregivers have a number of important implications for children's growth and development. In particular, it is evident that parental and caregiver perceptions of and intentions for child education strongly influence when or if children attend school (Ames et al, 2009; Woodhead, 2009). High value placed on education in India has prompted impoverished parents to pursue private education in Andhra Pradesh (Vennam et al, 2009). On the other hand, households in Ethiopia have lower educational aspirations for orphaned children in their care, and tend to demonstrate less investment and commitment to their education (Himaz, 2009b).

We must consider the influence and variability of wider norms, beliefs and assumptions that inform everyday life. Parents in a remote village of Ethiopia maintained that girls who stay in school through seventh and eighth grade may be seen as too old to marry well and hence are liable to become an economic and social burden on their families (Tafere and Camfield, 2009). Therefore, some parents choose not to encourage girls' education past this point and expect young girls' time out of school to be spent on household chores that will help the family and prepare them for marriage and families of their own. This work demonstrates the significance of culture and particular social structures for poverty transmission.

Individual factors

The influence of intra-household level factors is not a one-way channel of asset conveyance. Rather, household-level factors interact with individual children and wider social realities to contribute to poverty transmission. Individual factors concern those qualities and characteristics housed within the individual that influence and are influenced by systems outside the self.

Gender significantly influences educational trajectory. We have seen that boys have more access and opportunity for education than girls. So, while parents may invest in girls in other ways, as in buying jewellery for their dowry, more money is spent on boys' education than on girls in Andhra Pradesh, mostly likely because education is perceived as crucial to employment and girls are expected to marry rather than work when they grow up (Himaz, 2009a). Boys are often selected for private education while girls tend to be enrolled in public schools that are perceived as lower quality (Vennam et al, 2009; Woodhead, 2009). Instruction in private schools is in English and hence private education is seen as offering significant employment advantages to boys, with attendant opportunities for climbing out of poverty.

Many rural girls have less access to pre-school due to safety concerns. Small children, particularly girls, are considered too vulnerable to walk long distances to school. Ames et al (2009) observe that this causes an age delay for girls in beginning education, and notes that delayed and often disjointed educational participation leads to early drop-out. What we know is that the educational level achieved by their mothers influences the health and educational achievement of Young Lives children. As we look ahead, the future appears less promising for young women who are unable to attend school and reach higher grade levels.

Extra-household factors

The evolution of educational policy in India over the last 50 years has made a substantial contribution to impeding transmission for young children, as evidenced in our research in Andra Pradesh. India's goal of universal primary education up to age 14 is finally being realised 50 years after its inception (Vennam et al, 2009; Woodhead, 2009). The empowering influence of education is by now irrefutable. Children are more likely to be healthy, educated and better prepared to live productive lives when their parents and caregivers are also better educated.

Sociocultural structures have perhaps an even greater influence on poverty transmission. These affect the underlying values and beliefs that inform interaction and behaviour in a given community, and broadly, within a society as a whole (Sewell, 1992; Lieblich et al, 2008). For example, despite the political agenda to make education available for all a priority at the policy level, a gender bias remains in many households, limiting access of many girls whose families invest in issues other than their education (Himaz, 2009a; Tafere and Camfield, 2009).

Just as policies can make a profound difference on the lives of future generations, we see the significant impact of extra-household shocks on the well-being of successive generations in our study. These may be economic or environmental shocks that cause significant disruption in a household's ability to survive and protect its members. As Le Thuc (2009) points out, in Vietnam the economic crisis of the 1980s seems to have had a direct influence on the prenatal and early childhood nutrition of the parents of Young Lives children. Such shocks significantly influence health and cognitive development – thus their own ability to survive, cope and bring up their own children. Examples like this one demonstrate the importance of taking a life course perspective, and of considering the profound influence that a short-term situation can have on the long-term development and well-being of more than just one generation. The consequences of poor nutrition in early childhood can limit the capability of parents to adequately care for and provide for children of their own.

Conclusion

What we have sought to do in this chapter is to introduce our approach to, and preliminary results from, a longitudinal study of the dynamics of childhood poverty in four developing countries. We have laid out key findings from the various research papers, making use of two waves of data (a third was being collected at the time of writing). As more rounds are collected and analysed, the Young Lives dataset will grow in potential. Young Lives seeks not only to build and consolidate research evidence around childhood poverty but to examine what policies can work to reduce it. The contexts of each study country are very different, but here we conclude with four emergent policy-relevant conclusions.

First, *economic growth will not by itself solve the problems of childhood poverty and it can worsen inequality.* Our evidence to date (from the first two waves, both collected before the current economic crisis) shows intensifying social and economic inequalities between children (including by ethnicity, parental education level and the urban/rural divide), even in national contexts of economic growth. This demonstrates that intervention is required to ensure economic change delivers an equitable distribution of life chances for all and that untrammelled inequality will waste talent by building barriers in the way of some children achieving their potential.

Second, *living conditions experienced in very early life cast a long shadow.* Previous research has highlighted how precious the early years are to children's development. We reinforce those findings by demonstrating the impacts of anthropometric indicators, including stunting, on later cognitive development. We also reveal new evidence that poor nutrition early in life detrimentally affects children's psychosocial well-being later on. As Young Lives children age we will see the long-term implications of this early damage. Here we have promising evidence of the protective impacts of a school feeding programme in India to reduce the effects of poor nutrition and to support wider learning. That enrolment in primary education has risen so quickly and that engagement in pre-school education is fast becoming the norm for many children, suggests significant potential for policy makers to affect children's development by connecting well-designed nutrition supplementation schemes to education.

Third, Young Lives demonstrates *there is real potential for social protection schemes to improve children's well-being and life chances, although these need to be well designed.* Young Lives data on three countries (Peru, Ethiopia and Andhra Pradesh in India) cover the extension or introduction of social protection measures. This evidence reinforces the message that social protection schemes can support children's well-being and nutrition and can affect patterns of time use (for instance, the balance between school and children's work). Our evidence suggests social protection measures are of particular value where families experience shocks, and so it will be particularly important to evaluate the effects of these schemes on child and household well-being during the current economic and food price crisis. The analysis shows that design affects the performance of schemes and can have important intra-household impacts, including over allocation of children's time. We need both wider coverage and careful design of social protection measures.

Fourth, our evidence reinforces that *debates around education need to go well beyond enrolment.* In the Young Lives sample enrolment at primary level education has increased rapidly. This is a success. However, it says little about educational quality or attendance, later drop-out or the differential experience of, or parental investment in, girls and boys. Enrolment is important but not as much as education impact and outcome. Young Lives is finding startling evidence of variations in educational quality and increasing evidence of school performance varying by ethnicity (with both hours and language of tuition emerging as important considerations). Where inequalities widen through the school experience, school is acting to reinforce these differences not to open up life chances – policy makers need to know more about which children get what experience from school and with what result.

Finally, as the Young Lives children grow up we will be able to learn more around how transmission of poverty occurs between generations and therefore what might be done to break poverty cycles. However, one area which already seems clear is how high family and child hopes and aspirations often are compared to the reality of their lives, particularly in relation to the opportunities offered by education. Our next round of data will give us more insights into these issues, as the school, work and family responsibilities of the younger cohort children increase and as the older children start to move from school into the world of work, as their social relationships change and some become betrothed, get married or become parents themselves.

Notes

[1] Young Lives is an international collaboration of research institutes in the four study countries, together with the University of Oxford, the Open University and the international NGO, Save the Children UK. It is core-funded by UK aid from the UK Department for International Development (DFID) from 2001 to 2017, and co-funded by the Netherlands Ministry of Foreign Affairs from 2010 to 2014. Sub-studies are currently funded by the Bernard van Leer Foundation and the Oak Foundation. The views expressed are those of the author(s). They are not necessarily those of, or endorsed by, Young Lives, the University of Oxford, DFID or other donors.

[2] www.esds.ac.uk/international/access/I33379.asp

[3] There is a burgeoning literature that focuses on intergenerational transmission of psychological and psychosocial characteristics, tendencies and behaviours (see Caspi, 2004; Rutter, 2004; Serbin and Karp, 2004). While we recognise the significance of psychological disorders and illnesses on human health, well-being and functioning, we have not chosen to pursue an extensive investigation of mental health, so do not engage these aspects in our focus on contributing factors to intergenerational poverty transmission.

[4] We also have a methodological strand that critically examines our integrated, mixed-methods longitudinal research approach, with an emphasis on the sample frame, ethics, tracking and other elements of design.

[5] Measured by applying the Andhra Pradesh absolute poverty lines from the National Sample Survey Organisation (NSSO) to Young Lives consumption data. Note that this does not necessarily replicate the same level of poverty as in the state since Young Lives captures only households with children and is a pro-poor study.

[6] We are interested in learning about children's well-being in each of these spheres, but also recognise the synergistic relationships between them, for example, the extent to which physical health has an impact on cognition or psychosocial well-being and vice versa to better understand the different outcomes for children.

[7] The majority of child work among Young Lives children involves domestic work within the household, with some participating in paid work.

[8] The trends in pre-school enrolment may seem quite surprising given that our sample is pro-poor, but it needs to be kept in mind that the

age of entry into primary school is quite late in some of our country contexts.

Bibliography

Adler, P.S. and Kwon, S. (2002) 'Social capital: prospects for a new concept', *Academy of Management Review*, vol 27, no 1, pp 17-40.

Allais, F.B. and Hagemann, F. (2008) *Child labour and education: Evidence from SIMPOC Surveys*, IPEC Working Paper, Geneva: International Labour Organization.

Ames, P., Rojas, V. and Portugal, T. (2009) *Starting school: Who is prepared? Young Lives' research on children's transition to first grade in Peru*, Young Lives Working Paper 47, Oxford: Young Lives.

Barnett, I. (2011) *Co-existence of child undernutrition and maternal overweight within the same household: Is it a concern in a pro-poor sample from Ethiopia, India, Peru and Vietnam?*, Young Lives Working Paper 67, Oxford: Young Lives.

Bird, K. (2007) *The intergenerational transmission of poverty: An overview*, ODI Working Paper 286, London: Overseas Development Institute.

Bolin, I. (2006) *Growing up in a culture of respect: Child rearing in Highland Peru*, Austin, TX: University of Texas Press.

Bolt, V.J. and Bird, K. (2003) *The intra-household disadvantages framework: A framework for the analysis of intra-household difference and inequality*, CPRC Working Paper 32, Manchester: Chronic Poverty Research Centre.

Boyden, J. (2009) 'Risk and capability in the context of adversity: children's contributions to household livelihoods in Ethiopia', *Children, Youth and Environments*, vol 19, no 2, pp 111-37.

Boyden, J. and Cooper, E. (2007) *Questioning the power of resilience: Are children up to the task of disrupting the transmission of poverty*, CPRC Working Paper 73, Manchester: Chronic Poverty Research Centre.

Bronfenbrenner, U. (1979) *The ecology of human development: Experiments by nature and design*, London: Harvard University Press.

Camfield, L., Himaz, R. and Murray, H. (2009) *The impact of parental death on child outcomes: Evidence from Ethiopia*, Young Lives Policy Brief 7, Oxford: Young Lives.

Caspi, A. (2004) 'Life-course development: the interplay of social selection and social causation within and across generations', in P.L. Chase-Lansdale, K. Kiernan and R.J. Friedman (eds) *Human development across lives and generations: The potential for change*, Cambridge: Cambridge University Press, pp 8-27.

Corcoran, M.E. (1995) 'Rags to rags: poverty and mobility in the United States', *Annual Review of Sociology*, vol 21, pp 237-67.

Corcoran, M.E. and Chaudry, A. (1997) 'The dynamics of childhood poverty', *Children and Poverty*, vol 7, no 2, pp 40-54.

Crivello, G. (2009) *'Becoming somebody':Youth transitions through education and migration. Evidence from Youth Lives, Peru*, Young Lives Working Paper 43, Oxford:Young Lives.

Crivello, G. and Boyden, J. (2011) *Situating risk in young people's social and moral relationships:Young Lives research in Peru*,Young Lives Working Paper 66, Oxford:Young Lives.

Cueto, S., Guerrero, G., Leon, J., Seguin, E. and Munoz, I. (2009a) 'Explaining and overcoming marginalisation in education: a focus on ethnic/language minorities in Peru', Background Paper to the *Global Monitoring Report 2010*, Paris: UNESCO.

Cueto, S., Guerrero, G., Leon, J., Zevallos, A. and Sugimaru, C. (2009b) *Promoting early childhood development through a public programme: Wawa Wasi in Peru*,Young Lives Working Paper 51, Oxford:Young Lives.

Dawes, A. and Donald, D. (2005) *Improving children's chances: Developmental theory and effective interventions in community contexts*, Virginia, TX: Christian Children's Fund.

Dercon, S. (2004) 'Growth and shocks: evidence from rural Ethiopia', *Journal of Development Economics*, vol 74, pp 309-29.

Dercon, S. (2005) *Vulnerability: A micro perspective*, QEH Working Paper 149, Oxford: Queen Elizabeth House, University of Oxford.

Dercon, S. (2008) *Children and the food price crisis*, Young Lives Policy Brief 5, Oxford:Young Lives.

Dercon, S. and Krishnan, P. (2009) 'Poverty and the psychosocial competencies of children: evidence from the Young Lives sample in four developing countries', *Children, Youth and Environments*, vol 19, no 2, pp 138-63.

De Silva, M. and Harpham, T. (2007) 'Maternal social capital and child nutritional status in four developing countries', *Health and Place*, vol 13, pp 341-55.

DFID, HelpAge International, Hope & Homes for Children, Institute of Development Studies, ILO, Overseas Development Institute, Save the Children UK, UNDP, UNICEF and the World Bank (2009) *Joint statement on advancing child-sensitive social protection* (www.unicef. org/socialpolicy/).

Elder, G.H. (1994) 'Time, human agency, and social change: perspectives on the life course', *Social Psychology Quarterly*, vol 57, no 1, pp 4-15.

Engle, P. (2009) 'Poverty and child development', Paper presented at Young Lives Conference, Focus on Children, Oxford, March.

Escobal, J., Ames, P., Cueto, S., Penny, M. and Flores, E. (2008) *Young Lives: Peru Round 2 survey*, Young Lives Country Report, Oxford: Young Lives.

Filmer, D. (2000) *The structure of social disparities in education: Gender and wealth*, World Bank Policy Research Working Paper 2268, Washington, DC: World Bank.

Galab, S., Prudhvikar Reddy, P. and Himaz, R. (2008) *Young Lives Round 2 survey report initial findings: Andhra Pradesh, India*, Oxford: Young Lives.

Garbarino, J. (1999) 'What children can tell us about the trauma of forced migration', Seminar presented at the Refugee Studies Programme, University of Oxford, November.

Grantham-McGregor, S., Cheung, Y.B., Cueto, S., Glewwe, P., Richter, L., Strupp, B. et al (2007) 'Child development in developing countries 1: developmental potential in the first five years for children in developing countries', *The Lancet*, vol 369, no 9555, pp 60-70.

Harper, C., Marcus, R. and Moore, K. (2003) 'Enduring poverty and the conditions of childhood: lifecourse and intergenerational poverty transmissions', *World Development*, vol 31, no 3, pp 535-54.

Hart, J. (2008) Business as usual? The global political economy of childhood, Young Lives Technical Note 13, Oxford: Young Lives.

Himaz, R. (2009a) *Is there a boy bias in household education expenditure? The case of Andhra Pradesh in India based on Young Lives data*, Young Lives Working Paper 46, Oxford: Young Lives.

Himaz, R. (2009b) *The impact of parental death on schooling and subjective well-being: Evidence from Ethiopia using longitudinal data*, Young Lives Working Paper 44, Oxford: Young Lives.

Ko, I. and Xing, J. (2009) *Extra classes and subjective well-being: Empirical evidence from Vietnamese children*, Young Lives Working Paper 49, Oxford: Young Lives.

Le Thuc, D. (2009) *The effect of early age stunting on cognitive achievement among children in Vietnam*, Young Lives Working Paper 45, Oxford: Young Lives.

Le Thuc, D., Nguyen Phuong, N., Tran Minh, C., Nguyen Van, T. and Vo Thanh, S. (2008) *Young Lives: Vietnam Round 2 survey*, Oxford: Young Lives.

Lieblich, A., Zilber, T.B. and Tuval-Mashiach, R. (2008) 'Narrating human actions: the subjective experience of agency, structure, communion, and serendipity', *Qualitative Inquiry*, vol 14, pp 613-31.

Luthar, S.S., Cicchetti, D. and Becker, B. (2000) 'The construct of resilience: a critical evaluation and guidelines for future work', *Child Development*, vol 71, no 3, pp 543-62.

Mann, G. (2003) *Family matters: The care and protection of children affected by HIV/AIDS in Malawi*, Stockholm: Save the Children Sweden.

Mayer, S.E. and Lopoo, L.M. (2005) 'Has the intergenerational transmission of economic status changed?', *Journal of Human Resources*, vol 40, no 1, pp 169-85.

Moestue, H. and Huttly, S. (2008) 'Adult education and child nutrition: the role of family and community', *Journal of Epidemiology and Community Health*, vol 62, pp 153-9.

Moestue, H., Huttly, S., Sarella, L. and Galab, S. (2007) '"The bigger, the better": mother's social networks and child nutrition in Andhra Pradesh', *Public Health Nutrition*, vol 10, no 11, pp 1274-82.

Moore, K. (2001) *Frameworks for understanding the intergenerational transmission of poverty and well-being in developing countries*, CPRC Working Paper 8, Manchester: Chronic Poverty Research Centre.

Morrow, V. and Vennam, U. (2009) *Children combining work and education in cottonseed production in Andhra Pradesh: Implications for discourses of children's rights in India*, Young Lives Working Paper 50, Oxford: Young Lives.

Nair, A. (2009) *Disadvantaged at birth? The impact of caste on the cognitive development of young children in Andhra Pradesh, India*, Young Lives Student Paper, Oxford: Young Lives.

Nieuwenhuys, O. (1994) *Children's lifeworlds: Gender, welfare and labour in the developing world*, London: Routledge.

Patterson, J.M. (2002) 'Integrating family resilience and family stress theory', *Journal of Marriage and Family*, vol 64, pp 349-60.

Pepper, J.V. (2000) 'The intergenerational transmission of welfare receipt: a nonparametric bounds analysis', *Review of Economics and Statistics*, vol 82, no 3, pp 472-88.

Pollitt, E. (1994) 'Poverty and child development: relevance of research in developing countries to the United States', *Child Development*, vol 65, no 2, pp 283-95.

Popkin, B.M. (2001) 'The nutrition transition and obesity in the developing world', *Journal of Nutrition*, vol 131, pp 871-3.

Popkin, B.M. and Gordon-Larsen, P. (2004) 'The nutrition transition: worldwide obesity dynamics and their determinants', *International Journal of Obesity*, vol 28, pp 2-9.

Ranjan, R. (2009) 'Education and child labor: a global perspective', in H.D. Hindman (ed) *The world of child labor: A reference encyclopedia*, New York: M.E. Sharpe.

Rodgers, J.R. (1995) 'An empirical study of intergenerational transmission of poverty in the United States', *Social Science Quarterly*, vol 76, no 1, pp 178-94.

Rodgers, J.R. and Rodgers, J.L. (1993) 'Chronic poverty in the United States', *The Journal of Human Resources*, vol 28, no 1, pp 25-54.

Rogoff, B. (2003) *The cultural nature of human development*, Oxford and New York: Oxford University Press.

Rose, P. and Dyer, C. (2008) *Chronic poverty and education: A review of the literature*, CPRC Working Paper 131, Manchester: Chronic Poverty Research Centre.

Rutter, M. (2001) 'Psychosocial adversity: risk, resilience and recovery', in J. Richman. and M. Fraser (eds) *The context of youth violence: Resilience, risk and protection*, Westport, CT: Praeger, pp 13-42.

Rutter, M. (2004) 'Intergenerational continuities and discontinuities in psychological problems', in P.L. Chase-Lansdale, K. Kiernan and R.J. Friedman (eds) *Human development across lives and generations: The potential for change*, Cambridge: Cambridge University Press.

Sanchez, A. (2009) *Early nutrition and cognitive achievement in pre-school children in Peru*, Young Lives Working Paper 57, Oxford: Young Lives.

Serbin, L.A. and Karp, J. (2004) 'The intergenerational transfer of psychosocial risk: mediators of vulnerability and resilience', *Annual Review of Psychology*, vol 55, pp 333-63.

Sewell, W.H. (1992) 'A theory of structure: duality, agency, and transformation', *Journal of American Sociology*, vol 98, no 1, pp 1-29.

Shetty, P.S. (2002) 'Nutrition transition in India', *Public Health Nutrition*, vol 5, no 1(A), pp 175-82.

Singh, A. (2008) *Do school meals work? Treatment evaluation of the Midday Meal Scheme in India*, Young Lives Student Paper, Oxford: Young Lives.

Tafere, Y. and Camfield, L. (2009) *Community understandings of children's transitions in Ethiopia: Possible implications for life course poverty*, Young Lives Working Paper 41, Oxford: Young Lives.

Tanner, E.M. and Finn-Stevenson, M. (2002) 'Nutrition and brain development: social policy implications', *American Journal of Orthopsychiatry*, vol 72, no 2, pp 182-93.

Truong, C.H. (2009) 'Schooling as lived and told: contrasting impacts of education policies for ethnic minority children in Vietnam seen from Young Lives surveys', Background Paper to the *Global Monitoring Report 2010*, Paris: UNESCO.

Uppal, V. (2009) *Is the NREGS a safety net for children? Studying the access to the National Rural Employment Guarantee Scheme for the Young Lives Families and its impact on child outcomes in Andhra Pradesh*, Young Lives Student Paper, Oxford: Young Lives.

VanderKloet, M. (2008) *Dual burden of malnutrition in Andhra Pradesh, India: Identification of independent predictors for underweight and overweight in adolescents with overweight mothers*, Young Lives Student Paper, Oxford: Young Lives.

Vennam, U. and Crivello, G. (2009) 'Children's perspectives on risk and vulnerability in contexts of poverty and change', Paper presented at conference on 'The Impact of the Global Food, Fuel, and Financial Crises and Policy Responses', London, 9-10 November.

Vennam, U., Komanduri, A., Cooper, E., Crivello, G. and Woodhead, M. (2009) *Early childhood education trajectories and transitions: A study of the experiences and perspectives of parents and children in Andhra Pradesh, India*, Young Lives Working Paper 52, Oxford: Young Lives.

Victora, C.G., Adair, L., Fall, C., Halla, P., Martorell, R., Richter, L., Saxhdev, H.S. and the Maternal and Child Undernutrition Study Group (2008) 'Maternal and child undernutrition: consequences for adult health and human capital', *The Lancet*, vol 371, no 9609, pp 340-57.

Walker, S., Wachs, T., Meeks Gardner, J., Lozoff, B., Wasserman, G., Pollitt, E. and Carter, J. (2007) 'Child development: risk factors for adverse outcomes in developing countries', *The Lancet*, vol 369, no 9556, pp 145-57.

Walters, L.H. (2007) 'Intergenerational inheritance of poverty: bad news for children, challenges for policy', *Przeglad Socjologiczny (Sociological Review)*, vol 56, no 2, pp 27-42.

WHO/UNICEF (United Nations Children's Fund) (2000) *World report on child injury prevention*, Geneva: World Health Organization.

Wilson, W.J. (1987) *The truly disadvantaged*, Chicago, IL: University of Chicago Press.

Woldehanna, T. (2009) *Productive Safety Net Programme and children's time use between work and schooling in Ethiopia*, Young Lives Working Paper 40, Oxford: Young Lives.

Woldehanna, T., Jones, N. and Tefera, B. (2008a) 'The invisibility of children's paid and unpaid work: implications for Ethiopia's national poverty reduction policy', *Childhood*, vol 15, pp 177-201.

Woldehanna, T., Mekonnen, A. and Alemu, T. (2008b) *Young Lives: Ethiopia Round 2 survey report*, Oxford: Young Lives.

Woldehanna, T., Mekonnen, A. and Jones, N. (2009) 'Education choices in Ethiopia: what determines whether poor households send their children to school?', *Ethiopian Journal of Economics*, vol 17, no 1, pp 43-80.

Woodhead, M. (2009) *Pathways through early childhood education in Ethiopia, India and Peru: Rights, equity and diversity*, Young Lives Working Paper 54, Oxford: Young Lives.

Woodhead, M., Ames, P., Vennam, U., Abebe, B. and Streuli, N. (2009) *Equity and quality? Challenges for early childhood and primary education in Ethiopia, India, and Peru*, Working Papers in Childhood Development 55, The Hague: Bernard van Leer Foundation.

TWENTY

Policy implications of multidimensional poverty measurement in Morocco

Hicham Ait Mansour[1]

Background

During the past 20 years, official poverty rates have changed significantly in Morocco. They increased from 13% to 16% between 1991 and 2001 and then fell to 9% by 2007 (HCP, 2009). The increase between 1991 and 2001 was partly a result of slow economic growth and a decline in household expenditure (World Bank, 2001). Faster economic growth in the following decade coincided with increased household expenditure, and therefore a significant drop in the poverty rate. Total annual household expenditure increased by 2.7%, and total annual expenditure per capita by 5% between 2001 and 2007 (HCP, 2009).

Even though poverty declined significantly during the last decade, tackling poverty remains a policy priority in Morocco. In 2005, Morocco Government launched a National Human Development Initiative,[2] and a National Observatory for Human Development was created in 2006 to monitor human development policies, to strengthen the evaluation of public social policies and to recommend any necessary changes.

Poverty statistics are regularly updated in Morocco providing estimates of the number of people living below the national poverty line and those classified as vulnerable to poverty. However, there are two main problems with these official data: one is the limited unidimensional monetary approach that assumes that the whole population experiences poverty in the same way; the second is a complete absence of data on child poverty. The official national poverty line approach assumes that income is shared equally among all household members, regardless of their age, gender, etc.

Except for a recent Social Policy and Child Rights Forum held by the National Child Rights Observatory and UNICEF, child poverty has never been publicly discussed by policy makers. (UNICEF, ONDE, 2009)

This research represents the first analysis of child poverty in Morocco based on three methods for identifying poor children: a monetary approach using the national poverty line methodology; a deprivation approach based on a child deprivation index; and a combined multidimensional measure including both monetary and deprivation dimensions. The results are based on a secondary data analysis of the 2001 Household Expenditure and Consumption Survey (HCP, 2001a).

Poverty measurement practice in Morocco

Since gaining independence in 1956, poverty in Morocco has been measured using a monetary approach, based on expenditure per capita (Touhami, 2005). The current official methodology for measuring poverty was described in a report published by the Haut Commissariat au Plan (High Commission for Planning, HCP) in 2001. It is a two-stage budget standards method, which consists of first establishing a food poverty line and then a non-food poverty line as a second step. The food poverty line is constructed using the daily food energy intake recommended by the Food and Agriculture Organization (FAO) and the World Health Organization (WHO), which was estimated at 2,400 kcal as an average level of nutritional needs for an adult person.[3] A food basket is constructed and priced which meets this calorific threshold, based on the kinds of foodstuffs purchased by households in the second quintile of total expenditure per capita distribution. According to the HCP, this basket is compatible with the consumption habits of a disadvantaged population, and this method was used to estimate food poverty lines in 1984/85, 1990/91 and 1998/99.

The non-food poverty line is estimated using an Engel coefficient (multiplier) of food consumption (Rao, 1981). The food ratio multiplier is based on the ration of food to non-food expenditure of those households in the bottom quintile of the per capita expenditure distribution who also manage to meet the food poverty line. The poverty line is then established by simply multiplying the food poverty line by the Engel coefficient. Thus a household is considered to be poor when its average total annual expenditure per person is below this poverty amount.

Separate poverty lines are calculated for urban and rural areas, that is, 3,922 dh per person and per year for urban area and 3,037 dh per person and per year for rural area in 1999 (HCP, 2001b).

Lanjouw (2004) described these thresholds as being too conservative. In the geographical poverty mapping conducted by the HCP in 2004 with the technical assistance of the World Bank, the extent of poverty was re-estimated based on alternative poverty lines approximately 50% higher than the national ones (Lanjouw, 2004, p 6).

Poverty in Morocco has fallen significantly since independence in 1956, from 56% in 1959/60 to 18% in 2001. However, due to population growth, the number of poor people has remained virtually unchanged, that is, between four and five million Moroccans have been classified as poor since independence (Touhami, 2005, p 14).

In this research, child poverty in Morocco has been estimated using the same official monetary child poverty household expenditure per capita thresholds. Thus a child is assumed to have the same per capita expenditure needs as an adult.

A breakthrough in international child poverty measurement

Unlike poverty measurement in general, where there is an abundant literature on the different measures that can be applied to distinguish the 'poor' from the 'non-poor', there are very few studies on child poverty measurement (see, for example, Gordon et al, 2003; Minujin et al, 2006).

One of the best-known studies of child poverty supported by UNICEF is *Child poverty in the developing world* (Gordon et al, 2003). It used data from Multiple Indicator Cluster Surveys, Demographic and Health Surveys and similar national surveys, to develop a deprivation scale ranging from 'no deprivation' to 'severe deprivation' based on seven indicators.[4] This study inspired UNICEF's Global Study on Child Poverty and Disparities launched early in 2007, in more than 40 countries in the world.

Methodology used in the present research

This research used a similar methodology to the 1999 Poverty and Social Exclusion Survey (Gordon et al, 2002) to construct a child deprivation index. To date, the measurement of child deprivation has received little attention in Morocco. Therefore, the present research has pioneered the use of the Household Expenditure and Consumption Survey of 2001, which was, at the time of the research, the latest available dataset, to identify indicators that can form a child deprivation index.

An initial list of 18 indicators was identified and these are listed in Table 20.1.

Only the first nine indicators were included in the initial analysis (see the pre-final list below). Of course, other indicators can be relevant to our index but were not included either because data were not available or the way it was collected could bias the analysis. For example, economic and social conditions, as well as perception of head of household indicators, as listed above (9-18 in Table 20.1), were excluded because the survey respondents were asked to choose only three items they thought they would have difficulty in affording, compared to the last 10 years; it is not possible to have data on all items households cannot or think they cannot afford, and among the three items they reported, it was not possible to determine the items' order of importance.

The final index was tested to assess its validity and reliability. A reliability analysis was run on the nine-deprivation index, resulting in

Table 20.1: Domains and indicators of child deprivation in Morocco, 2001

Domains	Indicators
Housing	1. Live in a household with three people per room (UN Habitat definition)
	2. Live in a household without a toilet
	3. Closest water source within 30 minute distance or unimproved source (WHO/UNICEF definition)
	4. Live in a household without electricity
	5. Live in a shack or a slum or a room in an establishment or premises not for residential use
Employment	6. All working-age people within the household unemployed
Education	7. Children aged 6-15 who are not in school or have never been to school (primary, secondary). (Moroccan law states that education is compulsory for all children up to 15 years old)
Health	8. Has not seen a doctor while sick in the last two months
	9. Does not have access to social security (medical insurance)
Economic and social conditions	10. Has difficulties buying food compared to the last 10 years
	11. Has difficulties buying clothes compared to the last 10 years
	12. Has difficulties paying for rent/accommodation cost or purchase household equipment
	13. Has difficulties paying school fees
	14. Has difficulties paying for medical care and medication costs
	15. Has difficulties paying for transports fees
	16. Has difficulties paying for entertainment
	17. Anxious about cost of living
	18. Anxious about shortage of money

Source: HCP, Household Expenditure and Consumption Survey, Questionnaires, 2001

a Cronbach's alpha of 0.57. After removing two items from the scale, the overall alpha rose to 0.6, which is the highest value that can be obtained with a seven-item scale. The two indicators removed were:

- All working age within the household unemployed.
- Have not seen a doctor while sick in the last two months.

The final index was constructed using the seven following indicators:

- Closest water source within 30-minute distance or unimproved source.
- Lives in a household without electricity.
- Lives in a household without a toilet.
- Children aged 6-17 who are not in school or have never been to school.[5]
- Does not have access to social security (medical insurance).
- Lives in a shack or slum.
- More than three people per room.

Even though the final value of alpha was lower than 0.7 (regarded by social scientists as the desirable level to classify a given index as 'reliable'),[6] we believe the resulting seven-item index to be reliable, as 0.6 reflects the highest possible value obtainable with currently available data and a balanced trade-off between validity and reliability. It can therefore be used to assess child poverty in terms of multiple deprivations in Morocco.

The percentage of children living below the official food ratio poverty line was 21%, as shown in Table 20.2.

In terms of multiple deprivations, Figure 20.1 shows that deprivation increases with expenditure poverty. For example, 21% of children who are expenditure poor (the percentage of children below the poverty line) also suffer from two deprivations, 29% from three deprivations, 36% from four deprivations and 45% from five deprivations. There is a low correlation between expenditure poverty and deprivation. Spicker (2007, p 36) argues that no clear threshold or cut-off points can be established with certainty for any deprivation measure; however, it is recognised that, where there is poverty, there will be more than one problem or deprivation. In this research, given the high rates of deprivation using

Table 20.2: Expenditure child poverty line in Morocco, 2001 (%) (*n*=35,017)

	%
Not poor	79
Poor	21
Total	100

Source: Household Expenditure and Consumption Survey 2001 (weighted)

Figure 20.1: Poverty line and deprivation score, 2001 (%) (*n*=35,017)

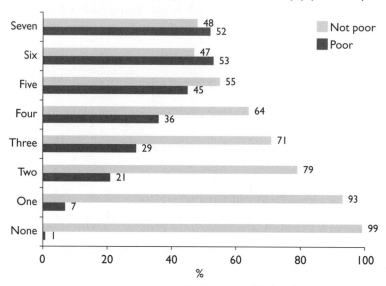

Source: Household Expenditure and Consumption Survey, 2001 (weighted)

a threshold established at two deprivations or more (about 60%) and relatively low child expenditure poverty, the cut-off is rather established at three deprivations or more.

Source of data

This research used the Household Expenditure and Consumption Survey 2001, which was the latest available at the time. The final datasets include 14,243 completed questionnaires, with a non-response rate of 5% (nearer 8% in urban areas and less than 2% in rural areas). The file includes information on 85,412 individuals, of which 35,017 were under 18 years old. As the focus of this research is on child poverty, the final selected and merged files included 35,017 children aged from 0 to 18.[7]

Summary of findings by sociodemographic characteristics

Figure 20.2 shows that gender is not a determinant of child poverty in Morocco – both boys and girls had similar poverty rates with all three measures. Children aged between 15 and 18 were slightly less likely to be poor than those aged between 0 and 5 years old, 19% compared with

Figure 20.2: Monetary, deprivation and multidimensional child poverty by sex, age group and area of residence in Morocco, 2001 (%) (n=35,017)

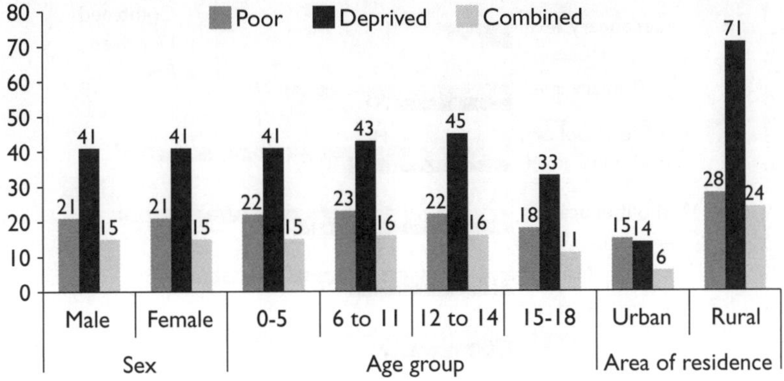

Source: Household Expenditure and Consumption Survey, 2001 (weighted)

22% for expenditure poverty, 33% compared with 41% for multiple deprivation, and 12% against 15% for combined multidimensional poverty. Children living in rural areas were much more likely to be poor than those living in urban areas across all three measures, at 28% against 15% for expenditure poverty, 71% against 14% in terms of multiple deprivation and 24% against 6% for combined poverty. This shows the huge disparities between rural and urban areas especially in terms of multiple deprivations.

In terms of head of household characteristics, Figure 20.3 shows that poor children across the three measures were more likely to live with a married, male and 'with no education' head of household. The poorest children also lived in large households of more than seven people, although this pattern was not as strong for the combined multidimensional poor compared with multiple deprivations where the rates were the highest.

As far as the regional distribution of poverty is concerned, Table 20.3 shows that this differs depending on which measure is used. For expenditure poverty, the three poorest regions were Meknes Tafilalet at 32%, Gharb-Cherarda-Benihssen at 30% and Oriental at 27%, whereas the most deprived regions were Taza-Al Hoceima-Taounate at 67%, Doukkala-Abda at 54% and Gharb-Chrarda-Beni Hssen at 52%. On a multidimensional measure of poverty, the worst regions for children were Gharb-Chrarda-Beni Hssen at 24%, Marrakech-Tensift- Al Haouz at 20% and Meknes Tafilalet at 19%. The three regions with the lowest

Figure 20.3: Expenditure poverty by head of household characteristics in Morocco, 2001 (%) (*n*=35,017)

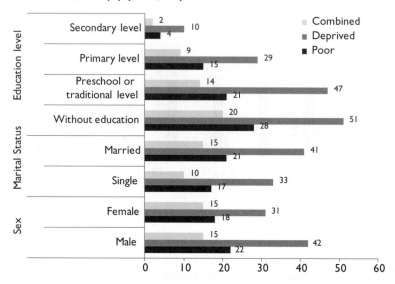

Source: Household Expenditure and Consumption Survey, 2001 (weighted)

Table 20.3: Monetary, deprivation and multidimensional child poverty by region in Morocco, 2001 (%) (*n*=35,017)

	Poor		Deprived		Combined	
Region	%	Rank	%	Rank	%	Rank
Meknes Tafilalet	32	12	36	5	19	7
Gharb-Chrarda-Béni Hssen	30	11	52	10	24	9
Marrakech-Tensift-Al Haouz	27	10	50	9	20	8
Oriental	27	10	37	6	17	6
Souss-Massa-Draâ	25	9	36	5	17	6
Fès-Boulemane	24	8	29	4	12	3
Doukkala-Abda	22	7	54	11	17	6
Chaouia-Ouardigha	20	6	49	8	15	5
Tanger-Tétouan	20	6	43	7	14	4
Taza-Al Hoceima-Taounate	18	5	67	12	17	6
Tadla Azilal	15	4	49	8	12	3
Rabat-Salé-Zemmour-Zaer	13	3	27	3	8	2
South Provinces of Sahara	11	2	21	2	4	1
Grand Casablanca	7	1	16	1	4	1

Source: Household Expenditure and Consumption Survey 2001 (weighted)

poverty rates, regardless of the measure applied, were Grand Casablanca, Rabat-Salé-Zemmour-Zaer and South Provinces of Sahara.

Except for the regional distribution of child poverty, most sociodemographic predictors used in this research identify the same groups as being poor. However, the rates of child poverty varied significantly from one measure to another. For example, when we used the deprivation approach, 41% of children were poor against 21% living in expenditure poverty. Area of residence was an important determinant of child poverty from a deprivation perspective since 71% of rural children were deprived against only 14% for those living in urban areas. Also, 51% of deprived children lived with an uneducated head of household against 28% for those classified as monetary poor and 20% for children suffering from combined poverty.

Generally speaking, the combined poverty measure shows relatively lower child poverty rates than with the other two measures. However, unidimensional measurements might obscure the number of children who might not be poor in terms of monetary approach but who are living in deprived circumstances. Figure 20.4 shows that 15% of children were both monetary and deprivation poor, 7% were monetary poor but had better living conditions (not deprived), whereas 26% of Moroccan children were not monetary poor, thus did not appear in official poverty statistics but their living conditions had deteriorated (deprived). Their families might have had financial resources to spend but they and the government did not invest in a better standard of living for their children. Therefore, these children need policies that

Figure 20.4: Combined child poverty estimates in Morocco, 2001 (%) (n=35,017)

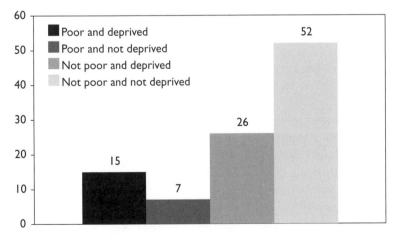

Source: Household Expenditure and Consumption Survey, 2001 (weighted)

focus on improving standards of living, in particular access to quality social services. These results are discussed below.

Policy implications

As shown above, children experience poverty differently. Some are monetary poor but are not deprived, some are deprived but are not monetary poor and others are both monetary poor and deprived. This requires child poverty targeting offering different policy options for these different groups.

However, before presenting policy recommendations, it is important to acknowledge the limitation of data from cross-sectional surveys, which provide only an overall picture of the proportions of the population living in poverty but do not allow us to identify changes over time. These limitations have implications for poverty targeting, thus the following recommendations should be understood bearing these limitations in mind (see also the recommendations related to data and further analyses).

For children who are 'monetary poor' but not deprived

Children (and their families) identified as monetary poor but not deprived might actually have seen their income dramatically decrease at the time of the survey but their living conditions had not yet deteriorated. If they did not increase their income, they would become extremely poor (in terms of both income and living conditions). For this group, the best policy would be to help these families to raise their income as soon as possible. For example, targeted income generation activities can be designed as well as enhancing child benefit schemes to make sure children from these households continue to access quality basic social services. Social protection schemes are vital to protect children's rights, because families who lose their income might stop sending children to school and encourage them to engage in child labour.

Furthermore, in the absence of a well-designed social protection policy with a sophisticated targeting methodology, this group of children should also be eligible for conditional cash transfers which are currently being tested in Morocco. This is important because, while many children within this group might still be going to school, they should be prioritised by these kinds of social protection programmes to protect them from dropping out of school.

The government should also consider establishing a child benefit scheme for children whose parents are self-employed or work in sectors where this kind of scheme does not exist (agriculture, informal sector, etc). The largest proportion of these children lives in rural areas. Child benefits could significantly improve the standards of living of families and allow children to enjoy their rights.

For children who are deprived but are not monetary poor

This group of children and their families might have increased their income but still need time to improve their living conditions and should be supported substantially to raise their living conditions and prevent them entering into monetary poverty. They should be targeted by human development programmes, for example, the National Human Development Initiative[8] launched in 2005 to reduce extreme poverty and vulnerability in both rural and urban areas. This initiative was based on 'expenditure' poverty mapping and did not use any deprivation index or variables that were child-centred; it is therefore likely that many communes and districts with large proportions of deprived children are excluded from the initiatives and programmes of the National Human Development Initiative. So the poverty map should be updated by including a child deprivation index and extending future human development policies to deprived children. Even if they are not poor, this group of children is not enjoying their rights to basic social services and to activities that enable them to be active players in their society. If their needs are not addressed they will be chronically excluded which will affect their development and this will also end up affecting wider society.

To take the discussion about deprivation reduction policies a bit further, simulations were run on the child deprivation index to test the effect of fixing each deprivation (giving the value of 0 = eradicated) on the overall child deprivation rate. In the original deprivation index, the absolute deprivation rate, with a threshold of three or more deprivations, was 41%. Table 20.4 shows how the estimate of absolute poverty might change if no children were exposed to particular deprivations, that is, if individual deprivations were eradicated.

Table 20.4 shows that if overcrowding (more than three people per room) deprivation was eradicated, the overall 2001 deprivation rate would have dramatically decreased from 41% to 29%. With medical insurance deprivation eradicated, this rate would have fallen to 31%; with education deprivation eradicated, the absolute poverty estimate would have decreased to 34%. Since 2001 and given different policies

Table 20.4: Absolute poverty rates after simulations of each deprivation eradicated

	%
Absolute poverty with all deprivations (+3)	41
Absolute poverty with dwelling deprivation eradicated	38
Absolute poverty with water deprivation eradicated	35
Absolute poverty with sanitation deprivation eradicated	35
Absolute poverty with education deprivation eradicated	34
Absolute poverty with electricity deprivation eradicated	31
Absolute poverty with medical insurance deprivation eradicated	31
Absolute poverty with density (nppr[a]=3+) deprivation eradicated	29

Source: Household Expenditure and Consumption Survey 2001 (weighted)
Note: [a]number of people per room.

which have been designed and implemented, poverty in general and deprivation in particular might have been reduced significantly (monetary poverty dropped from 15% to 9% between 2001 and 2007) (HCP 2009). However, the simulations presented above show that it is possible to prioritise some areas (that is, housing, medical insurance and education) that have a greater impact on overall child well-being.

For children who are both poor and deprived

Pantazis et al (2006) defined poverty as a situation which combines both monetary poverty and low living conditions. This group of children and their families, who are both monetary poor and deprived, suffer from an extreme form of poverty. These children need to be targeted both in terms of income generation for their families and in terms of living standards by enabling them to access quality social services and activities that are likely to improve their development at all levels. This group should obviously be the top priority in any anti-poverty policy both at central and subnational level.

For geographical distribution of child poverty

The findings of this research showed great variations in child poverty estimates among different regions in Morocco. Regions identified as being the poorest in terms of expenditure poverty are sometimes different from those identified by the child deprivation and multidimensional child poverty measure. Therefore, a combined child poverty measure should be constructed that takes into account the context of each region and subregion. This might have significant implications in terms of resource allocation to anti-poverty programmes among regions, provinces and communes. This becomes increasingly important given the advanced regionalisation being implemented in Morocco to create 12 regions instead of 16, which will have stronger policy attribution at regional level, as well as greater accountabilities (that is, presidents of regions will be elected through universal direct suffrage).[9]

For child poverty data collection and analysis

In general terms, every policy that aims to target the right groups identified as living in poverty should be based on evidence. As demonstrated in this research, expenditure poverty measurement is not sufficient to identify poor children. A move towards a more comprehensive measure of poverty, including both monetary and non-monetary dimensions, is essential.

It should be noted that child poverty has received little attention in Morocco so far, except for a study conducted by UNICEF in 2009 and presented in the first Social Policy and Child Rights Forum[10] and an ongoing research study by the HCP, in collaboration with UNICEF (2010-11), official poverty statistics are being collected, analysed and published in terms of the overall population including children. There are no child poverty estimates published regularly, and children appear only in age categories tabulations using the same definition (that is, household expenditure thresholds) applied to adults to identify the poor and non-poor within the Moroccan population.

Also, it is widely accepted that children experience poverty differently to adults and even within different groups of children (that is, urban−rural, level of available resources to the family, etc). In order to ensure than no child is left out, child poverty estimates should be produced separately using a combined method to make children living in poverty visible.

Further pre-requisites for child poverty measurement

A review of existing resources in terms of poverty research in Morocco shows that the only measure of poverty being used to identify the poor is the monetary approach (expenditure-based measurement). In order to allow a more appropriate measure of poverty in general and child poverty in particular, further work should be done to construct deprivation indices adapted to the Moroccan context, and these should be incorporated into national surveys. It was also mentioned in the beginning of this section that cross-sectional surveys only provide an overall picture of the poor population at a given point in time but not who is entering or exiting from poverty and who is persisting in poverty. The Household Panel Survey that will be launched early in 2012 by the Human Observatory of Human Development[11] will fill this knowledge gap in the next few years.

A second aspect is related to the necessity of making datasets available to researchers, encouraging a national research agenda on poverty. This is important in order to increase the evidence base on poverty in Morocco and to establish a culture of using research to inform policy making. So far very little academic research exists that has affected the quality of analysis and measurement and the national debate on poverty in general.

Further work to be done

Although the present research pioneered a combined measure of child poverty including both monetary poverty and multiple deprivations, it did not explore all potential dimensions of child poverty. Future research needs to investigate the dynamics of child poverty. This will help evaluate public policies targeting children and particularly anti-poverty policies.

To explore in-depth causes of child poverty, qualitative research should be undertaken involving children to see how they experience poverty and how they define it, and these views should be incorporated into the definition and measurement of child poverty. An appropriate child deprivation index for Morocco should therefore be constructed using both qualitative and quantitative methods.

Finally, this research was the first study to explore multidimensional child poverty using both monetary and multiple deprivation dimensions[12] that gave place to a closer collaboration with the HCP to institutionalise multidimensional child poverty measurement in Morocco. This collaboration was recently expanded to a much larger study between UNICEF Morocco, the UNICEF Innocenti Research Centre in Florence, Italy and the HCP.

Notes

[1] This chapter is based on research undertaken as part of a postgraduate degree at the School for Policy Studies, University of Bristol, while I was working for the United Nations Children's Fund (UNICEF) Morocco as Monitoring, Evaluation and Social Policy Specialist. I

would sincerely like to thank Professor Dave Gordon from the School for Policy Studies, who supervised this research and provided me with substantial advice, orientation and constant support. Thanks to him I was able to gain confidence in doing research in the difficult and complex area of poverty measurement. Very special thanks also to Dr Shailen Nandy, also from the School for Policy Studies, who provided informed and useful feedback through all the stages of the research, with rare patience and also friendship. I am grateful to Dr Mohamed Taamouti, Director of Statistics, High Commission of Planning (Haut Commissariat au Plan) in Morocco, and Professors Abdelkhalek Touhami and Abdeslam Fazouane from the National Institute of Statistics and Applied Economics in Rabat, Morocco, who provided invaluable advice in the dataset cleaning stage and feedback on earlier analyses. Finally, many thanks to the British Council Morocco for funding the first year of my postgraduate studies in Bristol.

[2] The INDH was launched following a speech by King Mohamed VI about the seriousness of the social situation in Morocco. For details about the National Human Development Initiative, see www.indh.ma

[3] The latest Household Living Standards Survey (2007) used 1,984 kcal, instead of 2,400 used in 2001; both food energy intake thresholds were referred to by the HCP as recommended by the FAO and WHO and no explanation was provided to justify this adjustment of threshold. To allow accurate comparison with previous years, poverty thresholds from 1984 to 2007 were revised accordingly as follows: 1984 (urban: 1,760 dh, rural: 1,604 dh), 1991 (urban: 2,725 dh, rural: 2,439 dh), 1999 (urban: 3,700 dh, rural: 2,921 dh), 2001 (urban: 3,421 dh, rural: 3,098 dh), 2007 (urban: 3,834 dh, rural: 3,568 dh). This research maintained the old 2001 threshold as mentioned above.

[4] See Chapter Four, this volume.

[5] Children aged from 0 to 6 were given the value of 0 (not deprived) as they were too young to go to school. They were not removed from the definition to avoid problems of missing data on the overall deprivation score. Children aged 15 to 18 were also kept in the analysis for the same purpose; the proportion of those deprived within this category are less 2%.

[6] For example, Garmines and Zeller (1994, p 41) state that it is believed reliability should not fall below 0.8 for widely used scales but mention that it is costly to try to obtain a higher level value. They stressed that it is more important to report how it was calculated to allow other

researchers to make their judgement whether the scale was appropriate or not for any given purpose.

[7] An analysis file was created by merging the household and individual datasets using SPSS Version 16, which includes demographic characteristics, housing, energy use, education and health as well as economic and social conditions.

[8] www.indh.ma

[9] www.regionalisationavancee.ma

[10] http://sites.google.com/site/globalstudy2/moroccosocialpolicy

[11] www.ondh.ma

[12] UNICEF conducted a first study in 2007-08 using a multiple deprivation approach applied to Multiple Indicator Cluster Survey 2006 datasets that did not include all relevant indicators and did not have a monetary component.

References

Bland, J.M. and Altman, D. (1997) 'Statistics notes: Cronbach's alpha', *British Medical Journal*, vol 314, p 572.

Carmines, E.G. and Zeller, R.A. (1994) Reliability and validity assessment. In: M.S. Lewis–Beck (ed) *Basic Measurement*. London Sage Publications, pp 1–58.

Gordon, D. (2002) 'The international measurement of poverty and anti-poverty policies', in P. Townsend and D. Gordon (eds) World poverty: New policies to defeat an old enemy, Bristol: The Policy Press, pp 53-80.

Gordon, D., Nandy, S., Pantazis, C., Pemberton, S. and Townsend, P. (2003) *Child poverty in the developing world*, Bristol: The Policy Press.

HCP (Haut Commissariat au Plan) (2001a) *Rapport de synthèse de l'Enquête des Dépenses et de Consommation des Ménages*, Maroc: Direction de la Statistique.

HCP (2001b) *Analyse du profil et de la dynamique de la pauvreté: Un fondement, de l'Atténuation des Dénuements*, Maroc: Direction de la Statistique.

HCP (2009) *Evolution des niveaux de vie, des inégalités et de la pauvreté au Maroc Enquête des niveaux de vie des ménages, 2007, Résultats préliminaires*, Maroc: Direction de la Statistique.

Lanjouw, P. (2004) *The geography of poverty in Morocco: Micro-level estimates of poverty and inequality from combined census and household survey data*, Washington, DC: Development Research Group, World Bank.

Minujin, A., Delamonica, E.E. and Komarecki, M. (eds) (2006) *Poverty and children: Policies to break the vicious cycle*, New York: The New School and the United Nations Children's Fund.

Pantazis, C., Gordon, D. and Levitas, R. (2006) *Poverty and Social Exclusion in Britain: The millennium survey*, Bristol: The Policy Press.

Rao, V.V. (1981) 'Measurement of deprivation and poverty based on the proportion spent on food – an exploratory exercise', *World Development*, vol 9, no 4, pp 337-53.

Spicker, P. (2007) *The idea of poverty*, Bristol: The Policy Press.

Touhami, A. (2005) 'La pauvreté au Maroc', in 50 ans de développement humain et perspectives 2025, Maroc: Rapports Thématiques, Pauvreté et Facteurs d'Exclusion Sociales (www.rdh50.ma/fr/gt07.asp).

UNICEF (United Nations Children's Fund) and Observatoire National des Droits de l'Enfant (2009) *Impact de la pauvreté et des disparités sur l'enfant au Maroc*, Maroc: Résultats Préliminaires.

World Bank (2001) *Poverty update, Morocco, Volume 1: Main report, Middle East and North Africa*, Washington, DC: Human Development Sector.

TWENTY-ONE

A multidimensional response to tackling child poverty and disparities: reflections from the Global Study on Child Poverty and Disparities

Gaspar Fajth, Sharmila Kurukulasuriya and Sólrún Engilbertsdóttir[1]

This chapter describes the United Nations Children's Fund's (UNICEF) Global Study on Child Poverty and Disparities, a coordinated international effort to highlight the nature and extent of multidimensional child poverty, and explores how national policies can address poverty and disparities.

Introduction

Despite strong economic growth in many developing nations over the last decade, progress towards the Millennium Development Goals (MDGs) has been uneven. Inequities have persisted or even increased, in part because economic and social policies and programmes have not always reached disadvantaged communities and vulnerable groups, particularly children. The recent global economic crisis has exacerbated these trends. Emerging evidence suggests setbacks in human development gains among the poorest communities. Since children experience all forms of poverty more acutely than adults, there needs to be greater understanding of how child deprivations relate to family and community deprivations, as well as how child deprivations are linked to weaknesses in public policies.

There is a critical time in childhood where failure to intervene can have irreversible impacts on capabilities and quality of life. Although protecting the rights of all children and reducing social inequities in progress towards the MDGs are acknowledged needs, strong evidence on how to do so is sparse. It is against this backdrop that UNICEF initiated the Global Study on Child Poverty and Disparities.[2]

The study commenced at the end of 2007. It was intended to speak on behalf of the world's most vulnerable children, and to leverage evidence, analysis, policies and partnerships to deliver results for them. In accordance with the principle of equity for all children, the study has had the following objectives:

- to identify disadvantaged and vulnerable children using a comprehensive framework that captures the most significant deprivations;
- to better understand the determinants of child poverty and underlying disparities; and
- to influence economic and social policies that will reduce child deprivations.

The Global Study began in 39 countries. Since then, it has spurred further interest − as of 2012, 54 countries are participating (see Figure 21.1).[3] They represent over 1.5 billion children under the age of 18, or approximately 60% of the child population in the developing world. In many participating countries, the study is the first comprehensive look at child poverty and disparities.

Figure 21.1: Countries participating in the Global Study on Child Poverty and Disparities

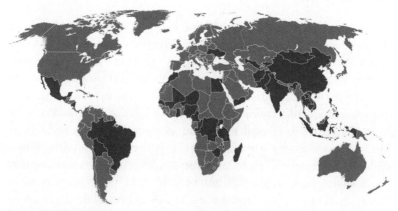

Source: UNICEF (2010b)

Defining child poverty

It is well documented that poverty has detrimental impacts on children, who have greater vulnerabilities due to their age, special development needs and dependency. The first step to address child poverty is to define and measure it. *The State of the World's Children 2005* report, *Childhood under threat*, set the precedent for UNICEF's focus on child poverty, presenting the following definition:

> Children living in poverty experience deprivation of the material, spiritual and emotional resources needed to survive, develop and thrive, leaving them unable to enjoy their rights, achieve their full potential or participate as full and equal members of society.[4] (UNICEF, 2005)

This conceptualisation is intrinsically multidimensional. Although research has shown striking effects from substituting love and stimulation for material needs among young children, it is clear that the three distinct resources in the definition are not entirely fungible, and that children need each type to survive and develop normally. The UNICEF understanding of child poverty, therefore, goes beyond the traditional material concept of poverty and resists a unidimensional scale.[5]

Since these three key elements influence children's well-being, it is critical to measure each. Given limits on the availability of data and ability to measure some dimensions, both qualitative and quantitative methods are important. The more accurate the measurement of child poverty, the more likely that policy makers will focus their attention on issues relevant to the rights and well-being of children. A focus on generating economic growth may have some impact on income poverty, for example, but may not necessarily reduce the multiple deprivations that children face or address the links among them.

The Global Study on Child Poverty and Disparities has worked towards applying the UNICEF definition of child poverty by combining income–consumption poverty and multiple deprivation concepts. For measuring multidimensional poverty, the Global Study guide recommends that participating countries combine income poverty figures with the University of Bristol approach to child poverty, which looks into child deprivations through the following critical dimensions: shelter, sanitation, safe drinking water, information, food, education and health. The study uses newly generated evidence on child poverty and disparities from sources such as the UNICEF-supported Multiple Indicator Cluster Surveys and the Demographic and Health Surveys.

Figure 21.2 illustrates links among the multiple deprivations and household income. Out of these eight dimensions, three provide insights into individual deprivations – health, food and education. The other five measure child deprivations at the household level. These show a

Figure 21.2: Eight dimensions of multidimensional child poverty

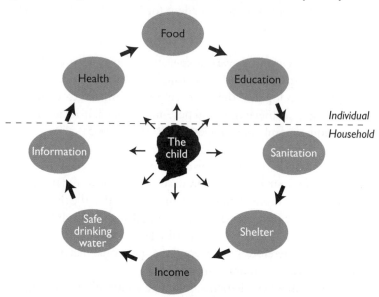

Source: Global Study on Child Poverty and Disparities

higher or lower *probability* of intergenerational effects, for example, lack of safe drinking water or adequate income in a household where a child lives is a deprivation in its own right. It also increases the probability that children will have poor nutrition, health or education outcomes.

Unlike individual deprivations, household deprivations may have varying impacts on individuals. Other factors in child well-being (including non-material factors such as cohesion, care, love, inspiration and stimulation) could neutralise their influence.

By making a distinction between individual and household level child poverty, the Global Study encourages participating countries to explore different perspectives (Fajth and Holland, 2007) and policies best suited to addressing different deprivations. A related issue is the overlap of multiple deprivations. Understanding their compounding effects is a powerful way to identify the most vulnerable populations and the underlying reasons for inequities.

To address links between outcomes and policies, the Global Study looks at gaps and opportunities in National Poverty Reduction Strategies, demographic and economic contexts, employment, public and private social expenditures, fiscal space and foreign aid. The study considers how public policies could more effectively reduce child deprivations by providing better services and protection for all families caring for children. It assesses which policies and programmes most effectively support the rights of all children, girls and boys, in different contexts (UNICEF, 2007).

In promoting stronger national policy responses and international collaboration to reduce and eventually eliminate the strikingly high levels of child poverty and deprivation, the study makes two assumptions: (a) that political will and domestic and/or external resources could be mobilised through concrete proposals and initiatives to improve, within a reasonably short time, the lives of vulnerable children and disadvantaged communities; and (b) that such interventions would be politically, financially and technically easier to achieve for children than for the population in general. The country level analyses aim to explore a comprehensive policy approach where progress in different sectors would have a synergistic effect on other sectors, and reduce inefficiencies and gaps.

The fact that the Global Study guide starts with an analysis of macroeconomic policies underscores that a child focus should influence decisions even at this level. Such an emphasis is rare, as those who make decisions at that level may not be aware of the potential impacts on children.

Another challenge comes from the methodological difficulties of operationalising a global concept. In many middle-income countries, for example, deprivation thresholds developed for low-income countries do not adequately capture the problems children experience. Under the Global Study, country analyses provided critical inputs into making methodological adjustments so that available child poverty measures would be more robust.

Guiding principles

The Global Study has become far more than a research exercise over its lifetime. It has spurred a dynamic process involving government partners, academia, civil society and other stakeholders, as well as other international agencies and providers of international development assistance.

Its four central tenets are:

- *Ownership:* although children's rights are universal, every country participating in the study has its own history, culture and sense of responsibility for its citizens. The analyses aim to stimulate discussion and provide evidence on how best to realise child rights in each country.

- *Multidimensionality:* no single measure can fully reflect the poverty that children experience. A multidimensional approach is therefore imperative to effectively understand and measure children's well-being, and the various forms of poverty that they experience.
- *Equity:* the analysis aims to encourage policies that reduce disparities, in order to protect the future of children living in poor, vulnerable households, unsafe circumstances and/or disadvantaged communities.
- *Interconnectedness:* today's world is increasingly interconnected through economic, social, technological, environmental, epidemiological, cultural and knowledge exchanges. These exchanges have important implications for child poverty and can also help provide avenues for its reduction.

The focus on national ownership allows the Global Study to extend far beyond UNICEF, advancing work with colleagues and partners who engage in and shape different aspects of national policy-making processes. Ultimately, the initiative has generated evidence, insights and networks that can be used to influence national development plans, poverty reduction or sector-wide strategies, common country assessments and other development instruments. In this way, the study helps bring a child's face into fora essential for progress towards the MDGs (UNICEF, 2007).

In each country participating in the study, a national statistical and policy team, in collaboration with the UNICEF country office, carries out evidence-based analysis as part of a national study summarised in a country report. New partnerships with representatives from the ministries of finance and planning, national statistical offices and national universities have been fostered through this process. The country teams enhance technical capacities through various national, regional and global initiatives.

To achieve national ownership and capacity development, participating countries identified several important elements:

- From the onset, the study needed to be conducted in a participatory manner; it is essential to include policy makers in particular. This helps increase the relevance of the study recommendations.
- Buy-in from relevant line ministries is essential, including through a focal point within each ministry. This helps sensitise key stakeholders on the purpose of the study.
- Analysis should be adapted to the country context, which may involve modifying the deprivation thresholds, adjusting the statistical and policy templates, and so on.

- A technical/steering committee comprised of key stakeholders needs to be involved throughout the process, not only for review and endorsement of a final product, but also to regularly meet and review progress made.
- The composition and reputation of the research team are key factors in ensuring the study reaches its advocacy goals (UNICEF, 2010a).

A number of Global Study country teams were able to effectively follow participatory processes to ensure national ownership of the study findings (see Box 21.1).

Box 21.1 The centrality of national ownership

A strong and vibrant working group was crucial for the study in *Bangladesh*. The group consisted of government officials (particularly from the Ministry of Planning), UNICEF staff, representatives from development organisations and the analytical team. From this working group, a smaller core group was formed, which helped expedite the study.

In *Thailand*, the study is fully 'owned' by the government within the National Economic and Social Development Board (NESDB). From the onset, NESDB senior officials encouraged staff to actively participate in the study as an opportunity to build their research capacities, and enhance their knowledge on child and youth issues. Focus group meetings were organised with key government agencies, academia, non-governmental organisations (NGOs) and youth groups. They made recommendations on plans and programmes most relevant to child and youth development.

In *China*, government partners supported by UNICEF's technical team organised and implemented the study. The process developed capacities among government counterparts, who agreed on a new concept of child poverty and initiated a process to advocate that top leaders incorporate child sensitive programmes in the next 10-year national poverty alleviation strategy, which has been positively received.

In the *Democratic Republic of Congo*, the study was carried out in a participatory process where a team of four national experts, coordinated by a senior researcher from the University of Kinshasa, worked together with UNICEF staff. The Ministry of Planning took the lead and managed the study, involving the Ministries of Education, Health, Social Affairs, Budget and Finance. Additionally, experts from the National Institute of Statistics were involved. UN agencies participated throughout the process.

(continued)

Nepal's steering committee demonstrates how heavily involved government counterparts can be. The National Planning Commission is the lead government agency; representatives come from the Ministry of Women, Children and Social Welfare; the Ministry of Health; the Central Child Welfare Board; the Ministry of Local Development; and the Ministry of Home Affairs.

Forging strategic partnerships

The Global Study has provided a platform for new strategic partnerships around addressing child poverty and disparities. In most countries, this work has helped bring key stakeholders together, both governmental and non-governmental, and strengthened collaboration across line ministries.

Regional partnerships have also developed. In Latin America and the Caribbean, UNICEF joined the UN Economic Commission for Latin America and the Caribbean (ECLAC) to carry out the 'Child poverty in Latin America and the Caribbean' study, the first comparative report on child poverty in the region (UNICEF, 2010i). UNICEF joined the Indian Ocean Child Rights Observatory to produce a comprehensive study on child poverty and disparities in Comoros, La Reunion, Madagascar, Mauritius and Seychelles.

A number of high-level policy fora have referred to study findings. The 2009 regional conference 'Achieving Child Well-being and Equity in South Asia' emphasised that regional analysis of child poverty and disparities is paramount to advocating for child well-being. In China, an international policy seminar, 'Anti-poverty and Early Childhood Development', and the 'Child Poverty and Development Training Seminar' helped promote understanding of the multiple dimensions of poverty and remaining child poverty challenges as observed by authors of this chapter.

Efforts to create a dynamic community of practice on child poverty have included launching a number of platforms, such as a blog for exchanging country experiences, useful resources and tools for analysis (UNICEF, 2010b). In 2008, UNICEF's Division of Policy and Practice launched a Child Poverty Network that encourages discussions on approaches, analytical frameworks and measurement issues surrounding child poverty and disparities in varying country contexts. It draws on cutting-edge research on child poverty and disparities, and facilitates the exchange of news and information on workshops, meetings, publications and other resources. The network now links over 1,200 members from over 150 countries. Members comprise development professionals from national governments, UN agencies and other international organisations, academia, NGOs and research institutes.

A new bimonthly online publication, *Child Poverty Insights*, explores key issues related to understanding the underlying causes of child poverty, its measurement and related policy responses.

Using a multidimensional lens

The findings of the Global Study have provided compelling evidence for measuring child poverty using a multidimensional approach. Initial findings from Morocco show that 17% of children there suffer from at least two deprivations, while only 9% are poor using the national income poverty line. The findings were disseminated in Morocco's first Social Policy and Child Rights Forum, which marked a shift in the national debate on child poverty. As a result, a Memorandum of Understanding was signed in 2010 between the High Commission for Planning, UNICEF and the National Observatory for Children's Rights to start incorporating child poverty estimates and analyses into the national monitoring system (UNICEF, 2010b). In addition, Tanzania has been able to demonstrate that the incidence and impact of poverty on children is far greater than indicated by conventional income–consumption measures, especially in rural areas (UNICEF, 2009a).

While countries have generally included income–consumption data in their analyses, and most of them have looked at multidimensional poverty data by wealth quintiles, only a handful have examined non-income deprivation data alongside income–consumption poverty figures to highlight direct overlaps between them. Household surveys developed by demographers (such as the Multiple Indicator Cluster Survey and Demographic and Health Survey) generally do not include information on income and consumption. Standard surveys used by economists, on the other hand, rarely capture a comprehensive picture of health, and other vital statistics on deprivations. It is consequently difficult to compare income poverty and deprivations of basic needs.

Some countries have attempted to work around this limitation. In order to measure the school attendance of elementary and secondary school-age children against income deciles, the Philippines research team merged the Labour Force Survey (which includes indicators on school attendance) with the Family Income and Expenditure Survey (which includes income data) (UNICEF, 2010c). The Thailand country team looked at overlapping data from a deprivation index developed from the Multiple Indicator Cluster Survey and monetary poverty from the Household Socioeconomic Survey (UNICEF, 2010d).

A number of countries conducted qualitative research to enhance their understanding of child poverty. This can provide strong advocacy messages that go far in shaping responses to fulfilling child rights, and provides an opportunity for children to express themselves. In Kosovo, the country team carried out a qualitative study using focus group discussions and a psychological test. At the heart of the findings is children's clear recognition that poverty is damaging, both personally and socially. For the most part, all of the informants – children, parents and a variety of stakeholders – recognised that growing up in poverty is a strong predictor of disadvantage in educational performance and the attainment of life goals. There was also an acute awareness that some minority children, such as the nine-year-old Ashkali boy cited here, have experiences that dramatically contrast with those of other children:

> 'Sometimes poor children don't know how to write while the rich ones know how to write. Children who don't know how to write are yelled at by the teacher. The teacher beats them with a stick. There are cases when the teacher throws pupils out of class when they did not know how to write, and tells them not to come back without their parents.' (quoted in UNICEF, 2009b)

The study in Bhutan demonstrated that 23% of school-aged children are severely deprived of education. The analysis draws on a 2004 qualitative study conducted by the Centre for Bhutan Studies that presents views of children on how poverty limits their educational opportunities:

> 'The worst thing that happened to me was the loss of my father.[...] My mother and grandpa decided to send me to a school. I was so excited, but on reaching the school for admission, the headmaster did not accept me, as I could not present my health card. My health card got burnt down along with my house. That day onwards, I gave up the hope for getting educated. My mother sent me here in Bumthang to work as a domestic worker. At least, I am free from the stepfather's cruel treatment. I am quite happy here.' (R. Namgay, age 10)

> 'When I was about seven, I was in the village looking after the cattle. Those were the most difficult part of my life. I had to walk in the forests without any slippers looking after the cattle. My father always promised me that he would

send me to school, but he never did that. When he got a work in Bumthang, he even bought me school uniform to get admitted in Wanduecholing School, but by that time I was considered too old for the school.' (T. Jamtsho, age 14) (quoted in UNICEF, 2010e)

The Sierra Leone country team conducted focus groups discussions with 140 children. The majority indicated that poverty was widespread in Sierra Leone, as they saw poor people in their families and communities, and they themselves experienced the effects of poverty. What many of the children most strongly emphasised as an indicator of poverty was the inability of parents to send their children to school (UNICEF, 2010f).

Highlighting the importance of equity

Study results from many countries stress the importance of going beyond national averages. The report from Ghana reveals that 48% of children in the Upper East region were experiencing at least one severe deprivation in 2006, compared to 3.1% of children in the Ashanti region. Disparities are evident across ethnic lines: 43.5% of children belonging to the Mole/Dagbane ethnic group were experiencing at least one severe deprivation, compared to 9% of children of the Akan ethnic group (UNICEF, 2009c). Likewise, the Philippines study highlights wide disparities across and within regions, and by urban and rural areas. The poverty incidence, according to income poverty measures among children living in rural areas, was more than twice that of children living in urban areas. Seven out of 10 poor children were from rural areas (UNICEF, 2010c).

The South Asia regional analysis stresses that despite strides in economic growth, inequities have persisted. Poverty Reduction Strategies have not been effective in lifting the most deprived populations out of poverty. The region still shows poor health indicators and high levels of illiteracy. Child malnutrition and mortality rates remain among the highest in the world. A large proportion of children in South Asia, between 20% and 60%, suffer from multiple severe deprivations, particularly in Bangladesh, India and Nepal. Bhutan, on the other hand, has been successful in bringing down the level of multiple child deprivations, in part due to innovations in extending public services to remote locations.

The data from the region illustrate that addressing one deprivation without due attention to associated deprivations can be less efficient and effective. The highest incidence of a single severe deprivation measure for most countries is shelter, for example. Children who face that deprivation tend to suffer other deprivations at the household level. In Bangladesh, 90% of children who experience shelter deprivation also face deprivations in sanitation, water and information. The same pattern can be seen in other countries: among children deprived of shelter, 75% in India, 80% in Nepal and 86% in Pakistan are simultaneously deprived of sanitation, water and information.

Social exclusion is a major challenge in South Asia. Accordingly, various exclusion vectors seem to be strong determinants of child poverty and deprivation. Children in lower-caste families, the lowest income quintiles, and ethnic and religious minorities experience the highest rates of deprivation. In India, twice as many children under age three are underweight in the poorest quintile compared to the richest quintile. Regional analysis brings attention to the role of social protection in addressing inequity in access, quality and provision of basic services. It emphasises firmly grounding strategies to address child poverty and disparities in the human rights framework, as it requires special attention to the well-being of marginalised and excluded groups (UNICEF, 2009d).

Addressing impacts of the global economic crisis

The Global Study was launched prior to the financial, fuel and food crises that escalated during 2008. Participating countries subsequently incorporated analysis of structural poverty and the effects of the crises on poor and vulnerable children in their studies.

The Mexican study points out that past crises have led to significant and lasting increases in poverty. For example, following the 1994 crisis, it was not until 2002 that the levels of poverty returned to pre-crisis levels (UNICEF, 2010g). The Jamaica study stresses that modest gains in human development are under threat as a result of sharp economic decline. Consequently, the report predicts that child poverty rates two to three years from now are likely to be much higher than currently reported (UNICEF, 2009e).

The Senegal study stresses the importance of investing in innovative social protection systems. Surveys conducted in rural and urban areas show that child malnutrition worsened in the months after the onset of the global financial crisis. Economic instability has caused slower growth, cuts in social spending, a reduction in remittances from abroad and a decline in job opportunities. All of these factors could reverse gains made in health, education and child protection in earlier years (UNICEF, 2009f).

Linking budgets to child outcomes

Despite challenges in accessing data, many country studies analyse if resources are allocated to programmes and regions in ways that benefit the most deprived families. The analyses look at public budget size, financing, social expenditures, sustainability and implementation, and point out evidence of existing good governance and commitments in favour of children, or the lack thereof.

The Egypt study shows that budget allocations directed to childhood development have increased in absolute terms, but decreased in relative importance. From 2000 to 2010, total spending by public and civic authorities to directly or partially benefit children increased less than total spending on the population at large; 30.9% against 82.4% (National Council for Childhood and Motherhood Egypt, nd). Health and nutrition expenditure constituted only 1% of GDP (2006-07) despite some alarming nutrition deprivation figures: 17% of children were nutritionally deprived in 2005 (UNICEF, 2010h). Consequently, one of the main recommendations from the study is that public policies aiming to improve the well-being of Egypt's children need to be adequately financed.

According to Kyrgyzstan's study, investments should be made in improving the quality of education. The Kyrgyz Constitution and the Law on Education stipulate that all children have the right to a free and compulsory nine-year school education. About 99% of Kyrgyzstan's population is literate, and secondary education coverage remains high. There is an alarming deterioration in the quality of education and a reduction in attendance at educational institutions, however. According to the Programme for international student assessment 2006 survey to determine functional literacy, carried out in 57 countries around the world, Kyrgyzstan was in the last position (UNICEF, 2009g, p 8). Disparities exist in access to education: 7.1% of children from the poorest quintile attend nurseries or pre-school institutions, compared to 47.4% of children from the richest quintile.

The Kyrgyzstan study notes that from 2005 to 2007, public spending on the education sector increased from 4.9% to 6.6% of gross domestic product (GDP), but the financing mechanism for education does not allow for flexible and efficient resource utilisation and improvement in quality. In the three provinces with the highest child poverty rates, Osh, Jalalabad and Batken, financing of secondary education per capita decreased in comparison with the national average. In an attempt to address these inequities, the government, in 2007, subdivided secondary education into two programmes, 'Urban Secondary Education' and 'Rural Secondary Education' (UNICEF, 2009g).

Key policy messages

In general, country studies recognise that while numerous social policies important for children are already in place, without proper implementation, budgeting, scaling up, monitoring and evaluation, they may not produce desired results. Some common policy recommendations emerging from the national studies involve the following.

A multifaceted policy response: understanding the multidimensional aspects of child poverty leads to direct, specific, focused and most importantly holistic interventions to enhance child well-being. A first step towards this is to adopt the concept of child well-being and deprivation in national poverty measures that call for concerted policy responses to simultaneously address multiple child deprivations.

Well-designed social protection systems: in the past decade, social protection schemes have received increasing recognition as effective mechanisms for reducing vulnerabilities and ensuring stability. Furthermore, comprehensive social protection systems can address the multidimensional nature of child poverty.

Accounting for inequities: alarming intra-country disparities in child well-being are evident in the majority of participating countries. Policy recommendations stress the importance of promoting inclusive policies, implementing programmes that foster the equitable distribution of returns from economic growth and prioritising access to social services for the most deprived communities.

Safeguarding families most affected by economic crises/shocks: policies should prioritise protecting children at greatest risk of falling into poverty, along with those families experiencing structural poverty. As was the case in the 1980s, with its emphasis on structural adjustment with a human face,[6] there is a need to promote social and economic recovery for all following the global economic crisis. This strategy emphasises a minimum set of crucial actions to mitigate negative effects on children's well-being. The actions include scaling up quick-impact social protection initiatives, maintaining/increasing social expenditures that benefit children and promoting economic recovery that raises household living standards. To facilitate national responses, UNICEF has also presented a set of alternative policy options for social and economic recovery.[7]

The value-added of the Global Study depends on various factors, most importantly the receptiveness of individual governments to exploring poverty from a child-centred, multidimensional angle. It is far simpler for policy makers to look at stand-alone social indicators, such as which children are nutritionally deprived, and which nutrition-related policies might address this, or to identify children deprived of education and the appropriate policy response from the education portfolio. When children are deprived on multiple fronts, the corresponding policy responses need to be multifaceted – and may be a harder 'sell' to different ministries. One challenge countries face in analysing multidimensional child poverty entails bringing together descriptive analysis of child outcomes and policies in ways that highlight causality and policy responsiveness. The true end result is an intellectual influence that permeates national institutions and systems.

Advocating for change

From the onset, participating countries were encouraged to finalise a comprehensive advocacy plan for disseminating their findings and translating their analysis into concrete impacts. This entails both a short-term plan focused on dissemination strategies, and long-term plans for policy reforms and/or the creation of new policies that address disparities and child deprivations. The involvement of national decision makers, providers of development assistance, UN agencies, NGOs and civil society constituencies including youth, media and other key stakeholders, has proven essential to progress. The studies have moved from providing diagnostic analyses to becoming critical policy advocacy tools that identify vulnerable communities and provide concrete recommendations on how legislation, policies and programmes can best support child rights.

The Global Study has so far helped motivate several important national policy interventions. In Mali, the national study, combined with additional analytical work, led to the first National Forum on Poverty, which was followed by the formulation of an action plan on social protection. In Kosovo, child poverty analyses prompted further investigation of appropriate social protection systems to address poverty, which led to a study on the impact of cash assistance on children. The Tanzania study emphasised the need to develop legislation on children's rights. Consequently, the Law of the Child Act was adopted by the

Tanzanian government at the end of 2009. It provides the legislative framework to address study recommendations and identified gaps.

The studies have provided valuable inputs for several national development plans. In Cameroon, findings have been reflected in the Growth and Employment Strategy Paper for 2010-20.The Government of Lao PDR has expressed interest in integrating key findings into the 7th National Socioeconomic Development Plan. The study in Ukraine provided the country team with a platform to actively participate in the development of the 2010-15 Poverty Reduction and Prevention Programme. Senegal's study has opened numerous advocacy opportunities to place children at the centre of policy discussions; some study results were used in the recent Poverty Reduction Strategy Paper (PRSP). Nonetheless, the end result of the study goes beyond providing inputs into development policies and plans.

A number of UNICEF country offices have adopted the study methodology, fully or partially, for ongoing initiatives such as the situation assessment and analysis of children and women's rights that guides country programme planning.

Country findings consistently reaffirm the central tenet of the Global Study: it is insufficient to look at poverty through an income lens alone, as multiple dimensions of poverty, including those reflecting lack of access to service delivery, paint a complete picture. Those countries able to effectively address the multidimensionality of poverty through comprehensive policies are more likely to be successful in advancing children's rights (Kurukulasuriya and Engilbertsdóttir, 2011).

The knowledge amassed through the national studies provides a baseline for further research and analysis, and creates demand for increased quality and timeliness of data collected on child deprivations. Under a global umbrella, coordinated, substantive and original work rooted in national level analysis offers a unique opportunity for advocacy on child poverty and disparities.

Notes

[1] The findings, interpretations and conclusions expressed in this chapter are entirely those of the authors and do not necessarily reflect the policies or views of the United Nations Children's Fund (UNICEF). For questions and comments, please contact gfajth@unicef.org, skurukulasuriya@unicef.org or sengilbertsdottir@unicef.org. Editorial suggestions from Gretchen Luchsinger are gratefully acknowledged.

[2] UNICEF's *Global Study on Child Poverty and Disparities guide (2007)* provides a framework for national teams participating in the study –

it includes the proposed report outline and templates teams may use for country-level data and policy analysis (http://unicef.globalstudy. googlepages.com/UNICEFGlobalStudyGuide.pdf).

[3] The countries participating in the Global Study (2011) include: Afghanistan, Bangladesh, Bhutan, Bolivia, Brazil, Burundi, Cambodia, Cameroon, China, Congo Brazzaville, Democratic Republic of Congo, Djibouti, Egypt, Ghana, India, Indian Ocean Islands (Comoros, La Reunion, Mauritius and Seychelles), Indonesia, Jamaica, Kazakhstan, Kiribati, Kosovo, Kyrgyzstan, Lao People's Democratic Republic (PDR), Lesotho, Madagascar, Malawi, Maldives, Mali, Mexico, Mongolia, Morocco, Mozambique, Myanmar, Nepal, Nicaragua, Niger, Nigeria, occupied Palestinian territory, Pakistan, Philippines, Senegal, Sierra Leone, Solomon Islands, Sri Lanka, Tanzania, Thailand, Togo, Uganda, Ukraine, Uzbekistan, Vanuatu, Vietnam, Yemen and Zimbabwe.

[4] According to this definition, material resources refer to income, food, access to education or health services and protection from health risks; spiritual resources include stimuli, meaningfulness, expectations, role models and peer relationships; and emotional resources include love, trust, feelings of acceptance, inclusion and protection from abuse.

[5] UNICEF is not alone in such conceptualisations. the World Bank's *World Development Report* on Poverty (World Bank, 2000-2001) for example, portrayed poverty as voicelessness and powerlessness. The empowerment/voice angle was operationally championed through the participatory angle of the Poverty Reduction Strategy process and through qualitative surveys, but income–consumption poverty measures continue to dominate the World Bank's quantitative indicators.

[6] Cornia, Giovanni Andrea, Jolly, Richard and Frances Stewart. (1987) This recognised that certain core investments need to be made during a time of economic adjustment.

[7] UNICEF Social and Economic Policy Website. Read more about UNICEF's work on mitigating the negative effects of the financial crisis on children's well-being at www.unicef.org/socialpolicy/ index_economiccrisis.html

References

Cornia, G.A., Jolly, R. and Stewart, F. (1987) *Adjustment with a Human Face: Protecting the Vulnerable and Promoting Growth*, Clarendon Press, Oxford.

Fajth, G. and Holland, K. (2007) *Child poverty: A perspective*, UNICEF DPP Working Papers, New York: UNICEF.

Gordon, D., Nandy, S., Pantazis, C., Pemberton, S. and Townsend, P. (2003) *Child poverty in the developing world*, Bristol: The Policy Press, Bristol (www.bristol.ac.uk/poverty/child poverty.html).

Kurukulasuriya, S. and Engilbertsdóttir, S. (2011) *A multidimensional approach to measuring child poverty*, UNICEF DPP Working Brief 2011, New York: UNICEF (www.unicef.org/socialpolicy/index_57664.html).

National Council for Childhood and Motherhood Egypt (nd) 'Government budget 2006-07: towards child rights budget', Unpublished report.

UNICEF (United Nations Children's Fund) (2005) *The State of the World's Children 2005: Childhood under threat*, New York: UNICEF (www.unicef.org/).

UNICEF (2007) *Global Study on Child Poverty and Disparities guide*, New York: UNICEF.

UNICEF (2009a) *Childhood poverty in Tanzania: Deprivations and disparities in child well-being*, Dar Es Salaam: UNICEF.

UNICEF (2009b) *Child Poverty Network consolidated reply – Undertaking qualitative research as part of the Global Study on Child Poverty and Disparities*, New York: UNICEF (https://sites.google.com/site/consolidatedreplies/).

UNICEF (2009c) *Child poverty and disparities in Ghana*, Accra: UNICEF.

UNICEF (2009d) *Child poverty, deprivation and disparities in South Asia: Some preliminary findings and recommendations, A discussion note (forthcoming)*, Kathmandu: UNICEF.

UNICEF (2009e) *Child poverty and disparities in Jamaica*, Kingston: UNICEF.

UNICEF (2009f) *Etude mondiale sur la pauvreté et les disparités chez les enfants au Sénégal*, Dakar: UNICEF.

UNICEF (2009g) *Global Study on Child Poverty and Disparities: Kyrgyzstan national report*, Bishek: Institute of Strategic Analysis and Evaluation under the President of the Kyrgyz Republic.

UNICEF (2010a) *Progress survey for participating Global Study teams*, New York: UNICEF.

UNICEF (2010b) The Global Study on Child Poverty and Disparities blog, 'Morocco: Institutionalizing child poverty measurement for long-term impact on children's lives' (www.unicefglobalstudy.blogspot.com).

UNICEF (2010c) *Global Study on Child Poverty and Disparities: The case of the Philippines*, Makati: UNICEF.

UNICEF (2010d) *Global Study on Child Poverty and Disparities: Child wellbeing in Thailand*, Bangkok: UNICEF.

UNICEF (2010e) *Child poverty and disparities in Bhutan: Towards betterment of child well being and equity (forthcoming)*, Thimphu: Centre for Bhutan Studies.

UNICEF (2010f) *Study on Child Poverty and Disparities in Sierra Leone (forthcoming)*, Freetown: UNICEF.

UNICEF (2010g) *Study on Child Poverty and Disparities: The case of Mexico*, Mexico City: UNICEF.

UNICEF (2010h) *Child poverty and disparities in Egypt: Building the social infrastructure for Egypt's future*, Cairo: UNICEF.

UNICEF-Economic Commission for Latin America and the Caribbean (ECLAC) (2010i) *Child poverty in Latin America and the Caribbean'*, Santiago: ECLAC-UN/UNICEF.

UNICEF Social and Economic Policy Website www.unicef.org/socialpolicy/index_economiccrisis.html

World Bank (2000/2001) *World Development Report 2000-2001: Attacking poverty*, Washington DC: World Bank.

TWENTY-TWO

Investment in social security: a possible United Nations model for child benefit?

Peter Townsend

We live in a world where children are accorded priority emotionally and politically. Five of the eight Millennium Development Goals (MDGs) of the United Nations (UN) are directed at children: one is to eradicate extreme poverty and hunger, another to drastically reduce under-five mortality, a third to reverse the spread of HIV/AIDS, malaria and other diseases, and the fourth and fifth to ensure full and gender-equal schooling (UN, 2000). Yet international leaders have conceded that declared progress is too slow to meet the goals by 2015.

The policies offered to protect children's welfare have been ineffective (UNICEF, 2004, 2005) – most are over-generalised and indirect or selectively helpful only to very small numbers. Children's social security is not defined precisely but often wrapped up in the 'family' or 'household' benefits to which their parents may or may not be entitled. The scale of their rights to income in developing countries has still to be defined, categorised for different age groups in different locations, and endorsed by representative government.

Previous work has shown the viability and affordability of social security in national economies, and illustrated promising initiatives in middle- and low-income countries to accelerate the growth of social security systems. This chapter aims to take three steps further: (a) to focus on children, who have a greater risk of being in poverty than adults and no opportunity to contribute to their own social security; (b) to pin down the nature and causes of child poverty to improve policy effectiveness; and (c) to demonstrate that international funds have to be found, and can be found quickly, to match national resources to meet child poverty directly. In this chapter I discuss:

- the consequences of poverty and multiple deprivation for child survival and health;

- child rights as the appropriate framework for measurement, analysis and the construction of policy;
- the need to reveal the extent of international responsibility for funding anti-poverty strategies;
- the recent disappointing history of international finance;
- and, as the most practical alternative, the use of a currency transfer tax to build up a UN Investment Fund for child benefit.

Consequences of child poverty and multiple deprivation

A special investigation for the United Nations Children's Fund (UNICEF) found that 56% of children in developing countries – 1.2 billion – experienced one or more forms of severe deprivation, over half of them (674 million) at least two forms of severe multiple deprivation such as total absence of toilet facilities, lack of nearby clean water, malnutrition and extreme overcrowding and poor shelter (Gordon et al, 2003; UNICEF, 2005). This is more potent evidence of child poverty than the (very crude, and unreliable) estimates by the World Bank of the numbers of children in households with less than US$1 per capita per day.[1] Over 10 million children in developing countries die each year, mainly from preventable causes, including malnutrition, pneumonia, diarrhoea, measles and malaria. Poverty, whether measured by household income or multiple material and social deprivation, and early child mortality, are intertwined. The World Health Organization (WHO) found that as many as seven out of every ten childhood deaths can be attributed to these five causes or their combination. Three in every four children seen by health services are suffering from at least one of these conditions. Many of these deaths could be prevented using readily available medical technologies at comparatively little cost and many more by providing resources for shelter, clean water, sanitary facilities, food and fuel. Thus, the free issue of mosquito nets, as illustrated in one initiative in different areas of Kenya (Rice, 2007), could dramatically reduce rates of malaria among children. Again, public provision of shelter, food and sanitary facilities and basic income as well as access to services for those widowed or orphaned by HIV/AIDS could save many from a miserable existence and early painful death (Akwanalo Mate, 2006). The number of children in Sub-Saharan Africa orphaned by HIV/AIDS is expected to rise to 15.7 million, or a quarter of all children, by 2010 (UNICEF, 2007, p 42). Globally, 1,800 children are newly infected every day by HIV/AIDS (UNICEF, 2005, p 16).

The accumulating studies of enforced child deprivation are calling sharp attention to mass violations of child rights that for many children maintain, and for some, increase, the risks of survival (Pemberton et al, 2007). For health professionals this has led recently to fuller acknowledgement of the positive relationship between human rights and health (Pemberton et al, 2005; Gruskin et al, 2007; R. MacDonald, 2007; T.H. MacDonald, 2007; Singh et al, 2007).

The WHO and other international agencies have been unable until now to distinguish rates of child mortality and malnutrition in richer and poorer households. The use in representative country surveys of questions about assets owned by households has led to a breakthrough.[2] In Table 22.1 I have drawn from the WHO's *World Health Statistics* 2007, in which it has proved possible for the first time to measure ownership of assets, albeit crudely, to compare children in the poorest 20% with the richest 20% of households in the country. In countries where there is mass poverty it should be noted that asset impoverishment may still apply to some among the richest 20%. Table 22.1 shows that 58% of under-fives in the poorest 20% of households in India, compared with 42% in Sub-Saharan Africa and 36% in Latin America, are physically stunted for their age, compared with 27%, 23% and 4%, respectively, in the richest 20% of households. Mortality rates of under-fives in the poorest households in these three regions are also disproportionately high, being 14%, 16% and 9% respectively. And, as another indicator, 72%, 46% and 34% of one-year-olds in the poorest households in these three regions have been found not to have been immunised against measles.

Table 22.1: Child mortality and poor health conditions, three regions (%)

Indicator	India	Sub-Saharan Africa (25 countries)	Latin America (8 countries)
Under-fives stunted for age			
– poorest 20%	58	42	36
– richest 20%	27	24	4
Mortality under five years			
– poorest 20%	14	16	9
– richest 20%	5	10	4
One-year-olds not immunised against measles			
– poorest 20%	72	46	34
– richest 20%	19	22	16

Source: WHO (2007)

Data for individual countries in these regions are to be found in the Appendix to this chapter. The highest percentages of children found to be stunted in Sub-Saharan Africa (50% or more) were in Rwanda, Malawi, Chad, Zambia and Madagascar. The highest percentage in Latin America was 65% in Guatemala. In India this percentage must have been matched or exceeded in some deprived areas.

Using child rights to construct policies to defeat child poverty

Using human rights as a methodology to pin down major patterns of development and to assess policy is of growing importance. For the first time *multiple* deprivation as reflected in numerous statements in a number of the human rights treaties can be expressed in precise statistical and empirical terms using random but coordinated national surveys, namely the Demographic and Health Surveys and the Multiple Indicator Cluster Surveys which have been and are being conducted in countries covering more than 85% of the developing country populations. Beginning in the last decade, a practicable method of constructing a measure of the economic and social conditions of small and large populations, so that they can be compared, has evolved. For example, during 2002-08 one research team based at the University of Bristol has been able to produce the first reliable global estimates for children, young people and all adults (Gordon et al, 2003, 2009; UNDESA, 2007).

The methodology draws on the analytical frameworks of the human rights treaties. Human rights have come to play a central part in discussions about economic and social development, and have been ratified by the great majority of governments in the world. There are rights to income and to social security enshrined in Articles 22 and 25 of the Universal Declaration of Human Rights; 9 and 11 of the International Covenant on Economic, Social and Cultural Rights; and 26 and 27 of the UN Convention on the Rights of the Child (UNCRC). But in the UNCRC there are also elaborate injunctions to protect children from malnutrition, maltreatment, neglect, abuse and exploitation and to ensure they are not deprived of access to clean water, sanitary facilities, shelter, healthcare services, education and information: governments are enjoined to 'recognize the right of every child to a standard of living adequate for the child's physical, mental, spiritual, moral and social development' (Article 27, and also see Articles 13, 17, 19, 20, 23, 24, 26, 28, 31, 32, 34, 37 and 39).

The statements, ratified by nearly all of the 191 nation states in the world, allow single but also multiple measures or indicators of the denial or fulfilment of the specified rights to be devised and tracked. Social science therefore has a considerable role to play in coordinating the collection and analysis of such evidence and evaluating policy impact.

There are two particular arguments in favour of using this methodology in relation to poverty and social security. First, all the human rights treaties allow multiple indicators of violations of those rights to be constructed. The UNCRC, for example, does not contain an explicit human right to freedom from poverty. However, statements about the conditions of material and social deprivation underlying poverty and characterising ill health, as specified above, occur in a number of different articles of the UNCRC, and have become the subject of national and international survey investigation. The rights are interrelated, and therefore deliberate action to fulfil a particular right is relevant to the realisation of other rights. So the progressive realisation of human rights will depend on the prior clustering of rights. Policies designed to implement a particular right have to be tested in relation to the outcomes for other rights. This is the source of scientific confirmation of the problem to be addressed, and of greater public confidence in policies designed to deliver human rights.

Second, human conditions are rarely one thing or the other – either good or bad. For example, there is under-nourishment but also extreme malnutrition. There is poverty but also extreme poverty. Empirical inquiry can trace a continuum from one extreme to the other, and thresholds of severity of conditions experienced by humans found. The advantage of empirical surveys of population conditions is that moderate needs can be distinguished from severe or extreme needs and doubts about over-generalised evidence removed. Another advantage is that by measuring severity as well as multiplicity of condition, cause can be more exactly unravelled and priorities for remedial policy demonstrated. There is a gradient or continuum ranging from complete fulfilment to extreme violation of rights – for example, on the continuum ranging from 'good health' to 'poor health/death' (see Gordon et al, 2003, pp 7-8). Courts make judgments in individual cases about this gradient to establish the correct threshold at which rights have been either violated or fulfilled. Correspondingly, scientists and policy analysts can demonstrate the point on the gradient at which there are severe or extreme violations, so that grey areas of the interpretation of mild or moderate violation can be set aside, and governments and international agencies persuaded that there are grounds for institutional action.

The language of rights therefore changes the analysis of world conditions and the discussion of responsible policies. It shifts the focus of debate from the personal failures of the 'poor' to the failures to resolve poverty of macroeconomic structures and policies of nation states and international bodies (agencies such as the World Trade Organization [WTO], the World Bank, International Monetary Fund [IMF] and UN, but also the most powerful transnational corporations [TNCs] and alliances of groups of governments). Child poverty cannot then be considered as a parental problem or a local community problem but a 'violation of rights' that nation states, and international agencies, groups of governments and TNCs, have a legal and institutional obligation to remedy (Chinkin, 2001). And violations of the rights of children to health, including problems like malaria and HIV/AIDS, would more easily be seen to be socio-structural problems and not only medical or healthcare problems.

Two 2007 examples may be given. The free issue of mosquito nets to selected populations (as in Kenya) can dramatically reduce rates of malaria among children (Rice, 2007). The problem is the scale of the issue – so that the children's needs are covered universally – rather than a small-scale scheme piloted by NGOs or governments in a few selected areas. Second, public provision of shelter, food and sanitary facilities and basic income as well as access to services for those widowed or orphaned by HIV/AIDS can save many from miserable existence and early painful death. This includes many among the nearly 16 million children, orphaned in Sub-Saharan Africa by HIV/AIDS. Resources have to be mobilised for population care and especially material resources that directly reach children (Akwanalo Mate, 2006). Again, the problem is to ensure universal coverage so that children in extreme need do not slip through grudgingly devised nets.

International responsibility for funding

Transnational corporations

Who is responsible for ensuring these policies are universal? The argument developed here is that TNCs and international agencies can work wonders by committing a tiny percentage of their growing resources to social security in the low-income countries, and also by moving towards acceptance of minimum standards of monthly or weekly income on the part of wage earners and those not in paid employment who are entitled to social security.

Both the Organisation for Economic Co-operation and Development (OECD) and International Labour Organization (ILO) have issued guidelines on 'corporate social responsibility' (ILO, 2001; OECD, 2001). Both organisations have sought to fill a growing gap left upon the termination by the UN in the early 1990s of substantial monitoring and reporting of the trends in TNC practices. In 2003 the UN produced draft norms on the responsibilities of TNCs and other business enterprises with regard to human rights. It may be the first document to place human rights at the core of its mandate (UN, 2003; Vagts, 2003, p 795; and see de Schutter, 2006) but it remains a generalised draft. The guidelines issued by the OECD and ILO are not yet attracting vigorous debate. The desirability of universal rules of practice for TNCs and international agencies is missing from much current commentary and analysis.

The growing bargaining power of the TNCs in headquarter locations in the rich countries is creating social and economic disequilibrium. This 'institutional hierarchy of power' has to be taken seriously. Recent failures of privatisation schemes, and of major TNCs such as Enron, WorldCom, ImClone, Credit Suisse First Boston, Hollinger International, Adelphi Communications, Martha Stewart Living Omnimedia and parts of the financial services industry, provide lessons that have to be learned and acted on internationally to restore structural stability. Recurring reports of instances of corporate corruption have paved the way for calls for collective approaches to be made through law and regulation (see, for example, Scott et al, 1985; Lang and Hines, 1993; Hudson, 1996; Korten, 1996; Kozul-Wright and Rowthorn, 1998; Madeley, 1999; Hertz, 2001; Hines, 2001; Sklair, 2001; Watkins, 2002) that go a lot further than the minimal and highly variable expressions so far of the unenforceable appeals for the observance of 'corporate social responsibility', as contained in the OECD and ILO guidelines or in the UN's Corporate Citizenship Initiative, 'the Global Compact', launched in June 2000.

Low-income countries are heavily dependent on trade with corporations with far larger resources than they possess. Through subsidiaries and subcontractors controlled from far away they are restricted in the employment that can be found, the wages that can be charged, the taxes that can be raised and the conditions of life that have to be protected for national populations. The poorest countries have too few resources to make swift headway in reducing poverty and creating real opportunities for enterprise on behalf of the great majority of their populations (see, for example, Watkins, 2002). The hierarchy of power is illustrated by elaborate stratification of wages, conditions of work and access to social security from the executive boards of TNCs in the US, Japan, Germany and the UK through to the 70 or 100 countries in which they operate. There has been a huge upsurge in transnational resources without corresponding modernisation of company law to adapt to the new social conditions and responsibilities for economic and social development and to impose particular obligations on corporations.

Through its Tripartite Declaration of Principles concerning Multinational Enterprises and Social Policy, first adopted in 1977, the ILO has sought to encourage governments to reinforce corporate responsibility to pave the way for more specific potentially binding international standards, turning codes of conduct into the seed of customary rules of international law (ILO, 2001). The problem is that as they stand, these guidelines have no teeth and are not routinely publicised and discussed. Observance is voluntary and not dependent on national or international sanctions or law. Some corporations and companies are concerned about their image and good name, and are prepared to moderate their practices, and profits, in consideration of the rights of their workers. Others take advantage of non-existent or inconsistent law.

A starting point might be an agreement about children. One serious and continuing embarrassment for many TNCs are charges that children are involved in extreme forms of labour by subcontractors and subsidiaries in locations remote from TNC headquarters (ILO, 2005). There is evidence of children as young as seven who are involved in producing paving stones, footballs, clothing and carpets, operating with dangerous pesticides and other chemicals, digging trenches, picking cotton and working in mines – often for 10 or more hours a day. A common corporation plea is that illegal practices, or violations of child rights, along the production line were unintended and unknown, and abhorrence of such practices by headquarters would now be passed down the chain of command. The problem is that the conditions of payment and the standards expected of the finished product are imposed. These inevitably affect incentives and lead to extreme practices. Accountability for such practices could be ensured by legal and other means – particularly through monitored reports and statistics for which headquarter organisations must be held routinely responsible (in the same way as nation states) and that would have to be submitted for public scrutiny. Agreement reached by the UN and TNCs about their accountability for severe deprivation among children engaged in forms of bonded labour connected with their trade represents one useful future development.

Perhaps the key element in taking such a step would be to concentrate on company responsibility for social security. In the late 19th century and throughout the 20th century employers came to accept provision of a 'social wage' as a condition of making profit. Laws were enacted to provide for temporary and long-term unemployment, and contributions by employers for illness and disability and other dependencies of family members, especially children, were expected. There were insurance payments for specific contingencies and taxes to meet shifts in economic conditions that could not be predicted. The social wage was one of the rules of economic operation that became widely accepted. New global conditions in the 21st century have transformed that responsibility and a new legal and social responsibility for impoverished conditions in low-income countries has to be accepted throughout the hierarchy of power exerted by headquarters corporations. The income rights of children could lie at the core of discussions to make globalisation work socially.

Employers who were expected or compelled in the OECD countries at early stages of the industrial revolution to make substantial contributions to social protection were national rather than transnational employers. People with hard-earned professional skills built on minimum standards of living and universal access to public social services were not at that time tempted overseas from national service or careers in the national economy, and neither were they given extensive opportunities to leave chosen countries of domicile. Cross-border social security is one burning question for the 21st century, but only one example of the urgent need to develop basic universal social security.

Children have been placed at the centre of this analysis. Transnational employers can add, or be obliged to add, 1 or 2% of wage costs in different countries for a child benefit to help banish malnutrition, poverty and premature child death, and also to encourage more schooling. At the same time, extreme forms of child labour would become less necessary as well as made illegal. Standard contributions towards social insurance for sickness, disability, bereavement and ageing, or represented in new taxes, could follow. The question of social protection or social security in the national interest has become one of social protection in the *international* interest.

International agencies

What cannot be disregarded in this discussion of children's needs is international funding. The responsibility of the UN and other agencies in funding social security, especially child benefit, requires urgent review. What conclusions can be drawn from present international funding, and how much of that funding actually reaches children in extreme poverty? When questions are asked about global, as distinct from national, anti-poverty measures, international agencies stress the importance of three sources of aid: economic growth, debt relief and overseas aid. Box 22.1 summarises these sources and criticisms of these sources of aid remain largely unanswered. Added lately as a fourth element of international anti-poverty strategy has been fairer trade, through reform of the WTO. In practice all four measures are principally dependent on the big economic powers, including TNCs, in the modern global economy. In working out what this means for children we need to understand that the four types of international funding are relatively indiscriminate and unpredictable in their distributional effect on populations. Success depends on whether a sufficient share of additional cash income and income in kind from these sources happens to reach the poor and how quickly.

Box 22.1: The current orthodox funding strategy for low-income countries

The strategy has been threefold:

- broad-based economic growth
- debt relief
- overseas aid.

Drawing on evidence of the trends over 30 years, the outcome of this strategy can be judged unsuccessful for several reasons:

- 'trickle-up' growth;
- conditionality policies for loans;
- cost-recovery policies in basic social services;
- cuts in public expenditure;
- lack of social security systems;
- excessive privatisation;
- unregulated globalisation and unequal terms of trade;
- enhancement of the power of the global 'triumvirate' (G8, TNCs and International Finance Agencies).

The absence of social security systems in many low-income countries means that 'trickle-down' from economic growth, or indeed most forms of overseas aid and debt relief, does not arise. These forms of funding have 'indirect' social outcomes. They are intended to reach the poorest, but measures of trends in extreme poverty, and not only the lack of investigative precise follow-up, cast doubt on the intended outcome. The over-generalised, and indirect, strategy has contributed to the failure to reduce poverty, especially child poverty.

What different forms of funding have been examined? The scale of resources to be made available has now become an acute problem. In September 2000 the lack of significant progress in reducing poverty, together with severe delays in implementing funding agreements, led the UN General Assembly to ask for 'a rigorous analysis of the advantages, disadvantages and other implications of proposals for developing new and innovative sources of funding'. A panel was set up under the chairmanship of Ernesto Zedillo and its report was issued in 2001 (UN, 2001).

On the question of scale, the Zedillo panel estimated conservatively that an additional US$50 billion was required annually to reach the MDGs. The World Bank estimated that additional overseas development aid (ODA) of US$60 billion over 2003 allocations would be needed in 2006, and US$83 billion by 2010 (World Bank, 2005, p 162). These estimates were unrealistically low, since they depended on making up the incomes of population below US$1 a day and not on the relatively indiscriminate indirect funding provided by economic growth, overseas aid, debt relief and fairer trade. Instead, the necessary increase in ODA was projected as US$20 billion for 2006 and US$50 billion for 2010 – and even these underestimates leave a gap of more than US$30 billion. By that year the total is estimated to reach an average of 0.36% gross national income (GNI) (OECD, 2005) but 'it is not clear that this is realistic' (Atkinson, 2005, p 6). The Netherlands, Denmark, Sweden, Norway and Luxembourg are the only countries to have reached the UN's 0.7 target for ODA. In 2004 the UK stood at 0.36% and the US at 0.16%.

By 2003 the UN inquiry about alternative funding had lost momentum. A parallel inquiry by the Helsinki-based World Institute for Development and Economic Research (WIDER) was mapping out alternative sources of funding (see Box 22.2). Because the UN process had offered little guidance, the alternatives were presented cautiously in 2004 (Atkinson, 2004). The seven alternatives are of course different in scale as well as likely support. The International Finance Facility was planned to reach a flow of US$50 billion for 2010-15. Private donations, that is, from NGOs, totalled US$10 billion in 2003, and might be increased, but on past evidence it is unlikely that in the foreseeable future they will provide the predominant share of the resources needed.

Box 22.2: New sources of development finance

- Global environment taxes
- Tax in currency flows (for example, Tobin)
- New 'special drawing rights'
- International Finance Facility (UK government)
- Private development donations
- Global lottery or premium bonds
- Increased remittances from emigrants

Source: Atkinson (2004)

They can be expected to fill only a small proportion of the funding gap. The creation by the IMF of Special Drawing Rights has been opposed by the US, and since any new issue has to be approved by an 85% majority, the US alone can veto progress. The two most promising alternatives for serious examination seem to be a global environment tax and a currency transfer tax (CTT). The former is usually illustrated by a tax on hydrocarbon fuels with high carbon content – or by a tax on airline travel. The 'Tobin' tax alternative is a tax on foreign currency transactions (covering different types of transaction – spot, forwards, swaps, derivatives and so on).

Both these taxes have been vigorously opposed on economic grounds. As Atkinson has pointed out, both need not necessarily be of a scale to warrant hostility, and could be reduced even further to produce substantial funds without adverse reactions in different markets. A small-scale initiative could, of course, be criticised, on the one hand, for failing to reduce global warming or pollution, and on the other hand, for failing to reduce currency speculation. But even small-scale taxes could produce substantial sums for international investment in development and the elimination of poverty. Such an investment could also be used to partially fund investments in a social security system by low-income countries. Even a tiny CTT of 0.02% is estimated by Atkinson to raise US$28 billion, and a small energy tax twice this sum, giving figures from three to five times the value of all private donations.

The energies of international bodies were diverted from consideration of the CTT. Two new issues were brought up in 2003. First was the possible creation of an international tax organisation. After the UN International Conference on Financing for Development in Mexico in March 2003, the Zedillo panel recommended creating within the UN an agency called the International Tax Organization (ITO) and an 'adequate international tax source' for global spending programmes (High-Level Panel on Financing for Development (2001). Second was to explore how multinational business might promote strong domestic private sectors in the developing world. In June 2003 a Commission on the Private Sector and Development, co-chaired by Ernesto Zedillo, was convened by the UN Development Programme (UNDP) at the request of Kofi Annan to recommend 'how to promote strong domestic private sectors in the developing world as a key strategy towards the achievement of the Millennium Development Goals' (Annan, 2004). There was no reference back to the simplicity and affordability of a single form of international tax in relation to that aim. In particular, the Commission looked at how multinational business could become a supportive partner for local entrepreneurs in the developing countries. The discussion of these issues at the World Conference in Davos in 2004 was inconclusive. The case for a CTT was effectively kicked into touch.

A currency transfer tax: new resources for child benefit and social security

Since the mid-1990s there has been a groundswell of support for the Tobin tax, particularly in Europe,[3] as a source of international finance for aid and economic stabilisation.

James Tobin put forward the idea of such a tax first in 1972 and then it was resurrected in the UNDP's *Human Development Report* for 1994. The rate of tax lately suggested is in the range 0.1 to 0.5% of currency transactions. If applied universally, a tax of 0.1% on all currency transactions, including the charge for changing different currencies for travellers, was estimated in 2002 to be likely to raise US$400 billion a year (see Townsend and Gordon, 2002, p 369) – or five times higher than the low target of debt relief and aid advocated for low-income countries by the International Financial Agencies and members of the G8.

Eighty per cent of exchange transactions currently involve only eight industrialised countries (with the UK and the US accounting for about 50%). Eighty-eight per cent of transactions also take place between five currencies: the dollar, the pound sterling, the euro, the yen and the Swiss franc (Harribey, 2002). Thus, agreement among a bare majority of the G8 countries would be sufficient to ensure large-scale implementation at a first stage.

The key question is taxation for what? In the first years of the millennium, progress in implementing international taxation to pump-prime social security systems has made very little progress. In 2002 the UN General Assembly considered a report prepared at the instigation of Kofi Annan. The Zedillo panel (the UN High-Level

Panel on Financing for Development) had been appointed in 2001, as stated above (UN, 2001), to 'recommend strategies for the mobilisation of resources required to accelerate equitable and sustainable growth in developing countries as well as economies in transition, and to fulfil the poverty and development commitments enshrined in the UN Millennium Declaration'. The Zedillo panel reported an annual shortfall of US$15 billion for the provision of global public goods, in addition to the extra US$50 billion per year needed to meet the MDG targets. A number of governments had been pressing for consideration of the recommendation by James Tobin of a CTT. Thus, a 2002 report from the Federal Ministry of Economic Cooperation and Development in Bonn explained that the tax was feasible and could even be introduced right away by the OECD or EC countries. The European Parliament carried out a feasibility study, with France, Germany and Belgium in favour, and the Vatican coming round to acceptance. Outside the European Union (EU), Canada also offered its active consent. Poor countries saw the Tobin tax as something which rich countries could implement straightaway,[4] a domestic taxation control that had very small financial drawbacks for the donors but large benefits for the potential recipients. At a UN conference on 'Finance for Development' in April 2002 in Monterrey, Mexico, a number of countries pressed for the CTT. The report to be submitted to the General Assembly was signed by 113 countries, but innovative mechanisms of financing were given only one paragraph and were left open for further consideration.

The Zedillo report had described the merits of a CTT as 'highly controversial' and concluded that 'further rigorous study would be needed to resolve the doubts about the feasibility of such a tax'. The Zedillo authors claimed to have examined a range of proposed mechanisms including a carbon tax, a currency transactions tax and a new allocation of Special Drawing Rights, concluding that 'new sources of finance should be considered without prejudice by all parties involved'.

However, there is no evidence that the issues were examined in any depth. Surprisingly, the Zedillo panel made no attempt to consider alternative practicable models of the Tobin tax, and to compare them, or to deal with the difficulties said to be involved in implementing such a tax. They did not compare its merits with other methods of raising funds for overseas development, or give persuasive estimates of costs and outcome. The uses to which the tax might be put or what social benefits might be derived were not discussed.

A CTT of 0.2%, compared with a standard fee of 2% or 3% charged by firms for currency exchange at airports, would raise US$280 billion.

A start would be feasible for those OECD countries prepared to introduce a CTT for travellers. Compared with an existing charge of 2% or 3%, it seems likely that the travelling public would accept an additional charge for an international investment tax of 0.2%. The social use of such a tax also deserves searching investigation. This has not, hitherto, attracted any attention.

Like a corporation 'tax' of 1% of turnover, a CTT could directly benefit children. The potential use of the tax was not considered by Tobin when introducing his idea in 1972, nor in the 1990s when publicity was again attracted to his proposal and, despite the terms of reference agreed by the Zedillo panel, the idea was not given serious attention in 2001 or subsequently. Interpreted and administered in the name of the world's impoverished children, for example, the tax could have considerably more public appeal and therefore potential acceptance. The proceeds of a tax – introduced severally or collectively by the richest countries – could be used to set up an international investment fund for children. Following its initiative in introducing the MDGs the UN would be the obvious international organisation to administer the fund. A universal benefit for children, in cash or in kind, would attract worldwide support. It could prove to be not just a salvation for the world's children, but regain public respect for the work of the international agencies on world social development and the fulfilment of the MDGs.

Grants from that fund to governments could be made conditional on, say, payments by each government and by the UN of 50% of the cost of the programme, as well as evidence of payment. The scheme would be monitored by a representative UN committee as well as individual governments.

This chapter has pointed up the fragile condition of a fifth of the world's children and has sought to recommend a change of strategy to bring resources directly to children, and to seek substantial funding from international bodies. The current threat to global economic and social development because of the financial downturn obliges the largest economic powers, international agencies and TNCs to reconsider their agreed commitments and obligations to human rights in all parts of the world. The governments of the 'developed' countries have to consider sharing the responsibility for the establishment and emergency reinforcement of social security systems to meet declared goals to eliminate world poverty. It is not just administrative know-how and domestic taxation that count, but also participatory international funding.

The use of a CTT for universal child benefit would immediately improve the life chances of hundreds of millions of children, and pave the way for the emergence of social security systems in low-income countries on a scale that will eventually compare with that of the OECD countries and therefore radically reduce mass poverty.

The priority recommendation is for an international child benefit that once administratively in place has a direct and immediate effect in bolstering family purchasing power and reducing child poverty. Because the circumstances of countries differ widely, a new child benefit would necessarily take a variety of forms and be introduced progressively. It could be a weekly allowance in cash or kind for children under a given age – say 10, or 5, or infants under 2. A low birth weight baby allowance is an example of a measure that could be applied in rich and poor countries alike. The scheme could be phased in, depending on available resources – maybe starting with infants – so long as it is introduced country- or district-wide. Conditional cash transfer schemes that have started in recent years, especially in parts of Latin America and Africa, could be merged or treated as preliminary or complementary stages of a process of rapid extension of entitlement to all children.

A second priority recommendation is a categorical child benefit for children with a severe disability. Whether parents are in paid employment or not, the costs of caring for a child with a severe disability often account for family poverty. And the market does not recognise this form of dependency. While some forms of congenital or disabling long-term illness may be declining, there are the disabling conditions of the major problems of the last two decades, such as HIV/AIDS, oil, nuclear and chemical pollution, and armed conflict, including landmines.

Notes

[1] There is good reason to question whether the World Bank had technically achieved accurate updating of its 1985 US$1 per person per day poverty line (see, for example, Pogge and Reddy, 2003; Wade, 2004; Kakwani and Son, 2006) and why the admitted insufficiency of the threshold had not been made good in later research, as promised by the Bank in the early 1990s (see in particular Chapter 14 in Townsend and Gordon, 2002).

[2] There are now two principal sources of standardised cross-national survey data, Demographic and Health Surveys and Multiple Indicator Cluster Surveys, the latter sponsored by UNICEF.

[3] For example, a report commissioned by the Federal Ministry for Economic Cooperation and Development, Bonn (2002), concluded that the Tobin tax is feasible and does not need global ratification, but could be started by OECD or EU countries.

[4] See *The view from the South on the Tobin Tax*, (Afrodad, 2000) for a really good overview of where African countries stand on the Tobin tax.

References

Afrodad, B.F.A. (2000) *The View from the South on the Tobin Tax Consolidated*. Report of Study on the Tobin Tax in Selected African Countries (www.ppp.ch/devPdf/TobinTaxAfrika.pdf).

Akwanalo Maté, F. (2006) *Children's Property and Inheritance Rights: Experience of orphans affected by HIV/AIDS and other vulnerable orphans in Africa*, London: London School of Economics and Political Science

Annan, K. (2004) Secretary-General of the UN, Address to the World Economic Forum, Davos, Switzerland, 23 January.

Atkinson, A.B. (ed) (2004) *New Sources of Development Finance*, UNU-WIDER, Oxford: Oxford University Press.

Atkinson, A.B. (2005) 'Global public finance and funding the millennium development goals', Jelle Zijlstra Lecture 4, Amsterdam, 12 December, Netherlands Institute for Advanced Study in the Humanities and Social Sciences (NIAS).

Chinkin, C. (2001) 'The United Nations Decade for the Elimination of Poverty: what role for international law?', *Current Legal Problems*, 54, 553-89.

De Schutter, O. (ed) (2006) *Transnational Corporations and Human Rights*, Oxford: Hart.

Federal Ministry for Economic Cooperation and Development, Germany (2002) *On the Feasibility of a Tax on Foreign Exchange Transactions*, Bonn: Federal Ministry.

Gordon, D., Kelly Irving, M., Nandy, S. and Townsend, P. (2009) *The Extent and Nature of Absolute Poverty Final Report to DfID: R8382* Bristol: Townsend Centre for International Poverty Research.

Gordon, D., Nandy, S., Pantazis, C., Pemberton, S. and Townsend, P. (2003) *Child Poverty in the Developing World*, Bristol: The Policy Press.

Gruskin, S., Mills, E.J. and Tarantola, D. (2007) 'History, principles and practice of health and human rights', *Lancet,* 370, 9585.

Harribey, J.-M. (2002) *The Seven Mistakes of the Opponents to 'The Tax'*, Paris: Scientific Committee of ATTAC.

Hertz, N. (2001) *The Silent Takeover: Global Capitalism and the Death of Bureaucracy*, London: William Heinemann.

High-Level Panel on Financing for Development (2001) *Report of the High-Level Panel on Financing for Development*, 28 June, New York: UN Headquarters (www.un.org/reports/financing/).

Hines, C. (2001) *Localization: A Global Manifesto*, London: Earthscan.

Hudson, E. (ed) (1996) *Merchants of Misery: How Corporate America Profits from Poverty*, Maine: Courage.

International Labour Organisation (ILO) (2001) *Social Security: A New Consensus*, Geneva: ILO.

International Labour Organisation (2005) 'Social protection as a productive factor', GB.294/ESP/4 November, Geneva: ILO (www.ilo.org/public/english/standards/relm/gb/docs/gb294/pdf/esp-4.pdf).

Kakwani, N. and Son, H.H. (2006) *New Global Poverty Counts*, Working Paper No. 20, Brasilia: UNDP International Poverty Centre.

Korten, D.C. (1996) *When Corporations Rule the World*, London: Earthscan.

Kozul-Wright, R. and Rowthorn, R. (1998) *Transnational Corporations and the Global Economy*, Helsinki: UNU World Institute for Development Economic Research.

Lang, T. and Hines, C. (1993) *The New Protectionism*, London: Earthscan.

MacDonald, R. (2007) An inspirational defence of the right to health, *Lancet*, 370, 379-380.

MacDonald, T.H. (2007) *The Global Human Right to Health: Dream or Possibility?*, Oxford: Radcliffe Publishing.

Madeley, J. (1999) *Big Business, Poor Peoples: The Impact of Transnational Corporations on the World's Poor*, London/New York: Zed Books.

OECD (2001) *The OECD Guidelines for Multinational Enterprises 2001: Focus: Global Instruments for Corporate Responsibility*, Paris, OECD.

OECD (2005) 'DAC Members' net ODA 1990–2005 and DAC Secretariat simulations of net ODA in 2006 and 2010' (www.oecd.org/dataoecd/57/30/35320618.pdf).

Pemberton, S., Gordon, D., Nandy, S., Pantazis, C., and Townsend, P. (2005) 'The Relationship between child poverty and child rights: the role of indicators', in A. Minujin, E. Delamonica and M. Komarecki (eds) *Human Rights and Social Policies for Children and Women: The MICS in Practice*, New York: UNICEF/New School University.

Pemberton, S., Gordon, D., Nandy, S., Pantazis, C. and Townsend, P. (2007) 'Child Rights and Child Poverty: Can the International Framework of Children's Rights be used to Improve Child Survival Rates?', *PLos Medicine*, 4 (10): doi:10.1371/journal.pmed.0040307.

Pogge, T. and Reddy, S. (2003) 'Unknown: the extent, distribution and trend of global income poverty', (www.socialanalysis.org).

Rice, X. (2007) 'Net giveaway halves Kenya's child deaths from malaria', *Guardian*, 17 August.

Scott, J., Stokman, F.N. and Ziegler, R. (1985) *Networks of Corporate Power*, London: Polity.

Singh, J.A., Govender, M. and Mills, E.J. (2007) 'Do human rights matter to health?', *Lancet*, 370, 9586.

Sklair, L. (2001) *The Transnational Capitalist Class*, Oxford: Blackwell.

Townsend, P. and Gordon, D. (eds) (2002) *World Poverty: New Policies to Defeat an Old Enemy*, Bristol: The Policy Press.

UN (2000) *United Nations Millennium Declaration*, (www.un.org/millennium/declaration/ares552e.htm).

UN (2001) *Report of the High-Level Panel on Financing for Development*, 28 June, New York: UN.

UN (2003) Sub-Commission on the Promotion and Protection of Human Rights, 55th Session, Agenda Item 4, 'Economic, social and cultural rights: norms on the responsibilities of transnational corporations and other business enterprises with regard to human rights', E/CN.4/Sub.2/2003/12/Rev.2, 26 August, (www.unhchr.ch/huridocda/huridoca.nsf).

UNDESA (United Nations, Department of Economic and Social Affairs) (2007) World Youth Report 2007 – Young People's Transition to Adulthood: Progress and Challenges, New York: UNDESA.

UNDP (United Nations Development Programme) (1995) *Human Development Report 1994 – New Dimensions of Human Security*, New York: Oxford University Press (http://hdr.undp.org/en/reports/global/hdr1994/chapters/).

UNICEF (2004) *State of the World's Children 2005*, New York: UNICEF.

UNICEF (2005) *State of the World's Children 2006*, New York: UNICEF.

UNICEF (2007) *State of the World's Children 2008*, New York: UNICEF.

Vagts, D.F. (2003) 'The UN norms for transnational corporations', *Leiden Journal of International Law*, 16, 795-802.

Wade, R.H. (2004) 'Is globalisation reducing poverty and inequality?', *International Journal of Health Services*, 34 (3): 381-414.

Watkins, K. (2002) *Rigged Rules and Double Standards: Trade, Globalisation and the Fight Against Poverty*, New York: Oxfam International.

World Bank (2005) *World Bank Development Report for 2005*, Washington D.C.: World Bank.

World Health Organization (2007) *World Health Statistics 2007*, Washington D.C.: WHO.

Appendix

Table 22A.1: Child mortality and poor conditions of health – countries in Sub-Saharan Africa

Country (year data collected)	Under-5s stunted for age		Mortality under 5		1-year-olds not immunised against measles	
	Poorest 20%	Richest 20%	Poorest 20%	Richest 20%	Poorest 20%	Richest 20%
Benin (2001)	35	18	20	9	43	17
Burkina Faso (2003)	46	21	21	14	52	29
Central African Republic (1994–95)	42	25	19	10	69	20
Chad (2004)	51	32	18	19	92	62
Comoros (1996)	45	23	13	9	49	14
Eritrea (2002)	45	18	10	6	16	4
Ethiopia (2005)	48	35	13	9	75	48
Gabon (2000)	33	11	9	5	66	29
Ghana (2003)	42	13	13	9	25	11
Guinea (2005)	41	22	22	11	58	43
Kenya (2003)	38	19	15	9	45	12
Madagascar (2003–04)	50	38	14	5	62	16
Malawi (2004)	54	32	18	11	33	12
Mali (2001)	45	20	25	15	60	24
Mauritania (2000–01)	39	24	10	8	58	14
Mozambique (2003)	49	20	20	11	39	4
Namibia (2000)	27	15	5	3	24	14
Niger (1998)	42	32	28	18	77	34
Rwanda (2005)	55	30	21	12	15	12
South Africa (1998)	–	–	9	2	27	16
Togo (1998)	24	15	17	10	66	37
Uganda 2000–01)	40	26	19	11	51	36
United Republic of Tanzania (2004–05)	40	26	14	9	45	9
Zambia (2001–02)	51	37	19	9	19	12
Zimbabwe (1999)	29	21	10	6	20	14

Table 22A.2: Child mortality and poor conditions of health – countries in Latin America

Country (year data collected)	Under-5s stunted for age		Mortality under 5		1-year-olds not immunised against measles	
	Poorest 20%	Richest 20%	Poorest 20%	Richest 20%	Poorest 20%	Richest 20%
Bolivia (2003)	42	5	10	3	38	26
Brazil (1996)	23	2	10	3	22	10
Colombia (2005)	20	3	4	2	36	10
Guatemala (1998–99)	65	7	8	4	21	9
Haiti (2000)	31	7	16	11	57	37
Nicaragua (2001)	35	4	6	2	24	6
Paraguay (1990)	22	3	2	2	52	31
Peru (2000)	47	4	9	2	19	8

Source: WHO, 2007, pp 74–7

TWENTY-THREE

Conclusion

Shailen Nandy and Alberto Minujin

This book has presented examples of ongoing work around the world that focus on the conceptualisation and measurement of child poverty and well-being. To this end, individual chapters reported findings of country-level case studies from Bangladesh, Congo Brazzaville, Haiti, Iran, Morocco, South Africa, Tanzania, the US and Vietnam. Chapters also presented regional case studies, with material and data from the European Union (EU), Latin America, Central and Eastern Europe, Sub-Saharan Africa and South Asia. Authors of all these chapters are currently involved in, and represent most of the key international research on, the measurement of multidimensional child poverty. Each contributor discussed the implications of child-sensitive poverty measures for policy making in different settings and, by placing children, and their particular needs, at the centre of poverty analyses, we believe the approaches presented in this book will benefit ongoing and future anti-poverty policies. The United Nations' (UN) adoption of a formal international definition of child poverty in 2006 lent considerable weight to the UN Children's Fund's (UNICEF) now decade-long call for poverty reduction programmes to begin with children (UNICEF, 2000).

As the focus of the book has been the measurement of child poverty and well-being, chapters have covered a combination of theoretical, methodological and policy-relevant material. The considerable potential of using multidimensional indicators to examine child poverty not only within countries, but also between them and also over time, should be apparent. In addition, the methods and data presented can also be used to examine disparities and inequities *within* and *between* countries. Both are critical issues in poverty research (see Chapter Three), as they result from disparities in power which perpetuate poverty (Townsend and Gordon, 2002). With survey data continually becoming available (for example, UNICEF is currently running a fourth round of Multiple Indicator Cluster Surveys in over 45 countries),[1] poverty researchers can now detail and track outcomes for different socioeconomic groups and areas over time, to show whether or not gaps between the haves and the have–nots are closing. If, as has happened in some rich countries (Milanovic, 2005), incomes and outcomes improve faster for the rich than for the poor, then this would prove a damning indictment for the development strategies of the last few decades. In the run-up to the 2015 target date for meeting the Millennium Development Goals (MDGs), the methods and data discussed in this book will provide clear evidence of how countries have fared. Given that the MDGs lack direct child-specific indicators of poverty, the methodologies set out here can be used to assess changes in multidimensional child poverty, and reasonable forecasts made of whether or not child poverty will be halved by 2015.

Key areas of debate among poverty researchers have concerned the choice of indicators (that is, monetary versus non-monetary, direct versus indirect) and unit of analysis. Ideally, analyses should be run at the level of individuals (Rio Group, 2006), and this has been true for most of the chapters in this book, with children being the units of analysis. This is due, in no small part, to the availability of high quality, nationally representative household and individual level survey micro data. The best known sources include the United States Agency for International Development's (USAID) Demographic and Health Surveys, UNICEF's Multiple Indicator Cluster Surveys, the World Bank's Living Standards Measurement Surveys and the World Health Organization's (WHO) World Health Surveys. Some authors have used other surveys (see Chapters Twelve, Thirteen, Fourteen and Twenty) that include monetary data, and thus have been able to develop monetary and non-monetary indicators. These, in turn, have been used to examine overlaps between different dimensions of child poverty and well-being in low-income countries, as has been done by others for rich countries (Bradshaw and Finch, 2003). While the Demographic and Health Surveys and Multiple Indicator Cluster Surveys do not include monetary data, we expect child poverty research in the coming years to make much greater use of overlaps analyses, to demonstrate the links between multiple disadvantage and deprivation, and poor outcomes for children.

The choice of which dimensions of child poverty should be reflected is probably not as contentious as it has been previously for wider poverty research. One reason for this is the availability of, and agreement on, a clear definition of child poverty (and also for absolute and overall poverty). Each chapter in this book reflects to some degree the sentiments of both the 1995 World Summit for Social Development and the 2006 UN General Assembly definitions of poverty. Both of these are unequivocal about the need for measures to reflect more than just monetary dimensions, as they detail the non–monetary dimensions of importance. Some would rightly argue that these definitions neglect important social needs, and Peter Townsend noted over 30 years ago that 'people do not live by bread alone ... sometimes they are prepared to forego bread to meet a more pressing social need' (Townsend, 1979, p 915). Research using consensual methods to establish socially perceived necessities (see, for example, Chapter Six) shows the importance that children place on *social* activities like play, having friends visit and being able to participate in school trips with their peers. Projects like Young Lives (see Chapter Nineteen) are now producing in–depth longitudinal data on poverty. These data are being used to examine the development of resilience strategies to cope with different economic and social risks, the extent of intergenerational transmissions of poverty between parents and children and also the importance of intra–household dynamics, particularly for girls and orphans.

A common finding in all chapters is that child poverty (with its inevitable negative impact on child well-being) is very prevalent. Not only is it widespread, in some instances it is on the increase (see, for example, Chapter Seventeen). Given current (2011/12) economic and political instabilities around the world, widely predicted cuts in public expenditure for basic services (on which children and the poor are most reliant) will exact a grim toll. Over a decade ago, UNICEF demonstrated, with abundant evidence, the importance of basic services to children (Vandemoortele, 2000). Today's politicians' insistence on massive and rapid reductions in public spending after will not be able to claim ignorance about the likely impact of their decisions. We have been in a similar situation before, and know for a fact that children and their families will be on the receiving end of any major economic adjustments and restructuring (Jolly and Cornia, 1984; Cornia et al, 1987, 1992; Mehrotra and Jolly, 1997; Mehrotra et al, 2000; Mehrotra and Delamonica, 2002; Mendoza, 2010).

There are, however, some differences between this crisis and previous ones. It is now more than two decades since the UNCRC was almost universally ratified by the governments of the world. Since 1989, the UNCRC's binding nature has placed clear obligations on governments (and also other actors) to ensure children's rights are met; Pemberton and colleagues (Chapter Two) showed how in some countries, judiciaries (rather than politicians) have begun to take responsibility for setting minimum welfare standards which governments are required to meet by law. UNICEF's Global Study on Child Poverty and Disparities is systematically detailing the extent of child poverty around the world and its impact on their well-being. Importantly, it is also collating detailed information about what national social and economic policies exist for ensuring children's welfare. Such exercises provide valuable direct evidence for assessing the commitment of governments to ensuring children's needs are met, and their rights fulfilled. Campaigners and advocates, in earlier times of crisis, lacked these tools and resources. We can only hope that things are different this time around.

Governments, international agencies, major aid donors and recipients and non-governmental organisations (NGOs) have all made strong commitments to ensuring the rights of children, by agreeing to try and meet the MDGs by 2015. Doubts as to whether *any* of the MDGs will really be met have already been expressed (Sahn and Stifel, 2003; UNDP, 2003), suggesting conditions for children are not improving as rapidly as they should. This is frustrating, given that the resources to deal with mass poverty already exist (Vandermoortele, 2002). No new scientific or technological breakthroughs are needed to deal with any of the deprivations or domains of poverty identified by international definitions; governments already know how to provide their populations with safe water, sanitation and adequate housing (Nandy and Gordon, 2009). What is lacking (as it always has been) is the necessary *political* will to prioritise children's needs and to choose to spend the resources required. Competing priorities undoubtedly play their part, as rapid and massive government bailouts of private banks in rich countries demonstrated so clearly in 2008 and 2009. The potential imminent economic collapse of some EU countries, such as Greece, certainly diverts attention (and resources) away from the poorest countries and, by definition, the unmet needs of children in poverty.

History shows how international aid has often been used, in part, as a tool of influence. Policy regimes and processes, demanded by international organisations in return for funds, hint at a not so subtle agenda of business as usual (Deacon, 2000; Wade, 2002; Mehrotra and Delamonica, 2005). This implies that real effort in the design and implementation of redistribution policies is unlikely, making it difficult to be optimistic about the future (Hall, 2007). Despite ample evidence of their shortcomings, it appears the neoliberal mantras of unregulated free markets continue to be propounded, with the likely outcome being increased inequality, inequity and poverty. We wait and hope to be proved wrong.

One example of radical change and action needed to tackle international poverty is the *Manifesto of international action to defeat poverty* (Townsend and Gordon, 2002). Set out nearly a decade ago, it identified 18 courses of action that, if acted on, would mean key elements of international legal conventions such as the UNCRC and

International Covenant on Economic, Social and Cultural Rights could be implemented, and by doing so, put into action policies that would reduce global poverty. These included the:

- introduction of schemes to ensure universal social security;
- strengthening of the legal right to universal child benefit;
- legal enforcement of the right to an adequate standard of living;
- establishing universal rights of access locally to publicly provided basic healthcare and education services.

Explicit demands were also made of donors and international organisations. They were urged to:

- agree an international poverty line, 'subject to demonstrable scientific, not politically convenient, consensus';
- adopt legally binding minimum levels (1%) of gross national product (GNP) for overseas development assistance;
- introduce new international company law, 'to curb anti-social activities and curb excessively high profits from poor countries';
- extend measures for full employment, and establish an International Full Employment Agency;
- establish strong regional policy alliances;
- further the democratisation of the UN, giving poor countries representation on UN committees;
- rebuild and/or strengthen tax administration;
- agree with the UN and national governments an action plan for staged greater equalisation of resources within and between countries.

Of particular relevance to child poverty was the recommendation to introduce an international financial transactions tax, akin to that recommended in the 1970s by James Tobin (Tobin, 1978; Ul Haq et al, 1996), to be administered by the UN (see Chapter Twenty-Two). The revenue raised could be used to subsidise the establishment of universal child benefit for all developing countries, particularly those lacking the resources to do it for themselves. Peter Townsend actively pursued the idea with the International Labour Organization, noting '... a tiny automatic tax on all financial exchanges, say 0.1%, could raise up to $400 billion annually...' (Townsend, 2002, p 369). He estimated that this amounted to around five times more than the low target of debt relief and aid for low-income countries advocated by the G8 rich countries and the World Bank (Townsend, 2008).

The *Manifesto* requires action on the part of all those working in international development – the governments of rich and poor countries, international agencies and financial institutions, and also the private sector multinational corporations. Social science researchers also have a duty to act, not least by developing valid, reliable and meaningful indicators against which national (and international) performances can be judged. This book presents an overview of new research on child poverty and some of the leading approaches to its measurement. We hope readers will build on and test the methods presented, and so contribute further to the development of valid and reliable indicators of child poverty. Based on sound methodological approaches to measuring child poverty, and clear evidence of the impact of poverty on children in rich, middle-income and poor countries, this book calls for immediate action by policy makers, researchers and activists to make child poverty reduction and equity central issues in their agendas, and to use their influence and power to ensure children receive the priority they deserve in international, regional and national policies.

Note

1 www.childinfo.org/mics4.html

References

Bradshaw, J. and Finch, N. (2003) 'Overlaps in dimensions of poverty', *Journal of Social Policy*, vol 32, pp 513-25.

Cornia, G.A., Jolly, R. and Stewart, F. (1987) *Adjustment with a human face: Protecting the vulnerable and promoting growth*, Oxford: Oxford University Press.

Cornia, G.A., van der Hoeven, R. and Mkandawire, T. (1992) *Africa's recovery in the 1990s: From stagnation to adjustment to human development*, Florence: UNICEF International Child Development Centre.

Deacon, B. (2000) *Globalization and social policy: The threat to equitable welfare*, Occasional Paper No 5, Geneva: United Nations Research Institute for Social Development.

Hall, A.J. (2007) 'Social policies in the World Bank: paradigms and challenges', *Global Social Policy*, vol 7, pp 151-75.

Jolly, R. and Cornia, G. (1984) *The impact of the world recession on children*, Oxford: Pergamon.

Mehrotra, S. and Delamonica, E.E. (2002) 'Public spending for children: an empirical note', *Journal of International Development*, vol 14, pp 1105-16.

Mehrotra, S. and Delamonica, E.E. (2005) 'The private sector and privatization in social services: is the Washington Consensus dead?', *Global Social Policy*, vol 5, pp 141-74.

Mehrotra, S. and Jolly, R. (1997) *Development with a human face: Experiences in social achievement and economic growth*, Oxford: Clarendon Press.

Mehrotra, S., Vandermoortele, J. and Delamonica, E.E. (2000) *Basic services for all: Public spending and the social dimensions of poverty*, Florence: UNICEF Innocenti Research Centre.

Mendoza, R. (2010) *Two years into the crisis: Signs of severe coping strategies that are impacting on children*, Social and Economic Policy Working Briefs, New York: United Nations Children's Fund.

Milanovic, B. (2005) *Worlds apart: Measuring international and global inequality*, Princeton, NJ: Princeton University Press.

Nandy, S. and Gordon, D. (2009) 'Children living in squalor: shelter, water and sanitation deprivations in developing countries', *Children, Youth and Environments*, vol 19, pp 202-28.

Rio Group (2006) *Compendium of best practices in poverty measurement*, Rio de Janeiro: Expert Group on Poverty Statistics, IBGE.

Sahn, D. and Stifel, D. (2003) 'Progress towards the Millennium Development Goals in Africa', *World Development*, vol 31, pp 23-52.

Tobin, J. (1978) 'A proposal for international monetary reform', *Eastern Economic Journal*, vol 4, pp 153-9.

Townsend, P. (1979) *Poverty in the United Kingdom*, Harmondsworth: Penguin Books Ltd.

Townsend, P. (2002) 'Human rights, transnational corporations and the World Bank', in D. Gordon and P. Townsend (eds) *World poverty: New policies to defeat an old enemy*, Bristol: The Policy Press, pp 351-76.

Townsend, P. (2008) *The abolition of child poverty and the right to social security: A possible UN model for child benefit?*, London: London School of Economics and Political Science.

Townsend, P. and Gordon, D. (2002) *World poverty: New policies to defeat an old enemy*, Bristol: The Policy Press.

Ul Haq, M., Kaul, I. and Grunberg, I. (eds) (1996) *The Tobin tax: Coping with financial volatility*, Oxford: Oxford University Press.

UNDP (United Nations Development Programme) (2003) *Human Development Report 2003*, New York: Oxford University Press.

UNICEF (United Nations Children's Fund) (2000) *Poverty reduction begins with children*, New York: UNICEF.

Vandemoortele, J. (2000) *Absorbing social shocks, protecting children and reducing poverty: The role of basic social services*, United Nations Children's Fund (UNICEF) Working Papers, New York: UNICEF.

Vandermoortele, J. (2002) *Are the MDGs feasible?*, New York: United Nations Development Programme Bureau for Development Policy.

Wade, R. (2002) 'US hegemony and the World Bank: the fight over people and ideas', *Review of International Political Economy*, vol 9, pp 215-43.

Index

Page references for notes are followed by n

Global child poverty and well-being

socially perceived necessities approach
135–49
  adults' views 139–42, 144
  challenges 146–8
  children's views 142–6
  data and methods 137–9
Society at a glance (OECD) 247
Somalia 21
South Africa 135–7
  child benefit 373
  child mortality and poor health
    conditions 564
  economic and social rights 27, 28
  Measures of Child Poverty Project 93
  socially perceived necessities approach
    137–49
South Asia 532
  child poverty and deprivation 420,
    429–33, 435–9, 441–2
  child poverty measurement 421–3
  gender disparities 433–5
  inequality 535
  social exclusion 536
  see also individual countries
Spain
  child poverty 210, 211, 212, 213, 222,
    223, 225, 228
  government intervention 220
  labour market situation of parents
    217, 218
  large families 215
Spearman, Charles 74
Special Drawing Rights 556, 558
Spicker, P. 380, 511
standard of living 66–7, 68–9, 70, 78
  American HDI 157, 158, 162,
    169–70
  socially perceived necessities approach
    136, 137–49
State of the World's Children, The
  (SOWCR) (UNICEF) xxx, 5, 247,
  248, 251, 252, 340, 350n, 382, 527
Statistical Information and Monitoring
  Programme on Child Labour
  (SIMPOC) 259
story-telling 168, 172
structural adjustment policies (SAPs)
  439–40
Structural Equation Modelling (SEM)
  78
stunting 481, 484, 546, 547, 564–5
Sub-Saharan Africa
  child mortality and poor health
    conditions 547, 564
  child poverty and deprivation 420,
    423–7, 435–42
  child poverty measurement 421–3
  gender disparities 427–9

HIV/AIDS 546, 550
  see also individual countries
subjective poverty 199
Sunstein, C. 27
Suriname 390
sustainability 465, 469
Sweden
  at-risk-of-poverty rates 236
  child poverty 211, 213, 222, 223, 227,
    228
  government intervention 220
  labour market situation of parents
    219
  lone-parent households 215
  material deprivation rates 236
  overseas development aid 555
  socially perceived necessities approach
    136

T

Tajikistan
  child well-being 190, 191, 192, 202–6
  education 186
  family situations 188
  health 185
  housing 184
  material well-being 183
  personal and social well-being 187
  risk and safety 189
Tanzania 263
  altering thresholds 277–9
  child mortality and poor health
    conditions 564
  child poverty 267–77, 279–80, 533
  child poverty measurement 265–7,
    284–6
  child rights 539–40
Tárki 216, 217, 220, 229, 238
teen births 156
Thailand 42, 531
Tobin, James 557, 558, 559
Tobin tax 556, 557–60, 571
Togo 564
Tomasevski, K. 28
Total Social Organisation of Labour
  (TSOL) 462–3
Tots Index 157, 167
  access to knowledge indicators 168–9
  attachment indicators 171–2
  health indicators 167
  prevention of harm indicators 170–1
  standard of living indicators 169–70
Townsend, Peter 4–5, 14, 20, 58, 63–4,
  65–6, 289, 456–7, 459, 467–8, 569,
  570–2
transition countries 179–80
  child well-being 182–93
  methods 181–2, 193–4

588